# Epics
## *for Students*

# Epics
## *for Students*

**Presenting Analysis, Context and Criticism on
Commonly Studied Epics**

*Marie Lazzari, Editor*

*Meg Roland, Columbia Gorge Community College, Advisor*

*Foreword by Helen Conrad-O'Briain,
Trinity College, Dublin, University College, Dublin*

GALE

DETROIT • NEW YORK • TORONTO • LONDON

# STAFF

Marie Lazzari, *Editor*

Catherine C. Dominic, David Galens, Diane Telgen, Kathleen Wilson, *Contributing Editors*

Aarti D. Stephens, *Managing Editor*

Jeff Chapman, *Programmer/Analyst*

Susan M. Trosky, *Permissions Manager*

Kimberly F. Smilay, *Permissions Specialist*

Diane Cooper, Edna Hedblad, Michele Lonoconus, Maureen Puhl, Sarah Chesney, *Permissions Associates*

Steve Cusack, Kelly Quin, *Permissions Assistants*

Victoria B. Cariappa, *Research Manager*

Barbara McNeil, *Research Specialist*

Laura Bissey, Julia Daniel, Tamara C. Nott, Michele P. Pica, Tracie A. Richardson, Cheryl Warnock, *Research Associates*

Alfred Gardner, *Research Assistant*

Mary Beth Trimper, *Production Director*

Evi Seoud, *Assistant Production Manager*

Shanna Heilveil, *Production Assistant*

Randy Bassett, *Image Database Supervisor*

Mikal Ansari, *Macintosh Artist*

Robert Duncan, Mike Logusz, *Imaging Specialists*

Pamela A. Reed, *Photography Coordinator*

Library of Congress Cataloging-in-Publication Data

Epics for Students : presenting analysis, context, and criticism on
commonly studied epics / Marie Lazzari, editor.
    p.   cm.
Includes bibliographical references and indexes.
ISBN 0-7876-1685-0 (alk. paper)
1. Epic literature--History and criticism.   I. Lazzari, Marie.
PN56.E65E67   1997
809.1'32--DC31

97-27859
CIP

This book is printed on acid-free paper that meets the minimum requirements of American National Standard for Information Sciences—Permanence Paper for Printed Library Materials, ANSI Z39.48-1984.

Library of Congress Catalog Card Number
ISBN 0-7876-1685-0

Printed in the United States of America

10 9 8 7 6 5 4 3 2 1

# *Table of Contents*

# Guest Foreword

The death of the epic, like that of Mark Twain, has been greatly exaggerated. Derek Walcott's *Omeros* and the still-living oral epic of Mali are neither its ghosts nor its last survivors. Closer to our own experience, *The Lord of the Rings, Star Wars,* and *Star Trek* prove that the epic, with its crowds of striking characters and sprawling action, is alive, vigorous, and popular.

How can we bridge the gap between these popular modern epics, often with special effects thrown in, and the older, more formal epics for a new audience? The epics themselves are their own best advocates. Unread, epics seem distant and difficult, the tedious doings of the dead. Read, the dead live again, and distances of time and space dissolve.

The epic has action and tension. It has passion and thought. Above all, it has men and women, facing circumstances and choices of their own and others' making. The epic plunges into the timeless struggle of the needs of the individual to be true to self and still reach some sort of equilibrium with society and what each perceives to be the universe and the divine. It celebrates human achievement and the human yearning for achievement. It celebrates human dignity as often in defeat as in victory.

The epic was meant not merely to be read, but to be heard. Read aloud short scenes from the epics covered in this book. Face their problems and their world and ask the people around you for a moment to do the same. Get into the skins of these characters. You will see that the skin is not so different from your own, and that the differences may be enriching. Transpose epics into your own world, and see the constants of human nature and societies. It is the form of the epic, rather than its content, which can put off a modern reader. Try rewriting an episode from any one of the following epics as a scene from a movie or television show. Try recreating for the screen the special effects that these men and women produced with words. Nothing will make you appreciate their talent and craftsmanship more. Casting even *Paradise Lost* (maybe especially *Paradise Lost*) is guaranteed to provoke rowdy discussion.

However elevated the language, however alien the setting, when you open one of the following epics you enter the human heart—and all the world is before you.

*Helen Conrad-O'Briain*
*Trinity College, Dublin*
*University College, Dublin*
*Dublin, Ireland*

# Introduction

## Purpose

*Epics for Students* (*EfS*) is designed to provide students with a guide to understanding and enjoying epic literature. Part of Gale's "For Students" Literature line, *EfS* is crafted to meet the curricular needs of high school and undergraduate college students and their teachers, as well as the interests of general readers and researchers. This volume contains entries on the works of epic world literature that are most studied in classrooms.

## Selection Criteria

The epics covered in *EfS* were selected by surveying numerous sources on teaching literature and analyzing course curricula for various school districts. Some of the sources surveyed included literature anthologies; *Reading Lists for College-Bound Students: The Books Most Recommended by America's Top Colleges;* and textbooks on teaching literature.

The editor solicited input from an advisor, high school teachers and librarians, and from the educators and academics who wrote the entries for the volume. From these discussions, the final entry list was compiled, featuring the epic works that are most often studied in high school and undergraduate literature courses. If a work was not selected for the present volume, it was noted as a possibility for a future volume. The editor welcomes suggestions for titles to be included in future volumes.

## Coverage

Each entry includes an introduction to the epic and its author, when known, and discussion of authorship controversies or speculation in the case of anonymous works. A plot summary helps readers follow the often complicated series of events in the epic. Character sketches include explanations of each character's role in the epic and relationships with other characters. Separate essays provide analyses of important themes and of literary techniques.

In addition to this material, which helps readers understand and analyze the epic itself, students are provided with meaningful information on the literary and historical background of each work. This includes an essay on the historical context of the epic, comparisons between the time and place of the epic's setting and modern Western culture, an overview essay surveying the course of commentary about the work, and excerpts from critical essays on the epic.

## Special Features

*EfS* includes a foreword by Helen Conrad-O'Briain, Trinity College Dublin, University College Dublin. This essay provides an enlightening look at how readers interact with literature and how teachers and students can use *EfS* to enrich their own experiences with epic literature.

A unique feature of *EfS* is a specially commissioned essay on each epic by an academic expert, usually one who has taught the work extensively, targeted to the student reader.

To further aid the student in studying and enjoying each epic, information on media adaptations is provided, as well as reading suggestions for works of fiction and nonfiction on similar themes and topics. Each entry also features illustrations, such as maps and depictions of key scenes. Classroom aids include ideas for research papers and lists of critical sources that provide additional scholarly information on each work.

## *Organization*

Each entry in *EfS* focuses on one work. The heading lists the title of the epic, the author's name (when known), and the date that the epic first appeared. In some cases, this date is known; in others, a range of dates is provided. The following elements appear in each entry:

- **Introduction:** A brief overview which provides general information about the epic, such as its place in world literature, its significance within its national culture, any controversies surrounding the epic, and major themes of the work.

- **Author Biography:** Includes basic facts about the author's life. In the case of anonymous works, speculative scholarship about the anonymous author or authors is summarized here.

- **Plot Summary:** A description of the major events in the epic, with interpretation of how these events help articulate the primary themes.

- **Characters:** An alphabetical listing of the epic's main characters. Each character name is followed by a description of that character's role, as well as discussion of the character's actions, relationships, and motivations.

- **Themes:** A thorough overview of how the principal themes, topics, and issues are addressed within the epic.

- **Style:** This section addresses important stylistic elements, such as setting, point of view, and narrative method, as well as literary devices such as imagery, foreshadowing, and symbolism. Literary terms are explained within each entry and can also be found in the Glossary.

- **Historical and Cultural Context:** This section outlines the social, political, and cultural climate in which the author lived and the epic was created. Descriptions of related historical events, pertinent aspects of daily life in the culture, and the artistic and literary sensibilities of the time in which the work was written are provided here.

- **Critical Overview:** Supplies background on the critical and popular reputation of the epic. Offers an overview of how the work was first received and how perceptions of it may have changed over time.

- **Criticism:** This section begins with an essay commissioned for *EfS* and designed to introduce the epic work to the student reader. This section also includes excerpts from previously published criticism that has been identified by subject experts as especially useful in explicating each work to students.

- **Sources for Further Study:** Alphabetical list of critical material quoted in the entry and other critical sources useful to the student who wants to read more about the epic. Full bibliographical information and descriptive annotations are provided for each source.

- **Media Adaptations:** A list of film and television productions of the epic, as well as information about stage adaptations, audio recordings, and musical adaptations.

- **Compare and Contrast Box:** "At-a-glance" comparison of some cultural and historical differences between the epic's time and culture and late twentieth-century Western society.

- **What Do I Read Next?:** A list of works that complement the featured epic or serve as a contrast to it. This can include works by the same author and works from other authors, genres, cultures, and eras.

- **Study Questions:** Questions designed to spark classroom discussion or research paper topics. This section includes questions related to other disciplines, such as American history, world history, science, math, government, business, geography, economics, and psychology.

## *Indexes*

A **Cumulative Author/Title Index** lists the authors and titles covered in the volume.

A **Nationality/Ethnicity Index** lists the authors and titles by nationality and ethnicity.

A **Subject/Theme Index** provides easy reference for users studying a particular subject or theme within epic literature. Significant subjects and themes are included. Boldface entries in this index indicate in-depth discussion of that subject or theme.

Each entry features **illustrations,** including author portraits, depictions of key scenes, and maps.

## *Citing* Epics for Students

When writing papers, students who quote directly from *Epics for Students* may use the following general forms. These examples are based on MLA style. Teachers may request that students adhere to a different style, so the following examples may be adapted as needed.

When citing text from a section of an *EfS* entry, the following format should be used:

*Aeneid, Epics for Students.* Ed. Marie Lazzari. Detroit: Gale, 1997. 11–13.

When quoting the signed commissioned essay from an entry in *EfS,* the following format should be used:

Looper, Jennifer E. Essay on *Cantar de mio Cid (El Cid). Epics for Students.* Ed. Marie Lazzari. Detroit: Gale, 1997. 62–5.

When quoting a journal or newspaper essay that is reprinted in *EfS,* the following format should be used:

Sasson, Jack M. ''Some Literary Motifs in the Composition of the *Gilgamesh* Epic.'' *Studies in Philology* LXIX, No. 3 (July, 1972), 259–79; excerpted and reprinted in *Epics for Students,* ed. Marie Lazzari (Detroit: Gale, 1997), pp. 165–69.

When quoting material reprinted from a book that appears in *EfS,* the following format should be used:

Williams, R. D., and Pattie, T. S. ''Virgil Today,'' in *Virgil: His Poetry through the Ages* (British Library, 1982, 57–67); excerpted and reprinted in *Epics for Students,* ed. Marie Lazzari (Detroit: Gale, 1997), pp. 18–22.

## *We Welcome Your Suggestions*

The editors of *Epics for Students* welcome your comments and ideas. Readers who wish to suggest epic works to appear in future volumes, or who have other suggestions, are cordially invited to contact the editor. You may contact the editor at:

Editor, *Epics for Students*
Gale Research
835 Penobscot Bldg.
645 Griswold St.
Detroit, MI 48226-4094
1-800/347-4253

# Literary Chronology

**1250 B.C.–1184 B.C.:** Traditional (approximate) dates during which the Trojan War, chronicled in the *Aeneid* and alluded to in the *Odyssey,* probably took place.

**850 B.C.–700 B.C.:** The *Iliad* and the *Odyssey* were probably composed during this span of time, as part of a long tradition of bardic composition.

**c. 500 B.C.:** Approximate date of the setting of *Beowulf.*

**400 B.C. 300 B.C.:** The development of literary criticism in Greece, typified by Aristotle's *Poetics,* features frequent references to the works of Homer.

**70 B.C.:** Publius Maro Vergilius, known as Virgil, born at Andes, near Mantua in northern Italy.

**60 B.C.:** Formation of the First Triumvirate: Julius Caesar, Pompey, and Crassius.

**44 B.C.:** Assassination of Julius Caesar on the Ides of March (March 15).

**43 B.C.-42 B.C.:** Civil war breaks out between Caesar's heirs (Octavian, Antony) and his assassins (Brutus, Cassius).

**42 B.C.:** Brutus and Cassius are defeated at the Battle of Philippi.

**37 B.C.:** Publication of Virgil's *Eclogues.*

**29 B.C.:** Publication of Virgil's *Georgics.*

**19 B.C.:** Publication of Virgil's *Aeneid.*

**19 B.C.:** Virgil dies at Brindisi.

**1 B.C.-1 A.D.:** Approximate range of dates of the composition of the *Mahabharata.*

**735:** Traditional dating of the composition of *Beowulf.*

**757–796:** Reign of King Offa of Mercia, proposed by some scholars as a possible alternate era for the composition of *Beowulf.*

**778–803:** Period of historic unrest between Emperor Charlemagne and Suleiman ibn-al-Arabi of Spain which provides some historical foundation for events in *The Song of Roland.*

**c. 1000:** Approximate date of transcription for the only extant copy of *Beowulf.*

**1098–1100:** Probable range of dates for the oral composition of *The Song of Roland.*

**1130–1170:** Probable range of dates for the manuscript of *The Song of Roland.*

**1201–1207:** Estimated range of dates during which *El Cid* was probably composed.

**1265:** Dante Aligheri born (probably in May).

**1289:** Dante fights in the Battle of Campaldino.

**1300:** Dante becomes a Prefect, or civic governor, of Florence, Italy. His *Divine Comedy* is set in this year.

**1307:** Dante probably begins writing the *Divine Comedy* this year.

**1321:** Dante dies at Ravenna, 14 September.

**1481:** Publication of the Christophoro Landino edition of the *Divine Comedy,* including Antonio Manetti's detailed maps of Hell based on Dante's descriptions.

**1488:** The first printed edition of Homer's works appears.

**1596:** Only extant manuscript of *El Cid* is copied by Juan Ruis de Ulibarri y Leyba.

**1608:** John Milton is born on 9 December in London, England.

**1628:** Publication of John Milton's poem ''On the Death of a Fair Infant Dying of a Cough.''

**1641:** Publication of Milton's anti-episcopal pamphlets as *Of Reformation in England, of Prelatical Episcopacy, Animadversions upon the Remonstrant's Defense.*

**1649:** In the year that rebels execute King Charles I of England, Milton publishes his *The Tenure of Kings and Magistrates,* which defends the rights of citizens to kill tyrant rulers. This same year, Milton is appointed Latin Secretary of Foreign Affairs in Oliver Cromwell's interregnum government.

**1652:** In February or March, Milton becomes totally blind.

**1658:** Milton probably begins writing *Paradise Lost.*

**1660:** Milton is imprisoned for his role in the overthrow of King Charles I.

**1667:** Milton's *Paradise Lost* is published in a 10–volume edition.

**1671:** Publication of Milton's *Paradise Regained* and *Samson Agonistes.*

**1674:** John Milton dies in London. Later this year, *Paradise Lost* is published in its final form in 12 volumes.

**1802:** Elias Lönnrot, the folklorist who compiled the *Kalevala,* is born in Sammatti, Finland (then Sweden).

**1815:** First printing of an edition of *Beowulf.*

**1833–1834:** Lönnrot prepares an early manuscript version of the *Kalevala* (published as the *Proto-Kalevala* in 1929).

**1835:** Publication of *Kalewala, taikka Wanhoja Karjalan Runoja Suomen kansan miunosista ajoista (The Kalevala; or, Old Karelian Poems about ancient Times of the Finnish People).*

**1837:** Francisque Michel publishes *La Chanson de Roland ou de Roncevaux (The Song of Roland).* This is the first published edition of the epic, although it has been known for more than 700 years.

**1849:** An enlarged second edition of the *Kalevala* is published.

**1871:** Archaeological excavations near Hissarlik, Turkey, reveal what may be the ruins of Troy.

**1884:** Elias Lönnrot dies.

**1929:** Publication of the *Proto-Kalevala.*

**1930:** Derek Walcott is born on the island of St. Lucia, the site of his later epic poem *Omeros.*

**1939:** Archaeological dig at an Anglo-Saxon burial site from approximately 625 B.C. at Sutton Hoo, England, yields armaments that resemble those mentioned in *Beowulf.*

**1990:** The poem *Omeros,* one of a few twentieth-century works in the epic form, is published.

# *Acknowledgments*

The editors wish to thank the copyright holders of the excerpted criticism included in this volume and the permissions managers of many book and magazine publishing companies for assisting us in securing reproduction rights. We are also grateful to the staffs of the Detroit Public Library, the Library of Congress, the University of Detroit Mercy Library, Wayne State University Purdy/Kresge Library Complex, and the University of Michigan Libraries for making their resources available to us. Following is a list of the copyright holders who have granted us permission to reproduce material in this volume of *EfS*. Every effort has been made to trace copyright, but if omissions have been made, please let us know.

**COPYRIGHTED EXCERPTS IN *EFS* WERE REPRODUCED FROM THE FOLLOWING PERIODICALS:**

*Critical Inquiry,* v. 12, Autumn 1985 for ''The Moor in the Text: Metaphor, Emblem and Silence'' by Israel Burshatin. Reproduced by permission of the publisher and the author. *Dante Studies,* Vol. LXXXVII, 1969. Reproduced by permission. *Of Poetry and Politics: New Essays on Milton and His World,* v. 126, 1995. Reproduced by permission. *Studies in Philology,* Vol. LXIX, 1972. Copyright © 1972 by The University of North Carolina Press. Reproduced by permission of the publisher. *The French Review,* v. LIV, April, 1981. Copyright © 1981 by The American Association of Teachers of French. Reproduced by permission of the publisher.

*The New Yorker,* Feb, 1991 for ''Ancestral Rhyme,'' by Brad Leithauser. Copyright © 1991 by Brad Leithauser. Reproduced by permission of the publisher and the author. *World Literature Today,* v. 67, Spring, 1993. Reproduced by permission.

**COPYRIGHTED EXCERPTS IN *EFS* WERE REPRODUCED FROM THE FOLLOWING BOOKS:**

Anderson, William S. From *The Art of the Aeneid.* Prentice-Hall, Inc, 1969. Copyright © 1969 by Prentice-Hall, Inc. All rights reserved. Reproduced by permission of the author.—Biebuyck, Daniel P. From *Heroic Epic and Saga: An Introduction to the World's Great Folk Epics.* Edited by Felix J. Oinas. Indiana University Press, 1978. Copyright © 1978 by Felix J. Oinas. All rights reserved. Reproduced by permission of the Indiana University Press.—Bradley, S. A. J. From *Anglo-Saxon Poetry.* David Campbell Publishers, Ltd. 1982. Copyright © 1982 by David Campbell Publishers, Ltd. All rights reserved. Reproduced by permission.—Clark, George. From *Beowulf.* Twayne Publishers, 1990. Copyright © 1990 by G.K. Hall and Company. All rights reserved. Reproduced by permission.—Duggan, Joseph J. From *A New History of French Literature.* Harvard University Press, 1989. Edited by Denis Hollier. Copyright © 1989 by Harvard University Press. All rights reserved. Reproduced by permission.—Duggan, Joseph J. From *Oral Traditional Litera-*

*ture: A Festschrift for Albert Bates Lord.* Slavica Publishers, 1981. Edited by John Miles Foley. Reproduced by permission of the author.—Gray, Wallace. From *Homer to Joyce.* Macmillan Publishing Company, 1985. Copyright © 1985 by Wallace Gray. All rights reserved. Reproduced by permission of the author. —Griffin, Jasper. From *Homer on Life and Death.* Clarendon Press, 1980. Copyright © 1980 by Jasper Griffin. All rights reserved. Reproduced by permission of the Oxford University Press.—Griffin, Jasper. From *Homer: The Odyssey.* Cambridge University Press, 1987. Reproduced by permission of the publisher and the author.—Hatto, A. T. From *The Nibelungenlied.* Translated by A. T. Hatto. Penguin, 1969. Reproduced by permission.—Hutson, Arthur E. and Patricia McCoy. From *Epics of the Western World.* J. B. Lippencott Company, 1954. Copyright © 1954 by Arthur E. Hutson and Patricia McCoy. Renewed 1982 by Eleanor Hutson. Reproduced by permission of HarperCollins Publishers, Inc.—Jacobson, Thorkild. From *The Treasures of Darkness: A History of Mesopotamian Religion.* Yale University Press, 1976. Copyright © 1976 by Yale University Press. All rights reserved. Reproduced by permission.—Jones, Peter V. From *The Odyssey.* Edited by Homer, translated by E. V. Rieu. Penguin Classics, 1991. Reproduced by permission.—Magoun, Francis Peabody Jr. From *The Kalevala: or Poems of the Kalevala District.* Edited by Elias Lonnrot, translated by Francis Peabody Magoun, Jr. Harvard University Press, 1963. Copyright © 1963 by The President and Fellows of Harvard College. All rights reserved. Reproduced by permission.—Mookerjee, Arun Kumar. From *Hindu Spirituality: Vedas through Vendanta.* Edited by Krishna Sivaraman. Crossroad, 1989. Copyright © 1989 by the Crossroad Publishing Company. All rights reserved. Reproduced by permission.—Oinas, Felix J. From *Heroic Epic and Saga:* An Introduction to the World's Great Folk Epics. Indiana University Press, 1978. Copyright © 1978 by Felix J. Oinas. All rights reserved. Reproduced by permission of the Indiana University Press.—Rexroth, Kenneth. From *Classics Revisited, New Directions.* New Directions Publishing, 1968. Copyright © 1968 by Kenneth Rexroth. All rights reserved. Reproduced by permission of New Directions Publishing Corporation.—van Nooten, B. A. From *Mahabharata.* Edited by William Buck. University of California Press, 1973. Copyright © 1973 by The Regents of the University of California. Reproduced by permission.—Williams, R. D. and T. S. Pattie. From

*Virgil: His Poetry through the Ages.* London, British Library, 1982. Reproduced by permission.

## PHOTOGRAPHS AND ILLUSTRATIONS APPEARING IN *EFS* WERE RECEIVED FROM THE FOLLOWING SOURCES:

A map of Asia Minor in Homer's time, illustration. From *A Short History of Greek Literature,* by Jacqueline de Romilly. Translated by Lillian Doherty. The University of Chicago Press, 1985. Reproduced by permission of the publisher.—Ajax defending the Greek ships against the Trojans, illustration. Archive Photos, Inc. Reproduced by permission.—Beowulf beheads Grendel, illustration. Corbis-Bettmann. Reproduced by permission.—Bhisma on a bed of arrows, illustration by Shirley Triest. From *Mahabharata,* edited by William Buck, introduced by B. A. van Nooten. University of California Press, 1973. Reproduced by permission.—Charlemagne holding orb and scepter, (742-814), Woodcut by Risson and Cottard. Corbis-Bettmann. Reproduced by Permission.—Sundiata's family approaches the city of Mema. King Maghan Kon Fatta. Cut-paper illustrations from *Sundiata*, by David Wisniewski. Copyright © 1992, by David Wiesniewski. Reprinted by permission of Clarion Books/Houghton Mifflin Co. All rights reserved.—Connolly, Peter, illustrator. From an illustration in *Homer's Odyssey* (City of Troy beside the sea). George G. Harrap & Company, 1911.—Dante Alighieri, photograph of illustration. The Bettman Archive. Reproduced by permission.—Dante's Inferno, Canto XXII, illustration, Gustave Dore Corbis-Bettmann. Reproduced by permission.—Dante's Inferno, Dante and Pope Adrian V., illustration, Gustave Dore. Corbis-Bettmann. Reproduced by permission.—Funeral of Hector, illustration. Archive Photos, Inc. Reproduced illustration by Shirley Triest. From *Mahabharata,* edited by William Buck, introduced by B. A. van Nooten. University of California Press, 1973. Reproduced by permission.—Map of Ancient Mesopotamia, illustration. From *Voices From the Clay: The Development of Assyro-Babylonian Literature,* by Silvestro Fiore. Copyright © 1965 by the University of Oklahoma Press.—Map of the voyage of Aeneas, line drawing. *From The Greater Poems of Virgil, Vol. I.* Edited by J. B. Greennough and G. L. Kittredge. Ginn and Company, 1895. Copyright, 1895, by J. B. Greenough and G. L. Kittredge.—Milton, John, photograph of a illustration. International Portrait Gallery. Reproduced by permission.—Patten, Wilson, illustrator. From an illustration in *Homer's Odyssey* (in the underworld).—Siegfried and the dragon, illustrated by Julius Hubner.—The Gods looking at Krsna and Arjuna, illustration by Shirley Triest. From *Mahabharata,* edited by William Buck, introduced by B. A. van Nooten. University of California Press, 1973. Reproduced by permission.— The Underworld Inferno as depicted in Virgil's *Aeneid,* copper engraving, 1655. Corbis-Bettmann. Reproduced by permission.

# Aeneid

## Virgil
## c. 29 B.C.-19 B.C.

When Virgil was dying in 17 BC he asked for the unfinished *Aeneid* to be destroyed. The emperor Augustus refused the request. This decision affected the course of literary history and the development of western culture. Even in his own lifetime Virgil's poetry had become a school text. Early Christian writers who attempted to reject Virgil could escape neither his style nor his attitudes. Christian thought assimilated them both. The *Aeneid* and the Bible were probably the two most consistently read books in Western Europe for two thousand years.

The *Aeneid* was composed at least in part to celebrate "truth, justice, and the Roman way" and to promote the rebirth of the Roman way of life under Augustus. The *Aeneid* also universalises Roman experience, ideals, and aspirations. The *Aeneid* represents a pivotal point in western literature: Virgil drew on the whole of Greek and Latin literature to create this epic. He expanded the range of the Latin epic, using elements from most types of late classical literature, while refining the linguistic and metrical possibilities of the epic genre. Because of its generic inclusiveness and linguistic brilliance, the *Aeneid* spread its influence across every form of written discourse for centuries.

In the last two thousand years the *Aeneid* has been a pagan bible, a Latin style manual, a moral allegory, a document of European unity, a pacifist document—and one of the most-read and studied

works of world literature of all time. Entering its third millennium, the *Aeneid* can still speak immediately to the reader.

## Author Biography

Virgil, full name Publius Vergilius Maro, was born near the village of Andes not far from Mantua in northern Italy on October 15, 70 BC. He died on September 21, 19 BC at Brindisi on the heel of Italy. The earliest biography of the poet, written by Suetonius, in the second century AD, says that he was from a poor and obscure family. It is clear, however, that Virgil was a Roman citizen. Circumstances pieced together from contemporary sources and from Suetonius make it seem likely that his family was at least of the landowning class. Further, Virgil was given an excellent and expensive education, including training for the Roman bar. This suggests that he might have been of the equestrian (middle) class and that his family was ambitious for political and social advancement. In fact he was preparing for the same sort of career which earlier brought Cicero, the great master of Roman oratory and Latin prose, from a country town to the consulship. Virgil gave up legal practice after pleading one case and began to study philosophy with an Epicurean master

Virgil was described by Suetonius as ''tall, raw-boned and dark, always rather countrified in his manners.'' He was sickly and so shy that he was nicknamed ''the maiden.'' At least one modern biographer has suggested that he was invalided home from the army of Brutus and Cassius before the battle of Philippi.

Virgil's family property was confiscated to help settle war veterans. He had friends in high places, however, who intervened with the young ruler Octavian Caesar (later called Augustus) to restore the property. Virgil's *Eclogues,* were written between 42 and 37 BC, partially in gratitude to his friends and the young Octavian. He followed with the *Georgics,* written between 36 and 29 BC, a long poem on farming and the country life. Virgil lived most of his later life near Naples. He became ill on a trip to Greece and returned to Italy only to die there. Suetonius suggests that Virgil was acutely concerned with leaving behind an unrevised *Aeneid.* He asked his friend Varius to burn the work if he died before it was finished. Varius emphatically refused. Augustus, who had heard parts of it read, ordered

its preservation. He delegated Varius and another of Virgil's friends, Tucca, to edit the poem for publication.

Virgil was a painstaking writer. He described his method as ''licking the verses into shape.'' Suetonius records that Virgil wrote out the whole of the *Aeneid* in prose and then worked it up into verse.

## Plot Summary

### Book 1
Aeneas and his Trojans are seven years into their journey home from the Trojan War to Italy when Juno, queen of the gods and arch-enemy of the Trojans, has Aeolus, god of the winds, blow up a violent storm which drives their ships off course. Aeneas, with some of the Trojan fleet, lands in North Africa. Aeneas is a nearly broken man, but he pulls himself together and encourages his people.

The scene switches to the home of the gods on Mount Olympus. Aeneas's mother, the goddess Venus, begs Jupiter, her father and king of the gods, to aid her son. Jupiter replies with serene optimism. He promises the Trojans, through their descendants, not only empire, but a new golden age. Venus departs from Olympus and, disguised as a huntress, meets her son. She sends him to Carthage. There he finds the Trojans who were separated from him in the storm and meets Queen Dido, the founder of the city. Dido takes pity on the Trojans. Meanwhile, Juno and Venus, each for their own purposes, scheme to have Aeneas and Dido fall in love.

### Book 2
At a banquet given in his honor, at Dido's request Aeneas narrates the story of Troy's last day and night. He tells the famous story of the Trojan Horse, left outside the city gates when the Greeks were supposedly departed, but actually filled with Greek warriors. The Trojan priest Laocoon warned ''I fear the Greeks even when bearing gifts.'' When Laocoon and his young sons were crushed by two enormous serpents who came out of the sea, the Trojans took this as a sign from the gods and brought the horse into the city during their celebration of what they thought was the Greek withdrawal. That night the Greek warriors emerge from the horse and open the gates to their returned comrades.

Aeneas is warned by the ghost of his cousin Hector, the greatest of the Trojan warriors (killed by Achilles in the *Iliad* ), who tells him to flee the city. As this section ends, Aeneas watches helplessly as Pyrrhus kills King Priam's youngest son before his father, and King Priam himself in front of his daughters and wife, Queen Hecuba.

Aeneas returns home to persuade his father to leave the city. He carries the crippled Anchises. Ascanius, his son, holds his hand while his wife Creusa and the servants follow. When Aeneas reaches the refugees' meeting point he finds Creusa has been lost in the confusion. He rushes back into Troy frantically looking for her. Finally he is met by her ghost. The ghost tells him that the mother of the gods (Cybele) has taken her under her care.

## Book 3

Aeneas continues the story of the Trojans's wanderings. Slowly Anchises and Aeneas learn more about the promised land of Italy and the future that the gods predict for them there. The book ends with the death of Anchises. Aeneas is left alone with his young son to carry out the will of the gods as best he can.

## Book 4

Aeneas's story is done. Dido, under the influence of Venus, is now hopelessly in love with him. Her sister Anna persuades her to forget her vow of fidelity to her dead and dearly beloved husband, Sychaeus. She loses all interest in governing her city. The ongoing construction of Carthage comes to a halt. Juno and Venus arrange for Dido and Aeneas to have to shelter together overnight in a storm-bound cave. Jupiter sends Mercury, the messenger of the god, to remind Aeneas of his duty to travel on to Italy. Aeneas is miserable, but accepts that he must follow the will of the gods. Dido begs him not to leave her, and ultimately commits suicide as the Trojans set sail, cursing them with her last breath and vowing her people to eternal war with those of Aeneas.

## Book 5

The Trojans land in Sicily and hold commemorative games. Aeneas relaxes briefly, but disaster strikes again. Juno, in disguise, leads the Trojan women to burn the ships. At Aeneas's prayer Jupiter quenches the fire, but four are destroyed. Aeneas is broken by this blow. He wonders whether he should give up trying to reach Italy. The ghost of his father appears. He tells him to continue and to visit him in

the underworld. Leaving behind four boatloads of families who have decided to settle where they are, the remains of the Trojan fleet again sets sail.

## Book 6

At this halfway point in the epic the Trojans reach the promised land of Italy. This book falls into three parts: the preparations for the descent into the land of the dead, a tour of the land of the dead, and the meeting between Aeneas and the ghost of his father Anchises. In the first part, Aeneas seeks out the Sibyl of Cumaea, a priestess-prophetess of Apollo who will be his guide into the underworld. He finds her at Apollo's temple. There she gives him instructions. He must first bury his comrade Misenus who has just died. Then he must find a talisman, the golden bough, to present to Persephone, Queen of the Dead.

In part two, Virgil sends Aeneus through the traditional geography of the underworld. Aeneas and the Sibyl enocunter the three-headed guard dog Cerebrus, the river Styx, the boatman Charon, Tartarus, the abyss of hell for the vilest souls, and finally the fields of Elysium, where he meets the ghost of his father. On the way he meets three recent ghosts: Palinurus, Dido—who refuses to speak to him and pointedly returns to the ghost of her husband—and Deiphobus, his cousin who was killed on the night of Troy's fall. These meetings fill Aeneas with sorrow, guilt, and remorse for what his mission has already cost in human terms.

In part three Aeneas meets Anchises. His father explains to Aeneas how the souls of all but the very evil and the very good are purified of their sins and reincarnated for another chance. Those who have lived lives of exceptional goodness and benefit to humanity are allowed to remain forever in Elysium. Finally he shows Aeneas the souls who will return to the upper world to become the great figures of Roman history. It is for these souls and what they represent that Aeneas has suffered and will continue to suffer.

## Book 7

This book opens peacefully, building to an incident of tragic reversal of fortune. The Trojans are welcomed by King Latinus, who sees their arrival as the fulfilment of a prophecy that foreigners will come to intermarry with the Latins and found a great empire. Latinus promises his daughter Lavinia to Aeneas in marriage. Juno, however, stirs

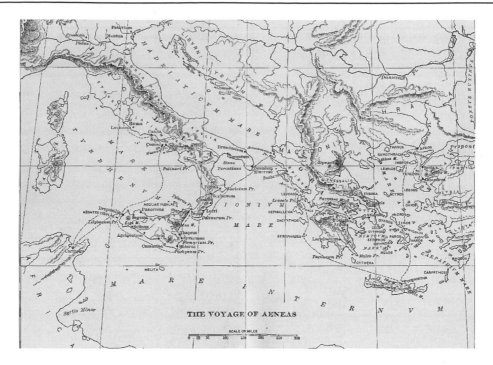

*Map of the voyage of Aeneas.*

up Turnus, a local chieftain and Lavinia's suitor, against the Trojans and the proposed marriage. She also influences Lavinia's mother, Queen Amata, who had favored Turnus for her daughter's hand, to reject her husband's decision. Juno organizes an incident to spark fighting between the men — the accidental killing of a pet deer by Ascanius. Virgil, however, leaves in question how much of the subsequent action is due to Juno's meddling and how much is due to humans giving in to their anger. After war has broken out between the Italians and Trojans, the poet lists the Italian armies opposing the Trojans, in celebration of local traditions and heroes of Italy.

### Book 8

Fighting is at a standstill. Aeneas visits Evander, King of Pallanteum, a little settlement on one of Rome's seven hills. Aeneas is shown the wild landscape where the great civic landmarks of Rome will be. Evander as a teenager had met and admired Aeneas's father, Anchises. He offers Aeneas help, and sends his son, young Pallas, with a band of warriors. The book ends with Venus having new armaments made for her son by her husband, the smith god, Vulcan. Vulcan makes Aeneas a great shield on which are pictured the major events of Roman history with the battle of Actium, where

Augustus defeated the forces of Antony and Cleopatra, in the center.

### Book 9

The war begins in earnest. In Aeneas's absence, Turnus attacks the Trojan camp with great success.

### Book 10

Aeneas and Pallas return to the Trojan camp. Pallas enters the fighting on the Trojan side. Turnus immediately singles him out for single combat. Pallas, promising and courageous, but still hardly more than a boy, is killed. Turnus exults over his death, wishing Evander were there to see the deed. This recalls Neoptolemus killing Priam's youngest son before his father and mother in Book 2. Aeneas goes into a rage when he learns of Pallas's death. He behaves as savagely as Turnus, mowing down all who stand before him, taunting them as they die, deaf to pleas for mercy in a passion of bloodlust. Revulsion finally recalls Aeneas to reason. A young man, Lausus, attempts to defend his father against Aeneas's onslaught. Aeneas kills him, but as he does he realizes that he would have done exactly the same. Full of anguish and regret, Aeneas carries the boy's body to his comrades.

## Book 11

The book begins with Aeneas presiding over the funeral of Pallas. A messenger comes from the opposing Italian forces asking for a truce to bury the dead. Aeneas replies that he wishes for a truce not just for the dead, but for the living. He wants to come to some sort of accommodation with the Italians. The action of the poem is now dominated by Turnus. He debates with his allies, defending his determination to destroy the Trojans. The battle begins again and focuses on the warrior-maid Camilla, one of Turnus's chief allies. When she is killed the Italian allies fall back in retreat.

## Book 12

When Book 12 opens, Turnus welcomes the challenge of settling the whole war in single combat with Aeneas. He rejects the pleas of King Lavinius and Queen Amata and arms himself with eager anticipation. Aeneas promises that if he is defeated he will leave Italy and if he wins he will not seek dominion over the Italians, but the two peoples will be united under the same laws. The Rutilians, Turnus's people, feel it is shameful to commit their fortunes to what they believe is an unequal combat and break the truce. General fighting begins again. Aeneas tries to stop the renewal of hostilities. His attempts are ended when a chance arrow wounds him. The wound is healed by divine intervention, but it enrages him. He rages over the battlefield. Turnus does the same in a different part of the field. The description of the slaughter they make leaves very little difference between them.

Juno, still protecting Turnus, keeps him away from the worst fighting. In his absence the Trojans surround the Latin capital. Queen Amata commits suicide. Turnus becomes aware that his chariot is being driven by his disguised sister, the nymph Juturna, who with Juno's help is keeping him away from real danger. Turnus learns of the queen's suicide and the siege of the city. The single combat between Aeneas and Turnus begins, but is suspended in mid-narrative as the scene switches to Olympus and a confrontation between Juno and Jupiter.

Jupiter forbids Juno to intervene any further against the Trojans. She accepts this order, but she begs Jupiter for three things. She asks that the eventual descendants of intermarried Trojans and Italians be called Latins, that they speak the native language, Latin, and that they wear the native Latin dress, the toga. Jupiter grants this and more, promising that not only the Latin mode of dress but the whole way of life will be derived from the native

Italians. Juno, then, is described is being responsible for the particular character of the Romans, and the audience understands at last that this is the reason for all the horror and bloodshed she caused.

The narrative returns to the combat between Aeneas and Turnus. Aeneas wounds Turnus and he begs for mercy. Aeneas is about to spare him when he notices that Turnus wears the best of his victim Palla. Overwhelmed by a rage for vengeance, Aeneas kills Turnus.

## Characters

### Adromache

Widow of Hector, given as a prize of war to Pyrrhus, the son of Achilles. She later marries Helenus. In a twist of fate, they come to reign over part of Pyrrhus's kingdom after Pyrrhus is killed by Orestes, son of Agamemnon. She never forgets either her adored Hector, or their little boy Astyanax, whom the victorious Greek threw from the walls of Troy for fear he would grow up and avenge his father.

### Aeneas

Prince of Troy and chief protagonist of this work. There are as many readings of his character as there are readers of *The Aeneid.* Virgil's narrative repeatedly puts Aeneas into situations in which he finds his duty to the gods and to the future in conflict with his own personal desires, freedom, and autonomy—when he wants to stay with Dido, Queen of Carthage, for example, and the god Jupiter sends a messenger reminding him that it is his destiny to leave and lead his people on to Italy.

Aeneas often seems to be confused about what he should do. He sometimes makes choices that seem clearly wrong to many readers. The classic epic pattern generally shows its protagonist becoming a true hero by learning through experience the importance of wisdom, tolerance, compromise, and justice. While Aeneus shows these qualities intermittently, some interpretations of *The Aeneid* indicate that at the end all his painfully acquired knowledge is thrown away in an act of bloody and violent revenge when he slays Turnus in a rage.

### Aeolus

The god of the winds. He is indebted to Juno for his role among the gods, and at Juno's request

# Media Adaptations

- For centuries the *Aeneid* was an enormously popular source of ideas for other writers and artists. The first medieval romance was an adaptation of the *Aeneid*. Hundreds or thousands of paintings have been based on scenes and episodes from the poem. The *Aeneid* was the basis for many operas; the two most famous being Purcell's *Dido and Aeneas* and Berlioz's *Les Troyens.*

- The *Aeneid* provides a story outline and a collection of characters and incidents that have become an integral part of popular culture. We see the dilemma of Aeneas and Dido recreated over and over in novels, movies, and on television. In novels and movies of the American westward expansion and in such "revenge" films as Sam Peckinpah's *Straw Dogs* and the "Deathwish" series starring Charles Bronson, audiences see a quiet hero roused to action when someone young

and vulnerable is killed, much as Aeneas is at the end of the Virgil's epic.

- The early television series *Wagon Train* has been compared to the *Aeneid*, with its similar small band of people leaving behind one way of life and traveling in search of a place where they can make another. It has been suggested by recent scholars that the television series *Star Trek*—which has been called "*Wagon Train* to the stars," also closely resembles Virgil's basic plot. Captain Kirk recreated the Aeneas and Dido episode regularly, for example, romancing and ultimately abandoning a lovestruck woman (or alien) on every planet.

- In the spring of 1997, NBC television presented a 2-part miniseries based on Homer's *Odyssey*, an important primary source for Virgil's *Aeneid*.

---

causes the storm that drives Aeneas's fleet onto the coast of North Africa in Book I.

### Amata

Lavinius's wife. The goddess Juno encourages her to think of Aeneas and the newly-arrived Trojans as dangerous interlopers on Italian soil. She opposes the proposed match between Aeneas and her daughter Lavinia.

### Anchises

A prince of Troy, Aeneas's father and Priam's second cousin. Aeneas is the son of a union between Anchises and the goddess Venus. One tradition holds that Jupiter crippled Anchises with a thunderbolt when he boasted of being Venus's lover.

### Anna

Dido's sister. She persuades Dido that an alliance with Aeneas is in her own best interests as well as those of her city, Carthage.

### Ascanius

The son of Aeneas and Creusa. The Roman tribe (extended family) of Julius claims him as an ancestor. He is the founder of Alba. His boyish joke in Book VII about the Trojans eating their tables together with their food recalls Anchises's prophecy that his people would find their foretold home in Italy only when they were reduced to eating their tables.

### Cacus

The monstrous son of the smith god Vulcan, he terrorizes the kingdom of Evander from a cave on the Aventine hill. He is killed by Hercules.

### Camilla

A warrior maiden, Camilla is the child of an exiled tyrant, Metabus. Her father pledged her life in service to Diana, goddess of the hunt. The goddess Diana protected Camilla when Metabus bound her to his spear and threw her across a river as he fled from pursuers. She is an ally of Turnus. Her death in battle is a severe blow to the Italian cause.

## Cerberus

The three-headed watchdog of the underworld. When the Sibyl escorts Aeneas through the underworld, she throws the dog a drugged honey-cake so that they can pass him safely while he sleeps.

## Charon

The ferryman of the dead. Souls of the dead must cross the River Styx to enter the underworld. If they have been properly buried, with coins on their eyes to pay him, Charon will ferry them across the river.

## Creusa

The first wife of Aeneas, she is killed when Troy falls to the Greeks.

## Deiphobe

*See* Sibyl

## Dido

Phoenician princess who flees with many of her people from the tyranny of her ruling brother. She founds the city of Carthage and is a capable ruler until, under the influence of the love-goddess Venus, she falls in love with Aeneas. When Aeneas deserts her to continue his journey to Italy on the orders of Jupiter, she kills herself, cursing Aeneas and the nation he will found. Her disintegration from a strong, virtuous, and capable woman and ruler to a distraught, love-sick suicide is based in her character, circumstances, and the interference of the gods in her life.

## Evander

King of Pallanteum, a small city on one of Rome's seven hills. When he was a teenage prince of Arcadia in Greece, he met Aeneas's father Anchises and was deeply impressed by him. His Arcadians are at constant war with the Latins, but they enjoy good relations with the Etruscans. Evander brings the Etruscans into the war on Aeneas's side partly out of respect for the memory of Aeneas's father.

## Ganymede

Trojan prince whom Jupiter abducts to be the cup-bearer of the gods.

## Hector

The greatest of Priam's son, a loving husband and father, generous and conscientious, a great warrior who does not glory in war, he is the bulwark of the Trojans until he is killed by Achilles. Aeneas in many ways takes on some of his dead cousin's attributes as well as his position of leadership among the Trojan refugees.

## Hecuba

The queen of Troy, wife of King Priam, she is forced into slavery after the city of Troy falls to the Greeks and she has witnessed the deaths of her husband and son.

## Helenus

Son of Priam, he is enslaved by Pyrrhus after the Trojan war. When Pyrrhus is killed by Orestes, son of Agamemnon, Helenus comes into possession of part of his kingdom. He and his wife Adromanche recreate the city of Troy on a small scale. Helenus is a prophet who assures Aeneas that he will eventually reach Italy and make a home there.

## Hercules

A great hero, the son of Jupiter and a mortal woman named Alcmena. He is known for his great feats of strength and bravery. He rescues the people of Evander from the monster Cacus.

## Iulus

*See* Ascanius

## Juno

Queen of the gods, both wife and sister of Jupiter. She is the patroness of married women and of the cities of Argos and Carthage. Juno sided with the Greeks in the Trojan Wars because she was offended when the Trojan warrior Paris pronounced Venus rather than Juno the most beautiful of the goddesses.

## Jupiter

"Father of gods and men," Jupiter is the king of the gods and the most powerful among them. He is bound only by his own word and by fate.

## Juturna

Turnus's sister, the spirit of springs. She is given immortality by her lover Jupiter.

## Lausus

A young Italian killed by Aeneas as he defends his father, the tyrant Mezentius. Aeneas regrets this killing immediately, realizing that he would have defended his own father Anchises with the same valor. When Aeneas carries the boy's body to his companions, this act of compassion leads to a temporary truce between the warring Trojans and Italians.

## Lavinia

She is the only child of Lavinius and Amata of Italy. Queen Amata hoped that Lavinia would marry Turnus, but the gods send signs that show she is fated to marry Aeneas, thus founding the Roman line.

## Lavinius

King of the Italians, he welcomes Aeneas and the Trojans. He offers his daughter Lavinia to Aeneas in marriage because he believes that it is the will of the gods.

## Mezentius

An Etruscan king, whom Virgil calls a ''scorner of the Gods.'' He rules Argylla until his incredible cruelty causes his people to drive him from the city. Turnus shelters him. The Etruscans join Aeneas, urged by Evander, in order to be revenged on Mezentius.

## Misenus

Aeneas's trumpeter, killed when he challenges Triton's pre-eminence on the trumpet. Aeneas must bury him and ritually purify the fleet before he can descend to the underworld.

## Neoptolemus

*See* Pyrrhus

## Neptune

God of the sea, he favors the Trojans in their attempt to reach Italy. He is annoyed when he finds that Juno and Aeolus caused the storm at sea that shipwrecks Aeneas's fleet on the African coast without consulting him.

## Palinurus

Aeneas's helmsman. He is washed overboard just as the Trojan fleet reaches Italy and is murdered when he reaches the shore. His death is described by Neptune in Book 5 as a sacrifice to guarantee the safe landing of the rest of the Trojans: ''One shall be given for the many.'' His shade (spirit or ghost) meets Aeneas in the underworld and begs for his help is crossing the River Styx—he was not properly buried and does not have money to pay the boatman Charon. The Sibyl who is guiding Aeneas through the underworld promises that the people who killed Palinurus will come to understand their error and will bury him with the necessary honors—and coins—to ensure his passage across the river.

## Pallas

Evander's son, a young man on his first real battle campaign. Aeneas is drawn to the father and son, and acts as a mentor and protector of Pallas. When Pallas is killed in the climactic battle between the Trojans and Italians, Aeneas goes wild with grief. He had been about to spare Turnus's life, but when he is reminded that Turnus killed Pallas, he in turn butchers Turnus savagely.

## Paris

A prince of Troy, son of King Priam and Queen Hecuba of Troy. At his birth it was prophesied that he would someday cause the destruction of Troy, so his parents sorrowfully abandon him as an infant to die on Mt. Ida. He is found and raised by a shepherd. Paris grows to be an exceptionally handsome young man, and the goddess Venus offers him his choice from among the most beautiful woman in the world. He selects Helen, unfortunately already married to Menelaeus of Greece, and abducts her. Helen's former suitors, who include all the major warriors of Greece, had sworn an oath to her husband to always protect their beloved lady. The Trojan War begins when Greek troops attack Troy to recover Helen.

## Persephone

Pluto's wife, queen of the underworld and of the dead.

## Pluto

The king of the underworld and of the dead. Pluto is the brother of Jupiter and Neptune.

## Polydorus

A son of Priam who is sent abroad to be raised in the court of the king of Thrace. When Troy falls, the king of Thrace kills him for his treasure. His ghost appears to Aeneas when the Trojans stumble upon his burial mound.

## Priam

King of Troy. He dies at Pyrrhus's hands while defending his family on the night Troy falls to the Greeks.

## Pyrrhus

Son of the famous Greek warrior Achilles, the hero of the *Iliad*. During the fall of Troy, Pyrrhus kills Priam's son Polites and then Priam himself with great cruelty in the presence of Queen Hecuba and her daughters. Adromanche, widow of Hector, is forced to become his mistress. When he is killed by Orestes, part of his kingdom comes into the hands of his slave, Helenus, a brother of Hector.

## Sibyl

The sibyls were priestesses and prophetesses of Apollo. Aeneas visits the Sibyl of Cumaea in southern Italy before his trip to the underworld .

## Sychaeus

Dido's first husband, murdered by her brother.

## Turnus

Prince of the Rutulians, a brilliant young warrior deeply conscious of his honor and standing. The Sibyl compares him to Achilles. He is a descendant of the royal house of Argos and is a favorite of the goddess Juno. Turnus seems to find war his most natural and satisfying occupation.

## Venus

The goddess of love and of beauty. In the *Aeneid*, she is also the mother of the Roman people. It is her son, Aeneas, who leads his Trojan fleet to Italy, where he intermarries with the Italian princess Lavinia, thus beginning the Roman ancestral line. Venus is a devoted mother in the distant way that many of the gods who have children with mortals remain somewhat involved in the lives of their offspring.

# Themes

In the *Aeneid* Aeneas travels from his lost home in the destroyed Troy to the land of Italy where the gods have promised him a new home for his people and a future empire. During his travels he encounters much danger. He must learn to think and act less for himself than for his people and their destiny.

## Roman History

The *Aeneid* quickly achieved a pre-eminent position in Latin literature and eventually in world literature and culture. Thanks to the *Aeneid's* enormous popularity and its immediate adoption as a school text, it became the standard for the epic in Western Europe. The work of Virgil's predecessors was almost completely lost. For these reasons it is difficult to properly appreciate Virgil's originality. The early Roman epics of Naevius and Ennius were essentially history, at times current events, written in the epic form. Virgil's *Aeneid* is equally concerned with Roman history, but handles it in a radically different way.

To handle both the flaws and the real, if frustrated, virtues and promise of the Roman way, Virgil used a legend for the main line of narrative in the *Aeneid*. History was relegated to digressions. In the *Aeneid,* legend was treated like real life, history was insinuated into prophecy, visions and into the descriptions of objects (ecphrasis). This means that the main narrative can be understood both as explicating the ancient source of the Roman way of life and as a commentary on the present as Virgil experienced it. The protagonist Aeneas both is and is not equated with the ruler Augustus (who may have commissioned or requested the work).

Virgil connects ancient legendry with his modern reality. Aeneas's legendary struggles are paradoxically the reality from which the Roman people, their history, and their institutions came. Aeneas and his history forge the Roman character for better and worse. In the *Aeneid,* all the dangers and all the glories of the Roman way of life resonate from their origins through the nation's whole history into Virgil's present.

## Right Conduct, the Roman Way of Life, and Roman Destiny

The moral center of the *Aeneid* is the Roman way of life which Augustus was attempting to revitalize in Virgil's own time. This system was ideally based on duty to the gods, to country, and to family and friends. It was powered by a deep sense of humanity. Virgil is aware of the social cohesion, order, even the personal happiness, which this ideal could produce. He is equally aware of the sorrows and cruelties which could result from the clash of these duties. Private experience and duty are often placed in tension against public duty. This tension is at the heart of the parting of Dido and Aeneas. On a historical level, Virgil expresses this tension with an allusion in to Brutus, the first consul, who drove the

# Topics for Further Study

- The Etruscans, who join Aeneas as allies, also claimed to have come from Asia Minor. Research the Etruscans and the ways in which they influenced the essential character of Roman society.

- Can the wanderings of Aeneas and his Trojans be found to have any basis in fact? There are strong archaeological indications that many established kingdoms were in fact destroyed around the traditional date of the fall of Troy (circa 1193). Research this period and try to determine if there is any archaeological evidence for the legends of the Trojan refugees.

- Virgil locates the origins of Rome and Carthage's long period of warfare in the goddess Juno's spiteful actions and Queen Dido's broken heart and suicide when Aeneas leaves her. Compare and contrast Virgil's imaginative account with the more concrete historical reasons behind the three Punic wars between Rome and Carthage.

- Define the concept of a "hero" from your own point of view. Give historical or contemporary examples if they help explain your concept. Compare your idea of what it takes to be a hero with some traditional literary, legendary, or mythic considerations of what a hero must be, think, or do (handbooks of literary terms will supply some definitions). Discuss ways that Aeneas either lives up to or falls short of both your idea of a hero and the traditional view of one.

- Virgil used plot elements and even characters from the earlier *Odyssey* and *Iliad* of the Greek poet Homer. Different generations of readers and critics have responded differently to this "borrowing." Discuss it from your own point of view. Are the events both wrote about large enough to support more than one literary retelling? Cite examples of this kind of "recycling" of themes and subjects from your own time.

---

tyrant king Tarquin out of Rome and ordered his own sons executed for attempting to reinstate Tarquin. These tensions are foregrounded throughout the poem. Nevertheless, it remains clear that Virgil believes that the ideals of Roman life and public service remain worth the often difficult struggle with self. In Book I the god Jupiter summarizes what the Roman way of life could and would give not only Rome, but all of humanity, a world-rule which brings universal peace and humane civilization. This world is not expressed in political terms, but ethical ones. It is available to all who follow the Roman way. Without this and similar prophecies the suffering of Aeneas, Dido, Creusa, Palinurus, Pallas and others are nearly unbearable. Aeneas must be brought to understand the promise which is given through him. The pageant of Roman history in Book 6 and the pictures on his shield illustrate the moral qualities of the Roman way of life. Nevertheless, Virgil often undercuts this glorious possibility:

in the lament for Marcellus in Book 6, for example, and in the end of the poem itself when Aeneas abandons his highest principles in grief for Pallas and kills Turnus, to whom he had considered granting mercy.

## *The Sorrows at the Heart of Things*

The theme which dictates the tone of the *Aeneid* for modern readers is that of human loss and regret. The theme can be defined by two remarks in Book 1. In line 203 Aeneas says, "Perhaps even this will be something to remember with joy." In the most quoted passage of of the *Aeneid,* Aeneas exclaims, "Here are tears for things and human mortality touches the heart." The first passage, however, is set in the context of promised destiny of Aeneas and his followers in lines 204-7: "Through many circumstances and various troubles we travel towards Italy where the fates point out a place of rest. There it is decreed for Troy to rise again. Endure and keep yourself for prosperity!'' In the second passage the tears and thoughts of which Aeneas is conscious are themselves a reflex of fame. ''What region is not full of our distress? Here,'' he says in lines 460-1, '' is the reward of praise.'' The sorrows of the individual heart caught in conflicting duties are seen in the setting of a divinely granted destiny and the immortality of fame.

### Private and Public Ideals

There is a strong sense of tension between Virgil's two ideals of individual human felicity and the mission of Rome. This has sometime been characterized as the tension in Virgil's own ethical ideals between Stoic and Epicurean philosophy. Stoicism was a philosophy of self-sacrificing public service, of a heart unmoved yet rationally compassionate. Epicureanism was a form of philosophical quietism, a retreat from the world. It was not a search for sensual pleasure, as is sometimes suggested, but for an absence of pain. The tension in the poem, however, is more complex. There is a tension between individual happiness and public mission. There is a frightening tension between the ideal and its fulfilment. Roman history was not a litany of broken loves, abandoned friends, and rage. Conjugal love, friendly fidelity, justice, and magnanimity towards the stranger were, for the Roman, what characterized the essence Roman way of life. The Romans never deluded themselves about the difficulty of this life of family and commonwealth. Aeneas is on one level the symbol of the difficulties which beset even an essentially decent man in maintaining the humanity which was necessary if Rome was going to be the great civilizing force the gods intended rather than simply another great power in a long line of great powers.

## Style

### Point of View

The particular literary character of the *Aeneid* derives from its double point of view. The personal vision, from Aeneas's point of view, emphasizes the human element in the story. The patriotic vision, concerned with both human and divine events combining to form the genesis of the Roman empire, is concerned with presenting a mythic and idealized view of Roman history. The tension between these two approaches creates a sense of breadth which affects both the work at hand and, because of its

*The underworld as depicted in the ''Aeneid.''*

importance to world culture, the development of western literary expectations.

### Setting

The action of the *Aeneid* ranges across the entire Mediterranean region. The most important geographic site is, of course, Italy—the final destination of the wandering Trojans. Virgil includes elements of the history, culture, and legends of many Mediterranean countries, however, so that even though this epic is about the founding of what became the Roman empire in Italy, the work is not narrowly nationalistic in focus.

### Imitation

Virgil drew heavily on Homer's *Iliad* and *Odyssey* in composing his own epic. Almost the whole of the first book is constructed from the *Odyssey*. The storm, the despair of Aeneas, the landing on a strange shore, the meeting with a disguised goddess, the reception by the ruler of the foreign land, the banquet, the minstrel's song leading up to the hero's narration of his adventures—all these elements are patterned on events in *Odyssey*. The two works share both similarities and differences. In the *Odyssey,* Odysseus is trying to return home from the

Trojan war to reunite with his wife and to take up his old and much-missed way of life. He succeeds, as his followers do not, by showing great resources and endurance. He is the ultimate individualist. Aeneas, however, is fleeing his home after the city's destruction in that same war. He loses wife, family, and home, and starts out to find the place ordained by the gods to build a new life and found a new empire. His first duty is to bring his people to that haven. Underscoring the connection between the two works, Virgil even has Aeneas rescue one of Odysseus's men on his way. Virgil's original audience knew Homer's narratives very well. They had their memories of and opinions about the Greek poet's earlier work to supplement their understanding and enjoyment—or criticism—of the *Aeneid*. This practice of building on an established tradition still takes place in popular entertainment today: modern audiences, for example, will watch a movie sequel or a televison show featuring a ''crossover'' guest performer from another series partly because they already know what to expect and enjoy seeing the familiar in a new setting.

### *Divine Intervention*

The gods have a number of roles in the *Aeneid*. Jupiter represents the providential divine intention for the human characters, while his wife Juno represents the seemingly irrational hostile forces that stand between the characters and their goals. Venus represents the divine nurturing of the Roman people and state. Sometimes gods are the direct motivation behind actions, and they are seen to always have some influence on events, which never unfold purely by coincidence or chance. Whether Virgil's audience actually believed in them or not, the gods were a tremendously powerful artistic symbol. The entire body of Greek and Roman art and literature is infused with demonstrations and explanations of the role of the gods in the affairs of humankind. This shared cultural referent was reinforced by a nostalgic affection among Virgil's audience for the ancient faith of their ancestors, with its overtones of rural simplicity and straightforward vigor.

### *Imagery*

Virgil's imagery in the *Aeneid* derives power from the repetition and sometimes startling variation of particular images through one or more books. Virgil exploits the repetition of imagery to constantly recall past events from the narrative. In the present, the past is being repeated or the future foreshadowed. The use of serpent and fire imagery in Book 2 provides an excellent demonstration of this facet of Virgil's technique

### *Structure*

The structure of the *Aeneid* has interested a number of critics in the twentieth century. It has been suggested that the poem is divided between books of intense action (even numbered books) and diffuse action (odd numbered books). In this view Books 3 and 5 function partly to release the tension of Books 2 and 4. The *Aeneid* has been described as a trilogy, with the tragedy of Dido, told in Books 1-4, and that of Turnus, in Books 9-12, flanking a central Roman section in Books 5-8. Another way of looking at the structure of the *Aeneid* suggests that the first six books are patterned after Homer's *Iliad* and the second six resemble his *Odyssey*.

### *Diction, Rhetoric, and Meter*

Virgil's word choices and meter have been constantly studied and copied for nearly two thousand years. It is hard to understand this aspect of the *Aeneid* without having also studied Latin, but it is possible to make a few basic generalizations.

Quantity is the time it takes to pronounce a syllable. In Latin, a long syllable takes twice as long to pronounce as a short one. The *Aeneid* is written in quantitative hexameters; that is: each line has six metrical feet. These feet are a combination of short and long syllables. A hexameter line is made up of dactyls—one long syllable followed by two short syllables (the name '' Ludwig van Beethoven'' is an English double dactyl, for example) and of spondees—two long syllables (''blackboard'' is an English spondee). This may sound restrictive, but within this relatively narrow rhetorical structure the *Aeneid* displays great variety. Lines can be jagged and abrupt. They can flow with a lulling smoothness of sound.

Virgil often uses commonplace words in fresh ways. Sometimes he deliberately used outdated terms that would attract attention because of their quaintness. Virgil chose and combined words which enlarge the reader's range of perception. His essential tool is variation within a symmetrical pattern, even within individual lines. Adam Parry, in his essay ''The Two Voices of Virgil'' (see Bibliography) demonstrates some of the effects that occur in less than two lines with an example from Book 7: ''For you Angitia's woods wept, For you Fucinus's glassy waters, For you the transparent lake.'' Here he has used repetition (of the phrase ''for you,'') personification (the weeping of the woods and the lake), and levels of variation (first: woods, then water; second, water, mentioned first by proper name ("Fucinus's glassy waters") and then by the common noun "lake".

## Historical Context

### *Roman Government*

Rome was founded in 753 BC. For nearly 250 years it was a monarchy. The last king was a tyrant whose son Tarquin raped the wife of a Roman noble. (One of the most famous accounts of this is found in the long narrative poem "The Rape of Lucrece" by William Shakespeare.) Outraged by this crime, the Romans, lead by L. Junius Brutus (an ancestor of the Brutus who assassinated Julius Caesar), drove the Tarquin family out and set up a republic. For the next 450 years Rome was ruled by the senate and consuls. The senate, chosen from the highest class of citizens (patricians) decided on government policies and the use of public money. The equites (middle class) and plebians (working class) had their own assembly which could accept or reject the proposals of the senate. After 287 B.C., Senate proposals had the force of law. The executive posts in the government from the consuls down were elected by the vote of all male citizens. The consuls were elected in pairs for one year only to protect against the rise of another tyrant. Later they were joined by the tribune of the people, who looked after the interests of the equite and plebian classes. Even after Rome entered a period of imperial rule (ruled by emperors), some forms of republicanism were maintained.

### *Rome and War*

Roman history during the Republic is full of wars. Some of these wars were fought simply for survival. Many, however, were wars of expansion. Military achievements were important to all levels of Roman society. Upper-class men who hoped for political careers needed to demonstrate personal courage and organizational ability in the ultimate test of war. Men of the lower classes could improve their place in society with a reputation for courage, loyalty, and intelligent obedience in warfare.

Of all the wars Rome fought, few were as important as the three Punic wars against Carthage, the city founded by Dido. These wars saw Rome's greatest triumphs as well as greatest defeats. Even when Italy itself was invaded by the Carthaginian general in 218 BC, the Romans refused to capitulate. After over a century of warfare, Roman forces eventually destroyed Carthage. Virgil constantly alludes to these ongonig wars in his narrative. Roman commentators believed that Dido's death scene in Book 4 was full of references to the Punic wars.

### *Roman Society under Pressure*

At the end of the Punic Wars Rome was the major power in the Mediterranean. The Romans themselves believed that as long as Carthage had remained a threat, Rome was strong because of the need to stay united in the face of this powerful enemy. Social problems were quickly dealt with so that the city could focus its attentions on opposing the Carthaginian threat. When this single-minded focus was removed, Rome began to fall apart.

Originally, most Roman citizens had at least a small farm that could generally support a family. The wars devastated these family holdings. Many men were away for long periods of fighting. Many never returned. It was difficult for the women and children left behind to do heavy farm work. Further, many Romans had to flee the countryside and band together in the safety of the cities when Hannibal invaded Italy. Further, international trade sprang up in the peace that followed the Punic Wars, and many small family farms could not compete with a flourishing trade in agriculture. Returning Italian soldiers, as well as the wealthy Roman senators, were able to buy up failed farmland cheaply and to amass huge estates. Instead of planting grain, they chose to raise sheep, grapes, or olives, all of which needed fewer farmhands. The collapse of traditional Roman agrarian (or agricultural) society and the enlargement of the empire made it more and more difficult for the government to function effectively. Civil disturbances between various factions grew worse and worse. By the time Julius Caesar assumed personal control with the grudging acceptance of the senate after a bloody civil war, Roman society needed drastic action.

### *Renewal under Augustus*

Julius Caesar's assassination threw Rome and her empire back into civil war, which continued until Caesar Augustus's defeat of Antony and

# Compare & Contrast

- **Legendary Period:** Aeneas and the Trojans are only one of the many peoples who legend records as being driven from their homes in this period. Men, women, and children, bringing with them only the possessions they can carry, search desperately for some haven where they can restart their lives. They often meet with serious resistance from the inhabitants of places where they come ashore.

  **Late twentieth century:** Recent history is full of instances of people being driven from their homes by war. Often reduced to poverty, few find their integration into other societies easy or even peaceful.

- **First century BC:** There is enormous interest in poetry among the literate. The Roman tradition of patronage and the lack of copyright law means that poets are almost always subsidised by wealthy and politically powerful men. Even under the patronage system, some exceptional poets, such as Virgil and Horace, can have both financial independence and comparative artistic freedom to create their works.

  **Late twentieth century:** Poetry is no longer a common medium for conveying history, ideas, or elements of a shared cultural experience. Most poets depend on university appointments or grants from various cultural bodies. Others hold down full-time jobs to support their writing.

- **Legendary Period:** All free men are soldiers when the need arises. Political leaders are expected to take part in the fighting to prove that they are worthy to lead in both war- and peacetime.

  **Late twentieth century:** The armies of most industrialized nations are professional. Politicians are no longer expected to necessarily have served in the military—although this is still a recommendation to some voters. The military's highest leaders and officers are not expected to take part in actual combat.

---

Cleopatra at Actium in 31 BC. Augustus attempted to revitalize the traditional Roman way of life and recruited poets to help. Virgil was commissioned to write in part to remind the Romans of the circumstances which created them and their society and the part of the gods in it. He defined their sense of having been chosen and lead by a divine wisdom. It has been suggested that Virgil knew Jews living in Rome and that his view of history was affected by their own sense of mission as ''chosen people'' with a specific preordained destiny.

## The Roman Way of Life

The Roman way of life, the *mos maiorem* (''manners of the ancestors'') had both a religious and a social aspect. Roman religion was based on two sets of gods. There were the Olympian gods, of whom Juno, Jupiter, Venus, Neptune, Vulcan, Diana and Pluto play a role in the *Aeneid*. The *Lares* and the *Penates,* or ''household gods,'' were the protective spirits of the family, the hearth (emblematic of the center of the household), the storeroom, and the countryside. Each family had its own personal household gods. Like the brownies or elves of fairy tales, but much more powerful, the household gods watch over each family. In the *Aeneid,* Aeneas's father is described carefully carrying his family's household gods away from the destroyed city of Troy. Traditional Roman families prayed to their *Lares* and the *Penates* every day.

Roman society was based on family and friends bound by mutual ties of respect and aid, and on the patronage system. Patronage may seem strange or even distasteful to a twentieth-century sensibility. To the Romans, it was perfectly honorable and practical way of life. A patron stood by his clients, ensured that they always received justice under Roman law, offered advice, and helped their careers. Clients of a patron in turn would support and advise him and live up to the recommendations he had given them. This pattern of give and take was expected at all levels of society. Aeneas and Misenus can be seen as an example of a patron and a client. Letters of recommendation from Roman patrons promote their clients as personal assistants, political candidates, even as potential sons-in-law. These young men would be expected to live up to their patron's recommendations. Prominent and powerful men expected to be asked to serve as mentors to promising young men, just as had been done for them in their youth. This practice connected families in a web of mutual responsibility and gratitude. A man might be asked to help the career of the nephew or son of a man who had done the same for him or his father years before. The connections down the generations among Anchises, Evander, Aeneas, and Pallas in the *Aeneid* offer examples of these kinds of continuing relationships. Further, the emperor Caesar Augustus functioned as a patron of the poet Virgil himself. Virgil's great epic is a preeminent example of a kind of work-for-hire that served the purposes of his patron while enabling the poet to advance his own career. The system was clearly open to misuse, but it served Roman society and administration well for nearly a millennium.

# Critical Overview

Virgil's earliest critics concentrated on discussing the style in which he wrote and the sources from which he drew his material. The *Aeneid* was written for a cultured and educated, extremely well-read audience, and almost immediately became a school text. Many Roman critics wrote treatises explaining the book's historical, religious, philosophical, and literary allusions to make it easier for teachers and students alike to understand. Others wrote explanations of difficult words or unusual grammar. In the fourth century, a teacher named Donatus published excerpts from many of these works to produce a kind of general reader's guide. A generation later, another teacher, Servius, relying in part on Donatus, produced a similar commentary for schools.

Macrobius's *Saturnalia* written in the first half of the fifth century, treated Virgil as a Roman bible. Macrobius depicted actual historical figures, including Servius, discussing the *Aeneid*. These figures were members of the last generation of educated Roman pagans, attempting to defend their gods, their way of life, the very nature of Rome, from the growing cult of Christianity.

Early Christian reaction to Virgil was mixed. On one hand, he was the poet of the Roman state and religion, which Christianity sought to usurp. On the other hand, his work was an essential part of a complete education, and he was widely considered the finest poet writing in Latin. Christian poets like Prudentius used Virgil as a model. Saint Augustine of Hippo admitted crying over Dido's tragic end when he read the *Aeneid* as a schoolboy. In the end, western Christianity simply co-opted Virgil. In his Fourth *Eclogue* Virgil had written about the birth of a wonderful child who would end war and bring back the golden age. For this, Virgil was popularly (if not officially) accepted as a prophet of Christ.

During the early middle ages, the *Aeneid* was used as a schoolbook for the study of Latin. Servius's commentary, with or without extra material from Donatus, was reprinted many times. In the late fifth or early sixth century, a Christian wrote a short treatise in the form of a rather humorous vision of Virgil in which the poet explained the *Aeneid* as an allegory—an extended narrative metaphor— about the soul's growth to maturity and virtue. From the late eleventh century on, Virgil's reputation for enormous learning, a few allegorical passages in Servius, and the popularity of allegory as a literary form changed the way people read the *Aeneid*. It was often treated as a sort of coded message, full of deep, hidden meanings. This approach was popular until the time of Shakespeare. It had a big impact on how other epic works were written. Writers like Torquato Tasso or Edmund Spenser wrote epics according to this allegorical model, with the action and even characters all serving as metaphors or symbols for something else. Throughout all the changes in literary and critical fashion, the *Aeneid* remained popular simply as a story. The earliest French romance was not about Lancelot and Guinevier, but Aeneas and Lavinia.

Modern criticism of the *Aeneid* began in the seventeenth century. Late seventeenth- and early eighteenth-century French and English critics began to interpret the *Aeneid* not as an allegory, but as a narrative which conveyed meaning in the same way as history. The narrative provided models of the highest qualities of conduct for both princes and their subjects. In the dedication to his translation, the poet John Dryden stressed these elements, which appealed to the readers of his time, who were looking for royal leadership into an era of national renewal.

Proponents of literary Romanticism in the late eighteenth- and early nineteenth centuries reacted against the classicism of the 1600s and 1700s, when Greek and Latin texts from Virgil's era were highly praised and imitated. The Romantics found Aeneas a poor hero and were not impressed with Roman destiny as a theme. When they praised Virgil at all, they did so for his style or for the same emotional sensitivities they admired in their own poetry. This approach lead readers to examine what critics have come to call Virgil's ''private voice.'' For much of the nineteenth century, Romantic critics and commentators focused on examining Virgil's treatment of individual human beings caught up in the larger issues of Rome's destiny.

In the twentieth century, criticism of the *Aeneid* has become increasingly more sophisticated in its understanding of the literary, social, and political realities of Virgil's world. Modern critics still reflect as much of their own world as of Virgil's. Two world wars and the end of colonialism have affected reader responses to the events depicted in the work. A critical arena which has shown great development is the continuing study of readers' changing attitudes about Virgil over the centuries. Kenneth Quinn's observation that Virgil ''is rarely completely for a character or completely against the character opposing him'' is one of the most important ideas that any reader can bring to the *Aeneid.*

## Criticism

### Helen Conrad-O'Briain

*In the following essay, Conrad-O'Briain offers a general assessment and an overview of the* Aeneid.

It is impossible to imagine western literature without Virgil's *Aeneid.* Outside of the Bible, perhaps no other book has had more direct effect on our writing and thinking. For four hundred years the *Aeneid* had the place in Latin education that could be compared to the King James Bible and the works of Shakespeare in English. Virgil's language, presentation, the things he found important, even the

things over which he simply lingered, sank deep into the heart of Latin literature. The *Aeneid* became a part of the Christian tradition. Even in the so-called Dark Ages in European history students were exposed to Virgil. Education in Europe and later the Americas meant: Virgil.

Whenever writing about the *Aeneid,* a critic is writing about ideas and forms which have application for all areas of western literature. The story of Aeneas offered real possibilities. It was a story involving big ideas, in the distant past. Its main outlines were fixed, but many of its larger details were fluid. Material could be added or subtracted. It could be used to reflect on recent events, but was far enough in the past to be neutral. The *Aeneid* is characterized by inclusiveness. It is a public Roman epic for a very particular audience. It is also Virgil's epic. It represents a series of rapprochements between what the establishment wanted and what Virgil the thinking Roman wanted. In the process of fulfilling both sets of expectations Virgil wrote an epic not just for Rome, but for humankind.

Virgil's epic is on one level a conflation of the *Iliad* and the *Odyssey,* but a conflation that is radically re-oriented away from largely self-centered, self-sufficient heroes to a hero and a chosen people. Virgil had re-invented the epic for an exploration of human nature in a social and political situation. Virgil and his original audience would have been conscious of a sense of coming age of Latin literature with such a controlled and masterful re-use of Homer, but this was not poem's real purpose nor even his main reason for echoing Homer. Virgil manipulated the earlier material to write a commentary on the heroic life into his own poem.

The *Aeneid* was written to explore the source and meaning of the Roman way of life, the tool of divine providence. Against this providential social history is the history of the heart—and not Aeneas's heart alone. All the private human plans and hopes of characters great and small are caught within the larger sweep of the will of the gods. It is these personal passages of the *Aeneid* which have always maintained interest because paradoxically Virgil's treatment of the individual simultaneously stresses the particular and the universal.

The vision of what the providential role of Rome in human history could achieve is just and dignified. It was the gods's offer of a humane

# What Do I Read Next?

- The *Eclogues* (often called the *Bucolics*) is Virgil's first published collection of poetry. It consists of ten selections, (*eclogues,* in Greek). The word *Bucolics* comes from the Greek word for cowherd. These are pastorals, poems set in a idealized countryside among herdsmen and small landowners. Reality intrudes in *Eclogues* 1 and 9, which concern the confiscation of Virgil's farm.

- Virgil wrote the *Georgics* in four sections. This handbook of agriculture was also intended to promote the revival of traditional Roman pastoral and agrarian life, with an emphasis on family life, hard work, practical patriotism and simplicity of manners and pleasures. Commissioned by Caesar Augustus in an attempt to make Rome's pastoral and agrarian past seem like an attractive and viable way of life for the population to continue to follow, the vision put forward in the *Georgics* is in many ways like that of Thomas Jefferson's for the new nation of the United States of America that he helped found.

- Lucan's *Pharsalia* also known as the *Bellum Civili,* is an epic written during the reign of the Emperor Nero. It is about the civil war between Caesar and Pompey a hundred years earlier. Unlike the *Aeneid,* it takes place in known historical times. It uses Fate rather than the intervention of the gods to explain events. For these reasons, its earliest critics claimed it was not an epic.

- Livy wrote at the same time as Virgil and for many of the same reasons. In his history, *Ab urbe conditor*, he reminds his Roman readers of their great heritage. Not all of Livy's work survives, but it was almost as influential as that of Virgil.

- David Wishart's *I Virgil* published in 1995, is a fictionalized biography of Virgil. It assumes that Virgil was ambivalent toward his protagonist Aeneas and the scope and plot of the *Aeneid* because he had reservations about Caesar Augustus's rule of Rome. In this account, Virgil is poisoned by Augustus when he realizes that the *Aeneid* is an indictment of his character.

---

society for the world, in which evil would be overcome by the concerted physical and ethical courage of the Roman people. Unfortunately it remains through out the poet, even in the poem's projected future only a possibility which seems doomed to be frustrated, not only by those who do not understand it, but by the character who is expected to bring it into being, Aeneas. The reader is constantly confronted with the paradox that in pursuit of this humane ideal, Aeneas becomes less than he was.

Quinn wrote in one of the most perceptive and simplest sentences in the history of Virgilian criticism that Virgil is "never completely for a character or completely against the character opposing him" (see Sources for Further Study). It is impossible to find a character in the epic who does not show some ambiguity. Nevertheless, criticism, particularly of the major characters, has too often attempted to read characters as either good or bad, and not as Virgil meant them to be read, human and fallible.

The characters make their own lives and deaths with their decisions. Like all great literature, the *Aeneid* is about characters's reactions to events and to each other. In it moral responsibility cannot be shirked. The tears are not only shed by men and women, they are caused by them.

Presiding over human action and choices are the gods. Divine providence is as ambiguous and dark as human nature in the *Aeneid.* Critics and readers focus on Juno's rage. More disconcerting is the chilling picture of the gods destroying Troy on the night of the city's fall. There is something cold and deeply frightening in that scene, like something out of a monster movie, for a modern reader in the vision of these vast beings pulling up the walls of Troy, while antlike humans fight and flee. There is a legendary streak of perfidy and disrespect for the gods in the history of Troy, but Virgil does not make this clear. Troy is not innocent, but on that night it hardly seems to matter. Only Jupiter rises above this divine terror. His is the vision, his is the disposition of all things towards a plan, but it is only late in the poem that he masters the other divine powers in the poem's universe. The new world order is being mapped out not merely on earth, but in heaven.

Thematic discussions take up a large part of critical analysis, particularly those aimed at first-time readers who meet the poem in translation. Virgil's characters and themes are memorable both because they seem to tap into constants of the human situation, but also because of his technique. For readers who do not know Latin, a good entry into Virgil's technique is his use of imagery. It has been remarked that Virgil has very small vocabulary of images. What Virgil does with that relatively restricted range of images is important.

Virgil in his chosen dactylic hexameter was perhaps the most technically perfect poet in the history of western literature. It has even suggested that Virgil's perfection exhausted the possibilities of the hexameter at the same time as it created an overwhelming audience expectation for it. We cannot experience this perfection in a translation. What we *can* see in a good translation, and even more clearly with a good translation and a little Latin, is the way Virgil chooses and arranges his words and ideas within a pattern of symmetry and variation. The meaning of the whole is always greater than the meaning of the individual words. From individual lines up to the poem as a whole, Virgil constantly balances ideas, images, characters and actions against one another. Within that balancing he uses variety. This variety is not an exact one on one replacement. Instead Virgil's variation extends meaning and action a little at a time. It occurs from the level of the line to the level of verse paragraphs to whole books and in the poem as a whole.

If we look at one short passage in Book 1 (lines 1.490-504) which introduces Dido for the first time, we can see Virgil at his best. Aeneas is looking at a representation of Penthesilea, an Amazon queen who died helping her Trojan allies. This work of art begins to function as a simile as the narrative moves on to the approach of Dido. Dido appears exactly in the center of the 15-line passage. Her appearance is accompanied by a another simile comparing her to

Diana and her followers dancing through the wilderness. Penthesilea is used to bring Dido on the stage since she too is a queen who will die because of helping the Trojans. The image of the Amazon moving through the armies like fire begins the passage and Dido's radiance as she moves through the crowd ends it. The comparison with Diana looks positive, but it is subtly dangerous. There is an ironic resonance in the line which records the happiness in Latona's heart for the grace of her divine daughter, since Latona's children had been known to destroy those who thought themselves happier than the gods.

**Source:** Helen Conrad-O'Briain, for *Epics for Students,* Gale Research, 1997.

## *R. D. Williams and T. S. Pattie*

*In the following excerpt, the authors note Virgil's significance as a writer who has had a profound influence on all subsequent Western culture, and examines those qualities of his writing that they believe make his poetry still relevant to modern readers.*

Perhaps more than any other Roman writer, Virgil has expressed the achievements, and the shortcomings, of that civilization of which we are the children, in a way that has led to his being called 'the father of the western world'. But supposing that we were not his children, supposing that we were people from Mars freshly arrived on this planet and able to read Latin, would we find in him qualities to ensure his continued survival? I think that we would.

Those qualities that make Virgil's poetry relevant today, two thousand years after his death, can be assessed by looking at two main aspects of a poet's work: technical skills in poetic craftsmanship, and the exploration of the underlying meanings and potentialities of human existence.

Technical skills mean the ability to use words in poetic composition—as a carpenter uses wood or a potter clay or an architect space—to produce something which has an aesthetic impact by its mastery of technique. The most obvious of these skills is the ability to produce word-music—'the sweetness of the sound' as Dryden called it—and here it has been universally agreed, even by those few who have been unreceptive towards him otherwise, that Virgil was pre-eminent. He was helped in this by having available as the appropriate metre for epic poetry the Latin hexameter, adapted from Greek by Ennius, and developed by Cicero, Catullus,

Lucretius, and others, until in Virgil's hand it became what Tennyson called 'the stateliest measure ever moulded by the lips of man'. The full elaboration of this would involve a lengthy technical discussion, and suffice it to say here that Virgil explored to the full the sonorous beauty of the Latin language so that the sound of his words could echo, and indeed express, the sense of the meaning. In particular the nature of the hexameter (a metre based on quantity) and the pronunciation of Latin (based like English on accent) gave two rhythms which could be employed in harmony or counterpoint as the mood and sense required.

This sense of word-music contributed greatly to a second technical requirement in poetry, descriptive power, and Virgil's word-music was supported by his almost unique imaginative visualization. He loved to depict scenes which the human eye does not see: the imaginary Golden Age in *Eclogues* 4, Orpheus and Eurydice in the underworld in *Georgics* 4, the Olympian gods in the *Aeneid* going about their business in the halls of heaven. We see this kind skill right at the beginning of the *Aeneid* in the mythological description of the winds imprisoned in Aeolus's mountain:

> *Hic vasto rex Aeolus antro luctantis ventos tempestatesque sonoras imperio premit ac vinclis et carcere frenat. illi indignantes magno cum murmure montis circum claustra fremunt: celsa sedet Aeolus arce sceptra tenens mollitque animos et temperat iras; ni faciat, maria ac terras caelumque profundum quippe ferant rapidi secum verrantque per auras.*

(*Aeneid* 1. 52–59)

> Where in a spacious cave of living stone,
> The tyrant Aeolus from his airy throne,
> With power imperial curbs the struggling winds,
> And sounding tempests in dark prisons binds.
> This way and that the impatient captives tend,
> And pressing for release, the mountains rend:
> High in his hall the undaunted monarch stands,
> And shakes his sceptre, and their rage commands;
> Which did he not, their unresisted sway
> Would sweep the world before them in their way:
> Earth, air, and seas through empty space
> would roll,
> And Heaven would fly before the driving soul.

(tr. Dryden)

This sort of imaginative description colours the whole of the *Aeneid.* We are invited to visualize Juno striding majestically through the halls of heaven, Jupiter smiling at his daughter Venus, Neptune driving over the sea in his chariot with his retinue of strange sea-deities, Iris descending to heaven on her own rainbow:

> *Ergo Iris croceis per caelum roscida pennis mille trahens varios adverso sole colores devolat.*

(*Aeneid* 4. 700–702)

> Downward the various goddess took her flight,
> And drew a thousand colours from the light.

(tr. Dryden)

Another essential technical skill for an epic poet is the ability to tell a story in an exciting way. In this respect Virgil is often compared unfavourably with Homer, and most people would agree that in sheer narrative speed and excitement Homer takes the palm. Virgil's epic method (like Milton's) is different, but that is not to say that he does not hold us with bated breath on occasion; for example, the story in Book 2 of the wooden horse, the treachery of Sinon, the last hours of Troy, moves with a verve which is breathtaking.

One might continue with other instances of technical skill in poetry, for example, Virgil's use of brilliant rhetoric in speeches. Those between Turnus and Drances, or especially between the goddesses Juno and Venus, enable us to relax emotionally, and enjoy intellectually the brilliant firework display of exaggerated oratory, in which Cicero would have revelled.

Or again we might consider the structure of Virgil's poetry. The *Eclogues* are symmetrically and elegantly organized in the Alexandrian mode, sometimes with balancing verses from two competitors in a song contest, sometimes with repeated refrain. The first two and the last two books of the *Georgics* cohere in their content, but in mood Books 1 and 3 correspond, and Books 2 and 4. Descriptive passages throughout are interspersed with didactic information in order to give variety of structure. The *Aeneid* especially shows architectural construction on a large scale. This is clearly a requirement of epic above all other kinds of poetry: the epic poet must be a builder on a large scale, able to handle his masses of material. Symmetries and contrasts may be seen between the two halves of the poem, between the first third and the last third, between the different books, and between the different sections of each book. Much has been written about Virgil's skill in structure during recent years, so much so that one should enter a *caveat* and say that however important the structure of poetry may be, it differs from architecture in that structure should be subservient to the poetic message; it is not an end in itself.

This brings us to the second main aspect of a poet's work: the underlying significance of the poetry in relation to human experience. The message conveyed by means of technical skills is obviously deeper in some poets than in others. Most of us could name poets whom we greatly enjoy solely or very largely because of the technical skills just mentioned, and we derive aesthetic rather than intellectual pleasure from their poetry. Virgil, however, is one of those poets who used his aesthetic skills not only for their own sakes, but in order to explore human behaviour in its most crucial aspects.

In the *Eclogues* some critics have put their greatest emphasis on the pure loveliness of the poetry, but increasingly in modern times these poems have been seen as explorations of an idyllic world to which mankind could attain but from which he may be excluded by the social and political pressures of real life. The fourth *Eclogue* is a vision of such a golden world; the first and ninth show the agony of the loss, through dispossession, of the happiness which the idyllic countryside offers. Here is a part of the first *Eclogue,* conveying the envy of the dispossessed for the shepherd who still retains his pastoral world:

> *fortunate senex, hic inter flumina nota et fontis sacros frigus captabis opacum; hinc tibi quae semper vicino ab limite saepes Hyblaeis apibus florem depasta salicti saepe levi somnum suadebit inire susurro; hinc alta sub rupe canet frondator ad auras: nec tamen interea raucae, tua cura, palumbes nec gemere aeria cessabit turtur ab ulmo .*

#### (*Eclogues* 1. 51–58)

Ah, fortunate old man, here among
    hallowed springs
And familiar streams you'll enjoy the longed-for
    shade, the cool shade.
Here, as of old, where your neighbour's land
    marches with yours,
The sally hedge, with bees of Hybla sipping
    its blossom,
Shall often hum you gently to sleep. On the
    other side
Vine-dressers will sing to the breezes at
    the crag's foot;
And all the time your favourites, the husky-voiced
    wood pigeons
Shall coo away, and turtle doves make moan in
    the elm tops.

#### (tr. Day Lewis)

The *Georgics* too have had, and still have, a great appeal purely because of their descriptive power, and the best-known parts have always been the most brilliant of the descriptive passages, like the praises of Italy (2.136ff.) or the activities of the bees (4.67ff.). But again modern criticism has concentrated on the concept in the poem of man as part of nature, divinely created, and on his successes and failures. The poem is seen as a presentation of the positive achievements of man in fitting himself in to the world of nature, and of the disasters which sometimes seem inexplicable (like flood or fire or the plague) and which sometimes are due to man's own folly in the neglect of his duty towards 'the divine countryside'. Above all the life of the countryman is extolled as a religious communion with nature, calling for 'unremitting toil' and resilience, but offering the richest of rewards. Here is a passage contrasting the ambitious, wealth-seeking town-dweller with the contented farmer:

> *condit opes alius defossoque incubat auro; hic stupet attonitus rostris, hunc plausus hiantem per cuneos geminatus enim plebisque patrumque corripuit; gaudent perfusi sanguine fratrum, exsilioque domos et dulcia limina mutant atque alio patriam quaerunt sub sole iacentem. agricola incurvo terram dimovit aratro: hic anni labor, hinc patriam parvosque nepotes sustinet, hinc armenta boum meritosque iuvencos.*

#### (*Georgics* 2. 507–515)

One piles up great wealth, gloats over his
    cache of gold;
One gawps at the public speakers; one is worked
    up to hysteria
By the plaudits of senate and people resounding
    across the benches:
These shed their brothers' blood
Merrily, they barter for exile their homes beloved
And leave for countries lying under an alien sun.
But still the farmer furrows the land with his
    curving plough:
The land is his annual labour, it keeps his
    native country,
His little grandsons and herds of cattle and
    trusty bullocks.

#### (tr. Day Lewis)

The *Aeneid* differs from the *Eclogues* and the *Georgics* with regard to its underlying significance in that it deals with man's problems by presenting and developing individual characters in constantly changing situations. The characters of the *Eclogues* are in a sense static pictures in a given situation; the characters of the *Georgics* (except for the Orpheus and Eurydice story) are not individuals at all, but generalized types. The *Aeneid,* however, as is appropriate for an epic poem, dwells at length on character, and this is best illustrated by focusing on the hero of the poem.

First and foremost Aeneas is a man who has accepted a divine mission which dictates the whole of his actions. He would have preferred to die at Troy among his friends, he would have preferred to stay with Dido, but because he has received intimations by means of visions, dreams and oracles that he has been chosen as the agent of Providence to fulfil a destiny which will bring great benefits to mankind, he devotes himself to this mission. Throughout the poem Virgil explores the effect which such a calling has upon an individual, and many readers of the *Aeneid* have thought that it causes Aeneas to be a puppet-like creature in whose activities it is hard to take an interest. This is a wholly mistaken view: he is in fact free at any time to cry 'Enough', to decide that his mission is too hard or too uncertain or too unconvincing for him to continue. That he does continue—often by the skin of his teeth—is due to a series of acts of his own free-will. This is explicitly shown, as we have seen, in a passage already referred to (5.700–703) where he ponders on two possible courses of action: continuing with his mission, or abandoning it, 'forgetting' the fates. Thus the fascination of Aeneas lies in the character study of a man whose actions are guided by a sense of divine duty, which he has to struggle to obey, falteringly at first but then with increasing confidence as he becomes more aware of the nature of his calling. Throughout the poem he is devoutly religious in prayer and sacrifice, but increasingly he begins to understand God's purpose for the world and his part in it.

This devotion to the divine will, involving often the sacrifice of personal wishes, covers a large part of Virgil's frequent epithet for Aeneas—*pius,* 'devoted', 'ready to accept responsibility', 'aware of his duty'. But there are other aspects of this specially Roman virtue which affect his actions. Patriotism is one, and in Aeneas's case this merges with his devotion to the gods whose intention it is to found the Roman race. Care for his family is another, and this is a powerful motivation for his actions. He saves his father from the burning ruins of Troy, and pays the utmost attention to his advice until the very moment of his death. His concern for his son Iulus is evident throughout, and his last words to him are the poignant ones:

> *Disce, puer, virtutem ex me verumque laborem, fortunam ex aliis.*

(12. 435–436)

> Learn, my son, valour from me and the reality of toil, but good luck from others.

Care for his friends and his fellow-soldiers is a part of *pietas,* and here again Aeneas does all he can to safeguard his followers (unlike Turnus, whose rash impetuousness leads to many unnecessary deaths). Aeneas is the group hero, the social man.

To achieve this object (which he does not always succeed in doing) Aeneas has to sacrifice something of himself—he gives away something of his own personal individuality in the interests of his duty. In this he contrasts with the vivid personalities of Homer's heroes; they shine more brightly than Aeneas because they are always themselves, seeing life very clearly, understanding their obligations clearly, but not having to struggle inwardly with themselves in order to try to determine the right course of action. They know instinctively what the right course is, and to the best of their ability they set about doing it. But Aeneas is always groping for a way of life which he does not fully understand, and in the course of it tragedies and disasters befall him and others for which he feels guiltily responsible. In a paradoxical way it is his *pietas* which is responsible for the cruelty with which he treats Dido (indeed Virgil implies as much, 4. 393): he sacrifices his own personal wishes (and with them hers) to what he sees to be a higher responsibility.

In contrast with Aeneas both Dido and Turnus are characters drawn very simply, on Homeric lines. Dido knows exactly what she wants, and is not swayed from her personal desire by any other considerations at all. Her duty towards the city of Carthage is forgotten and she alienates her subjects by her disregard of all her queenly duties. She is completely unable to understand Aeneas's arguments that he would like to stay with her but cannot; for her 'like to' and 'can' are the same. Similarly, Turnus is not confused in his attitude by any attempt to weigh up the requirements of Fate, or the wishes of his king, against his own personal determination to have his own way if he possibly can. With both Dido and Turnus we feel that they have been treated scurvily by the force of events—but they are neither of them prepared to compromise in any way with what they want to do.

Aeneas for the most part is very different— thinking always of the implications of a situation and often deciding to act against his own personal wishes. But there are moments when he loses this rational control and lets himself be swayed by his personal instincts—as when he hears of the death of Pallas in Book 10 and rages wildly over the battlefield dealing indiscriminate slaughter; or again after he has been wounded in Book 12; or finally at the end of the poem when he kills Turnus in hot anger. The last adjective to be applied to him in the poem is *fervidus,* 'in a passion'. In founding Rome he has not trodden an easy path, and he has left it bestrewn with the corpses of those who wished to help as well as those who wished to hinder.

Very many critics in the two thousand years of the *Aeneid*'s existence have found it above all a poem of sadness, of the world's tragedies, of this our vale of sorrow, and Virgil is often thought of as the poet of the 'tears in things', *lacrimae rerum*. To a very large extent this is true; and yet the vision of a Roman Empire spreading peace and civilization to a war-weary world never fades altogether, and in the attempts of Aeneas, very imperfect though they are, to set in motion the beginnings of this worldly paradise we see something of mankind's indomitable spirit, through mistakes and setbacks and calamities, to press onwards: 'to strive, to seek, to find, and not to yield'.

**Source:** R. D. Williams and T. S. Pattie, "Virgil Today," in *Virgil: His Poetry through the Ages,* pp. 57–67. London, British Library, 1982.

## William S. Anderson

*In the following excerpt, Anderson discusses the significance of the opening line of the* Aeneid: *"I sing of arms and of the man."*

It is not enough . . . to describe Vergil's opening ["I sing of arms and of the man"] as a skillful allusion to inevitable rivalry with Homer. To be sure, he used two nouns of different orders, one referring to a person, one to a thing, and the nouns suggest main elements of the two Homeric narratives. Two nouns together, however, interact; they cannot be absorbed separately as mere equivalents to separate Greek epics. When George Bernard Shaw entitled his comedy *Arms and the Man,* he knew exactly what he was doing and exactly what Vergil meant with his pair of nouns: they affect each other. Shaw humorously explores some of the paradoxical ways in which warfare affects the personality of the warrior. One appreciates the comedy all the more if he has read the *Aeneid* and grasped the near-tragic vision which Vergil presents of Aeneas the man of arms. Homer knew that warfare can turn a man into a beast, but in the *Iliad* war remains a fact with which men must deal; within the limited context of battle, men can become heroes. It is part of Achilles' tragedy that he can no longer accept the war as a necessary fact for himself. Vergil goes beyond Homer, since he does not present war as a necessary or desirable fact, and furthermore he shows not only that war brutalizes men, but also that men alter the meaning of war. Note, however, that he does not define Aeneas from the beginning as a tragic warri-

or, as Homer does Achilles. Instead of the negative term "anger" (later elaborated for its ruinous effects), Vergil uses the neutral word "arms," which he explains in the next lines as crucially important for the establishment of Rome. Together, "arms and the man" could be viewed as positive words, interacting creatively to make possible the good that undoubtedly existed in Rome. So from the beginning Vergil has started a theme of rich ambiguity, a theme which runs through the poem and remains provocatively rich even after the last lines.

This Vergilian theme of arms and man is so crucial that the reader should be prepared for it a little more elaborately. Vergil narrates two distinct occasions of war: the fall of Troy and the conquest of Latium. In the first, Aeneas meets defeat; he battles heroically—and his triumphs are not neglected—but the gods do not permit him to die, with conventional heroism, fighting for Trojan home and country. Although briefly bestialized by the exigencies of desperate resistance to the Greeks, Aeneas remains uncompromised; and it is evident that the gods have selected him because he has more importance as man than mere warrior. The second war is more complex. It starts under checkered circumstances, not without some responsibility on the Trojan side. It continues despite many cruel losses on both sides. Aeneas loses control of his passions and slaughters indiscriminately until at last he vents his anger on the guiltless Lausus and the guilty, but devoted, father Mezentius. Neither of these victories is clean and glorious, neither entirely tarnished by circumstances, but our uncertainty as to the attitude to adopt toward them applies to Aeneas as well. What is this war doing to him and to his ultimate goal? We see now that Vergil never intended to limit our sight to arms and Aeneas in themselves. We are always concerned, as we were but rarely in the *Iliad,* with the ultimate purpose to which this warfare is instrumental. Aeneas while being a man, also stands for Rome itself. If his victories are compromised, what happens to the Rome he founds? That is the tragic question which Vergil makes us face in Book Twelve, as we watch the encounter between Aeneas and Turnus. Without any obvious guilt on his part (such as Achilles' anger), Aeneas becomes so involved in the Italian war as to render his final victory equivocal.

A few words about Vergil's verb "I sing." Just as Vergil felt free to exploit Homeric convention and to present a theme of complexity that accorded with the new complexities of civilization seven centuries after Homer, so he altered somewhat his relation to material and reader. I have already emphasized the tradition of *impersonality* and insisted that Vergil could not have begun with a set of autobiographical lines. Now it is time to note the other facet of the poem: with all its impersonal narrative devices, it is also highly personal. A recent writer has used the term "subjective," and perhaps that is more serviceable here, to avoid the awkwardness of the pair "impersonal" and "personal." Vergil's subjectivity is developed from a post-Homeric attitude in Greek and Roman writers, who openly placed themselves in their poetry, expressing attitudes toward narrated events and openly influencing readers. It is too much to detect in "I sing" an assertion of this artistic method. The reader, however, will do well to notice how often and ambiguously Vergil suggests attitudes, especially sympathy for Aeneas' victims. . . .

In the myths about Troy, there is little doubt that the city deserved its destruction. A heritage of deceit and ruthless exploitation culminated in the selfish lust of Paris, who stole Helen, the wife of the man who was his host in Sparta, and heedlessly took her back to Troy, where the Trojan leaders permitted him to enjoy his criminal passion. Homer adds to this heritage of evil by staging a violation of truce negotiations: Pandarus shoots Menelaus, the injured husband, at the moment when a carefully arranged duel has promised to settle the war with a minimum of bloodshed. Thus, although the individual Trojan might feel deeply the defeat of his country, it was conventional to depict the end of Troy as an event favored and promoted by gods as well as men. To escape from Troy, defeated but alive, would mean to leave behind the sinful taint of the past and to seek some new, creative future. And since Aeneas was permitted to escape, it should also follow that he himself was hardly tainted by the misdeeds of Paris and other members of Priam's family. In Italy, destiny had chosen a new environment for the Trojans under Aeneas; there, the good aspects of the Trojan heritage could flourish, stimulated by the change of milieu and the proximity to the new Italian culture.

At one level, then, the flight from Troy to Rome signifies the abandonment of a corrupt past and dedication to a creative future in a new land—all this happening far back in the mythical past just after the Trojan War, that is, around 1200 B.C. But Vergil saw more immediate, contemporary relevance in the Trojan theme, and he shared his insight with other writers of the period. Also writing in the 20's, Horace published a poem in which he made

much of the Trojan War, the move to Italy, and the hostility of Juno . . . . Horace's theme concerns the absolute and necessary break between guilty Troy, which must remain ruined and uninhabited, and the new land founded by the Trojan survivors. To this extent, his short Ode 3.3 parallels Vergil's epic. Horace also links this remote mythical past with the present by comparing the reward of apotheosis won by Romulus, Aeneas' descendant who founded Rome, with the divinity to be granted Augustus for his heroic achievements. For Horace the myth of Troy-Rome was a symbolic story which could be applied fruitfully to contemporary history. Vergil made a similar application on a larger epic canvass.

**Source:** William S. Anderson, "Virgil Begins His Epic," in *The Art of the Aeneid,* pp. 1–23. Englewood Cliffs, NJ: Prentice-Hall, Inc., 1969.

## Sources for Further Study

Anderson, William S. *The Art of the Aeneid,* Prentice-Hall, 1969, 473 p.
    An introductory study of the *Aeneid* which discusses themes, images and technique in the context of a broad synopsis. It is a good accessible running commentary to all aspects of the poem.

Bernard, John D. ed. *Vergil at 2000: Commemorative Essays on the Poet and his Influence,* AMS Press, 1986.
    A collection of essays on Virgil and his influence, many of which are listed below.

Boyle, A. J., ed. *The Roman Epic,* Routledge, 1993.
    A good new collection of essays placing the *Aeneid* in the setting of its Latin predecessors and descendants.

Boyle, A. J. "Roman Song." In his *The Roman Epic,* Routledge, 1993, pp.1-18.
    Perhaps the best short English introduction to the tradition of the Latin epic. Boyle briefly covers the form from Virgil's earliest predecessors, Livius and Naevius to the Renaissance epic.

———. "The Canonic Text: Virgil's Aeneid." In his *The Roman Epic,* Routledge, 1993, pp. 79-107.
    A solid discussion of all aspects of Virgil's epic from his sources through literary style to its political and moral implications. Boyle offers an essentially negative reading of Aeneas's character.

Commager, Steele. ed. *Virgil: A Collection of Critical Essays,* Prentice Hall, 1966.
    A good introductory collection for student use.

Curtius, Ernest Robert. *European Literature and the Latin Middle Ages,* trans. Willard R. Trask. Bollingen Series 36, Princeton University Press, 1973.
    This classic study explains how Latin literature affected the development of literature all over Europe.

Curtius pays special attention to the influence of Virgil.

Dominik, William J. "From Greece to Rome: Ennius *Annales*" in Boyle, A. J. ed. *The Roman Epic,* Routledge, 1993, pp. 37-58.
An important and revealing study of the poet who was Rome's epic poet before Virgil.

Dryden, John. Introduction to *Virgil: The Aeneid,* translated by John Dryden, Heritage Press, pp. ix- xliii.
The founder of modern English criticism gives his reading of the *Aeneid.* This introduction was the most influential reading of the poem in English for over a hundred years. It formed every educated English speaker's view of the poem.

Freeman, Charles. *The World of the Romans,* Cassell, 1993.
A very thorough and well-written description of every facet of Roman life. It includes the essentials of Roman history. The illustrations are very good. An excellent student resource.

Goldberg, Sander M. "Saturnian Epic: Livius and Naevius," in Boyle, A. J., ed. *The Roman Epic,* Routledge, 1993, pp. 19-36.
A good study of the features of these two early Roman writers of epic which most influenced Virgil. A fascinating example of scholarship as detective work, piecing together literary history from fragments.

Graves, Robert. "The Virgil Cult," *The Virginia Quarterly Review,* Vol. 38, No. 1, Winter, 1962, pp. 13-35.
Perhaps the best known modern attack on Virgil, it is as much an attack on T. S. Eliot and C. S. Lewis and their conversion to Christianity. Wishart offers a fictionalized autobiography of the poet.

Hadas, Moses. *Ancilla to Classical Reading,* Columbia University Press, 1961.
A good place to find biographical sketches of all those ancient writers that Virgilian critics assume everyone knows.

Jones, J. W. "The Allegorical Traditions of the Aeneid" in Bernard, John D., ed. *Virgil at 2000: Commemorative Essays on the Poet and his Influence,* edited by John D. Bernard, AMS Press, New York, 1986, pp. 107-32.
A worthwhile study of the allegorical readings of the *Aeneid* and of the medieval treatment of the poem.

Le Bossu, Ren. "On the Fable of the Aeneid," in *Le Bossu and Voltaire on the Epic,* Scholars Facsimiles and Reprints, 1970, pp. 26-31.
A short statement of the main ideas of this important early modern critic of the *Aeneid.*

Mackail, J. W. *Virgil and his Meaning to the World of To-Day,* Marshall Jones Co., 1922.
A popular introduction, most useful for its discussion of Virgil's technique.

Marks, Anthony and Tingay, Graham. *The Romans,* Usbourne Publishing Ltd., 1990.
This book is for young readers, but it's layout makes it a good source for presentations. Handouts and charts can be simply made by enlarging pages.

Miles, Gary B. and Allen, Archibald W. "Virgil and the Augustan Experience," in *Vergil at 2000: Commemorative Essays on the Poet and his Influence,* edited by John D. Bernard, AMS Press, New York, 1986, pp. 13-41.
Conveys the complexity the period's ideals and realities.

Miola, Robert. "Vergil in Shakespeare: From Allusion to Imitation," in *Virgil at 2000: Commemorative Essays on the Poet and his Influence,* edited by John D. Bernard, AMS Press, New York, 1986, pp. 241-58.
A wide-ranging study of the influence of Virgil on Shakespeare. This article would be the perfect place to begin a paper comparing the two poets.

Otis, Brooks. "The Odyssean Aeneid and the Iliadic Aeneid," in Commager, Steele. ed. *Virgil: A Collection of Critical Essays,* Prentice Hall. Inc. Englewood Cliffs, New Jersey, 1966, pp. 89-106.
Otis concentrates on the ways that Virgil adapted Homer's epics. He shows Virgil transforming Homer rather than simply imitating. He traces the way this builds in a sort of Homeric commentary within the *Aeneid.*

Quinn, Kenneth. *Virgil's Aeneid: A Critical Description,* Routledge and Kegan Paul, 1968.
A somewhat more demanding read than Anderson's introductory book, filling in the fine detail. The first chapter, "The Heroic Impulse," gives a balanced introduction to modern critical treatment of Virgilian heroism and covers the heroic impulse in heroism in the minor as well as the main characters.

Reynolds, L. D. "Vergil," in *Texts and Transmissions,* Clarendon Press, 1986, pp. 433-36.
A clear and fascinating introduction to the manuscripts which preserved the text of the *Aeneid.*

Virgil. *The Aeneid,* 2 Vols., trans. H. Rushton Fairclough. Loeb Classical Library, Harvard University Press, 1978.
A good plain translation of the poem with the Latin text on the facing page.

———. The Aeneid, trans. David West, Penguin Books, 1990.
A popular modern translation with useful maps and appendixes.

Williams, R. D. *Virgil,, Greece and Rome: New Surveys in the Classics* 1, Clarendon Press, 1967.
The journal *Greece and Rome* is geared towards secondary school teachers of classical literature and interested, but serious amateurs. This booklet gives a good serious overview of criticism on the *Aeneid.*

Williams, R. D. and Pattie, T. S. *Virgil: His Poetry through the Ages,* London, British Library, 1982.
This introduction is carefully geared to the first-time reader of the *Aeneid.* It includes a full synopsis of the epic. The chapter "Virgil Today" is probably the best place to begin reading criticism on the *Aeneid.*

Wolverton, Robert E. *An Outline of Classical Mythology,* Littlefield Adams and Co., 1966.
A short and occasionally funny introduction to mythology. There are family trees and useful lists of types of stories.

# *Beowulf*

## Anonymous
## c. 1000

The Old English poem *Beowulf* follows Beowulf from heroic youth to heroic old age. He saves a neighboring people from a monster, Grendel, eventually becomes the king of his own people, and dies defending them from a dragon. It is a great adventure story, and a deeply philosophical one. Scholars differ over the poem's original purpose and audience, but *Beowulf* probably appealed to a wide audience and garnered a range of responses.

*Beowulf* survives in one manuscript, which is known as British Library Cotton Vitellius A. 15. At least one scholar believes the manuscript is the author's original, but most scholars believe it is the last in a succession of copies. *Beowulf* may have been written at any time between circa 675 A.D. and the date of the manuscript, circa 1000 A.D.

No one knows where the manuscript was before it surfaced in the hands of a man named Laurence Nowell in the sixteenth century. An edition of *Beowulf* was published by G. S. Thorkelin in 1815, but for over 100 years study focused on *Beowulf* not as poetry, but on what it revealed about the early Germanic tribes and language (philology).

J. R. R. Tolkein's ''The Monsters and the Critics'' moved study on to the poem as literature. The excavation of the Sutton Hoo ship burial and Tolkein's own popular *Lord of the Rings,* influenced by his lifelong study of *Beowulf,* helped to interest general readers in the poem. Since then translations and adaptations of the poem have in-

creased the poem's audience and recognition. It has influenced modern adventure fantasy and inspired at least two best-sellers, comic books, and even a *Beowulf/Star Trek Voyager* cross-over.

In 1939, an important archaeological discovery was made which contributed to the twentieth-century understanding of *Beowulf*. The remains of a ship burial were uncovered at Sutton Hoo, an estate on the estuary of the Deben river in Suffolk, England. Some of the objects in the grave included a sword, shield, and helmet, a harp, and Frankish coins which date approximately to 650-70 A.D.— the presumed date of the action of the epic.

## Author Biography

There is no indication of who wrote *Beowulf;* scholars have suggested at least two possible candidates, but neither of these identifications has been generally accepted.

Many dates and places have been suggested for the composition of *Beowulf*. Most of the theories suffer from wishful thinking: scholars connect it to a favorite time and place. It is no use, however, to show where and when it *might* have been written. It must be shown that it could not have been written anywhere else at any other time in order for a theory to be conclusive. Early critics often stressed the antiquity of the poet's material and attempted to break the poem down into a number of older "lays" (see Style section below). Northumbria during the lifetime of the scholar Bede has often been suggested because it was culturally advanced and Bede was the greatest Anglo-Saxon scholar. The kingdom of Mercia during the reign of Offa the Great (756-798) has been suggested, partially because the poet included 31 lines praising Offa's ancestor, also named Offa. Recently a late date has become popular. Kevin Kiernan believes that the existing manuscript may be the author's own copy. This would mean the poem was written very close to 1000 A.D. An early date for Beowulf (675-700) is now usually connected with East Anglia. It has been suggested that the East Anglian royal family considered themselves descended from Wiglaf, who comes to Beowulf's aid during the dragon fight.

The main argument for this early date, however, is based on archaeology. The poem's descriptions of magnificent burials reflect practices of the late sixth and seventh centuries, but this does not mean that the poem was written then. A person witnessing such a burial might describe it accurately fifty years later to a child, who might then repeat the description another fifty years later to the person who would then write it down a century after it happened. Some scholars assume that the poem, celebrating the ancestors of the Vikings, could not have been written after their raids on England began. Others suggest that a mixed Viking Anglo Saxon area or even the reign of the Danish Canute (King of England when the manuscript was written) would have been the most obvious time and place. It has also been suggested that the poem might have been written to gain the allegiance of Vikings settled in England to the family of Alfred, since they claimed Scyld as an ancestor. On the other hand, Alfred's family may have added Scyld to their family tree because he and his family were so famous through an already existing *Beowulf*.

## Plot Summary

### Narrative in Beowulf

The action of *Beowulf* is not straightforward. The narrator foreshadows actions that will occur later, talking about events that are yet to come. Characters talk about things that have already happened in the poem. Both narrator and characters recall incidents and characters outside the poem's main narrative. These "digressions" (see Style section below) are connected thematically to the main action. Critics once saw the digressions as flaws. The poet, however, was consciously using them to characterize human experience, stressing recurring patterns, and to represent the characters' attempts to understand their situation (see Themes section below).

### The Kings of the Danes and the Coming of Grendel

Scyld was found by the Danes as a small boy in a boat washed ashore. The Danes at this time were without a leader and oppressed by neighboring countries. Scyld grew to be a great warrior king and made the Danes a powerful nation. Dying, he ordered the Danes to send him back in a ship to the sea from which he came. They placed him in a ship surrounded by treasures and pushed it out to sea— and "no one knows who received that freight."

Scyld's son, Beowulf Scylding, becomes king in his turn. Next, his son Healfdene takes the throne, and then Healfdene's son, Hrothgar, succeeds him. Hrothgar builds a great hall, Heorot, to entertain and reward his people. There are festivities at its opening, but the music and laughter enrage Grendel, a human monster living underwater nearby. That night Grendel breaks into Heorot, slaughters and eats thirty of Hrothgar's men (the king's warriors would normally sleep in the hall). This happens again the next night. After that, "it was easy to find him who sought rest somewhere else."

Grendel haunts the hall by night for twelve years. The Danes despair of ridding themselves of him. They can neither defeat him nor come to terms with him.

### Beowulf Comes to the Kingdom of Hrothgar

Danish sailors bring news of Grendel to King Hygelac of the Geats whose nephew (also named Beowulf, like King Hrothgar's father Beowulf Scylding) has a growing reputation for strength and monster-killing. Beowulf, supported by the wisest of his people, resolves to go to Hrothgar's aid and sets off by ship with fourteen companions. They land in Denmark and are met and questioned by a coast guard who, impressed with Beowulf, sends them to Heorot. Hrothgar receives them and accepts Beowulf's offer of help. Hrothgar knew Beowulf as a child, and interprets Beowulf's arrival to his court as an act of gratitude. He had sheltered Beowulf's father, Ecgtheow, when he was an exile and made peace for him with his powerful enemies.

Unferth, an official of the court, attempts to discredit Beowulf with the story of a swimming match Beowulf had as a boy with another boy, Breca. Beowulf exonerates himself with his version of the swimming match. Wealtheow, Hrothgar's queen, welcomes Beowulf. The young man tells her that he would lay down his life to defeat Grendel. She thanks God for his resolve.

### Beowulf's Fight with Grendel

Hrothgar gives Beowulf and his companions the duty of guarding Heorot that night. The young man decides to face Grendel without weapons since Grendel does not use them. He tells those around him that the outcome of the fight is in the hands of God. The Danes leave the hall, Beowulf and his companions bed down for the night. When darkness falls, Grendel comes stalking across the empty moors. Intent on slaughter and food, he has no idea what is waiting for him in the hall. He bursts open

Heorot's heavy iron-bound doors with the touch of his hand and rushes in, grabs one of the sleeping Geats, eats him, greedily gulping down the blood, and then grabs Beowulf. Beowulf has had a moment to orient himself, however, and wrestles with Grendel. Grendel is taken aback by his strength and tries to get away, but cannot. They struggle, Beowulf refusing to break his grip. Beowulf's companions try to wound Grendel, only to find he is impervious to their weapons. In the end, Grendel manages to pull away from Beowulf, leaving his arm in the hero's grasp. He flees, bleeding, to his lair.

### The Morning after the Battle

With morning the Danes come to see the huge arm, its nails like steel, and the bloody trail of the dying monster. Some of them follow the trail to the water's edge and come back singing Beowulf's praises. One of the king's men compares Beowulf to the great dragon-slayer Sigemund. (In the legends on which the epic the *Nibelungenlied* is based, it is Sigemond's son, Siegfried, who is the dragon-slayer.) Hrothgar thanks God that he has lived to see Grendel stopped. He publicly announces that he will now consider Beowulf his son. Beowulf tells Hrothgar that he wishes the king had seen the fight. He says that he had hoped to kill Grendel outright, but it was not God's will.

### Celebrations in Honor of Beowulf's Victory

There is a celebration in honor of Beowulf and his companions. Hrothgar gives him magnificent gifts including a golden banner, sword, and armor. The other Geats are given rich gifts too. Hrothgar gives treasure for the man whom Grendel had eaten. (This probably represents his *wergild* or "wergyld," literally "man-price," the payment made to a man's lord or his family by someone responsible for his death as an indemnity.) A lay, or short narrative poem, of a famous battle is sung as entertainment.

Wealtheow acknowledges Beowulf's great deed, but counsels her husband not to alienate his nephew Hrothulf by adopting Beowulf. She hopes aloud that Hrothulf will remember all she and the king did for him when he was young, and will treat his young cousins, their sons, well. Wealtheow then gives Beowulf a magnificent golden necklace (worn at that time by both men and women). Wealtheow asks Beowulf to be a good friend to her sons. She ends by saying that in Heorot all the men are loyal to one another and do her will. The original Anglo-Saxon audience knew from existing legends and stories that Hrothulf would later kill his two cousins.

## Grendel's Mother Comes for Vengeance and Beowulf Tracks Her to her Lair

The Geats are given new quarters for the night and Danish warriors sleep in the great hall for the first time in many years. While the Danes are sleeping, Grendel's mother comes to avenge her son. She carries off Aeschere, Hrothgar's friend and counsellor, a man who had always stood at his side in battle. Beowulf finds Hrothgar broken with grief over the loss of his friend. Hrothgar tells Beowulf everything that the Danes know about the monsters and the wilds where they live. Beowulf offers to track Grendel's mother to her underwater lair, remarking that it is better to perform noble deeds before death, and better to avenge a friend than mourn him too much. Hrothgar, Beowulf and their men ride to the sea where they find Aeshere's head at the edge of the overhanging cliffs. Unferth, now deeply impressed by Beowulf's generous heroism, loans Beowulf his sword. Beowulf asks Hrothgar to take care of his companions and to send Hygelac the treasures he had been given for killing Grendel if he (Beowulf) dies.

## Beowulf's Fight with Grendel's Mother

Beowulf enters the water and is seized by Grendel's mother, who drags him to her den, which is dry despite its underwater entrance. Unferth's sword is useless against this monstrous hag. Beowulf wrestles with her. The woman trips him and tries to stab him with her dagger, but the blade is turned away by his chainmail (a mesh tunic of fine interlocked metal rings). He struggles away from her, grabs a great sword hanging on the wall, and strikes off her head. He sees the body of Grendel and cuts off his head too, the sword blade melting in his blood. Carrying Grendel's head and the sword's hilt, Beowulf swims back to the surface.

## Beowulf Returns from the Fight in Triumph

Meanwhile, from the cliffs above, the waiting men see blood welling up to the surface of the water. Hrothgar and the Danes assume the worst and make their way sorrowfully back to the hall. Beowulf's companions linger, grieving and forlornly hoping for his return. Beowulf comes to the surface. He and his men return to the hall. He presents Grendel's head and the hilt of the ancient sword to Hrothgar. Beowulf recounts his underwater fight to the court,

acknowledging the grace of God. Hrothgar praises Beowulf and counsels him to use his strength wisely. He warns him of the temptations of prosperity which lead to arrogance and avarice. Beowulf returns Unferth's sword. He thanks Hrothgar for his great kindness and promises him that if Hrothgar ever needs him, he shall come to his aid with a thousand warriors. Beowulf and his companions return to their ship, and Beowulf presents the kindly coast guard with a sword.

## Beowulf's Return to his Uncle's Court

Beowulf and his companions return home and go immediately to his uncle's hall. Hygelac's young queen, Hygd, is presiding with her husband. Hygelac welcomes his nephew back with great warmth. Beowulf narrates his adventures. In particular he talks about Hrothgar's daughter, Freawaru, who is engaged to Ingeld, a prince whose people are hereditary enemies of the Danes. Beowulf fears the marriage will not end the feud, and that Ingeld will have to decide between his people and his young wife. This was a moving passage for the original audience, since this is exactly what happens in the Ingeld legend. Thus the epic's original listeners are moved by Beowulf's wisdom and prescience in predicting the strife that is to come. Beowulf presents Wealtheow's and Hrothgar's gifts to his uncle and aunt. In return Hygelac gives his nephew a princely estate and his grandfather's sword.

## The Treasure and the Dragon

Years pass. Beowulf's uncle and his uncle's son, Heardred, die in battle. Beowulf becomes king of the Geats, and rules well for fifty years. Then a dragon begins to threaten the land. The dragon had been sleeping on a treasure, deposited in a barrow above the sea centuries before by the last despairing survivor of a noble family. A desperate man stumbles upon the treasure and steals a golden cup from it to regain his lord's favor. The dragon, in revenge, terrorizes the countryside, burning Beowulf's hall in the old king's absence. Beowulf decides to fight the dragon. He orders an iron shield made and assembles an escort of twelve warriors plus the thief, brought along as a guide. They arrive on the cliffs above the barrow. Beowulf, feeling his death near, looks back over his life and recounts the tragic history of his family and people. He speaks affectionately of his grandfather and the old man's grief over the accidental death of his eldest son. He speaks bluntly of the warfare between the Geats and Swedes. He recalls his adventures in Denmark. He speaks of his loyalty to his uncle Hygelac. Finally he remembers his uncle's disastrous raid to the Rhine and his own part in it. He recalls defeating Daegrefn, champion of the Franks, in single combat before both armies by crushing him in a bear hug. Beowulf then announces that he intends to fight the dragon alone. He goes down the path to the treasure barrow and attacks the dragon, but cannot manage to kill it. Only one of his men, the young warrior Wiglaf, comes to his aid. Together they kill the dragon, but Beowulf is fatally wounded. He dies saying he has no fear in God's judgment of him and thanking God for allowing him to trade his old life for a great treasure for his people. He tells Wiglaf to take care of the Geats. Finally, he asks that they build a barrow for him on the cliffs where it will be seen and he remembered. The Geats build the barrow, place the treasure in it, and mourn their lost king as the kindest and most worthy of rulers.

*Beowulf preparing to decapitate Grendel.*

## Characters

### Aeschere

Hrothgar's councillor and friend, his "wing man" in battle. Grendel's mother murdered him in revenge for the death of her son. Hrothgar is broken with grief when he learns of Aeschere's death.

### Beowulf

The son of Hrethel's daughter and Ecgtheow. From the age of seven he was raised by his maternal grandfather. He is first and foremost the hero who kills the monsters no one else can face, but he is more than a fighter. Beowulf is a strong man who thinks and feels. His deep affection for his grandfather, Hrethel, and uncle, Hygelac, lasts to the end of his long life. He is capable of discernment, sensitivity, and compassion. He is concerned for what Freawaru may face in her political marriage. He understands and sympathizes with Wealtheow's concern for her sons. He, more than any other character, has a sense of God's hand in human affairs. He alone talks about an afterlife. His impulses are not merely courageous, they are gener-

ous. As a young man he comforts Hrothgar at Aescere's death, saying that glorious deeds are the best thing for a man to take into death. Dying, he thanks God that he has been allowed to trade his old life for a treasure for his people and commits their welfare to Wiglaf.

Beowulf is not merely an incredibly strong man skilled in hand-to-hand combat, he is equally skilled with words. His defence of himself against Unferth is a brilliant exercise in oration. His conversation with his uncle on his return home is a formal "relatio," an official report of an ambassador. When he looks backward on his life and times before his final fight, he produces the sort of historical memoir that was long the literary hallmark of the elder statesman. His choices may not have always been what people around him wanted, whether in his decision not to take the throne over his young cousin or in his decision to fight the dragon. His choices, however, are never without reasons to which the narrator and the audience can feel sympathy.

Except for monsters, Beowulf, although he was always his uncle's foremost fighter, kills only two human beings in the poem: Daegrefn, the champion

# Media Adaptations

- After being the preserve of specialists for the first 150 years after its rediscovery, *Beowulf* began to catch the attention of general readers after the second world war. This is partially the result of the popularity of J. R. R. Tolkein's *Lord of the Rings*. Partially it is the result of a shift in attitudes concerning the bizarre and the marvellous. For whatever reasons, late twentieth-century audiences are willing to take seriously stories which pivot on human responses to monsters. *Beowulf's* monsters may be terrestrial, but they are essentially the terrors of modern science fiction, and of horror stories even closer to daily life. Many of the fears that *Beowulf* expressed and sublimated for its original audience are those which are similarly expressed and sublimated by the television series *X-Files* or the movie *The Creature from the Black Lagoon* or even *Independence Day*. We may even note that in the *X-Files*, the character Fox Mulder, like Beowulf, draws much of his motivation from his love of his family, a family which has grown to include his partner Dana Scully, just as Beowulf's

grew to include Hrothgar. Many of the ideals which we find in *Beowulf* and other Old English and Old Norse heroic poetry have made their way into the fictional development of Klingon culture in the various *Star Trek* television series and movies.

- *Star Trek Voyager* used a holodeck setting of *Beowulf* as a plot line in the first-season episode ''Heroes and Demons.''

- John Gardiner adapted *Beowulf* as a novel, *Grendel*, published by Knopf in 1972.

- *Beowulf* was adapted as a feature-length animated film, *Grendel, Grendel, Grendel* by independent Australian director and producer Alexander Stitt in 1981. The film is narrated by Peter Ustinov as the voice of Grendel.

- In 1982 Kenneth Pickering and Christopher Segal adapted *Beowulf* as a rock musical. The book and music were published as *Beowulf: A Rock Musical*, London: Samuel French, Inc., 1982.

---

of the Franks, during his uncle's disastrous raid to the lands at the mouth of the Rhine, and Onela, who was responsible for his cousin Heardred's death. Except for an expedition against the Swedes, Beowulf does not engage in any wars during his reign.

### Beowulf Scylding

Son of Scyld, father of Healfdene, grandfather of Hrothgar.

### Breca

A boy who has a swimming match with Beowulf. Beowulf admits it was a foolish thing to do. They are separated by a storm at sea. Breca reaches shore in Finland. Beowulf comes ashore after killing nine sea monsters who tried to eat him.

### Daegrefn

The champion of the Franks. Beowulf defeats him in single combat before the armies of the Geats and the Franks, crushing him in a bear hug.

### Dragon

As late as the sixteenth century, writers assumed that dragons still existed in out-of-the-way places. The dragon in this epic is only an animal–unlike many other dragons in northern legends, it does not speak. Traditionally dragons lived in caves or burial mounds, guarding treasure which they had either found or somehow accumulated. An Anglo-Saxon would probably expect Fort Knox to have a real dragon problem.

## Eadgils

Son of Othere, grandson of the Swedish king Ongetheow. He and his brother Eanmund rebelled against their uncle King Onela. They were sheltered by Heardred and the Geats. Beowulf, to avenge his cousin, supports him in a successful attempt to take the throne.

## Eanmund

Son of Othere, grandson of the Swedish king Ongetheow. He and his brother Eadgils rebelled against their uncle King Onela. They were sheltered by Heardred and the Geats.

## Ecglaf

Unferth's father.

## Ecgtheow

Beowulf's father, married to the unnamed daughter of Hrethel, king of the Geats. It is likely that Ecgtheow was related to the Swedish royal family. This would explain why the Swedish king, Onela, does not dispute Beowulf's control of the Geat kingdom after Beowulf's cousin Heardred dies in battle with the Swedes. Ecgtheow was involved in a feud so violent that only Hrothgar would shelter him. Hrothgar was able to settle the feud.

## Freawaru

Hrothgar's daughter, engaged to Ingeld in the hope that this would end the recurring war between the Danes and Ingeld's people, the Heathobards. Beowulf's prediction of what is likely to happen is uncannily like what the legends say did happen. The passage characterises Beowulf as perceptive and sympathetic.

## Grendel

With characters like Hannibal Lector and Eugene Victor Toombs appearing in popular novels, movies, and television series, readers are less likely to dismiss a story whose hero has to defend his society against an immensely strong cannibal like Grendel. Whatever Grendel and his mother may have been in the traditions behind the present poem, in *Beowulf* they are descendants of Cain, the eldest son of Adam and Eve, and the first murderer. Placing Grendel and his mother in a biblical context made them even easier for the original audience to accept. They live in the wilds, cut off from human society. Grendel's attack on the hall is motivated by his hatred for joy and light. The Danes cannot hope to come to terms with Grendel or his mother since they are completely outside of normal human society.

## Haethcyn

Second son of Hrethel, he accidentally kills his older brother in an archery accident. Haethcyn is killed in the border warfare between the Geats and the Swedes. Hygelac, his younger brother, leads the relief party which saves the remnants of the Geatish army at the battle of Ravenswood.

## Halga Til

Halga the good, Hrothgar's younger brother, father of Hrothulf. He is only a name in the story, as this character does not appear or take part in the action.

## Healfdene

Beowulf Scylding's son, the father of Hrothgar.

## Heardred

The son of Hygelac and Hygd. Beowulf refuses to take the throne before him and acts as his guardian. Heardred is killed in the fighting which follows his intervention in a power struggle between two branches of the Swedish royal family.

## Heorogar

Healfdene's second son.

## Herebeald

Hrethel's eldest son, killed by his younger brother Haethcyn in an archery accident.

## Heremod

A king of the Danes who reigns before Scyld. Despite his great promise he grows cruel and avaricious, murdering his own supporters. Both Hrothgar and the retainer who first sings Beowulf's praises use him as an example of an evil leader.

## Hondscio

Beowulf's companion. He is eaten by Grendel.

## Hrethel

Beowulf's maternal grandfather, Hrethel raises Beowulf from the age of seven. He dies of grief after his second son accidentally kills his eldest son. Fighting between the Geats and Swedes begins after Hrethel's death. Beowulf remembers his grandfather with great affection.

### Hrothgar

Great-grandson of Scyld, Hrothgar is a successful warrior king. He has built the greatest hall in the world and finds himself unable to defend it or his people from Grendel. Only once does his dignity and patient endurance break down, when he is faced with another monster and the death of his closest friend just when he thought his hall and people were finally safe. Hrothgar recovers his composure and gives Beowulf a philosophy of life that, while austere and pessimistic, is fitted to the world in which they live. As hinted in the poem, he will be killed by his son-in-law, Ingeld, and Heorot will be burned.

### Hygd

Wife of Hygelac, represented as a perfect queen. She offers the throne to Beowulf after her husband's death because her son is too young. It is interesting to note that while Hygd's name means "thought", her husband's means "thoughtless."

### Hygelac

Hrethel's youngest son, hero of the battle of Ravenswood. He dies on a raid that is initially successful, but ends with the annihilation of the Geatish forces.

### Ohtere

Son of Ongentheow. His sons Eadgils and Eanmund unsuccessfully rebel against his brother Onela.

### Onela

King of the Swedes, son of Ongentheow. His nephews Eadgils and Eanmund unsuccessfully rebel against him. They then seek refuge with Heardred and the Geats. Onela exacts vengeance on the Geats, killing Heardred, but he does not interfere when Beowulf takes the throne. Beowulf helps Eadgils take the Swedish throne and kills Onela in vengeance for his cousin's death.

### Ongentheow

King of the Swedes, killed at the battle of Ravenswood.

### Scyld

Often called Scyld Scefing, the first king of his line. In other ancient accounts, Scyld is said to have arrived alone in a boat as a small child. One tradition holds that he is the son of the biblical Noah, and was born aboard the ark. Scyld appears in the genealogy of the West Saxon kings.

### Unferth

Unferth is characterized as Hrothgar's "thyle," but modern scholars are not exactly sure what this means. In glossaries from the Old English period, the word is defined by the Latin word *rhetor* or *orator*. Unferth may be the king's "press officer," a source of official information about the king and his policies, or he may be a scribe or a sort of jester. He is initially envious of Beowulf's reception at court and his reputation, but later offers him his friendship.

### Wealtheow

A princess of the house of the Helmings and the wife of Hrothgar. She is a woman of great dignity, political sense, and status among her husband's people. She addresses Hrothgar like a counsellor.

### Wiglaf

A young warrior who comes to Beowulf's aid when he fights the dragon. He is a relative of Beowulf, probably on his father's side since his connections are Swedish. His father, Weohstan, fought on the Swedish side during their invasion of the Geats following Heardred's meddling in the internal feuds of the Swedish royal house.

## Themes

The young Beowulf saves the Danes from two monsters. After a long and noble life, he dies defending his own people from a dragon.

### Fortitude and Wisdom

For narrator and characters, wisdom and fortitude represent an ideal to which every man aspires and every society needs. Physical bravery was most appreciated when accompanied by understanding and discernment. This discernment was not merely practical, it was supported by a larger spiritual understanding of God and the human condition. This is the point of Hrothgar's "sermon" in lines 1700-82.

The Danish coast guard, for example, (lines 229-300) respects and demonstrates these qualities in his treatment of Beowulf and his men. Beowulf is

# Topics for Further Study

- Research the finds of the Sutton Hoo Burial excavated in 1939 and compare the burial and the treasures found to the burials and treasures in *Beowulf*.

- Investigate the recent research done on the development of kingship in the seventh and eighth centuries and compare the findings to the presentation of kingship in *Beowulf*.

- Read J. R. R. Tolkein's *Lord of the Rings*, particularly the chapters dealing with the Riders of Rohan. How is *Beowulf* reflected in the work?

- Investigate the new *Beowulf* manuscript project and report on the scientific tests which are used to investigate manuscripts, including infra-red photography and chemical analysis. Information on the project is available on the world wide web at http://www.edu/~kiernan/BL/kportico.html.

- *Beowulf* is a poem almost exclusively concerned with the upper end of society. Investigate the economic basis of migration-age tribes or early medieval kingdoms.

- The society which created *Beowulf* accepted the importance of the desire to be remembered. Investigate how modern psychology views this need.

- Metal-working was an important Anglo-Saxon craft. Although they could not achieve the high temperatures used in steel-making until the later middle ages, they had developed techniques to make small quantities of usable steel. Investigate these techniques and the physical properties of iron which make them possible.

---

a fearless master of hand-to-hand combat. He demonstrates discernment in his understanding and treatment of men and women and in his sense of God. Even if his decision to fight the dragon is questionable, the narrator underlines the reasonableness of its basis. Beowulf's uncle Hygelac, on the other hand, while having great courage, lacks wisdom and falls victim to his own folly and the greater military resources of the Franks.

### Glory and Treasure

The characters in *Beowulf*, and its original audience, wanted glory, the immortality of good fame, to remain alive in human memory across time and space. Glory in *Beowulf* is usually connected with heroism in battle or with generosity. Treasure was the outward manifestation of glory. Men were anxious to receive gifts of fine weapons, armor, and jewellery—and, much as today's athletes look on their salaries relative to those of other athletes, warriors compared their gifts with those given to others. Such visible wealth advertised a warrior's worth and a people's strength.

Devout Christians, however, would have tried to seek the glory which God gave to those who did his will, the imperishable treasure laid up in the heaven of the Gospels. They would seek to do their duty, and more than their duty, purely for the love of God and neighbor rather than for earthly fame. Earthly treasure was to be used to do good, not as a display.

The narrator's and the characters' view of glory is a point of contention among critics. Some commentators think that *lofgeornost,* ''most desirous of praise,'' the poem's last word, which is applied to Beowulf, as well as Beowulf's own words to Hrothgar ''Let him who can, gain good repute before death— that it is the finest thing afterwards for the lifeless man'' (lines 1384-89) reflect badly on Beowulf. It may not be so simple.

In the last lines of the poem (3180-82) the qualities for which Beowulf's people praise him are not a warrior's, but those of a kindly friend. He is, they say, ''of all the kings of the world, the gentlest of men, the kindest and gentlest to his people, the most eager for glory.'' Because of the qualities the Geats link with Beowulf's eagerness for glory and fame, some readers believe that *lofgeornost* is specifically divine and not human.

### Wyrd (fate) and Providence

In lines 1055-58 the narrator says Grendel would have killed more men if he could ''except God in his wisdom and the man's (Beowulf's) courageous spirit had withstood that wyrd and him. The lord ruled all the human race as he still does.''

Both the narrator and individual characters talk about both God's providence and a concept the Anglo-Saxons called *wyrd.* Providence is the will of God moving in the affairs of men. It means that there is a plan and meaning behind what happens. It does not mean that men are coerced by God. Their wills are their own, but the ability to carry out their intentions is given by God.

*Wyrd* is usually translated as ''fate.'' Many critics have assumed that it means a blind force which predetermines the outcome of everything. There are one or two places in the poem where this may be its meaning. In others it is a word for ''death''. In most cases *wyrd* appears to mean the normal or expected pattern of cause and effect.

### Loyalty, Vengeance, and Feud

Loyalty is one of the greatest virtues in the world depicted in *Beowulf.* It is the glue holding Anglo-Saxon Society together, but it brought with it the darker duties of vengeance and feud.

Today injustice and victimization are often presented as lesser evils than ''taking the law into your own hands,'' but in Anglo-Saxon society order was maintained by just that, the concept that all free men had a duty to see justice done. It was a duty to punish the murderer of family, friends, lord, or servant. One deposed West Saxon king was killed by a swineherd in retribution for the king's murder of his lord. It was possible to accept one's guilt and pay compensation, the *wergild,* or ''man-price.'' The guilty person's family or lord had a duty to see that it was paid. Christians were encouraged to offer and accept these fines, but no one was forced to. In some circumstances it was considered dishonorable to accept—if the killing was generally considered justified, for example.

Feuds were often the result of tit-for-tat vengeance. The feud is a constant unspoken theme in *Beowulf* since Anglo-Saxons understood conflict generally in terms of the feud. In *Beowulf* Grendel is said to be feuding with God and with the Danes. To stress Grendel's alienation from human society the poet writes that the Danes could not expect a ''wergild'' from him (lines 154- 58). When Grendel is killed, his mother comes to avenge his death. Hrethel, Beowulf's grandfather, grieves bitterly because he cannot seek vengance for his eldest son's accidental death. The presentation of the wars between the Geats and Swedes stress elements which recall the feud, particularly the killing of kings.

### Evil and the Monsters

The monsters in *Beowulf* are thought by some to represent the evil of human suffering caused by natural disasters. This is not an entirely adequate explanation. Grendel and his mother are essentially human even if they are monstrous. Although it does not excuse them, each monster's predatory activities are motivated first by human actions. Grendel's envy is aroused by the sounds of human joy. The dragon is only following its nature when it enters the open barrow and nests on the hidden treasure. The dragon is disturbed by a thief who was himself driven by necessity.

Hrothgar locates evil within man himself. In lines 1700-82 he sums up all that can go wrong when a warrior forgets that God is the source of everything that he has and is. Beginning with the example of Heremod, a Danish king turned tyrant, Hrothgar asks the young Beowulf to remember the source of his strength and to be wary of the greed and hunger for power that destroys the generosity that binds society together. Finally he begs him to recall that good fortune and life itself are transitory; sickness, the sea, the sword, or old age will eventually take his strength and life. Beowulf takes Hrothgar's word to heart. He refuses to accept the kingship of his people until there is no other choice. He dies thanking God that he was able to win a treasure that will be of use to his people.

## Style

### Narrative Voice

*Beowulf* has an omniscient (''all-knowing'') narrator. The narrative voice comments on the character's actions, and knows and is able to report on what they think. The narrator is aware of things—for example, the curse on the dragon's treasure (lines 3066-75)—that are not known to the epic's characters. *Beowulf* shares this omniscient narration with other epics, such as the *Iliad,* the *Odyssey,* and the *Aeneid,* but remains subtly different. The narrator of *Beowulf* makes an explicit connection with the audience, acknowledging a shared background of cultural knowledge, in the opening lines of the poem: "*We* have heard of the thriving of the throne of Denmark" (emphasis added). The narrator's voice is also intimately connected with those of the characters. Both use narratives in the same way, to point a moral or to project future events.

## Characterization

The poet used several methods to create character. The narrator describes characters. The poet uses direct speech, a popular method in Germanic poetry to develop character. Characters define each other, as when the coast guard (lines 237-57) or Wulfgar (lines 336a-70) speak of their impressions of Beowulf and his men. More striking is the poet's careful development of characters through their own speeches. The voices of the individual characters are just that, the voices of individuals. Beowulf's speeches could not be confused with Hrothgar's.

## Alliterative Verse

Old English poetry is different from that of most English verse written since the Norman Conquest. It is based on a pattern of stressed syllables linked by alliteration (the repetition of identical initial consonant sounds or any vowel sounds appearing close together) across a line of verse divided by a distinct pause in the middle.

Old English Verse follows these basic rules:

1. The basic unit is the half line. Each half line has two stressed syllables and up to six unstressed syllables.

2. In a full line the two half lines are divided by a pause (called a caesura). They are joined by alliteration, the repetition of the initial consonants or vowels of stressed syllables, as: Anna angry, Arthur bold.

Two or three (never all four) stressed syllables alliterate with one another. They may be the first and/or the second and the third. The third stressed syllable must alliterate. The fourth stressed syllable does not.

## Episodes and Digressions

One of the most characteristic features of *Beowulf* is the use of shorter narratives embedded in the main action of the poem. They are not part of the main narrative, but they can be part of its past or present. These narratives can be divided into two types, episodes and digressions. An episode is a narrative which is complete in itself, but merged one way or another into the main narrative. An example is the Finnsburg Tale (lines 1063-1159a), which is sung during the celebration after Beowulf kills Grendel's mother. A digression is much shorter, allusive rather than entire and complete, and it breaks the flow of the main narrative. Episodes and digressions often illustrate good or bad conduct or suggest to the audience a particular way of looking at the main action.

## From Lay to Epic

Except for *Beowulf,* existing secular narrative poetry in Old English, like "The Battle of Maldon," "The Battle of Brunnanburh," and the "Finnsburg Fragment" are all lays, or fairly short narratives telling the story of one event. Only the "Waldhere Fragment" (sixty-three remaining lines) may have been part of a poem as long as *Beowulf.* The lay seems to have been the usual native narrative poem. Longer, more complex epic structure appears to have come into existence with the introduction of Christian Latin culture, whose educational system included the *Aeneid* as a school text for study. For this reason, nineteenth-century scholars assumed that *Beowulf* was made up of earlier lays. Scholars now accept that *Beowulf* is not a patchwork of older material stitched together, but an original composition using completely recast older material from a variety of sources.

## Formulaic Style

Many scholars have attempted to demonstrate that *Beowulf* was composed orally. Whether the poet wrote or spoke, the Beowulf poet did use a traditional stock of words and patterns of composition used by all Anglo-Saxon poets and recognized and appreciated by their audiences.

The poetic formula used can be broken down into 3 parts:

1) Epithets and short modifying formulas

2) Sentence formulas

3) Formulaic elaboration of themes

1. One kind of epithet, the kenning, is a kind of condensed or boiled-down metaphor: *isern-scur* ("iron shower") for a flight of arrows; *hildegicelum* ("battle-icicle") for sword. Another kind of epithet

is a literal description similarly reduced to its essentials: *hildebord* ("battle board," a shield). The difference between a kenning and a normal noun compound can be seen by comparing *hilde-mece* ("battle sword") with *hilde-leoma* ("battle light"). There are many different compounds for warriors, weapons and relationships in a heroic culture. By varying the first word of the compound, the poet could make different alliterative patterns. Thus *hilde* can be varied with *beado, guth, wael.* The words formed do not necessarily mean exactly the same thing. *Hilde* means battle, but *wael* means specifically "slaughter."

2. Sentence formulas provided summaries and transitions. Many are short, half-lines: "I recall all that," line 2427. There are also sentence patterns, for instance those beginning "not at all" or "not only" which then go on to "but," "after," "until," "then." These are often used for ironic understatement, another characteristic of Anglo-Saxon verse. For example: "*Not at all* did the personal retainers, the children of princes stand about him in valour, *but* they ran to the woods" (lines 2596-9a). Sentence formulas were developed to allow quick shifts of action and to carry the parallels and contrasts which are characteristic of Old English style.

3. Certain themes were addressed through the use of specific words, images, and symbolic objects. These words and ideas had an understood meaning among Anglo-Saxons. Using such words invoked their understood meaning, so that the themes they referred to need not be further elaborated by the poet. A good example is the group of words and images used to develop battle descriptions: the "beasts of battle," the wolf, the raven and the eagle, who, it was understood, traditionally fed on the bodies of those slain.

# Historical Context

## Introduction

The historical Hygelac died circa 521. The *Beowulf* manuscript was written about 1000 A.D. In the intervening centuries there was both change and continuity in every area of Anglo-Saxon life. Because we cannot date *Beowulf* with certainty, we cannot draw specific parallels. We do not know if the society the poet described is the one he or she knew at first hand and projected into the past from his or her present, or if it was a poetic reconstruction, pieced together from memories, older Anglo-Saxon and Latin poetry.

## The Origins of the Anglo-Saxon Kingdoms

The Germanic peoples arrived in Britain over a period of perhaps a century and a half. They did not always arrive in tribal or family groups. They do not seem to have brought their kings with them. Only the Mercian royal family claimed to be descended from a continental king. Certainly groups based on kinship or on loyalty to a military leader—whether one of their own or a Roman-Britain—began to coalesce into proto-kingdoms. The wars between the Geats and the Swedes in *Beowulf* may represent remembered incidents on the continent. At the same time the wars may represent the continual struggle among the kingdoms of Anglo-Saxon England.

These areas absorbed one another and Romano-British areas until at the time of the Viking invasions (circa 800) there were three major kingdoms: Mercia, Northumbria, and Wessex, and two smaller ones, Kent and East Anglia. When Alfred had fought the Vikings to a standstill circa 890, Wessex alone was left. Through all these centuries government, society, and culture was changing and developing

## Loyalty and Society

Throughout this period, however, some things remained constant. One is the personal loyalty which held society together. The mutual loyalty within the kindred and within the war band was at the heart of Anglo-Saxon social organization. Institutions were centered on individuals. A noble, even a royal household was held together by loyalty to a lord who was generous and worthy of respect. Within this relationship the *beotword'* was important. It was not a boast, as we understand it, but a formal statement of intention.

## Learning, Literature and Craftsmanship

Life in Anglo-Saxon England had few of the comforts which we take for granted, but it was not without achievement and personal satisfaction. Anglo-Saxon society appreciated craftsmanship and was open to new ideas and technologies. Within a century of the arrival of Roman and Irish missionaries among them, the Anglo-Saxons had mastered the manufacture of parchment, paint and ink, glass and masonry. By the eighth century they had several kinds of watermills with relatively elaborate wood-

# Compare & Contrast

- **Anglo-Saxon period:** The pre-electrical world was a world of darkness. People got up and went to bed with the sun. Artificial lighting consisted of firelight and candles or small lamps burning whale or olive oil, or rushes dipped in animal fat. On a clear night in Anglo-Saxon England the sky would have been powdered with stars.

  **Late twentieth century:** Today earth's great urban centers can light up the night. Airplane travelers can see the lights of towns, cities, and interstates. Relatively few stars can be seen.

- **Anglo-Saxon period:** The population of Britain in the early Middle Ages was probably under three million people. Land was still being re-claimed for farming, difficult in a country where most of the native trees will readily regrow from stumps. In Anglo-Saxon England wolves still roamed the countryside. The edges of forests were important for game, wood, and food for foraging semi-domesticated animals. Wetlands were important for fish, waterfowl and basketry materials, such as alder, willow, and rushes.

  **Late twentieth century:** Today the population of Britain is over fifty-seven million. Most people live in cities. There is a constant struggle to save woodlands, wetlands, and areas of tradi-tional agriculture.

- **Anglo-Saxon period:** Most Anglo-Saxons lived in largely self-sufficient communities. People grew what they ate, made what they needed, built their homes out of local materials, and traded for goods made locally. Local or traveling smiths made up knives and tools to order. Salt and millstones and luxury goods, like wine, spices, and silk, would be bought at fairs. Items such as swords, and gold and silver jewellery, were less the objects of commerce than of socially meaningful gift exchange.

  **Late twentieth century:** Modern consumers buy nearly everything they use in daily life. Very few subsistence cultures are left. Even food is often bought already prepared. Many, if not most, consumer goods originate hundreds or thousands of miles from where they are sold and used.

- **Anglo-Saxon period:** Most Anglo-Saxons died before the age of forty. Some people lived into their sixties and seventies, but the average age of death for those who lived passed infancy was probably between thirty-five and thirty-eight. Medicine was primitive. Herbal remedies had limited effectiveness. There was no clear idea of how diseases were contracted or how they could be prevented. There were few ways of deadening pain. Many common ailments were fatal because of ineffective treatments. Blood-poisoning and death in childbirth were both frequent.

  **Late twentieth century:** Today people in indus-trialized nations can expect to live into their seventies and even beyond. Most of the illnesses and conditions which killed Anglo-Saxons are no longer a threat to people with access to basic modern medicine. Improved hygiene, abundant clean water supplies, the ability to preserve food safely, and greater knowledge about the causes and prevention of communicable illnesses have all contributed to longer and healthier lives.

---

en machinery, monumental sculpture, and the pot-ter's wheel. By the eighth century Anglo-Saxons were producing literature in Latin and carrying Christianity to related tribes on mainland Europe. The love of craftsmanship, learning, and literature survived the greatest hardships. When the educa-tional base was nearly wiped out by the Viking raids in the ninth century, Alfred of Wessex, in the middle of his struggles to defend his kingdom, set about re-establishing schools and encouraging scholarship. He encouraged translators, even translating texts himself, so that those who did not know Latin could still have access to "the books most necessary for men to know."

The Germanic immigrants from the continent who became the Anglo-Saxons brought a writing system—runes—with them from the continent. Runes were used for short inscriptions, occasionally magical, usually merely a statement of who made or who owned an object. Their literature and history were preserved orally using an elaborate poetic technique and vocabulary. Even after the introduction of Latin learning, this poetry held its own and began to be written using the Latin alphabet. Nevertheless, literature was still heard rather than read, even when the text was a written one. The difficulties of book production meant that multiple copies of anything except the most basic religious books were a luxury even in monasteries. Whether literate or illiterate, men and women would rely on hearing books read aloud. Even when reading privately people read aloud. This made them conscious of the rhythm of poetry and even prose.

Beside their love of literature, the Anglo-Saxons had a passion for music. Small harps, called lyres, are even found in warriors graves, and in *Beowulf* at least one warrior is also a poet-singer. Songs and chants were popular among the Anglo-Saxons, and some of the earliest manuscripts of chant still in existence are from Anglo-Saxon England. There are even mentions of large organs in the tenth century.

### The Hall

Halls like Hrothgar's mead-hall or drinking hall Heorot, if not so magnificent, were the normal homes of wealthier land-owners. A great deal like the old fashioned wooden barns still seen in parts of the United States, they had great central open fires and beamed roofs. The walls were hung with woven and embroidered hangings. By the tenth century some halls had an upper floor. Some had smaller attached rooms or halls to give the women of the family some privacy.

### Women in Anglo-Saxon Society

The hall was in many ways a men's club, but the owner's wife and her eldest daughter would extend hospitality to guests and retainers, offering them a drink from a special cup. The word "Wassail," an early English toast that later came to be applied to a hot alcoholic brewed drink, derives from *Waes thu hael,* "Be you healthy," which was said as a drink was handed to a guest.

Women were active in dairying and textile production. Wool and linen were spun by hand and woven on upright frames. English woollen cloth and fine embroidery were already prized on the continent by the end of the eighth century. Women, particularly from ruling families, could have considerable power, influence, and education.

### Weapons

Every Anglo-Saxon man and woman carried a plain practical knife for work and eating. Men who could be called up for military service would be equipped with a spear and shield. Warriors and nobles would also own a sword. Swords were very expensive, worth as much as the price of a small farm, and armor even more so. They were important possessions often handed down from father to son. To bury them with a man was a great mark of honor and a display of wealth and status.

## Critical Overview

If the *Beowulf* manuscript is not the author's autograph (the author's own handwriting), as claimed by Kevin Kiernan, then the first critical appreciation we have of the poem is the manuscript itself. Someone thought enough to copy it down or to have it copied on good vellum by two fairly good scribes—incuring a sizable expensive for the year 1000. Another indication of early popularity may be in its apparent influence on another Old English poem, *Andreas,* which survives in a manuscript kept at Exeter Cathedral in Devon since the mid-eleventh century. After that there is no sign of the poem for well over five hundred years.

Laurence Nowell acquired the eleventh-century manuscript in the 1560s and wrote his name and date on the top of the first page. The manuscript eventually appeared in the library of a family named Cotton, but it does not appear in either of the library's two catalogues (1628-29 and 1696). In 1704, Humfrey Wanley, however, recorded it in his published catalogue of manuscripts containing Old English. A century later Sharon Turner published illustrative citations and very inaccurate translations. The effective re-discovery of the poem was the work of an Icelander, G. S. Thorkelin, and a Dane, N. S. F. Grundtvig. Thorkelin had a transcription of the poem made and made a second himself. He published his edition in 1815. Grudtvig worked on and published an edition of the poem between

1815 and 1861. Perhaps the greatest single scholar of the poem, Grudtvig proposed many of the now accepted restorations of the text (emendations) and proved that Beowulf's uncle Hygelac was in fact a historical figure. For Grundtvig the poem's greatness lay in its sense of moral purpose. He approached the poem as a unified work of literature in its own terms, anticipating the major topics of modern *Beowulf* criticism.

After Grudtvig, scholars concentrated on clearing up problems of the poem's language and allusions. Others mined the poem as a historical and social document in the hopes of proving their often politically inspired theories about ancient Germanic life. Still others attempted to identify still older poems (lays) within it or to discover a nature myth or allegory in its action. By the opening years of the twentieth century, *Beowulf* was a synonym for undergraduate literary boredom. In 1915, novelist D. H. Lawrence used it in *The Rainbow* as a symbol of aridity and meaninglessness in education. Robert Graves, just back from front-line battle in World War I in 1919, disagreed: ''*Beowulf* and *Judith* [another Old English poem] seemed good poems to me. Beowulf lying wrapped in a blanket among his platoon of drunken thanes . . .—all this was closer to most of us at the time than the . . . eighteenth century.''

It was another returned soldier, J. R. R. Tolkein, who, in writing ''*Beowulf:* The Monsters and the Critics,'' made it impossible to treat the poem simply as a resource for the study of language or anthropology. Some thirty years earlier, W. Kerr had complained that the monsters cheapened the poem. Tolkein insisted that the evil which the monsters represented was a central part of a profound commentary on the human condition. Many critics agree that Tolkein redirected readers of *Beowulf* from what the poem is not to what it is. His powers as a writer, not only in his lecture but also in his use of *Beowulf* in *The Lord of the Rings,* mean that *Beowulf* came to be accepted not only as literature, but as great literature.

Criticism in the 1930s was dominated by discussions of lyric poetry. Tolkein's elegiac reading of *Beowulf,* although not entirely convincing in its details, was popular among critics, and re-focused critical attention away from the problems of narrative momentum and on to the poem's humanity. Although F. Klaeber had established the poem's essential Christianity over twenty years before, critical tendencies were also now sympathetic

*A manuscript page from Beowulf.*

to Tolkein's identification of a Christian reading beneath the surface action. The horrors of war, too, had made monstrous and unreasoning evil at the heart of the human situation a compelling subject.

Klaeber saw Beowulf as a real, even Christlike, hero. Tolkein, like many writers and film makers of the middle of the century, was uncomfortable with ''traditional'' heroes. Eric Stanley, John Leyerle, and others developed a vision of the man Beowulf flawed by his desire for praise or treasure or even being born before the arrival of Christianity. Leyerle and Halverson, and even more thoroughly Berger and Leicester, tend to relocate the flaw from the character to his society. In its most developed form, this view says that the heroism the characters see as necessary for personal worth and social solidarity are destructive of both. These studies are often selective in their presentation, out of touch with historical reality and full of special pleading. In them Beowulf is, as the saying goes, ''damned if he does and damned if he doesn't.'' Kemp Malone and others rebutted at least the more extreme of these arguments.

Many recent readers have struggled with the assumption that since Beowulf is not Christian the poet must have assumed that he was damned. This does not seem to fit with what actually goes on in the poem. Some critics have flirted with the idea of a slightly heretical or at least theologically confused poet. For much the same reason, Margaret Goldsmith proposed an allegorical reading of the poem. More recently, beginning with a collection of articles edited by Colin Chase in 1981, *Beowulf* criticism has been re-focused on the manuscript itself and the question of dating. In the last fifty years hundreds of articles and books have been written on *Beowulf*, of them perhaps the most influential have been Adrien Bonjour's 1950 *The Digressions in Beowulf*; E. B. Irving's two books *A Reading of Beowulf* (1968) and *Rereading Beowulf* (1989); and John Nile's *Beowulf: The Poem and its Tradition* (1984).

## Criticism

### Helen Conrad-O'Briain

*In the following essay, Conrad-O'Briain discusses the epic elements of and analyzes the Anglo-Saxon epic techniques the Beowulf poet used in the poem. She also compares the character of Beowulf with other epic heroes and reviews several of the themes of the work, including the role of God and providence and the futile, transitory nature of human existence.*

Michael Alexander, a translator of *Beowulf*, begins his entry on the epic in *A Dictionary of Modern Critical Terms* with Milton's "great argument" and "answerable style," that is, an important theme and a style to match, to define epic. He continues, "classically trained critics, expecting art to see life steadily and see it whole, look for an idealized realism and debar folklore and romance elements." Paraphrasing and then quoting the critic Northrup Frye, Alexander accepts that "these stories recapitulate the life of the individual and the race. The note of epic is its objectivity: "'It is hardly possible to overestimate the importance for western literature of the *Iliad's* demonstration that the fall of an enemy, no less than of a friend or leader, is tragic and not comic.'" According to this definition, *Beowulf* somehow combines the elements which define the epic with other elements which seem to come from the world of "Jack the Giant Killer" and "Three Billy Goats Gruff."

*Beowulf* is, indeed, on one level a very simple story told with great elaboration, A man of great strength, courage, and generosity fights three mon-

sters, two when he is a young man, the third in his old age. Other more complicated human events precede these, others intervene, others will follow, but those more realistic events are all essentially background. To some earlier critics as to W. P. Kerr in *Epic and Romance*, the choice of a folktale main narrative was a serious fault. Monsters lacked the dignity to carry the "great argument" with "answerable style."

But *Beowulf* is a true epic in its breadth of interests and sympathies, even though it is centered on the career of one man killing three monsters. The action and the characters of this apparently simple story have the strength to embody the experience and ideals of the original audience. The monsters participate in evil and disorder as no human, even Heremod, could, but the evil that originates purely within the human heart is not overlooked. Transforming both the fairy tale monsters and the sordid power politics of the background is the objective recognition of human struggle for understanding and order. This is the hallmark of human experience seen through the lense of epic technique. In *Beowulf* the narrator and characters use human experience to understand the human condition and to find the noblest way to live their lives.

In part *Beowulf's* epic inclusiveness comes from the narrator's often short observations, which place the poem in a larger, transcendent context. The narrator periodically reminds the reader of the over-arching providence of God as in lines 1056-58: "except that God in his wisdom and the man's courageous spirit withstood him. The Lord God ruled over all men, as he now yet does." In part the epic breadth comes from the characters, particularly Beowulf and Hrothgar. It is Beowulf's generosity of spirit and imaginative sympathy for individuals, which introduce characters like the old man mourning his executed son or the young girl Freawaru facing a political marriage. It is that same generosity of spirit and sympathy which allows him to speak objectively of the "sin and crime on both sides" in the war between the Geats and Swedes (lines 2472-73). Hrothgar, the old king of the Danes, a man who has known triumph and disaster, looks back across his long life and reaches into the workings of the human heart and out into the realities of time and circumstances to understand human sorrow and evil.

The inclusiveness of *Beowulf* reaches backwards and forwards in time. The short narratives embedded in the main narrative (digressions), reflect on the main action as Adrien Bonjour demon-

# What Do I Read Next?

- The anonymous Old English poem *The Battle of Maldon* was composed close to the time the *Beowulf* manuscript was being transcribed. It recounts the death in 991 A.D. of Byrhtnoth, ealdorman (governor) of Essex, and his men while fighting the Vikings. It is filled with the heroic commonplaces of Germanic literature: the courageous and still active old war leader who makes one miscalculation, but dies shoulder to shoulder with his men, the retainers who die one by one standing by their dead lord. Modern readers will see in it formulas of another kind, the voices and characters of the men in the ranks, the career soldier as well as the civilian volunteer. *Maldon* and its characters could easily be transposed to a Hollywood platoon or bomber crew movie.

- The anonymous Irish epic *Tain Bo Cualgne* (*The Cattle Raid of Cooley*), available in a translation by Thomas Kinsella (1969), is unusual in that it is composed in prose with inset short verses. Like *Beowulf* it is difficult to date, the language of the oldest version is probably eighth century although some passages of inset verse may be older. The focus of the story fluctuates between two characters, Queen Maeve of Connacht, who begins the war, and the Ulster hero Cuchulainn. During the period in which the *Tain* and *Beowulf* were written, England and Ireland enjoyed close cultural relations.

- Felix's *Life of Guthlac*, translated by Bertram Colgrave (1956), was written in Latin sometime after 714 and before 749 A.D. Guthlac (circa 674-714 A.D.) was an adventurous young Anglo-Saxon nobleman. After successfully leading a war band, he was moved in his early twenties by "the miserable deaths of kings of his race" to enter a monastery. There he read of the heroism of the "desert fathers," the monks who had gone into the wilderness to be alone with God, and decided that he would attempt to be such a spiritual warrior. He became a hermit in the East Anglian fens, living in an old burial mound, which he held against the onslaughts of demons. Although he was a hermit he was often visited by people seeking spiritual comfort. As well as being a constant friend to his fellow humans, animals trusted him implicitly.

- John Gardner's *Grendel*, published in 1972, is an imaginative retelling of *Beowulf* from Grendel's point of view. *Grendel* made the *New York Times* best-seller list.

- Tom Holt's "Who's Afraid of Beowulf" (1989) is a fantasy comedy which mixes satire, heroic virtues, and computers. The hero, whose generosity of spirit seems to be based on one strain of critical analysis of Beowulf's character, leads his loyal band and a young woman archaeologist from Long Island to save a world which is superficially utterly alien from his own, yet essentially unchanged.

- In the three books of *The Lord of the Rings* (1954-55), J. R. R. Tolkein's reading and teaching of *Beowulf* shaped the characters, action and society of his famous fantasy. The influence of *Beowulf* is strongest or most obvious in the "Riders of Rohan" who play a large part in Book 2, *The Two Towers*, and Book 3, *The Return of the King*. Their society and culture is clearly based on the Anglo-Saxon heroic ideal.

strated in the *Digressions in "Beowulf."* They also create a sense of continuity and universality in the situations the characters face. Character by character, incident by incident, they create the society and the universe in which the great tests of the monsters are set. They define the limits of the heroic heart and heroic society, the ideals which characters like Hrothgar and Beowulf fulfill and in some ways transcend. In these narratives, as in the poem, as Alexander writes in his translation's introduction, the operations of cause and consequence, however mysterious to the characters, whether deriving from natural forces or human will, are inescapable.

*Beowulf* is a carefully designed poem. A heroic king comes from the sea and is given back to the sea in death. Generations later another heroic king is buried on the cliffs overlooking the sea. Between them vengeance and feud, despair and generosity weave their way through the human life. Every idea, every theme is examined from one angle after another, with all the techniques available to the poet from an Anglo-Saxon poetic tradition rich in irony and understatement. Treasure is the lifeblood of heroic society, fame made tangible, but the poet links it with death and despair. Love of kin motivates Beowulf throughout his life, but in the society around him families destroy themselves. Song and generosity wake a monster. Just when safety seems assured the best and truest friend and councillor dies.

The fineness of the poet's application of technique make the poem a sustained high point in Anglo-Saxon poetry. Although these techniques are specifically Anglo-Saxon, they can be broadly paralleled in all western epics. The poem uses an elaborate vocabulary dictated, at least in part, by the alliteration and stress patterns of Old English verse. This vocabulary, although largely that of everyday speech or prose, includes words which are rarely used outside of poetry. It is quite possible the poet has even coined words for *Beowulf*. The poet presents the material in carefully structured sentences and equally structured verse paragraphs. This structure, with its emphasis on defining things by what they are not, and by understatement, produces pointed juxtapositions of characters, themes and action. It clarifies cause and effect. It produces clear and swift narrative movement. It can be a potent source of irony.

Alexander in the introduction to his translation, draws the reader's attention to the use of constant basic values in *Beowulf*. Sunlight is good, cold is bad. The words do not refer to symbols but to reality. Alexander's observations are a good introduction to the poet's use of description. The poem gains immediacy from simplicity and universality, qualities it shares with the Homeric epic. The poet always seems to find the best and fewest words to make objects real to us. Landscapes resonate with atmosphere: grey, cold and threatening as in the

description of the wild lands which Grendel haunts (lines 1357-76 and 1408-23), or full of light and life, like the landscape of the creation song (lines 90-98). Sometimes space is defined by the quality of movement through it, like the landscape through which the Danish retainers ride back after tracking Grendel's last bloodstained retreat or Beowulf's two sea voyages (lines 210-24 and 1903-12).

The poem's characters, particularly Beowulf himself, are molded by the needs and aspirations of the poet and audience's society. This is true to some extent of all literature, but particularly of the epic. Beowulf, however, is different from other northern heroes and from the heroes of Greek and Roman epics. He is radically different, not just from Heremod, but from Ing and Scyld and Sigemund. He is unlike Achilles, unlike Odysseus, except in his love of family. He is a hero driven not by personal glory but by affection and duty. He seems largely untouched by the darker emotions which dog Aeneas and betray him into fury at the end of the *Aeneid*. Only the doomed Hector of Homer's *Iliad* seems to be a hero of the same clay. Personal glory is not without meaning to Beowulf. He tells Hrothgar that the best thing men can do is to lay up fame before death (lines 1386-89). He happily accepts treasure and just as happily passes it on to others. Nevertheless, duty and sympathy and generosity are his primary motivations. Despite his great strength, he is a man with limitations, in each of his fights he is seriously challenged and clearly sees himself as relying on the help of God.

Beginning with J. R. R. Tolkein's "The Monsters and the Critics," many critics have stressed a sense of futility in *Beowulf*. This reading arose partially from factors within the poem and partially from factors external to it. These critics had lived through two world wars. Many of them had served as soldiers and known violent, often pointless, death, often the death of friends. They did not cease to admire heroism, but they balanced it against what they knew of war's futility. *Beowulf* is not a pacifist's poem, but these critics have made readers more aware of the problems and fragility of its warrior society and standards. Beowulf and the rest of the characters are never allowed the luxury of assuming that any victory earns more than a respite. The poem is full of a deep sense of the fragility of human institutions and of human hopes. Good men and women can do their best, their fame is assured, but not necessarily their works. The whole action of the poem happens within historical patterns where families and kingdoms rise and fall.

This sense of the transitory nature of human life is part of the critical re-evaluation of the implications of the poem's Christianity. J. D. A. Ogilvy and Donald Baker have suggested that Beowulf's death is like a saint's death, and the parallels, particularly with that of Bede's death are closer than even they suggest. Other critics have explored similar implications in Beowulf's burial. The real tragedy of the poem may lie not in Beowulf's own death, which transcends the tragic through his faith in God, but in his people's despair which leads to the re-burial of the treasure. He gives his life to save them from the dragon, but he cannot save them from themselves. The Geats, even Wiglaf, refuse more than his dying wish, they refuse to accept Beowulf's view of them, a people worthy of the real treasure of an old king's life.

**Source:** Helen Conrad-O'Briain, for *Epics for Students,* Gale Research, 1997.

## George Clark

*In the excerpt that follows, Clark discusses the world of* Beowulf *as it is presented by the poem's narrator. Clark explains that the society of the Danes is first shown to be a prosperous and successful one, until Grendel's attacks, after which it becomes paralyzed for twelve years. By contrast, demonstrates Clark, the Geatish society is one of action, and Beowulf, as a member of that society coming to aid the Danes seems to be surrounded by ''an aura of good luck and good intentions.'' In the book's ''Afterword,'' Clark discusses briefly the Sutton Hoo ship burial discovery, and predicts the avenues by which new criticism will likely approach the poem.*

### Discovering the Poem's World

The poem imposes many delays on its central story and includes many explorations not directly related to its main business, but despite an indirect movement and moments of leisure, *Beowulf* creates a powerful impression of a great action moving irresistibly forward, advancing not steadily but abruptly in sudden lurches and turns toward a fearful event. Brief summaries of the ''basic story'' of *Beowulf* conceal its rich variety of forms and matter; the poem captures a vast historical scope, includes a variety of genres or modes of composition, and reveals a constant interplay of tones. The prologue separates the poem's audience from the story—long ago in another country—then presents the audience with a gratifying account of heroic success, of heroism leading to national success, of

the hero as founder of a great dynasty. At the height of Scyld's brilliant career, a kingdom won, an overlordship established, and an heir engendered, the narrator proposes as a universal truth the rule that in every nation the successful aspirant to honor must do praiseworthy deeds. On these words, the narrator announces Scyld's death at the fated time; the prologue closes with his people's grief for the great king's passing.

Scyld earned the narrator's accolade—. . . that was a good king! (11)—early in the prologue which ends with the universal truth of mortality and an unanswerable question. Scyld returns to the mystery from which he came after his richly laden funeral ship is launched on the unknowable deep. Still, the succession of fortunate generations of Scyld's line contrasts the mystery and the blunt fact of death with an unfolding story of dynastic prosperity extending for generations until the crowning of the Scyldings' success with the building of Heorot. Mortality presses in on the line of Scyld Scefing and the first celebration at Heorot awakens a monster who seems to embody or to represent the force of chaos and old night. That scene, dramatically reversing the stately tone of the poem's prologue, begins with the monster's anger at the sound of joy in Heorot, then traces that joy to the poet's song celebrating the creation of the world, then leaves the Danish ruling elite living in those joys until the monster, Grendel, begins his raids.

Grendel's first raid turns all the successes of the triumphant line of the Scyldings into horror, pain, and humiliation. After Grendel's second raid, the night after his first, the narrator notices that:

> Then it was easy to find the man who got himself a more distant resting place, a bed in a private dwelling, when the hall-thegn's hatred was manifested to him, plainly declared by a sure sign; whoever escaped that enemy kept himself farther away and safer. (138–43)

Six full lines remorselessly detail the humiliation of noble warriors among the Danes who, in the face of certain death there, give up sleeping in the royal hall, a kind of mens' lodge, and seek out a more domestic safety. The Danes become double victims, of Grendel's wrath and of the poem's irony; the monster diminishes their manly status; the poem makes that diminishment public and thus real. The audience is drawn toward Grendel, it accepts a certain complicity in calamity to savor the poem's detached irony at the cost of Danish manliness. Warrior societies in many cultures segregate men and women; apparently the all-male fellowship of such lodges contributes to the aggressive spirit a warring society requires. Grendel's interruption of the regular practice unmans the Danish warrior class, calls their heroic status into question, and damages the means of sustaining their traditional calling and their honor.

As the poem moves from the Danes to the Geats, a series of contrasts in the character and tone of the narrative become apparent. The Danish scene represents a whole society in paralysis, the Geatish a man in action. The Danes meet frequently, consider deeply, risk their immortal souls searching for supernatural help, and lament their losses in an agony of helplessness. Immediately following the report of Grendel's first and second raids, the narrator adds that this calamity persisted for twelve years; that the lord of the Scyldings suffered great sorrows; that songs sadly revealed to the world that Grendel waged cruel war against Hrothgar for many years. The narrator (or those songs) reports that Grendel intended never to make a truce with the Danes. The narrator sums up: Grendel performed "many crimes . . . cruel humiliations," many powerful men among the Danes often considered what should be done, and Hrothgar's sorrows burned continually in his heart.

In the Danish setting some forty lines report the unending succession of humiliations and sorrow heaped upon the hapless people and above all their king, but restated among the Geats, the long story of passive suffering and helplessness amounts only to a clause. The Danish complaint ends with Hrothgar's sorrow and inaction:

> the wise man was unable to ward off that misery; that distress, that cruel and violent, hateful and long-drawn-out onslaught, that cruel distress, which had fallen upon the people, was too severe.

The scene abruptly moves to the Geats, where the strongest man living on earth, Hygelac's retainer, hears of "Grendles dæda" (195), Grendel's deeds. The strong man at once commands that a ship be readied and announces his intention to visit the famous king of the Danes who has need of men. Between the hero's command, his announcement, and his selection of his companions for the exploit, the Geatish councillors consult the omens and approve his plans even as he leads his picked company to the sea and the ready ship.

The pagan and superstitious practice of consulting omens evokes no negative comment in the poem, though Anglo-Saxon sermons strongly condemned such time-honored observances. From Beowulf's first introduction into the poem to the moment Grendel realizes his impending doom, all signs agree that the hero's victory is certain. The alacrity of the hero's decision, preparations, and setting out bespeaks a self-confidence that seems itself a token of victory. The voyage is swift and easy, which requires strong winds from the right quarter and confirms the favorable omens. The supernatural sign vouchsafed the Geatish councillors and the disposition of nature agree in pointing toward Beowulf's success. The wisdom of the Danes concurs: the coast guard who challenges Beowulf and the Geats at the Danish shore seems to respond to an aura of good luck and good intentions manifested in Beowulf's appearance when he breaks off his formal challenge to observe that one of the seafarers seems a man of unique qualities and exceptional status and to wish: "may his look, his matchless appearance, never belie him". Given the Danes' dearest wish of the past twelve years, the coast guard must see a resolve to destroy Grendel and the tokens of success in the foreigner at the Danish coast.

. . . . .

## Afterword

In the coming decades, *Beowulf* scholarship will almost surely be deeply influenced by the findings of archaeological research and especially by the excavation at Sutton Hoo. Students of the poem have hardly digested the importance of the original Sutton Hoo excavation of 1939, definitively published in a massive study by Rupert Bruce-Mitford and others (1975–83). Already the new excavations at Sutton Hoo have offered some surprises. While archaeologists extend our knowledge of the material culture of the Anglo-Saxon world, lexicographers are doing the same for the word-hoard of the Anglo-Saxons. *The Dictionary of Old English* project at the University of Toronto has already produced a microfiche concordance of the corpus of Anglo-Saxon texts, an immensely valuable tool for the study of *Beowulf*. The project has published the letters C and D in microfiche and at some point in the twenty-first century we will have a better dictionary of the Old English or Anglo-Saxon language than most of us dreamed possible when the late Angus Cameron began the work.

The study of the poem itself will surely develop in some directions already partially mapped out. The poem's psychological and social realism has already become a topic of critical inquiry that will continue to prosper in an age that can accept or even value mixtures of realism and fantasy. A renewed effort to reconstruct the poem's social and cultural milieu seems likely: reader-response criticism and the new historicism alike will demand a vigorous inquiry into the poem's origins and attempt to discover what the poem meant to its earliest audiences and what the place of poetry was in the Anglo-Saxon world. The poem's idea of the basic social institutions needs a deeper reading against what we know of those institutions in the Anglo-Saxon age. The questions of the poem's date and place of origin will burn strongly for some decades to come. We are likely to find too many rather than too few answers, and the profusion of seemingly contradictory solutions may strengthen the case for the poem's oral transmission and for its susceptibility to at least some reworking even after being committed to parchment.

The poststructuralist new criticisms and formalist approaches to narrative texts will try (and have tried already) their strength with *Beowulf.* The possibility of a deconstructive reading of *Beowulf* may fill some philologists with horror, but such a reading may be illuminating. The concentration of the newer critical schools on narrative will almost surely benefit the study of the greatest poem in English before the *Canterbury Tales.*

**Source:** George Clark, ''The Heroic Age, Ideal, and Challenge,'' and ''Afterword,'' in *Beowulf,* Twayne Publishers, 1990, pp. 51–54, 143–44.

## S. A. J. Bradley

*In the following excerpt, Bradley discusses the controversy over the dating of* Beowulf *and comments on its oral tradition. Bradley notes that the early criticism of* Beowulf *focused on the work as a source of information regarding early Germanic culture rather than as a poem.*

The date of the poem remains an unsettled problem. A *written* version of it preceding the uniquely surviving MS may safely be postulated; and beyond doubt is the likelihood that a form of the poem was in circulation among poets of the *oral* tradition for some centuries before the known MS version was made. Indeed, the principal motifs of the poem's plot are motifs of widespread folklore, and parts of the story, and the figures of Beowulf and of the monsters, have analogies elsewhere in the ancient literature of North-West Europe. But the story as it survives embodies, unless we have misunderstood it, a strikingly sophisticated and deliberately structured philosophical statement which is surely the

construct of one creative mind presiding in literary manner over the traditional material.

Concern with locating the elements of this traditional material in the context of early Germanic culture has characterized the preliminary stages of *Beowulf* criticism; but it is the location of that artistically and didactically sovereign mind in a plausible intellectual and social milieu within the evolving culture of the Anglo-Saxons to which much *Beowulf* scholarship continues to address itself. Though it is conventional to regard the poem as early — first, because of the obvious antiquity of some of the traditional content, then because the relatively clear landmarks of the age of Bede, or of Offa's Mercia, or of Rædwald of East Anglia and the Sutton Hoo ship-burial inevitably tempt scholars to take all other bearings from them — the early dating has always had its strenuous opponents. It must indeed be acknowledged that the arguments insisting on a seventh- or eighth-century date remain, after all the discussion, barely more absolute and compelling than arguments placing the poem after the start of the Danish invasions, in the ninth or tenth century, or even as late as the likely date of the unique MS itself, which palaeographers place about the year 1000. It is well to bear in mind what the very nature of the oral mode of transmission of poetry makes probable: that the broad narrative of *Beowulf* had served many generations as a vehicle for their current values and tastes long before a version was composed in writing, and that however ancient in origin the narrative may be, however antique some of the elements surviving from earlier stages, the particular re-telling recorded in the Cotton MS may have been shaped to articulate philosophical and literary purposes much more 'modern' than the world of ship-funerals and dragon-tales preserved in its plot. What we can most confidently say of the poem as we have it is that it represents a literary judgment of the late tenth or early eleventh century.

Over generations of critical attention, *Beowulf* has proved its stature as a literary classic — as a major monument to an historic culture and as a visionary statement of issues of abiding relevance to people living in community at any time. The literary appreciation of the poem benefited little from nineteenth-century scholars who quarried it for Germanic antiquities, or subjected it to drastic editorial restoration in quest of a prototype text, or used it as grist to the mills of anti-clericalism, of nationalism, and of the cult of Aryanism. It fared little better when early twentieth-century critics tested it by standards of classical literary structure and taste, and found it wanting. But what scholars of that period derided as the chimera of a 'literary' *Beowulf* has since been claimed by many to be a substantial reality — though even if there is wide agreement that the surviving version is the creative work of a single poet, and is therefore amenable on that basis to literary critical analysis and judgment, the poem continues to speak differently to different readers. One may do worse than look back for guidance to the pioneering assessment of the Dane, N. F. S. Grundtvig — largely ignored, particularly by English scholars, in his day — who published a Danish translation and a study of the poem in 1820, not long after the first printed edition of the whole text had been made, in 1815, by the Icelander, G. J. Thorkelin, on behalf of his Danish patron.

The language of the poem, Grundtvig says, is of the finest, compared with any other example of the rich corpus of early Germanic poetry. Though the poem's structure, he thought, was not so beautifully coherent as that of Greek epic poetry (but later critics have drawn attention to the differently conceived, but nonetheless distinctive structural principles of *Beowulf,* to the symmetries, parallels and contrasts, large and small, of theme, imagery and diction), the English poem had in his view far more to say. He found it a poem whose liveliness and entertaining qualities enhanced its high ethical integrity. He evidently understood it to speak from deep poetic insight about humanity, not merely about men and women. He identified in it a fundamental religious tone, and saw that the poet desired to represent his hero's struggles as being part of the cosmic contest between good and evil which is a characterizing element in the Christian view of history. He recognized that the monsters represented the powers of darkness striving against the light with which God penetrated the primordial darkness; and he understood the stakes to be the survival and thriving of human community, through which mankind had best hope of realizing the Godward-aspiring part of its flawed human nature. He acknowledged the sombre view taken by the poet, who chose no refuge in literary escapism, but compelled his audience to contemplate the sacrifice when heroes lay down their life for their friends. But Grundtvig found final optimism in the poem, an optimism determined not by literary convention but by Christian philosophy: that though the powers of darkness are potent to kill mankind's worthiest champions, God will not let such champions bear witness in vain. In Grundtvig's view, Beowulf *succeeds* in saving the dying life of the community.

Thus, Grundtvig's reading implies, sacrifice of oneself for the life of civilized community, imperfect though it may be, is not an act of vain and self-deluding heroics, but a responsibility which the strong and the gifted may not repudiate, and which is in itself a victory against anarchy and elemental evil; such is the poet's understanding of the testimony of history, and he endorses his view by appeal to divine authority. We may cite St Augustine in his support: 'It is wrong to deny that the aims of human civilization are good, for this is the highest end that mankind of itself can achieve. For, however lowly the goods of the earth, the aim, such as it is, is peace.' (*CG*, Bk.XV, ch.4, pp.419–20).

Such a reading gives full credit to the secular heroic material of the plot, which the poet has evidently drawn from Germanic tradition. But it does not see these elements as bringing with them the heathen implications which no doubt many of them had when first they were coined. They are rather exploited so as to express in terms challengingly meaningful to an audience nurtured on secular heroic narrative poetry the larger philosophy of Christianity — at least as it related to questions of heroic altruism in defence of the common good, and of the virtues of (Christian) civilization, specifically defined in the poem as awareness of the source of good and of happiness, sanctity of familial bonds and the brotherhood of nations, mutuality of respect between ruler and ruled, communality, order, harmony, beauty, peace, the innocent pursuit of happiness, generosity, magnanimity and wisdom.

The prescriptions and warnings of this highly ethical work speak relevantly to any period of AS history one chooses to consider; and they remain a preoccupation of significant literature through the whole English literary tradition.

**Source:** S. A. J. Bradley, *"Beowulf,"* in *Anglo-Saxon Poetry,* translated and edited by S. A. J. Bradley, David Campbell Publishers Ltd, 1982 , pp. 408–11.

## Sources for Further Study

Alexander, Michael. "Introduction," in *"Beowulf": A Verse Translation,* Penguin Books, 1973.

Alexander offers a detailed introduction to the poem, discussiong the history of the manuscript, the epic tradition, and the characters and plot of the poem.

Alexander, Michael. "Epic," in *A Dictionary of Modern Critical Terms,* edited by Roger Fowler, Routledge and Kegan Paul, 1987, pp. 73-75.

Alexander provides a short, clear introduction to the western epic with brief, well-integrated extracts from important critical texts.

Backhouse, Janet, D. H. Turner, and Webster, Leslie. *The Golden Age of Anglo-Saxon Art: 966-1066,* British Museum, 1984.

Provides marvellous illustrations of Anglo-Saxon art, fine and applied, covering the period in which the *Beowulf* manuscript was written.

Basset, Steven. ed. *The Origins of Anglo-Saxon Kingdoms,* Leicester University Press, 1989.

Provides a discussion of the political and social circumstances which may be reflected in *Beowulf.*

Benson, L. D. "The Originality of *Beowulf,*" in *The Interpretation of Narrative: Theory and Practice, Harvard Studies in English,* Vol. 1, edited by M. W. Bloomfield, Harvard University Press, 1970, pp. 1-43.

An excellent discussion of the originality of the poem and its the characters.

Bessinger, Jess B. and Robert F. Yeager. *Approaches to Teaching "Beowulf,"* Modern Language Association, 1984.

Essentially a teacher's guide. Includes an excellent bibliography and list of derivative works which may be of use to students.

Bonjour, Adrien. *The Digressions in "Beowulf,"* Medium Aevum Monographs 5, Basil Blackwell, 1950.

Bonjour studies the workings and implications of the "digressions," the short narratives and allusions which are embedded in the main narrative.

Boyle, Leonard. "The Nowell Codex and the Poem of *Beowulf,*" in *The Dating of "Beowulf,"* edited by Colin Chase, University of Toronto Press, 1981, pp. 23-32.

An excellent short study of the *Beowulf* manuscript. It challenges Kevin Kiernan's theory that the manuscript is the author's copy.

Bradley, S. S. J., trans. *Anglo-Saxon Poetry,* Everyman Books, 1992.

A good prose translation of the poem with a short and useful beginners' introduction.

Brown, Michelle. *Anglo-Saxon Manuscripts,* British Library, 1991.

A good beginners' introduction to the process of making a manuscript. It covers the materials used in a manuscript, how the writing was done, how a page and a text were laid out, and finally discusses individual manuscripts made by Anglo-Saxons.

Chambers, R. W. *"Beowulf:" An Introduction to the Study of the Poem,* 3rd Supplement by C. L. Wrenn, Cambridge University Press, 1963.

Chambers' book remains one of the most valuable studies of the poem's background. It is a scholarly

book, but user-friendly, clearly and even entertainingly written.

Chase, Colin, ed. *The Dating of "Beowulf,"* University of Toronto Press, 1981.

This collection of essays restarted the controversy over the dating of *Beowulf* and redirected interest back to the manuscript of the poem.

Clark, George. *Beowulf,* Twayne Publishers, 1990.

A first–class beginners' introduction to the poem. There are chapters on the history of *Beowulf* criticism, the other legends embedded in the poem, the ethics of heroism, the monsters and kingship.

Curtius, Ernest. *European Literature and the Latin Middle Ages,* translated by Willard R. Trask, University of Princeton Press, 1973.

A study of the ways medieval writers absorbed and used the heritage of Greece and Rome in their writing. It stresses the importance of this process to the formation of the western mind. It pays particular attention to the idea and presentation of the hero.

Engelhardt, George J. "*Beowulf:* A Study of Dilation," *PMLA,* Vol. 70 , 1955, pp. 269-82.

Very technical, but an excellent discussion of how the poet organised and developed his material.

Evans, Angela. *The Sutton Hoo Ship Burial,* British Museum, 1994.

A richly illustrated introduction to the splendid Anglo-Saxon ship burial first excavated in 1939. The objects uncovered and the burial itself have been an important factor in *Beowulf* studies since the poem was quoted by the inquest which sat in 1939 to decide the treasure's legal ownership.

Garmonsway, G. N., Jacqueline Simpson, and Hilda Ellis Davidson. *"Beowulf" and its Analogue,* E. P. Dutton and Co, Inc., 1971.

This is a collection of translations of northern tales similar to the poem and to the oldest forms of the stories and characters which are alluded to or used in *Beowulf.* However, the chapter on archaeology is now out of date.

Goldsmith, Margaret. *The Mode and Meaning of "Beowulf,"* Athlone Press, 1975.

The high-water mark of allegorical interpretations of the poem, Goldsmith's book studies the biblical and theological texts which may have influenced the poet of *Beowulf* leading to the poem's identification as an allegory.

Irving, E. B. *A Reading of "Beowulf,"* Yale University Press, 1968.

A sober, close reading of the poem of great insight. Written without pretensions and enviable clarity, there is something in Irving for every reader of the poem from beginner to professional scholar.

Jack, George. *"Beowulf"; A Student Edition,* Clarendon Press, 1994.

One of the best introductory texts in Old English. There are very full marginal vocabularies and equally extensive footnotes on the text. Jack provides an excellent introduction to the poem and its criticism. The bibliography is particularly good.

Kerr, W. *Epic and Romance: Essays on Medieval Literature,* 2nd edition, Eversley Series, London and New York, 1908.
One of the classic discussions of *Beowulf.* J. R. R. Tolkein's "Beowulf: The Monster's and the Critics" is in many ways specifically an answer to Kerr.

Kiernan, Kevin S. "The Eleventh Century Origin of *Beowulf* and the *Beowulf* Manuscript," in *The Dating of "Beowulf,"* edited by Colin Chase, University of Toronto Press, 1981, pp. 9-22.
Kiernan argues that the *Beowulf* manuscript in the British library is the author's own working copy.

Kirby, D. P. *The Earliest English Kings,* Unwin Hyman, 1991.
A study of the development of kingship and kingdoms among the Anglo-Saxons. Kirby offers insights into the circumstances which formed the poet's and his audience's view of the political world.

Klaeber, Friedrich. *Beowulf and the Fight at Finnsburg,* 3rd edition, D. C. Heath and Co., 1950.
Still the standard edition of the poem, Klaeber's introductory material is still useful nearly fifty years after the last edition was published.

Leyerle, John. "Beowulf the Hero and King," in *Medium Aevum,* Vol. 34, 1965, pp. 89-102.
Leyerle argues that Beowulf fails to understand that the responsibilities of kingship must override the personal desire for glory and that Beowulf destroys himself and his people by insisting on fighting the dragon.

Malone, Kemp. "Beowulf the Headstrong," in *Anglo-Saxon England,* Vol. 1, 1972, pp. 139-45.
Malone argues that Beowulf, in facing the dragon, takes the only realistic course available to him. Malone forcefully explains that the modern distinction between king and hero would be incomprehensible to the poem's original audience.

Nicholson, Lewis E. *An Anthology of "Beowulf" Criticism,* University of Notre Dame Press, 1963.
One of the most cited critical anthologies, this volume includes Tolkein's "Beowulf: The Monsters and the Critics."

Niles, John D. *"Beowulf": The Poem and its Tradition,* University of Harvard Press, 1983.
A detailed discussion of all aspects of the poem. Niles believes that *Beowulf* is an essentially "middle brow" work of the tenth century.

Ogilvy, J. D. A. and Donald C. Baker. *Reading "Beowulf,"* University of Oklahoma Press, 1984.
Another excellent beginners' introduction to the poem. There are chapters on *Beowulf* and other Germanic poetry, its date and authorship, versification and style and modern interpretation and criticism, as well as a detailed synopsis of the story.

Robinson, Fred C. "History, Religion, Culture: The Background Necessary for Teaching *Beowulf,*" in *Approaches to Teaching "Beowulf,"* by Jess B. Bessinger and Robert F. Yeager, Modern Language Association, 1984, pp. 107-22; reprinted in his *The Tomb of Beowulf and Other Essays on Old English,* Blackwell Publishers, 1993, pp. 36-51.
Another overview of the poem, concentrating on the culture in which the poem is set.

———. "An Introduction to *Beowulf,*" in his *The Tomb of Beowulf and Other Essays on Old English,* Blackwell Publishers, 1993, pp. 52-67; reprinted from *"Beowulf": A Verse Translation with Treasures of the Ancient North,* by Marijane Osborn, 1983, pp. xi-xix.
A brief introduction to the poem by a noted scholar. Most of the articles in this collection are meant for specialist students of Old English literature, but they are written in a clear and unassuming style that makes *Beowulf* scholarship accessible to the general reader.

Short, Douglas D. *"Beowulf" Scholarship: An Annotated Bibliography,* Garland, 1980, 538 p.
The annotations make this bibliography indispensable to the beginner. It also includes useful indices.

Tolkein, J. R. R. "The Monsters and the Critics," in *Publications of the British Academy,* Vol. 22, 1936, pp. 245-95.
The granddaddy of modern *Beowulf* criticism, this is essential reading. It is reprinted in both the Nicholson and Tuso anthologies listed here.

Tuso, Joseph F. *Beowulf,* W. W. Norton and Co., 1975.
This book from the Norton series of Critical Editions includes the Donaldson translation and a good selection of criticism through the late 1960s. There is very little overlap with the Nicholson collection.

Whitelock, Dorothy. *The Audience of "Beowulf,"* Clarendon Press, 1951.
A classic study of what the original audience of the poem might have been like in their culture, tastes, and expectations.

Whitelock, Dorothy. *The Beginnings of English Society, The Pelican History of England* 2, Penguin Books, 1968.
An introduction to Anglo-Saxon society and institutions enlivened with anecdotes and historical examples.

Wilson, David M. *Anglo-Saxon Art from the Seventh Century to the Norman Conquest,* Thames and Hudson, 1984.
Lavishly illustrated, this is an excellent introduction to what sort of mental pictures the descriptions in *Beowulf* must have conjured up to its Anglo-Saxon audiences.

Wilson, David M. *The Anglo-Saxons,* Penguin Books, 1971.
One reviewer called this the best introduction to Anglo-Saxon archaeology ever written. It has served students for well over twenty-five years. The line illustrations are very useful.

# Cantar de mio Cid (El Cid)

**Anonymous**

**c. 1201–1207**

The *Cantar de mio Cid (El Cid)* recounts the heroic deeds of the Cid, an exiled member of the lower nobility who wins back his king's favor by battling the Islamic inhabitants of Spain. Based on the exploits of a historical personage, Rodrigo (Ruy) Díaz de Vivar, who lived from 1040-1099, this epic offers an important example of the interaction of history and literature in the Middle Ages.

The *Cid* is best known for its interweaving of irony, heroic drama, and a rare strain of realism that incorporates multifaceted portraits of Moors, Jews, and Christians. One of the oldest Spanish documents in existence, it is also the only Spanish epic to have survived almost intact. It is contained in a fourteenth-century manuscript, which bears the date 1207, most likely referring to an earlier version of the poem that was copied in the later book. Several accounts of the Cid's life, however, exist before this epic poem was written in manuscript form. Two Latin poems, one written before the Cid's death, and the other just after, chronicle his life. He is mentioned in Arabic sources, and his fame endured throughout the Middle Ages, in works of varying quality.

The *Cantar de mio Cid* has been well-received as a work of literature for several centuries. The French dramatist Pierre Corneille's famous version of the poem (*Le Cid,* 1637) demonstrates its lasting popularity in Europe. Printed editions of the poem have existed since the eighteenth century; a ground-

breaking newer edition (1908) was published by the prominent Spanish medievalist Ramón Menéndez Pidal. Menéndez Pidal's influential work on the *Cid* ensured an international critical audience for this epic. A poem which treats basic themes such as national and religious identity, family honor, and personal prowess, the *Cid* has earned a lasting place in the ranks of great world literature.

## Author Biography

Intense scholarly debate has raged over the question of the identity of the *Cid*'s author. Critics are divided into two camps, the "traditionalists" and the "individualists." The former group, led by Ramón Menéndez Pidal, believes that the poem was composed as an oral composition soon after the historical Cid's death, and was written in a manuscript only later, thus negating the importance of the idea of a single author for the poem. The "individualists," on the other hand, (championed most recently by Colin Smith) insist that a single, brilliant author wrote the poem in 1207. Some critics point to Per Abbad, the name that appears at the end of the poem, as the author, although the text states that this personage "wrote" the text (*escrivó*), indicating that he was the copyist rather than the author. Opinion on the subject is so divided that individualists tend to call the work the "Poema" of the Cid, whereas traditionalists entitle it the "Cantar," or Song of the Cid, to emphasize its oral origins. The interpretation of the text varies widely according to the stance of a given critic with regards to the text's authorship and the author's intentions.

The person who wrote the 1207 version of the text was undoubtedly a talented author. The individualist school (especially the British Hispanists) insists that the author had extensive knowledge of the law and the Bible, and used written historical documents to bolster the more historically sound sections of the epic. Traditionalists tend to discount all three of these claims, maintaining the oral nature of the transmission of this information during the presumed era of composition, which, for Menéndez Pidal, was around 1140. In addition, they note the archaic nature of the language of the 1207 text itself. Despite the quality of this literary text as it has come down to us in its single manuscript, the traditionalist viewpoint has prevailed in recent years. This view is bolstered by research by "neo-traditionalist" scholars who draw on new findings in the oral tradition in

literature by scholars such as Albert Lord and Milman Parry, who suggest that the written versions of the most famous epics that we possess are but one manifestation of a chain of oral versions. The debate about authorship has dominated epic research during the past century, but with increased understanding about the role of orality in medieval literature and new scholarship about the status of the author in this era, the problem can be approached in new ways.

## Plot Summary

### First Cantar

The unique manuscript of the *Cantar de mio Cid* is missing its first folio (manuscript page), and so the poem begins by describing the Cid's reaction to the news of his banishment. From contemporary Latin histories and from a note later in the poem (laisse 9), we discover that the reason for the Cid's banishment is the accusation by King Alfonso VI that the Cid had embezzled money collected from the Moors for the king. This is the second time that Alfonso banished the Cid, and the missing folio might have described this event. The manuscript text itself begins by showing the Cid weeping when he leaves his home village, Vivar, and enters Burgos, a town to the south. He sees crows flying and interprets them as an omen of his ill fortune. The townspeople of Burgos watch him ride by with his ally, Minaya Alvar Fáñez. A nine-year-old girl is the only person who dares to address him, telling him that the townspeople have been forbidden by the king to offer aid to the Cid. After praying at the church of Saint Mary, the Cid leaves Burgos, and pitches his tent outside the city walls. The "worthy citizen of Burgos," Martín Antolínez, provides supplies for the party and joins the Cid. Together they plan how to get money to support themselves, deciding to take advantage of two Jewish moneylenders, Rachel and Vidas. Martín Antolínez returns to Burgos, finds the moneylenders, and gives them two beautifully-decorated chests filled with sand. He proposes to pawn these chests for a sum of money, and the moneylenders agree to give 600 marks, and to not look into the chests for a year. Gleeful at having tricked the moneylenders, the Cid and his companions head to San Pedro de Cardeña, where they meet Doña Ximena (the Cid's wife) and the Cid's daughters. The Abbot of the abbey (Abbot Don Sancho) is delighted to see the Cid, and promises to care for the ladies until the Cid can return. At the abbey, he is joined by 115 knights. Doña Ximena prays for her husband's safety, and the Cid parts from his family with great sadness. With promises of great rewards to all, the Cid and his party leave the abbey and travel through Castille, gathering great numbers for their army. During the voyage, the Cid is visited by the angel Gabriel in a dream, who tells him that he will be successful in his campaigns. After crossing a mountain range, they leave Alfonso's lands and thus enter Moorish territory.

When the Cid and his army arrive at the Moorish town of Casejón, they ambush the residents and capture the town. Minaya, in particular, distinguishes himself. After dividing the wealth between his men, the Cid and his army leave Casejón, partly to avoid border conflicts with Alfonso. When they arrive at the town of Alcocer, they again decide to invade it. The Cid's army besieges the city for fifteen weeks, and then, short of food and water, they pretend to give up and strike camp. When the inhabitants of Alcocer see the army leaving, they are delighted and leave the city to pursue them. The Cid seizes the opportunity and attacks the Moors, thereby winning the town. His army occupies the town and forces the Moors to serve them. Inhabitants of the neighboring towns, frightened, tell the Moorish king of Valencia that the Cid threatens their safety, and the king sends an army to attack and besiege the Cid for three weeks. The Cid's army prepares for battle, and Pedro Bermúdez is given the honor of carrying the Cid's flag. Pedro disobeys the Cid's orders to wait until given the command to attack the Moors, and charges into battle. The Cid and his army follow, and the Moors are defeated, leaving great wealth in horses and armor for the Cid. The hundred horses and a large quantity of silver that the Cid wins is immediately sent to Alfonso, as tribute, and to the abbey at Cardeña for the care of the Cid's family. The Cid then sells Alcocer back to the Moors and continues to Valencia. En route, he captures several more towns, and is distinguished by his generous treatment of his victims. In the meantime, Minaya has brought the horses to Alfonso, who is duly impressed but refuses to pardon the Cid. The count of Barcelona hears of the Cid's exploits and wrongly believes that he is despoiling the count's territory. He attacks the Cid, but is captured. The count, deeply embarassed, refuses to eat until the Cid releases him.

## Second Cantar

The second third of the *Cid* begins with the capture of several more towns, including Murviedra, before the Cid turns his attention to Valencia. The people of Valencia attempt a pre-emptive strike against the Cid, but he is assured of his God-given victory, and summons every ally he can to combat the people of Valencia. He captures more towns, plunders the countryside for three years, and finally attacks Valencia itself. He invites anyone who wants to participate in taking the city to join him, fights a great battle, and wins the city. After dividing the booty, the Cid sends Minaya again to visit Alfonso and the abbot of Cardeña. At the same time a French churchman, Don Jerome, joins the Cid, who appoints him bishop of Valencia. As a reward for the capture of Valencia, the king agrees to allow the Cid's family to join him in exile. The Cid's growing reknown in Alfonso's court, however, provokes the jealousy of Count García Ordóñez. The high-born Infantes de Carrión, on the other hand, consider marriage with the Cid's daughters an advantageous match, and send their greetings to him via Minaya. Minaya takes the ladies from the abbey and escorts them to Mendaceli where they are met by the Cid's Moorish ally, Abengalbón, who takes them to Molina, where he is governor. They then travel to Valencia, where the Cid welcomes them. The Cid makes a great impression on onlookers with his flowing beard and marvelous horse, Babieca.

King Yusuf of Morocco, in the meantime, is furious when he hears of the capture of Valencia, and brings an army from Morocco to retake the city. With his wife and daughters as witnesses, the Cid with his four thousand knights defeats the fearsome army of fifty thousand. The Cid wins an immense amount of wealth from this battle, including the Moroccan king's cloth-of-gold tent. Minaya once again goes to Alfonso to beg pardon for the Cid. Alfonso is delighted at the news of the Cid's victory and by the fantastic present of two hundred horses, which again annoys García Ordóñez. The king, this time, pardons the Cid and annuls his banishment. The Infantes, in their turn, decide to marry the daughters of such a wealthy and successful man, and ask the king to speak on their behalf with the Cid. Minaya reports this news back to the Cid, who agrees reluctantly to the marriage. All the parties agree to meet on the banks of the Tagus river. When the Cid arrives in front of the king, he dismounts, kneels, and pulls up a mouthful of grass with his teeth as a sign of his great humility before his lord. Alfonso is greatly affected, and pardons the Cid publicly. The marriages are subsequently arranged, and great festivals are organized in honor of the marriages. The Cid gives the Infantes swords to symbolize his kinship with them, and the marriages are thus begun with great promise.

### Third Cantar

The Infantes, married for several months, are deeply embarrassed when a captive lion belonging to the Cid escapes in his palace. While they hide under a couch and behind a wine press, the Cid catches the lion with his hands and puts it back into captivity. The court subsequently jeers at the Infantes for their cowardice. In the meantime, King Búcar of Morocco attempts to renew the failed attempt to retake Valencia. The Cid sees the coming battle as a chance for the Infantes to distinguish themselves and regain their lost prestige, but they are only able to do so by convincing Pedro Bermúdez to support their falsely boastful claims of prowess (this passage is missing in the manuscript, but can be reconstructed through consulting other sources). In the battle, Bishop Jerome proves his bravery, and the Cid wins the battle and kills Búcar. The Cid praises God when he hears the reports of his son-in-laws' bravery in battle, but his followers remain skeptical of their courage and continue to tease them. Frustrated and angry, the Infantes plot revenge, and ask permission to leave the court, ostensibly to return to Carrión so as to show their lands to their wives. The Cid agrees to their request, and the two couples leave the court with a suitable retinue.

Their first stop is at Molina, where they meet the Moor, Abengalbón. Although Abengalbón treats them with great respect, the Infantes plot to kill him. The plot is foiled, and Abengalbón expresses his disappointment with the Infantes. The party continues, and soon the Infantes send their travelling companions ahead so as to carry out their plot against the Cid's daughters. When they are alone with their wives, the Infantes beat them senseless and leave them for dead. Félez Muñoz, the Cid's nephew, is suspicious of the Infantes' intentions, and returns to find the Cid's daughters unconscious in the woods. He quickly takes them back to the town of San Esteban where they regain their health. In the meantime, the Infantes have returned to Alfonso's court, where the king is greatly disturbed

by their boasting of their humiliation of the Cid through beating his daughters. The Cid hears the news, and mulls it over for a long time before swearing vengeance. The Cid's daughters return to Valencia via Molina, where they are again hosted by Abengalbón. The Cid sends his vassal Muño Gustioz to present the Cid's claim to King Alfonso. The king is considered to be responsible for the situation, since he had recommended the marriage. The king agrees to summon the Infantes and order them to give satisfaction to the Cid, which takes place in a court of justice in Toledo. Here, a great company of legal scholars, high government officials, and court members assemble to seek justice. The Cid arrives with his most faithful retainers, and enters the court, making a favorable impression on the onlookers. He has tied a cord around his long white beard so that no one can pluck it—a mortal insult—on purpose or accidentally. Thus the proceedings begin.

The Cid first demands the return of his swords, to thus annul this symbol of kinship. He gives these swords to Pedro Bermúdez and to Martín Antolínez. Although the Infantes believe that this is the only price they will have to pay, the Cid then continues. He demands the return of the money that was given to the Infantes when the marriage was contracted, and they reimburse him by giving him horses and property, borrowing what they no longer own. Then the Cid states his final claim: he challenges the Infantes to a duel against his own champion. At this point, many insults are flung by both sides, accusing the Infantes of cowardice and the Cid of his low birth. According to the Infantes, the Cid's daughters were of too low birth to marry those of the house of Carrión. Finally, the challenges are met, and on a field umpired by specially-chosen judges, the Infantes meet the Cid's champions. Pedro Bermúdez first defeats the Infante Fernandez, who surrenders. Then Martín Antolínez defeats the Infante Diego, who fears the Cid's sword, Colada. Finally, Muño Gustioz nearly kills Ansur González, brother of the Infantes; the latter's father is obliged to intercede to save his son's life. With the field won, the Cid declares himself satisfied, and returns to Valencia. Seeing his good fortune, the high-born princes of Navarre and Aragon negotiate with Alfonso to marry the Cid's daughters. This marriage is carried out, to the benefit of the entire family of the Cid. The kings of Spain, according to the author, are all related to the Cid through these marriages. The scribe completes the manuscript by signing himself

"Per Abbat," who finished the text in the month of May, 1207.

## Characters

### Per Abbat

Although some critics consider Per Abbat the composer or author of the *Poema de mio Cid,* it is generally accepted that he was more likely the scribe of the work, either of the fourteenth-century manuscript, or, more likely, of the 1207 copy. The term *escrivó* ("wrote out" or "copied down"), which is used in the last segment of the poem, seems to uphold this interpretation.

### Abengalbón

Abengalbón is the Cid's Moorish ally. He helps the Cid by protecting his wife and daughters when they travel to Valencia. In another appearance, he hosts the Cid's daughters while they travel to Carrión with their husbands, and discovers a plot hatched by the Infantes to kill him. His noble behavior as a Moor functions as a comparison with that of the cowardly Infantes, and serves as an example of the complex relations between Moors and Christians in Spain during the Middle Ages.

### King Alfonso

Although King Alfonso VI of León is portrayed as a harsh ruler at the beginning of the poem, when he banishes the Cid, his image gradually improves until, by the end of the text, he proves the Cid's advocate. According to historical sources, their uneasy relationship stemmed from the Cid's alliance with Alfonso's enemy and brother, Sancho. Alfonso banished the Cid twice: once for arriving late to battle, and a second time for allegedly embezzling funds he was in charge of collecting for the king. The second exile forms the background of the epic. The relationship of the Cid with his ruler, dominated by exchanges of services and money, provides an interesting example of a Spanish nobleman's evolving relationship with his king.

### Martín Antolínez

Martín Antolínez, the "worthy citizen of Burgos," is another of the Cid's military allies, and has no historical counterpart; he is probably a poetic creation intended to emphasize the town of Burgos's support of the Cid's campaigns. In the final duel, Martín defeats the Infante Diego.

*Ttile page of the 1546 edition of "Poema de mio Cid."*

### Count Ramón Berenguer

Ramón is the count of Barcelona, who fights the Cid (in the first Cantar) for allegedly having damaged his territory in his march to Valencia. When Ramón is captured by the Cid, he refuses to eat until he is freed. The episode of the count's imprisonment, which has a historical basis, is used to demonstrate the Cid's great generosity with his (Christian) victims, whom he frees once they have guaranteed a cessation of hostilities.

### Pedro Bermúdez

Pedro "the mute" appears in the poem as another of the Cid's allies and nephews. He is the Cid's standard-bearer. He is known for his stutter, but he delivers an eloquent speech in which he challenges Fernando, one of the Infantes de Carrión, to a duel. A Pedro Vermúdez is listed in a document of c. 1069, but not in this capacity.

### King Búcar of Morocco

In a second attempt to recapture Valencia from the Cid, another Moorish king fails in his attack and is killed by the Cid.

# Media Adaptations

- The best-known modern media adaptation of the *Cantar de mio Cid* is *El Cid,* the 1961 film produced by Anthony Mann and starring Charlton Heston and Sophia Loren. It draws on later romance versions of the Cid legend, and is considered one of the finest epic films ever made. It was restored and re-released by Martin Scorsese for Miramax films, and is available on home video.

- Another famous adaptation of the *Cantar,* also drawing on later texts, is the play *Le Cid* by Pierre Corneille, written in 1637 and published in translation by John Cairncross. See *The Cid Cinna; The theatrical illusion, by Pierre Corneille,* Penguin Classics, 1975.

- Corneille, in turn, drew from the Spanish playwright Guillen de Castro's 1618 play *The youthful deeds of the Cid,* available in translation from Exposition Press, 1969.

- At least two operas also drew on the Cid legends, including Antonio Sacchini's *Il Cidde* of 1784, available from T. Michaelis, 1880; and Jules Massenet's 1885 opera *Le Cid,* Columbia Records, 1976.

---

### El Cid Campeador
*See* Rodrigo (Ruy) Díaz de Vivar

### Infantes de Carrión
The deceitful Infantes are portrayed as cowardly members of the upper class who, seeing the Cid's swift rise in the king's favor, contract marriages with the Cid's daughters, Elvira and Sol. After being embarrassed and subsequently taunted by the Cid's court when they are frightened by a lion and hide under a couch, the Infantes take their wives from Valencia, then beat them and leave them for dead in the woods. When the Cid obtains justice for this insult, his family is assured a place in the heirarchy of lineage that makes up Spanish medieval society. The historical González brothers actually did not belong to this high level of society and were not married to the Cid's daughters.

### Doña Ximena Díaz
*See* Ximena

### Rodrigo (Ruy) Díaz de Vivar
Modeled after a historic personage who lived from c. 1043 to 1099, Rodrigo Díaz is the hero of this epic poem. Named the Cid, for the Arabic word *Sayyidī,* or "leader," with the epithet "campeador," meaning "master of the field," Rodrigo Díaz appears in the poem as an invincible military leader. He was born into the lower nobility (*infanzon*) in the small town of Vivar, near Burgos, and was a vassal to the king of Spain. In the poem, this low social status is of great importance, for the Cid is a true social climber, gaining social status by successfully amassing wealth and thus power. When he marries his daughters to the high-born *infantes* and later to the kings of Aragon and Navarre, successfully fighting for his family's honor in the third *cantar,* his success as the founder of a new and great lineage is guaranteed. Unlike most epic heroes, he is depicted as an older man, with a white beard that is a source of great pride and prestige. He is portrayed not only as a military hero, but also as a family man, during tender scenes with his wife, Ximena, and his daughters, Elvira and Sol. Generous with his retainers, who join him so as to take part in the amassing of wealth that comes with winning battles against the Moors, the Cid also wins back favor with his king, who had banished him, by sending him extremely valuable gifts. Rodrigo is also a Christian hero in the poem and is shown to be victorious as a Christian who struggles righteously against the "infidel," although the historical Cid once was allied with a

Moorish emir. By drawing on all the qualities of a traditional epic hero: generosity, religious superiority, clannishness, military prowess, and loyalty, the author of *El Cid* is able to enhance the already stellar status of a historical hero.

## Elvira

Elvira is one of the Cid's daughters, who is married to one of the Infantes de Carrión, and then to the king of Navarre. In fact the historical Cid's daughter was named Cristina, and it was her son who became king of Navarre.

## Doña Elvira

*See* Elvira

## Minaya Alvar Fáñez

Minaya is the Cid's ''good right arm,'' and is yet another of his nephews. He is the first of the Cid's allies to be mentioned, but his historical counterpart did not accompany the Cid into exile, but rather remained in Alfonso VI's court.

## Ansur González

Ansur is the brother of the Infantes. He appears during the final duel to support his brothers' claims and he criticizes the Cid for his low birth.

## Diego González

*See* Infantes de Carrión

## Fernando González

*See* Infantes de Carrión

## Muño Gustioz

Muño Gustioz is an ally of the Cid, his ''criado'' or member of his household, and, historically, Ximena's brother-in-law. In the final duel, he defeats Ansur, the Infantes' brother.

## Don Jerome

The historical Bishop Jerome was Jérôme de Périgord, who was brought to Spain by the bishop of Toledo to help reform the Spanish church. He became the bishop of Valencia in 1098. In the poem, Jerome is a fighting bishop who, like Archbishop Turpin in the *Song of Roland,* takes part in the battles while guaranteeing eternal salvation to the fighters.

## Pedro Mudo

*See* Pedro Bermúdez

## Félez Muñoz

Félez is one of the Cid's nephews, and is his ally and champion. He is the character who first discovers the Cid's daughters after their beating, and takes them back to their father. There is no historical record of this character.

## Count García Ordóñez

Ordóñez is the ally of the Infantes and the bitter enemy of the Cid, rather like Ganelon in the *Song of Roland.* Although he boasts of his noble lineage, the Cid reminds him that he pulled the count's beard in the past, a mortal insult.

## Rachel

One of the two moneylenders who provide the initial source of money for the Cid, who needs capital for his period in exile. The Cid tricks them into believing that he has placed all his wealth in two sand-filled chests, and they are persuaded to lend him money while being forbidden to open the chests. The antisemitic portrayal of the Jewish moneylenders is a commonplace in medieval texts.

## Sol

The Cid's second daughter, who also marries one of the Infantes de Carrión, and then the king of Aragon. The historical Sol, named María, married the count of Barcelona and perhaps the son of the king of Aragon. She died around age 25.

## Doña Sol

*See* Sol

## Vidas

One of the two moneylenders who provide the initial source of money for the Cid, who needs capital for his period in exile.

## Ximena

The Lady Ximena is the virtuous wife of the Cid. Although she is left behind in the Abbey of Cardeña with her daughters during the first part of the epic, she later joins her husband in Valencia, where she is met with a joyful welcome. The unusually close relationship between the Cid and his wife is expressed when they first are separated: ''Weeping bitterly, they parted with such pain as when the fingernail is torn from the flesh.'' Ximena is portrayed as a devoted wife who prays for her husband's safety in an eloquent speech early in the poem. The historical Ximena was the daughter of the count of Oviedo and first cousin of King Alfonso VI, although this is not mentioned in the text. She brought her late husband's remains to the monastery of San Pedro de Cardeña near Burgos in 1102. In later versions of the Cid legend, it is Ximena who attracts the most attention; in Pierre Corneille's *Le Cid,* she is the epitome of the tragic heroine.

### King Yusuf of Morocco

King Yusuf comes from Morocco to fight the Cid and thus to regain Valencia, a plan which fails. The historical Yusuf was Yusuf ibn Tesufin, first Almoravid caliph of Morocco (1059-1106), and he did not come to Valencia to recuperate it, but rather sent his nephew. The author is clearly amplifying the action to make the Cid's deeds appear even more stunning.

## Themes

The *Cantar de mio Cid* tells the story of a Spanish warrior who, disinherited by his king and driven from his lands, finds wealth, social success, validation, and acceptance through his great military prowess and strength of character.

### Nobility and Class

An epic about a highly successful social climber, the *Cantar de mio Cid* has much to say about the concept of nobility. For example, the Infantes de Carrión are characterized as members of the upper nobility; they have vast land-holdings and enjoy high status in King Alfonso's court. They marry the Cid's daughters for their money, but later describe these marriages as "concubinage," implying that this match is null and void because of the vast difference in class between the Infantes and the Cid. According to medieval Spanish law, those of illegitimate birth cannot legally marry, and can only be concubines, rather than legitimate wives. The hint of illegitimacy can be found in lines 3377-3381, where the brother of the Infantes, Ansur, implies that the Cid is the son of a miller. In the later romances of the Cid, the tradition notes that the Cid's father raped a miller's wife, who gave birth to the Cid. The allusion to bastardy on the part of the Cid and, by extension, his daughters, makes the theme of nobility even more dramatic, especially when someone of such low birth garners enough allies and supporters to challenge the insults to the Cid's family's legitimacy flung at them by the

highest stratum of society. When, by the end of the poem, we are informed that, after the Infantes are soundly defeated, the Cid's daughters' marry princes whose alliance causes them to be related to subsequent kings of Spain, we know that the Cid, as a self-made man, has "arrived." Nobility, then, does not simply stem from one's birth into a social class. An individual, according to the *Cid,* can work to augment one's status as a person of quality. One way to do this, in medieval Spanish society, is to demonstrate great generosity.

### Generosity and Greed

The definition of a "gift economy" is an economy in which an individual gains prestige by giving gifts. These economies are illustrated, for example, by the "potlatch" festivals in which the chief of certain Native American tribes of the Pacific Northwest gives away huge amounts of money and other forms of wealth. In the *Cid,* the hero proves his worth by, literally, giving it away. This epic is filled with itemized lists of each piece of war booty that the Cid and his followers win after each battle; the Cid himself is careful to use his fifth of the winnings to send magnificent presents to the king to, essentially, buy back favor. The Cid also is generous with the Church, sending money regularly to the Abbey of Cardeña to assure God's favor. In addition, he is generous even with his victims, allowing the residents of one of the cities that he conquers to return to their homes, and freeing Ramón Berenguer, count of Barcelona, from captivity. An interesting exception to the Cid's generosity is the repayment of Rachel and Vidas, the Jewish moneylenders who are themselves shown to be especially greedy, and whom it seems the Cid never pays back. The Infantes of Carrión, the Cid's typological opposites, are noted for their lack of princely generosity. By the end of the epic, however, the Cid is proven to be a man as worthy as King Alfonso when the king is forced to admit that the Cid's generosity embarrasses him (l. 2147). It is more noble to give than to receive in this society.

### Cowardice and Bravery

Just as generosity is the mark of a noble man, bravery in battle is likewise an important characteristic of the ideal hero. The Cid, of course, is the epitome of the brave warrior, using tactics and courage to defeat armies of superior numbers. Bravery, like generosity, is not necessarily linked with one's inherited social status. The comic episode in which the Infantes de Carrión hide under a couch

# Topics for Further Study

- When the apparently advantageous marriages between the Cid's daughters and the high-born Infantes de Carrión have been contracted, the daughters thank their father, saying, "Since you have arranged these marriages, we are sure to be very rich." What is the place of women in the society described in the *Cantar de mio Cid*? Compare the different women in the epic, including Ximena and her ladies in waiting. What is the traditional role of women in epics? How is the *Cid* different? Why do you think later interpretations of the legend of the Cid concentrated so intensely on Ximena as a heroine?

- The *Cid* is well-known for its relativistic portrayal of Muslims and Christians, especially compared to the contemporary epic the *Song of Roland*, where "the Christians are right and the pagans are wrong." Research the intercultural relationships between Christians, Jews, and Muslims in Spain in the Middle Ages. Try to present the points of view of each of these groups about the other communities. Have some of the stereotypes about Christian, Muslim, and Jewish cultures persisted in the twentieth century?

- The *Cantar de mio Cid* displays a restless "frontier spirit" in which a growing population turns its attention to new lands to conquer. Find narratives of the American West and compare them to passages in the *Cid* that demonstrate similar attitudes towards a frontier.

- The Cid, as a character, is sometimes called the "most successful medieval outlaw." Compare the legends of other outlaws, such as Robin Hood, Jesse James, Billy the Kid, Blackbeard, Jean Lafitte, Joachim Murieta, to the Cid. What is their relation to authority figures, such as King Alfonso? What function might these legends play in a given society? What constitutes a "successful" outlaw, and does the Cid qualify?

---

and behind a wine cask when a lion escapes illustrates the importance of bravery in this epic. The Cid is able to tame the lion—the symbol of courage itself—because he is a personage of extraordinary bravery himself. The cowardly Infantes, on the other hand, shirk their duties in battle and invent lies to cover their own lack of courage in episodes that demonstrate how unworthy they are as knights.

## Honor

The important traits of courage and generosity fall under the general rubric of a noble man's honor. A man of worth, according to the *Cid,* must work to preserve his honor. In the Cid's case, he has lost a certain amount of honor by being banished by his king, but he manages to recuperate it by being extraordinarily generous and courageous in battle against the Moors. On a more symbolic level, a man's honor can be seriously damaged if personal insults pass unavenged. The Cid's long, flowing beard is so impressive because it has never been

pulled—a mortal insult punishable by death. He notes with pleasure that Count García Ordóñez's beard has not grown back after suffering pulling by the Cid, implying irreparable damage to his personal honor. The Cid is careful, in public appearances, to keep his beard tied with a cord so as to avoid even accidental pulling. Honor is not only a masculine trait: women such as Ximena and her daughters are portrayed as honorable ladies through their religious faith and their faith in the Cid. The daughters, although they are humiliated by being beaten by the Infantes, regain their honor when it is defended in duels by the Cid's men against the Infantes. The proof that their honor has been regained is revealed in the subsequent advantageous marriages which have been arranged for them.

## Race Conflict

One of the most curious themes of the *Cid* is the problem of race relations, in particular the coexistence of Christians and Moors in Spain under the

Reconquest. The Cid's conquest of Valencia was a somewhat isolated success against the Moors during Alfonso VI's reign, which was characterized by a general gaining of ground on the part of the Moors after initial Christian successes. Moors in the *Cid* are portrayed alternatively as the fearsome pagans who prove terrifying in battle with their war-drums, or as the magnanimous Abengalbón, the Moorish governor who welcomes the Cid and his family and who proves a useful ally. The relativistic treatment of the Moors, some of whom revere the Cid as much as the Christians, stands in contrast to other portrayals of Christians and pagans, as well as to the treatment of Jews in the *Cid,* who are depicted as stereotypes. In a text told by a Christian narrator, it is interesting to discover a measure of cultural relativism.

# Style

## Meter

Discussions of the *Cantar de mio Cid* 's narrative technique tend to revolve around the unusual irregularity of the epic's meter. French epic, for example the *Song of Roland,* is characterized by its regular, assonanced ten-syllable lines. The French epic is organized in "laisses," or unequal blocks of text that are grouped by their assonance, that is, the similarity of the last vowel of the line. Additionally, each line has a strong hemistich, also known as the "caesura," or pause between the first four syllables and the final six. Thus, in *The Song of Roland:*

Rollant est proz / e Oliver est sage; Ambedui unt / merveillus vasselage (ll. 1093-94)

The narrative technique of the *Cid* does share some similarities with this pattern. The epic is constructed of 152 assonanced laisses with a strong hemistich. Thus:

De los sos ojos / tan fuertemientre llorando, tornava la cabeça / e estávalos catando (ll. 1-2)

However, as this example indicates, the length of the verse is extremely irregular, and is termed "anisosyllabic." The verse length in this poem can vary from eight to twenty-two syllables. This irregularity has puzzled critics who attempt to locate the variance in meter to the original source of the epic. P. T. Harvey and A. D. Deyermond compare the epic to the oral literature researched by Milman Parry and Albert Lord. When collecting epic songs from the "singers of tales" in Yugoslavia, these scholars noted that, while the meter of the songs remained regular when they were sung, when the researcher requested that the singers recite the works without singing, the meter became irregular. Harvey and Deyermond theorize that the *Cid* may have been originally collected from a recited, rather than a sung, source, which might explain its metrical irregularity.

## The Epic Epithet

The epic as a performed literary form tends to present characters as representatives of certain human traits. One technique that works to emphasize these specific characteristics is the epic epithet. This technique forces the reader/listener to concentrate on the most important traits of a given personage. The Cid, for example, is "El de Bivar," "the man from Vivar," emphasizing the importance of the Cid as a landowner and locating him within a matrix of local politics. He is the good "Campeador," "master of the battlefield." King Alfonso, interestingly, recieves few epithets while his relations with the Cid are antagonistic. When he pardons the Cid, he receives more favorable epithets. Important places, such as Valencia, can also receive epithets.

## Ring Composition

The form of many epics, as oral literature, is shaped, according to some scholars, by the characteristics of oral memory and composition. Specifically, patterns of repetition, formulaic expressions, standard themes such as battles, marriages, and reconciliations emerge. Often, a circular pattern that serves as a frame adds shape and clarity to the narrative. The *Cantar de mio Cid* has such a shape according to Cedric Whitman and Walter Ong. The first Cantar, for example, reveals ring composition. In line 1, we learn of the adversities and anguish resulting from the Cid's exile and of the convocation of vassals; and later, in lines 48 through 63, we hear of the benefits and jubilation resulting from the Cid's conquests and of the increase in number of his vassals. Similarly, this type of repetition of themes and ideas can be seen in lines 2 through 22, with the departure from Castile accompanied by ill omens and the promise of masses, and in lines 40 through 47, which depict the return of Minaya Alvar Fáñez to Castile with favorable omens and masses paid. Ring composition draws the listener's attention to important parallels in the work, and is a device commonly used in oral literature.

# Historical Context

## Spain and Feudalism

The shape of Spanish society, as opposed to the situation in France, was not strictly or formally organized by feudal ties that linked a lord to a vassal who, in return for protection, provided military services. Although the social structure in Catalonia (the northeastern corner of Spain) was influenced by France, the northwest was original. The fine gradations of northern feudal society in Spain, become a more or less direct relationship between a man and his king. As the *Cantar de mio Cid* shows, the sign of the lord-vassal relationship is the kissing of hands. The reason for this less-stratified shape of society has to do with the Reconquest of Moorish Spain and with the resettlement of the lands taken from the Moors. Peasants occupied these frontier lands, often taking up arms to defend their new territory, militia-style. The king, on the other hand, retained his power as warlord, as the organizer of these campaigns against the Moors. The kings of the Spanish provinces ruled effectively over their comparatively small kingdoms, thus remaining in touch with their subjects. Northern feudal society is characterized by two factors: the vassal-knight's monopoly of military duty, and the dominance of the various ties of vasselage—the dependance and reliance of one man on another—over other forms of government. Spanish society, organized to combat a numerous and formidable enemy, rather than to maintain interior peace, took on a different shape. In the *Cid,* written down in the early thirteenth century, the emergence of the state as a larger organizing force can be charted in the evolution of the portrayal of King Alfonso who, once he pardons the Cid, acts as an arbiter between warring clans. The people who made up Spanish society then included the Christians, who organized themselves in "households" (made up of *criados*), and who were classified as *ricos hombres* or wealthy men; *infanzones* , also called *caballeros* (the Cid is an *infanzon*); and knights. There were two types of peasants: the serfs, or *solariegos,* were tied to the land and were not free to move, whereas the *behetrías* were freemen, and sometimes moved to the borderlands to become "peasant knights."

## Late Twelfth-Century Politics and the 1207 Cid

One of the most important recent studies of the cultural context within which the *Cantar de mio Cid* was written is María Lacarra's 1980 study on history and ideology in this epic. She considers the poem a frankly propagandistic work that functions as a denunciation of an important Leonese family whose ancestors were hostile toward the Cid. The historical background of the tension between the powerful Beni-Gómez family and the historical Cid seems to uphold this theory. During the eleventh, twelfth and thirteenth centuries, a power struggle developed between the provinces of Castile and Leon. The historical Cid was involved in one phase of these developments. The Cid was the head of the armies of King Sancho II of Castile, but upon Sancho's death, his brother, Alfonso VI, became king of Castile and Leon. Alfonso cultivated relations with the obviously talented Cid, marrying his cousin Ximena to the Cid and verifying his land holdings in Vivar. Alfonso sent the Cid to collect tribute from the Moorish king of Seville in 1079. While in Seville, the Cid confronted García Ordóñez, who was attacking Seville in the company of the king of Granada. The tension between the Cid and García Ordóñez is charted in the epic, and is expanded to reflect the clan feud that marked Castillian politics of the late twelfth century.

When the young Alfonso VIII of Castile ascended the throne in 1158, as often happens when a child becomes king, a struggle ensued for control over his education and for control over the government. The Lara clan, staunch supporters of Alfonso VIII, were soon embroiled in a feud with the powerful Castro family, whose interests were not served by Alfonso VIII's lifelong program to unite Castile and Leon against the Moorish threat to the south. A critical moment was reached in 1195, when Alfonso VIII of Castile attacked the Moorish stronghold of Toledo. Alphonso VIII suffered a monumental defeat at the hands of the Moorish Almohad caliphs. Importantly, Pedro Fernández de Castro, head of the Castro family, who were related to the Infantes de Carrión and the Beni-Gómez clan, fought on the Moorish side in this battle. The Lara family, who had remained loyal to Alfonso VIII of Castile, saw Pedro's actions as traitorous to the cause of Castile and Leon. Joseph Duggan, a noted *Cid* scholar, sees the 1207 *Cantar de mio Cid* as a praise poem for the historical Cid that is also a shame poem for the Beni-Gómez family, a representative of whom was considered a traitor to Alfonso VIII, who was a descendant of the Cid himself. The Lara family, in addition, benefitted from a praise-poem about the Cid since they were also related to him through marriage. By writing a poem about the exploits of a famous fighter of Moors who, in the process of

# Compare & Contrast

- **1090s:** The primarily agricultural economy of medieval Spain was influenced by the *Reconquistà*. The repopulation that accompanied the capture of Moorish territory led to the establishment of fortified Christian towns which became economic centers for international trade. The *Cid*, however, depicts an archaic gift economy, in which a man's status depends on how much wealth he can win and then distribute.

  **1207:** Towns garner increasing population and importance, trade increases, and commerce expands. The expansion of the market economy, dominated by monetary exchanges, credit, and international commerce, characterizes this period.

  **1990s:** Spain's inclusion in the European Union shows that it has a strong economy. However, unemployment remains around 21%, the near-worst rate in Europe in 1996.

- **1090s:** Christian culture was in the process of a great renewal, which started with the Church reforms begun in the monasteries of Cluny and Cîteaux in France. Bishop Jerome, in the *Cid*, is a figure linked to these reforms; in the epic, his arrival in Spain demonstrates the effect of the French reforms on the Church of Spain.

  **1207:** A new wave of reforms, including the movement headed by the Spaniard Domingo de Guzmán, established the Dominican Order in 1215. The Dominicans were later instrumental in the administration of the Spanish Inquisition.

  **1990s:** Spain has no state religion, but the Roman Catholic Church receives state support. The vast majority of Spaniards are Catholic.

- **1090s:** The feudal system of government, characterized by a personal relationship between a vassal and a lord, gained ground in the eleventh and twelfth centuries in Spain. Spanish feudalism, as is demonstrated in the *Cid*, consisted of the promise of service to a lord, and was sealed by kissing the lord's hand. In Spain, however, the triangular shape of feudal society was overshadowed by the role of the king as military leader; in the epic, the Infantes and the Cid all work for the king, although they are of unequal rank.

  **1207:** The rise of towns in the thirteenth century added a new aspect to the relationship between king and vassal, as towns demanded increasing governmental autonomy.

  **1990s:** Spain is a constitutional monarchy, led by the popular King Juan Carlos I, who regained the throne after the dictator Franco died in 1975.

- **1090s:** Spain in the eleventh century is noted for the sometimes uneasy cohabitation of Muslims, Jews, and Christians. The *Cid* chronicles the efforts of Christians to reclaim Muslim lands, lost in the eighth century. In Christian territory, Jews were isolated, but were also under the protection of the king. Muslims were distrusted, and were also isolated in ghettos in the cities. In Muslim territory, whose inhabitants had constructed a specific culture, Jews and Christians enjoyed relative lenience. The relativistic attitude towards Muslims is demonstrated in the *Cid*, for example in the depiction of the Cid's moorish ally Abengalbón. The Jews, on the other hand, are shown in harsher light.

  **1207:** The thirteenth century and the later Middle Ages are generally considered to be a period of increased oppression of minority groups in Spain. An important Church council decreed that Jews wear a distinctive dress in 1179 and 1215. A great pogrom against the Jews erupted in 1351, and the Muslims were also oppressed. In 1492 the Jews were expelled from Spain.

  **1990s:** Today, there are about 250,000 non-Catholic Christians, around 12,000 Jews, and a growing Muslim community of over 300,000 whose numbers are increasing because of immigration from North Africa.

winning lands and booty, caused a rival clan to lose face, the author of the 1207 *Cid* might have been writing a propagandistic poem which praised an ancestor of Alfonso VIII and the Lara clan while functioning to incite renewed efforts against the Moors after a dramatic defeat during the darker days of the Christian Reconquest of Spain.

### The Reconquistà

Never far in the background of the *Cantar de mio Cid* is the long history of the Spanish Reconquest of Muslim territory, which began in the early Middle Ages and was nearly completed by the middle of the thirteenth century. The last Muslim enclave, Grenada, was annexed by Ferdinand and Isabella of Spain in 1492, thus completing a long and painful reordering of the Spanish peninsula. In the early history of the Reconquest, Christian success came in direct proportion to the strength of Islamic Spain. Tension between the kings of Asturias, Castile, and Leon and the rulers of Portugal, Navarre, and Aragon-Catalonia often undermined the Christian program to gain territory, but by the end of the Middle Ages, only Portugal remained separate. With the Reconquest and the resettling of territory came accelerated development of the towns, with the consequence, among others, that Christian religious centers were reestablished, restored, and expanded. With the expansion of Christian territory, many Muslims and Jews came under Christian rule. For the most part, a relatively stable coexistence was maintained; Muslims and Jews were allowed freedom of religion and their own law codes as long as they paid regular fees (tribute) to the Christians.

## Critical Overview

The critical reception of the *Cantar de mio Cid* must be studied in two parts: first, the evolution of the epic itself, and how the story was retold in the Middle Ages and in later literary periods, and second, the reception of the epic by modern critics.

The Cid's heroic deeds were recorded in a Latin poem, entitled the *Carmen Campidoctoris,* around 1093, and in a shorter Latin chronicle, or historical document, the *Historia Roderici,* around 1110. Although other fragments of the story of the Cid exist in several chronicles, including the prose *Primera Crónica General*, the *Cantar de mio Cid* is the only Spanish (Castilian) epic to have survived in near-entirety. A later text, written around 1250, bridges the gap between the epic and the romance tradition of literature: the *Mocedades del Cid* tells of the deeds of the Cid during his youth. This text is full of fanciful and romantic anecdotes about the Cid, contrasting strongly with the heroic, venerable Cid of the epic tradition. Interestingly, the epic version of the Cid's legend had almost no effect on later literature; it is the romance tradition that fed the fanciful ballads of the fifteenth and sixteenth centuries. The Spanish playwright Guillén de Castro's 1618 play, *Las Mocedades del Cid,* inspired Pierre Corneille to compose *Le Cid* in 1637, which provoked an important literary discussion in France about appropriate literary subject matter. In these romantic versions of the Cid legend, the authors focus on the relationship between Doña Ximena and Rodrigo, with the larger historical question of the battles between Christian and Moors relegated to the background.

While the epic was never entirely forgotten—the manuscript was rediscovered in Vivar in the sixteenth century and was passed among scholars for many years—it was not until the late nineteenth century that it began to receive serious scholarly attention. The single extant manuscript is now in very bad condition, due to the use of reagents, or acids, which were applied to places in the manuscript where the ink had faded (ultraviolet lamps and infrared photography are now the preferred methods to decipher difficult–to–read documents). In the late nineteenth century, the Spanish scholar Ramón Menéndez Pidal turned his attention to the work, publishing a three-volume edition in 1908-11. Menéndez Pidal's dominant position in Cidian scholarship ensured the duration of critical topics that he thought were important. A scholar of the "generation of 1898," an intellectual movement that opposed the restoration of the monarchy and favored a political return to the "purified" origins of Spain, Menéndez Pidal believed that the *Cid,* as the "national epic of Spain," reveals the origin of Spain's national character. He also believed that the *Cid* should be studied as an accurate historical document. Finally, he supported the "traditionalist" viewpoint that the epic had been composed gradually in the oral tradition by generations of folk poets. The search for origins, with an interest in seeking the roots of European culture, and which often led to fanciful reconstructions of literary texts, was an important characteristic of nineteenth-century philology.

Menéndez Pidal's nationalist, historicist, and traditionalist views dominated the shape of Cidian

*Title page of the 1498 edition entitled "Coronica del cid."*

scholarship for many years. The sharpest debate about this epic has involved the battle between the "individualist" belief in a single author of the epic, versus the "traditionalist" approach, which, following Menéndez Pidal and, later, Milman Parry and Albert Lord, insists that all epic literature has oral coposition at its core (see the "Author" section above). Although the "individualist" thesis has lost ground, Colin Smith's recent book (1983) demonstrates that it is not yet dead. Other scholarly problems that have attracted attention revolve around the date of composition of the poem and of its manuscript; problems of authorship; origins and influences (especially French) of the themes in the epic; the relation of the *Cid* to other types of medieval Spanish literature, including the *Romanceros* and the *Crónicas;* aesthetic evaluation of the epic as literature; mythic or folkloric aspects of the *Cid;* and finally, the application of social science methodology to the study of this epic.

Menéndez Pidal's nationalism, the result of his political ideology, has not affected subsequent scholarship as much as his historicism. An important debate between this scholar and another eminent medievalist, Leo Spitzer, revolved around the place of history in this epic, which contains much accurate historical detail. While Menéndez Pidal thought that the *Cid* could be read as an historical document, Spitzer disagreed, writing that the fictional events (almost the entire second half of the poem) of the epic are as important as the historical elements, and must be weighed as such. In recent years, new historicist treatments have added an important facet to Cidian studies. María Lacarra, in particular, characterized this epic as a propagandistic poem in which history is rewritten in order to better present a particular clan's interest. More recently, Joseph Duggan and Michael Harney have studied larger social structures of the era, linking them to problems that are raised in the text itself. Cidian criticism seems to have nearly surpassed the individualist/traditionalist battle, and is headed in a direction that can shed light on the cultural function of literature.

## Criticism

### *Jennifer Looper*

*In the following essay, Looper analyzes the "propagandistic element of epic literature," explaining how the* Cantar de mio Cid *was used as a means of promoting the political and economic*

# What Do I Read Next?

- The *Song of Roland*, an epic roughly contemporaneous with the *Cantar de mio Cid*, takes place on the frontier between France and Spain, in an atmosphere of impending doom which contrasts strongly with the exhuberant conquests of the *Cid* .

- Pierre Corneille's *Le Cid*, written in 1637, reflects the turbulence of France under Cardinal Richelieu and Louis XIII, more than the turmoil of Reconquest Spain.

- The twelfth-century *Pilgrim's Guide to Compostela* offers a different view of medieval Spain: that of the pilgrim who traveled to Compostela on the Western coast of Spain to visit the famous shrine of Saint James.

- Ibn Hazm, a theologian from Cordoba (994-1064), wrote the *Ring of the Dove*, a treatise on love. This work provides a view of the unique Arab culture that developed in Spain before the Reconquest.

- The famous novel by Miguel de Cervantes, *Don Quixote* (1605-15), tells the story of a very different kind of knight than the Cid. This novel illustrates the death throes of the chivalric romance—the descendant of the feudal epic—as a literary genre.

---

*aims of medieval institutions long after the death of the historical Cid.*

As an epic, compared with other examples from the genre, the *Cantar de mio Cid* stands out not so much in its form as in its content as a literary reflection of history. A text that probably underwent many transformations as oral literature before it was written down by a talented poet, the *Cantar de mio Cid* shares the epic epithets, stock themes, and formulas typical of other early epics. As the tale of a heroic individual whose existence is well documented, the *Cantar* offers a unique example in the epic genre of the relationship between literature and history. The link between the Cid as a man, the legend that quickly evolved about his deeds even during his lifetime, and the use of this story as a political tool during the turbulent twelfth century in Spain, during which time the descendants of the Cid won the throne of Castile, lends itself to a fascinating reconsideration of the way literature is used to change history.

Since the *Cantar de mio Cid* does recount the tale of a famous historical figure who is also well-documented, one of the most important questions to ask about the epic surrounds the cultural and historical impetus behind its composition. Why, in 1207, was the epic first written down? Why was it again recopied 100 years later? With regards to the events that are recounted in the epic itself, one can ask why certain fictional elements were added to the historical narrative, as well as why certain historical elements were retained while others were omitted. Two interesting phenomena illustrate the way this epic was used to promote the political and economic interests of certain medieval institutions many years after the Cid died. One example of the way that the poem was used to promote the political interests of King Alfonso VIII of Castile and his allies in the late thirteenth century demonstrates the propagandistic element of epic literature. A second example of the exploitation of the epic illustrates its "commercial" use: the development of a tomb-cult, a sort of tourist site at the Abbey of Cardeña, where the Cid was buried.

The hypothesis that the *Cantar de mio Cid* was written as a praise-poem for the king of Castile's (Alfonso VIII) ancestor and the king's allies, the Lara family, who were related to the Cid by marriage, has been discussed above (see the "History" section above) and is best summarized by J. Duggan, who follows María Lacarra in much of his argument. Duggan explains that the question of family integrity and illegitimacy, which dominates the narrative even over the conquest of Valencia—a monumental historical event—is related to the twelfth-century political struggle between Castile and Leon. It is important to remember that the historical Ximena, the Cid's wife, was of royal blood, cousin to Alfonso VI of Castile. In the epic, however, no mention is made of this, and the poet concentrates on the insults that are hurled at the Cid by the Infantes de Carrión, who maintain that the Cid is a member of the lower class: ''Who ever heard of the Cid, that fellow from Vivar? Let him be off to the river Ubierna to dress his millstones and collect his miller's tolls as usual. Who gave him the right to marry into the Carrión family?'' (ll. 3377-81) The Infantes insist that the Cid's daughters are not wives, but concubines, suggesting that they are illegitimate, or are born of an illegitimate parent. Duggan shows that the poet's insistence on ''clearing the Cid's name'' relates to a crisis that centered on the marriages of Alfonso IX of Leon and Alfonso VIII of Castile.

A common practice in the Middle Ages was to marry a member of an opposing family to restore peace between two warring clans; the historical Ximena was married to the Cid in a peacemaking gesture on the part of Alfonso VI. At the height of the tension between Alfonso IX and Alfonso VIII, after the disastrous battle of Toledo in 1195, the pope stepped in to try to restore peace between the Christian kings so as to better combat the Muslim presence. He excommunicated Alfonso IX of Leon and his counselor Pedro Fernández de Castro (the man considered a traitor by the Lara clan). Excommunication was a terrible punishment in this period; the victim was essentially ejected from the Christian community. Faced with this threat, in 1199 Alfonso IX agreed to marry Alfonso VIII's daughter, Berenguela, to make peace. This match, however, although it brought peace, was problematic in that Alfonso IX and Berenguela were first cousins, and thus the marriage was considered incestuous. The new pope who entered the scene at that moment, Innocent III, was particularly stubborn on the matter of incestuous marriages, and insisted that it be annulled, imposing the interdict on Leon and Castile, another terrible punishment in which no sacred services could be performed.

Alfonso IX and Berenguela refused to separate, and Berenguela eventually bore five children. These children were judged illegitimate by the pope, but Alfonso IX ignored this, naming his son, Fernando, heir to the Leonese throne. After a period of intense crisis, Fernando, the son of a daughter of Castile and the king of Leon, finally was given legitimacy by the pope in 1218, and the tension between Castile and Leon was finally ended, as it had been planned by Alfonso VIII, when Fernando became Fernando III, king of Castile and Leon. A crisis that threatened regional stability when popes and kings clashed is reflected and resolved in a work of fiction, in which the Cid is represented as illegitimate, but manages to earn, through his intrinsic worth, the approbation of his peers and, more importantly, the approval of God. It is important to note that the Cid's champions, in the final three duels, fight for the Cid and his family's honor and win, not because of their skill in fighting, but because God wills it. The clash of church and state, illustrated by the series of interdictions imposed on Spanish regions by various popes in the late twelfth century to force them to change their dynastic politics, is resolved in the epic when God remains consistently on the Cid's side throughout his struggle with the Moors and with those who would insult his family. A political and moral message is thus sent by this text, which works to uphold the prestige of a ruler who is tainted by the hint of illegitimacy.

The link between the Church and the Cid's descendants becomes clear when one takes into account the importance of churches and monasteries for royal families in the Middle Ages. In exchange for political and spiritual support in the form of sermons preached and masses said for the benefit of a powerful family, these families often donated great sums of money for the maintenance of the resident monks. Two institutions figure importantly in the history of this epic; the first is San Pedro de Cardeña, and the second is, according to Duggan, Santa María de Huerta. The former was powerful during the reign of Alfonso VI (the king who interacted with the Cid) and the latter was a newer institution, established by Alfonso VIII, who himself placed the keystone of the building in the ground. Huerta was also patronized, or given financial support, by the Lara family, allies of Alfonso VIII. Alfonso visited Huerta several times, and Duggan suggests that one of these occasions may have been commemorated by the composition of the 1207 manuscript of the *Cantar de mio Cid.* The mysterious ''Per Abbad'' who ''wrote down'' the text may refer to the Abbot Pedro I, who was Abbot at Huerta around 1203 through 1210. He might have presented it to Alfonso VIII on one of his visits in 1207.

Although the thirteenth-century copy of the text, which is now lost, may have been composed at the Abbey of Huerta, the fourteenth-century copy of this manuscript was discovered in the sixteenth century in the archives of the city hall of Vivar, the Cid's home town. Later it was borrowed by an eighteenth-century scholar and subsequently was passed around Spain for two hundred years. The history of Cardeña differs from that of Huerta in that it was a Benedictine institution, rather than a monastery such as Huerta, built on a newer, reformed model. It consequently enjoyed less royal favor than Huerta in this period, since Alfonso VIII favored the reformed model. Even a slight lessening of royal favor had serious financial ramifications for any given religious institution, and the monks of Cardeña took action. P. E. Russell states that "Cardeña enjoyed the favour of Alfonso VIII (1158-1214), though, in common with the other Benedictine foundations, it was now no longer closely connected with the life of the court. The monks began to elaborate, with small regard for historical probability, legends designed to keep alive memories of the part they had once played in the early days of the Castilian nation." ("San Pedro de Cardeña and the Heroic History of the Cid," *Medium Aevum,* Vol. 27, no. 2, 1958, p. 68)

One method that these monks used to maintain the prestige of their Abbey was the production of manuscripts, which served as valuable tools in the process of generating support for an element that the Abbey wanted to promote. In the case of Cardeña, it was a well-known fact that the Cid had been buried there after his wife Ximena brought his embalmed remains to the Abbey in 1102. The monks of Cardeña worked to aggrandize the Abbey's link with the Cid: stories circulated that not only the Cid was buried there, but also his wife Ximena and his famous horse, Babieca. The Cid's body, like that of a saint, was reported to be "incorrupted," or in perfectly preserved condition. In the *Cantar de mio Cid* itself, many unlikely details were either added or retained from the earlier version to emphasize Cardeña's helpful role in the Cid's campaigns. Ximena and her daughters, for example, were housed at the Abbey in defiance of the king's orders, according to the text. The Cid is depicted as donating vast sums of money to the Abbey in his lifetime. Even the general region in which the Abbey was situated is glorified by the invention of Martín Antolínez, the "worthy citizen of Burgos," who likewise defies the king and joins the Cid in exile.

These stories can be seen as a carefully orchestrated "advertising campaign" that resulted in attracting tourists who brought much-needed revenue

to a religious institution that enjoyed less royal favor than their newer counterparts. A tomb-cult quickly developed at Cardeña: people flocked there to view the tomb of the Cid, elevating his legend to the status of a saint by retelling the tales of his heroic deeds. This phenomenon is not an isolated one: Russell notes that "The gradual turning of a lay (e.g. not religious) figure into a hagiographical (e.g. saintly) one as a result of a tomb-cult was clearly a general phenomenon." ("San Pedro de Cardeña and the Heroic History of the Cid," *Medium Aevum,* Vol. 27, no. 2, 1958, p. 67). The steady stream of pilgrims to visit the tomb of a popular hero or a saint generated considerable wealth for the church or monastery that housed the relics, or remains, of a popular hero. These pilgrims also ensured the survival and elaboration of these heroic legends, in that they learned the story of the hero during their pilgrimage and returned home to retell it. Perhaps the manuscript was produced as yet another piece of written—and thus more plausible—proof that the relics were indeed worthy of popular veneration.

The *Cantar de mio Cid* offers a unique demonstration of how literature about a historical figure can reflect and even influence local politics and, later, generate revenue for a medieval tourist site. Heroic stories continue to be used to draw parallels between the present and the past. The 1961 Hollywood movie *El Cid* could be interpreted as a reflection of the American public's veneration of their own heroic leader, John F. Kennedy, who, with his wife, shed glory on an empire of their own. Thus an epic can be generated for the most self-serving of reasons.

**Source:** Jennifer Looper, for *Epics for Students,* Gale Research, 1997.

### Israel Burshatin

*In the following excerpt, Burshatin examines the status of Moors as portrayed in the epic and the metaphoric and symbolic roles filled by Moorish characters in the work.*

The image of the Moor in Spanish literature reveals a paradox at the heart of Christian and Castilian hegemony in the period between the conquest of Nasrid Granada in 1492 and the expulsion of the Moriscos by Philip III in 1609. Depictions fall between two extremes. On the "villifying" side, Moors are hateful dogs, miserly, treacherous, lazy *and* overreaching. On the "idealizing" side, the men are noble, loyal, heroic, courtly—they even mirror the virtues that Christian knights aspire to—

while the women are endowed with singular beauty and discretion.

Anti-Muslim diatribes are fairly common and predictable: they are flat and repetitive in their assertion of Old Christian superiority over every aspect of the lives of Muslims or crypto-Muslims. Any sign of cultural otherness is ridiculed; the conquering caste, insecure about its own lofty (and, more often than not, chimerical) standards of *limpieza de sangre* (''purity of blood''), laughs away whatever trace of old Hispano-Arab splendor might remain in the Morisco. Or, conversely, the uneasy master recasts wretched Moriscos as ominous brethren of the Ottoman Turk.

The truly vexed problem, however, consists in determining the meaning of idealized Moors in historiography, ballads, drama, and the novel. Roughly speaking, modern criticism divides into two camps in attempting to explain this curious phenomenon of literary infatuation with a cultural and religious minority subjected to growing popular hostility, Inquisitional hounding, and economic exploitation. I will call one camp ''aestheticist'' and the other ''social.''

In the ''aestheticist'' view, what counts above all else is the expansiveness of the Spanish soul, which is so generous to its enemies of eight centuries' standing that it buries the hatchet and fashions them into models of the courtly and chivalric. No Christian knight is more adept at arms than Abindarráez; no lady is ever lovelier than Jarifa, Daraja, or Ana Félix.

The ''social'' interpretations render literary phenomena as pamphlets for ''peaceful coexistence.'' They argue, often persuasively, that chivalric or sentimental narrative in Orientalist garb hides a subversive message available only to the *cognoscenti*—New Christians, crypto-Muslims, and crypto-Jews—in need of consoling or intent on dismantling the dominant culture. This literary fashion may well have been encouraged by aristocratic patrons wary of sacrificing faithful and hard-working vassals to the Church-inspired zealotry of Charles V's heirs. Some of the strongest dissenting voices belonged to Aragonese seigneurial patrons, whose fondness for *Maurophilie littéraire* may have come from a political conservatism rooted in profitable *mudéjar* traditions. Aragonese lords of Morisco vassals may thus have nurtured the proliferation of Moorish ''positive role models.'' Some scholars argue that seigneurial protectors of Morisco traditions might have sought to lift the sagging image of their New Christian subjects by conjuring up aristocratic Moors of yore. Still, the Morisco was as much of an outsider in sixteenth-century Spain as he would have been in the golden Nasrid Granada romanticized in literature.

Turning from the ''social'' aperçus on the possible origins of the sixteenth-century Moorish novel to the earliest vernacular instances of the discourse on the Moor, we find one of the most uncanny expressions in premodern literature of the power of representations. In the *Poema de mio Cid,* composed some time around 1207, the exiled hero's return to the fold takes the form of an ever widening but essentially redundant displacement of the Moor. And, as in the sixteenth century, the Moor in the *Poema de mio Cid* falls between extremes of the dehumanizing and the fanciful: either he is reduced, metonymically, to an item of value in the booty lists carefully drawn by the hero's *quiñoneros* (''officers in charge of counting and distributing booty''), or he is the reassuring and Orientalized projection of the hero's sway over reconquered lands. Grounded in conquest and reiterated tests of valor on the battlefield, the discourse of the conqueror also displays a twofold drift: on the one hand, writing is an instrument of surveillance, the means of recording all the wealth taken from Moors and then allotted to the Cid's fighters; on the other hand, the conqueror produces a poetic language belonging to the class of propagandistic gestures and calls to arms (*pregones*) which is essential to the seizure and, later, to the defense of Valencia.

The Cid is a soldier turned poet when he describes an army of Moors as a pageant of Moorish service that proclaims the Cid's presence—and not the Moors'—in a reconquered landscape. This metaphoric transformation of a Moorish menace into a hyperbolic statement of Moorish devotion to the conqueror takes place in Valencia, at the tower of the alcazar, where the proud conqueror has taken his wife and daughters to contemplate their vast estates. But into their vision of wealth and familial pleasures now intrude King Yúçef's North African hordes, encamped around the city they hope to seize for Mafomat (''Muhammad''). The threat is a Moorish version of the Christian Reconquest, and it is therefore all the more horrifying to the women after their uncertain years in the monastery at Cardeña, outside Burgos, away from the Cid. Model father and husband that he is, the Cid soothes the women by translating his proven force of arms into a reassuring metaphor of Moorish service:

Su mugier e sus fijas subiolas al alcaçar, alçavan los ojos, tiendas vieron fincadas: ''?Ques esto, Çid? !Si el Criador vos salve!'' ''!Ya mugier ondrada non ayades pesar! Riqueza es que nos acreçe maravillosa e grand; !a poco que viniestes presend vos quieren dar; por casar son vuestras fijas: aduzen vos axuvar!''

(He led his wife and daughters up into the castle; they raised their eyes and saw the tents pitched. ''What is this, Cid, in the name of the Creator?'' ''My honored wife, let it not trouble you! This is great and marvelous wealth to be added unto us; you have barely arrived here and they send you gifts, they bring the marriage portion for the wedding of your daughters.'')

Confident of his military and political savvy, the warrior as poet turns an image of Moorish force into a projection of his own overwhelming presence. Moorish weapons, tents, and horses exist in the poem only to be detached from armies whose defeat is episodic and invariable. In the Cid's proleptic metaphor, ''Riqueza es que nos acreçe maravillosa e grand,'' the tension between the ominous beating of Moorish battle drums and the hope of making worthy marriages for his daughters in the court of Alfonso VI of Castile and León is swiftly resolved in the ensuing battle, which bears out what the poem's implied audience has come to expect of its hero.

The Cid's metaphor makes two rhetorical thrusts. One is the proleptic shorthand that captures the development of the plot it describes. The second is the metonymic reduction of the Moor, whose presence (''riqueza es (''this is . . . wealth'')'') in the conqueror's universe of discourse is illusory, relegated to the spoils that *quiñoneros* can describe in their lists. But the heuristic fiction, which the metaphor gives rise to, dresses epic force in Orientalized garb. Once the Moor is defeated in battle, the role of the Moor in discourse is to enhance the prestige of the hero and his world. Not for nothing does the adjectival form *morisco* undergo a semantic shift in the work. First, it describes a coveted cloak which one of the duped Jewish moneylenders requests:

Rachel a mio Çid la manol ba besar: ''!Ya Campeador en buen ora çinxiestes espada! De Castiella vos ides pora las yentes estrañas; assi es vuestra ventura, grandes son vuestras gananças, una piel vermeja *morisca e ondrada* Çid, beso vuestra mano en don que la yo aya.'' (my emphasis)

(Raquel has kissed the hand of My Cid: ''Ah, Campeador, in good hour you girded on sword! You go from Castile forth among strangers. Such is your fortune and great are your gains; I kiss your hand, begging you to bring me a skin of crimson leather, *Moorish and highly prized.*'') (my emphasis)

Later, as the hero sweeps over Muslim lands, the adjective *morisco* aptly describes the manner in which the Cid puts his own stamp on booty and people: beaten *moros* point to *moriscos,* and both are the undifferentiated names for the Islamic defenders which the *Poema de mio Cid* marks for defeat.

Esta albergada los de mio Çid luego la an robada de escudos e de armas e de otros averes largos; de los *moriscos* quando son legados ffallaron .dx. cavallos.(my emphasis)

(My Cid's men have looted from this camp, shields and arms and many other things; they counted sixty horses in the booty taken from *Moriscos.*) (My translation; my emphasis)

Thus, the idealized Moor and the items listed by *quiñoneros* —congener to the romanticized Moor— presuppose one another in the conqueror's metaphoric language. The Cid's exemplary Moorish vassal Avengalvón, probably the first of a long line of idealized Moors in Spanish literary history, also displays elements of this complex interplay between the logic of the poet and that of the *quiñonero.*

To imagine the besieging Almoravides at the walls as an already beaten yet prestigious foe is a powerful device, but it becomes more vividly so when seen in the wider context of the Western epic tradition. The exchange of words between the Cid and his wife, Ximena, as they watch the armies below is a discrete reworking of the classical *teichoskopia*—the view from/on the wall. This topos, as in the *Iliad,* marks a shift in point of view, emphasis, and theme. In the *Poema de mio Cid* the broadening effect of the classical *teichoskopia* is masterfully turned into an Orientalizing trope. As viewed from the walls, the besieging warriors— shouting heretical war cries of ''Mafomat!'' and beating thousands of battle drums— are turned, simultaneously, into chattel *and* romanticized subjects not to be feared but counted and possessed. In the guise of a poet, the hero produces a powerfully self-centered caption to the fearsome sight below. The *teichoskopia* thus furnishes the privileged vantage point from which the hero enacts his sway over Muslim adversaries. High above the enemy, within sight of vast land-holdings and wealth, the hero now empowers his discourse with the ability to redefine, at will, bristling motifs of Moorish force and to imbue them with ''Cidian'' meaning and a reassuring sense of harmony and continuity.

This total dominion over the Moor—the linking, through *teichoskopia,* of metaphor and sword, the Moor as chattel *and* as romantic Other—is a key moment, both in shaping the Spanish Orientalist tradition and in fostering the ideological solidarity characteristic of the epic. All those who participate in the social mobility and expansiveness of the vigorous frontier world of Castile and its hero feed on the beaten Moors: the townspeople of Burgos, the fighting bishop don Jerome, the Cid's intrepid followers, and even Avengalvón, the Cid's ever loyal Moorish vassal. Catalans, Leonese, members of the old aristocracy, duped Jewish moneylenders, and Moorish enemy all constitute an opposition handily negated by the Cid and his band, exiles whose ostensible return to the fold actually initiates a new society and an ethos nurtured by "object values" taken from their antagonists and reinscribed in their own—the conqueror's—universe of discourse. The univocity thus achieved also manifests in the continuity of language and world: mobility over vast stretches of frontier territory coincides with the frequent *pregones* ("recruiting propaganda"); booty lists are homologous to epic catalogs of warriors; and narrative equivalence of wealth and authority, the forceful and the sacred, displays the scope of epic consolidation.

**Source:** Israel Burshatin, "The Moor in the Text: Metaphor, Emblem, and Silence," in *Critical Inquiry,* Vol. 12, No. 1, Autumn, 1985, pp. 98–118.

## Joseph J. Duggan

*In the following excerpt, Duggan traces the action in this epic work and discusses differences between it and other Romance epics, concluding that the heroes of such epics, though they possess less than ideal lineage, attain nobility and legitimacy through their actions.*

The *Chanson de Roland* and the *Cantar de mio Cid* are often compared, but usually for the wrong reasons. The Spanish poem has a documentary quality about it, and the single poetic version which has survived the Middle Ages, in a manuscript identified as the product of one Per Abbat, a scribe, was composed within a hundred and eight years of the hero's death The *Cid* is thus much closer in narrative type to, say, *Garin le Loherain* or to the *Canso d'Antiocha* than it is to the *Roland,* which in its earliest extant form is at least three hundred years removed from the historical events it reflects and which is marked by notable geographical and temporal distortions. What justifies considering these two poems together is that they both incorporate myths looking back to a foundation, the *Cid* for the Spanish kingdom born of the union of Leon and Castile, and the *Roland* for the Carolingian Empire.

The relationship between literature and history underlies notions of the epic to a greater extent than it does conceptions of other genres. During the last hundred and fifty years certain models of that relationship have been dominant. For the Romantic critics, the people spoke by and large as if with one voice, and the role of individual poet-craftsmen who gave form to that voice was usually passed over. More than any other type of poetry, the epic embodied the people's sentiments, preserving the memory of heroes to whose model it had looked in the past for leadership in life and an exemplary way to die. Because of constant rivalry between modern France and Germany, two powers which were at least theoretically united in Charlemagne's empire, the question of whether the French populace was more closely linked to a Germanic or to a Roman ancestry preoccupied scholars who were concerned with the origins of the French epic. Even those who were cognizant of the Franco-Prussian War's distorting effects on French intellectual life may register surprise at the formulation found in the second edition of Léon Gautier's *Les Epopées françaises:* the French epic is surely of Germanic origin, Gautier tells us, because its leading female characters are utterly without shame and their actions must thus be based on Germanic models of womanhood. The myth of origins itself—and here I use "myth" in the pejorative and popular sense of a belief which is not backed up by verifiable facts—is a historical concept conditioned by political and intellectual categories which are now outmoded. It is no secret that questions formerly asked about origins are now more often framed in terms of manifestation or development.

But all too often the issues posed by the giants of nineteenth-century and early twentieth-century scholarship—Gautier, Gaston Paris, Joseph Bédier, Ramón Menéndez Pidal, and others—are still being discussed in the same terminology which they bequeathed to us. In particular the perception of history as a sequence of striking events brought about by the potentates of this earth has survived largely intact in the work of many literary scholars concerned with the relationship between epic and history in western Romania. In the framework of their interpretations, great personages manipulate the epic to support their own drive for hegemony. Bédier's idea that the French epics were first created in the eleventh century through a collaboration between clerics and poets seeking to promote the fame of certain shrines situated along the great pilgrimage routes derives from a related view of history in that it posits that the motivation and working habits of medieval poets did not differ from those of later and better documented authors: witness Bédier's pronouncement that a masterpiece begins and ends with its author, his comparison of the *Roland* with Racine's *Iphigénie,* and his citation of La Bruyère's statement that making a book is no less a feat of craftsmanship than making a clock. But eleventh- and twelfth-century poets could not have worked in the same ways as those of the seventeenth, because the processes of poetic creation are a function of social, economic, and intellectual circumstances which vary from period to period and from one type of society to another. The manner in which a poet creates is conditioned above all by what French historians of the *Annales* school call *mentalités,* perceptual categories which shape the way in which phenomena are viewed. Substantial though they be, differences in educational background and in political and social milieu are less important than diversity in mental framework, a basic and all-pervasive variance that prevents us from reconstructing adequately the world view of medieval poets.

In studies on the *Cid,* a similar reliance on the concept of history as a sequence of noteworthy occurrences prevailed. While Menéndez Pidal appreciated the import of political events and the effects of Muslim pressure on the kingdoms of northern Spain, he gave less attention in *La España del Cid* to social and economic forces; although he took great pains to establish the geography of the epic Cid's progress from Burgos to Valencia, he seldom referred to medieval conceptions of time and space which contribute to the skewing of geographical reality. Pidal's achievements in filling in the backdrop against which the historical Cid acted are undeniable, and even his detractors make use of the data he collected. His discussion of the *Chanson de Roland's* manuscripts is a masterful treatment of how medieval texts recorded from oral tradition differ radically from what we in the twentieth century normally mean when we speak of a text, and as such it contributes in a major way precisely to that history of mentalities which is so regretfully lacking in the *España del Cid.* In reading the *Cantar de mio Cid* with greater attention to its social aspects and to the relationship between political and economic history, I believe one can approach with greater hope of success a realization of the poem's significance.

Dealings between men as they are represented in the *Cid* cannot all be subsumed under the terms "vasselage" or "feudalism." Social relationships are marked by an economic give and take which mirrors a particular state of society best qualified as a "gift economy" in which exchanges of money and goods take place continually, but not under the conditions which one normally calls "economic" in the modern sense. The historian Georges Duby has drawn upon ideas developed by the socio-anthropologist Marcel Mauss to sketch out a description of exchanges in the early and high Middle Ages which can illuminate the meaning of gift-giving and other processes of the eleventh- and twelfth-century economy as they are reflected in the *Cantar de mio Cid.* Conquests and the payment of various types of feudal dues and rents supplied political leaders and fighting men of that period with an abundance of wealth beyond what was needed for their sustenance. The economic workings of society required that such wealth be circulated to others, with the result that generosity in its distribution was not merely an option open to the powerful, but an uncodified obligation. Recipients of seignorial largess were not all of a lower rank then benefactors: gifts from inferior to superior were also immensely important. At the top of the social pyramid the king was forced to have at his disposal sources of wealth which he could dole out to those who came to test his liberality, and while conquest and plunder provided much of this wealth, so did the offerings of lesser men. The relationships whose existence was fueled by these gifts were of a mutually beneficial nature. Gift-giving was probably never considered to be disinterested. Between military men and their followers, of course, service was commonly exchanged for largess; tributes guaranteed against attacks; even stipends and legacies made in favor of the Church brought a return, in the form of divine favor. The economic system sustained by this movement of commodities and coin in many cases had no relation to mercantile trade, but nevertheless effected a flow of goods which maintained the poor, supported significant numbers of able-bodied if occasionally idle monks, provided motivation for the warrior class, and acted in general as a cementing element in the social edifice.

While the gift economy dominated in the early Middle Ages, its main traits were still present in the period 1050 to 1207, that is during the Cid's career and the time in which the poem in all probability took shape in something close to the form in which we have it. More than one observer has called the Cid a bourgeois hero, the poem a bourgeois epic. Such a formulation could only be based upon the conviction that obsession with wealth is a monopoly of the city-dwelling, mercantile class; as Duby has shown, this is manifestly untrue for the eleventh and twelfth centuries. No hero in all of epic literature is as concerned with money and possessions of various kinds as is the Cid, but his insistence on the prerogatives of nobility is unmistakable. Even the most cursory recital of the poem's themes confirms that economic interests dominate the *Cantar de mio Cid* to an extent unmatched in the Romance epic, and yet the outcome of the social process set in motion by the hero's acquisition of wealth is attainment of the very highest level of the aristocracy.

In tracing the motivations for actions in the *Cid,* one is forced to consult the prose version found in the *Cronica de Veinte Reyes,* since the poetic text as found in Per Abbat's manuscript lacks a beginning. The chronicle tells us that King Alfonso of Leon and Castile believed the accusations of evil counsellors to the effect that his vassal Rodrigo Diaz of Vivar was withholding from him tribute that was supposed to have been delivered subsequent to a mission to Seville and Cordova. While he was in Seville, Rodrigo had defended Alfonso's tributary against an attack from Cordova, and had earned by his prowess and magnanimity the honorific "Cid Campeador." Whatever the historical Alfonso's motive for exiling the Cid, the poet responsible for the Per Abbat text assumes that popular opinion lent credence to the accusation that the hero had profited at his lord's expense. After receiving six hundred marks from the Jewish money-lenders Rachel and Vidas in exchange for two chests which supposedly contain money but are actually full of sand, the Cid is financed and ready to face his exile which he will begin with a series of raids.

That an epic poem should devote any attention at all to how a military campaign is funded is extraordinary, let alone that negotiations should occupy a major scene. Why is the poem anomalous in this respect? In placing the *Cid* in the context of medieval Romance epic, one must refer primarily to the one hundred or so French works which are extant, a preponderance of evidence against which the three fragmentary Spanish poems and the half-dozen Provençal titles represent comparatively little. Allowance should be made, first of all, for differing social conditions. Undoubtedly the landed estate, the classic base for feudalism of the French variety, played a lesser role in Spain than it did north of the Pyrenees. In addition, whatever benefit might accrue from possession of a territorial foothold was denied to the Cid in his exile. A more important factor is also at work, deriving both from the particular circumstances of peninsular history and from the epic's role as a genre which holds up models for emulation. In the expanding world of northern Spanish Christendom, in which land was available for capture by force from the Arabs and in which one of the chief political problems was how to motivate fighting men to leave familiar surroundings so as to take advantage of the military inadequacies of weak and fragmented Muslim principalities, the *Cantar de mio Cid* furnishes the exemplary model of a noble of relatively low rank rising to the highest level of the social hierarchy without having at his disposal the power base of the landed estate. The poem is both an entertaining tale of military prowess and an economic and social incentive for ambitious Castilian knights of low rank and narrow means.

The acquisition of booty, its proper distribution among the knights and soldiers, the appraisal of precious objects, and the use to which wealth is put join together to form one of the poem's major thematic complexes. The poetic Cid achieves his reintegration into the social fabric directly through economic power, and succeeds in proportion to his personal enrichment, beginning with the unhistorical raid on Castejón. Time and again, the type and quantity of booty are enumerated: coined money, shields, tents, clothing, slaves, camels, horses, beasts of burden, and other livestock. At times the amounts are stated to be beyond reckoning, but this type of comment is only a figure of speech since the poet also depicts the tallying up of loot by the *quiñoneros,* officials whose job it was to divide and count the spoils. Repeatedly and as early as the first major engagement the fighting men are termed *ricos.* As lord, the Cid receives a fifth of all plunder.

The relative worth of objects is of less interest than what their possession connotes in social terms. In the *Cid,* wealth and fame are closely linked, from the hero's first proclamation inviting others to join him in his exile, which frankly appeals to the desire for *rritad,* through the marriage of his daughters Elvira and Sol with the heirs of the house of Carrión, to the climax at the court scene in Toledo where the Cid is dressed in his most luxurious finery. Throughout the poem he displays his wealth by bestowing gifts on those who surround him, although he is never seen receiving them. The outstanding examples of interested gift-giving are the three embassies which carry extravagant offerings to King Alfonso. In return the Cid receives first the lifting of the king's official displeasure, then that his wife and daughters be allowed to join him in Valencia, and finally full pardon and, without his having requested it, his daughters' marriage to the heirs of Carrión.

The link between wealth and honor is nowhere more apparent than in the hero's dealings with the heirs. The villainous motives of this pair are epitomized when they accept booty from the victory over King Búcar in spite of having acted in a cowardly fashion on the battlefield. The five thousand marks that come to them on this occasion lead them to the mistaken belief that they are now rich enough to aspire to marriage with the daughters of kings and emperors. Whereas for the Cid courage brings material benefits in the form of possessions which can then be exchanged for the prerogatives of birth and can even, in a sense which I will discuss shortly, compensate for the inadequacies associated with doubtful lineage, for the heirs of Carrión high birth conveys an intrinsic value which makes it unnecessary for them to put themselves to the test of battle. As they leave Valencia supposedly to escort their wives to Carrión, the Cid gives them more wealth in the form of a bride-gift: three thousand marks and the precious swords Colada and Tizón. That this contrast is essential rather than coincidental is seen in the aftermath of the incident at Corpes in which the brothers beat the Cid's daughters and leave them for dead. Surprisingly for the modern reader, the hero places loss of the wealth he has distributed to the heirs of Carrión on the same level as his daughters' dishonor: ''*Mios averes se me an levado que sobejanos son, / esso me puede pesar con la otra desonor*.'' This preoccupation with worldly goods as a symbol of intrinsic worth continues during the court scene at Toledo. The Cid makes three legal points against the heirs of Carrión, of which the first two concern possessions: that they return the two swords, and that they give back the bride-gift of three thousand marks. The third point is a moral accusation, but it is framed in an economic metaphor: the brothers are worth less, since they struck their own wives. The key term *menosvaler* sums up emblematically the relationship between wealth and honor, economic and moral ''worth.''

The poem ends in a curiously unhistorical fashion. The Cid's daughters will become queens of two kingdoms, according to the poet, who returns to this theme just before he refers to the Cid's death:

Los primeros (casamientos) fueron grandes mas
    aquestos son mijores;
a mayor ondra las casa que lo que primero fue:
!ved qual ondra creçe al que en buen ora naçio
quando señoras son sus fijas de Navarra e
    de Aragon!
Oy los reyes d'España sos parientes son.

The Cid's historical daughters, Cristina and María, married respectively Ramiro, lord of Monzón in Navarre, and Ramón Berenguer III, Count of Barcelona. Thus neither of his daughters became queen, and they did not marry the infantes of Navarre and Aragon, although confusion on these points is conceivable in a poet composing in the mid-twelfth century or later since the son of Cristina and Ramiro became King of Navarre in 1134 and Barcelona was united to Aragon in 1137. Questions of title are not generally obscure to contemporaries, so that it is likely the poem was composed in a form not too far from the one in which we have these lines long enough after 1137 for people's memories to have become clouded regarding the chronology. In any event it is more than surprising that a poet who knows the names of the Cid's minor historical associates, such as Pero Vermúdez, Muño Gustioz, Martin Muñoz, Alvar Salvadórez, and Diego Téllez, should err on whether the hero's daughters were queens, and of what political entities. His inaccuracy on these points, although partly justified by later historical developments, at the very least exaggerates the Cid's rise to respectability among the very highest class of nobles. Why should a singer of the twelfth or early thirteenth century be so intent on depicting his hero's meteoric ascent as to represent the Cid's immediate progeny as queens at the risk that some members of the audience would recognize the error? The answer to this question provides an explanation for the poet's concern with the acquisition of wealth, gift-giving, and other economic phenomena.

Let us return to the court scene. There are two heirs of Carrión, each of whom is challenged to single combat by one of the Cid's men, who will use the swords Colada and Tizón in their respective duels so that, fittingly, the two brothers will be tested by the very instruments which they received under the false pretense of marriage-alliance with the Cid. But unexpectedly a third duel is proposed, provoked by Asur Gonçález, elder brother to the heirs of Carrión, who enters the palace and flings an apparently gratuitous insult at the Cid:

''!Hya varones! ?Quien vio nunca tal mal?
!Quien nos darie nuevas de mio Çid el de Bivar!
!Fuesse a Rio d'Ovirna los molinos picar
e prender maquilas commo lo suele tar!
?Quil darie con los de Carrion a casar?''

This curious intervention might at first seem to be only an attack on the hero's position at the low end of the noble hierarchy, since as an infanzón he was entitled to collect feudal dues on the use of mills which came under his jurisdiction. But as Menéndez

Pidal points out, mills were prized possessions of the seignorial class. Asur Gonçález is probably not simply assimilating the Cid's possession of a mill to the actual operations performed by the miller, for as rude as such a quip might be, it would hardly justify a challenge to mortal combat such as Muño Gustioz subsequently proffers, nor is it equal in weight to the outrage of Corpes which will be avenged by the other two duels which are to be fought on the same occasion. The *maquila* was a portion of wheat given to the miller in return for his services, and the Cid as an *infanzón* would hardly be expected to receive recompense under that rubric, although he would take other types of payment from a miller working under his jurisdiction. Asur Gonçález's words convey a far greater affront, an innuendo about the Cid's birth, suggesting that he is descended from a miller and thus entitled to a miller's pay. Verse 3379, scornfully exhorting the Cid to go to his mill on the river Ubierna, the location of Vivar, and roughen the millstones, can only mean that for Asur Gonçález the Cid *is* a miller. A person of such low rank would indeed be ill-advised to aspire to a marriage tie with the powerful combat family of the Vani-Gómez.

An obscure legend, preserved primarily in the *romancero,* has it that the Cid was the illegitimate son of Diego Laínez, and one version reports that his mother was a *molinera.* The agreement between this detail and Asur Gonçález's otherwise senseless insult can hardly be coincidental. Acceptance of the Cid's daughters as queens of Aragon and Navarre would be convincing proof that his accomplishments transcended and annuled the disadvantages of his bastardy. Asur Gonçález's defeat at the hands of the Cid's vassal shows that God approves of the hero's deeds in spite of the fact that he was conceived out of wedlock, for the duel takes the form of an ordeal.

The *Cantar de mio Cid* differs from the other extant Romance epics in its author's obsession with the acquisition of wealth, then, not only on account of the differing social and political conditions of Reconquest Spain, but because, unlike most of the heroes whose legends are recounted in poems belonging to this genre, the Cid does not enter the struggle with his honor intact. The amassing of riches and their proper use allow him to rise to the dignity and rank which great nobles of unblemished descent, such as the heirs of Carrión, could claim by birth. He is a king by right of conquest, excelling in knightly virtues that might well have been called into doubt by his maternal ancestry. Seen in this light, the *Cantar de mio Cid* is the story of how courage and prowess are transmuted into economic power, and wealth into lineage, the highest in Spain. As such it is a message to the lesser nobles of Castile, because if the Cid, whose line of descent was in question and whose king exiled him from his land, could raise his kin to the level of royalty through his participation in the Reconquest, then other nobles of his class could legitimately aspire to the same heights of success in invading Arab-controlled lands which enjoyed, despite their political troubles, the most prosperous economy in medieval Europe at this time.

The obscure allusion to Rodrigo of Vivar's bastardy calls to mind a similarly fleeting reference in the Carolingian foundation myth as it is found in the Oxford manuscript of the *Chanson de Roland.* I refer, of course, to Charlemagne's Sin. As with the Cid ..., the question of Roland's parentage is clouded. Neither the poet of the Oxford *Chanson de Roland* nor the one who composed the extant *Cantar de mio Cid* devotes more than a passing allusion to the issue of the respective hero's birth; it is nonetheless intriguing that in each case the problem of illegitimacy surfaces. In societies such as these where kinship is a pervasive social bond, and in which a person is considered to be legally responsible for acts committed by his kinsmen—above all in a genre in which lineage, one of the two principal meanings of the term *geste,* is one of the most important determinants of character—illegitimacy, whether it results from royal incest or simply from a paternal liaison with a commoner, represents a most serious deficiency. Roland's case differs from the Cid's in obvious ways. Nevertheless I believe that as with the *Cantar de mio Cid,* the meaning of the Oxford *Chanson de Roland* in its social context is closely linked with the theme of the hero's birth.

While historians of the Romance epic, dominated by a concern for origins, formerly sought to isolate the historical kernel preserved in each work, a focussing of attention on *how singers have distorted history* and on the circumstances or purposes which have led them to do so will undoubtedly teach us more about the genre's function in society. Modern political forces tend in sometimes subtle ways to appropriate for themselves the "tale of the tribe," as Ezra Pound characterized epic. This deformation of the past is an interesting phenomenon in itself, and its study will enable us to compensate in part for a collective wish to see the past in certain ways. The philologist's task is to appreciate medieval uses of epic legends, although at the same time he realizes that total awareness of them is unattainable. No one knew the Cid tradition as manifested in epic, chronicle, and *romancero* better than Menéndez Pidal, but he failed to see the meaning of a key element in the *Cantar de mio Cid,* one without which the poem's ending is a puzzle. Bédier was aware of the motif of Charlemagne's Sin, but, oblivious to the Oxford poet's admonition against ignoring it, he did not consider it to be an important theme. One cannot help thinking that these giants of scholarship were little inclined to pursue clues leading to revelations which might be considered unflattering for the foundation myths of their respective nations. Not that either one was consciously engaged in obfuscation. Rather in one instance the political and intellectual climate fostered by the Generation of '98, and in the other a propensity to identify Roland's Franks with the French, may have left no scope for the idea that the greatest of heroes were tainted by the circumstances of their birth or that the "national" epics, *nos épopées* as both Gautier and Bédier preemptively referred to them, could have such a theme among their key interpretive elements.

The different versions of the *Chanson de Roland* have taken on various meanings for their singers and audiences. To the late eleventh-century noble French public, however, about to heed Urban II's exhortation that it follow in the footsteps of the epic Charlemagne to recover the Holy Land from the Arabs, Roland is an exemplary hero because he was able to overcome the impediments of his birth. To Castilian singers whose lords had to resort to unique forms of land tenure in order to encourage repopulation of border territory vacated by the retreating Muslims, the Cid represented an ideal model, achieving for his descendants access to the highest level of society although he may himself have been a bastard. Both these heroes, deprived of the privileges of irreproachable ancestry, acquired legitimacy in the eyes of the epic public through their own actions. (pp. 231–32)

**Source:** Joseph J. Duggan, "Legitimation and the Hero's Exemplary Function in the 'Cantar de Mio Cid' and the 'Chanson de Roland'," in *Oral Traditional Literature: A Festschrift for Albert Bates Lord,* edited by John Miles Foley, Slavica Publishers, 1981, pp. 217–34.

## Ramón Menéndez Pidal

*In the following excerpt, Menéndez Pidal examines the similarities and differences between the historic Cid and the title character of the epic. He also comments on the historical and literary contributions of both figures.*

As an epic hero the Cid stands in a class by himself. History has little or nothing to say about the protagonists of the Greek, Germanic or French epics. From the ruins revealed by learned excavators we know that the Trojan War was an event that actually took place at Troy, so that the excavations confirm and illustrate the veracity of Homeric poetry. But we shall never know anything about Achilles, nor, for that matter, about Siegfried, whom we can only suspect to have been an historic personage, as Günther, the King of Burgundy, at whose Court Kriemhild's husband loved and died, undoubtedly was. The historians of Charlemagne assure us that Roland, Count of Brittany, really existed; but beyond this fact all we know of him is his disastrous end. Those heroic lives will for ever remain purely in the region of poetry and intangible for the purpose of historical analysis. The Cid, however, is a hero of a very different type. From the height of his idealism he descends with a firm step on to the stage of history to face unflinchingly a greater danger than had ever beset him in life, that of having his history written by the very people on whom he had so often waged war and by modern scholars who as a rule show even less understanding than the enemies he humiliated.

For the Cid, unlike the other heroes, did not belong to those early times when history still lagged far behind poetry. The broad stream of poetic creation along which Achilles, Siegfried and Roland glide, may be likened to a mysterious Nile whose sources have never been explored; whereas the epic river of the Cid may be traced to its earliest origins, to the very heights above their confluence, where poetry and history rise. Philological criticism enables us to explore primitive history and takes us back to the poetry of the hero's own age, the works inspired either by his deeds or by a vivid recollection of them. This contemporary poetry, which has come down to us about the Spanish hero but not about the others, may help to complete our historical knowledge of the heroic character, just as, when it agrees with the records, that poetry has helped us to establish the facts of the hero's life.

Renan is utterly mistaken when, in docilely acknowledging the divorcement by Dozy of the poetic from the historic Cid, he considers that "no other hero has lost so much in passing from legend to history." For the truth is that history and poetry, if taken to mean duly documented history and primitive poetry, show rare agreement in characterization, in spite of the fact that on no other epic hero has the light of history shone more relentlessly. Often, indeed, the character of the real Cid is found to be of greater poetical interest than that of the traditional hero. Legend achieved much that is of poetic value, but it left unworked many veins that appear in the rock of the hero's real life in the rough, natural state in which the beauties of nature occur.

Much has been written about the "heroic age" and the society and culture of those barbaric and lawless times, when pride in personal glory and lust for wealth overruled all other feelings. Yet to my mind, the heroic age, in the widest sense of the term, is distinguished by one essential characteristic only, and that a literary one; it is the age in which history habitually takes on a poetic shape, the age in which an epic form of literature arises to supply the public want of information about events of general interest either of the time or the recent past. This epic form of history, of course, only appears in primitive times, before culture has reached the stage of producing erudite works in prose; as historiography advances, the epopee loses its pristine vigour.

But in Spain, the scene of the last heroic age of the western world, that age coincided with the historic age, and epic poetry continued to be the vehicle for conveying the news of the day down to the time of the Cid despite the fact that history had already reached a fair stage of development. Thus, in view of the difference in time and circumstance separating the heroic age of Spain from that of other countries, it is not to be expected that the mind of the Campeador would work in unison with that of Beowulf. And so it is that we do not claim to have discovered in the Cid *the* heroic, but merely *an* heroic, character. Our main interest will lie in obtaining a close view of a hero, the last hero to cross the threshold from the heroic to the historic age.

The most modern trait in the character of the hero, who lived during this period of transition, is his loyalty. His is not the loyalty of a vassal in the rude heroic ages to the lord for whom he fought; it is the loyalty of a vassal to a king who persisted in persecuting him, a virtue that none of the other persecuted heroes of epic poetry possessed. The Cid of reality, though exiled, remained true to his king; though grossly insulted by Alphonso, he bore with him and treated him with respect. According to law, he owed no fealty to the King, and yet his loyalty was unswerving. Though the King was openly

hostile to his occupation of Valencia, he placed the city, to use his own phrase, "under the overlordship of my lord and king, Don Alphonso." These words are recorded by the Arab historian and are echoed in the old *Poem,* where Alvar Hañez is sent by the Cid to offer the conquered city to the King in spite of his having obstinately refused to lift the ban of exile.

This attitude would be incomprehensible if, as is possible, we were to assume that the motives of the Spanish hero were purely personal. True, all heroes, whether of Greek, Teutonic, or Romance poetry, act under the impulse of personal honour and glory; indeed, the personal motive is so strong that, in the French epic, notwithstanding the highly developed national spirit, the hero who rebels against the King when offended by him, is constantly glorified. But if, on the other hand, the Cid of poetry is on all occasions respectful towards his royal persecutor, it is because the longed-for pardon means reconciliation with "fair Castile," which he puts before his personal pride. The King and his country, his native land, to him are one and the same thing. And so the Cid of history appears eager and, at times, over ready to be reconciled with Alphonso and at the same time distrusts Berenguer and is slow to accept his proffered friendship.

The fact that, contrary to the custom established in the law and poetry of the time, neither the Cid of history nor the Cid of fiction makes war on his king but remains loyal to him, shows the extent to which the hero subordinated personal motives to love of country, thereby betraying a spirit practically unknown to the heroic types of older epic poems. This same patriotism also finds expression in his famous resolve to reconquer the whole of Spain and even, as the old poem maintains, lay Morocco under tribute to King Alphonso.

The Cid, who refrains from retaliating against his king although authorized by mediæval law to do so, and who ignores the monarch's insults at Ubeda, is equally anxious to avoid an encounter with the King of Aragon or Berenguer, to each of whom he makes friendly overtures before adopting an aggressive attitude. He grants generous terms to the defeated Valencians, in spite of their repeated infringements of the treaty of surrender; he returns a lawful prize taken from the Moorish messengers when on their way to Murcia; and finally, he refuses presents of doubtful origin when proffered by Ibn Jehhaf.

The Cid of poetry, coming at a later time than the other epic heroes, also displays this moderation, which is the outstanding virtue of the *chivalrous* type that succeeded the *heroic* type of the earlier ages.

But, in depicting him as constantly moderate, poetry diverges from fact. For when the real Cid's patience was exhausted, his violence knew no bounds. When he realizes that loyal submission is all in vain, he devastates the lands of Alphonso's favourite vassal; when repulsed by Berenguer, he sets the etiquette of the Court of Barcelona at naught; when the Valencians persist in siding with the Almoravides, he passes from the greatest clemency to the greatest severity. He was, indeed, ever apt to go to extremes. As soon as he had captured Berenguer, his attitude to him at once changed from rancour to the utmost generosity. Enigmatic and capricious, he loved to play with an adversary, as when he scorned the offer of the royal gardens at Valencia, only to seize them later at a most unexpected moment.

The thirst for treasure which he shares with the heroes of barbaric times, has already been referred to; it forms a strange contrast to the generosity he showed on other occasions.

The Cid, as a representative figure of his race, was tightly bound by atavistic ties of both ritualism and superstition. History and poetry agree that he was guided by omens. The birds of prey that crossed his path foretold to him the result of his exile, of the fording of a river, of his daughters' journey. This superstitiousness was deeply engrained in men-at-arms, though it frequently gave rise to rebuke, such as that which Berenguer hurled at the Cid at Tevar.

According to the *Poem*, the Cid was addicted to ritual. In a moment of great emotion, on his return from exile, he does homage to the King by biting the grass, which is a very ancient symbol of submission. To publish the grief he felt at his unjust banishment, he swore he would never again cut his beard, well knowing that thereby he would make both Moors and Christians talk. To go unshorn as a sign of grief was an old and common custom, but the Cid observed it so faithfully that he came to be called "Mio Cid, el de la barba grant." The whole Court of Toledo was astonished to see him appear with his beard pleated, a well-known though rare sign of deep mourning; then, hardly has justice been done to him, when he unravels his beard and resumes his normal appearance. Not that he was ever a slave to tradition. He was an innovator in all he did, whether in combating the traditionalism of Leon, abandoning the tactics generally adopted by Spaniards and Burgundians, in order to overcome the Almoravides,

in promoting the reform of the clergy, or in revolutionizing, as he actually did, heroic poetry.

The Cid's detractors paint him as a mere outlaw, a bandit who knew no honour; but both the Arab and the Latin historians agree with the early poets that his whole career was governed by his attitude to the law. Here again we find the Cid combining the characteristics of the two epochs, the heroic age and the chivalrous age that followed it.

When the chivalrous ideal had been perfected and formulated, it was held to be the duty of a knight to defend the rights of the weak, with the result that a knowledge of legal matters became a knightly accomplishment. Chivalric literature, from its birth to its death, bears this out. Old Gonzalo Gustioz of Salas, in enumerating the attainments of his deceased son, speaks of him as "learned in the law and fond of judging," and the last perfect knight, Don Quixote, also acts as a judge and shows that he possessed a thorough knowledge of the law.

The Cid on several occasions gave evidence of this knightly accomplishment: when acting as counsel for the monastery of Cardeña; as judge at Oviedo, where he interpreted Gothic law and inquired into the authenticity of a deed; and again when drawing subtle distinctions in the drafting of a fourfold form of oath. The Cid of poetry likewise pleaded his cause with skill and method before the court of Toledo.

The Cid always applied the law, according to its loftiest conception. In his youth, as champion of Castile, he fought out the legal duel against Navarre, and at Santa Gadea he exacted the oath, no doubt in the same capacity. Later, when aggrieved by Alphonso, as an exile, he had two legal courses open to him, to make war on his sovereign or to seek reconciliation. He chose the second course throughout. Availing himself of the means afforded by mediæval law for regaining royal favour, he twice hastened to the aid of his king; on a third occasion, he attempted to clear himself by the ordeal of a legal oath. It is only when all these attempts at reconciliation have failed and he has been made to suffer fresh and more grievous wrongs, that he exercises his right to make war on the King's lands; and, when this time comes, the heavy hand of the Campeador achieves what his moderation had steadfastly failed to do. But to call the Cid an enemy of his country, as Masdeu and Dozy call him, is simply absurd.

Owing to this failure to recognize his two distinct lines of conduct, the Cid's relations with the

Moors have also been misunderstood. His attitude to the Spanish Moslems may be summed up in his own declaration: "If I act lawfully, God will leave me Valencia; but if with pride and injustice, I know He will take her away from me." Even the usually malevolent Ibn Alcama admits that the Cid dealt very fairly with the Valencians. But when, in their anxiety to remain under Islam, the Moors of Spain called in the Africans, the Cid perforce took up a different stand: thenceforth the war could only end in the expulsion of the invader and the complete submission of the Spanish Moors.

The contrast between these two lines of conduct is most pronounced during the Valencian revolution, when on the assassination of his protégé King Al-Kadir, the city was handed over to the Almoravides. The Cid launches forth on the siege of Valencia, his greatest military enterprise, as an act as much of justice as of policy, and he determines not to rest until he has punished the regicide and driven out the African intruders. On the expulsion of the Almoravides and the surrender of the city, he begins by treating the Valencians with benevolence; but, when he finds that they continue to intrigue with the Africans, he ceases to respect Moslem law and resorts to the mailed fist of the conqueror. His detractors attribute this change of conduct to mere arbitrariness, but the fact remains that it was based on political justice.

Although poetic exaggeration clothes all heroes in the mantle of invincibility, it is surprising to find that, so far as the Cid is concerned, fact agrees with fiction.

The fame that the Cid enjoyed amongst his contemporaries is expressed in the name of *Campeador* or "victorious," given him by Moors and Christians alike; in the phrase "invictissimus princeps" used in the Valencian charter; and in the "invincibilis bellator" of the *Historia Roderici,* which adds that he "invariably triumphed." Further, the *Poema de la conquista de Almeria,* composed in Latin some fifty years after his death, says of the hero: ". . . of whom it is sung that no foe ever overcame him."

Ibn Bassam himself emphasizes the Cid's extraordinary victories, typical instances of which were the combats at Tamarite, where he overcame odds of twelve to one, and at Zamora, where alone and unaided he defeated fifteen knights. But the exceptional superiority of the Campeador was never more patent than when he tackled the Almoravides as an entirely new and hitherto invincible military

organization. He alone, at Cuarte and Bairen, was successful against the invaders, routing their armies and taking a great number of captives; he alone was able to conquer Valencia, Almenara and Murviedro in spite of their determined opposition. This contrast is in itself sufficient to bring out in full relief the military genius of the ever victorious Cid.

At times the hero found himself in situations so desperate that to all others everything seemed lost, when of a sudden his keen vision would descry the hidden opportunity that led to success. In emergencies such as a surprise attack by night he would tremble with excitement and grind his teeth; whenever there was the prospect of a battle his heart would leap with joy ("gaudenter expectavit"). The poet is at one with the historian when he tells of the hero's fierce glee on sighting the imposing array of the Almoravides: "Delight has come to me from overseas."

The Cid's infallible tactics on occasions struck panic into his enemies. Latin and Arab historians relate how the host of García Ordoñez at Alberite, the mighty *mehalla* of the Almoravides at Almuzafes, and the knights of Ramon Berenguer the Great at Oropesa were all routed without daring even to face the Cid. The battle of Cuarte also suggests panic among the enemy. Legend seized upon this terror-striking ascendancy of the hero to suggest that no Saracen could meet the eye of the Cid without trembling.

The Cid's chroniclers narrate the personal share he took in all his enterprises. The extent to which he exposed himself upon the field of battle is shown by the many mishaps he suffered and the narrow escapes he had. In the sphere of government, he assumed many duties; he administered justice at Valencia several times a week and he it was who exposed the bad faith of the envoys sent to Murcia. His extraordinary powers of organization are seen in the rapid rise of Juballa from a smouldering ruin to a flourishing city and in the way he rebuilt and enlarged the suburb of Alcudia.

His prodigious and unremitting energy enabled him to master the highly complex problems of Eastern Spain that had baffled the Emperor, Alvar Hañez, the Kings of Aragon, Saragossa and Denia and the Counts of Barcelona. In face of their futile claims, he established and tenaciously maintained his protectorate over the coveted and disunited region. When his work had been twice undone, he patiently built it up again in spite of seemingly insuperable difficulties presented, in the first place, by the jealous rage of Alphonso and, in the second, by the ambition of Yusuf.

It savours of madness that a single man, unsupported by any national organization and lacking resources even for a day, should appear before Valencia determined upon restoring a rule that had been overthrown this second time by an enemy who had proved irresistible to the strongest power in Spain; that he should dream of doing what the Christian Emperor had failed to do, and in the teeth of the Moslem Emir's opposition. That memorable day in October, 1092, when he pitted his will-power against all the chances and changes of fortune, marks the zenith of heroism.

From which it may be gathered that, even more noteworthy than the Cid's activity and success, is his exceptional firmness of purpose. Indeed, when he first left for exile, he conceived a plan of action in the East and to its execution he devoted the rest of his life.

Ten years after the hero's death, Ibn Bassam, in a passage vibrant with mingled hate and admiration, pays the highest tribute to the superhuman energy of the Campeador:

> The power of this tyrant became ever more intolerable; it weighed like a heavy load upon the people of the coast and inland regions, filling all men, both near and far, with fear. His intense ambition, his lust for power . . . caused all to tremble. Yet this man, who was the scourge of his age, was, by his unflagging and clear-sighted energy, his virile character, and his heroism, a miracle among the great miracles of the Almighty.

Thus, like Manzoni in his famous ode on the death of Napoleon, the Moslem enemy bowed reverently before a creative genius that bore the imprint of God.

Nemo propheta acceptus est in patria sua.

The Cid was first active in promoting the aims of Castile against Leon and Navarre. His action was decisive at a critical period of Spanish history, for thanks to his victories as the ensign of Sancho II, the political hegemony passed from Leon to Castile.

King Sancho and his ensign made an admirable combination: the king, exuberant and ambitious, his vassal restrained and capable. Together, they set out to change the map of Spain. And, although the course of history is shaped more by collective than by individual effort, had this happy association not been brought to an untimely end by the murder at Zamora, it may safely be assumed that the African invasion would have been stayed and the Reconquest expedited by further immediate successes such as Coimbra, Coria and Toledo. This was clearly seen by the men of the time, to whom the hero's exile appeared a grave blunder on the part of the monarch. This feeling is voiced in the famous line of the old poem: "Lord, how good a vassal, were but the liege as good!"

But the King was not the only one to blame. When Alphonso was enthroned in Castile, the barons curried favour with him and turned against the Cid, refusing to admit the exile's worth. Rejected by Castile, the Campeador had to seek an outlet for his energy elsewhere. After great pains, he succeeded in forging an alliance, first with the Count of Barcelona, and afterwards, with the King of Aragon. Thus, his sometime opponents, the Catalans and the Aragonese, came to appreciate the hero before Alphonso and his Castilians.

Literature bears out this shifting of the Cid's activity and fame. As Du Meril and Milá indicate, the earliest known song of the Cid, the *Carmen Roderici,* is of Catalan and not of Castilian origin. Later, and working on independent lines, I proved—I think, conclusively—that the second poetic record, the *Poema del Cid,* was not of Old Castilian origin either, but was composed in the "extremaduras" or borderlands of Medinaceli by a *jongleur* whose pronunciation was different from that of the Castilians. Now, on deeper research into the historical sources (and again independently of the former investigations) I find to my surprise that the first historical text, the *Historia Roderici,* is also foreign to Castile. It was written on the borderland between Saragossa and Lerida, the scene of the Cid's activities in the second part of his life; and the author even accuses the Castilians of being envious of the hero and incapable of understanding him.

The important inference to be drawn from these facts is that admiration for the Cid was first awakened, not at Burgos, but in the more distant lands of Saragossa and what was later known as Catalonia, on the borders of that eastern region which he had made safe during the latter years of his life. It was during these years that Castile, which had witnessed his first exploits, yielded to the all-absorbing character of the Emperor, and the less pliant spirits of Burgos, such as Martin Antolinez, chose to follow the Cid into exile. Thus it came about that officially Burgos only recognized the heroism of her son after his fame had reached her from abroad. True, indeed, it is that "no man is a prophet in his own country," except he be some local celebrity, quite unknown outside his own narrow circle.

The idea of a united Spain, which apparently obsessed the Cid, was, as has been shown above, not of Castilian, but of Leonese origin. A change came, when a new conception of nationhood arose in the minds of Basques and Castilians, to take the place of the Leonese imperial idea, and for this change the Cid was largely responsible.

If we were to take the usual view that the idea of Spanish unity was purely Castilian, we should have to regard the Cid, as Masdeu and his followers did, solely from a Castilian angle, and, like them, we should fail to understand him. It may be true that he is the hero of Burgos, but his heroism is displayed in non-Castilian as well as Castilian aspects, and it is wrong to regard these as antagonistic. Unquestionably the Cid was the first to abandon the already worn-out idea of a Leonese empire and embrace the new Castilian aims that were to usher in the modern Spain. But when Castile, after the assassination at Zamora, bowed to King Alphonso of Leon, the Cid was compelled to strike out in a fresh direction; and it was as an exile that he outstripped his own country in fighting for the national ideal.

In spite of many vicissitudes, the Cid embodied that ideal throughout his exile, from the time when he withdrew before Alphonso, who was working for the old Leonese empire, to the time when he broke the force of the African invasion in campaigns that were frowned upon by the King of Leon and Castile.

The exclusion of the Cid from the Court and Castile served but to accentuate his position as a truly national figure; and it is significant that he should have had fighting side by side with his Castilians, the Asturian Muño Gustioz, the Aragonese knights of Sancho Ramirez and Pedro I, and the Portuguese followers of the Count of Coimbra and Montemayor. This co-operation in the common cause is recognized by the early *Poem:*

> How well he fights in saddle set in gold,
> My Cid, the mighty warrior, Ruy Diaz;
> Martin Antolinez, the worthy Burgalese,
> Muño Gustioz, brought up by him,
> The good Galin Garcia, of Aragon,
> Martin Muñoz, the count of Mont Mayor!

These lines, brief as an heraldic motto, are to Spaniards what Homer's list of ships was to the Hellenes. The fact that knights from so many parts of the Peninsula fought under his banner renders the Cid's campaigns real campaigns of Spain, and,

despite the envy of the barons of Burgos, of Castile as well.

But, neither love of his home land nor his wider patriotism made the Cid narrow-minded. The appointment of a Cluniac monk to the see of Valencia shows that he welcomed western ideas as an influence that would lift Spain out of her former isolation. Such an attitude on the part of the most typical hero of Spain may give food for thought to those who, in a spirit of bigoted nationalism, would close the door to all foreign influence as being detrimental to "the descendants of Pelayo and the Cid."

The Cid was extolled, not so much for promoting Castile's hegemonic aspirations, as for his conquest of Valencia. In the early *Poem* he is frequently alluded to as "My Cid, who won Valencia."

Dozy, in an access of Cidophobia less virulent than usual, sought to belittle this conquest by saying: "The Cid took the proud and rich city of Valencia, but what advantage did the Spaniards gain from its capture? The Cid's followers certainly won a great deal of booty, but Spain won nothing; for the Arabs regained the city on the death of Rodrigo." Nevertheless, although he never amended the passage, the author seems to have been so convinced of its absurdity that he deleted it from the second edition of his work (1881).

In the first place, the conquest of Valencia set a great example of heroic effort. According to the Aragonese historian, Zurita, it was the most extraordinary achievement ever performed in Spain by anyone but a king. He adds that, even had the King of Castile, the most powerful monarch in Spain, engaged his whole forces in the effort, he would have found it extremely difficult to conquer so populous a city in the very heart of the Moorish country. Alphonso did, in fact, throw his whole strength into the attempt, and failed.

In the second place, Dozy, in likening the conquest of Valencia to a mere marauding expedition, is greatly in error. It was far different from the conquest of Barbastro, where the troops of the papal standard-bearer abandoned themselves to plunder and sensuality. The Cid's work was one of reconquest, and he carried it out after the manner of the Spanish kings; he reorganized the lands that he had won, restored the ancient bishopric, and established himself in the city with his family. Had he been granted the normal span of life, Castile would have seen her dream of consolidating her hold upon the old Carthaginian Province realized, and there would have been a totally different distribution of the realms throughout the Peninsula.

In spite of the hero's premature death, the results of the conquest were highly important. An extraordinary revival was then taking place in Islam. Whilst the Turks in the East were routing the Byzantines and, having captured their Emperor, were depriving him of provinces as large as Spain, the Berbers in the West were defeating and driving back the Emperor of Leon. Once again, as in the early days of Arab expansion, the Mediterranean was assailed at either end, but Europe saved the situation by the agency of the Cid in the West and the crusaders in the East.

The anxiety of Urban II at the Almoravide invasion of Spain has led to the belief that the crusades were originally planned by the Pope, in ignorance of the divided state of Islam, as a military diversion. However this may be, there is no denying that, whereas the Turks were causing concern in the East alone, the Almoravides were reckoned a powerful danger to Europe, as was proved by the great French expedition to the Ebro valley in 1087. It is clear also that the Cid, in founding his Valencian principality amidst the Moors, anticipated what the crusaders did at Jerusalem, Antioch, Edessa and Tripoli. True, the Valencian principality did not long survive its founder; but then those other Christian principalities were also ephemeral and only lasted longer because the crusaders had all Europe behind them, whereas the Cid could not even count on the help of his king. Moreover, the crusaders established their States in opposition to emirates that were considerably smaller than the Taifa kingdoms, and they soon succumbed when confronted by a coherent power such as that of Saladin; nor could the united forces of England, France and Germany, even under leaders like Richard Cœur de Lion and Philip Augustus, regain Jerusalem or Edessa. The Cid, on the other hand, built up and held his dominions in the teeth of the bitterest opposition on the part of the Taifas and Yusuf ibn Teshufin, one of Islam's greatest conquerors and head of a huge empire, then at the height of its power. The comparison remains striking even when other factors, such as the distance of the crusaders' field of operation, are taken into account.

Finally, the dominion of the Cid at Valencia was of more immediate importance to Europe as a dam against the Almoravide flood. It is significant, though the fact has hitherto passed unnoticed, that both Ibn Bassam and the *Historia Roderici* agree that his conquest of Valencia stemmed the African invasion and prevented it from reaching the most outlying Moslem Kingdoms of Lerida and Saragossa. That was the spring-tide of the invasion and, had it flooded the Ebro basin, Aragon and Barcelona, being much weaker states than Castile, would both have suffered a greater disaster than Sagrajas. The threat of invasion held out by Alphonso VI as a warning to the French barons, might then have been fulfilled. Indeed, the German historian, V. A. Huber, though unaware of that warning, stresses the importance of the conquests by the Cid as a barrier protecting, not only Spain, but the whole of Western Europe from the Moslem peril. And from all accounts that seems to have been the general impression at the time. (pp. 418–35)

We have already pointed out how concerned the Cid was that the law should at all times be observed. That this alone surrounded him with a halo in the eyes of the people is shown by the fact that the most artistic episodes of the two principal early poems are based on a lofty conception of the law.

The final scene of the *Cantar de Zamora* depicts with great dramatic effect the taking of the oath at Santa Gadea. If there the Cid imposed his will upon Alphonso VI, it was not in defence of any personal right or privilege, such as so many mediæval barons exacted of their king, but to protest against the usurpation of the throne and insist upon the fulfilment of the laws of succession. This scene, therefore, endured, not because of the events that gave rise to it, but because of its capital importance in characterizing the hero. As late as that tragic period of transition from the last century to the present, Joaquin Costa, while denying the Cid of armour and Tizon for fear lest his memory should again plunge Spain into warlike adventure, did not hesitate to invoke the Cid of Santa Gadea and would gladly have seen every Spaniard equally solicitous to uphold the law and at the same time demand satisfaciton from his rulers.

The *Poema del Cid* presents the great scene of the Cortes at Toledo, where, in striking contrast to the general custom of mediæval epic, the Cid is shown forgoing vengeance in favour of the legal satisfaction afforded by the court. In my work, *Poema de Mio Cid,* I have pointed out the revolution that choice occasioned in the poetry of the time. There can be no doubt that it reflects the real outlook of the Cid and reveals in him the moral characteristics that inspired the poets.

It is astonishing to find moderation poetized as a characteristic of the most redoubtable of warriors; and yet, not only did he always subordinate his own strength to the law, but he knew how to temper justice with mercy.

The *Poema del Cid* shows a keen perception of the value of this self-restraint as a poetic theme and even suppresses the traces of violence to be found in the hero's true character. The Cid of fact, who waives his right as a nobleman to fight against his lord, provides one of the main inspirations of the poem: the loyalty of the hero, despite the unjust harshness of the monarch. Even with the great insult still smarting in his brain, the Cid speaks ''well and in measured language.'' In this connection, the *Poem* again strikes a singular note; for, whereas the Spanish *cantares* and French *chansons* glorify the rebel exile who rode rough-shod over all who came his way, the *jongleur* of the Cid, true to the grave conception of life held by his hero, sought ideality in another direction and produced an exile of perfect bearing, moderate at all times, and showing the greatest respect for those social and political institutions that might well have trammelled his heroic energy. The hero and his poet, in imbuing the epic with this ideal, show themselves to be far ahead of their time. For centuries nobles continued to take private vengeance and make war upon their king and country, and the poets kept pace with them by singing of the violence of their heroes and even inventing, in the *Mocedades,* an insolent and over-bearing Cid.

Again, the Cid of the *Poem* forbears to insist on his rights as a victor; witness his treatment of the Count of Barcelona. Anxious to make a good impression on the vanquished Moors, he treats them with generosity, ''lest they speak ill of me,'' and, when he leaves them, they are sorry to lose his protection:

> The Moorish men and maids
> Bless him and wish ''God speed.''
> But, must thou go, My Cid?
> Our prayers do thee precede.

How different a character from the Charlemagne of the *Chanson de Roland* who calls for the conversion of the Saracens by fire and sword!

The high principles of the Cid, especially at a time of resurgence of spiritual values, are thus one of the main reasons why he was sung, both at home and abroad. Already in the second half of the twelfth century German poets (informed no doubt by pilgrim *jongleurs* from Compostela) had made an obvious copy of Rodrigo de Vivar in the figure of the margrave Rüdiger, who was later embodied in the *Nibelungenlied* as a model of chivalry, brave, triumphant, and loyal: Rüdiger, the good, the true, the noble, who gave his life fighting for his principles against an overwhelming force.

Further evidence of the base upon which the idealization of the Cid as a hero rests, is furnished by the *Poema de la conquista de Almeria,* written about 1150, when the early gests appeared. The author, after extolling the Cid's invincibility, proceeds to show that he used his strength, not only against the threat of foreign danger, but also against the intrigues of the counts at home:

> ipse Rodericus, mio Cidi saepe vocatus,
> de quo cantatur quod ab hostibus haud superatur,
> qui domuit mauros, comites domuit
>     quoque nostros.

The banishment of the Cid furnishes a typical instance of the instability of the social fabric. The age produced the man required, but Society banned him from his natural sphere. A really invincible captain had arisen in Spain, only to find his efforts frustrated by the antagonistic counts of Najera, Oca and Carrion; he could obtain neither the co-operation of the Count of Barcelona to help him dominate the East, nor that of the Emperor of Leon to prevent the disasters of Sagrajas, Jaen, Consuegra and Lisbon.

So far as the Cid was concerned, envy acted as the most powerful dissolvent of the social bonds. The Cid was envied by many of his peers and even by his kinsmen; he was envied by the greatest men at Court, even by the Emperor himself; one and all, they rejected him from motives of pure spite to, as events soon proved, their own detriment. The charge of *in-vidia,* so often preferred by the Latin historian, connotes a lack of vision: ''castellani invidentes.'' Such an *in-vidente* was Alphonso, who found it convenient to promote García Ordoñez in preference to the Cid; such also was the Count of Najera himself, who supplanted one who was better than he; such, in short, were all the counts whom the Cid had to subdue. Thus, the phrase of the *Poema de la conquista de Almeria,* ''comites domuit nostros,'' acquires a general significance by extolling the Cid as the hero of the struggle with the jealous nobles.

In face of this blind, malignant envy, the Cid showed neither discouragement nor rancour. When exiled, he sought no direct vengeance, however much he was entitled to do so; nor did he, like Achilles, sulk in his tent and hope for the defeat of his detractors. On the contrary, he repeatedly went to the help of the King who had exiled him and, in spite of a series of rebuffs from his countrymen, took the only dignified course left open to him; he withdrew his invaluable energy to a distant field where envy and mortification could not reach him, but where he could still co-operate, whether they wished it or not, with his backbiters.

The Cid sought and found his support among the enthusiastic and loyal countrymen of the outlying districts and in the spirit of comradeship he instilled into the motley crowd that flocked to his standard; courteous towards the humble, he showed himself as deferential to his cook, when the occasion demanded, as he was firm, though respectful, in the presence of the Emperor of the two religions. In the midst of that strange host he displayed his heroism, and no sooner had he conquered a kingdom than he presented it to his unjust sovereign, by recognizing "the overlordship of his King, Don Alphonso." In seeking reconciliation with the King and humbling himself before him at Toledo in a scene to which the early poet attaches capital importance, the Cid reaches the apogee of heroism by achieving a victory over his own unruly spirit. Though his great victories had rendered him immune from his enemies, he indulged in no vain contempt, but was willing to efface himself before his mean and little-minded opponents, for he desired no more than to take the place in the social order allotted to him, as it is to every man, however eminent. Far from thinking that the sole purpose of things is to pave the way for the superman, he felt that the strongest individuality would be nothing were it not for the people for whom it exists.

**Source:** Ramon Menendez Pidal, in *The Cid and His Spain* , translated by Harold Sunderland, John Murray, 1934, 494 p.

## Sources for Further Study

Bloch, Marc. *Feudal Society,* 2 vols. University of Chicago Press, 1961.
  Marc Bloch's classic study of the society of the Middle Ages in the West includes a useful discussion of feudalism in Spain, in Volume I, pp. 186-87.

Clissold, Stephen. "*El Cid:* Moslems and Christians in Medieval Spain," *History Today,* Vol. 12, no. 5, May, 1962, pp. 321-28.
  This article, written for the popular press and including interesting illustrations, was written after the 1961 film brought renewed attention to the Cid.

De Chasca, E. *El arte juglaresco en el "Cantar de mio Cid,"* 2d ed. Gredos, 1972.
  De Chasca offers in-depth studies of the structure, form, and meaning of this epic, with chapters on the epic epithet, number symbolism, the role of time, and the epic's cultural context.

Deyermond, A. D. "The Singer of Tales and Medieval Spanish Epic," *Bulletin of Hispanic Studies,* Vol. 42, no. 1, 1965, pp. 1-8.
  This article can be read as a companion to Harvey's 1963 article on orality and the *Cid.*

———. "Tendencies in *Mio Cid* Scholarship, 1943-1973," in his *"Mio Cid" Studies,* pp. 13-48, Tamasis Books, 1977.
  Deyermond presents a useful survey of Cidian scholarship in this article.

Duggan, Joseph J. "Formulaic diction in the *Cantar de mio Cid* and the Old French Epic," in his *Oral Literature: Seven Essays,* Barnes and Noble, 1975, pp. 74-83.
  Duggan shows how the formula, a key aspect of oral literature, is present in the *Cid* as a vestige of its oral sources.

———. *The "Cantar de mio Cid": Poetic Creation in its Economic and Social Contexts,* Cambridge Studies in Medieval Literature 6, Cambridge University Press, 1989.
  In this important book, J. Duggan studies the economy that is depicted in the *Cid,* a text obsessed with money, populated by characters who are "surely the most acquisitive heroes in any epic poem composed in a Romance language" (p. 37) and the economy of Spain during the central Middle Ages. He also discusses the importance of lineage and legitimacy in the epic, as well as the social milieu of the poet and the possible reasons behind his choice of events to include in his text.

Hamilton, Rita. "Epic epithets in the *Poema de mio Cid,"* *Revue de Littérature Comparée,* Vol. 36, no. 2, 1962, pp. 162-78.
  Hamilton's article is an in-depth study of the epic epithets in the *Cid.*

Harney, Michael. *Kinship and Polity in the "Poema de mio Cid,"* Purdue Studies in Romance Literatures 2, Purdue University Press, 1993.
  Harney fills an important scholarly gap with this book, in which he draws on social science to study the idea of social class in this epic. According to Harney, the *Cid* chronicles not the emergence of one social class but of the idea of class itself. In the process it also demonstrates how the invocation of transcendant power to put clans in their place indicates the emergence of the state.

Harvey, P. T. "The Metrical Irregularity of the *Cantar de mio Cid,"* *Bulletin of Hispanic Studies,* Vol. 40, 1963, pp. 137-43.
  Following Lord's suggestion that metrical irregularities in the *Cid* may be a sign of oral composition, Harvey explores the meter of this epic.

Lacarra, María Eugenia. *El Poema de mio Cid: realidad histórica e ideologíca,* Ediciones José Porrúa Turanzas, 1975.

In an important thesis, Lacarra portrays the *Cid* as a politically slanderous poem, written to debase the Beni-Gómez clan, including García Ordóñez, Alvar Díaz, and the Infantes de Carrión, who were the historical ancestors of the Castro family, a powerful force in twelfth- and thirteenth-century Castilian politics, to the benefit of their rivals, the Lara family, who were related to the Cid.

Lord, Albert B. *The Singer of Tales,* Harvard University Press, 1960. Reprint, 1971.
This classic study of epic performers in Yugoslavia gave rise to the field of oral literature; "neo-traditionalists" or "oralists" such as Duggan owe much to Lord. Note: This work was carried out under the guidance of Milman Perry, an eminent scholar of orality in the Homerian epic tradition.

Menéndez Pidal, Ramón. *The Cid and his Spain,* J. Murray, 1934.
Although parts are outdated, this history of the Cid and his cultural context is another seminal work by the great Spanish scholar.

————. ed. *Cantar de mio Cid. Texto, gramática y vocabulario,* 3 vols., 3rd ed., *Obras completas,* Vols. 1-3, Espasa-Calpe, 1954-56.
This edition of the poem is a classic, and has been used by generations of Cid scholars.

Michael, Ian, ed. *The Poem of the Cid: A Bilingual Edition with Parallel Text,* Penguin Books, 1984.
Michael's edition of the epic is one of the most accessible for students, and contains a useful introduction.

O'Callaghan, J. F. *A History of Medieval Spain,* Cornell University Press, 1975.
Offers an in-depth analysis of the history of the periods during which the *Cid* was composed and written.

Ong, Walter J. *Orality and Literacy: The Technologizng of the Word,* Routledge, 1982.
This is Walter Ong's seminal work in which he studies how oral literature is transformed when it is written down, and how literature which is composed as a written document differs from oral literature.

Russell, P. E. "San Pedro de Cardeña and the heroic history of the Cid," *Medium Aevum,* Vol. 27, no. 2, 1958, pp. 57-79.
Russell demonstrates the ties between the tomb cult of the Cid at San Pedro de Cardeña and the *Cantar de mio Cid.*

Smith, Colin. *The Making of the "Poema de mio Cid,"* Cambridge: Cambridge University Press, 1983.
Smith's book offers the most radical and recent exposé of the "individualist" theory of the *Cid*'s authorship.

Spitzer, Leo. "Sobre el carácter histórico del *Cantar de mio Cid,"* *Nueva Revista de Filología Hispánica ,* Vol. 2, 1948, pp. 105-17.
In this article, an eminent literary scholar contests Menéndez Pidal's approach to the *Cid* as a historical document, later obliging the latter to somewhat amend his position. Spitzer points out the unhistorical aspects of the poem, especially the episode of the beating of the Cid's daughters by the Infantes, and suggests some reasons for this fictionalization.

Webber, Ruth House. "The *Cantar de mio Cid:* Problems of Interpretation," in *Oral Tradition in Literature: Interpretation and Context,* edited by John Miles Foley, University of Missouri Press, 1986, pp. 65-88.
This article includes a useful overview of the "individualist" and "traditionalist" controversy in Cidian scholarship.

West, Geoffrey. "Hero or Saint? Hagiographic Elements in the Life of the Cid," *Journal of Hispanic Philology,* Vol. 7, no. 2, Winter, 1983, pp. 87- 105.
West suggests that the Cid, as a character, shares some aspects with saints whose lives are described in hagiographical legends.

Whitman, Cedric H. *Homer and the Heroic Tradition,* Harvard University Press, 1958.
This study of Homer contains interesting discussions of ring composition, a characteristic technique of oral literature.

# Chanson de Roland (The Song of Roland)

## Anonymous

## c. 1130—1170

*The Song of Roland,* generally believed to have been composed around 1130, is the oldest surviving French epic. It is the preeminent example of the *chanson de geste,* or "song of great deeds," a poetic form usually used to tell stories of heroism rather than the accounts of love relationships that became more popular later in the twelfth century. The work knew an astounding success throughout the Middle Ages. Versions of the tale were popular in England, Italy, Germany, the Netherlands, Scandinavia, and Wales until about 1500, but the story languished during the Renaissance (1500-1700). Starting in the late nineteenth century, scholars in France and Germany began to study the tale, noting its relevance to the formation of modern-day France. The epic draws a line between France and Islamic Spain By describing "la douce France" (sweet France) as consisting of a particular people, faith, and territory, the anonymous author lays the foundation for the emerging French nation-state.

The story establishes the eighth-century Charlemagne as the father of France. Particular attention is giving to naming specific barons who were, in fact, not contemporaries of Charlemagne but twelfth-century feudal lords, contemporaries of the anonymous author or authors of the *Song.* The story glorifies these barons by contrasting their honor, valor, and courage against the treachery of the Muslims, then called Saracens. The Christian forces of the French defeat the Muslims with divine intervention and great determination.

The characters of the story are still revered in French culture today. The treasonous French baron, Ganelon, who betrays the noble Roland to the enemy, embodies deception. Roland, Charlemagne's nephew, serves as a model of obedience and bravery in the face of overwhelming odds. *The Song of Roland* serves as the foundation of French literature, giving modern readers insight into the inception of the cultural life of France.

## Author Biography

Little is know about the anonymous author or authors of the *Song of Roland*. The oldest surviving manuscript, the Oxford Digby 23, is signed ''Turoldus'' and written in Anglo-Norman, a language predominant in England following the Norman invasion from France in 1066. Few people outside the clergy in medieval France and England were literate, so Turoldus may have been a monk. One school of thought argues that the tale shows signs of being composed orally, perhaps copied down by Turoldus and other scribes when the story was performed at a feast or celebration. The extent to which the text's first scribes might have added their own creative touches to the story is not known, but scribes are generally considered to be recorders of traditional tales, and not authors of original ones.

Another theory maintains that the legend, existing from the time of Charlemagne, was put into poetic form by a single individual in the late eleventh century. The debate over the authorship of the *Song of Roland* probably can never be resolved.

## Plot Summary

### Part I: The Betrayal of the Peers

The *Chanson de Roland* begins at the close of Charlemagne's seven-year campaign against the Saracens, or Muslims, in Spain. The Frankish (French) forces have conquered all of Spain except for the city of Saragossa, ruled by the Saracen King Marsile. Charlemagne's men are weary from their long battles and yearn to return to their lands in France. Likewise, the Saracens are eager for the French to leave them in peace. Knowing that his army is no match for the French forces, Marsile

holds a council to ask his men for advice. The knight Blancandrin suggests that they play upon the French desire to return home by paying Charlemagne rich tribute and promising to follow him back to France and convert to Christianity—never intending, of course, to do so. This way the Saracens will rid Spain of the French army. The Saracens agree that this is an excellent plot, and they send an envoy and a caravan loaded with riches to the French king with the proposal. Charlemagne calls a council of the Peers, his twelve most trusted advisors, to decide what to do.

The Peers encourage Charlemagne to accept Marsile's offer and end the war. Only Roland speaks out against the plan, reminding the French of past incidents of Saracen treachery. His is the lone dissenting voice, and he is disregarded. Several men volunteer to serve as Charlemagne's envoy back to Marsile, but are rejected because of the danger of the mission. Roland proposes his stepfather, Ganelon, and all the Peers agree that he would be a good choice. Ganelon, angered at Roland for putting him in such a perilous position, denounces him and names Roland's supporters among the Peers as his enemies now.

As Ganelon rides off with the Saracen envoy, Blancandrin, the two plot to kill Roland. Blancandrin will be glad to rid himself of a formidable enemy, and Ganelon will have his revenge. Roland and the other Peers will be found in the rear guard of the departing French forces, and Ganelon tells the Muslims exactly when to attack. For his efforts, Ganelon is well-rewarded with gifts by Marsile, Queen Bramimonde, and the Saracen court.

When Ganelon returns, he convinces the French of the good intentions of their enemy, encouraging Charlemagne to accept Marsile's offer and return to Aix. The next day, preparations are made for the trip, and Roland and the Peers are appointed to the rear guard at Ganelon's suggestion. Charlemagne, deeply upset by the danger to which he is exposing his nephew and favorite knight, nonetheless agrees to the arrangement. Charlemagne and his men pull away, leaving the rear guard.

### Part II: The Last Stand of the Peers

On the other side, the Saracens are preparing for the attack. Marsile gives his nephew the honor of leading the raid against the French rear guard. Like the French forces, the Saracen contingent includes

Marsile's twelve most trusted and valiant warriors. The Saracens, who vastly outnumber the French rear guard, outfit themselves richly for battle in gleaming golden armor, and the sound of their battle trumpets is heard by the French rear guard. Olivier, Roland's closest friend, sees the Saracens approaching, armed for battle, and declares Ganelon a traitor, but Roland will hear no evil of his stepfather. Olivier encourages Roland to blow the horn that will call the rest of Charlemagne's forces back to help defeat the Saracens. Roland contends that to call for help would dishonor him as a knight. He vows to kill all of the Saracens, singlehandedly if necessary. Olivier continues to beg Roland to blow his horn, as the enemy approaches. Finally, when it is too late for Charlemagne to come to their rescue, Archbishop Turpin blesses the French barons so that they will die as holy martyrs, and they engage the Saracens.

With their battle cry of "Montjoie," the French barons confront the Saracens, described by the author as a series of one-to-one combats. The carnage is great on both sides, and the Saracens call for reinforcements. Roland announces his intention to sound his horn to call Charlemagne. Olivier now objects, saying that because they are clearly doomed, it is wrong to call the rest of the French forces back to fight in what is now a lost cause. Turpin intervenes, pointing out that despite the fact that the rear guard cannot be saved, Charlemagne should be called to come and take revenge for them.

Roland blows the horn with all his might, so hard that he bursts a vessel in his brain, which will eventually lead to his demise. Charlemagne hears the horn and knows that his men are in mortal danger. He and his men wheel about to rush to their aid, and Ganelon is arrested and tortured as a traitor. The rear guard continues to fight their hardest, down to the last man. Olivier is struck down, and in his pain does not recognize Roland and almost kills him. The two are reconciled as Olivier dies. Finally, only Roland and Turpin remain standing, fighting the Saracen army. The remaining Saracens flee the approaching French forces as Turpin dies from his wounds. Close to death, Roland arranges the bodies of the French dead, turning them to face the retreating Saracen army so that it will not appear that any French fighters tried to run from the battle. Determined not to let his sword, Durendal, be taken by a pagan, Roland tries to break it on a stone. The mighty sword, however, will not break. Roland retreats beneath a pine tree, hiding both the sword

and the horn underneath his dying body. Three angels sent by God come to escort Roland's soul to paradise.

Charlemagne and his men arrive, too late to aid the Peers. The French fear that they will be unable to avenge their men since they cannot pursue the Saracen forces with night falling. Charlemagne prays, and God causes the sun to stop in the sky, giving the French the light they need to ride on. They overtake and decimate the fleeing Saracens. The French make camp, planning to return to France the next day. In the night, Charlemagne has a vision, announcing a great battle. In yet another dream, a chained bear is attacked by a greyhound.

Marsile had sent for Baligant, the Emir of Babylon (Cairo) to help fight Charlemagne. Charlemagne, meanwhile, is overcome with grief at Roland's death. Only with the encouragement of his men is he able to pull himself together for the burial of the Peers and the great battle to come. Baligant's men attack the French, and great valor and destruction ensue for both armies. Finally, the Emir and Charlemagne meet in one-to-one combat. Baligant calls for Charlemagne to capitulate and become his vassal. Charlemagne refuses and is almost killed. With the aid of God's angel, Gabriel, Charlemagne regains his strength and strikes a mortal blow. The remainder of the Saracen army flees.

## *Part III: The Trial*

Victorious, but at a great price, the French army returns home. The bodies of Roland, Olivier, and Turpin are laid to rest. Aude, the sister of Olivier and fiancee of Roland, learns about their deaths from Charlemagne. She asks God not to let her live on without Roland, and she falls dead at Charlemagne's feet.

Ganelon stands accused of treason to Charlemagne. His argument is that he indeed plotted revenge on Roland, but that he always remained faithful and loyal to Charlemagne. He thus pleads vengeance, which is legal, and not treason, which merits death. Ganelon is seconded by thirty of his relatives, with the mighty warrior Pinabel as his champion. Pinabel will fight Charlemagne's representative, and the warrior who wins proves the case for his side. None of Charlemagne's barons, however, will stand up to the mighty Pinabel. A small, slight warrior named Thierry approaches, volunteering to fight the giant Pinabel. Thierry feels that

Charlemagne's accusation of treason is just, since Roland was in Charlemagne's service at the time the vengeance was carried out. God helps Thierry to slay Pinabel, and Ganelon and his thirty relatives are put to death for the treason.

The tale closes with a conversion. The wise Queen Bramimonde, brought to France as a captive of war, converts to Christianity. The narrative stresses that the conversion is not forced, but is her choice, which for the twelfth- century transcriber of the account is a further sign of Bramimonde's wisdom and righteousness. The ancient Charlemagne goes to his room to rest. Hardly does he fall asleep when God send the angel Gabriel to bid Charlemagne go and rescue a Christian king who has been attacked by Saracens. With great regret, the weary king will go to their aid. The battle will never cease for the defender of Christianity.

## Characters

### Archbishop Turpin
*See* Turpin

### Aude
Aude is Roland's fiancee and the sister of his best friend Olivier. When she hears from Charlemagne that Roland is dead, she rejects his offer of his own son Louis as a husband. She asks God that she not live on after Roland's death, and in a display of ultimate loyalty, she falls dead at Charlemagne's feet.

### Baligant
Baligant is the Emir of Babylon, or Cairo. Marsile calls on him to come and help him defeat Charlemagne. Baligant makes the long trip in record time, and his troops fight valiantly against Charlemagne's forces. Although a Saracen, Baligant is a fine and noble warrior, and that the epic implies that he surely would have won the battle if he had been a Christian. Only with the help of the angel Gabriel is Charlemagne able to kill Baligant in the decisive battle.

### Blancandrin
Marsile's most trusted advisor, Blancandrin is described as wise, valiant, and a worthy soldier. It is

he who hatches the plot to betray the French and trick them into leaving Spain, and he acts as King Marsile's emissary to the French to carry the sham proposal that the Saracens do not intend to honor. He and Ganelon devise the plan to annihilate Roland and the Peers who make up the French rear guard.

### Bramidonie
*See* Bramimonde

### Bramimonde
Queen Bramimonde is the wise wife of the Saracen King Marsile. In several passages she is shown functioning effectively as a ruler in the Saragossan court, and she displays knowledge of the deployment of both the French forces and her own country's defending army. She predicts doom for the Saracen forces. Captured by the French, Bramimonde converts to Christianity when taken to France. While this may be offensive to a twentieth-century reader, to the author of the epic it was intended to show the Saracen queen's noble qualities, inherent goodness, and wisdom.

### Bramimunde
*See* Bramimonde

### Carlemagne
*See* Charlemagne

### Carlemagnes
*See* Charlemagne

### Charlemagne
Charlemagne is the venerable leader of the Frankish (French) forces. When the epic opens, he has been in Spain for seven years, at war with the Saracens, as Spanish Muslims (and many other foreigners) were termed by the Franks. Defender of the Christian faith, his purpose is to travel from place to place, fighting to regain lands lost to "the infidel," that is, to non-Christians. The character is based on the actual historical figure of Charlemagne (742-814), King of the Franks (768-814) and Emperor of the Holy Roman Empire. The epic's unknown author or recorder took some liberties with historical fact: Charlemagne is said to be 200 years old, for example, and in *The Song of Roland*

# Media Adaptations

- *Le mystère de Roncevaux* is a stage adaptation written by Adolphe, Baron d'Avril, and published in 1893 in Paris. The play was republished in 1993 by Troyes.

- Peter Racine Fricker wrote three fragments from the *Song of Roland* for unaccompanied chorus in London, published by Schott in 1955.

- Edward MacDowell, 1860-1908, wrote *The Symphonic Poems* which include two fragments from the *Chanson de Roland*, one called "The Saracens," and the other called "The Lovely Alda."

- A full-length feature movie directed by Frank Cassenti, *La Chanson de Roland*, appeared in France in 1978 from Z productions.

- Greg Roach created the award-winning multimedia interactive book CD-ROM called *The Madness of Roland* from HyperBole.

- A World-Wide Web site containing an electronic edition of the *Song of Roland* (1995) was produced, edited and prepared by Douglas B. Killings. It can be found at URL http://sunsite.berkeley.edu/OMACL/Roland.

---

he is presented as the contemporary of French nobles who actually lived hundred of years after him. The central event of *The Song of Roland*—the ambush and slaughter of the Frankish rear guard by Spanish forces at Roncesvalles—is also based on historical fact

At times Charlemagne seems almost weak. The barons who are among his followers make most of the important decisions for the group. He has strong objections to putting his favored nephew, Roland, at the head of the rear guard because of the danger of the position, yet he is unable to prevent it. Charlemagne is almost killed by the Emir of Babylon, Baligant, and only wins the battle with the help of God. In the final conflict, when Charlemagne accuses Ganelon of treason, none of Charlemagne's strongest soldiers will stand up for him in combat, acting as his champion. Only the weak Thierry will step forward to profess his belief in Charlemagne and champion his lord. Despite his age and a hint of frailty, both the French and the Saracens speak of Charlemagne in reverent terms. At the close of the text, as Charlemagne finally lies down for a well-deserved rest, God calls to him, telling him to go and regain another Christian land lost to the infidel. The weary, reluctant, and weeping Charlemagne does as he is told.

### Charles the Great
*See* Charlemagne

### Charles I
*See* Charlemagne

### Durendal
Roland's famous sword, Durendal, has a golden hilt and a blade of steel. Sacred relics, including the teeth, hair, and blood of saints, and fabric from a garment worn by the Blessed Virgin, are enclosed in the hilt. The sword's strength is such that Roland cannot even dull the blade as he tries to break it on a rock to prevent it from falling into enemy hands. Roland hides the sword under his body as he dies.

### Gabriel
Gabriel is god's emissary and the leader of the angels that help the French army. Gabriel leads Roland's soul to Paradise after his death and helps Charlemagne and Thierry triumph in combat.

### Ganelon
Roland's stepfather Ganelon is one of Charlemagne's most trusted advisors. When the

Franks debate the merits of the Saracen peace plan—to pay rich tribute and to become French vassals and Christian converts if the French forces will leave Spain—Roland reminds the group that the Saracens have broke such promises before, and advises an immediate attack on their forces. Ganelon scornfully rejects Roland's suggestion, even going so far as to term it the advice of a fool. He urges strongly that the French accept the terms and leave. His arguments convince Charlemagne and his advisors. When Roland proposed that Ganelon undertake the dangerous mission of carrying the French response to the Saracen peace proposal, Ganelon denounces Roland angrily in front of Charlemagne and his gathered advisors, and curses those Franks who support Charlemagne's decision to send him on the mission. Ganelon admires Charlemagne, and he deems himself loyal to his ruler even after he betrays Roland and the Peers to the Saracens. Ganelon's betrayal of Roland for goods and money echoes the betrayal of Jesus Christ by Judas Iscariot in the Bible. Because of this association, Ganelon's name now represents the arch-traitor.

### Guenelon

*See* Ganelon

### Guenelun

*See* Ganelon

### Guenes

*See* Ganelon

### Karlemagne

*See* Charlemagne

### King Marsile

*See* Marsile

### Marsile

King Marsile rules Saragossa, the only Spanish city that has not fallen to Charlemagne's forces in seven years of fighting. In many ways, Marsile's rule parallels that of the French leader. He is well respected by his people, and he, too, seeks the counsil of twelve trusted advisors in planning his strategy. His treachery: promising to become Charlemagne's vassal and then attacking the rear guard, leads ultimately to the annihilation of his troops. The French only attain their victory with the help of God, implying that while the forces of goodness are on the side of the French, the Saracens were their equals in strength and bravery in battle. Marsile's ruthlessness is underscored by the fact that he pledges to send his own son Jurfaleu as a hostage in order to guarantee the promise he intends to break, knowing that Jurfaleu will be executed when the treachery is discovered.

### Marsilie

*See* Marsile

### Marsilies

*See* Marsile

### Oliver

*See* Olivier

### Olivier

Roland's best friend, fellow soldier, and the brother of Roland's fiancee Aude, Olivier represents wisdom where Roland stands for bravery. Olivier encourages Roland to call back the main body of Charlemagne's forces as soon as Ganelon's treachery is discovered and the French rear guard is attacked by the Saracens. Had Roland followed this advice, Charlemagne's men could have returned to aid the outnumbered rear guard and their destruction would have been avoided. The struggle between these two close friends over blowing the horn to call for help comprises a central theme of the epic. The intervention in their dispute by the archbishop Turpin helps the friends to reconcile before they die.

### Pinabel

Pinabel is a formidable French warrior and a relative of Ganelon's. He volunteers to defend his relative against Charlemagne's accusation of treason, facing Thierry in the bout of judicial combat that will determine Ganelon's guilt or innocence.

### Roland

Eclipsing Charlemagne in this epic, the emperor's nephew Roland takes center stage. He is renowned for his phenomenal bravery, always volunteering for the most difficult and dangerous assignments. His bravery and pride in his abilities as a soldier ultimately bring about his death and the deaths of the men he leads. Roland proposes that his stepfather, Ganelon, take the dangerous role of carrying Charlemagne's answer to the Saracen envoy when the Saracens propose a diplomatic end to the war. This begins the central conflict of the story. Roland had wanted to undertake the mission, but Charlemagne refused to risk one of his best soldiers. Roland may have thought that his stepfather would be happy to accept such an honorable assignment, but Ganelon does not seem to share his stepson's love of danger. Ganelon avenges himself by choosing Roland to lead the dangerous rear guard as the French return to Aix, a mission that Ganelon believes will result in Roland's death: Ganelon has already betrayed this contingent of the French forces to the Saracen envoy, Blancandrin. When the Saracens attack the rear guard, Roland refuses to blow the horn that would call Charlemagne and the rest of the French troops to their aid, believing that it would be dishonorable. The outnumbered French contingent is wiped out by the Saracens. After an argument with his friend Olivier that is settled by Archbishop Turpin, Roland finally calls on Charlemagne to avenge the deaths of his fellow fighters, blowing the horn so forcefully that he bursts a blood vessel in his brain and falls, mortally wounded. He arranges the bodies of the dead to face toward the Saracen army, so that it will not appear than any of them fled from battle. He dies from the brain injury sustained as he blows the horn to call Charlemagne.

### Thierris

*See* Thierry

### Thierry

Although short and slight, Thierry, Duke of Argonne, is the only one of Charlemagne's followers who will fight with the might warrior Pinabel to determine the outcome of the charge of treason against Ganelon. During their battle, he commends Pinabel's bravery and physical prowess, and asks him to consider halting their combat and requiring Ganelon to answer the charge of treason. Thierry appears to be no match for the huge warrior Pinabel, but with the aid of God Thierry wins the bout of judicial combat.

### Tierri

*See* Thierry

### Turpin

An archbishop fighting with the French forces, Turpin excels in warfare even as he tends to the souls of Charlemagne's men. Turpin's prayers before battle and his blessings over fallen men guarantees martyrdom for them. Side-by-side with Roland, Turpin makes a brave last stand against the Saracen sneak attack. His wise intervention between the quarreling Roland and Olivier helps them to reconcile before both die on the battlefield.

## Themes

The *Chanson de Roland* tells of the decisive battle at Roncesvalles, Spain, between Charlemagne's Christian forces and the Saracens, or pagans, led by King Marsile of Saragossa. The knight Roland's bravery and his betrayal by his stepfather, Ganelon, are of central interest in the tale.

### Culture Clash

As the Saracens and Franks encounter each other, differences in culture and religion come to the foreground. The French admire the Saracens for their prowess, the beauty of their armaments, and, at times, their valor. However, Charlemagne's sole purpose in life according to the epic is to defend the Christian religion. As such, all non-believers must be converted or destroyed. Since the Muslim Saracens control Spain, which was formerly Christian, Charlemagne's special mission is to drive the Muslims from Christian lands. The epic shows no real understanding of Islam by the medieval, presumably Christian, author of the text.

### Duty and Responsibility

Charlemagne is the venerable lord of the French fighters. They must serve him, even if this means personal danger or hardship. Roland, eager to serve, tries to volunteer for every mission. When he is appointed to head the rear guard, he vows to protect Charlemagne from all harm. Thus, he refuses to blow the horn that will summon Charlemagne when the rear guard is attacked. Even the treacherous Ganelon accepts his duty to act as emissary to the Saracens when Charlemagne orders it, but because of the danger involved he harbors resentment against Roland, who encouraged his appointment. Ganelon

# Topics for Further Study

- Many commentators on *The Song of Roland* debate the question of Roland's character. Does his refusal to summon help for the rear guard support an interpretation of Roland as a brave and noble man, or does it mark him as guilty of the sin of pride? Can a case be made for both interpretations?

- The character of Ganelon claims that he always remained loyal to his lord and king, Charlemagne, even though he betrayed another of Charlemagne's knights to the Saracens. Can Ganelon's claim be justified? Compare his actions with incidents from modern history in which highly-placed officials broke laws or caused harm while claiming to keep faith with a leader. Examples might include: the Watergate conspirators, Colonel Oliver North, German army officers during World War II, or Soviet and U.S. double agents during the Cold War.

- *The Song of Roland* is said to be the written form of an oral story. Read about oral performance and investigate ways that the text of *The Song of Roland* might demonstrate its oral origin.

- Research the early history of France and look at the ways that *The Song of Roland* reflects more about eleventh-century France than the France of the eighth century in which it is set.

- Roland's fiancee, Aude, prefers death to living without her beloved. This was considered an honorable and desirable choice for a woman of her time. How is this choice viewed by a twentieth-century reader of this work?

- The trial of Ganelon gives us a picture of medieval justice. Compare this system of justice with that of the late twentieth-century United States.

- Toward the end of *The Song of Roland,* the captive Saracen Queen Bramimonde voluntarily renouces her Muslim faith and is baptized as a Christian. To the anonymous author of this epic, this is proof of her wisdom and goodness. Offer another explanation of why a foreign prisoner of a war in which her husband was killed might choose to accept the belief system of her captors.

---

tries to separate his duty to Charlemagne from his duty toward Charlemagne's men. He contends that he remained faithful to Charlemagne even while betraying Roland. Charlemagne and the knight Thierry, who fights on his behalf, believe that the duty owed to Charlemagne includes protection of his men. The fact that an angel of God helps Thierry to defeat the knight who fights for Ganelon suggests that God, too, agrees that Ganelon's duty was to Roland as a representative of Charlemagne.

## Friendship

Olivier and Roland present a model friendship of men brought together in battling a common enemy. They have fought together for many years, and Roland is engaged to marry Olivier's sister. Olivier does not hesitate to criticize Roland for not blowing the horn to summon Charlemagne, and their differing views on calling for help lead to a serious argument. While Roland represents sometimes heedless bravery, Olivier represents a more considered wisdom. Together they form a perfect union, and their reconciliation in the final hour attests to the strength of their friendship and the necessity that the qualities of bravery embodied in Roland be tempered with the kind of wisdom held by Olivier.

## Good and Evil

The characters of the *Chanson de Roland* are aligned starkly on the side of either Good or Evil. Individual Saracens are acknowledged to possess qualities of bravery, wisdom, skill in battle, and even physical attractiveness—but for the epic's author, the fact that they are ''pagan'' and not Christian relegates them to damnation. Conversely, some Christian characters are shown to have faults. Most notably, Roland's excessive pride leads to an angry exchange with his best friend, the massacre of the rear guard, and his own death. But, as a Christian crusader, Roland is on the side of good, and at his death angels escort his soul to heaven. Marsile, when killed, is ushered away by demons. God intervenes several times in the French cause and to ensure that Ganelon is punished for betraying Roland. In the end, Good will always triumph over Evil.

### Honor

Roland struggles with the issue of honor as he decides whether to blow the horn or not. He deems it dishonorable to blow the horn call the main body of the French forces back to help him fight the Saracens, yet once the French rear guard is massacred, honor dictates that Charlemagne be called to avenge the death of the Peers.

### Justice and Injustice (Right and Wrong)

Each action in the epic falls on the side of right or wrong. Because the Christians believe in God, their actions are viewed as essentially right, whereas the non-Christian Saracens cannot be other than wrong. Individuals may present qualities that differ from this mold. For example, Ganelon, though French, acts wrongly toward Charlemagne in betraying Roland. The Babylonian Baligant, though a pagan, is regarded as a valiant and courageous warrior by both sides. Nonetheless, the essential conflict between Muslim and Christian is one of right versus wrong, and the Christians, being on the side of right, are destined to win the battle. Medieval man believed that God would intervene on the side of right. Therefore, in the narrative, God intervenes to help the French defeat Marsile's army, to enable Charlemagne to slay Baligant, and to make it possible for the weak knight Thierry to strike down the giant Pinabel.

### Memory

The role of the epic is to establish the memory of the origins of the French nation. Charlemagne emerges as father of the French, and the recounting of his battles in the *Chanson de Roland* writes the earliest history of France. Many of the characters in the text are not historical contemporaries of

*Woodcut of the crusading Emperor Charlemagne, in whose service Roland fought and died.*

Charlemagne but, rather, lived at the time that the text was first written down. By using their names in the epic, the author ensures that the memory of their names is admirable, linked with that of the national hero Charlemagne and to the very beginnings of France as a nation. The importance of memory—of how the story of the battle will be recalled and retold— is found within the text. The dying Roland turns the bodies of the French dead to face the retreating Saracen army. He does this to make sure that since no one survives to tell of the battle, Charlemagne will know that no French man turned and fled. The stories told after death, the memory of the battle, are of utmost importance to the fighters.

### Race and Racism

The question of race and racism in the epic is a confused one. While the Saracens are described at times as black as coal and monstrous in appearance, at other times the author lauds the beauty of an individual Saracen warrior, complete with flowing blonde hair. The Saracens fight as well as, and sometimes even better than, the French. The main issue is the religious differences between the two forces. The Saracens are Muslim and the French are

Christian. To the epic's author (and, presumably, to its first audience), this difference means that the Saracens are destined to lose, God being on the side of the French.

### Treason

The question of Ganelon's treason is central to the work. By betraying Roland, Ganelon also betrays his lord, Charlemagne. The final battle between Thierry and Pinabel serves to establish Ganelon's guilt, making him stand in French culture as an archetypal traitor.

## Style

*The Song of Roland* comes to the present in many varied hand-copied manuscripts from the Middle Ages. Each manuscript alters the story slightly and uses a somewhat different literary technique or style. Most modern editions of the epic are taken from the manuscript called Digby 23, housed in the Bodleian Library in Oxford, England.

### Poetic Form and Rhyme

*The Song of Roland* is written in poetic form. The verse paragraphs are called *laisses,* and they are of varying length. The rhyming scheme is assonance, meaning that only the final stressed vowels are identical. Most lines have 10 syllables, with a break, or caesura, after the fourth syllable.

### Language

The author of the Digby 23 manuscript penned this epic in Anglo-Norman. This was a form of French spoken in the region that is now England about 100 years after the Norman invasion of 1066. The story existed in oral form long before this, and the original language of the epic is unknown.

### Point of View

The story is told by an omniscient, or "all-knowing," third-person narrator. The author is not involved in the story, but is very clearly on the side of the French. Authorial asides criticize the treachery of Ganelon or the frightfulness of the Saracens, for example, while praising the bravery of Roland and the wisdom of Olivier.

### Foreshadowing

From the beginning of the tale, the author lets the audience know the essential elements of the story. Ganelon is called a traitor long before he actually betrays Roland to the enemy. Roland and the Peers proclaim their own death and martyrdom before the battle even begins. Charlemagne cries when Roland is appointed to the rear guard, knowing somehow that he will not see this favorite knight alive again. The technique of foreshadowing points to the oral nature of the test: traditionally, in this kind of oral narrative, the audience hears the outcome, or importance of the story, then hears the story itself. Foreshadowing helps set the stage for the performance that most likely accompanied the reading or reciting of the story.

### Symbolism

As in most medieval texts, symbolism is an important part of *The Song of Roland.* Charlemagne's dreams are full of symbols, mainly animals. Medieval bestiaries, or animal dictionaries, attributed certain characteristics to each animal. These characteristics transfer to the animals in Charlemagne's dreams, each of which represents an important character in the story. Another example of symbolism: Ganelon drops the glove and baton ceremonially given to him as emissary from his ruler, Charlemagne. By dropping these tokens of trust, Ganelon's treachery is symbolically revealed even before it takes place.

### Setting

The setting of *The Song of Roland* serves as more symbolic than picturesque. Rarely is the landscape described. In a rare exception, the author notes that Charlemagne sits under a pine tree during one of his council meetings. The pine tree acts a symbol. The triangular shape of the pine was thought to represent the Holy Trinity, central to the Christians' system of belief. Tellingly, Roland drags himself beneat a pine tree to die. The skies themselves reflect the action of the epic. Charlemagne prays for help in defeating the fleeing Saracens, and God stops the sun in the sky so that the French will have the daylight they need to pursue their enemy. While nature is rarely described except for its symbolic importance, the author details the armor and outfitting of the troops with gusto. Each knight bests the next in the quality of his weaponry and the luxury of his gem-encrusted armor. For the medieval author, the setting of a text privileged the man-made world over nature.

## Historical Context

### Charlemagne's Reign

The historical Charlemagne was born in 742, about 300 years before *The Song of Roland* was first recorded in a manuscript. Descended from Germanic tribesmen, Charlemagne possessed a remarkable love of learning for a ruler of his time. He learned to read and tried, without success, to learn to write. In addition to his local Germanic dialect, he spoke old Teutonic, literary Latin, and understood Greek. Charlemagne, like his literary image, fought to defend the Christian faith in foreign lands, including the regions that are now Spain, France, Germany, and Italy. His success on the battlefield unified the peoples of these countries, who had been torn apart by tribal conflict for centuries.

Charlemagne's administrative expertise provided a structure to his vast empire. He made military service codified and mandatory. To increase the sense of public participation in government, he fostered assemblies in which landowners came together and made suggestions to be brought before the king. Under his rule, the beginnings of the modern jury system were formed. The empire was divided into counties for administrative purposes, and local assemblies served as governing bodies and courts for the region. He shared his love of learning by bringing in foreign scholars to his realm and establishing schools. At his direction, monks began to make more accurate and legible copies of the Bible, the writings of the Church Fathers, and Latin classics. This renewal of learning, often termed the Carolingian Renaissance, helped reintroduce much of the literature of the Ancients to Europe.

In 800, Charlemagne was crowned Emperor of the Romans by Pope Leo III. This first coronation had for effect the subordination of temporal power to the Church, as the Emperor had to look to the Pope for justification of his power. On the other hand, this act greatly increased the power of the king, since his power was deemed to have come from God, thus establishing a precedent for rule by Divine Right. In 806, Charlemagne divided his empire among his sons. Charlemagne died in 814 at the age of 72, leaving a legacy that his son and only remaining heir, Louis, was unable to maintain.

### Women's Lives under Charlemagne's Rule

Marriage was a central question during the late eighth century. The Catholic Church had one set of rules while Carolingian society had others. During this period, the two models of marriage moved closer to each other. Charlemagne prohibited remarriage after divorce and declared that adultery could not be considered a cause for dissolution of a marriage. Wives were generally chosen by the husband's father. Among nobility, women had a degree of security because of the stricter marriage and divorce laws, but they also gained new responsibility. Charlemagne's queen had the power to rule in his absence. She also had Charlemagne's backing on any requests made of his judges and ministers. All women were concerned with child-bearing and rearing. Noble women provided religious instruction to boys until they left home at the age of seven to go to another lord's court, and they taught daughters until they married somewhere between twelve and fifteen. Because of a high incidence of death in childbirth, women lived only an average of thirty-six years, whereas men generally reached almost fifty. The peasant women of Charlemagne's realm owed services to their overlords, just as their husbands did. In an unusually thoughtful document for the period, Charlemagne decreed that these women had rights to a certain standard of living, including heat and security.

### The Battle of Roncesvalles

In 773 Charlemagne took on the role of protector of the Catholic Church. Charlemagne fought the enemies of the Church for most of his reign. At that time, the non-Christian threat included Muslims (called Saracens in *The Song of Roland,* Bavarians, and Saxons, among others. In 777, the Muslim governor of Barcelona, Ibn al-Arabi, asked Charles to aid him against the emir or caliph of Cordoba. Charlemagne crossed the Pyrenees into Spain, captured Pamplona and advanced on to Saragossa. En route, he treated the Christian Basques, living in Northern Spain, as enemies. His campaign into Spain, though somewhat successful, did not unseat the caliph of Cordoba, largely because the reinforcements expected from Ibn al-Arabi did not materialize. Realizing that he would never be able to take on the formidable caliph alone, Charlemagne began his return to France. Traveling back through the Pyrenees in 778, he was attacked by the Christian Basques whom he had mistreated on his entrance into Spain. The route through the Pyrenees was made of long, narrow passes through the high mountain range, and, in one of these passes, the Basques swooped down on Charlemagne's rear

# Compare & Contrast

- **700s:** During this century Charlemagne expanded his empire to include all of present-day France and Germany, as well as parts of Spain, Italy, Slovenia, Hungary and Croatia. His seat of power was Aachen, in present-day Germany.

  **1000s:** France was divided into small houses of power, ruled by local lords. Henry II's marriage to Eleanor of Aquitaine made the king of England the most powerful ruler in what is present-day France. The French king controlled the area around Paris, but his influence was slight outside the immediate area. The barons in the *Chanson de Roland* exert considerable influence over Charlemagne's actions.

  **Late twentieth century:** France, though divided into departments for administrative purposes, has a highly-centralized government located in Paris. Attempts to spread power and influence throughout the country are underway in the late twentieth century, but Paris remains the political and cultural center of France.

- **700s:** The Islamic empire expanded as conquests begun by Muhammad in 622 continued throughout this century. The Arabs met little organized resistance until they pushed well into France and were stopped and driven back by Charles Martel in 732.

  **1000s:** The Islamic empire, like the Christian one, was divided into two parts; the Shiites with a capital in Cairo, and the Sunni caliphate centered in Baghdad. Baligant comes from Cairo to aid his vassal, Marsile.

  **Late twentieth century:** The Muslim world, never reunited, is still divided among Sunnis and Shiites. No central power exists as each country in the Islamic world has its own spiritual and temporal rulers.

- **700s:** In Europe, marriage laws based on Christian doctrine are passed, providing women with a degree of security and added responsibility.

  **1000s:** Women, left behind as their husbands went on crusade, control lands and run households. Marsile's wife Bramimonde rules in her husband's absense.

  **Late twentieth century:** Women enjoy equal protection under the law and hold positions of power in local and national governments in many countries, though some feel there is still progress to be made in the campaign for women's rights.

- **700s:** The French language was emerging as a combination of Latin and the tongues of the Germanic tribes. No literary works in this tongue have been found.

  **1000s:** Old French has evolved into an entirely separate language. *The Song of Roland* marks the beginning of a literary explosion in the vernacular.

  **Late twentieth century:** France continues to cherish its literary heritage, encouraging young writers and making French literature a central element in its national curriculum. The Academie Française is charged with maintaining the purity of the French language. In the late 1990s laws and regulations have been put in place to restrict the use of non-French-language words in advertising, public interchange (such as television programming), and even the ratio of French to non-French language songs that can be broadcast on the radio.

---

guard and annihilated it to the man. Within the ranks of the rear guard, historians tell us there was one "Hruodland," and it is believed that the heroic Roland is based on this historical person.

## Christians and Muslims in the Middle Ages

The Muslim invasions of Spain and even France in the eighth century thrust Western Europeans into close contact with another culture and religion. Christians and Muslims remained enemies on the battlefield for another 700 years, but their rapport changed significantly during this period. Early fighting was focused mainly on stemming the seemingly endless flood of Muslim invaders into Christian lands. National boundaries were fairly firmly fixed, however, by 732, when Charles Martel drove advancing Muslim troops from established Frankish territories back into Spain, where they made their stronghold for many centuries to come. These lands were always coveted, but to those living in present-day France the threat of loss of further life and property had diminished. The dream of reconquest was ever-present, however, spurred by the Catholic Church, which promised martyrdom for those who died trying to recapture Christian lands. The Crusades—military actions against non-Christians with the dual purpose of winning converts and seizing land— were common from the eleventh through the thirteenth centuries. While this cultural contact was hostile by definition, other practical relationships had begun to form that would continue to flourish until the end of the Reconquest in 1492. Trading relationships, ambassadorial envoys, cross-cultural education, and even cohabitation exposed those north of the Pyrenees to a way of life quite different from their own. The Muslim culture had developed art and learning to a much higher degree than their counterparts in the West. Exquisite fabrics and spices were the envy of many a Christian who profited through commerce and trade with the Infidel. Christian noblemen sent their sons to learn in the courts of Muslim Spain, where the finest teachers could be found. Intermarriage became a theme in the literature of the high Middle Ages, suggesting that some such marriages between Christian and Muslim did indeed take place. While the differences in religion provided for an uneasy and sometimes tumultuous coexistence, even during the period of the Crusades Christians and Muslims forged alliances that have not since been repeated.

## Critical Overview

The Song of Roland was largely ignored by critics and the reading public until the nineteenth century. In their cursory examinations of the French epic, the first commentators on the work considered it lacking in emotionalism, primitive, and inferior to Greek and Latin epic. The first real interest in the text stemmed from a debate between Gaston Paris, the most illustrious professor of medieval French literature in late nineteenth-century France, and his student, Joseph Bédier. Paris claimed that *The Song of Roland* was an essentially oral text, having been sung by minstrels since the battle of Roncesvalles. The written text, he contended, was simply a version of the oral story copied down by a cleric. This critical approach is called ''traditionalism.'' Bédier contended that, while the story of Roland and Olivier was a popular legend, the cleric who found in the legend material for an epic poem added the detail and complexity that make it a significant literary work. This is called the ''individualist'' approach to *The Song of Roland.*

This critical debate, never resolved, has given way to different readings and debates, making *The Song of Roland* arguably the most analyzed work in the French literary tradition. Many essays closely analyze the actions and character of Roland. Should he have blown the horn or not? Is he guilty of the sin of excessive pride in refusing to call for help, or is such reckless bravery the hallmark of the worthy soldier? Critic Alain Renoir sees Roland's internal conflict as a religious one, and several commentators have noted that Roland's final prayer is followed by the approach of angels who take his soul to heaven, indicating that he has found redemption. D. D. R. Owen and others, however, maintain that the motivation for Roland's conduct is non-religious, based on ''a triple sense of duty: to king and country, to family, and to self.'' Roland's refusing to blow the horn is not a sin of pride but rather an admirable trait of bravery that came from his utter devotion to the feudal political system. The question of Roland as hero or as redeemed recalcitrant yet remains, as does the dispute between traditionalist and individualist interpreters, unresolved and probably unresolvable.

Yet another trend in *Song of Roland* criticism reads the epic for the insight it provides into late eleventh-century French life. While at first glance the tale seems far from realistic, many of its episodes recount events common in eleventh-century life. Emanuel J. Mickel has found that Ganelon's trial by judicial combat between his representative and a representative of his accuser is an accurate account of such medieval trial. For Eugene Vance the story illustrates a political conflict that preoccupied eleventh-century France. According to Vance, the author writes to explore the questions ''How to tame the barons?'', ''Where does power reside?'' and ''Where is loyalty due?''

*The Song of Roland* lends itself as well to postmodern criticism. In a foray into psychoanalytical criticism, R. Howard Bloch finds the hostility between Roland and Ganelon to be an expression of the oedipal archetype. Ganelon, married to Roland's mother after the death of Roland's father, represents the wicked stepfather, while Charlemagne, Roland's maternal uncle, is Roland's spiritual father. This psychoanalytic reading explores the many twisted and complicated familial relationships found in *The Song of Roland.* Feminist critic Ann Tukey Harrison looks at the women in the text, finding that Aude is essentially passive and defined by her relationship to male characters (Roland's fiancee, Olivier's sister), whereas Queen Bramimonde functions independently: she is active in ruling Saragossa and guiding court business.

The many and varied approaches to reading *The Song of Roland* demonstrate the work's timeless appeal. The epic is sufficiently complicated and vague to allow multiple readings that have significance for audiences of all times. Each reader can find a lesson, a moral, or an example that is appropriate to his or her own experience. As long as *The Song of Roland* is read, new audiences will bring new ideas and approaches to the text. Some of these notions will no doubt share much with those of the eleventh- century audience, while others will be unique to the reader's time and place.

## Criticism

### *Lynn T. Ramey*

*In the following essay, Ramey discusses such aspects of the epic as its basis in historical fact, as well as the national, political, religious, and racial biases of the anonymous author.*

The oldest known epic in France, *The Song of Roland,* which dates from around 1100, bears traces of the battles that had taken place about 200 years earlier. While ostensibly telling the story of Charlemagne at Roncesvalles in 778, the events of *The Song of Roland* have been shifted into a contemporary setting, superimposing a long history of concerns about the Muslim upon the palpable fear of Muslim invasion that gripped France in Charles Martel's and Charlemagne's time. The historical basis of the battle, most likely a decimation of Charlemagne's rear guard in 778 by Basques, then in control of the mountains separating present-day France and Spain, is transformed to make it more understandable, even more tragic, for the early twelfth-century audience. While it would no longer make sense for Charlemagne to be fighting what were now Christian brothers in Spain, the threat of the Muslim infidel had very real meaning and a long history of representation to the listeners. Charlemagne's struggle with the Saracen forces could thus take on the guise of good versus evil, right versus wrong, that makes ideal material for an epic tragedy.

Yet this tale that would seemingly be made up of straight-forward dichotomies of black versus white encounters ambiguities at each turn. When Roland decides not to blow the horn, his action could be interpreted as a mistake due to excessive pride, as Janet Boatner deems. At the same time, his refusal to summon Charlemagne can be viewed as Christian and Germanic bravery, as Constance Hieatt asserts. T. Atkinson Jenkins reads Charlemagne as heroic, while Eugene Vance counters that Charlemagne embodies disillusionment with the whole ideal of heroism. We cannot say that the author shows a progressive view of the role of women, for as Ann Tukey Harrison shows, Aude retires while Bramimunde acts. Apparently almost every question that is asked of the characters of the *Chanson de Roland* can be answered both one way and with its opposite. Nowhere does this statement hold truer than in the picture the author draws of the Muslim.

In the early twelfth century concrete knowledge about the customs, habits and religion of the Muslims was little or non-existent. One of the problems when dealing with these invasions is precisely what to call the peoples who invaded Spain and the south of France. While the impetus certainly came from the extraordinary success of the followers of Muhammad, the people who actually carried out the invasions were not a homogenous bunch. Having come via Morocco and the Straits of Gibraltar up through Spain, the invaders included Arabs (both Muslim and non-Muslim), as well as a strong contingent of Berber tribesmen who had not yet converted to Islam. The victorious group did not even speak the same language, some conversing in Berber and others in Arabic. In many ways then, the medieval term of Saracen to refer to this disparate group of peoples embodies a generalizing, and therefore more accurate, terminology appropriate for the period.

# What Do I Read Next?

- Other medieval French epics have survived. They were grouped by twelfth-century scribes into cycles. *The Song of Roland* is part of the Cycle of the King *(Geste du roi),* which also includes *The Pilgrimage of Charlemagne (Le pelerinage de Charlemagne* or *Le voyage de Charlemagne).* Other epic poetry cycles included the Feudal Cycle *(Geste de Doon de Maiance)* and the William cycle *(Geste de Guillaume d'Orange* or *Geste de Garin de Monglane.*

- Italian Renaissance poet Luidi Pulci wrote a burlesque version of the Roland story in 1470 entitles *Il Morgante maggiore (The Great Morgante),* retelling the story of the ambush in the valley of Roncevalles.

- The romantic poem *Orlando Innamorto (Roland in Love),* by Matteo Maria Boiardo, blends the heroic ideal of the Roland epic with the courtly love motif of later French epic poetry.

- Lodovico Ariosto's *Orlando Furioso (Roland Mad)* adds many episodes to the account of the heroic knight Roland, including his amorous adventures.

- Defiance and courage characterize the quest of the knight portrayed in Robert Browning's poem ''Childe Roland to the Dark Tower Came'' (''Childe'' is an archaic term for ''knight'').

- Norman Daniel's 1984 study *Heroes and Saracens* looks at the portrayal of Christians and Muslims in medieval literature.

- *A History of Women: Silences of the Middle Ages,* edited by Christiane Klapish-Zuber in 1992, provides essays that give a good overview of what life was like for medieval women.

- Jamaica Kincaid's short story ''Song of Roland'' appeared in the *New Yorker* magazine on April 12, 1993.

---

The term Saracen probably comes from the Greek, *sarakenos,* the word used to describe the Arab invaders following the precepts of Muhammad. ''Saracen,'' however, was used to describe all foreign enemies, even those residing in Hungary or the Holy Land, and even the Normans, with apparently no need for justification on the part of the author of a text. Saracen is used interchangeably with ''pagan.'' In the late Middle Ages, the remains of Roman architecture, long-since unused and of forgotten origin, were sometimes termed Saracen'' The term Saracen seems to hold the same place in the medieval imagination that ''foreign,'' ''exotic,'' or ''outlandish'' represents for a late twentieth-century reader.

*The Song of Roland* undoubtedly speaks of the Saracen as Muslim, yet understanding of Islam plays no role in the text. In a piece of Christian crusade propaganda such as this epic, one would not necessarily expect the author to take a great interest in truthfully exposing the tenets of Islam and the differences between this faith and Christianity. However, even very basic, accurate information about Islam is lacking. The poet credits the infidels with numerous gods, contrary to the monotheism that makes ''There is no god but God'' the first and most fundamental belief of Islam. Examples of this misunderstanding include the author's assertion that Marsile worships three gods: Muhammad, Apollo and Tervagant. Likewise, when the Saracens wish to swear an oath to do their best to kill Roland, they swear it on their holy book, mistaking Muhammad and Tervagant as the authors of, presumably, the Koran, whereas Islam holds the book to be the literal word of God. The Saracens, anticipating the return and vengeance of Charlemagne, pray to one of their gods, Tervagant, who predictably does not come to their aid. Angry with the non-response of their gods, the Saracens desecrate their own temple, cursing and tearing down the statues of Tervagant, Muhammad and Apollo. This scene reflects perhaps the ultimate sacrilege to the Christian community, which believed quite strongly in icons, but it makes no sense in Islam as images and pictorial representations were and are not permitted.

The Saracen warrior mirrors the Christian quite frequently throughout the text. Charlemagne retires to an orchard, underneath a pine tree, following his initial defeat of the Saracens. Here his 15,000 soldiers gather around, but most notably present are the Peers, Charlemagne's closest men and advisors with whom he proceeds to discuss plans for leaving Spain. Marsile, the Arab ruler, also goes into an orchard following the same battle and is described as sitting in the shade. His 20,000 men surround him, and he takes this moment to call his closest advisors to brainstorm on how to finally crush the French. The political and governing strategies of the two groups are the same. Both leaders are greatly respected by their men, yet their best ideas and future directions come from a select group of noble advisors (dukes and counts), many of whom are related to each other and to the king. As Marsile and his men seal their treachery, the parallelism is complete; twelve chosen from the Saracens, led by the nephew of Marsile, will go head to head with the twelve companions of Charlemagne, led by Roland, his nephew. The glove that the Saracen carries as representative of his ruler will be the same emblem that Ganelon, ambassador of Charlemagne, accepts from his king.

The Saracen doubles the Christian in other aspects of the epic as well. During the battle, as is the convention in most battle scenes of the chansons de geste, each Christian knight meets individually with a Saracen knight. Blows are exchanged and one knight emerges victorious, having killed the other. The two armies are equipped identically, though a certain exoticism dominates the description of the Saracen outfit. The armor remains essentially western, as does the basic riding techniques (on a special war-horse, in tight lines). Yet, the Saracen is distinguished from the French by the provenance of his weaponry. The author gives the impression that excellent, perhaps the best, armor comes from far away, from the pagan lands of Saragossa and Valencia, in addition to Venice. No doubt about it, the Saracen is regally equipped. The shield of an Emir holds fascination and beauty, encrusted in stones, amethyst, topaz, diamonds, and a brilliant carbuncle.

Admiration for the Saracen is not limited to his armor. The Saracen knight can be noble, handsome, loyal and bold. In short, all the same characteristics admired in the Christian knight can be found in certain Saracen knights as well. The author highlights the prowess and beauty of the Saracen Margarit. Baligant, the Emir of Babylon serves as a prime example of the knight that would be perfect, were he only a Christian. Physically, even, this Saracen shares the traits of the Christian. His skin, most noticeably, is white.

The author is able to step back from the good versus evil dichotomy that forms the basis of the epic in order to admit a certain similitude and even admiration. The armor of the Christian knights is not quite so fabulous as that of the Saracen. Baligant distinguishes himself as almost a true baron, to be compared with the treasonous French renegade, Ganelon. By bringing the two armies together in moments of similarity, an implicit examination of the values and culture of the Christian results. Better weaponry can be found in other cultures. Superior knights are not limited to the French, and indeed certain Christian knights fall short of their Saracen counterparts.

The Saracen is not without his abominable traits, however. Roland sees the approaching hordes through a literal perspective of black versus white, noting that they "are blacker than ink and have no white except for their teeth alone." Just as the Emir epitomized the almost-ideal knight, the appropriately named Saracen, Abyss, serves as the stereotypical concentration of French fears of Arabs. Not only is Abyss morally corrupt, he is also physically repulsive. His very humanness is called into question by his inability or unwillingness to laugh and play. The archbishop/knight Turpin, symbolizing Christianity and Good, takes it upon himself to destroy the personified evil, Abyss. The fight is nothing other than good versus evil, right versus wrong, truth versus lies.

The portrait of the Saracen in the *Chanson de Roland* vacillates between the positive and the negative. At the same time that the audience of the 1100s feared the Saracen, and thus pictured him in monstrous terms, they also coveted the refinements of Muslim culture, many of which were totally lacking in the West. The Saracen characters of the epic echo this movement between fear and envy. As Joseph J. Duggan relates, the *Chanson de Roland* and other militant poems "helped shape the mentalities that made the crusades possible." Not simply by opposing Christians and Muslims, but also by constructing a Saracen who was frightening and inhuman enough to kill at the same time that he possessed objects and characteristics worthy of appropriation. The epic battle satisfied both these urges.

**Source:** Lynn T. Ramey, for *Epics for Students,* Gale Research, 1997.

## Joseph J. Duggan

*Below, Duggan provides an historical overview of the beginnings of French literature in the* chansons de geste, *or "songs of great deeds," the great epic poems of which* The Song of Roland *is the "acknowledged masterpiece of the genre." He notes the origins of this form in oral, or recited, poetry, and notes that these works were often based on actual events and individuals. Duggan discusses the way that epic poems were used propagandistically, to glorify national heroes, to find historical precedence for current events, and to popularize specific social, political, or religious points of view. Duggan comments that* The Song *contributed to the mindset that let to the Crusades and served as a "foundation myth" about the beginnings of French nationalism.*

When Pope Urban II preached the First Crusade to the Orient in 1095 at Clermont, the vernacular literature of France consisted of epic poems (*chansons de geste*), saints' Lives, and lyric poetry. Most of these works were still being passed on orally rather than being written down. The immensely popular *chansons de geste* include several of the finest works in medieval French literature: the *Chanson de Roland* (ca. 1100; *Song of Roland*), *Raoul de Cambrai, Garin le Lorrain* , the *Chanson de Guillaume, Girart de Roussillon* , and *Huon de Bordeaux.* They were sung at fairs, weddings, and coronations, in public squares and in castles. Over 120 of them have survived, and the corpus totals more than a million lines. Many of the poems were translated into other medieval languages. In the 14th and 15th centuries, the most popular were reworked in prose, and several of these were among the first texts to be printed in the late 15th century. They continued to be read well into the 1800s in the Bibliothèque Bleue and other popular collections.

The French epic was largely the creation of jongleurs, itinerant performers who not only composed *chansons de geste* and performed the lyric poetry of the trouvères (inventors) of northern France and the troubadours of the south, but also juggled, did acrobatic tricks, exhibited trained animals, played instruments, and staged mimes and other entertainments. Jongleurs depended for their livelihood on the generosity of audiences; thus their songs can be taken to reflect the types of narrative diversion that the public desired. From the pronouncements of ecclesiastical officials, it is obvious that jongleurs belonged to the lowest level of medieval society. Female jongleurs, for example, were routinely assumed to engage in prostitution. Since literacy was confined almost entirely to the clergy and the higher nobility in the period in which the *chansons de geste* flourished, it appears that most jongleurs were illiterate. In any case, in medieval iconography jongleurs are never seen using books in their performances. Apparently they were able to perform *chansons de geste* of considerable length—examples of the genre range from 800 to 35,000 lines—through the use of an improvisational technique that has been solidly documented in other preliterate cultures: jongleurs developed a repertoire of stock scenes and phrases to aid them in reproducing, often in more or less the same form but sometimes with considerable modification, the songs that they heard others perform. In keeping with this oral and traditional transmission, the vast majority of the poems are anonymous.

Medieval illuminations show jongleurs playing a stringed instrument called the *vielle,* and treatises report that they sang the entire story to a chantlike melody. *Chansons de geste* are divided into *laisses,* stanzas of varying length, each characterized by a single assonance or rhyme; the lines are ten or twelve syllables long (though in one text, *Gormont et Isembart,* eight), and each is marked by a pause, or caesura. Variations in melody probably marked the first and last lines of the *laisse,* and the hiatus between *laisses* may have been filled with instrumental music.

Evidence for the existence of a thriving literature of epic song before the First Crusade is found in several precious texts: in his chronicle of the abbey of Saint-Riquier (completed in 1088), the monk Hariulf incorporates into his narrative an event from *Gormont et Isembart* ; the Nota Emilianense, from the third quarter of the 11th century, summarizes a version of the *Chanson de Roland* ; and the Fragment of the Hague, an attempt around the year 1000 to render into a nostalgically classicized Latin the story of a fictional siege of Gerona, places there a number of heroes from what was later to be the cycle of epic poems recounting the deeds of Guillaume d'Orange, his forebears, and his nephews. The two other major epic cycles of *chansons de geste* (so divided by the 12th-century poet Bertrand de Bar-sur-Aube) are that of the kings of France, sometimes referred to as the cycle of Charlemagne, and that of the rebellious vassals, treacherous or recalcitrant barons who are conceived as having all belonged to the same lineage. Several indications, including references to episodes from other songs in the early 12th-century *Chanson de Guillaume* and the presence of Guillaume-cycle heroes in the Fragment of the Hague, lead to the conclusion that the cycles had begun to develop well before the earliest *chanson de geste* to be preserved, the Oxford *Chanson de Roland* (Bodleian Library Ms. Digby 23), was copied in the second quarter of the 12th century. Not mentioned by Bertrand is the cycle that purports to give an account of the First Crusade: its content is, with the notable exception of the *Chanson d' Antioche ,* almost entirely fictitious.

As a body of literature, then, the *chansons de geste* were conceived of genealogically. Typically each of the great heroes was the subject of a major song: examples are the *Chanson de Roland,* the *Chanson de Guillaume, Renaut de Montauban, Girart de Roussillon,* and *Raoul de Cambrai.* The process of cyclical development led to the composing of songs that told of the heroes' childhood exploits, or *enfances* (the *Enfances Guillaume,* the *Enfances Vivien*); their young manhood or *chevalerie* (the *Chevalerie Ogier de Danemark ,* the *Chevalerie Vivien*); their conversions to the monastic life, or *moniage* (the *Moniage Guillaume,* the *Moniage Renouart*); and their deaths (the *Mort Charlemagne;* the *Mort Aimeri de Narbonne,* which recounts the demise of Guillaume's father). The deeds of great heroes are set in the context of their kinship alliances, reflecting the medieval legal principle that one was responsible for the acts of one's relatives: thus in the Oxford *Chanson de Roland,* Roland is the son of Charlemagne as well as his nephew; Guillaume is the brother of six other heroes, each of whom sets out to conquer a different land (*Les Narbonnais* ), and the uncle of the tragic Vivien; the traitor Ganelon of the *Roland* is viewed as having been related to other untrustworthy knights, like him descended from the eponymous hero of *Doon de Mayence.* This emphasis on genealogy in the *chansons de geste* is hardly surprising: *geste* signifies not only ''deeds'' and ''tale about a hero's exploits'' but also ''lineage'' and ''cycle of songs about a lineage.''

The seemingly sudden profusion of French texts after the First Crusade has frequently been viewed as the product of a great burst of authorial energy. Much of that textual production, however, resulted simply from the writing down of an oral literature that was in full blossom long before the crusade got under way. Although debates about the origins of French literature are often confined to the few hagiographic texts that were actually copied before the crusade, such as the late 9th-century *Cantilène* or *Séquence de sainte Eulalie (Sequence of Saint Eulalie)* and *La vie de saint Alexis* (ca. 1050), in a very real sense there were no discrete origins, since it appears that the oral literature of France came into being along with the French language as it developed out of popular Latin.

Viewed in that light, the relationship between the *chanson de geste* and history takes on added significance. Many of the earliest and most famous of the songs have at their center a historical kernel, frequently a great battle. Thus the *Chanson de Guillaume* recalls William of Toulouse's capture of Barcelona from the Moors in 803; the battle of Saucourt in 881, in which Louis III defeated a Viking force that had attacked and burned the monastery of Saint-Riquier, inspired the tradition that produced *Gormont et Isembart;* the attack of Raoul, son of a certain Raoul de Gouy, on the county of Vermandois in 943 is at the core of *Raoul de Cambrai.* Sometimes surprisingly accurate details are preserved in the epics, such as the name of William of Toulouse's wife, Witburgh, which comes down in works of the Guillaume cycle in the corresponding French form Guibourc. Generally the historical events found in the *chanson de geste* date from the Carolingian period, although names and occurrences from as early as the Merovingian monarchy and as late as the taking of Antioch in 1098 figure in the French epic, and the Occitan *chanson de geste,* composed south of the Loire, contains material from as late as the civil war in Navarre of 1276–77. The preservation of events for as long as 300 years says much about the conservatism of the oral tradition.

Nonetheless, only a modicum of the tens of thousands of events recounted in the epics have a basis in history, and even in those cases the facts have been adapted to the dramatic and mythical requirements of the genre. The poets appropriated the details of history to their own needs—compositional, socio-economic, and occasionally even propagandistic—shaping a vision of the French past that centered on the achievements of legendary figures from the formative period in which the consciousness of national identity had begun to appear. In the process, they sometimes merged the deeds of historical figures who shared the same name, assigned one person's actions to another, created independent heroes from the same historical prototype, ascribed straight-forward military defeats to the machinations of traitors, and took other liberties with the facts that had entered their ken. Still, they claimed that their songs were true, as a result of which the *chansons de geste* were viewed as history by many a medieval cleric; and modern readers have not been exempt from the tendency to accept their testimony. In fact the *chanson de geste* embodied a popular form of historiography that competed with both the official annalists and chroniclers and the ecclesiastical historians.

*Chansons de geste* were sometimes used to spread the news of great historical events. The late 12th-century chronicler of the house of Guines, Lambert d'Ardre, tells a revealing anecdote concerning Arnold de Guines, who took part in the siege of Antioch during the First Crusade. A jongleur singing a *Chanson d'Antioche* one day offered to include Arnold's deeds in his tale in exchange for a pair of scarlet shoes. When Arnold rejected the bargain, the jongleur excluded him from his version of the song. This example of the use of a *chanson de geste* to propagate the news of a recent event is also valuable for the insight it provides into the economic mentality of jongleurs, who did not hesitate to exact a price for the fame they were capable of spreading. That noble families did indeed pay attention to the songs that told of their putative ancestors' achievements is indicated by the fact that, from the last quarter of the 12th century on, the viscounts of Narbonne began to call their heirs "Aimeri" in obvious emulation of the epic—and probably fictitious—Aimeri de Narbonne of the Guillaume cycle.

Legends from the *chansons de geste* were also invoked for purposes of persuasion. The First Crusade offers a salient instance: the chronicler Robert of Reims, an eyewitness to Urban II's speech launching the idea of the crusade, reports that the pope called upon the assembled nobles to follow the example of their predecessors Charlemagne and his son Louis, who destroyed pagan kingdoms and extended the boundaries of the holy church. In the context of the struggle against Islam, this image of Charlemagne and Louis corresponds more closely to their deeds as transformed in the *chansons de geste* than to their historical undertakings, and suggests that the fictional story of Charlemagne's journey to the Holy Land, told in the *Pèlerinage de Charlemagne,* provided an ideal precedent for French knights to take the cross.

Thus it is very likely that the *Chanson de Roland* and similar militant poems helped to shape the mentalities that made the crusades possible. Struggles between paganism and Christendom are predominant themes in the *chansons de geste,* and the ways in which the French Crusaders imagined Islam and the Arabs could not help but be shaped by their depiction in the epics. Not that the forces who opposed the Crusaders can simply be equated with the Saracens of the *chansons de geste.* The inclusion among the latter of such diverse tribes as the Ireis (Irish), the Argoilles (Scottish Argyles), the Esclavon (Slavs), the Ermines (Armenians), the Avers (Avars), the "people of Samuel" (Bulgars of Macedonia), the Hums (Huns), and the Hungres (Hungarians) renders it plausible that the Saracens represent all the external forces of paganism that were perceived as threats in early medieval France. Understanding of the tenets of Islam did not figure in the stock of knowledge available to the Crusaders, most of whom probably held a notion of that religion informed by the *chansons de geste:* the Saracens are said in the epics to worship many gods in the form of idols and to keep pigs—characteristics that are not only alien to Islam but abhorrent to its followers. That Mohammed is included among the gods of the Saracens is perhaps the crowning distortion. But rather than an anti-Islam conceived in calculated fashion, this depiction of the pagans who held Spain, North Africa (whose chief city in the epics is "Babylone," that is, Cairo), and the Holy Land represents a failure to differentiate between, on the one hand, the Germanic, Scandinavian, and Slavic pagans, many of whom did indeed worship idols, and, on the other, the monotheists emanating from Arabia, Persia, and Turkey. These reminiscences of the earlier threat of northern and eastern paganism is an archaism in the epic conception of the world: just as many of the subjects of the *chansons de geste* hark back to the Carolingian era, when the poems presumably first began to take shape, so the view of the non-Christian world represented in them reflects a popular historiography of the 8th through 11th centuries rather than the view of Islam that men of learning began to develop in the 12th century.

The acknowledged masterpiece of the genre, the *Chanson de Roland,* has traditionally been viewed as the story of Charlemagne's nephew, but an obscure reference to the emperor's confessor, St. Giles, in lines 2096–98 reveals that the poet composed his work in full awareness of the legend that Charlemagne had committed incest with his sister, who as a consequence gave birth to Roland. These events are detailed in the First Branch of the *Karlamagnus Saga,* a Norse text of the mid-13th century that is based on lost French epics of the 11th and 12th centuries. The most renowned of the *chansons de geste* is thus the tale of the tragic death of Charlemagne's son, the genealogically pure offspring of the Frankish royal family, whose death, caused not by the Saracens but rather by his own extraordinary effort in sounding the horn to call for help after he and his men have fallen into a trap arranged by his stepfather Ganelon, is no doubt a punishment for his father's sin. Hence the *Chanson de Roland* belongs among a range of myths concerning heroes and gods born of incest—Heracles, Romulus, Mordred, Zeus, Apollo, Freyr, and in particular Sinfjotli in the *Völsunga Saga,* son of a brother (Sigmund) and a sister (Signy), who refuses to call for his father's help in a fight against overwhelming odds and who dies young and without offspring through his stepmother's treachery. The *Chanson de Roland* is a foundation myth, the story of the suffering and eventual triumph of Charlemagne, the figure who in the national consciousness is the founder of the French collectivity, on the occasion of his own son's death. In keeping with the character of the *chansons de geste,* however, the myth is anchored in a historical event, the defeat of Charlemagne's rearguard in the Pyrenees in the year 778. The evidence for Roland's historical existence is fragile and ambiguous.

The *Chanson de Roland* exemplifies the mutually beneficial relationship between the jongleurs and history: the poets preserved in their songs fragmentary memories of historical events, which they embellished for artistic purposes, while historical figures such as Urban II appropriated and exploited the epic legends to further their political and social agendas.

**Source:** Joseph J. Duggan, ''The Epic,'' in *A New History of French Literature,* edited by Denis Hollier, Harvard University Press, 1989, pp. 18–23.

## Ann Tukey Harrison

*In the following excerpt, Harrison compares the two main women characters from* The Song of Roland. *She notes that Roland's fiancee Aude is described as having typically desirable ''feminine'' traits: she is beautiful, faithful, and devoted, and is identified primarily in terms of her relationships with male characters. In contrast, the anonymous author depicted the Saracen queen Bramimunde as a strong, active, indepedent individual, who is in*

*fact the only surviving Saracen discussed by name in the* Song.

Modern students of the humanities in high school, college, and graduate school who study the history of western civilization in a wide variety of disciplines from anthropology to comparative literature and French are currently exposed to the *Chanson de Roland* (in English, modern French, or Old French); usually they read short passages of a hundred verses or so, and they are told about the content and emphasis of the work as a whole.

Such readers are led to two conclusions concerning women characters in French epic literature: 1) women are unimportant or even nonexistent in the French epic; 2) the major female character in the *Chanson de Roland,* Aude, Roland's fiancée, offers a typical feminine depiction: her appearance is brief, unusually beautiful, and poignant. The first premise does find corroboration in many *chansons de geste,* where women are secondary or tertiary figures, not major protagonists of heroic proportions. The French epic seems to have been written for, by, and about men.

The second premise, asserting the representative nature of Aude and the remarkable beauty of her few verses, continues to be popular, both in French and English-language scholarship. In some ways, this can be seen as a direct response to the intellectual currents of our own time, when women as students and scholars are increasingly interested in the roles of women in literature and in the cultures that produced such writings. Two questions are central to a balanced appraisal and understanding of women characters in the *Chanson de Roland:* how important to this work is Aude? are there other artistically interesting women characters in the poem?

Aude is first mentioned during the rearguard battle. When first named in verses 1719–1721, she is a relative latecomer to the story. The poet focuses at once on her relationship or kinship to both of the heroes, Roland *and* Olivier: she is fiancée to one, sister of the other. The two companions have disagreed vigorously earlier, and their debate is renewed at the turning point of the battle, when their heroism is at its apogee. Here the reader first hears of Aude, from Olivier, in the heat of anger.... Critics have observed the importance of the whole battlefield debate without much attention to its effect on the characterization of Aude. She is introduced at a privileged moment of high emotion, in a passage that circumscribes four traits essential to her character: her noble family lineage; her passive status therein dominated by their right of bestowal of her person in marriage; her prestigious betrothal; and her discreetly sexual role as bride-to-be. At this point, Aude's possession, within the limits of family and marriage—two of the primary circles of medieval woman's social existence—is a subject of a mild oath, uttered in anger, a corollary to the foremost male pursuit—warfare. It is not an exaggeration, within this context, to equate Aude with royal booty, one of the better prizes of conquest.

Aude's major episode, two thousand verses later, consists of a dialogue with Charlemagne, about Roland, followed by her death and interment. Described only as "une bele damisele" ["a fair damsel"], she meets the emperor on the steps of his palace, to ask: "Ço dist al rei: 'O est Rollant le catanie, / Ki me jurat cume sa per a prendre?'" ["She said to the King: 'Where is Roland, the captain, / Who gave me his solemn word he would take me to wife?'"] Charles, weeping and tearing his beard, tells her she inquires after a dead man, and he then offers her his own son Louis in marriage. Aude finds the offer "estrange," which I interpret to mean "incompatible or inconsistent with my nature and view of my life." Praying that it not please God, his angels, and saints for her to survive Roland, she drops dead. (The same idiom, *aler a sa fin,* is used to describe Roland also, right after his death.) Charlemagne, thinking she has fainted, attempts to revive her, then calls four countesses to carry the body to a convent, where, after a night's vigil, she is buried beside an altar. Finally, Charlemagne endows a convent in Aude's honor.

Aude is faithful, pious, beautiful, a noblewoman whose sacrifice is honored. Her status is thrice indicated: first, by her direct approach to the emperor, which is well received by him; second, by his reactions to her words, his deep concern for her and his marriage offer of his own heir; finally, by his endowment of the convent. Although Aude is here an initiator of action, a woman who speaks and acts, she does so only in relation to male characters. As her introduction as a character was defined by her relationship to Roland and Olivier, her deeds here are directly related to Charlemagne, her sovereign, with full power over her person. The poet implicitly suggests the spatial and legal constraints within which she exists (the palace and the arranged marriage), while explicitly stating the male dominance that circumscribes her life. Charlemagne's actions begin and end the episode, and his words or deeds

occupy seventeen of the twenty-nine verses. Aude's life has been one of honor, within the confines of family, betrothal, and church; although she is associated with the major heroic figures of the poem (Roland, Olivier, Charlemagne), she is sheltered, protected, bestowed. She is wholly dependent, and her honor, like her status, is reflected from male characters.

Some critics call her death a martyrdom, and both Réau and Brault associate her demise with the iconographic formula of the Death of the Virgin. As Brault writes: "Like Mary, Alda is a virgin, and her passing, which is so peaceful it completely deceives Charles into believing she has merely fainted, is an awe-inspiring dormition." Scholars have seen her as the last victim of the Battle of Roncevals, the most touching reminder of Roland, the incarnation of ideal love and the most moving of all tributes to Roland's glory, one of Roland's greatest claims to glory. Although her twenty-nine verses are surely not mere decoration, some of these claims on her behalf are hyperbolic and distorted. Her episode is woven well into the epic's action; she does contribute to the character development of both Roland and Charlemagne, but she does not directly reinforce the poem's central theme of Christian supremacy over the pagans. Beautiful Aude is tightly confined, subordinate, and supportive, and if that is typical of unmarried noblewomen of her time, then she can be called representative and, if not mimetic, at least *grosso modo* realistic.

A much more significant female figure is the Saracen queen Bramimunde, wife of Saragossa's King Marsile. By far the most developed woman character in this epic, she is an independent, active participant in four different passages, each of which is strategically located within the poem's action. Bramimunde first appears in the scene of treachery (when the betrayal of the French rearguard is planned by Ganelon and the Saracen leaders to whom he is an ambassador); she is next a central figure during the scenes showing the reactions to Marsile's defeat; she is prominent in three stages of the second half of the poem when Charlemagne as Roland's emperor and Christendom's champion defeats the Emir Baligant, sovereign of Marsile and ruler of Araby; and finally, her conversion to Christianity is reported by the poet as part of the poem's conclusion. In each instance she is directly and explicitly linked with the emperor Charlemagne. She is the sole individualized Saracen survivor, and by her baptism, arranged at Charles' behest, she embodies the primary theme of the *chanson:* the Christians are right, the pagans are wrong.

Laisse 50, within the section of the poem where Ganelon plans the Saracen ambush of the French rearguard led by Roland, contains a description of Bramimunde's gifts to the wife of the French ambassador and traitor. While Ganelon is in council with the enemy Saracens, Bramimunde comes to the gathering, declares her affection for the Frenchman, and states that she is sending two necklaces (with gold, amethysts, and sapphires) to Ganelon's wife. In this her first appearance, Bramimunde concludes with a formulaic, oblique reference to Charlemagne: "Vostre emperere si bones n'en out unches" ["Your Emperor never had such fine ones"]. The Queen is not the only pagan to give presents to Ganelon; Valdabrun has already offered his sword and Climorin his helmet, but the men's gifts are to the ambassador directly, and the men exchange kisses as well to seal the gift-giving. Bramimunde's gifts are non-military, for Ganelon's wife (a woman never mentioned again), and the feudal kiss is replaced by a statement that "Il les ad prises, en sa hoese les butet" ["He took them, he sticks them in his boot"]. The author of the *Roland* is fully cognizant of Bramimunde's femininity, and he depicts actions and statements that are appropriate for women.

Brault finds Bramimunde's words to Ganelon "bold and suggestive." . . . [He] explains that "the voluptuous and amoral Saracen lady is a stock character in epic literature." He also notes that in this passage, as elsewhere in the epic tradition, "diabolism and eroticism are closely intertwined." I find little substantiation for this interpretation, in this section of the text or in other appearances of Bramimunde in the poem. She is a Queen, with a political and religious role; her gifts are to Ganelon's *wife;* and nowhere else in the text does her conduct convey an erotic connotation, much less diabolism.

Bramimunde's second scene takes place in Saragossa, immediately after the defeat of Marsile. In laisse 187, she cries out, along with 20,000 men. They are reported to curse Charlemagne, then proceed to depose their gods while uttering blasphemous shouts and curses quoted by the poet directly. Although Bramimunde is the only individual of the stanza, her appearance is very short (three verses), and the actions and words are attributed to the mob as well. The next stanza, laisse 188, the last before the principal division of the poem (the second

part or Baligant episode), is devoted entirely to Bramimunde's outpouring of grief, in deed and word. . . . The Saracen reaction to Marsile's defeat is described in terms of the undifferentiated mob *and* Bramimunde, who is the only individual to speak for the infidel cause. She performs the ritual actions of grief and delivers a carefully balanced, eleven-verse speech of formal lamentation.

The third set of passages in which Bramimunde appears are the three stages of the Baligant section; she is still a part of the Saracen court. Marsile, her husband, was victorious over Roland's rearguard, but Charlemagne's army has destroyed the Saracen troops. Now Marsile's sovereign, the Emir Baligant, comes to do battle with the Emperor Charles, in the ultimate conflict between pagan and Christian. When the messengers from Baligant arrive at Saragossa, at the court of Marsile, his Queen receives them, and she counsels them twice. Neither speech is well received, and both times a male character virtually tells her to be quiet, in so many words. Their refusal to listen to her is, eventually, their undoing, for she has ended each statement of advice with a warning about the power of Charlemagne. . . .

Bramimunde is the official of the court to welcome the Emir Baligant, throwing herself at his feet, as she bemoans her pitiful situation, since she has lost her lord (Marsile being wounded and incapable of protecting her).

And finally, Bramimunde, from a tower, witnesses the Emir's defeat, called the confounding of Araby, and she invokes Mohammed while reporting the shame and death she sees. Upon hearing her words, her wounded husband Marsile turns his face to the wall and dies of grief.

Bramimunde is in evidence and speaks at three crucial moments during the Baligant encounter: the arrival of the messengers, the arrival of the Emir himself, and the defeat of Baligant along with the subsequent death of Marsile. She fills an official role, both as Queen and as witness.

The fourth stage of her role in the *Chanson de Roland* is her conversion to Christianity. It is annouced by the poet during the sack of Saragossa; each time the reader is told that it is the will of the king that she be converted, but by love and not by force, in France and not in Spain. She is to be taken, as a prisoner, to Aix. This information is conveyed directly twice. The first time, she is the only individual taken, unconverted, from Saragossa home to

France. . . . The second reference says that the Emperor wishes her only good.

After the trial of Ganelon and the execution of his kin (among whom there is no mention of his wife, to whom Bramimunde sent the necklaces), Charlemagne's first concern seems to be the conversion of his queenly captive. . . . [In the baptism scene, as] with the gift-giving scene, the poet is conscious that Bramimunde is a woman, and the ritual observed is appropriate for a nun, not a male convert.

The final stanza of the entire poem contains the reiteration of the conversion of Charlemagne's important prisoner; this is the third accomplishment of his mission—he has done justice, assuaged his anger, and given Christianity to Bramimunde. . . . Although converted and baptised Juliana, she is in the last reference known under the old, familiar Saracen name, and she here represents the Saracen community of which she is the sole individualized survivor.

A feminist appraisal of Bramimunde must answer at least three crucial questions: is she a full-fledged member of the society depicted? does she act outside of the love-marriage situation? is she a role model? Certainly Bramimunde's participation in her society is full, if not extraordinary. The gift scene, her role in the formal reception of Baligant's embassy and the Emir's arrival at Saragossa, and finally her conversion, at the singular behest of Charles: the importance of these episodes and her particular behavior in them show her as not only a full-fledged member, but, by the end of the *geste,* as the representative of the Saracen world. On two instances when she is rebuffed by Saracen men, rudely, the poet shows that Bramimunde is right and the pagans are wrong when they do not heed her warnings.

Though the reader would infer that her title Queen of Spain comes to her through marriage with Marsile, the author of the *Roland* only twice qualifies her as "his wife," both in stanza 187, in the scene where she sees and understands the severity of her husband's wounds. The poet far prefers to call her by name or royal title. Bramimunde is portrayed as a loyal wife, fulfilling the regal duties of her status, but after the mortal wounding of her spouse Marsile, her activity, prominence, and representative position increase, verse by verse. And long after her king-consort has died, Queen

Bramimunde is alive, a worthy convert, far beyond the love-marriage identification of other medieval women in other works of literature, such as Iseut.

The most important facet of Bramimunde's presentation by the *Roland* poet is her close association, specifically stated in each instance, with Charles. Every time she appears, without exception, she or the poet makes explicit reference to Charles the Emperor. And this link, forged from her debut as gift-giving queen, to the great king, with a divinely bestowed mission of subduing or converting the pagans, brings Bramimunde into contact with the major theme of the poem. Neither diabolic nor erotic, she is not a romantic foil for Charles, or a feminine counterpart, or a pseudo-consort; she is instead a living example of the most lasting and benevolent side of his assigned earthly task—the flower of the pagan world converted to Christianity, admitted in honor to the very center of Christendom, and the only preoccupation of Charles when the vengeance is over.

Aude and Bramimunde offer an interesting set of opposite characteristics; in some ways they are complementary to one another: Christian/Saracen, virgin betrothed/wife then widow, noblewoman/queen, representative of women left behind/representative of the Saracen political and religious community, inexperienced youth of uncompromising idealism/experienced middle age capable of compromise and conversion. Critics observe a religious association for both (Aude with the Virgin Mary in death, Bramimunde with St. Juliana in baptism), and both are clearly female, depicted as women in actions appropriate to women. Teachers who decide to emphasize Aude at the expense of Bramimunde are choosing to stress Roland's sacrifice as the central event of the epic, since Aude as a character serves, perhaps exclusively, to reinforce Roland's role. Bramimunde as a character is more full, much more active, and woven into the greater theme of the whole epic: Charlemagne's conquest of the pagans, as the champion of Christendom. Although the total number of verses devoted to both women is small (twenty-nine for Aude and one hundred forty-seven for Bramimunde, out of four thousand), these women are integral to the plot, character, and thematic development of the *chanson.* An examination of them both, in measured fashion, is but another way of observing the meticulous artistry of the *Roland* poet.

**Source:** Ann Tukey Harrison, "Aude and Bramimunde: Their Importance in the 'Chanson de Roland'," *The French Review,* Vol. LIV, No. 5, April, 1981, pp. 672–79.

# Sources for Further Study

Auerbach, Erich. "Roland against Ganelon," in *Mimesis: The Representation of Reality in Western Literature,* pp. 96-122. Princeton University Press, 1953.
  Examines and discusses the technical composition of The *Song of Roland,* focusing on the work's representation of reality.

Burgess, Glyn. Introduction to *The Song of Roland,* translated by Glyn Burgess, pp. 7-25. Penguin, 1990.
  Provides information about the provenance of the manuscript, the historical background of the poem, a plot synopsis, and a technical analysis of the verse and language of the poet.

Cook, Robert Francis. *The Sense of the Song of Roland.* Ithaca: Cornell University Press, 1987, 266 p.
  General reading with detailed analysis of key episodes.

Duby, Georges, and Perrot, Michelle. *A History of Women, Vol. II: Silences of the Middle Ages.* Belknap Press, 1992, 575 p.
  Essay collection treating the different roles for women during the Middle Ages.

Duggan, Joseph J. "The Epic," in *A New History of French Literature,* Harvard University Press, 1989, pp. 18-23.
  Study of the relationship between history and epic that examines the popularity of the epic form in the twelfth century.

Durant, Will. *The Age of Faith,* Simon and Schuster, 1950, 1196 p.
  Provides historical background for the period in which *The Song of Roland* is set and was written.

Emden, Wolfgang van, *La Chanson de Roland,* London: Grant & Cutler, 1995, 135 p.
  Critical guide.

Enders, Jody, "The Logic of the Debates in the *Chanson de Roland,*" in *Oliphant,* Vol. 14, No. 2, pp. 83-100.
  Looks at the use of rhetoric—the art of effective or persuasive speech—as practiced by major characters in *The Song of Roland.*

Jenkins, T. Atkinson, Introduction to *La Chanson de Roland,* edited by D. C. Atkinson, pp. 175-78. Heath and Company, 1924.
  Discusses the characters, style and themes of the poem, and concludes that the character of Roland is a hero in the traditional sense of the word.

Mickel, Emanuel J. *Ganelon, Treason and the Chanson de Roland,* University Park: Pennsylvania State University, 1989, 184 p.
  Examines the medieval legal system in France with application to the trail of Ganelon in *The Song of Roland.*

Renoir, Alain. "Roland's Lament: Its Meaning and Function in the *Chanson de Roland ,*" in *Speculum,* Vol. 35, No. 4, 1960, pp. 572-83.
  Bases an interpretation of *The Song of Roland* as an essentially Christian work on an explication of Roland's lament for the fallen French knights.

Uitti, Karl D., "'Co dit la geste': Reflections on the Poetic Restoration of History in the *Song of Roland,*" in*Studies in Honor of Hans Erich Keller,* edited by Rupert T. Pickens. Kalamazoo: Western Michigan University, 1993, pp. 1-27.
  Examines the historical sources of *The Song of Roland.*

Vance, Eugene, *Reading the Song of Roland,* Prentice-Hall, 1970, 118 p.
  Provides a detailed reading and interpretation of the epic that includes analysis of characters and the work's historical context.

# *Divina Commedia (Divine Comedy)*

Dante Alighieri (1265-1321) wrote his epic poem, the *Divine Comedy,* during the last thirteen years of his life (circa 1308-21), while in exile from his native Florence. There are three parts to this massive work: *Inferno, Purgatory* and *Paradise.* In each section Dante the poet recounts the travels of the Pilgrim—his alter ego—through hell, purgatory, and heaven, where he meets God face to face. The primary theme is clear. In a letter to his patron, Can Grande della Scala, Dante wrote that his poem was, on the literal level, about ''The state of souls after death.'' It is, of course, that and much more. The poem works on a number of symbolic levels, much like the Bible, one of its primary sources. Like that sacred text, Dante meant his work and his Pilgrim traveler to serve as models for the reader. He hoped to lead that reader to a greater understanding of his place in the universe and to prepare him for the next life, for the life that begins after death.

The greatness of the *Divine Comedy* lies in its construction as a *summa,* or a summation of knowledge and experience. Dante was able to weave together pagan myth, literature, philosophy; Christian theology and doctrine, physics, astrology, cartography, mathematics, literary theory, history, and politics into a complex poem that a wide audience, not just the highly educated, could read. For Dante boldly chose to write his poem of salvation in his own Italian dialect, not in Latin, which was the language of Church, State, and epic poetry during

## Dante Alighieri

## 1321

his time. Its impact was so great that Dante's Tuscan dialect became what we recognize as modern Italian.

As one of the greatest works, not just of the late Middle Ages, but of world literature in its entirety, the influence of the *Divine Comedy* has been incalculable. The poem was immediately successful—Dante's own sons, Pietro and Jacopo, wrote the first commentaries on it—and it continues to be read and taught today. Many of western literature's major figures were indebted to Dante's masterwork. A highly selective list includes: Giovanni Boccaccio (1313-75); Geoffrey Chaucer (circa 1344-1400); Don Iñigo Lopez de Mendoza, the first Marqués de Santillana (1389-1458); John Milton (1608-74); William Blake (1757-1827); Victor Hugo (1802-85); Joseph Conrad (Teodor Josef Konrad Korzeniowski) (1857-1924); James Joyce (1882-1941); Ezra Pound (1885-1972); Jorge Luis Borges (1899-1986); and Italo Calvino (1923-85).

If this impressive list were not testament enough, one has only to consider the four to five hundred manuscripts of the *Divine Comedy* in existence (an almost unheard-of number), the four-hundred-some Italian printed editions and the hundreds of English translations to get some idea of this work's impact on Western culture. Clearly, readers have found the *Divine Comedy* relevant to their lives since its composition nearly seven hundred years ago. Perhaps this is because Dante Alighieri, for all the differences between his era and subsequent ones, wrestled with and wrote about concerns that affect all people who have ever stopped to think about them: What is the purpose of this life? Is there an afterlife? If so, how should I prepare for it? Why, in short, am I here? Dante's answers to those questions will not necessarily be the same as those of each of his many readers, but by asking them he forces each reader to ask them, too, and to wonder how to answer them.

## Author Biography

As is often the case with medieval authors, we know relatively little about Dante Alighieri's personal life. In his *Convivio* (circa 1304-1307) (*The Banquet*), he tells us that he was born in Florence, Italy, and we now know that his birth probably occurred in late May or early June, 1265, in the San Martino district of that city. We know that his father, Alighiero di Bellincione d'Alighieri, was a notary. His moth-er, Donna Bella, was probably the daughter of the noble Durante degli Abati. She died before Dante was fourteen, and his father took a second wife, Lapa di Chiarissimo Cialuffi. They had a son, Francesco, and a daughter, Tana. Although the Alighieri family was noble by virtue of the titles bestowed upon it, by 1265 its social status and wealth seem to have declined. Nonetheless, when Alighiero Alighieri died around 1283, he left his children moderately well off, owners of city and country properties.

Around this time, Dante Alighieri followed through on the marriage arranged by his father in 1277 and took the gentlewoman Gemma Donati as his wife. They had two sons, Pietro and Jacopo, and at least one daughter, Antonia. (Dante and Gemma might have had a second daughter, Beatrice, although Beatrice could have been Antonia's monastery name.) Dante's marriage and family life seem to have had no impact on his poetry. He wrote nothing about his immediate family in the *Divine Comedy* (circa 1308-21), but there might be a reference to a sister in *La Vita Nuova* (*The New Life*) (circa 1292-1300).

As a youth, Dante might have attended Florence's Franciscan lower school and school of philosophy. Brunetto Latini (circa 1220-94), the distinguished scholar, teacher, statesman and author, encouraged him to study rhetoric at the University at Bologna. In *La Vita Nuova* Dante tells us that he taught himself to write verse. He became one of Florence's top poets, associating and exchanging work with other well-known writers like Guido Cavalcanti (circa 1240-1300), Lapo Gianni (circa 1270-1332) and Cino da Pistoia (circa 1270-1336). Dante was friendly with the musician and singer Casella (no dates) and might have known the artists Oderisi da Gubbio (circa 1240-99) and Giotto (circa 1267-1337).

In 1274, when he was nine years old, Dante tells us he met Bice Portinari, whom he later called Beatrice, ''bringer of blessedness.'' His love for this beautiful daughter of Folco Portinari was to become one of the strongest forces in his life. When she died suddenly in 1290, Dante collected the lyric poems he had written to her, linked them with prose commentaries and produced *La Vita Nuova,* the slim volume that is really the beginning of his masterwork, the *Divine Comedy*. Linking the two is Dante's love for and idealization of Beatrice, a love which Dante transformed from the physical to the spiritual. Indeed in the *Divine Comedy,* Beatrice prepares Dante the Pilgrim for and leads him to his final face-to-face meeting with God.

Dante was also a soldier, a politician, and a diplomat. Like other families of the lesser nobility and artisan class, the Alighieris allied themselves with the Florentine political faction called the Guelfs (or Guelphs). Their opposition, the Ghibellines, represented the feudal aristocracy. Dante saw military service as a member of the cavalry, which he joined in 1289. He fought with Florence and her Guelf allies against Arezzo, in their victory at the battle of Campaldino in 1289, and in the Guelf victory at Caprona in August of that year.

As a first step toward holding important public offices, Dante joined the Guild of Physicians and Apothecaries in 1295. That same year he served on the People's Council of the Commune of Florence and as a member of the council that elected that city's Priors. In 1296 we find him on the Council of the Hundred, an influential political body involved in Florentine civic and financial matters. He traveled as ambassador to San Gimignano in 1300 and was himself elected that year to the high office of Prior. Again as ambassador, the White Guelfs (his faction) sent him to meet with the Pope at Anagni. While he was away, the Whites lost power and their rivals, the Black Guelfs, exiled Dante for two years. They charged him with conspiracy against the Pope and Florence. Dante refused to appear at his hearing in 1302 or to pay his fines, since he thought doing so would be an admission of guilt. The Blacks told him that if he ever returned to Florence he would be arrested and burned alive. There is no evidence that he ever saw his beloved Florence again.

From 1303 on, Dante traveled extensively in northern Italy and lived the rest of his days as a courtier and teacher in exile. In 1303 he stayed in Verona with Bartolomeo della Scala, and in 1304 appeared in Arezzo plotting a re-entry into Florence with other exiled Whites and Ghibellines. This failed disastrously and Dante probably moved on to Lunigiana, where he performed diplomatic services for the Malaspina family from 1305-07. Some historians think he journeyed to Paris in 1309 to study at the University, although there is little evidence to support this. From 1312-18 he lived in Verona, again with the Scala family, this time under the patronage of Can Grande della Scala, to whom he dedicated his *Paradise,* the third volume of the *Divine Comedy.* While in Verona, the Florentine government again sentenced Dante to death and this time extended the threat to include his sons. From

1318-21 Dante was in Ravenna under the protection of Guido Novella da Polenta, surrounded by eager pupils and highly praised as the author of *Convivio*, *Inferno* and *Purgatory*. On September 13 or 14, in 1321, Dante died in Ravenna, where he is buried.

## Plot Summary

Dante's *Divine Comedy* is bewilderingly complex to the first-time reader, even on the literal level. (This complexity remains after many rereadings, but for many readers, it enhances the poem's appeal rather than hindering the reader's understanding.) Trying to keep track of the poem's more than five hundred characters often produces frustration, as do attempts to sort out thirteenth- and fourteenth-century Florentine politics and the city-state's conflicts with the papacy. However, Dante lived during a time when categorization—the orderly arrangement of knowledge—bordered on the obsessional, and his *Divine Comedy* is no exception. Indeed, it is a prime example of this drive to order. Therefore, its very structure helps the reader navigate and make sense of its complex world.

The poem is divided into three books or *cantiche*: *Inferno, Purgatory,* and *Paradise.* Each book is then broken down into *canti* or what we might call chapters: *Inferno* has thirty-four, *Purgatory* has thirty-three, and *Paradise* has thirty-three. There are, then, a total of one hundred *canti,* and each volume has thirty-three chapters. (The first one in *Inferno* introduces the entire poem and thus in a sense stands alone.) This ordering system is a prime example of medieval Christian numerology, the science of attributing religious significance to numerals. In this system, three is the ideal number, since it represents the Holy Trinity: God the Father, Christ the Son, and the Holy Spirit. One hundred, the number of *canti* in the poem, is the square of the perfect number 10. One hundred represents the belief that the Father, Son and Holy Spirit are individuals yet indivisible from one another: $100 = 1 + 0 + 0 = 1$. This simple example only hints at the extent to which *Divine Comedy* uses such tight structures to produce meaning and to deliver its message of salvation.

### *Inferno: Layout and Journey*

Dante's Hell is cone-shaped and points to the center of the earth. Dante divided his Hellish cone into a hierarchy, an orderly structure that he split into two major divisions, upper and lower Hell. Three rivers circle around three levels of the cone. As they circle, the rivers Acheron, Phlegethon, and Styx flow down to the pit at the bottom of Hell. There they become part of Cocytus, the ice lake which imprisons Lucifer.

Through this region (Hell) Dante sent his alter ego, the Pilgrim, and Virgil, the Pilgrim's guide. Virgil was one of the greatest classical Latin poets. He wrote the *Aeneid,* which starts after the Trojan War and tells the story of Aeneas, the Trojan hero who founded Rome—at least according to Virgil. In general, Virgil represents Reason, a quality the Pilgrim needs to get him through the first two regions, Hell and Purgatory. When he reaches the third, Paradise, his faith largely takes over, although he is guided there, too.

Upper Hell has a vestibule (an entry way) and nine levels around and down which the Pilgrim and Virgil travel. Upper Hell's five levels correspond to five of Christianity's seven deadly sins: lust, gluttony, greed, sloth, and wrath. Lower Hell holds the shades of those guilty of the other two deadly sins, envy and pride. Starting at the top, at ground level, and working downward, the divisions of upper Hell are: 1) the Vestibule, which holds the indecisive, including the angels who sided neither with God nor with Lucifer during his revolt; 2) Circle One, Limbo, where those, like Virgil and other Classical poets and philosophers, who lived before Christ's birth, are; 3) Circle Two, the lustful; 4) Circle Three, the gluttons; 5) Circle Four, the greedy and wasteful; 6) Circle Five, the wrathful. Here stands the City of Dis, which separates the upper and lower regions.

Circle Six begins lower Hell and is the level on which the heretics are punished. Circle Seven punishes three groups of sinners: those who were violent against their neighbors, against themselves (the suicides), and those who were violent against art, nature, and God. The Great Barrier, a sheer drop, separates Circle Seven from the rest of lower Hell, and Dante and Virgil descend to it on the back of Geryon, a fantastical, multicolored beast with the face of a man and a scorpion's tail. Circle Eight is divided into ten concentric circles. These circles are called ''evil ditches,'' or *malebolge,* and are crossed by seven bridges, which radiate out from the center like a spokes on a wheel. All seven bridges are broken over the sixth ditch. Into each ditch, or *bolgia ,* are placed sinners: 1) panderers and seduc-

ers; 2) flatterers; 3) those guilty of simony, of selling pardons for sins; 4) sorcerers; 5) barrators, those who provoked discord or division; 6) hypocrites; 7) thieves; 8) deceivers; 9) others who provoked discord or division; 10) falsifiers.

Circle Nine, the last, holds the worst group of sinners: traitors to family, country, guests, and lords. This vast ice lake, Cocytus, is divided into four Circles: 1) Caina; after Cain, the Bible's first murderer; 2) Antenora, after Antenor, the treasonous Trojan warrior; 3) Ptolomea, either after the biblical Ptolemy, who had his father-in-law and two sons killed; or after Ptolemy XII, the Egyptian king who invited Pompey to his kingdom and then killed him; 4) Judecca, after Judas Iscariot, who betrayed Christ. At the center of this lake stands three-headed, six-winged Lucifer, the arch-traitor, who rebelled against God and was banished from Heaven. He is frozen from the waist down. Each of his three heads chews on a legendary traitor: Judas Iscariot, Marcus Brutus, and Caius Cassius. These last two participated in the assassination of Julius Caesar and combine with Judas to create an evil perversion of the Holy Trinity.

On each level the Pilgrim and Virgil encounter the shades of sinners who have committed the sins for which they are being physically punished. The deeper into the cone the travelers descend, the more serious the sins become. As the Pilgrim sees and talks to these shades, he learns about the nature of sin and about using reason to avoid committing sins. Most importantly, he learns to hate the sin and not the sinner; he discovers the difference between feeling sorry for the sinners and pitying their plight.

In Dante's orderly system, all the sinners' punishments fit their crimes. Dante called this kind of punishment *contrappeso,* counterpoint or counterbalance. For example, in Canto 5 of the *Inferno,* the Pilgrim meets Francesca da Rimini and Paolo Malatesta. These two lovers committed adultery and were murdered by Francesca's husband. Their eternal punishment is to be blown round the fifth level by a hot wind that symbolizes passion—and they are joined together, inseparably, for all time. To show how much the Pilgrim has to learn at this point, Dante demonstrates the Pilgrim's sorrow for these sinners. The Pilgrim does not understand that Francesca lies when she claims that she and Paolo loved each another. He does not understand that it was the lust they felt, and acted on, and not love, that condemned their souls to damnation. The misguided Pilgrim is so affected that he faints after listening to Francesca's story. By the time he reaches Lucifer in Hell's pit in Canto 34, though, the Pilgrim has a fuller knowledge o the true nature of sin. Then, and only then, is he ready to follow Virgil, to climb out of Hell and up the Mountain of Purgatory.

## Purgatory: Layout and Journey

When they emerge from Hell's pit, the Pilgrim and Virgil find themselves at the foot of the Mountain of Purgatory. This very steep mountain rises at a more than forty-five degree angle, and the narrow paths that circle toward its summit are dangerously unrailed. Sinners are not condemned to Purgatory forever. They are there to do penance for their sins. As in Hell, these penances fit the sins. Penance is not punishment; it is remedial and corrective. This is the primary difference between Hell and Purgatory: the shades in Purgatory have time and the desire to learn from their sins. They know that they will someday rise to Heaven. Hell, on the other hand, is a hopeless place. At the Last Judgment it will be sealed forever, and its residents exist with no opportunity for repentance, completely without hope. This is the worst punishment possible in the Christian universe.

Dante invented the Mountain and placed it opposite Jerusalem, in what medieval mapmakers thought was the uninhabited southern hemisphere. Since these mapmakers thought this hemisphere was landless and covered with water, it makes sense that Purgatory is a mountain and an island. This region's layout is somewhat simpler than Hell's. Dante divided his Mountain into four levels: Antepurgatory, Lower, Middle, and Upper Purgatory. These last three make up Purgatory proper, and Antepurgatory is like Hell's vestibule or entryway. Atop it all sits the Garden of Eden. The four levels are further divided into circles and terraces. Antepurgatory at the bottom has two circles, and these regions have earthly landscapes. (The sun even rises and sets on the Mountain.)

Purgatory proper is made up of seven terraces, all of which are composed of nothing but bare stone. Counting the Garden of Eden at the peak, Antepurgatory's two circles and Purgatory proper's seven levels, there are ten levels in all. The most sinful inhabit the lower levels and are farthest from God.

The first and lowest level of Antepurgatory is home to two groups of sinners who have not yet begun their penance. This first group contains the excommunicated. The second group inhabits ter-

*Dante encounters Pope Adrian V in Hell.*

race two and contains three subgroups, all of whom lacked spiritual passion. They were, in a sense, spiritually indifferent. On the third terrace, just above these late repentants, is Peter's Gate, which an angel guards. The Pilgrim must pass through this gate before he moves to the seven upper terraces of Purgatory, each of which contains shades who committed one of the seven deadly sins. On these levels temporarily reside those who misused love: the proud, the envious, the wrathful, the slothful, the greedy, the gluttonous and the lustful. This order reverses that of Hell, which has the lustful at the highest level and the proud in the pit at the bottom. Therefore, the Pilgrim moves from worst sin in Hell to worst sin on the Mountain. When he reaches the peak, he meets Purgatory's least sinful souls and is closest to God.

The Pilgrim's education continues as he and Virgil wind their way around and up the Mountain to the Garden, much like the souls must do who are destined for Heaven. The Pilgrim participates in his instruction in much the same was as he does in Hell. On the Mountain he encounters various groups and individuals who sinned while alive and who interact instructively with him. From them he learns valuable lessons about, among other things, humility, love of God and misuse of reason, the power of prayer and the power of poetry. Early on an angel inscribes seven ''Ps'' (for the Latin for ''sin,'' (*peccatum*) on his forehead, one for each of the deadly sins. As the Pilgrim moves upward toward innocence, one ''P'' per level is removed by an angel. Reason can lead him only so far, and after crowning his student lord of himself (*Purgatory* 27), Virgil vanishes from the Garden of Eden (*Purgatory* 30). This signifies that the Pilgrim has ''graduated'' and is ready to move to the next and highest level. He has worked his way back to a state of innocence like that lost by Adam and Eve when they lived in the Garden. From Eden, Beatrice and his faith lead the Pilgrim the rest of the way and carry him on to Paradise.

## Paradise: Layout and Journey

The historical Beatrice died at a young age, in 1290, and Dante's earthly, physical love for her became intensely spiritual. In the epic work that Dante created, Beatrice's reciprocal spiritual love for the Pilgrim motivates her to lead him to God, source of all love. This she does, as the two travelers are transported heavenward. As they soar toward God, the Pilgrim is amazed to find himself moving through space and wonders if his body or just his soul has taken flight from the Garden at the the Mountain's summit.

Beatrice and the Pilgrim find themselves at the edge of another ten-level structure. This one is comprised of nine crystalline spheres, each one placed concentrically inside the other. All revolve, providing the seven ''planets'' set in the first seven spheres with motion. (During Dante's time, astronomers believed the moon and sun to be planets. Neptune, Uranus, and Pluto had not yet been discovered.) Moving outward from the earth, Dante's planetary spheres are those of: the moon, Mercury, Venus, the sun, Mars, Jupiter, and Saturn. Past Saturn are the spheres of the fixed stars and of the Primum Mobile, or ''Prime Mover.'' Medieval astronomers believed that the stars were stationary, fixed in place in the heavens. They posited that all the stars were embedded in the surface of an immobile crystal sphere which held them all in place. Beyond this eighth sphere of the fixed stars was the ninth, the Prime Mover. God sets the Prime Mover into motion, and it turns the eight spheres below and inside it. Beyond these nine spheres is the Empyrean, which is made of pure white light. This region surrounds all the spheres. It is where the Pilgrim meets God.

Each of the spheres is inhabited by a collection of saints. Like the lower regions, the heavenly spheres and their saints are arranged in a particular order. In Paradise the souls are ordered according to the states of grace they have achieved. Those on the outside rim partake of God's blessedness to a lesser degree than those in the inner circles. Nonetheless, all are happy to be in Heaven, and all partake of God's love . Moving from the outer rim of the first sphere, that of the moon, the first seven spheres and their blessed souls are: 1) the moon and the ambitious who broke vows on earth; 2) Mercury and those who loved glory on earth; 3) Venus and those who were lovers on earth; 4) the sun and the theologians; 5) Mars and those who died as martyrs and Crusaders; 6) Jupiter and the righteous rulers; 7) Saturn and the contemplatives, men like St. Benedict and St. Bernard. In the eighth sphere, that of the fixed stars, the Pilgrim has a vision of the Virgin Mary and of the light of Christ. In the ninth sphere, that of the Prime Mover, the Pilgrim has a vision of Christ. Finally, in the Empyrean the Pilgrim has avision of God.

In Paradise the Pilgrim's education proceeds in the same way it does in the lower two regions. There are two fundamental differences here, though. The souls that the Pilgrim encounters have all fulfilled their desire for God. They have nothing to strive for or to desire, nothing to do but gaze in rapture upon the light andlove of God. Unlike the concrete regions of Hell and Purgatory, Paradise's residents do not inhabit their fleshly bodies. Therefore, they appear to the Pilgrim as sparks or as light and communicate with him via signs or symbols. For example, when the theologians appear to him, they do so in the form of a circle, the symbol of perfection. When the souls in the sphere of Mars materialize, they take the shape of a brilliant cross. As the souls in the sphere of the fixed stars return to the Empyrean, they appear like snowflakes falling upward. The poet had so much trouble explaining such phenomena that he had to invent new words to describe them. Indeed, the closer the Pilgrim gets to God, the more the poet writes that words fail him.

Beatrice leads the Pilgrim through the nine spheres and leaves him with St. Bernard, who provides him with his last instructions (*Paradise* 31). Beatrice has also functioned as the Pilgrim's teacher in this region. For example, she explains that, since human capabilities are limited, Scripture describes God in human terms in order to make him comprehensible. Beatrice also introduces the Pilgrim to a variety of blessed souls, some of whom test him to see if he has made the necessary progress. St. Peter, for instance, asks the Pilgrim some rather difficult theological questions, which he answers perfectly, proving that he is becoming ready for the ultimate vision of God (*Paradise* 24).

In Canto 33 the Pilgrim has that vision, and it comes to him as a blinding flash of wisdom. In that brief moment, he experiences everything that the blessed experience in Heaven. Thus, all of his desires are momentarily fulfilled. He returns to earth, ready and anxious to write, for our benefit, the *Divine Comedy,* so that all people might have a brief glimpse of "the Love that moves the sun and other stars" which he has experienced (*Paradise* 33, l. 145).

*Engraving of a scene from the Inferno, Canto XXII.*

## Characters

### Beatrice

Beatrice summons Virgil from Limbo (*Inferno* 2) to lead Dante the Pilgrim through Hell, up the Mount of Purgatory to the Garden of Eden. She sits with the blessed in the heavenly rose, where she waits to replace Virgil as the Pilgrim's guide (*Purgatory* 30). Beatrice, "bringer of blessedness," is therefore largely responsible for the Pilgrim's (and the poet's) salvation. The historical Beatrice Portinari (1266-90) was the daughter of Folco Portinari, a wealthy Florentine, and the wife of Simone dei Bardi. In his *Vita Nuova* (*New Life*), Dante claims to have met and fallen in love with her when they were about nine years old. The *Vita Nuova* consists of love poems Dante wrote to Beatrice, which he connected with prose commentaries. The physical love he had for her, which is the subject of the *Vita Nuova,* was transformed into the spiritual love that enabled his salvation, which is the subject of the *Divine Comedy.*

### Bice

*See* Beatrice

### The Pilgrim

The Pilgrim is Dante the poet's alter ego, a kind of "Everyman" (someone whom everyone can relate to) whose travels the reader follows, experiencing the three regions while he does. Ideally, as the Pilgrim learns from his encounters with countless shades, the reader attains, along with him, a degree of enlightenment. Virgil, author of *The Aeneid,* traditionally seen as the voice of Reason, leads the

Pilgrim through Hell and Purgatory, where the Pilgrim learns about the nature of sin in all its guises. Through Virgil's instruction, which is sometimes imperfect, the Pilgrim learns, most importantly, not to pity sinners but to have compassion for them, not to hate the sinner but the sin. Virgil takes the Pilgrim to the Garden of Eden at the top of the Mountain of Purgatory, where Matelda becomes their guide (*Purgatory* 28). She leads them through the Garden and gives way to Beatrice (*Purgatory* 30), who takes the Pilgrim the rest of the way through Purgatory and up into Heaven. There St. Bernard (*Paradise* 31) replaces her and guides the Pilgrim until he is able to travel on his own.

Dante the poet and Dante the Pilgrim are not the same, at least not until the final few lines of the poem. Dante the poet tells us that he actually made this journey to God and was told to return to earth and write what he saw. Like his Pilgrim, the poet was naive and unschooled when he entered hell's mouth. He returns to his earthly life a wiser person, secure in the knowledge that there is a place reserved for him in Heaven (which he will occupy after spending time in Purgatory for being prideful). Only after the Pilgrim makes the journey and attains the poet's wisdom through experience, only after he

# Media Adaptations

- The *Divine Comedy*, or parts of it, has inspired a number of films: Giuseppe de Liguoro directed a silent feature in 1912, called *Dante's Inferno*; in 1924, Henry Otto directed another silent version with the same title. In 1935 Harry Lachman directed Spencer Tracy, Claire Trevor, Rita Hayworth, Yakima Cannutt and Dorothy Dix in a film called *Dante's Inferno*, about a carnival concession that shows scenes from Dante's poem. Peter Greenaway produced *TV Dante: The Inferno Cantos I-VIII*. Greenaway shot his film on video for Channel Four television in Great Britain, where it aired in 1989. Tom Phillips wrote the screenplay for this highly stylized, almost experimental, interpretation of the first eight cantos of the *Inferno*. It features Sir John Gielgud as Virgil, Bob Peck as Dante's Pilgrim, and Joanne Whalley-Kilmer as Beatrice. Hard to find since its television debut, Greenaway and Phillips' graphic version is available as a Films for the Humanities videocassette. It runs 90 minutes and has been retitled *The Inferno*.

- Dante's work has inspired classical composers. In 1980 Carlo Maria Guilini, Dame Janet Baker, the Philharmonia Chorus and Philharmonia Orchestra of London recorded Giuseppe Verdi's (1813-1901) *Four Sacred Pieces*. This work sets some of Dante's texts to music and is available on a His Master's Voice recording. The thirty-fourth and final canto of Dante's *Inferno*, along with poetry by Francesco Petrarch (1304-1374), e.e. cummings (1894-1962), and Ezra Pound (1885-1972), inspired Eric Ericson's modern choir music in 1987. Ericson's contemporary compositions are available on a compact disc produced by Phono Sueica in Stockholm.

- The tradition of illustrating Dante's poem goes back almost to its composition in the early fourteenth century. Peter H. Brieger's two volume *Illuminated Manuscripts of the Divine Comedy* includes commentaries by the eminent Dante scholar Charles S. Singleton, along with a wealth of manuscript illuminations. Princeton University Press published it in 1969. Giovanni di Paolo (1403-1482) illustrated the last section of Dante's epic, the *Paradise*. John Wyndham Pope-Hennessy edited and published these illustrations with Random House in New York in 1993 under the title: *Paradiso: The Illuminations to Dante's Divine Comedy by Giovanni di Paolo*. Sandro Botticelli (1444-1510) illustrated the entire *Divine Comedy*. Sir Kenneth Clark brought out an edition of Botticelli's work in 1976 with Thames and Hudson publishers in London. The English visionary poet, William Blake (1757-1827), did a famous set of illustrations for Dante's epic. In 1953 Albert S. Roe published these as *Blake's Illustrations to the Divine Comedy*. Greenwood of Westport Connecticut reissued Roe's 1953 collection in 1977. Paddington Press in New York reissued Gustave Dore's (1832-1883) famous 1861 illustrations of the *Inferno* in 1976. This large-format edition, *Inferno Dore: The Vision of Hell by Dante Alighieri* also contains Henry Cary's translation of the poem and is available in paperback.

- Students of Dante's work now have a variety of Internet sites to visit. A good place to start is the ILT Web Digital Dante Project. Jennifer Hogan of Columbia University in New York edits this wide-ranging page, which provides, among other things, the complete texts of the *Divine Comedy* in facing-page Italian and English format. The translation is by the American poet Henry Wadsworth Longfellow (1807-1882). Also available are links to sites providing: other works by Dante; images of medieval art; a variety of Bibles; classical, medieval and Renaissance writing connected to Dante and his work; Sandro Botticelli, Dante Gabriel Rossetti (1828-1882) and Gustave Dore's images. The site's address is: http://daemon.ilt.columbia.edu/projects/dante/index.html.

meets God face to face in *Paradise* , do the poet and Pilgrim merge. There, for a brief moment, the poem's past tense shifts to the present, to Dante's Florence, where the two become one, as the poet writes the Pilgrim's vision of God and his recounting that vision.

### Ulysses

Ulysses is the crafty hero of Homer's epic Greek poem, the *Odyssey*. Ulysses is the son of Laertes, King of Ithaca, and father of Telemachus. Homer's poem tells the tale of his wandering for twenty years after the Trojan War and of his return to Ithaca. Dante created the events he tells about Ulysses and his crew and places him in hell with his Greek warrior companion, Diomede (*Inferno* 26). There he has the proud Ulysses tell of how he disobeyed Hercules' instructions and convinced his men to sail beyond the Pillars of Hercules and the bounds of the known world. He explains how they sailed into the southern hemisphere, where they saw Dante's Mount of Purgatory just before their ship was pulled beneath the waves where they all perished. Dante uses the story as a contrast to his own, which was divinely sanctioned.

### Virgil

Publius Vergilius Maro (70-19 B.C.) was one of the greatest Roman poets and is Dante the Pilgrim's guide through Hell and most of Purgatory. Virgil's *Aeneid,* tells the story of Aeneas's founding of Rome after the Trojan War and was a major inspiration for Dante's *Divine Comedy*. In the famous Book 6 of the *Aeneid,* the pagan Aeneas travels to the underworld, where he sees the wicked suffering and the virtuous living a life of comfort and ease. This episode provided Dante, along with other literary accounts of underworld journeys, with the basic structure for his vision of the Christian Hell. During the Middle Ages, Virgil had a reputation as a magician and wizard. St. Augustine, the Emperor Constantine, and others thought Virgil's *Fourth Eclogue* prophesied Christ's birth. Dante the Pilgrim and Virgil encounter the Roman poet Statius (45-96) on the Mountain of Purgatory (*Purgatory* 21), where Statius claims that Virgil's *Fourth Eclogue* was responsible for his conversion to Christianity.

Virgil's *Aeneid* was the basic Latin textbook in medieval schools. Students learned grammar, rhetoric and the language by translating Virgil's Latin. Dante would have been no exception. Since Latin was the language of the literate in the Middle Ages and since most people learned it from Virgil, his *Aeneid* was one of the most well-known books. It is still used in many Latin courses today.

## Themes

The *Divine Comedy* recounts the travels of Dante Alighieri's Pilgrim, his alter ego and the reader's Everyman (a figure with whom every reader can relate ), through three regions: Hell, Purgatory, and Paradise. His goal is to reach spiritual maturity and an understanding of God's love. Having achieved his goal, the Pilgrim has the ultimate vision, a face-to-face encounter with God.

### Education and Salvation

Learning how to attain salvation is the main theme of Dante's epic and subsumes all its other themes. The *Divine Comedy* is, therefore, a tale of the Pilgrim's education and, by association, the reader's. The reader follows Dante's Pilgrim through Hell in *Inferno* and learns with him about sin's pervasiveness. The torments of the sinners, who exist forever without hope of redemption or of an end to their suffering, graphically illustrate sin's consequences. As the reader and Pilgrim move through the underworld, the shades they see and speak with provide physical examples of and exemplary lessons on the seven deadly sins. At the end of *Inferno,* the Pilgrim and reader are better able to recognize sin in its various forms and to avoid committing it. Salvation and further spiritual education are impossible without such knowledge.

In the second section, *Purgatory,* the Pilgrim and the pilgrim reader move up the Mountain of Purgatory to the Garden of Eden at its peak. Along the way they learn the value of contrition and repentance, of having to suffer for causing suffering and for disobeying God. They learn this again by seeing and interacting with shades who represent the Seven Deadly Sins but who here exemplify the desire for contrition and repentance.

The learning process concludes in the third section, *Paradise,* where a plethora of saved souls appear to the Pilgrim and explain the workings of grace and God's love to him. In this celestial region, the Pilgrim takes a series of what we might call oral exams which test his growing knowledge. Schooled by his experiences in the three regions, having gained a firm understanding of sin and grace, the Pilgrim passes his exams and graduates to the vision of God. He, then, becomes a teacher, because he returns to earth with instructions to write about his experiences for the benefit of others.

### Choices and Consequences: Providence and Free Will

Inextricably linked to the theme of education and to the soul's salvation is the theme of free will and its relation to God's Providence. Following the writings of Boethius and Thomas Aquinas, which permeate the *Divine Comedy,* Dante shows his Pilgrim and reader that God's Providence, his vision, encompasses all events and all of time. Since God knows and sees all simultaneously, he knows exactly what we will do and when we will do it. Dante's great-great-grandfather, Cacciaguida, explains to the Pilgrim in *Paradise* that this does not mean that our actions are predestined, only that God has full knowledge of them. We can and do choose how to act, how to employ our free will, and we must accept responsibility for those choices. As he does in the scene with Cacciaguida, over the course of the poem the Pilgrim comes to understand that his actions have consequences and that he bears ultimate responsibility for those consequences. This is of the utmost importance, for failing to understand this can damn one for eternity, as it has those in Hell.

### Art and Experience: The Power of Literature

Closely tied to the themes of education and the correct use of free will is that of literature's power to influence its readers' actions. Dante made the revolutionary decision to write his poem in Italian and not Latin—the language of epic, of the Church and of lofty themes—so that it would reach a wider audience. Among other things, he meant his *Divine Comedy* to be an example, to focus the reader on the next life and, if necessary, to change the way he or she was living this life. Some scholars have gone so far as to suggest that Dante expected his poem to be read with the same seriousness as Scripture.

Dante himself was profoundly influenced, poetically and spiritually, by sacred and secular texts from his own time and from the ancient past. Perhaps most telling for this theme was the impact Augustine's *Confessions* had on him. In Book 8 of that important work, Augustine (354-430) writes about the power of literature to convert and uses himself as a moving example. He tells of sitting in a garden during a time of intense emotional and spiritual turmoil. In his moment of greatest anxiety,

he heard a voice telling him to open the book he had with him to a random place and to read. Doing so, he finds St. Paul's Epistle to the Romans, the story of his conversion to Christianity (13.13). Paul's tale has such a profound effect upon Augustine that he puts down the book, reading no further. Immediately, his suffering is relieved and he converts to Christianity.

Dante used this episode from the *Confessions* to make a point about the power of literature and the need for correct reading. In *Inferno* (5), Dante has Francesca tell of the effect reading had on her and Paolo, her lover. They were not reading Scripture like Augustine, but a medieval romance, *Lancelot.* Francesca says that she and Paolo reached the place where the lovers in the tale kiss. Then, echoing Augustine, she says they read no further, implying that they consummated their adulterous relationship and that *Lancelot* inspired the act. The difference between these two reading episodes is clear: both readers were affected by the power of the tales they were reading, but Augustine read Paul's account correctly and took up the faith. Francesca and Paolo allowed the medieval romance to negatively affect their actions. For "misusing" the text and their free will, they must spend eternity in Hell.

The other major example of this theme, and one that counterbalances the Francesca episode, is the meeting between the Pilgrim, Virgil (70-19 B.C.), and Statius (61-96 A.D.), the poet in *Purgatory* 22. Ecstatic at meeting Virgil, the great pagan poet, Statius tells him that his *Fourth Eclogue,* a poem that the Middle Ages read as prophesying the coming of Christ, inspired him to convert to Christianity. Unlikely as this might seem, Dante uses it as another example of the power of literature and the need for right reading, for correctly employing free will in the service of salvation.

### Order and Disorder

Dante's age was a chaotic one, and his poem, particularly *Inferno,* takes the fourteenth century's sacred and secular strife as a dominant theme. He rails against corrupt popes and clergy and lashes out at politicians, assigning many of them permanent places in Hell. Nonetheless, we must understand that Dante did not hate the institutions of Church or State. As a political and religious conservative, he saw such institutions as vital to maintaining social and spiritual order. Indeed, Dante hoped for a reduction of papal political involvement and that an

# Topics for Further Study

- Compare Aeneas's encounter with the souls of the dead in Book Six of Virgil's *Aeneid* to Dante's Pilgrim's meetings with some dead souls in the *Inferno*. How are the encounters similar? How are they different? Why?

- Choose either *Inferno,* the Mount of Purgatory, or the heavenly rose in *Paradise Lost.* Following Dante's description, and consulting any modern illustrations you are able to find, redraw the levels. Choose five levels and put contemporary public figures on them. Give reasons for your choices and placements, according to Dante's explanation of what happens on each level.

- Dante lived in political exile while he wrote the *Divine Comedy*. Research the politics of early fourteenth-century Florence. Use your research findings to explain Dante's criticism of his own city in *Inferno* or *Purgatory*. Focus on no more than two characters.

- Dante's love for Beatrice Portinari was at first physical and earthly, and he wrote love poetry to her. He later idealized his love as something pure and holy, apart from physical attraction. Research their historical relationship. Explain how Dante in *Purgatory* and/or *Paradise* turned Beatrice into his teacher and guide to salvation.

omnipotent Christian emperor would arise and restore order to his chaotic world. He had great faith in Emperor Henry VII's ability to do so. Unfortunately, Henry was never able to overcome his political opposition nor to maintain papal support, and his unifying efforts failed.

A supporter of institutions in the abstract, Dante was angry with those individuals he thought abused their offices or who were corrupt in other ways. For example, he placed Pope Nicholas III (d. 1280) in Hell, angrily stuffing him upside–down in a hole, where tongues of fire eternally "baptize" the soles of his feet (*Inferno* 19). He then goes a step further and prophesies that Boniface VIII (1217-1303) and Clement V (d. 1314) will join Nicholas in his hellhole, where they too will pay for perverting the papacy. Politicians fare no better, particularly the Ghibellines, members of the political party that exiled Dante from Florence. For instance, the Pilgrim finds the Ghibelline leader, Farinata degli Uberti, entombed with other heretics in Hell (*Inferno* 10). Dante was not above condemning members of his own party, the Guelfs, to Hell either, as we see in the circle of violence. There Guido Guerra and Tegghiaio Aldobrandi run after the green flag with the other naked sodomites.

Dante's *Divine Comedy* is itself representative of the need he felt for the comfort that comes from order and stability. It is almost as if Dante, through the order he built into his poem, was trying to counteract the disorder he saw all round him. As the last great hierarchical epic of the Middle Ages, this intensely ordered poem attempts to synthesize and summarize the histories of pagan and Christian thought and to weave those systems into a cohesive whole. The sheer complexity of this whole, however, almost works against its author's need for order and desire for comfort by illustrating just how difficult—if not impossible—constructing and maintaining such a complex system can be.

## Style

Not all epics conform to one definition; however, they share enough of the same poetic characteristics so that we can group them under the genre label of epic. Traditionally epics deal with grandly important themes, often begin "in the middle of things," *in medias res,* take place over an extended period of time and a large area, have a large cast and involve heroic, often legendary, characters. In keeping with their serious subject matter, epics often involve the gods or God in some way. They are narrative in form; in other words, they tell a story. Epics are written in verse of a high register; that is, their authors use formal language and poetic devices like symbolism, metaphor and simile, which is a kind of metaphor or figurative language. Dante's *Divine Comedy* utilizes all of these characteristics.

Dante's epic tells the story of the Pilgrim's journey from sin to grace. For medieval Christians there was no loftier theme about which to write than the soul's salvation. As the poem opens, Dante the Pilgrim, the poet's alter ego, finds himself lost in sin, wandering ''in the middle of the road of our life'' (*Inferno* 1, l. 1). The Pilgrim is at the midpoint along the road of his life, a familiar metaphor. The plural pronoun ''our'' pulls the reader into the action and includes him or her as virtual pilgrims on this journey to God. Thus, the Pilgrim stands for all Christians, who may read and learn, as he learns, the nature of sin and how to overcome it.

Along with this lofty theme and beginning in the middle of things, the *Divine Comedy* takes place over a number of days and an infinitely large area. The narrative action stretches from Good Friday to Easter Sunday. The setting encompasses nothing less than the entire universe, and includes places like the Mountain of Purgatory that Dante invented specifically for the poem. Dante's Pilgrim travels with his guide, the classical epic poet Virgil (70-19 B.C.), through the depths of Hell, up the Mountain of Purgatory and through the heavenly spheres to meet God face to face.

The theme and scope of this epic are matched by its huge cast of characters, many of them legendary, even mythological. There are over five hundred characters in *Divine Comedy,* each of them somehow instrumental in the Pilgrim's theological instruction. There are countless Italian contemporaries of Dante the poet, pagan and Christian heroes and martyrs, kings, queens, emperors, empresses, devils, angels, saints, philosophers, theologians, the Blessed Virgin Mary, Christ and God the Father himself. There are also a number of poets, past and present. The most important, of course, is Virgil. What more important guide could an epic poet have than Publius Virgilius Maro, whose name—along with that of Homer—is virtually synonymous with the title of epic poet? Virgil's *Aeneid,* the tale of

Aeneas' wanderings after the Trojan War, remains one of the great epics of all times. Book 6 of the *Aeneid ,* in which the hero, who is predestined to found Rome, travels to the underworld was especially inspirational to Dante.

The *Divine Comedy*—like the *Aeneid* and Homer's *Iliad* and *Odyssey*—devotes a good deal of time to supernatural beings. Being a Christian epic, of course, Dante's divinities are saints, angels and the Trinity. All of these divine characters intervene in some way to speed the Pilgrim along on his trip to the Empyrean, that space of pure white light where God dwells. The Virgin Mary notifies St. Lucy that Dante is in spiritual trouble. St. Lucy, in turn, notifies the blessed Beatrice, who sends Virgil to guide her Pilgrim, the man who loved her on earth, through Hell and Purgatory.

Dante chose to tell this massive tale of his Pilgrim's trip through the three regions in verse, following the epic form. However, he did not write it in Latin, then the language of the Church and of most serious religious poetry. Dante wrote in the vernacular, in the Tuscan dialect of his people. He did so because he wanted his message to be available to a wider audience, to include more than just those who could read Latin. Even though he wrote in the common tongue, his diction, the type of speech he used, is of the highest register, which perfectly suited his purposes.

Flexible and expressive though it was (and is), Dante's Tuscan dialect was not completely up to the task. This is no criticism of the language, for it is doubtful whether Latin or any other language would have suited him any better. The problem was that many of the things Dante needed and wanted to represent were just too otherworldly. Put another way, he had trouble describing God and parts of his Creation. Dante invented words, most famously the nearly untranslatable *trasumanar,* and had to resort to metaphor, to figurative language, consistently as he tried to replicate Creation. The section in which *trasumanar* occurs stands as a good example of the poet's acknowledging his impossible task: ''The passing beyond humanity [*trasumanar*] may not be set forth in words'' (*Paradise* 1, l. 70). The closer his Pilgrim gets to God and the more he transcends (his) humanity, the more frequently Dante confesses that language fails him. Indeed, on a truly profound level, the entire poem is a metaphor, a figure for a journey that perhaps never happened but that seemingly had to have happened for Dante to write about it for his readers.

## Historical Context

### Papacy and Empire: The Decline

Dante Alighieri was born into one of the most chaotic periods of Western European history. His birth in 1265 and death in 1321 meant that he witnessed the decline of the two most powerful social institutions of the Middle Ages, the Holy Roman Empire and the papacy. This degeneration—this loss of power, control and respect—affected Dante emotionally, psychologically and politically. The conflicts between Church and State constitute a major thread in Dante's *Divine Comedy* and are the subject of his Latin treatise *De Monarchia* (*On Monarchy*). This work is his plea for a universal monarchy, one that would co-exist peacefully with a pope who would hold spiritual sovereignty over the same subjects.

The process of decline began well before Dante's birth and continued long after his death. By the thirteenth century, the papacy's interests had grown ever more political and less and less spiritual. As C. Warren Hollister writes, it was at this time that the papacy "[lost] its hold on the heart of Europe" (*Medieval Europe: A Short History,* p. 206). By moving into national and imperial power politics and business, it created and widened the gulf between its increasingly secular agenda and the increasing spiritual needs of its members. Not only had the Church lost the respect of its flock, it found itself constantly at odds with purely secular authorities. Kings of Western and Northern European countries were centralizing their power during the thirteenth century and felt threatened by the presence in their midst of this independent, very powerful institution. These monarchs found themselves in constant conflict with this massively influential power, an institution controlled from Rome and therefore less easy to control on a local level, for the hearts, minds and coffers of its subjects.

This was particularly true of the kings of England and France. After Boniface VIII passed the bull *Unam Sanctum* in 1302, declaring that all Christians concerned with the salvation of their souls owed allegiance to the papal monarchy, things decidedly took a turn for the worse. The king of France, Philip the Fair, captured Boniface at his palace in Anagni and tried to spirit him off to France for trial (Hollister 208). Philip's spiritual coup failed, but Boniface died in shame soon after. After Boniface's death, the body of cardinals elected the politically subservient Frenchman Clement V pope. Clement's mov-

ing the papacy from Rome to Avignon in 1309 instituted the so-called Babylonian Exile or Captivity, which lasted until 1377 and meant the end of the strong medieval papacy.

The secular empire fared no better. Moving back three decades or so before Dante's birth to the reign of the Sicilian-born Emperor Frederick II, it seems that chaos was the norm in the secular realm, too. Pope Innocent III was Frederick's mentor and supported his bid for the throne, thus demonstrating one significant instance of papal involvement in secular politics. Frederick's desire to unify a fractious Italy and to make it the imperial center earned him the hatred of the papacy, caused him to lose a good portion of his German holdings and set much of Italy against him in rebellion. His enterprises made particular enemies of Gregory IX and Innocent IV. These popes built political alliances and used all their powers and sanctions to thwart Frederick's plans, until 1245 when Innocent and a universal Church council excommunicated this enemy of the papacy, this "Antichrist." Frederick, deposed, died in 1250 and was not succeeded until 1273. In that year, Rudolph the Hapsburg was crowned Emperor after a nineteen–year interregnum that further weakened the already unsteady imperial monarchy. Like Frederick in Italy, Rudolph wanted to extend and solidify his holdings, and, like his predecessor, aroused nothing but princely discontent. This discontent and the events leading up to it meant the start of 600 years of German instability (Hollister, p. 205). Henry of Luxembourg followed as Emperor in 1308, submitted to papal authority and pledged to restore peace, beginning with Italy. Dante had high hopes for Henry's monarchy, hopes which were never fulfilled. By this time Dante had grown more and more critical of Florentine politics and of the papacy, and went so far as to urge Henry to attack Florence in 1311, when he was in Italy for his coronation. The Emperor marched on Florence, but his efforts failed and meant "the end of Dante's hopes for the reestablishment of effective imperial power in Italy in the foreseeable future" (Chiarenza, *The Divine Comedy: Tracing God's Art,* p. 3).

### Florence: Civic Strife

Before and during Dante's time, Italy was, as Charles T. Davis writes, "a peninsula united by language and history but not by any central government." Indeed, "Italy remained, after the failure of Frederick II's attempt to conquer her, in her habitual state of political chaos" (*Dante's Italy and Other Essays,* p. 1). Dante was intensely displeased with

# Compare & Contrast

- **circa 1300:** Dante's understanding of the universe, knowledge of which is key to understanding his work, was based upon the ideas of the Greek astronomer, mathematician and geographer, Claudius Ptolemy (circa B.C. 100-circa 178). Ptolemy asserted that the stars and planets were embedded in crystalline spheres that revolved around the earth. This geocentric (earth-centered) belief placed earth and humanity at the center of all creation, in the location of greatest importance.

  **Late twentieth century:** In 1543 the Polish scholar, Nicolaus Copernicus (1473-1543), published his theory that replaced Ptolemy's. Copernicus argued that the earth is not the center of the universe, but that it and all the planets in our solar system revolve around the sun. This heliocentric (sun-centered) system changed classical and medieval notions of humanity's importance in the grand scheme of creation and became the foundation of modern astronomy.

- **circa 1300:** Dante believed that the southern hemisphere was covered with water and therefore uninhabitable. World maps from the period illustrate this view and show only the inhabited northern hemisphere. Dante's creation and placement of the Mountain of Purgatory—with the Garden of Eden at its peak—in the apparently uninhabited southern region were original to him. Nonetheless, he followed mapmaking conventions, also illustrated on some medieval world maps, which held that the Garden was, although earthly, very hard to reach. Such maps usually place it in the east, sometimes as an island, and show it surrounded by stone walls and a ring of fire. This is the island Ulysses and his crew see (*Inferno* 26, ll. 133-42), the one Virgil describes to Dante the Pilgrim as they leave Hell (*Inferno* 34, l. 121) and is the one the two climb in *Purgatory.*

  **Late twentieth century:** Just after Dante's time, in the early fourteenth century, seamen began to travel more widely and mapped much more of the oceans, seas and shorelines. The Age of Exploration produced more accurate maps that changed dramatically the way people like Dante saw the earth. This image has changed even more with space exploration in the last decades of the twentieth century.

- **circa 1300:** Although Western Europe during Dante's time was changing and expanding rapidly, it was still fundamentally hierarchical in nature—highly ordered. Christians believed that God presided over all, much like a king or emperor, and that they and all things were arranged under him in order of descending importance. The world of Dante's *Divine Comedy,* his universe, owes its shape and structure to such hierarchical notions. Beatrice and St. Bernard explain this to Dante the Pilgrim, when they show him how God's love moves and orders the universe (*Paradise* 27-33).

  **Late twentieth century:** Social structures clearly differ in the late twentieth century, although traces of medieval hierarchies remain, as do systems of class. Since at least the Enlightenment of the seventeenth and eighteenth centuries, much of humanity has become more skeptical, less ready to put all its faith in a divinely-ordered universe like Dante's.

- **circa 1300:** During Dante's time, the Christian Church was perhaps the strongest institution in Europe. The Pope's power was rivaled only by that of the Emperor, and the two were often in conflict. Along with its spiritual duties, the Church was involved in world and local politics, and learned men in all regions the Church reached spoke its language, Latin.

  **Late twentieth century:** There is no comparable global power in the late twentieth century. No single institution has such a far-ranging spiritual and political reach. The United States perhaps comes closest as a world leader. English is fast becoming the global language, due early on to the scope of the British Empire and now to the strength of American business and tourism interests round the globe.

the state of Florentine politics. Although the Florentine city-state was one of the most prosperous of its day, and although it flourished artistically, intellectually and commercially, it had long been the site of intermittent civil war, gang violence and family feuds which took on regional and even international dimensions. This highly accomplished place was, then, something of an paradox: a thriving commercial and artistic center and yet a very dangerous place to be. This paradox produced Dante's love/hate relationship with his native city. It did not help that he thought of Florence as the "most beautiful and famous daughter of Rome," as he referred to it in *De Vulgari Eloquentia* (*On the Vulgar Tongue*). We have already seen what state Rome and her Empire were in at this time.

Much of the internal strife in Florence was caused by the Guelf and the Ghibelline parties, Italianized forms for the German *Welf* and *Weiblingen*. These groups had a long-standing adversarial relationship in Germany, dating to the twelfth century. Guelfs were traditionally associated with papal power and the French monarchy and the Ghibellines with Imperial power, although the situation is far more complex than that. They were introduced into Florentine politics following a quarrel arising out of the murder of Buondelmonte de' Buondelmonti by members of the Amidei family on Easter Sunday, 1215. The Buondelmonti family headed the Guelf faction and the Uberti the Ghibelline one. After the murder, the Guelfs reached out to the papacy for support, the Ghibellines to the Empire, and Florence became bitterly divided. Their struggles lasted in earnest (although did not really end) for sixty-three years, until 1278, and control of Florence shifted back and forth, from Guelf to Ghibelline hands. In 1266, one year after Dante's death, the Guelfs regained control of Florence and began nearly 30 years of peace and prosperity. They prevailed but in 1300 split themselves into factions, the White Guelfs and the Black Guelfs. The Whites were led by the rich and powerful Cerchi, a family of prosperous merchants who eventually associated themselves with the Ghibellines. The Blacks were led by the Donati, a family with banking interests all over Europe.

Dante was intimately involved in this conflict, and although he was born into a Guelf family, he came to side with the Whites and the Ghibellines in opposition to a papal monarchy and to Charles of Valois. Dante saw military service as a member of the cavalry, which he joined in 1289. He fought with Florence and her Guelf allies against Arezzo, in their victory at the battle of Campaldino in 1289, and in the Guelf victory at Caprona in August of that year. In 1295 he served on the People's Council of the Commune of Florence and as a member of the council that elected that city's Priors. In 1296 he was on the Council of the Hundred, an influential political body involved in Florentine civic and financial matters. He traveled as ambassador to San Gimignano in 1300 and was elected that year to the high office of Prior. Again as ambassador, he was sent by the Whites to meet with Pope Boniface at Anagni. While he was away, the Whites lost power and the Blacks exiled Dante for two years. They charged him with conspiracy against the Pope and Florence. Dante refused to appear at his hearing in 1302 or to pay his fines, since he thought doing so would be an admission of guilt. The Blacks told him that if he ever returned to Florence he would be arrested and burned alive. There is no evidence that he ever did return there.

## Critical Overview

Dante's poem, and particularly its allegorical qualities, provoked commentary almost from the moment of its completion. Indeed, Dante himself was perhaps its first critic. In a letter he wrote to his patron, Can Grande della Scala, the man to whom he dedicated the *Paradise* , Dante suggested that his poem should be read on four levels. The first level is the literal one. On this level, the poem is about a physical journey toward God taken by the poet himself. The other three levels are allegorical, abstractly symbolic, and very complex. From the beginning of its public life, commentators have extracted and studied these abstract allegorical meanings of Dante's epic, to dig deeper meanings out of its literal level just as they did with Holy Scripture. As Ricardo Quinones notes in *Dante Alighieri,* 1979, there were twelve commentaries written on the *Divine Comedy* from Dante's death in 1321 to 1400. Dante, a political exile, was praised in the year of his death by his fellow Florentine, Giovanni Villani, who included a biography and praises of Dante in his chronicle of Florence. Dante's sons Jacopo and Pietro were the first to write commentaries on the *Divine Comedy,* and their work, like that of other early commentators', is vital to our understanding of the socio-cultural references that pervade the work. (Many of these commentaries are now online and accessible through the Dartmouth Dante Project.)

The Florentine poet Boccaccio (1313-75) was the first real keeper of the flame, though. He wrote the first life of Dante and gave the first university lectures on the *Divine Comedy* in Florence during the academic year 1373-74. His correspondence with the poet Francesco Petrarch (1304-74) is particularly revealing, because it provides us with a glimpse of the beginnings of a poetical rivalry with Dante that was to continue for years and because the correspondences reveal that Petrarch felt rather envious of his contemporary's popularity. It was not until 1481, though, that Dante's name was fully restored in his native Florence. That year the city produced a major edition of Dante's poem in which Cristoforo Landino referred to him as "divino poeta," the divine poet. This adjective, as Quinones reports, was used in the 1555 Venetian edition of the work and applied to the title. From then on, the poem that Dante called his *Commedia* became known as his *La Divina Commedia,* the *Divine Comedy.*

Nonetheless, as Werner Friederich in *Dante's Fame Abroad ,* 1950, points out, such veneration was not sustained in Western Europe through the nineteenth century. Although Dante has been a major force of inspiration in English letters since Geoffrey Chaucer (circa 1345-1400), in countries where the Enlightenment took stronger hold, like France, his reception was less favorable. The predominance of rational thought there and a reliance on grammatical and rhetorical studies during the seventeenth and eighteenth centuries meant that Dante's poem fell from favor. German readers and critics valued him more during this time for his antipapal stance than as a poet, and in Spain after the fifteenth century, Friederich writes that he was "completely neglected." Dante does not seem to have made much of an impact in the United States during this time, although Thomas Jefferson was interested in his poetry. There was also the occasional article on Dante in American magazines. Interest in the United States really did not begin in earnest, though, until the nineteenth century with writers such as Ralph Waldo Emerson (1803-82) and Henry Wadsworth Longfellow (1807-82). The latter's magnificent translation of the *Divine Comedy,* published in 1867, is still read today.

In the nineteenth century, with the rise of Romanticism, things changed rather dramatically for Dante's epic. The literary-critical focus shifted from grammar and rhetoric to dramatic, historical and national concerns. Romantic critics tended to focus on the poem's drama, on the way Dante characterized the inhabitants of the three regions,

and to ignore the poem's allegorical and theological aspects. Dante's *Inferno* was the inspiration for a number of compassionate character studies. Francesco DeSanctis' famous essay on Francesca da Rimini, whom Dante placed in hell for adultery (*Inferno* 5), is a classic of the genre. For critics like DeSanctis, the value in the poem—particularly *Inferno*—derives from the pleasure the reader gets from its dramatic characterizations. This led to critical sympathizing with figures like Francesca and the belief that Dante, too, must have felt this way. Although not surprising, given the Romantics' emphasis on feeling and emotion in their own poetry, such readings of this medieval text are misguided. Using Francesca as an example, we can see that critics like DeSanctis were seduced by her poetic monologue, just as Dante's Pilgrim is. The latter faints out of sympathy with Francesca's plight because he misreads her lust for the adulterous Paolo as love.

In the early twentieth century, Benedetto Croce reacted to such Romantic readings by separating the poem's structure from its theology. Nonetheless, as Marguerite Mills Chiarenza says in *The Divine Comedy: Tracing God's Art,* 1989, Croce found Dante at his best when he was intuitive. This meant rather ironically that Croce legitimized the Romantics' focus on compassion and drama. After all, Croce argued, allegory is artificial and doctrinal—anything but intuitive—and a work that relies upon such artifice is not poetry. Although such assertions meant that Croce's theories were hard for many to accept, he did influence a large following.

Since Croce, two American Dante scholars greatly impacted readers in this country: Charles Singleton and John Freccero. Singleton's facing-page edition of the poem is the standard edition for American critics and offers a wealth of scholarship and interpretation. Singleton argued for what we might call an organic or holistic reading of *The Divine Comedy ,* and Freccero has gone even farther in this direction. According to this way of thinking, we cannot separate allegory from politics, poetic structure from theology and philosophy. We must read the poem as an allegory of creation, as Dante's attempt to mimic God's work in verse. Hence, Singleton and Freccero see and promote the importance of St. Augustine's (354-430) thought in understanding Dante's world and work. The saint's autobiographical *Confessions* stands as one of Dante's conversion models. For Freccero, seeing how Augustine turned his own conversion to Christianity and journey to God into literature, and recognizing that journey's impact on Dante, takes readers a long way toward a deeper understanding of Dante'spoem. Like Singleton, Freccero sees the poem as knowable. He thinks of it as an organic whole that readers can understand fully if they work at it .

Singleton, and Freccero after him, have revolutionized Dante studies, particularly in the United States. Their work and totalizing vision have legions of followers.

A growing number of younger scholars, like Teolinda Barolini and John Kleiner, are more skeptical of the poem's perfection. They point out what they see as cracks in its structural and allegorical armor and have produced insightful new readings of it. It seems likely that seven hundred years of study and commentary have not yet exhausted all the possible approaches to the poem.

## Criticism

### Daniel Terkla

*In the following essay, Terkla traces the Pilgrim's journey through Hell, Purgatory, and Paradise, focusing on one primary image in each of the poem's main sections to demonstrate that the Pilgrim attains wisdom (and that the reader may also do so).*

Dante's *Divine Comedy* is a poetical paradox, a brilliant failure. How can one of the great works of Western literature—one of the most innovative, profound and, in many ways, unsurpassed poems of the Middle Ages—be a failure? Put simply, neither Dante nor any poet before or after him was capable of accomplishing this impossible task: to use the imperfect medium of language to represent convincingly and accurately his journey to Paradise and, even more problematic, to write God, to represent the unrepresentable. Dante himself was aware of the impossibility of his undertaking, of course, and this drove him even harder, pushed him to lead his reader to that final, stunning vision of God. Most astonishingly, he very nearly succeeded.

As the Pilgrim travels toward God, the poet's task becomes increasingly difficult. The closer Dante moved his Pilgrim to his goal, the more regularly his language failed him, until he had to admit that his descriptive "wings were not sufficient for that," that his "power failed lofty phantasy" (*Paradise* 33, ll. 139, 142). In order to leave his reader with the essence of the moment when his "mind was smitten by a flash wherein its wish [to know the mind of God] came to it" (*Paradise* 33, ll. 141-42), Dante had to rely upon metaphor. This kind of figurative language is perhaps the most potent tool for image-making and asserts that A=B, that, for example, poem=journey. We know that Dante's poem is not a literal journey, but it is a figurative one, a metaphorical one. Seeing it in this way allows the reader to cross from A and B, to consider for him- or herself how and why this poetic pilgrimage is relevant to the road of life we all travel.

Dante's poem is fundamentally didactic, that is, instructive. In order to accommodate our low-level understanding of the poem's theological, philosophical and historical components, it guides its armchair pilgrims carefully through a plethora of unfamiliar images and mystical paradoxes. Dante managed this by constructing his world's three spaces in a logical order that is still unprecedented. As the Pilgrim experiences Hell, Purgatory and Heaven, he really re-experiences events Dante the poet claims to have had in this life. Thus, the reader follows the Pilgrim through spaces that present the poet's memories. As Frances A. Yates writes in his classic study, *The Art of Memory,*

> If one thinks of the poem as based on the orders of places in Hell, Purgatory, and Paradise, and as a cosmic order of places in which spheres of Hell are the spheres of Heaven in reverse, it begins to appear as a summa [a full collection] of similitudes and exempla, ranged in order and set out upon the universe (p. 95).

Taken together, then, Dante's remembrances, presented as striking poetic images, produce the world of the *Divino Comedy* and thus reproduce his supposed journey to Heaven.

The Pilgrim receives these images via his sight, which functions on three levels: the ocular or physical, the spiritual, and the intellectual. These levels derive from the writings of St. Augustine (354-430), which were a major influence on Dante's thought, and which correspond to stages of understanding and to *cantiche,* or what we might call books, of the *Divine Comedy:* ocular in *Inferno,* spiritual in *Purgatory* and intellectual in *Paradise.* The lowest level, the ocular, includes sensual experiences of things terrestrial and celestial. It therefore corresponds to the physical nature of *Inferno* and its closing view of "the beautiful things that heaven bears" (34, ll. 137-38). Level two, spiritual vision, and *Purgatory* mesh in the same way. In this second canticle, the Pilgrim's spiritual vision makes possible the encounters with the angels and the dreams he

# What Do I Read Next?

- *Vita Nuova* (*New Life*) is Dante's earliest major work. In *Dante's Vita Nuova: A Translation and an Essay* (Bloomington, Ind.: Indiana University Press, 1973), translator and editor Mark Musa combines 31 poems with explanatory prose and treats Dante's love for Beatrice Portinari.

- Reliable English translations of Dante's lyrics can be found in *Dante's Lyric Poetry* (2 volumes, translated and with commentary by Kenelm Foster and Patrick Boyde, Oxford: Clarendon Press, 1967).

- In *Literary Criticism of Dante Alighieri* (Lincoln: University of Nebraska Press, 1973), Robert S. Haller has collected, translated and edited Dante's own writings about literature, including the important ''Letter to Can Grande,'' in which Dante explains how to read and understand his *Divine Comedy.*

- Saint Augustine's *Confessions* had a profound influence on Dante. A wonderful translation of this work by R. S. Pine-Coffin (*Confessions,* by Saint Augustine (354-430), translated by R. S. Pine-Coffin, Harmondsworth: Penguin Classics, 1961) makes this work accessible to students.

- The *The Consolation of Philosophy* by Anicius Manlius Severinus Boethius (475?-525?), a Roman philosopher and statesman, is an important philosophical treatment of free will and predestination—issues examined by Dante in *Divine Comedy.* The translation of this work by Richard Green is the English standard for students (*The Consolation of Philosophy* by Boethius, translated and with introduction and notes by Richard Green, The Library of the Liberal Arts, Indianapolis: Bobbs-Merril Co., 1962).

- Giovanni Boccaccio and Leonardo Bruni Aretino, authors in their own rights, wrote early biographies of Dante. Boccaccio's came some fifty years after Dante died, and Aretino's followed soon after. The biographies have been translated by James Robinson Smith and can be found in *The Earliest Lives of Dante* (1901; rpt. New York: Ungar, 1963).

- Although Dante did not read Homer's epic *The Odyssey,* he knew its basic plot, was influenced by it and, like most readers, was probably awed by Homer's genius. Odysseus' trip to the Underworld, the realm of dead souls, influenced Virgil, whose *Aeneid* was Dante's poetic model. A good translation of *The Odyssey* is by Robert Fitzgerald (New York: Vintage Classics, 1961, 1963).

- John Milton's *Paradise Lost,* the great Protestant epic of the seventeenth century, tells the story of Adam and Eve's fall from grace and is in some ways a commentary on Dante's Catholic *Comedy.* Scott Eledge's edition of *Paradise Lost* is an excellent one (New York: W. W. Norton, 1975).

- Any reader of Dante's work needs a good Bible, one with solid notes and cross references. *The New English Bible with the Apocrypha: The Oxford Study Edition* (general editor, Samuel Sandmel, New York: Oxford University Press, 1976) is an excellent edition for student use.

- Virgil leads Dante's Pilgrim through Hell and to Beatrice in Purgatory. Virgil's own epic tale, *The Aeneid,* tells the story of Aeneas' founding Rome. This work, along with much of Virgil's poetry, had a profound impact on Dante. Aeneas' trip to the Underworld in *Aeneid* 6 was a model for Dante's Pilgrim's trip through hell. A fine translation of Virgil's epic is *The Aeneid of Virgil,* translated by Allen Mandelbaum, 1961 (reprint, New York: Bantam Books, 1985).

---

has. Finally, the Pilgrim's visions of the Earthly Paradise, Christ, and God in *Paradise* conform to Augustine's description of the third and highest level of vision, the intellectual.

---

The Pilgrim and reader take in images, store them in their memories, convert them to knowledge—to what Hugh of St.-Victor called "history"—and graduate to the next level of understanding. As the Pilgrim (and the reader following him) progresses from one spherical realm to the next, Dante's fictional faculty materialize, quiz and instruct him about what he has learned. Along with this instruction, Dante's unique metaphors accommodate the Pilgrim's and reader's weak understanding by converting difficult concepts into visual images that they can more easily decipher and more easily store in memory for later retrieval. These images accumulate as knowledge of sin and salvation, which Pilgrim and reader process into divine wisdom, all of which prepare them for the final vision of God in Paradise.

After graduating from each training level, the Pilgrim is ready to see with his mind, to link to the mind of God in the most profound way possible. The fact that the reader and the Pilgrim achieve one of these levels of vision in each of the three books, suggests that Dante saw them as plottable points upon an ascending scale that moves from potential damnation to certain illumination. The following three sections use this upward itinerary to demonstrate in small how wisdom is attained by focusing on one vibrant image from each canticle.

There are a number of places in the poem where one could begin to chart this progression, but the appearance of Geryon in *Inferno* 16 is the first instance of the truly outlandish. As such, it works nicely as an example of a visual image processed by the lowest level of vision, which is then firmly imprinted on the reader's memory. In this section, the Pilgrim and Virgil find themselves at the rim of the Great Barrier and in need of a way down to lower hell, the last of the three infernal regions, where sinners are punished for ever more serious levels of fraud. The travelers stand at "the verge" (*Inferno* 17, l. 32) that separates these regions. Virgil, the Pilgrim's guide and teacher, tosses his student's belt over the edge, causing the Pilgrim to wonder: "'Surely'. . . , 'something strange will answer this signal that my master follows so with his eye'" (*Inferno* 17, ll. 115-16). True to form, the strangest vehicle in the *Divine Comedy* swims into view, Geryon.

This bizarre image of fraud is a patchwork of man and painted serpent: "His face was the face of a man, so complaisant was its outward appearance, and all of the rest of his trunk serpentine; he had two paws which were hairy to his armpits; his back and chest and both sides were painted with knots and small wheels" (*Inferno* 17, ll. 10-15). Faced with this incredible apparition, the poet asks the reader to trust him, to trust this metaphorical voyage and all it represents. What better infernal example, with perhaps the exception of Lucifer, is there of Augustine's first level of vision? This is, after all, the creature on whose back the poet swears he flies down to Hell's depths: "I cannot be silent; and by the notes of this *Comedy,* reader, I swear to you, so that they may not fail of lasting favor" (*Inferno* 16, ll. 127-29). There was no need for "I swear to you," unless Dante knew or expected his reader to doubt his word—or unless he wanted to impress this image upon the reader's memory. Dante knew that the strangeness of this creature would be surpassed by the vision of Lucifer frozen in the pit of hell—not engulfed in flames as we might expect—and sets us up for it by challenging us with Geryon.

Dante's Lucifer is not just a perverted version of God; he is not the Trinity, not love, not hope, not charity, neither light nor any longer the bringer of light, not order, not calm, not peace, not harmony. The list of negative descriptors is as infinite as God is positively indescribable. Given these considerations and Lucifer's heavy corporeality, we can say with Francis X. Newman that, "The confrontation with Satan is the ultimate exercise of the [corporeal vision] since Satan is the ultimate center of corporeality" ("St. Augustine's Three Visions and the Sturcture of the *Comedy,*" *Modern Language Notes,* [1967]: 65). If we have little faith in the poet, what will we make of his final vision, of that moment when Dante writes God? Incredulous though we might be at this point, Dante schools us from his unique perspective and pulls us along with his Pilgrim, as he climbs to Heaven.

As his Pilgrim comes upon Lucifer, Dante again challenges his reader: "How frozen and faint I then became, ask not, reader, for I do not write it, because all words would fail. I was not dead nor did I remain alive: now think for yourself, if you have any wit, what I became, deprived of both the one and the other" (*Inferno* 34, ll. 22-27). This address to the reader is more intense, more insistent, than the one above. Here is no mere oddity like Geryon: this is the one and only Satan, "Belzebù" (*Inferno* 34, l. 127), cause of all the world's troubles. The address to the reader insures that close attention is paid to this dramatic manifestation of the ultimate corporeal vision. The sight of Satan is so horrific that the poet cannot explain his feelings. Language fails him and Dante tells the reader to "think for yourself"; make this image and moment yours; feel something of what I felt at the moment. Here the reader and the Pilgrim have experienced the worst of the corporeal universe; here poet, Pilgrim and reader momentarily merge in experience. After this profound encounter, we are ready to move with the Pilgrim to Augustine's second level of understanding, that of spiritual vision.

*Purgatory* 17, halfway through the *Divine Comedy,* is an excellent location from which to view this process of growth, change and education. In this section Virgil lectures on the crucial doctrine of love as driving force. This is also the point in the poem where the Pilgrim figuratively comes out of his fog to see the sun, a moment that foreshadows the poem's final vision. This is such a monumental occurrence that Dante again challenges his reader to confront a startling image and to participate in his Pilgrim's spiritual education:

> Recall, reader, if ever in the mountains a mist has caught you, through which you could not see except as moles do through the skin, how, when the moist dense vapors begin to dissipate, the sphere of the sun enters feebly through them, and your imagination will quickly come to see how, at first, I saw the sun again, which was now setting. So, matching mine to the trusty steps of my master, I came forth from such a fog to the rays which were already dead on the low shores. (*Purgatory* 17, ll. 1-9)

Dante expects the reader to match both imaginative power and figurative steps with his Pilgrim, to follow spiritually and "physically" as he ascends. Here he compares the Pilgrim's mental state to that of a man in an alpine fog, a state in which imagination cannot function because the fog of physicality and faulty vision block the light of God. A glimpse of the sun, of loving enlightenment, is necessary to drive away the confusion before the Pilgrim and reader can confront fully the solar brilliance of divine wisdom. By reading through the skin, so to speak, like Dante's mole, by seeing the through the parchment of the poem, the reader perceives a glimmer of this divine light.

Dante fittingly situates his foggy image here and requires his Pilgrim and reader to "see" at the spiritual level. This transitional space, midway through the poem, requires us to engage both our external and internal modes of sensory perception, if we are to rise to the middle level of understanding. To paraphrase Paul, here in Purgatory things are seen darkly through a glass. This is the realm of dreams, the shadowy zone where imagination holds sway:

> O imagination, which at times steals us from things outside, which does not leave man aware, even though a thousand trumpets sound, what moves you if the senses offer you nothing? You are moved by the light which is formed in heaven or by the will that sends it. (*Purgatory* 17, ll. 13-18)

Here we read as the poet calls upon his own "imagination," linking it to the reader's before wondering about its source. But what does he mean by imagination? Following Aristotle, Thomas Aquinas explained it as an interior sense, a kind of treasure chest, into which images are received through the physical senses and within which they are stored. The "light which is formed in heaven" sends down instructively helpful images to engage the reader's imagination. We store images of Geryon, Lucifer and the mole in the treasure chest of memory. As Charles Singleton notes, such "images descend into the mind directly from God, whose will directs them downward" to help us understand things divine (*Purgatory,* p. 379, n. 13-18). This fits nicely with the spherical universe in which Dante situates his *Divine Comedy.* The *Primum Mobile,* the First Mover, drives all of the other spheres, which it contains. In turn, the First Mover is contained by the Empyrean, that heaven which exists only in the mind—in the imagination—of God. This is the source of the poet's inspiration. After crossing from the sphere of the *Primum Mobile* to the Empyrean, the Pilgrim's interior vision takes over. He "sees" via his intellect, while the reader is left longing to duplicate his experience and Dante strives to write what he has seen. Fully aware of the task before him, he summons all his talent to write that final moment: "And I who was coming near the end of all I desired, as I should, raised high the desire burning in me" (*Paradise* 33, ll. 46-48).

Shifting to the present tense at the end of his poem, returning to his life in exile, Dante questions his memory before trying to describe his vision of God, the "infinite good" (*Paradise* 33, l. 81). Such a task not surprisingly brings with it descriptive failure, and Dante admits his shortcomings a number of times in *Paradise* 33: at lines 55-66, 67-75, 93-105, 106-08, 121-23, 139-41 and 142-45. In fact, Dante tells us that his memory is obliterated by this sight, and that it would be easier to remember 2500 years back to Jason's voyage with his Argonauts, the first ever: "One moment brings greater forgetfulness than twenty-five centuries. . ." (*Paradise* 33, ll. 94-96). But since the love of God survives even after human memory fails, Dante can—indeed, must—tell us of that instant when he achieved spiritual stasis, peace in God:

Therefore my mind, completely suspended, was gazing fixed, immobile and intent, and ever desirous to see more. In that light one becomes such that it would be impossible to think of turning from it for another sight; because the good, which is the object of the will, is completely gathered in it, and outside of this everything is defective that is perfect here. (*Paradise* 33, ll. 97-105)

As Mark Musa has written, here the Pilgrim witnesses "the conjoining of substance and accident in God and the union of the temporal and the eternal. . ." (*Paradise*, p. 397, n. 91-93). To depict as best he can the vision of God, Dante turns to the language of mathematics, to "Geometry, [which] is whitest, in as much as it is without error. . ." (*The Banquet* 2.13, l. 27). This is the goal toward which his massive poetic machine has moved, and the image of squaring the circle (a feat still unaccomplished) is the perfect figure for the immensity of his task:

> Like the geometer who completely sets himself to measuring the circle, and in thinking cannot find the principle which he needs, so was I at that new sight. I wished to see how the image came together in the circle and how it fit there; but my own wings were not sufficient for that, until my mind was smitten by a flash wherein its wish came to it. Here power failed lofty fantasy; but my desire and my will already were turned, like a wheel in balance that is moved by the love which moves the sun and the other stars. (*Paradise* 34, ll. 133-45).

Undaunted by his undertaking and driven by the impossibility of fulfilling it, Dante strove to mirror Creation and to lead his reader to see the "love which moves the sun and the other stars." Here Pilgrim achieves that full intellectual vision, brief but total and overwhelming understanding of the Godhead, and the reader should, ideally for Dante, desire the same. If this happens, if we experience a slight ray of this burst of light and love through Dante's 700 year-old text, we cannot but characterize the moment and the poem that led us there as brilliant.

**Source:** Daniel Terkla, for *Epics for Students,* Gale Research, 1997.

## Joan M. Ferrante

*In the following excerpt, Ferrante notes the relationship between human speech and sin in the Inferno. She notes in particular how the power of speech is distorted or entirely taken from some of the sinners who are suffering in Hell.*

In the *De vulgari eloquentia,* Dante reveals the high importance he attaches to human speech—it is the gift which distinguishes man from other creatures. Angels, with direct intuition, and animals, with natural instinct, have no use for it. Only man needs words to reveal his thoughts to others because only man has perceptions which differ from his fellow's and which, taken together, may add up to wisdom. By nature a social animal, man must draw on this wisdom in order to live in society. To have a workable government, he must be able to communicate effectively, hence speech is his most important tool.

Speech is a gift of God, like life itself, bestowed on man so that he can share in the joy of existence and the pleasure of expressing that joy. Although, as Dante points out, God knew what Adam would say, He wanted him to know the happiness of saying it. But because speech is the outward expression of man's reason, it is vulnerable to the same weaknesses of human nature—it is corruptible, always changing. As language moves further and further from its divine source, branching into various tongues and dialects, communication among men becomes increasingly difficult. This opens the way to war among nations, to strife within cities and families.

The connection between speech and sin is of ancient tradition. The confusion of tongues was visited on man at the tower of Babel as divine punishment for his pride. Echoes of this attitude towards language are to be found in the Fathers and in secular writers throughout the Middle Ages. Dante, however, is the first to use a man's speech dramatically as the symbol and betrayer of his sinfulness. ... I should like to suggest that in Dante's use of direct discourse can be seen a conscious artistic pattern which is based on the philosophic view of language expressed in the *De vulgari eloquentia.*

In Hell, the realm of sin from which the "ben dell'intelletto," God, and truth are absent, speech has lost the power to communicate in a normal way; men who have denied or abused the use of reason cannot control the outward expression of reason, speech. Either they make sounds without meaning or their words convey a meaning they did not intend. Conversely, in Purgatory, communication is facilitated by an apparent unification of language. . . . When Dante finds himself beyond the human experience in Paradise, words fail him and he begins to create new ones to describe mystical concepts, "s'india," "intrea," "s'inluia," etc. Thus we have the failure of language as a mode of communication in Hell, the unification of language in Purgatory, and the creation of language in Paradise.

The positive function of language to teach virtue and truth is seen particularly in the *Purgatorio* and *Paradiso*. The negative effects are found in the *Inferno:* the tongue as a harmful weapon, language as a means of deception, either consciously to harm or delude the hearer, or unconsciously to betray the speaker himself; we see the danger of too many words, the fear aroused by unintelligible sounds. As speech is what distinguishes man from other animals, the discourse of each sinner in Hell is what distinguishes him and his sin.

Hell itself is a great mouth, "l'ampia gola d'Inferno," as Dante calls it in the *Purgatorio* (XXI, 31–32). It is filled with horrid sounds, but its core is the terrible silence of Lucifer, parodying the perfect silence of the Trinity, in Dante's vision (*Par.* XXXIII). As we progress through Hell, we are assailed by disharmonies, wails, screams, curses, barking, hissing, but at the center, completely void of God, truth, good, there is no sound at all. Antithetically, in heaven, after the passage through realms of harmonious sound, which is increasingly difficult for the ear to apprehend, we reach perfect harmony in the utter quiet of the final vision.

The God Dante sees in *Paradiso* XXXIII is light, a light which in Hell is "silent" (*Inf.* I, 60; V, 28). What Dante hears instead as he enters Hell is a Babelic confusion of tongues and sounds: "Sospiri, pianti e alti guai . . . diverse lingue, orribili favelle, parole di dolore, accenti d'ira, voci alte e fioche, e suon di man" (III. 22–27). The sounds come from those who have lost "il ben dell'intelletto," without which language cannot function properly. The disintegration of communication is shown in various stages: it is total in the gibberish of Plutus and Nimrod, in the garbled sounds of the submerged, and in the animal noises of the monsters. Some souls can express only laments, some have lost the use of speech altogether, some, whose bodies are hidden in tombs or trees or flames, have nothing but speech left of their humanity and that speech betrays them, belieing the impression they wish to give; others seem normal in appearance and speech, but the very banality of their style reveals their state.

Since effective communication is essential to the proper working of any society, it is not surprising that Dante uses the most blatant examples of non-communication, the gibberish of Plutus and Nimrod, to enclose the sins that threaten the social order (Circles 4 to 8). Outside these circles lie

sinners who behaved like animals rather than men. Above Plutus' circle, there is only lust and gluttony, sins in which men surrendered to their animal instincts; beyond Nimrod are the traitors, men who, by consciously denying all human bonds to family, state, guest, benefactor, chose to be no better than animals. Plutus guards the circle of avarice, where men are punished for misusing material wealth. It is fitting that his incomprehensible invocation to Satan should introduce this circle, for coins, like words, are a basic medium of exchange in a civilized state—the misuse of either can disrupt the social order. Indeed, Dante often associates sinners with words and sinners with coins: users and blasphemers in the third ring of the seventh circle, falsifiers of coins and words in the tenth *bolgia* of the eighth circle. Plutus, as the classical god of wealth, represents the abuses of that means of exchange, while Nimrod, the biblical tyrant, is responsible for the confusion of tongues that resulted from his building the tower of Babel, according to medieval tradition . . . Dante's Nimrod guards a circle in which all human feeling is dead, frozen in a lake of ice. Thus, although speech remains, it no longer has power to move the hearer (cf. Dante's callous treatment of these souls). Here the intent of speech is betrayed not by the words but by the actions that precede and follow them, e.g., the cannibalism of Ugolino (XXXIII, vv. I and 76–77). Nimrod's non-words, which introduce this circle, prepare us for Lucifer who emits no sound but sends forth a silent and freezing wind of hate, a parody perhaps of the love-inspiring tongues of flame brought to the Apostles by the Holy Spirit.

Though Dante cannot make out the words of Plutus or Nimrod, he instinctively understands the threat in them and is frightened. He has the same reaction to the confused sounds that issue from the *bolgia* of the thieves (Circle 8, seventh *bolgia*); the voice he hears there is "not fit to form words" (XXIV, 65–66), but the sound is angry. The thieves of holy things, who do not recognize ownership, even of what belongs to God, and cannot, therefore, maintain possession of their own bodies, lose their power of speech periodically as they exchange shapes with serpents (the tongue, formerly "united and able to speak" [XXV, 133–134], splits and becomes forked). When they speak, their words are harsh in sound and meaning; they are an attack either on Dante (an ominous prophecy meant to distress him—"e detto l'ho perchè doler ti debbia," XXIV, 151), or on God ("Togli, Dio, ch'a te le squadro," XXV, 3). The wrathful, too, who are perceived at first by the bubbles they cause in the mud, have difficulty speaking; they "gurgle a hymn in their throats," since they cannot form complete words (VII, 125–126). When one of them does emerge from the mud, he also attacks Dante. We might note that the rivers of mud, blood, and pitch all discourage speech to some extent, perhaps to contrast with the "fountain that gives rise to a great river of speech," Virgil (I, 79–80).

The inability to express one's thoughts puts man on a level with beasts; animal-like sounds and actions, therefore, abound in Hell. Among the incontinent, the gluttons "howl like dogs," while their guardian, the mythological dog, Cerberus, barks from three throats; misers "bark" their shouts at the prodigals; the lustful are carried by a wind that "lows"—only when it is silent can they speak. Usurers lick themselves with their tongues (cf. the counterfeiters whose tongues burn; the thirst for wealth, never sated, led both groups to "make" money, figuratively or literally). Flatterers, whose tongues were "never sated with flattery" make sounds with their snouts.

Most of the sinners give vent to their feelings in moans (grief without words) or curses (a direct perversion of God's gift of speech), but there are others who are unable to make any sound at all: falsifiers of person, who gave up their own personalities to assume someone else's, have lost the expression of personality and rage through the tenth *bolgia* of fraud, silently biting and tearing at others. The false prophets can only weep silently while Virgil, the true prophet, names and describes them to Dante. These are allowed no opportunity to defend themselves or to request sympathy; indeed Virgil harshly condemns the pity Dante feels for their distorted bodies. Their heads are twisted so they face backwards, as if in an extreme "parlasía" (XX, 16), Dante says, using an odd word for paralysis, probably to incorporate the pun on speech. Some of the schismatics are also deprived of speech, which they had used to tear apart various human and social bonds, and in a particularly graphic way: one has his throat cut and his windpipe exposed, another a slit tongue; Bertran de Born carries his head (the source and outlet of words) in his hand. Dante is so appalled at the sights of this *bolgia* that words fail *him.*

In contrast to those who have lost the power of speech, some sinners—suicides, simoniacs, counselors of fraud—have nothing left of their human selves but speech. The suicides who destroyed their bodies have lost even the semblance of them and are confined within trees and plants. They still have speech, but only at the cost of great pain; when a branch is torn off or a wound made in the bark, blood and words pour out, hissing like sap in a burning green twig. Speech is the only relief they have, but it must be released through suffering.

Simoniacs (Circle 8, third *bolgia*) and counselors of fraud (eighth *bolgia* ), whose function on earth should have been to serve men with their tongues, the former to carry the message of love and truth, the latter to advise men towards justice and order, instead abused the highest trusts of church and state. In Hell, not only are they bodiless voices, but their infernal shapes are parodies of the organs of speech. The simoniacs are upside-down in holes that resemble baptismal fonts; their feet project from the "mouths" of the holes like tongues and, in their writhings, express the feelings of the soul. The counselors of fraud are themselves huge tongues of flame, projecting from the "throat" of the *bolgia* (XXVI, 40).

The tongues of flame in which counselors of fraud are enveloped, like the tongues of flame that lick the feet of the simoniacs, are probably another parody of the pentecostal tongues of flame through which the Holy Spirit bestowed the gift of language on the apostles, so they might spread the word of God with especial fervor . . . .

Those who surrender to the physical appetites, who ignore reason to indulge their passions, rely on words only when they cannot satisfy their physical desires: when the wind of passion stops, they talk; when they were unable to make love, they read about it. And they twist words to justify themselves.

We have seen how little control sinners in Hell have over their speech. They are unable to communicate as they wish, whether because they cannot form intelligible sounds or because their words say more than they intend them to, but the problem of communication is not restricted to sinners or to monsters. Dante, who is both an observer and a participant in the three realms he visits, also has difficulty in expressing himself to Virgil, or in describing what he has seen (XXVIII, 1 ff. and XXXII, 1 ff., though the latter is partly an artful pose—"*If* I had harsh rhymes," he says, using one), or what he thinks (II, 36 and XXX, 139), and sometimes what he hears (IX, 14–15 and XIX, 58–60) or reads (III, 10–12). When speech might be dangerous, distorted by the atmosphere of a certain circle, Virgil is made to understand Dante's thoughts without words (a Power Beatrice frequently exercises in Paradise): in the circle of the pagans, among the heretics, at the approach of fraud (Geryon), among the the hypocrites, and as they leave the falsifiers. In each case, this occurs in the sphere of sinners who dealt in falsehood or in limited truth, where words bear little relation to the truth. The one time Virgil fails to understand is as they enter the *bolgia* of falsifiers, where nothing can be trusted.

When Virgil speaks, his words are usually effective, for he is carrying out God's purpose and he has the command of language that Dante must develop and finally surpass. Virgil's assertion of the divine will that moves him is sufficient to control most of the guardians of Hell, the classical figures, although they have no power over the fallen angels. And his words have a double effect on Dante, they wound and heal XXXI, 1–3), correct and encourage. It is because of Virgil's "parola ??" (II, 67), his "parlar onesto" (II, 113), that Beatrice summoned him to help Dante. Beatrice, herself moved to speak by the force of love (II, 72), sends the most skillful poetic master of words, Virgil, to teach Dante what he must know in order to move others to good with his words. That, as Dante will learn from Beatrice in Purgatory and from Cacciaguida in Paradise, is the purpose of his journey.

**Source:** Joan M. Ferrante, "The Relation of Speech to Sin in the Inferno," *Dante Studies,* Vol. LXXXVIII, 1969, pp. 33–46.

## Dorothy L. Sayers

*In the following excerpt from an introduction written in 1948 and first published in 1949, Sayers mentions some of the factors that can make understanding* The Divine Comedy *difficult for a modern reader, and offers some pointers for understanding the work.*

The ideal way of reading *The Divine Comedy* would be to start at the first line and go straight through to the end, surrendering to the vigour of the storytelling and the swift movement of the verse, and not bothering about any historical allusions or theological explanations which do not occur in the text itself. That is how Dante himself tackles his subject. His opening words plunge us abruptly into the middle of a situation:

> *Midway this way of life we're bound upon*
> *I woke to find myself in a dark wood,*
> *Where the right road was wholly lost and gone.*

From that moment the pace of the narrative never slackens. Down the twenty-four great circles of Hell we go, through the world and out again under the Southern stars; up the two terraces and the seven cornices of Mount Purgatory, high over the sea, high over the clouds to the Earthly Paradise at its summit; up again, whirled from sphere to sphere of the singing Heavens, beyond the planets, beyond the stars, beyond the Primum Mobile, into the Empyrean, there to behold God as He is - the ultimate, the ineffable, yet, in a manner beyond all understanding, "marked with our image" - until, in that final ecstasy,

> *Power failed high fantasy here; yet, swift to move*
> *Even as a wheel moves equal, free from jars,*
> *Already my heart and will were wheeled bylove,*
> *The Love that moves the sun and the other stars.*

Yet the twentieth-century reader who starts out on this tremendous journey without any critical apparatus to assist him is liable to get bogged halfway unless he knows something of Dante's theological, political, and personal background. For not only is the poem a religious and political allegory— it is an allegory of a rather special kind. If we know how to read it, we shall find that it has an enormous relevance both to us as individuals and to the world situation of to-day. Dante's Europe—remote and strange as it seemed to the Liberals of the eighteenth and nineteenth centuries—had much in common with our own distracted times, and his vivid awareness of the deeps and heights within the soul comes home poignantly to us who have so recently rediscovered the problem of evil, the problem of power, and the ease with which our most God-like imaginings are "betrayed by what is false within". Moreover, Dante is a poet after our own hearts, possessed of a vivid personality, which flows into and steeps the whole texture of his work. Every line he ever wrote is the record of an intimate personal experience; few men have ever displayed their own strength and weakness so unreservedly, or interpreted the universe so consistently in terms of their own self-exploring. Nor, I suppose, have passionate flesh and passionate intellect ever been fused together in such a furnace of the passionate spirit. . . . .

But if Dante is to "speak to our condition", as the Quakers so charmingly put it, we must take him seriously and ourselves seriously. We must forget a great deal of the nonsense that is talked about Dante —all the legends about his sourness, arrogance, and "obscurity", and especially that libel . . . that he was a peevish political exile who indulged his petty spites and prejudices by putting his enemies in Hell and his friends in Paradise. We need not forget that Dante is sublime, intellectual and, on occasion, grim; but we must also be prepared to find him simple, homely, humorous, tender, and bubbling over with ecstasy. Nor must we look to find in him only a poet of ''period'' interest; he is a universal poet, speaking prophetically of God and the Soul and the Society of Men in their universal relations.

We must also be prepared, while we are reading Dante, to accept the Christian and Catholic view of ourselves as responsible rational beings. We must abandon any idea that we are the slaves of chance, or environment, or our subconscious; any vague notion that good and evil are merely relative terms, or that conduct and opinion do not really matter; any comfortable persuasion that, however shiftlessly we muddle through life, it will somehow or other all come right on the night. We must try to believe that man's will is free, that he can consciously exercise choice, and that his choice can be decisive to all eternity. For *The Divine Comedy* is precisely the drama of the soul's choice. It is not a fairy-story, but a great Christian allegory, deriving its power from the terror and splendour of the Christian revelation. Clear, hard thought went to its making: its beauty is of that solid and indestructible sort that is built upon a framework of nobly proportioned bones. If we ignore the theological structure, and merely browse about in it for detached purple passages and poetic bits and pieces we shall be disappointed, and never see the architectural grandeur of the poem as a whole. People who tackle Dante in this superficial way seldom get beyond the picturesque squalors of the *Inferno* . This is as though we were to judge a great city after a few days spent underground among the cellars and sewers; it would not be surprising if we were to report only an impression of sordidness, suffocation, rats, fetor, and gloom. But the grim substructure is only there for the sake of the city whose walls and spires stand up and take the morning; it is for the vision of God in the *Paradiso* that all the rest of the allegory exists.

Allegory is the interpretation of experience by means of images. In its simplest form it is a kind of extended metaphor. Supposing we say: ''John very much wanted to do so-and-so, but hesitated for fear of the consequences''; that is a plain statement. If we say: ''In John's mind desire and fear contended for the mastery'' we are already beginning to speak allegorically: John's mind has become a field of battle in which two personified emotions are carrying on a conflict. From this we can easily proceed to build up a full-blown allegory. We can represent the object of John's ambition as a lady imprisoned in a castle, which is attacked by a knight called Desire and defended by a giant called Fear, and we can put in as much description of the place and people as will serve to make the story exciting. We can show Desire so badly battered by Fear that he is discouraged and ready to give up, until rebuked by his squire, called Shame, who takes him to have his wounds dressed by a cheerful lady named Hope. Later, he is accosted by a plausible stranger called Suspicion, who says that the lady is much less virtuous and good-looking than she is made out to be.... And so forth, introducing as many personifications of this kind as may be needed to express John's successive changes of mind. In this way we can work out quite a complicated psychological pattern, and at the same time entertain the reader with an exciting and colourful tale of adventure. In this purest kind of allegory, John himself never appears: his psyche is merely the landscape in which his personified feelings carry out their manœuvres. But there is also a form in which John himself—or what we may perhaps call John's conscious self, or super-self—figures among the personages of the allegory, as a pilgrim or knight-errant, exploring the wildernesses of his own soul and fighting against opposition both from within and without. The earlier part of *The Romance of the Rose* is an example of the first kind of allegory and *The Pilgrim's Progress* of the second. In neither kind does the actual story pretend to be a relation of fact; in its *literal* meaning, the whole tale is fiction; the *allegorical* meaning is the true story.

Dante's allegory is more complex. It differs from the standard type in two ways: (1) in its *literal* meaning, the story is—up to a certain point and with a great many important qualifications—intended to be a true story; (2) the figures of the allegory, instead of being personified abstractions, are *symbolic personages*.

To take the second point first: In dealing with the vexed subject of symbolism, we shall save ourselves much bewilderment of mind by realising that there are two kinds of symbols.

A *conventional* symbol is a sign, arbitrarily chosen to represent, or ''stand for'', something with which it has no integral connection: thus the scrawl X may, by common agreement, stand, in mathematics, for an unknown quantity; in the alphabet, for a sound composed of a cluck and a hiss; at the end of a letter, for a fond embrace. The figure X *is* not, in itself, any of these things and tells us nothing about them. Any other sign would serve the same purpose if we agreed to accept it so, nor is there any reason why the same sign should not stand, if we agreed that it should, for quite different things: infinity, or a murmuring sound, or a threat. With this kind of symbol we need not now concern ourselves, except to distinguish it from the other.

A *natural* symbol is not an arbitrary sign, but a thing really existing which, by its very nature, stands for and images forth a greater reality of which it is itself an instance. Thus an arch, maintaining itself as it does by a balance of opposing strains, is a *natural symbol* of that stability in tension by which the whole universe maintains itself. Its significance is the same in all languages and in all circumstances, and may be applied indifferently to physical, psychical, or spiritual experience. Dante's symbolism is of this kind. To avoid confusion with the conventional or arbitrary symbol I shall follow the example of Charles Williams and others and refer to Dante's natural symbols as his "images".

We are now in a position to distinguish between a simple allegorical figure and a symbolic image. The allegorical figure is a personified abstraction. Thus, in an *allegorical masque,* Tyranny might be represented as a demon with a club in one hand and a set of fetters in the other, riding in a juggernaut chariot drawn by tigers over the bodies of Youth, Innocence, Happiness, and what-not, and declaiming sentiments appropriate to tyrannical passions. In a play using *symbolicimagery,* the dramatist might bring in the figure of Nero or Hitler, wearing his ordinary clothes and simply talking like Nero or Hitler, and every one would understand that this personage was meant for the image of Tyranny.

In the *Comedy,* Dante uses the allegorical figure only occasionally; by far the greater number of his figures are symbolic images. Thus, he is accompanied through Hell, not by a personified abstraction called Reason, or Wisdom, or Science, or Art, or Statecraft, but by Virgil the Poet, a real person, who is, by his own nature, qualified to symbolize all these abstractions. The characters encountered in the circles of Hell, Purgatory, and Paradise are similarly not personifications of Sin and Virtue, but the souls of real people, represented as remaining in, or purging off, their sins or experiencing the fruition of their virtues.

Being thus real personages, the images of the *Divine Comedy* are set in a real environment: Hell, Purgatory, and Heaven are not a fiction invented to carry the allegory, but a true picture of the three states of the life after death. I do not, of course, mean by this that Dante's description of them is meant to be physically accurate. He did not really suppose that Hell was a pit extending from a little way below the foundations of Jerusalem to the centre of the earth, or that Purgatory was a mountainous island in the Antipodes, or that a person could go from one to the other in his mortal body in the space of two and a half days; nor did he really imagine that Heaven was located among the celestial spheres. He takes the utmost pains to make his geographical details plausible and scientifically correct; but that is just the novelist's method of giving verisimilitude to the story. Dante knew better, and from time to time he warns his readers against mistaking a work of the imagination for a bald statement of material fact. He did, however, share the belief of all Catholic Christians that every living soul in the world has to make the choice between accepting or rejecting God, and that at the moment of death it will discover what it has chosen: whether to remain in the outer darkness of the alien self, knowing God only as terror and judgment and pain, or to pass joyfully through the strenuous purgation which fits it to endure and enjoy eternally the unveiled presence of God.

But although the *literal story* of the *Comedy* is (with the qualification and within the limits I have mentioned) a true one, and the characters in it are real people, the poem is nevertheless an allegory. The literal meaning is the least important part of it: the story with its images is only there for the sake of the truth which it symbolizes, and the real environment within which all the events take place is the human soul. . . .

We are apt to be astonished at first, in reading (say) the *Inferno ,* to find how little is actually said about the particular sin of which Dante and we are witnessing the retribution. Sometimes the souls relate their histories (as do Francesca da Rimini, for instance, and Guido da Montefeltro), but even then there is little or no moralizing on the subject. More often there is merely a description of the conditions in which the sinners find themselves, after which a character is introduced and talks with Dante upon some apparently extraneous matter which is closely related, indeed, to the subject of the *Comedy* taken as a whole, but has no special relevancy to the immediate circumstances. In showing us his images, Dante has already told us all we need to know about the sin. He has introduced us, for example, to Ciacco—a rich and amiable Florentine gentleman, well known and much ridiculed by his contemporaries for his monstrous self-indulgence: the familiar name is enough to remind contemporary readers of what Gluttony looks like to the world; he has also shown us the conditions of Ciacco's part of Hell—a cold wallowing in mud under the fangs and claws of Cerberus: that, stripped of all glamour, is what Gluttony *is,* seen in its true and eternal nature. Why waste more words upon it? Let Ciacco and Dante converse upon the state of Florence.

We now begin to see the necessity for all the notes and explanations with which editors feel obliged to encumber the pages of Dante. To the fourteenth-century Italian, the personages of the *Comedy* were familiar. To identify them, and to appreciate the positions they occupy in the Three Kingdoms of the After-world, was to combine an understanding of the allegorical significance with the excitement of a *chronique scandaleuse* and the intellectual entertainment of solving one of the more enigmatical varieties of cross-word puzzle. For us it is different. We do not know these people; nor indeed are we to-day quite so familiar with our classical authors, or even with our Bible, as a medieval poet might reasonably expect his public to be. . . .

We need to know what Dante's characters stood for in his eyes, and therefore we need to know who they were. But that is as much as we need. The purely historical approach to a work of art can easily be overdone by the general reader. Just because it puts the thing away into a "period", it tends to limit its relevance to that period. . . .

The poem is an allegory of the Way to God—to that union of our wills with the Universal Will in which every creature finds its true self and its true being. But, as Dante himself has shown, it may be interpreted at various levels. It may be seen, for example, as the way of the artist, or as the way of the lover—both these ways are specifically included in the imagery. . . . For many of us it may be easier to understand Hell as the picture of a corrupt society than as that of a corrupt self. Whichever we start with, it is likely to lead to the other; and it does not much matter by which road we come to Dante so long as we get to him in the end.

We cannot, of course, do without the historical approach altogether, for the poem is largely concerned with historical events. Neither can we do altogether without the biographical approach, since the poem is so closely concerned with the poet's personal experience. The allegory is universal, but it is so precisely because it is a man's answer to a situation—a particular man and a particular situation in time and place. The man is Dante; the time is the beginning of the fourteenth century; the place is

Florence. All Heaven and Earth and Hell are, in a sense, included within that narrow compass.

**Source:** Dorothy L. Sayers, in an introduction to *Dante: The Divine Comedy,* by Dante Alighieri, translated by Dorothy L. Sayers, Penguin Books, 1949, pp. 9–66.

## Sources for Further Study

Alighieri, Dante. *The Divine Comedy, Vol. I: Inferno; Vol. II: Purgatory; Vol. III: Paradise,* translated and with notes by Mark Musa, Harmondsworth: Penguin Classics, 1984.
Musa's unrhymed verse translation comes close to representing the meter and sense of Dante's difficult *terza rima.* This eminent Dante scholar provides a summary of each canto at its start, very thorough explanatory notes, illustrations and bibliography.

———. *The Divine Comedy,* translated and with notes and commentary by Charles S. Singleton, 3 vols, Bollingen Series 80, Princeton: Princeton University Press, 1970-75.
Singleton's facing-page, prose translation is considered by many to be the best and is therefore the critical edition of Dante's epic poem. His notes and commentary are the most thorough and provide full texts of all references, in both English and their original languages.

———. *The Portable Dante,* edited and with introduction and notes by Mark Musa, New York: Viking Penguin, 1995.
This single-volume paperback brings together Musa's earlier translations of *Inferno, Purgatory, Paradise* and the *Vita Nuova.* Like the earlier Penguin editions, this volume contains summaries of each canto, a select bibliography and illustrations. Unlike in the Penguin editions, Musa's commentary here appears in concise footnote form.

Bergin, Thomas G., ed. *Dante: His Life, His Times, His Works,* New York: American Heritage Press, 1968.
This older introductory study includes an anthology of excerpts from Dante's writings, along with a number of useful sections: a brief biography, a select chronology of the thirteenth and fourteenth centuries, a section on the arts of the time, and one on the characters in the *Divine Comedy.*

Bergin, Thomas G. *Dante,* New York: Orion, 1965.
A classic, scholarly study.

Chiarenza, Marguerite Mills. *The Divine Comedy: Tracing God's Art,* Boston: Twayne Publishers, 1989.
A study targeted to students who are new to the *Divine Comedy.* Chiarenza provides accessible information on historical context, reception, and theimportance of the poem, along with a reading of each canticle, a rather detailed chronology (1215-1321) and a nicely annotated bibliography.

Davis, Charles T. "Dante's Italy," in his *Dante's Italy and Other Essays,* Philadelphia: University of Pennsylvania Press, 1984, pp. 1-22.
Focuses upon Dante's views about language, in particular on his views about the power of Italian (not

Latin) poetry. His political and religious views are also discussed.

Demaray, John G. *The Invention of Dante's Commedia,* New Haven: Yale University Press, 1974.
> Demaray argues that Dante modeled his heavenly pilgrimage on real-life medieval pilgrimages to the Holy Land, and provides a good deal of historical and cultural information about such pilgrimages.

Fowlie, Wallace. *A Reading of Dante's Inferno,* Chicago: The University of Chicago Press, 1981.
> Fowlie provides an analysis of each canto from the first canticle of Dante's epic. Each entry concludes with a helpful section, "Principal Signs and Symbols," and the work as a whole ends with an instructive section entitled "Note on Reading Dante Today."

Freccero, John. *Dante: The Poetics of Conversion,* edited and with an introduction by Rachel Jacoff, Cambridge, Mass.: Harvard University Press, 1986.
> A difficult but valuable collection of essays by the premier American Dante scholar. Freccero's readings of selected cantos of Dante's poem offers unique and original insights.

Friederich, Werner P. *Dante's Fame Abroad: 1350-1850,* Studies in Comparative Literature 2, Chapel Hill, N.C.: University of North Carolina Press, 1950.
> A comprehensive overview of existing scholarship on Dante's infuence on the Poets and Scholars of the United States and Europe.

Giamatti, A. Bartlett, ed. *Dante in America: The First Two Centuries,* Medieval and Renaissance Texts and Studies 23, Binghamton, N.Y.: Medieval and Renaissance Texts and Studies, 1983.
> This collection of essays, edited by the eminent scholar and former Commissioner of Major League Baseball, gathers together important critical studies by American scholars from the nineteenth and twentieth centuries.

Kirkpatrick, Robin. *Dante: The Divine Comedy,* Cambridge: Cambridge University Press, 1987.
> A scholarly study that includes a section on Dante's development as a poet, an extended reading of each canticle, a short essay on Dante's "impact," and a useful "guide to further reading."

Kleiner, John. *Mismapping the Underworld: Daring and Error in Dante's "Comedy",* Stanford, Calif.: Stanford University Press, 1994.
> Kleiner investigates Dante's "enthusiasm for error," and fruitfully works against a critical tradition that seeks perfection in the *Divine Comedy.*

Mazzeo, Joseph Anthony. *Medieval Cultural Tradition in Dante's "Comedy."* Westport, Conn.: Greenwood Press, 1968.
> This fundamental collection of essays by a renowned Dante scholar deals with the structure of the *Divine Comedy* and solidly sets the poem in its cultural context.

Musa, Mark. "The 'Sweet New Style' I Hear," in his *Advent at the Gates: Dante's "Comedy."* Bloomington, Ind.: Indiana University Press, 1974, pp. 111-28.
> One of America's foremost Dante scholars explains the poet's *dolce stil novo,* the "sweet new style" of lyric poetry in which Dante and some of his contemporaries wrote.

Quinones, Ricardo J. *Dante Alighieri,* Boston: Twayne Publishers, 1979.
> Quinones discusses Dante's life and each work in the context of their cultural and historical events. Quinones' chronology (1215-1321) is less informative than Chiarenza's but provides a much more detailed history of Dante in his time.

Thompson, David. *Dante's Epic Journeys,* Baltimore: Johns Hopkins University Press, 1974.
> Accessible study providing a good discussion of Dante's use of workd by Homer and Virgil.

Toynbee, Paget. *Dante Alighieri: His Life and Works,* 4th ed., Gloucester, Mass.: Peter Smith, 1971.
> Toynbee's work, originally published in 1901, was long the standard biographical and historical study of Dante's life. It contains still-useful background information.

Toynbee, Paget. *Dante Dictionary,* rev. ed., edited by Charles S. Singleton, Oxford: Clarendon Press, 1965.
> Toynbee's original title, *A Dictionary of Proper Names and Notable Matters in the Works of Dante,* gives a general indication of its scope. First published in 1889, this work remains one the most valuable aids to the student of Dante's works.

Yates, Frances A. *The Art of Memory,* Chicago: Univ. of Chicago Press, 1966.
> Dated but still useful, especially for those interested in the role memory plays in texts like Dante's.

# The Epic of Gilgamesh

## Anonymous

## c. 1600–1000 B.C.

Although several thousand years old and written on tablets of clay, the *Epic of Gilgamesh* continues to fascinate contemporary readers with its account of Gilgamesh, ruler of Uruk; his companion, the "wild man" Enkidu; and their exploits together. Generally recognized as the earliest epic cycle yet known—prior to even *The Iliad* or *The Odyssey* —*Gilgamesh* was discovered and translated relatively recently. The *Epic of Gilgamesh* initially caught the attention of biblical critics for its episode of the "Mesopotamian Noah," that is, the character Utnapishtim, who, like his later biblical counterpart, was warned to build a great boat and stock it with animals and his family to avoid a disastrous flood. However, the epic is equally fascinating for the window it opens to the ancient and far-removed Sumerian and Babylonian cultures. Gilgamesh's struggle against the gods, the forces of nature, and his own mortality mirrors the always-contemporary endeavor to find one's place both in wider society and in the cosmos.

At the same time the *Epic of Gilgamesh* addresses these important metaphysical themes, it is equally a story of two friends, Gilgamesh and Enkidu, and their devotion to one another even after death. All in all, the *Epic of Gilgamesh* contains everything we have come to expect from great epic literature: fantastic geographies and exotic characters; exhausting quests and difficult journeys; heroic battles with monsters, supernatural beings and natural forces. It is, above all, the gripping story of

an epic hero who is driven to meet his destiny and who rises to every challenge with courage and determination.

## Author Biography

The *Epic of Gilgamesh* is not the product of a single author in the modern sense. It has come to us as the progressive creation of several ancient near-eastern cultures, specifically the cultures of the Euphrates River valley. Originally an oral composition recited by communal storytellers, perhaps priests, to a listening audience, portions of the Gilgamesh epic were repeated, probably for many generations, before being "written" by scribes in an archaic form of writing called "cuneiform." Scribes "wrote" the ancient oral stories into clay tablets with a sharply pointed, triangular stick, and the tablets telling the Gilgamesh story were kept in royal libraries. The most famous of these was the library of Ashurbanipal, king of Babylon during the seventh century B.C., but other portions of the *Epic of Gilgamesh* from different time periods have also been found. The individual stories of the Gilgamesh cycle were probably first written in cuneiform by ancient Sumerian scribes about 3,500 to 4,000 years ago. The story passed from the Sumerians through succeeding civilizations to the Babylonians, who added or otherwise adapted the Gilgamesh stories to their own culture until a so-called Standard Version of the story coalesced about 1500 B.C.

The *Epic of Gilgamesh* was lost for thousands of years until archaeologists began to discover the ancient tablets during the nineteenth century. Therefore, it is important to keep in mind that the English translation we now have of the *Epic of Gilgamesh* is the product of many scholars' work and many years of archaeological investigation, historical inquiry, and linguistic research. Even with all this academic reconstruction, we cannot be completely sure of all the details of the *Gilgamesh* epic. Some portions of the story are missing, lost on broken-off sections of the existing cuneiform tablets found buried in ancient ruins. Some aspects of its language are so obscure that modern translators cannot be sure of an exact meaning. At many points, the story we read is a reconstruction—the best guess of this or that scholar—of what the story said originally. As new tablets come to light—either containing more fragments of the *Gilgamesh* epic, or of other works in

the same language and from the same era—our knowledge of the *Epic of Gilgamesh* can grow.

Originally, the *Epic of Gilgamesh* was written as poetry, but not in the kind of rhyming verse commonly recognized as poetry by modern readers. The style was closer to the alliterative tradition of a poem like *Beowulf.* A readily available and easily readable translation of the *Epic of Gilgamesh* is the narrative version by N. K. Sandars, and many other editions are available. Sandars's translation has turned the poetic form of the so-called Standard, or Babylonian, Version of the *Epic of Gilgamesh* into a narrative or story form. Moreover, the *Epic* probably appeared originally as five or six separate Sumerian stories that were adapted by later cultures, especially the Babylonians. The current translation has divided the original story found in twelve tablets into eight sections: seven chapters and a prologue. Therefore, the *Epic of Gilgamesh* has been transformed once again in language, style, and structure for contemporary readers.

## Plot Summary

### *Prologue*

The Prologue establishes Gilgamesh's stature as the special creation of the gods: he is the son of a goddess and a human and thus partly divine. The strongest and wisest of all humans, he is also the renowned builder and king of the great city of Uruk. The Prologue sets the story in the distant past, in "the days before the flood" (l. 61), when Gilgamesh himself etched the whole story in stone.

### *1. The Coming of Enkidu*

Gilgamesh, king of Uruk, is the strongest of all men, but he is a harsh and unkind ruler. The people of Uruk describe his abuses to Anu, god of Uruk, who asks Aruru, goddess of creation, to create an equal or "second self" (l. 62) to oppose Gilgamesh and leave them at peace. Aruru creates Enkidu out of the raw stuff of nature. Enkidu is a fearfully strong, uncultured "wild man" with long hair and coarse features who runs with the beasts and eats grass. A trapper sees Enkidu at a watering hole, and tells his father about the wild man who disrupts his snares. The father advises the son to tell Gilgamesh about the wild man. Gilgamesh gives him a temple courtesan to tame the wild man. The woman embraces Enkidu, cleans and clothes him, and teaches him civilized behavior. When Enkidu is brought to

Uruk, Gilgamesh puts off his pending marriage to Ishtar, the goddess of love, and meets Enkidu, who has challenged him, in the street. They fight, and after Gilgamesh throws Enkidu, they embrace and become friends.

## 2. The Forest Journey

Enlil, father of the gods, establishes Gilgamesh's destiny to be king and achieve great feats, but Enkidu is "oppressed by [the] idleness" (l. 70) of living in Uruk. In order to establish his eternal reputation, to "leave behind me a name that endures" (l. 71), Gilgamesh purposes to travel with Enkidu to the Land of the Cedars and kill its guardian, the fearsome giant Humbaba. Gilgamesh prepares for the journey both by making a sacrifice to Shamash, who gives him the natural elements as allies; by forging a set of formidable weapons, including an axe, bow, and shield; and by seeking the intervention of his mother Ninsun, who adopts Enkidu as her own. Now brothers as well as companions, Gilgamesh and Enkidu begin their journey. On the way, Gilgamesh has three dreams, which though frightening portend a successful end to his quest. Humbaba, the guardian of the cedars, can hear an animal stir from many miles away, and he has seven fearsome "splendors" as weapons. After they arrive at the grove, Gilgamesh and Enkidu send Humbaba into a rage by cutting down one of the sacred trees. After a fierce battle, Gilgamesh defeats Humbaba, who begs for his life. Gilgamesh nearly relents, saving Humbaba momentarily, but acting on Enkidu's warning, Gilgamesh cuts off the giant's head. They present Humbaba's head to Enlil, who rages at them for their actions.

## 3. Ishtar and Gilgamesh, and the Death of Enkidu

After Gilgamesh slays Humbaba, Ishtar calls Gilgamesh back to be her groom by promising him many expensive gifts. Gilgamesh now flatly refuses her offer because of her "abominable behaviour" (l. 87), for he knows how badly Ishtar has treated her previous lovers, turning many of them into animals. Ishtar becomes angry and pressures her parents Anu and Antum to set loose the Bull of Heaven upon Uruk and Gilgamesh. Gilgamesh and Enkidu together slay the bull, proving again their great fame and prowess. Afterward, Enkidu has a dream in which a council of the gods has decreed that Enkidu must die for their deeds. Enkidu falls ill, cursing the trapper and courtesan who brought him to civilization, but Shamash reminds him how much good

came from the trapper's and harlot's action. Enkidu has a second dream about the underworld and its inhabitants, which Gilgamesh interprets as an omen of death. Enkidu languishes for days before he dies, and Gilgamesh, who mourns for seven days, offers a moving lament and builds a noble statue in tribute to his friend.

## 4. The Search for Everlasting Life

In his despair, Gilgamesh begins a lengthy quest to find the answer to life's mysteries, especially the mystery of eternal life. He decides to seek out Utnapishtim, "the Faraway," his ancient ancestor who "has entered the assembly of the gods" (l. 97) and received everlasting life. Sick at heart for the death of Enkidu and realizing for the first time his own mortality, Gilgamesh travels through the great mountains of Mashu, gate to the afterlife where the sun sets, where he defeats a band of lions. He then encounters the frightful Scorpion-Demon and his mate who guard Mashu. He persuades them to let him enter. Gilgamesh travels through twelve leagues of darkness (24 hours) until he enters the garden of the gods. There, in turn, he meets Shamash, the sun god; who discourages his quest; Siduri, goddess of wine and the vines, who encourages him to "dance and be merry, feast and rejoice" (l. 102); and finally Urshanabi, the ferryman of Utnapishtim, who at first tells him his quest is futile but then takes him to Utnapishtim. Gilgamesh recounts the story of his journey, Enkidu's death, and his quest. In response to Gilgamesh's questioning about eternal life, Utnapishtim replies flatly, "There is no permanence" (l. 196). Gilgamesh persists until Utnapishtim agrees to tell Gilgamesh "a mystery" (l. 107), the story of how he gained immortality.

## 5. The Story of the Flood

In the ancient city of Shurrupak on the Euphrates, according the Utnapishtim's tale, the clamor of humanity rises up to the gods and disturbs their peace. Enlil calls for the gods "to exterminate mankind" (l. 108). The council of the gods agree, but Ea warns Utnapishtim secretly in a dream that a flood is coming. To protect her favorite, Ea tells Utnapishtim to build a boat and "take up into the boat the seed of all living creatures" (l. 108). It takes Utnapishtim seven days to build a boat of seven decks, and after loading it with his family, wealth, craftspeople, and animals, he rides out a six-day storm. On the seventh day, the boat runs aground and Utnapishtim releases three birds in succession. A dove and swallow return, but a raven does not,

*Map of ancient Mesopotamia.*

indicating the presence of dry land. After Utnapishtim makes a sacrifice, over which the gods "gathered like flies" (l. 111), Ishtar presents her opulent necklace as a remembrance of the disaster, and Enlil makes restitution for his rash act by giving Utnapishtim and his wife immortality.

### 6. The Return

Utnapishtim puts Gilgamesh's desire for eternal life to the test: "only prevail against sleep for six days and seven nights" (l. 114). Gilgamesh, however, quickly falls asleep as the result of his exertions. To prove that Gilgamesh has slept, Utnapishtim has

his wife bake a loaf of bread for each of the seven days Gilgamesh sleeps. After Utnapishtim wakes Gilgamesh, Gilgamesh sees the proof and despairs, realizing more clearly than ever that "death inhabits my room" (l. 115). Utnapishtim then curses Urshanabi for bringing Gilgamesh to him and commands Urshanabi to bathe and dress Gilgamesh, who is covered in grime and clothed in skins. Utnapishtim's wife asks Utnapishtim not to send Gilgamesh away empty-handed. In response, Utnapishtim reveals the location to a secret underwater plant that will "restore his lost youth to a man" (l. 116). Gilgamesh harvests the plant and purposes to take it back to Uruk with him, but when Gilgamesh stops at an oasis to bathe, a serpent from the well steals and eats the plant, sloughs off its skin, and disappears again. Gilgamesh bewails the loss—his last chance for immortality—and returns to Uruk. There he engraves his exploits in stone to testify to his greatness.

## 7. Death of Gilgamesh

Gilgamesh has fulfilled his destiny to be king, but his dream of eternal life eludes him. The narration concludes with a lament on Gilgamesh's mortality, a description of the funerary ritual, and a paean of praise to Gilgamesh: his family, his servants, the city of Uruk, and the pantheon of gods all mourn his loss.

## Characters

### Adad

The storm god, who endows Gilgamesh with courage at his birth.

### Antum

Wife of Anu, the sky god or god of the heavens, and mother of Ishtar. Ishtar complains to her parents Anu and Antum when Gilgamesh refuses her offer of marriage and describes how she has abused her previous lovers.

### Anu

God of the firmament, the patron god of Uruk, husband of Antun, and father of Ishtar. The *Epic of Gilgamesh* opens with a description of "the temple of blessed Eanna for the god of the firmament Anu" (l. 61). Gilgamesh calls a meteor that falls in his dream portending Enkidu's arrival "the stuff of Anu" (l. 66).

### Anunnaki

Gods of the underworld or the seven judges of hell. Their sacred dwellings are in the Forest of Cedars guarded by Humbaba. They also appear in Utnapishtim's account of the great flood as forerunners of the storm.

### Apsu

The fresh or sweet waters beneath the earth, governed by Ea.

### Aruru

Goddess of creation, or Mother Goddess, who fashions Enkidu from clay.

### Aya

Goddess of the dawn and wife of the sun god Shamash.

### Belit-Sheri

The "recorder of the gods" (l. 92) and scribe of the underworld who "keeps the book of death" (l. 92). She appears in Enkidu's dream of the afterlife.

### Bow of Anshan

The great bow which was made for Gilgamesh's confrontation with Humbaba.

### Bull of Heaven

A legendary beast, the personification of seven years of drought unleashed upon Uruk by Ishtar in response to Gilgamesh's refusal to marry her. In one of their epic battles, Gilgamesh and Enkidu defeat the Bull of Heaven, who represents famine and natural disaster.

### Courtesan

Probably a temple courtesan in the cult of Ishtar at the great temple Eanna. The Courtesan is the woman Gilgamesh sends back with the Trapper to pacify Enkidu. She initiates Enkidu into the ways of sex and culture, teaching him to eat, drink, and clothe himself. After her ministrations, Enkidu is unable to return to the wilderness. She then takes Enkidu to Uruk where he challenges Gilgamesh.

### Dilmun

The distant abode of the gods; also where Utnapishtim resides.

### Dumuzi

God of shepherds and sheepfolds; god of vegetation.

### Ea

Called "the wise" (l. 66), god of the sweet waters and of the arts. He breaks rank with the council of the gods and warns Utnapishtim of the impending flood.

# Media Adaptations

- *The Epic of Gilgamesh* has not yet received the attention given to Greek and Roman epics like *The Odyssey* and *The Iliad*. However, Adapa Films (http://www.lightlink.com/offline/Adapa.html) has produced a video of the ancient Babylonian myth, ''The Descent of Ishtar,'' and is currently producing, ''The Epic of Gilgamesh Tablet XI: The Deluge.'' According to Adapa Film's own literature, ''Adapa Films . . . aims to bridge the ancient and modern worlds by creating a video archive of re-enacted stories and myths from the ancient world utilizing the languages of these most ancient texts, live actors, computer imagery, as well as reconstructed ancient musical scores. Adapa introduces the viewer to seldom heard stories and beliefs and provides a unique window into the mindset of our most distant ancestors.'' The actors speak Akkadian, and the films use English subtitles. ''The Descent of Ishtar'' has been well-received by scholars and critics alike, and ''The Deluge'' promises the same.

## Eanna

The great temple complex in Uruk dedicated to Anu and Ishtar. Probably a ziggurat, a monumental multi-level, pyramid-shaped building.

## Egalmah

The palace of Gilgamesh's goddess-mother, Ninsun, in Uruk.

## Endukagga

Underworld god, associated with the Nindukugga, governor of the underworld.

## Enki

*See* Ea

## Enkidu

Gilgamesh's ''second self'' and faithful companion. Arruru fashions Enkidu out of clay in the image of Anu. Enkidu is a ''wild,'' primitive, or uncivilized man who has both the hardened physique and virtue of Ninurta, the god of war; the long hair of Ninursa, goddess of corn; and the hairy body of Samuqan, god of cattle. Enkidu runs freely with the animals and lives in the wilderness until he meets a Trapper, whose snares Enkidu has destroyed, at a well. The Trapper's father suggests that the Trapper bring a woman appease the wild man sexually. After a courtesan initiates Enkidu into the ways of civilization, Enkidu is taken to Uruk, where the populace looks to him to deliver them from the abuses of the king. Having foretold Enkidu's arrival in a dream, Gilgamesh postpones his marriage to Ishtar, goddess of love, and meets Enkidu in the streets, where they fight. After a fierce struggle, Gilgamesh finally throws Enkidu but finds him a worthy opponent. The two become inseparable companions from that point on. Enkidu accompanies Gilgamesh on Gilgamesh's greatest quests: to the Forest of the Cedars to slay Humbaba and to Uruk to defeat the Bull of Heaven. After Enkidu and Gilgamesh kill Humbaba and the Bull of Heaven, Enkidu has a dream in which a council of the gods decrees that one of the two companions must die. Enkidu awakens, falls ill, and eventually dies. Seeing his own mortality in the death of his friend, Gilgamesh begins another series of adventures, this time in quest for eternal life.

## Ennugi

The ''watcher over canals'' and god of irrigation.

## Ereshkigal

The queen of the underworld, who appears in Enkidu's dream of the afterlife. She is the wife of Nergal.

## Forest of Cedars

The region guarded by Humbaba, the giant. It is the place to which Gilgamesh and Enkidu travel to establish their fame and gather the sacred cedars. Late twentieth-century scholars have suggested that "cedars" should be tranlated as "pines."

## Gilgamesh

The protagonist or main character of the *Epic of Gilgamesh*. An historical figure who ruled Uruk around 2700 B.C., Gilgamesh is the child of Lugulbanda, a divine king, and Ninsun, and in the *Epic's* famous words, "Two thirds they made him god and one third man" (l. 61). Gilgamesh is the semi-divine king of Uruk; the special charge of Shamash, the sun god; sometime consort of Ishtar, goddess of love; and builder of the mighty city of Uruk and its great temple Eanna. Originally the subject of at least five ancient Sumerian myths, Gilgamesh becomes the main character in a Babylonian revision of those earlier stories. In later myths he is a judge of the underworld and is sometimes called its king.

The *Epic of Gilgamesh* narrates the transformation of Gilgamesh from a selfish and thoughtless young ruler into a wise and well-loved king and reveals Gilgamesh's gradual understanding of his own mortality. Seeing that Gilgamesh mistreats his people, the gods create a companion for him, a "second self" (l.62), who will be his equal. This companion is Enkidu, the civilized "wild man" with whom Gilgamesh forms a powerful bond after defeating him in a wrestling match. The companions share extraordinary heroic experiences. Gilgamesh's first adventure is to defeat evil Humbaba, the guardian of the Cedar Forest, and capture the mighty cedars for his city. After a fierce struggle, and with Enkidu's encouragement, Gilgamesh kills the giant Humbaba. Soon thereafter, Gilgamesh defeats the Bull of Heaven, who represents famine and disaster.

The companions' defeat of these divinely-sponsored threats raises the gods against Gilgamesh, and a council of the gods announces that Enkidu must die. For the first time in his life, Gilgamesh faces human limitation in the death of his friend. From that point on in the story, Gilgamesh is haunted by the loss of Enkidu and by the presence of death. Paralleling his earlier quest to conquer the threats of the natural world, Gilgamesh embarks on a journey to find Utnapishtim, the only mortal ever to gain eternal life. From Utnapishtim, Gilgamesh seeks the secret of immortality, and Gilgamesh's quest takes him literally to the ends of the earth: the mountains of Mishu. There he battles a pride of lions and, unlike any other mortal, is admitted through the gate to the underworld by the Scorpion-Demons. He passes through twelve leagues of horrible darkness before he emerges, tattered and gaunt, on the other side. His mighty exertions have reduced the once haughty prince to a shadow of his former glory. Prodded on by the memory of Enkidu's death, Gilgamesh questions Shamash, the sun god, and Siduri, the goddess of wine, before he finds Ushanabi, Utnapishtim's ferry keeper, to take him across the waters of death. At first, Urshanabi is reluctant to carry Gilgamesh to Utnapishtim, but after Gilgamesh threatens him and destroys his sailing gear, Urshanabi enables Gilgamesh to pass over to Utnapishtim.

His goal finally within reach, Gilgamesh asks Utnapishtim the fateful question, in effect, "What is the secret to eternal life?" The far-flung king of Uruk does not get the answer he anticipates, for Utnapishtim responds: "There is no permanence" (l. 106). However, Gilgamesh does hear Utnapishtim's story of the great flood and how Ea saved his family from certain death. As a reward for his faithfulness, Utnapishtim and his wife were granted immortality. Utnapishtim does give Gilgamesh the chance to earn immortality by remaining awake for seven days and nights, but Gilgamesh, weary from his long journey, immediately falls asleep instead. Gilgamesh is given a second chance at eternity with a secret flower, but that is stolen from him. Ultimately, Gilgamesh, accompanied by Urshanabi, returns to Uruk as a kinder and wiser king.

## Hanish

The herald of storms and bad weather. He appears with Shullat at the beginning of the storm in Utnapishtim's story of the flood.

## Harlot

*See* Courtesan

## Humbaba

The fearsome monster appointed by Enlil to protect the Forest of Cedars. Enkidu, who knows Humbaba from his time in the wild, says memorably of the giant: "When he roars it is like the torrent of the storm, his breath is like fire, and his jaws are death itself. He guards the cedars so well that when the wild heifer stirs in the forest, though she is sixty leagues distant, he hears her" (l. 71). In a fierce battle, Gilgamesh and Enkidu ultimately kill Humbaba and cut down the sacred cedars.

## Irkalla

*See* Ereshkigal

## Ishtar

Goddess of love and daughter of Anu and Antun. She also is the patroness of Uruk, Gilgamesh's home city. She is fickle and at times spiteful, as deomonstrated in her treatment of her former lovers and her wrath at Uruk after Gilgamesh spurns her advances. She inhabits Eanna, Uruk's fabulous temple, or ziggurat.

## Ishullana

Anu's gardener, whom Ishtar loved and then turned into a blind mole after he rejected her.

## Ki

*See* Ninhursag

## Lugulbanda

One of the ancient kings of Uruk, Lugulbanda is Gilgamesh's guardian god and progenitor. As Gilgamesh prepares to fight Humbaba, he carries himself into battle with the cry, ''By the life of my mother Ninsun who gave me birth, and by the life of my father Lugulbanda . . .'' (l. 80). Lugulbanda is the subject of his own epic cycle.

## Magilum

The boat of the dead. It eventually carries all creatures to the land of the dead.

## Mammetum

The ''mother of destinies.'' Utnapishtim reveals that Mammetum, with the Anunnaki, ''together . . . decree the fates of men. Life and death they allot but the day of death they do not disclose'' (l. 107).

## Man-Scorpion

Described as ''half man and half dragon,'' the Man Scorpion and his mate are guardians of Mashu, the mountains of the rising and setting sun. They let Gilgamesh pass through to the garden of the gods.

## Mashu

The twin peaks where the sun sets and which house the gate to the underworld. Mashu is guarded by the Scorpion-Demons.

## Might of Heroes

The formidable axe Gilgamesh takes to slay Humbaba.

## Namtar

The ''evil fate who knows no distinction among men'' (l. 82), is the servant of Ereshkigal. As Gilgamesh lays dying, ''Inhuman Namtar is heavy upon him, Namtar that has neither hand nor foot, that drinks no water and eats no meat'' (l. 119).

## Nergal

Underworld god, husband of Ereshkigal. During Utnapishtim's flood, ''Nergal pulled out the dams of the nether waters'' (l. 110).

## Neti

Gatekeeper of the underworld.

## Nindukugga

Governor of the underworld with Edukugga.

## Ningal

Mother of the sun god, Shamash, and wife of the moon god Sin.

## Ningizzida

The god of the serpent and lord of the tree of life.

## Ningursu

*See* Ninurta

## Ninhursag

The goddess of growth and vegetation, and mother of Enlil.

## Ninki

*See* Ninhursag

## Ninlil

Wife of Enlil, and goddess of heaven, earth, and air or spirit.

## Ninsun

Called ''the well-beloved and wise'' (l. 66), mother of Gilgamesh and wife of Lugulbanda. Prior to Gilgamesh's and Enkidu's trip to kill Humbaba, Ninsun adopts Enkidu as her own, gives him a sacred necklace, and entrusts Gilgamesh's safety to him.

## Ninurta

A warrior god and god of wells and canals. In the story of Utnapishtim, Ninurta is one of those who caused the flood with Nergal.

## Nisaba

Goddess of corn; Nisaba gives Enkidu his long, flowing hair.

## Nisir

The mountain upon which Utnapishtim's boat settled after the flood.

## Old Men Are Made Young Again

The name of the secret flower Utnapishtim reveals to Gilgamesh: ''There is a plant that grows under the water, it has a prickle like a thorn, like a rose; it will wound your hands, but if you succeed in taking it, then your hands will hold that which restores his lost youth to a man'' (l. 116) Gilgamesh retrieves the flower, which a serpent later eats.

## Puzur-Amurri

The steersman and navigator of Utnapishtim's great boat.

## Samuqan

God of cattle and the god of herds; Samuqan gives Enkidu his rough, hair-covered hide.

## Scorpion-Demon

*See* Man-Scorpion

## Shamash

One of the chief gods, Shamash is the sun god, law-giver, and judge who is evoked in blessing and protection throughout the *Epic*. At Gilgamesh's birth, Shamash endows Gilgamesh with physical beauty. According to the Courtesan who helps to civilize Enkidu, Shamash has granted Gilgamesh his favor. During his search for everlasting life, Gilgamesh encounters Shamash in the garden of the gods. Although Shamash tells Gilgamesh that ''You will never find the life for which you are searching'' (l. 100), Gilgamesh begs the sun god, ''Although I am no better than a dead man, still let me see the light of the sun'' (l. 100). Shamash relents and sends Gilgamesh to Siduri and eventually to Utnapishtim.

## Shullat

With Hanish, heralds of the storm god, Adad, during the great flood.

## Shulpae

God of the feast. Sacrifices are made to Shulpae at funerals.

## Shurrupak

Utnapishtim's home city and one of the five most ancient cities, according to legend.

## Siduri

Goddess of the vine, who at first bars Gilgamesh from passage through the garden of the gods, but then tells him: ''When the gods created man they allotted to him death, but they retained life in their own keeping. As for you, Gilgamesh, fill your belly with good things; day and night, night and day, dance and be merry, feast and rejoice. Let your clothes be fresh, bathe yourself in water, cherish the little child that holds your hand, and make your wife happy in your embrace; for this too is the lot of man'' (l. 102).

## Sillah

The mother of one of Ishtar's lovers.

## Sin

The moon god, to whom Gilgamesh prays as he passes through dark mountain passes populated by lions on his way to Mashu.

## Tammuz

One of Ishtar's unfortunate lovers, whom she turned into a broken-winged bird.

## Trapper

The first person to encounter Enkidu, who had sabotaged his traps. Enkidu later curses the Trapper for introducing him to civilization and its difficulties.

## Ubara-Tutu

Ancient king of Shurrupak and Utnapishtim's father.

### Urshanabi

Boatman who takes Gilgamesh over the waters of death to Utnapishtim. Utnapishtim curses Urshanabi for bringing a mortal to him across the sea of death. After Urshanabi helps Gilgamesh back to health and vigor, he returns to Uruk with Gilgamesh.

### Uruk

Gilgamesh's home city, which houses the great temple Eanna.

### Utnapishtim

Favored by the god Ea, Utnapishtim is warned of Enlil's plan to destroy humanity through a flood. Utnapishtim, at Ea's command, builds a huge square boat, seven decks high and one-hundred twenty cubits per side, in seven days. He seals it with pitch, stores away supplies, and "loaded into her all that I had of gold and of living things, my family, my kin, the beast of the field both wild and tame, and all the craftsmen" (l. 109). He rides out the seven day storm and then sets three birds free—a dove, a swallow, and a raven. When the raven does not return, he knows the crisis is over and he offers a sacrifice to the gods. In restitution for his thoughtless punishment of humanity, Enlil blesses Utnapishtim and his wife, grants them immortality, and places them "in the distance at the mouth of the rivers" (l. 113). Thus, the once-mortal Utnapishtim, now called Utnapishtim the "faraway" or Utnapishtim the "distant," becomes immortal and the object of Gilgamesh's final quest.

After Enkidu's death, Gilgamesh seeks Utnapishtim for the secret of eternal life. As a test, Utnapishtim challenges Gilgamesh to remain awake for seven days and nights, which Gilgamesh cannot do. So, Utnapishtim gives Gilgamesh the location of a secret plant, "The Old Men Are Young Again" (l. 116), which will bring those who eat it back to their youthful state, and sends him home to Uruk. While Gilgamesh is resting at a well during the return trip, a serpent steals the flower, sheds its skin, and disappears.

### Vampire-Demon

A supernatural being who appears in Enkidu's dream of the underworld: "an awful being, somber-faced man-bird.... His was a vampire face, his foot was a lion's foot, his hand an eagle's talon" (l. 92). In the dream, he attacks and smothers Enkidu.

### Voice of Heroes

The imposing breastplate Gilgamesh wears into battle with Humbaba.

## Themes

The story of Gilgamesh, king of Uruk, and his companion, Enkidu, a civilized wild man, falls essentially into two halves: during the first half of the *Epic,* Gilgamesh meets Enkidu and the two defeat both Humbaba the giant in the land of the cedars and the Bull of Heaven, who Ishtar has sent to plague Uruk. After their victories the gods decree that Enkidu must die. In the second half of the epic, prodded by Enkidu's death, Gilgamesh pursues the secret of immortality first in the garden of the gods and then with Utnapishtim, the Mesopotamian Noah, who recounts his own story of survival during the great flood that destroyed humanity. Although Gilgamesh fails to gain eternal life, he ends his journeys a wise man and celebrated ruler.

### The Motif of the Journey and the Search for the Meaning of Life

On one hand, at its foundation, the *Epic of Gilgamesh* is a story of action in the world and of movement out into the physical realm. After their meeting, Gilgamesh and Enkidu travel out into the sacred and mysterious Forest of the Cedars to face Humbaba, the embodiment of evil. They then return to Uruk to face the Bull of Heaven, who comes as the wrath of Ishtar, goddess of love and war. Both Gilgamesh and Enkidu are men of action who define life according to the obstacles they overcome, and they find their greatest fulfillment in facing challenges. On the other hand, the outward journeys of Gilgamesh and Enkidu in the first half of the epic are matched by the internal struggle Gilgamesh faces in the second half of the story. After Enkidu dies at the will of the gods, Gilgamesh commences a parallel journey into the spiritual realm. He literally goes into the earth at the mountains of Mashu to find the realm of the gods, and although Enkidu is not physically present with Gilgamesh, the memory of his friend's death continues to impel Gilgamesh's search for meaning and immortality. Thus, the journeys that structure the *Epic of Gilgamesh* need to be read on two levels: first, at the narrative level of physical action in the

# Topics for Further Study

- Compare and contrast an episode in N. K. Sandars' narrative version of the *Epic of Gilgamesh* with David Ferry's poetic version or one of the versions that follow the original 12-tablet structure of the story. How do the versions differ in their use of language and their organization on the page. Do they differ in their symbolic or thematic emphases? Is one easier to read than the other? What other kind of differences occur when you read the *Epic* as poetry and as a story?

- Locate the five independent myths of the Sumerian song-cycle featuring Gilgamesh ("Gilgamesh and Agga of Kish;" "Gilgamesh and the Land of the Living;" "Gilgamesh and the Bull of Heaven;" "Gilgamesh, Enkidu, and the Netherworld;" and "The Death of Gilgamesh") in James Pritchard's *Ancient Near Eastern Texts Relating to the Old Testament*. Choose one, read it carefully, and see if you can identify which portion(s) or details of the Sumerian myth have been incorporated into the Babylonian Standard Version and which have been excluded. What changes did the later version make to the earlier Sumerian myths?

- Many contemporary movies feature a hero and counterpart, a sidekick or "buddy." Examples include "Thelma and Louise" and the "Lethal Weapon " and "48 Hours" movies. Often these two characters are as different as Gilgamesh and Enkidu, but together they make a complete team. Select a current "buddy movie"—a movie that feature two dissimilar characters who team up for some purpose—and, using the *Epic of Gilgamesh* as a guide, analyze the "epic qualities" of that movie. For example, you might ask: How are the buddies alike or different? How do they react to the opposite sex? What quest do they set out to achieve? What great enemy or evil do they face? Let your imagination guide you to new and outlandish parallels between the ancient story of Gilgamesh and these modern works.

- Drawing on such subjects of study as biology, geography, and history, create a collage depicting the elements of ancient Mesopotamian life depicted in the *Epic of Gilgamesh* or a diorama (picture box) of an ancient ziggurat or temple. From your research, can you reconstruct the architecture of the time; the kinds of people who inhabited the cities; and the kinds of crops, crafts, and clothing they wore?

---

world, and second, at the symbolic level of supernatural meaning and fulfillment.

## Culture and Nature

The internal balance between physical and spiritual journeys in the *Epic of Gilgamesh* is matched by the contrast in the two main characters, Gilgamesh and Enkidu. At the *Epic*'s opening, Gilgamesh embodies both the arrogance and the cultivation of high Sumerian culture. He is the king and the height of power, he is physically gifted and beautiful, but he is also haughty and abusive: he deflowers the maidens of his kingdom for his own pleasure and he presses the young men into his service. When Enkidu enters the story, he incarnates the coarse physicality and vitality of the natural world: He is immensely strong, he lives and runs with the wild beasts, and he destroys the traps set by hunters. At a crucial early juncture in the *Epic,* Gilgamesh, having heard about this "wild man," sends a Courtesan to Enkidu. She transforms Enkidu's wildness through her sexual charms and she teaches him table manners and correct behavior. Afterwards, the wild animals run away from Enkidu. The Courtesan thereby brings him into the civilized world, or as the *Epic* reads, "Enkidu had become a man" (l. 67). In contrast to Enkidu, Humbaba, the forest giant is considered a monster and enemy, for he says, "I have never known a mother, no, nor a father who reared me" (l. 82). Together, Gilgamesh, the cultivated ruler, and Enkidu, the civilized wild man, form an inseparable bond and begin a series of exploits to conquer Humbaba, that other forest creature, and the Bull of Heaven, the embodiment of natural disaster.

### Identity and Relationship

As the semi-divine creation of Shamash, the sun god, who gives him physical beauty, and Adad, the storm god, who gives him great courage, Gilgamesh is at the top of the human social ladder. As king of Uruk, Gilgamesh has access to all the riches and pleasures his society can provide. In his lofty and elevated station, Gilgamesh has no need nor desire for a relationship with others, for he seems to be complete in himself. However, Gilgamesh is also unsettled and ''a man of many moods'' (l. 65), an arrogant ruler who mistreats his people. He is, in other words, incomplete, lacking an ingredient essential to becoming fully human. The people of Uruk complain to Anu, god of Uruk, to intervene on their behalf, and Aruru, the goddess of creation, responds by creating Enkidu. As Anu tells the goddess, ''You made him, O Aruru, now create his equal; let it be as like him as his own reflection, his second self, stormy heart for stormy heart. Let them content together and leave Uruk in quiet'' (l. 62). Enkidu, himself ''innocent of mankind . . . [who knows] nothing of the cultivated land'' (l. 63), requires the moderating influences of civilization to become fully human. Incomplete when separated, but together and fulfilled in close relationship, Gilgamesh and Enkidu establish their true identities, or as the *Epic* puts it, their ''names,'' only through the bond of their companionship. Their identities are fulfilled through their relationship. Although Enkidu perishes before the end of the tale, the death of his friend haunts Gilgamesh and sends him on his arduous quest of immortality. Thus, Gilgamesh carries the legacy of his friend back to Uruk, where he dies a well-loved king.

### Humanity and Divinity

Human interaction with the gods, and the gods' intervention in human events, is a standard hallmark of epic literature, and the *Epic of Gilgamesh* is no exception. From beginning to end of the tale, the supernatural world intersects the physical plane. Persons, places, and all manner of things are closely associated with patron deities: Anu is god of Uruk; Shamash oversees Gilgamesh; Ishtar inhabits the temple precincts of Eanna, the great temple of Uruk;

Ereshkigal is queen of the underworld; and Ea favors Utnapishtim. The interplay of humanity and divinity is closely allied to the question of identity and relationship throughout the *Epic of Gilgamesh.* Characters take on the attributes of deities associated with them. Gilgamesh is a mixture of both human and divine, but emphasizing the divine: ''Two thirds they made him god and one third man'' (l. 61). Enkidu incarnates precisely the opposite proportions, favoring the human: two thirds natural and one third divine. Gilgamesh actualizes the beauty of Shamash, the sun god, and the ferocity of Adad, the storm god; Enkidu manifests the ferocity of Ninurta, god of war, and the long hair of Nisaba, goddess of corn. At the same time the *Epic* invokes the gods throughout the narrative, they seem distant from the action, interfering only when pressed or perturbed. The gods are also clearly anthropomorphic, seemingly very human in their petty jealously, bickering, and irritation with irascible humans like Gilgamesh, Enkidu, and the people of Shurrupak.

### Change and Transformation

Some readers of the *Epic of Gilgamesh* argue that Gilgamesh never really changes appreciably during the course of the tale; others find a gradual progression and deepening of his self-understanding. What is clear, however, is that although Gilgamesh remains a towering figure who seeks a secure reputation and eternal life, he finds the answer to his quest when he encounters Utnapishtim: ''From the days of old there is no permanence'' (l. 107). Strictly speaking in the context of the *Epic,* Utnapishtim is correct: Gilgamesh will not receive eternal life. However, Gilgamesh has two provocative encounters during his quest, two creatures of the natural world who change while remaining the same: the dragon-fly nymph and the snake. The insect nymph, says Utnapishtim, ''sheds her larva and sees the sun in his glory'' (l. 107); that is, she changes form but remains the same creature. Later, after Gilgamesh has recovered the magical plant of everlasting life, a ''serpent sensed the sweetness of the flower. It rose out of the water and snatched it away, and immediately it sloughed off its skin and returned to the well'' (l. 117). Like the insect larva, the snake sheds its exterior while remaining the same animal. At the end of his quest with Utnapishtim, Gilgamesh also literally ''sheds his skins'' (l. 115) and is given new clothing. Gilgamesh's lesson is that humans, though they cannot escape their mortality, can be transformed through experience.

## Mortality and Immortality

During the course of the *Epic,* Gilgamesh, as king of Uruk, progresses from the highest social station to the lowest example of a human being—pale, starved, and clothed in skins during his encounter with Utnapishtim. During each encounter with divinities in the garden of the gods, Gilgamesh hears the refrain: ''If you are Gilgamesh . . . why are your cheeks so starved and why is your face so drawn. Why is despair in your heart and your face like the face of one who has made a long journey? (L. 101). The crux of this journey is the death of Gilgamesh's beloved comrade, Enkidu. During the first half of the tale, Gilgamesh and Enkidu bring death to all enemies in their quest to establish their eternal reputations; during the second half, Gilgamesh lives with the haunting presence of Enkidu's death. As Gilgamesh tells Utnapishtim, ''Because of my brother I am afraid of death; because of my brother I stray through the wilderness. His fate lies heavy upon me. How can I be silent, how can I rest? He is dust and I shall die also and be laid in the earth forever'' (l. 106). Having turned to great exploits, huge building projects, and epic journeys to secure his immortality, Gilgamesh finds lasting reputation, his everlasting life, in the story of his life. As the *Epic* records in the final paragraph of chapter 6, ''The Return'' of Gilgamesh, ''He went on a long journey, was weary, worn out with labour, and returning engraved on a stone the whole story'' (l. 117). The gods do not give Gilgamesh immortality; immortality comes through the stone tablets of his epic adventure.

## Style

In *A Glossary of Literary Terms,* literary scholar M. H. Abrams lists five essential characteristics of epic literature: (1) ''The hero is a figure of great national or even cosmic importance;'' (2) ''The setting of the poem is ample in scale, and may be worldwide, or even larger;'' (3) ''The action involves superhuman deeds in battle;'' (4) ''In these great actions the gods and other supernatural beings take an interest or even an active part;'' and (5) ''An epic poem is a ceremonial performance, and is narrated in a ceremonial style which is deliberately distanced from ordinary speech and proportioned to the grandeur and formality of the heroic subject and epic architecture'' (p. 52). *The Epic of Gilgamesh* fulfills each of these characteristics in its own distinct way.

## Orality and Performance

One of the key attributes of the *Epic of Gilgamesh* is the sense of breathless immediacy of the story. The *Epic* achieves this effect by placing the story in a setting that simulates the oral performance in which the story was originally performed. The opening lines provide a sense that this is not an ancient story, but one just now occurring. The narrative ''I'' of the Prologue places the reader at Uruk's city walls and erases the distance between that ancient time and the present time of telling the story, inviting the hearer (and reader) to touch the walls, feel their strength, and sense their glory. These walls, the narrative voice proclaims, are those of the great Gilgamesh and now I will tell you his story. This sense of immediacy continues throughout the *Epic.*

## In medias res

Traditionally, epics begin ''in medias res'' or ''in the middle of things.'' Although this characteristic was originally applied to Greek and Roman epics like *The Odyssey* and *The Iliad,* it is equally true of *The Epic of Gilgamesh.* The story begins not at the beginning of Gilgamesh's life, but somewhere in the middle. He is initially portrayed as a young, hot-headed king, heedless of the effect of actions and desires on the well-being of his people. One of the effects of this technique is to allow the reader to gauge the extent of Gilgamesh's development as a character.

## The Epithet

Another key technique of the epic style is the use of ''epithets,'' usually adjectives or persistent adjective phrases that reveal the attributes or personality of people, places, and things in the story: ''strong-walled Uruk'' (l. 68), ''Humbaba whose name is 'Hugeness''' (l. 71), ''Shamash the Protector'' (l. 78), and Utnapishtim ''the Faraway'' (l. 97). Epic epithets provide a good way of keeping track of a character and that character's development.

## Literary Formulae and Set-Pieces in the High Style

A third literary characteristic of the epic style is found in the elevated, formal language and repeated formulaic phrases. In fact, the dialogue sounds stilted and rehearsed, as if read for a formal occasion. During chapter 2, ''The Forest Journey,'' Gilgamesh calls out for assistance: ''By the life of my mother Ninsun who gave me birth, and by the life of my father, divine Lugulbanda, let me live to be the wonder of my mother, as when she nursed me on her lap'' (l. 80). These formal invocations of deity give the task an elevated stature and a sense of being a holy mission which Gilgamesh undertakes for his city and his divine heritage. In another example, a bit later as he faces Humbaba in battle, Gilgamesh beseeches his patron god: ''O glorious Shamash, I have followed the road you commanded but now if you send no succor how shall I escape?'' (L. 81). The use of ''apostrophe,'' a figure of speech indicated by ''O,'' indicates a formal invocation of a person or personification who is not otherwise present.

Another important element of the elevated style of the *Epic* is its inclusion of ''laments,'' the formal poems of praise and songs of grief that the living give on behalf of the dead. The finest example in the poem is Gilgamesh's lament for Enkidu, which begins (on line 94):

'Hear me, great ones of Uruk, I weep for Enkidu, my friend, Bitterly moaning like a woman mourning I weep for my brother. You were the axe at my side, My hand's strength, the sword in my belt, the shield before me, A glorious robe, my fairest ornament; An evil Fate has robbed me.'

Gilgamesh's heart-felt lament concludes with the mournful lines, '''What is this sleep which holds you now? / You are lost in the dark and cannot hear me''' (l. 95). Nearly all of these formal speeches also serve to summarize or rehearse the characters' attitudes or even the action in the story up to that point in the narrative.

## Balance and Repetition

A fourth literary characteristic of *Gilgamesh* closely related to its often formal, even stilted language, is its carefully balanced structure and strategic use of repetition at all levels. There is hardly a moment, event, or speech that does not have a counterpart somewhere in the tale. Commonly called ''parallelism'' and ''antitheses,'' these repetitions and contrasting and balancing elements can indicate both a comparison and/or a contrast between the paired elements of the story. The repetitious elements can be examined in terms of structure, events, speeches, and numbers.

## Repetition of Structure

First, the entire *Epic of Gilgamesh* is split into two halves and is balanced along structural lines. The pivot of the story is Enkidu's death. In the first half of the narrative, Gilgamesh travels outward into the Forest of the Cedars to slay Humbaba; in the second half he journeys into the realm of the gods to find Utnapishtim. Gilgamesh's early successes and personal glory contrast the successive frustrations and individual hardships of the end of the tale, while Enkidu's physical presence contrasts with his later, but no less palpable, absence.

## Repetition of Events

The first section of the *Epic of Gilgamesh* is full of repetition: Gilgamesh and Enkidu are mirror images of one another; they slay two semi-divine monsters, Humbaba and the Bull of Heaven; and Gilgamesh has a series of dreams, matched by Enkidu's dreams later in the section. Events in the second half of the *Epic* are often repetitions of earlier affairs, as when Gilgamesh's twelve-league journey through the Mashu's darkness pales in comparison to his one-hundred and twenty pole voyage across the waters of death. Finally, events in the second half mirror those in the first: Enkidu's funeral and Gilgamesh's lament for his dead friend are matched by Gilgamesh's funeral and Uruk's praise for its dead king, and Gilgamesh's voyage to find Utnapishtim parallels the earlier journey to the Cedar Forest.

## Repetition of Speeches

Parts of a speech may be repeated from one character to the next or more tellingly, the entire speech may be repeated several times throughout a portion of the *Epic of Gilgamesh*. The most significant instance of this technique occurs in chapter 4, ''The Search for Everlasting Life.'' In his horrific journey from the Country of the Living to the abode of the gods, Gilgamesh encounters Siduri, goddess of the vine and of wine; Urshanabi, ''the ferryman of Utnapishtim'' who takes him across the waters of death; and finally Utnapishtim himself, the immortal human. Each encounter follows the same structure.

1. Each divinity initially opposes Gilgamesh, who responds with a summary of his deeds and identity: ''I am Gilgamesh who seized and killed the Bull of Heaven, I killed the watchman of the cedar

forest, I overthrew Humbaba who lived in the forest, and I killed the lions in the passes of the mountains.''

2. The divinity, in this case Siduri, repeats Gilgamesh's claim but asks: ''If you are that Gilgamesh who seized and killed the Bull of Heaven, who killed the watchman of the forest, who overthrew Humbaba that lived in the forest, and killed the lions in the passes of the mountains, why are your cheeks so starved and why is your face so drawn. . . .''

3. Gilgamesh's answer includes the divinity's questions and concludes with his ultimate rationale for making his journey: ''And why should not my cheeks be starved and my face drawn?'' for ''Enkidu my brother, whom I loved, the end of mortality has overtaken him'' (l. 101).

4. In each case, the divinity then offers Gilgamesh advice for his life—in effect, an entire worldview—and here the pattern breaks down, for each inhabitant of the domain of the gods gives Gilgamesh a different answer. Siduri tells him to eat, drink, and be merry. Urshanabi, whose sailing gear Gilgamesh has destroyed, tells Gilgamesh that he must create a new means of powering the ferry if he is to meet Utnapishtim. Utnapishtim himself finally reveals to Gilgamesh that, in fact, ''There is no permanence'' (l. 106). Thus, the *Epic of Gilgamesh* offers meaningful patterns of similarity and of repetition, but variations in the pattern can also reveal important insights to the story.

*Carved image of Gilgamesh from the eighth century B.C.*

## Repetition of Numbers

Repetitions in patterns of two (two halves to the story or two carefully balanced main characters) or three (Gilgamesh's series of three dreams or the three quests of the tale) are well-known characteristics of oral composition. An even more obvious symbolic number in the *Epic of Gilgamesh* is the number seven, sometimes in combination with two and three. Generally considered to be a ''perfect'' number or number of ''completion'' or ''wholeness,'' seven appears throughout the tale: the ''seven sages'' laid the foundations of Uruk (l. 61); Enlil gives Humbaba ''sevenfold terrors'' with which to guard the forest (l. 71); the gate of Uruk has seven bolts (l. 73); and during the climactic battle with Humbaba, the giant unleashes the ''seven splendors'' against the pair of warriors; they fell ''seven cedars'' to provoke Humbaba's wrath, and they kill

the giant with three blows to the neck, severing his head (l. 83). This symbolic numerology continues especially in the story of the flood and throughout the *Epic*.

## Annular or Ring Structure

One final, closely-related literary technique to note is the *Epic*'s ''annular'' or ''ring-like'' structure. Simply stated, the end of the story refers the reader back to the beginning by repeating key images and speeches. The Prologue begins: ''I will proclaim to the world the deeds of Gilgamesh. This was the man to whom all things were known; this was the man who knew all the countries of the world. He was wise, he saw mysteries and knew secret things . . .'' (l. 61). Chapter 6, ''The Return'' of Gilgamesh to Uruk, concludes, ''This too was the work of Gilgamesh, the king, who knew the countries of the world. He was wise, he saw mysteries and knew secret things . . . (l. 117). By referring the reader to the story's opening at its conclusion, the narrative gains a sense of wholeness or completion, and the *Epic* invites the reader to experience Gilgamesh's story once again.

## Historical Context

### Development of the Epic

The *Epic of Gilgamesh* is the product of several civilizations of ancient Mesopotamia, those city-states of the Tigris-Euphrates river valley, in present-day Iraq. These cultures are, in turn, the Sumerians, the Akkadians or Babylonians, and the Assyrians. Scholars of the ancient Near East have determined that the *Epic of Gilgamesh* probably began as five separate Sumerian Gilgamesh stories (called ''Gilgamesh and Agga of Kish;'' ''Gilgamesh and the Land of the Living;'' ''Gilgamesh and the Bull of Heaven;'' ''Gilgamesh, Enkidu, and the Netherworld;'' and ''The Death of Gilgamesh''). According to Jeffrey H. Tigay, who has written the standard account of the literary and historical development of the Epic, the ancient oral tales about Gilgamesh probably were first written down, in cuneiform, about 2500 B.C. by Sumerian scribes, although the earliest copies date from about 2100 B.C. or about 500 years after the historical Gilgamesh ruled Uruk. These separate Sumerian tales were drawn together by a later Akkadian author (or authors) who adapted elements of the early stories into a more unified, complete epic. By this time the *Epic* had been widely circulated throughout the ancient Near East, with copies being found in Hittite and Hurrian, and as far away as modern day Palestine and Turkey. The *Epic* underwent other minor changes until it became formalized in a Standard Version, according to tradition, by the scribe Sinleqqiunninni around 1300 B.C. This is the most completely preserved version of the *Epic,* which archaeologists discovered in Ashurbanipal's library in Nineveh (668-27 B.C.) (Jeffrey H. Tigay, *The Evolution of the Gilgamesh Epic,* [Philadelphia: University of Pennsylvania Press, 1982], pp. 248-50). This Standard Version is the basis for the

present translation by N. K. Sandars, but the text will continue to change as new archaeological discoveries are made and as scholars understand more fully the language, culture, and history of these antiquated cultures.

### Events Historical and Mythological

The *Epic of Gilgamesh* is marked by both the threat and the promise of its historical and physical setting. According to the famous Sumerian ''King-List,'' which traces the royal lineage from the time ''When kingship was lowered from heaven,'' through past the rulers during the time of the great flood, until the defeat of Uruk, Gilgamesh was an historical figure who reigned about 2700 B.C. He is called ''the divine Gilgamesh . . . [who] ruled 126 years'' (''Sumerian King-List,'' trans. A. Leo Oppenheimer, in *Ancient Near Eastern Texts Relating to the Old Testament,* ed. James A. Pritchard [Princeton: Princeton University Press, 1950], p. 266). Although it is impossible to know exactly, events like Gilgamesh's journey to the Forest of Cedars to defeat Humbaba may reflect the historical Uruk's trade relations, need for natural resources, and later struggles with neighboring city-states over vital resources like wood.

Other details of daily life emerge from the story of Enkidu's gradual humanization at the hands of the Courtesan: ''This transformation is achieved by eating bread, drinking beer, anointing oneself, and clothing oneself. . . . Bread, beer, oil, and clothing are the staples which were distributed as daily rations by the central institutions, such as the temple or palace, to a large segment of the population; these rations were their only means of subsistence'' (Johannes Renger, ''Mesopotamian Epic Literature,'' p. 44). Furthermore, the cultures of the Tigro-Euphrates river valley depended upon the rivers for the rich soil that sustained their agriculture; at the same time the rivers brought life, frequent floods also wrecked havoc upon their cities and people. The *Epic* reveals these horrors, for Gilgamesh himself ''looked over the wall and I see the bodies floating on the river, and that will be my lot also'' (l. 72). Even the gods are effected, for Ishtar ''cried out like a woman in travail'' when she sees her people floating in the ocean ''like the spawn of fish'' (l. 110) during Utnapishtim's flood. Likewise, Ishtar's Bull of Heaven represents another of the ancient world's great fears: drought, famine, and natural disaster. Anu reminds Ishtar, ''If I do what you desire there will be seven years of drought throughout Uruk when corn will be seedless husks'' (l. 87).

# Compare & Contrast

- **Ancient Mesopotamia:** Credited with the invention of the first writing system (cuneiform), the widespread use of wheeled transportation, sophisticated metalworking, extensive irrigation and agricultural production, and monumental building projects whose remains are still visible after four thousand or more years.

  **Modern Western Civilization:** Characterized by rapid technological change, creating a "global village," where travel to, or communication with, any part of the world (or even beyond the earth) is possible. Increased human intervention in natural processes (nuclear power and warfare, genetic engineering and cloning, disease prevention and pharmaceuticals, weather prediction and flood control, agricultural production and chemical treatments, etc).

- **Ancient Mesopotamia:** Highly stratified and essentially male-dominated politically and culturally, with the priestly caste and ruling elite controlling power and wealth. Power concentrated in individual city-states rather than larger administrative units and wielded by divinely instituted monarchy. Status determined by birth, with little chance for advancement or education. Warfare limited in scope and localized in space.

  **Modern Western Civilization:** Economically stratified, though birth and gender are somewhat less determinative for access to power and wealth. Political and religious leadership generally separated. Representative democracy rather than genetic monarchy; education widely available. The possibility for "total war" leading to widespread destruction.

- **Ancient Mesopotamia:** Farm-based, agrarian economy, based on domesticated livestock and on the yearly cycles of flood and soil replenishment. Supply of foodstuffs highly susceptible to ecological disruptions. Industry limited to traditional crafts (wood and metalworking, warcraft), but large-scale building projects of lumber and baked brick (city walls and gates, royal and religious structures). First large-scale urban centers in cities like Uruk and Ur (the Biblical Erech), with populations near 50,000 people.

  **Modern Western Civilization:** Highly competitive, diverse, interdependent global and local economies increasingly based upon information or communications rather than traditional commodities. Risk of famine minimized by chemical and genetic interventions. Large-scale industries with hugely complex inventory, production, and distribution systems. Some metropolitan areas exceed 20 million people.

- **Ancient Mesopotamia:** Pantheon of gods, related to natural phenomenon. Series of religious festivals keyed to yearly seasonal cycle. Religious and political systems highly inter-related, with local and patron deities celebrated in specific cities.

  **Modern Western Civilization:** Pantheon of faiths, largely dominated by different forms of Christianity. Religious festivals intact, but often secularized. Religious and political systems separated, but religious practice often determined by local custom and history.

---

Thus, the ancient Mesopotamians were caught between the bounty of their river valley and the misery of its floods and droughts.

Finally, the *Epic of Gilgamesh* does not encompass all the stories recorded about Gilgamesh. Gilgamesh himself is placed in the pantheons of gods as "an underworld deity, a judge there and sometimes called its king. His statues or figurines appear in burial rites for the dead, and his cult [official worship] was especially important in the month of Ab (July-August), when nature itself, as it were, expired" (William L. Moran, "Introduction,'' in David Ferry's *Gilgamesh: A New Rendering in English Verse,* [New York: Noonday Press; Farrar, Straus and Giroux, 1992], p. ix).

## Critical Overview

### History and Recovery of the Epic of Gilgamesh

The critical reception of the *Epic of Gilgamesh* parallels the history of ancient Near Eastern archaeology over the last 150 years. The *Epic* first came to light in tablets from the palace library of Ashurbanipal, King of Assyria (668-27 B.C.), in Nineveh. The *Epic* comprised twelve fragmented clay tablets inscribed with cuneiform. Since that initial discovery, portions of the tale have surfaced throughout the region, from different time periods, and in several different languages. By comparing the differences among the tablets and between various versions of the story, scholars have been able to reconstruct the history of the Epic's composition. Although the complete literary history of the *Epic* is quite complex, its formation can be divided into four main phases: (1) the period of oral composition and circulation, (2) the Sumerian tales of Gilgamesh, (3) the Akkadian and Babylonian epics, and (4) the Standard Version.

First, the historical Gilgamesh ruled Uruk, in southern Mesopotamia, around 2700 B.C., and a variety of historical artifacts confirm his existence. As is the custom of traditional cultures, stories of the king's exploits circulated among the populace and were repeated orally before being written down probably about 2500 B.C.

Second, the Sumerians inscribed into clay tablets at least five separate Gilgamesh stories, the earliest of which we have dates from around 2100 B.C. These stories are now known as ''Gilgamesh and Agga of Kish;'' ''Gilgamesh and the Land of the Living;'' ''Gilgamesh and the Bull of Heaven;'' ''Gilgamesh, Enkidu, and the Netherworld;'' and ''The Death of Gilgamesh.'' It is important to note that these stories shared little except the same main character. They were not joined together as a whole, nor did they share an overriding theme.

Third, these separate Sumerian stories became the raw material for the Babylonian (or Akkadian) *Epic of Gilgamesh,* composed about 1700 B.C. The Babylonian editor(s) combined aspects of the earli-

er Sumerian stories to create the unified story of Gilgamesh's search for the meaning of life and his struggle against death. This Babylonian edition also introduced several important changes, including: (1) turning Enkidu from Gilgamesh's servant, as he is in the Sumerian tales, to an equal and companion; (2) adding the hymn-like Prologue and conclusion and intensifying the use of formulaic sayings and set-pieces; and (3) incorporating the ancient legend of Utnapishtim and the great flood. This Babylonian version became known throughout the ancient Near East in a variety of languages.

Finally, rather than adding new stories or deleting old material, the *Epic* became fixed in the so-called Standard Version, attributed to the author Sinleqquinninni, who lived about 1300 B.C. This Standard Version is the one found in Ashurbanipal's library. See the introductions to the translations by N. K. Sandars, Maureen Gallery Kovacks, and Stephanie Dalley for succinct overviews of the *Epic*'s history of composition.

### Utnapishtim: The Mesopotamian Noah

Although at its discovery the *Epic* was immediately recognized for its literary and historical merit, it gained recognition especially for its account of Utnapishtim and the flood. The story of the flood is found in Tablet XI of the *Epic,* and is itself derived from an earlier story, ''The Myth of Atrahasis.'' What most intrigued reader's were the parallels between Utnapishtim and the Old Testament story of Noah and the Flood, found in Genesis 6:1-9:18. What shocked them even further is that the Utnapishtim episode predates, or is earlier than, the biblical account of Noah and the ark. Alexander Heidel, in *The Gilgamesh Epic and Old Testament Parallels,* 2nd ed. (Chicago: University of Chicago Press, 1949), pp. 224-69, compares and contrasts Noah's story and Utnapishtim's:

Utnapishtim: Flood decreed by an assembly of gods because of humanity's clamor: ''The uproar of mankind is intolerable and sleep is no longer possible by reason of the babel,'' says Enlil (l. 108). Emphasizes divine capriciousness (or arbitrariness) and polytheism, or the many gods of the Mesopotamian pantheon. Enlil motivates the action, but not all the gods agree, namely Ea and Ishtar.

Noah: Flood attributed to a single god because of humanity's wickedness: ''Now the earth was corrupt in God's sight, and the earth was filled with

# What Do I Read Next?

- Samuel Noah Kramer's *History Begins at Sumer: Thirty-Nine Firsts in Man's Recorded History*, (3rd rev. ed., Philadelphia: University of Pennsylvania Press, 1981) discusses a variety of Sumerian ''innovations''—common cultural, historical, scientific, and social trends or events that were first recorded in Sumeria. Kramer's book covers such topics as: ''Education: The First Schools,'' ''Medicine: The First Pharmacopoeia,'' ''Ethics: The First Moral Ideals,'' ''The Sacred Marriage Rite: The First Sex Symbolism,'' ''U-a a-u-a: The First Lullaby,'' and ''Home of the Fish: The First Aquarium.''

- James B. Pritchard's *Ancient Near Eastern Texts Relating to the Old Testament* (Princeton: Princeton University Press, 1950) offers an absolutely indispensable collection of literary, historical, religious, legal, and other cultural texts of the ancient Near East (Sumerian, Akkadian, Babylonian, Egyptian, and others), including the individual myths of the Sumerian Gilgamesh song-cycle; the *Enuma Elish* or the Mesopotamian Creation Epic, and other early mythological texts, and well-known sources like the Code of Hammurabi.

---

violence'' (Genesis 6:11). Emphasis on divine judgment and Hebrew monotheism, or worship of one all-powerful god.

Utnapishtim: Spared because he is a favorite of Ea, as demonstrated by his obedience to the god's command.

Noah: Spared because of his singular righteousness, as demonstrated by his obedience to the god's command.

Utnapishtim: Storm is immediate and devastating, with only a few days' warning.

Noah: Storm preceded by a long period wherein humanity could amend its ways.

Utnapishtim: Great boat is square shaped (120 x 120 cubits), with seven decks, symbolizing the design of the great Mesopotamian ziggurats, or step-temples. It is built in seven days out of wood and caulked with pitch and asphalt. Finally, Utnapishtim loads the boat with his family, kin, wealth, craftsmen, and ''the beast of the field, both wild and tame'' (l. 109).

Noah: Ark more realistically boat-shaped (300 x 50 x 30 cubits), with three decks and a door. It is built of wood and caulked with pitch. Finally, Noah loads food, his family, and ''of every living thing of all flesh, you shall bring two of every sort into the ark, to keep them alive with you; they shall be male and female (Genesis 6:19).

Utnapishtim: Storm persists for 6 days and nights; on the seventh day the storm breaks from above, all humanity is dead, and the world is desolate. According to Utnapishtim, after the flood, ''I looked at the face of the world and there was silence, all mankind was turned to clay. The surface of the sea stretched as flat as a roof-top; I opened a hatch and light fell on my face. Then I bowed my face and I wept, the tears streamed down my face, for on every side was a waste of water'' (l. 111). The boat comes to rest on ''the mountain of Nisir'' (l. 111).

Noah: Storm continues for 40 days and nights, and ''on that day all the fountains of the great deep burst forth, and the windows of the heavens were opened'' (Genesis 7:11). The flood covers the entire earth, killing every living thing, and the ark comes to rest on ''the mountains of Ararat'' (Genesis 8:4).

Utnapishtim: Seven days after the boat comes to rest, Utnapishtim releases a dove and swallow, who return to the boat, and finally a raven, who finds dry land and does not return. Afterward,

Utnapishtim makes "a sacrifice and pour[s] out a libation on the mountain top," and when "the gods smelled the sweet savour, they gathered like flies over the sacrifice" (l. 111).

Noah: Forty days after the ark comes to rest, Noah sends out at seven day intervals a raven and dove, who return to the ark. After seven days, he sends the dove out again, who returns with "a freshly plucked olive leaf" (Genesis 8:11), indicating dry land. Afterward, Noah "offered burnt offerings on the altar. And when the Lord smelled the pleasing odor, the Lord said in his heart, "I will never again curse the ground because of man, . . ." (Genesis 8:21).

Utnapishtim: Visited by Ishtar, who offers "her necklace with the jewels of heaven" as a remembrance of the flood and who bans Enlil from the sacrifice (l. 111-12). In restitution, Enlil blesses Utnapishtim and his wife and grants them immortality. "Thus it was," Utnapishtim says, "that the gods took me and placed me here to live in the distance, at the mouth of rivers" (l. 113).

Noah: God blesses Noah and his family and commands them to repopulate the earth. God offers the rainbow as "the sign of the covenant which I have established between me and all the flesh that is upon the earth" (Genesis 9:17). Prior to the flood, biblical characters were said to have lived for hundreds of years. After this point, the biblical generations live a more recognizably human life span.

The argument of "precedence," or which story came first, is still debated. While Heidel argues that the two stories could be derived from a common ancestor, most scholars accept that the Mesopotamian myth came before the Hebrew account. Since the cuneiform texts are much older than the biblical account, most scholars accept that the biblical writers drew from that account and adapted it to their own historical and theological circumstances.

## Criticism

### Daniel T. Kline

*In the following essay, Kline traces the action of the epic and the development of Gilgamesh as a character. Kline concludes that by the end of the tale, Gilgamesh has changed considerably: he has gained an understanding of himself and of the importance of relationships with others.*

In essence, *The Epic of Gilgamesh* is a story about Gilgamesh's search for identity and meaning, and readers of his story—both ancient and modern—have seen in Gilgamesh something of their own experience. These issues of identity and meaning are both personal and intimately related: if I know who I am, I can make better sense of the world in which I live; and if I can make better sense of my world, perhaps I can live a better, more satisfying life. Through its characters, themes, events, and structure, the story itself serves as a lens through which the reader may carefully examine his or her own experience. Although the specific historical, cultural, and social circumstances of the modern world differ vastly from the time of the *Epic*, Gilgamesh's quest to know himself and his world remains current even today.

We might view Gilgamesh's journey into self-knowledge and the meaning of life as a progression through a series of relationships, specifically his relationship to himself (the individual realm), to others (the social realm), to his kingdom (the political realm), and to the gods (the supernatural realm). Gilgamesh's experiences in each of these realms accumulates throughout the *Epic* and shape his development as a character.

### The Individual Realm: Gilgamesh's Relationship to Himself

Gilgamesh's self-understanding develops gradually throughout the *Epic*. As the *Epic of Gilgamesh* opens, the Prologue outlines all of the hero's extraordinary qualities. He is all-knowing, wise, and experienced; he is beautiful, courageous, and powerful; and he is a noble king and expansive builder. As testimony to Gilgamesh's greatness, the narrator points to the great temple Eanna and the walls surrounding Uruk itself. No "man alive can equal" Gilgamesh's great ziggurat (or temple). Nearly 5,000 years later, the narrator's verse is still true. The remains of the Uruk's great wall and temple still stand in present-day Warka (the biblical Erech) in the Iraqi desert as the confirmation of Gilgamesh's political ambition and devotion to Anu and Ishtar.

### Gilgamesh: An Arrogant King

The *Epic* which follows the Prologue recounts Gilgamesh's heroic deeds, but the hero we find at first does not measure up to these lofty goals. The most significant detail the Prologue gives us is that Gilgamesh is semi-divine: "Two thirds they [the gods] made him god and one third man" (l. 61). Rather than giving Gilgamesh a higher sense of purpose or calling as a king, his partial divinity seems to have unsettled him and given him the hallmark quality of an epic hero: pride or *hubris*. Thus, the reader is faced with a contradiction at the very outset of the *Epic of Gilgamesh:* in contrast to the glowing testimony of the Prologue, the young ruler of Uruk is arrogant, cruel, and heedless of the consequences of his actions. The reader is left with the tantalizing problem that motivates the rest of the action: What happens to transform this cruel young ruler into a wise and celebrated king?.

### Gilgamesh: An Abusive Ruler

The opening moments of the *Epic* make clear that Gilgamesh's self-understanding effects his relationships to others; that is, his pride in his semi-divine status elevates him above everyone else, convinces him that he needs no one else, and leads him to think only of himself and his selfish needs. Because he is so full of *hubris* and his abuses are so great, Gilgamesh even destroys the social and familial bonds of his subjects, isolating themselves from one another: "No son is left with his father, . . . . His lust leaves no virgin to her lover, neither the warrior's daughter nor the wife of the noble" (l. 62). Gilgamesh is not "a shepherd to his people" (l. 62), as he should be. Sheep were an important commodity in the ancient world, and the shepherd occupied an important place in the society, for the shepherd not only cared for the sheep, he or she kept the sheep together in a flock, kept headstrong sheep from going astray, and protected them for dangerous predators. In short, the shepherd and sheep formed a close-knit social bond. Gilgamesh, however, has become the predator rather than the protector.

### The Social Realm: Gilgamesh's Relationship to Others

Gilgamesh's pride and isolation threaten to rip his city apart, and as a last resort, his people cry out to the gods for help: "'You made him, O Aruru, now create his equal; let it be as like him as his own reflection, his second self, stormy heart for stormy heart. let them contend together and leave Uruk in quiet" (l. 62). Notice that their solution to Gilgamesh's abuse is to ask the gods to give him a companion and an equal—someone with whom he can have a relationship. By giving Gilgamesh a "shadow self," someone to match his strength and passions, Gilgamesh can then leave the city, its families, and its people in peace. Although Gilgamesh's contact with the social world begins

with just one other person, its effect changes Gilgamesh for the rest of his life and the rest of his story.

### Enkidu: Gilgamesh's "Second Self"

Gilgamesh's mirror image is, of course, Enkidu. Gilgamesh and Enkidu are antithetical or opposites in many ways. On one hand, Gilgamesh is the highest product of civilized society. He is a semi-divine king who lives in a palace and indulges himself in fine food and sensuality. On the other, Enkidu represents the basic attributes of the natural world. He is fashioned from clay, is enormously strong, and has never encountered the opposite sex; he runs with the wild animals, frees them from the hunter's snare, and eats wild grasses. The *Epic* says simply that Enkidu "was innocent of mankind; he knew nothing of the cultivated land" (l. 63). While Enkidu lives off the land and what it provides naturally, Gilgamesh and the archaic Sumerian civilization thrives because of its ability to control nature—or at least harness it—by domesticating herd animals, by cultivating crops in the rich soil, by directing the river through irrigation and channels. Enkidu, who needs the cultivating influence of civilization, represents "natural man" or "pre-civilized humanity," while Gilgamesh embodies his civilization's highest cultural attainments.

### Women in the Epic of Gilgamesh: The Courtesan and Ishtar

In addition, the companion's relationships to women are also different but strangely parallel. After Gilgamesh dreams of Enkidu's arrival and hears from the trapper about the wild man who runs with the animals, Gilgamesh sends a temple courtesan to initiate Enkidu into civilized society. The Courtesan "taught him the woman's art" (l. 64), and in addition to her sexual lessons, the Courtesan instructs Enkidu in the proper way to eat bread, drink wine, clothe himself, and bathe and anoint himself with oil and perfume. After Enkidu embraces the Courtesan and her civilization, he is forever changed, and when he attempts to return to the mountains, "when the wild creatures saw him they fled. Enkidu would have followed, but his body was bound as though with cord, his knees gave way when he started to run" (l. 65). Enkidu's "wildness" literally has been harnessed by the bonds of civilization. At the same time Enkidu joins with the Courtesan, Gilgamesh carries out his sacred duty as king to unite with Uruk's ruling goddess. The *Epic* here likely reflects an early stage of Sumerian development when the king embodied both the priestly and political functions. Representing the lowest scale of human development, Enkidu enters the human community through the ministrations of a courtesan, or temple prostitute, in Ishtar's sacred service. Representing the highest pinnacle of human attainment, Gilgamesh joins with Uruk's divine patroness, Ishtar.

### Intimate Bonds Between Men: The Homosocial

It is important to recognize that when Gilgamesh and Enkidu meet, fight, and become bound companions, their relationships to women in the story—whether divine or common women—virtually disappear. In his dreams of the meteor and the axe, Gilgamesh repeatedly emphasizes that he is drawn to these objects "and to me its attraction was like the love of a woman" (l. 66). Each time Ninsun interprets the dreams for her son Gilgamesh, she also repeats that "you will love him as a woman and he will never forsake you" (l. 66).

Contemporary readers are often uncomfortable with erotic language that is applied to same-sex relationships, and too often see strong bonds between men only in stereotypical terms like "homosexual." However, social scientists and literary critics use the term "homosocial" to denote the intense personal bonds between men. "Homosocial" also indicates the kind of behavior, social codes, and activities that unite groups of men together, and this "Heroic Code" often arises in the context of athletic competition, warfare, or survival.

Gilgamesh and Enkidu are united in this kind of homosocial bond, for they are faithful to one another, they are united in their dangerous quests and battles, and their relationships to others pale in comparison to their connection with one another. After their fierce struggle in the streets of Uruk, "where they grappled, holding each other like bulls," shattering the door posts and shaking the temple walls (l. 69), Gilgamesh abandons Ishtar and Enkidu leaves the Courtesan. Gilgamesh, once united to the divine goddess, and Enkidu, once coupled to the lowly temple courtesan, "embraced and their friendship was sealed" (l. 69). Gilgamesh's relationship to Enkidu frees Uruk from the abuse of its king, and together, Gilgamesh and Enkidu make a complete package. Ninsun completes their union by adopting Enkidu as her own child, thus making him Gilgamesh's brother (l. 75).

### The Political Realm: Gilgamesh's Relationship to His Kingdom

After finding a companion, someone whom he can accept as an equal, Gilgamesh's attitude toward the people of Uruk changes. He must then face two superhuman threats to his kingdom: Humbaba and the Bull of Heaven. Gilgamesh's campaign against Humbaba, the giant who protects the Cedar Forest, not only puts into action both Gilgamesh's renewed sense of self and his new relationship to Enkidu, it also reinvigorates his sense of kingship. Until their journey into the forest, Gilgamesh and Enkidu have grown complacent in Uruk. Once active and vital, Enkidu has become weak and is "oppressed by idleness" (l. 70). Gilgamesh also seeks new adventure, for he says, "I have not established my name stamped on bricks as my destiny decreed" (l. 70). In terms of the Heroic Code, only a battle in a distant and threatening place against a formidable and evil foe will secure Gilgamesh's lasting reputation and quest his thirst for esteem.

### The First Test: Humbaba of the Forest

Notice, however, that Gilgamesh's personal quest for everlasting fame is at the same time a royal mission to free the land of evil: "Because of the evil that is in the land, we will go to the forest and destroy the evil; for in the forest lives Humbaba who name is 'Hugeness,' a ferocious giant" (l. 71). Humbaba represents wild and destructive nature apart from any civilizing tendencies, for as Humbaba says as he begs for his life, "I have never known a mother, no, nor a father who reared me. I was born of the mountain" (l. 82).

Now, Gilgamesh's desires are no longer at odds with Uruk's needs. In contrast to his earlier abuse of his people, Gilgamesh, now a true shepherd to his people, seeks to protect Uruk from Humbaba's evil and secure the vital natural resources Uruk needs to thrive. Some scholars see in Gilgamesh's journey to the Cedar Forest the historical echo of the cities of southern Mesopotamia infiltrating the more mountainous north and west for the lumber and minerals necessary to support their thriving economies. In fact, the cedar timbers are used to create one of Uruk's monumental city gates, "Seventy-two cubits high and twenty-four wide, the pivot and the ferrule and the jamb are perfect. A master craftsman from Nippur has made you" (l. 90). The city gates of ancient cities served a dual purpose: In their size and strength they offered the city protection from invaders, and in their craft and beauty they advertised their city's wealth much in the same way a modern corporate tower might celebrate a company's affluence and status. The forest he protects thus provides the raw materials for Uruk's protection. Ancient cities like Uruk needed to harness both forest and flood in order to survive, and Humbaba's defeat marks both Gilgamesh's prowess and Uruk's prosperity.

## The Second Test: The Bull of Heaven

Although Gilgamesh and Enkidu defeat Humbaba, the fearsome giant of the forest, their success triggers another fateful test: the Bull of Heaven. Gilgamesh and Enkidu return to Uruk, and Ishtar wants Gilgamesh as her lover. However, much in the same way Enkidu could not return to the embrace of the wild, so Gilgamesh cannot requite to embrace of the goddess. Gilgamesh recognizes that Ishtar uses and discards her human lovers much in the same way he used and dishonored the women of Uruk, and he pointedly asks Ishtar, "And if you and I should be lovers, should not I be served in the same fashion as all these others whom you loved once?" (l. 87). In other words, his renewed sense of relationship with others has shaped his view of himself, and he is no longer willing to treat others badly or be abused himself.

In her rage at being turned down by a lesser being, Ishtar persuades Anu and Antun, her parents, to unleash the Bull of Heaven upon Uruk. Much in the same way that Humbaba embodied both the promise of mountain riches and the danger lurking in the deep forest, so the Bull of Heaven personifies the threat of prolonged drought and famine, or natural disaster. Anu reminds Ishtar that, "If I do what you desire there will be seven years of drought throughout Uruk when corn will be seedless husks" (l. 87). Ishtar intends the Bull of Heaven to punish both Gilgamesh and Enkidu, but it is let loose upon Uruk. The Bull goes first to the river, where "with his first snorts cracks opened in the earth and a hundred young men fell down to earth" (l. 88). With the Bull's second snort, two hundred fall to their deaths, and with his third, Enkidu is struck a blow. It is difficult not to see the in the Bull of Heaven's snorts the rumbling destruction of an earthquake, which would devastate Uruk's mud-brick walls and open up crevasses in the earth. But Gilgamesh and Enkidu work together to defeat this threat and this latest venture becomes their greatest glory. Thus Gilgamesh's great victories yield the double benefit of bringing him glory and his city peace and prosperity.

## Death and the Supernatural Realm: Gilgamesh's Relationship to the Gods

Unfortunately, Gilgamesh's remarkable triumph against Humbaba and the Bull of Heaven also enrage some members of the heavenly pantheon, and Enkidu has a dream that a council of the gods has decreed that "Because they have killed the Bull of Heaven, and because they have killed Humbaba who guarded the Cedar Mountain one of the two must die" (l. 89). The gods choose Enkidu to die, and his last words to Gilgamesh reflect the Heroic Code around which their relationship has revolved: "My friend, the great goddess cursed me and I must die in shame. I shall not die like a man fallen in battle; I feared to fall, but happy is the man who falls in the battle, for I must die in shame" (l. 93). The true warrior dies with his comrades in battle, not in bed, but Enkidu's death brings Gilgamesh face-to-face with his most difficult challenge: the inevitability of his own mortality. Together, Gilgamesh and Enkidu had done everything in their power to establish their reputations, their "names," but at Enkidu's death Gilgamesh realizes that even their heroic exploits do not hold the key to happiness, eternal life, or even ultimate meaning. In Enkidu's death Gilgamesh faces his own destiny, for as Gilgamesh dreamed and Enkidu interpreted, "'The father of the gods has given you kingship, such is your destiny [but] everlasting life is not your destiny" (l. 70). In his rage and grief, Gilgamesh laments the passing of his friend and faces life again alone.

Although Gilgamesh is isolated again after Enkidu's death, he is not the same person he was at the beginning of the *Epic*. His relationship to Enkidu has changed him irreversibly, for although death separates Gilgamesh and Enkidu physically, it seems that Gilgamesh carries Enkidu's memory with him throughout the rest of the tale. Often, when critics talk about the central theme of the *Epic of Gilgamesh,* they describe it in the abstract: the theme of mortality or the awareness of death. Yet Gilgamesh's understanding of his mortality emerges from a very concrete and personal loss. His best friend has died and left the great hero fearful, and that life-changing event sends him into an even more desperate quest for the answer to life's ultimate question: what will become of me?

## Gilgamesh's Search for Immortality and the Meaning of Life

Gilgamesh recognizes his own fate in his friend's death, and this awareness spurs him on to the ends of the earth to find Utnapishtim: "Despair is in my heart. What my brother is now, that shall I be when I am dead. Because I am afraid of death I will go as best I can to find Utnapishtim whom they call the faraway, for he has entered the assembly of the gods" (l. 97).

During Gilgamesh's search for Utnapishtim, the hero changes both emotionally and physically in ways that contrast his earlier elevated status. First, the great hero who defeated Humbaba and the Bull of Heaven is truly fearful for the first time in the tale. He is just as tentative and unsure after Enkidu's death as he was arrogant and abusive before Enkidu's coming. Second, he changes physically to the point that he appears to be a wild man just like Enkidu had previously. He roams the wilderness dressed in skins, just a haggard shadow of his former self. Furthermore, Gilgamesh's journey into the supernatural to find Utnapishtim and conquer death parallels his earlier quest into the natural world of the Cedar Forest to locate Humbaba and conquer evil.

### Gilgamesh in the Garden of the Gods

The earlier quest tested his divinity; this final quest tests his humanity. After passing through a great darkness into the garden of the gods, Gilgamesh encounters three supernatural beings in succession before reaching Utnapishtim. Shamash, appalled at Gilgamesh's appearance, tells him, "'You will never find the life for which you are searching'" (l. 100). Alongside the great sea of death, Siduri, goddess of wine, tells him to abandon his search and advises him instead to eat, drink, and be merry while he can (l. 102). Urshanabi, Utnapishtim's boatman, at first refuses to take Gilgamesh to Utnapishtim, but after Gilgamesh destroys Urshanabi's sailing gear, the boatman relents. Finally, Gilgamesh confronts Utnapishtim with a single question: "how shall I find the life for which I am searching?" (l. 106). At this moment of completion when Gilgamesh has reached the end of his final quest, Utnapishtim replies: "There is no permanence" (l. 106). Utnapishtim goes on to explain that death is humanity's great equalizer, for everything human will fall eventually and masters as well as servants face the grave.

Each of these four encounters is marked both by repetition and increasing complexity. It is as if the closer Gilgamesh gets to his goal, the more difficult his encounter. First, Shamash simply comments that Gilgamesh will not find what he's look-ing for. Next, Siduri supports her contention with illustrations from everyday life. Third, Urshanabi has to contend with the angry hero and give him the means to cross the waters of death to Utnapishtim. Finally, Utnapishtim not only answers Gilgamesh's query, Utnapishtim goes on to tell the story of the great flood and how he became immortal.

### The Quest for Meaning and the Process of Grief

At the same time, Gilgamesh's journey into the supernatural follows a numbing repetition. Each deity wonders how Gilgamesh came this way and into his deteriorated state; Gilgamesh responds each time that he is haggard and drawn because of his grief for his companion Enkidu—with whom he conquered Humbaba and the Bull of Heaven—that he fears death, and that he seeks Utnapishtim. Narratively, these repetitions summarize the action up to this point; psychologically, they recreate the haunting questions that persistently assail someone in grief. In fact, Gilgamesh's description—his "face like the face of one who has made a long journey" (l. 105)—captures the poignant weight of grief and its effects. Thus, we might view Gilgamesh's journey into the supernatural to find Utnapishtim equally as a psychological journey through grief toward understanding of his mortality and a reconciliation with his own limitations.

### Gilgamesh and the Loaves of Bread

Utnapishtim gives Gilgamesh a rather simple test to see if he is worthy of immortality: remain awake for seven days. However, sleep quickly overcomes the hero, and Utnapishtim's wife bakes a loaf of bread for each day Gilgamesh sleeps. In a fascinating descriptive sequence, the story describes how the loaves of bread age and decay over seven days (l. 114), paralleling Enkidu's seven-day spiral of decay "until the worm fastened on him" after his death (l. 96). The symbolic nature of the decaying bread is not lost on Gilgamesh, for it confirms again that "death inhabits my room" (l. 115).

### Gilgamesh, the Flower of Youth, and the Serpent at the Well

After Gilgamesh fails the test, the *Epic* presents two strangely parallel scenes. In the first, Utnapishtim give Urshanabi the charge to "take him to the washing place" (l. 115). There Urshanabi helps Gilgamesh clean himself up, literally sloughing-off "his skins, which the sea carried away, and showed [again] the beauty of his body" (l. 115). Despite Gilgamesh's apparent failure, the king of Uruk is once again transformed, and this physical metamorphosis hints toward his awareness of human limitation. Utnapishtim banishes Urshanabi, and at the urging of his wife, reveals to Gilgamesh the whereabouts of an underwater plant whose bloom can renew old people to their lost youth. Gilgamesh finds the plant and wants to share its benefits with the people of Uruk, but a snake hiding at the bottom of a well eats the bloom, sheds its skin, and returns to the well, leaving Gilgamesh bereft once again.

## The End is the Beginning: Gilgamesh in Relationship and in Death

Many critics believe that the story ends on a note of loss, for Gilgamesh loses the life-giving plant and returns to Uruk empty-handed. However, the tale leaves us with two more positive images. First, although Gilgamesh does not earn everlasting life, he is physically renewed like the snake that sloughs off its skin. The clothes Utnapishtim gives him "would show no sign of age, but would wear like a new garment till he reached his own city, and his journey was accomplished" (l. 115). Physical change and decay, like the loaves of bread, is inevitable, but change is not necessarily to be equated with death.

Second, Gilgamesh actually does not return empty-handed. Urshanabi returns to Uruk with him. Here we see the beauty of the *Epic's* consistently parallel but antithetical structure. In the first half of the story, Gilgamesh begins as a ruthless prince and ends as a grieving friend. The second half reverses the first. Gilgamesh begins as a haggard, wild wanderer and returns with a new companion. Gilgamesh may not have eternal life, the ultimate object of his quest, but he does have understanding and relationships with others, two things he lacked at the beginning.

The final chapter of the *Epic,* the brief "The Death of Gilgamesh" (ll. 118-19), completes Gilgamesh's cycle from haughty young king to beloved old ruler. The opening of the tale found Gilgamesh to be selfish and arrogant, using the women of Uruk for his own pleasure and the men for his ambitions. He lived outside of meaningful human relationships, and he was completely without companionship except for those he dominated. Gilgamesh was restless and "a man of many moods"

until he found an equal and a companion. Indeed, he was no shepherd to his people. The story's conclusion finds just the opposite. Gilgamesh has fulfilled the destiny which Enlil had decreed, and he has achieved great victories. But instead of dying alone on his bed, Gilgamesh is surrounded by love of his family; by his extended household, servants, courtiers, and friends; by the people of Uruk "great and small," and even by a host of gods, including "Dumuzi" the god of shepherds and sheepfolds (l. 119). All of creation is united in their lament for Gilgamesh's death, and although he did not find eternal life, his story has endured, etched in stone and now on the page, in the memory of his people and his readers alike.

**Source:** Daniel T. Kline, for *Epics for Students,* Gale Research, 1997.

## Thorkild Jacobson

*In the following excerpt, Jacobsen traces the course of Gilgamesh's quest for immortality.*

As the story begins Gilgamesh shares the heroic values of his times, and his aspirations to immortality take the form of a quest for immortal fame. Death is not yet truly the enemy; it is unavoidable of course but somehow part of the game: a glorious death against a worthy opponent will cause one's name to live forever. In his pursuit of this goal Gilgamesh is extraordinarily successful and scores one gain after another. He fights Enkidu and gains a friend and helper. Together they are strong enough to overcome the famed Huwawa and to treat with disdain the city goddess of Uruk, Ishtar. At that point they have undoubtedly reached the pinnacle of human fame. And at that point their luck changes. In ruthlessly asserting themselves and seeking ever new ways to prove their prowess they have grievously offended the gods, paying no heed to them whatever. Huwawa was the servant of Enlil, appointed by him to guard the cedar forest; their treatment of Ishtar was the height of arrogance. Now the gods' displeasure catches up with them, and Enkidu dies.

When he loses his friend, Gilgamesh for the first time comprehends death in all its stark reality. And with that new comprehension comes the realization that eventually he himself will die. With that all his previous values collapse: an enduring name and immortal fame suddenly mean nothing to him any more. Dread, inconquerable fear of death holds him in its grip; he is obsessed with its terror and the desirability, nay, the necessity of living forever. Real immortality—an impossible goal—is the only thing Gilgamesh can now see.

Here, then, begins a new quest: not for immortality in fame, but for immortality, literally, in the flesh. As with his former quest for fame Gilgamesh's heroic stature and indomitable purpose take him from one success to another. Setting out to find his ancestor, Utanapishtim, in order to learn how to achieve, like him, eternal life, he gains the help of the scorpion man and his wife, Sidûri, the alewife, and Urshanabi. When after great travail he stands before Utanapishtim it is only to have the whole basis for his hopes collapse. The story of the flood shows that the case of Utanapishtim was unique and can never happen again and—to make his point—Utanapishtim's challenging him to resist sleep, proves how utterly impossible is his hope for vigor strong enough to overcome death.

However, at the point of the seemingly total and irreversible failure of his quest, new hope is unexpectedly held out to Gilgamesh. Moved by pity, Utanapishtim's wife asks her husband to give Gilgamesh a parting gift for his journey home, and Utanapishtim reveals a secret. Down in the fresh watery deep grows a plant that will make an oldster into a child again. Gilgamesh dives down and plucks the plant. He has his wish. He holds life in his hand. Any time he grows old he can again return to childhood and begin life anew. Then on the way back there is the inviting pool and the serpent who snatches the plant when he carelessly leaves it on the bank.

Gilgamesh's first quest for immortality in fame defied the gods and brought their retribution on him; this quest for actual immortality is even more deeply defiant; it defies human nature itself, the very condition of being human, finite, mortal. And in the end it is Gilgamesh's own human nature that reasserts itself; it is a basic human weakness, a moment of carelessness, that defeats him. He has nobody to blame but himself; he has ingloriously blundered. And it is perhaps this very lack of heroic stature in his failure that brings him to his senses. The panic leaves him, he sees himself as pitiful and weeps; then as the irony of the situation strikes him, he can smile at himself. His superhuman efforts have produced an almost comical result. This smile, this saving sense of humor, is the sign that he has, at last, come through. He is finally able to accept reality

and with it a new possible scale of value: the immortality he now seeks, in which he now takes pride, is the relative immortality of lasting achievement, as symbolized by the walls of Uruk.

The movement from heroic idealism to the everyday courage of realism illustrated by [the hero of] the Gilgamesh story gains further in depth if one analyzes it not only positively as a quest, but also negatively as a flight, an avoidance. A flight from death rather than a quest for life—but a flight in what terms?

Throughout the epic Gilgamesh appears as young, a mere boy, and he holds on to that status, refusing to exchange it for adulthood as represented by marriage and parenthood. Like Barrie's Peter Pan he will not grow up. His first meeting with Enkidu is a rejection of marriage for a boyhood friendship, and in the episode of the bull of heaven he refuses—almost unnecessarily violently—Ishtar's proposal of marriage. She spells disaster and death to him. So when Enkidu dies, he does not move forward seeking a new companionship in marriage, but backward in an imaginary flight toward the security of childhood. At the gate of the scorpion man he leaves reality; he passes literally ''out of this world.'' In the encounter with the alewife he again firmly rejects marriage and children as an acceptable goal, and eventually, safely navigating the waters of death, he reaches the ancestors, the father and mother figures of Utanapishtim and his wife, on their island where, as in childhood, age and death do not exist. True to his images, Utanapishtim sternly attempts to make Gilgamesh grow up to responsibility; he proposes an object lesson, the contest with sleep, and is ready to let Gilgamesh face the consequences. The wife of Utanapishtim, as mother, is more indulgent, willing for Gilgamesh to remain a child, and she eventually makes it possible for him to reach his goal with the plant ''As Oldster Man Becomes Child.'' Gilgamesh is fleeing death by fleeing old age, even maturity; he is reaching back to security in childhood. The loss of the plant stands thus for the loss of the illusion that one can go back to being a child. It brings home the necessity for growing up, for facing and accepting reality. And in the loss Gilgamesh for the first time can take himself less seriously, even smile ruefully at himself; he has at last become mature.

> For whose sake, Urshanabi, did my arms tire?
> For whose sake has my heart's blood been spent?
> I brought no blessing on myself,
> I did the serpent underground good service!

The *Gilgamesh* epic is a story about growing up.

**Source:** Thorkild Jacobson, "Second Millennium Metaphors: 'And Death the Journey's End,' The Gilgamesh Epic," in *The Treasures of Darkness: A History of Mesopotamian Religion,* Yale University Press, 1976, pp. 193–219.

## Jack M. Sasson

*In the following excerpt, Sasson discusses the five separate, original Sumerian legends that were eventually combined into the unified Gilgamesh epic.*

As it is still preserved for us, the material in Sumerian dealing with Gilgamesh consists of five legends, each complete within itself. "Gilgamesh and King Agga of Kish" is probably the most "historical" text. It speaks of Gilgamesh's stouthearted refusal to submit to the mighty king of a neighboring kingdom and of his eventual triumph over the forces which threatened Uruk. "Gilgamesh and the Land of Living" is by far the masterpiece among the fragments in existence. Its mood is somber throughout, for it treats a poignant theme. These are the words of Gilgamesh to Utu the sun-god:

> Utu, a word I would speak to you, to my
>     word your ear!
> I would have it reach you, give ear to it!
> In my city man dies, oppressed is the heart,
> Man perishes, heavy is the heart,
> I peered over the wall,
> Saw the dead bodies floating in the river's water.
> As for me, I too will be served thus, verily it is so!
> Man, the tallest, cannot reach to heaven,
> Man, the widest, cannot cover the earth.
> Brick and stamp have not yet brought forth the
>     fated end,
> I would enter the "land," would set up my name;
> In its places where the names have been raised up,
> I would raise up my name.
> In its places where the names have not
>     been raised up,
> I would raise up the names of the Gods.

In order to accomplish this task, Gilgamesh and his servant Enkidu travel to the Cedar-forest, the land of the Living. There they attack and kill Humbaba, its monstrous guardian. But not before some of the most felicitous imageries in cuneiform literature were preserved on clay.

"Gilgamesh, Enkidu and the Nether World", sometimes called "Gilgamesh and the Huluppu-tree," begins with an act of creation. This is not especially remarkable, for to the Mesopotamian, as well as to the Hebrew, almost every existing element, be it animate or inanimate, resulted from a genesis that was tailor-made to fit its special nature. This, incidentally, helps to explain the many acts of creation, often clashingly different, that have been preserved in almost every Ancient Near Eastern civilization. To return to our story, a huluppu-tree, some sort of willow, had been nurtured by the goddess Inanna. Sadly enough it soon became the haunt of repulsive creatures. Gilgamesh is called upon to banish these intruders and is rewarded with same symbols of kingship produced from the huluppu's wood. When these objects accidentally fall into the Netherworld, heroic Gilgamesh sends his companion Enkidu to regain them. The latter's descent into Hades offers the Sumerian poet a chance to describe life among the dead. "The Death of Gilgamesh" and "Gilgamesh and the Bull of Heaven" are two additional tales from the Sumerian which exist in an extremely poor state of preservation.

Because of the episodic nature of the Sumerian material at our disposal, we are faced with yet another difficulty. Did the Sumerian poets know of a cycle of tales whose protagonist was Gilgamesh, or were they content just to chant his praises in a series of single, complete adventures? In other words, was there as early as Sumerian times a unified epic with a major theme woven within the succession of encounters? With the possibility that future discoveries may force drastic revision in current opinions, the answer will have to be "No!" A meticulous reading of the Sumerian fragments summarized above will show very little internal evidence to suggest that even the humblest idea was followed or elaborated. As a matter of fact, one suspects an ulterior motive to have influenced the forging of some of these songs. This is best noted in "Gilgamesh, Enkidu and the Netherworld," where the act of creating the huluppu tree and the subsequent conversion of some of its wood into symbols of kingship requires as many lines as the visit of Enkidu to the underworld.

It is nearly inescapable, one is forced to conclude, that man's first written epic was wrought by a Semitic genius who probably lived during the time of Hammurapi. To be sure, our poet must have been acquainted with some important emendations brought about by an Assyrian predecessor some generations earlier. The following will be no more than an educated guess, but it is ventured that some of the more bombastic episodes of far-away conquest, such as the expedition to the Cedar-forest to destroy Humbaba, may have been patterned after historical events which occurred around 2350 B.C. Then Sargon of Agade, a Semitic dynast, deeply penetrated the Amanus ranges and Anatolia. His exploits were remembered with special relish by the

Assyrians, one of whose famous kings took the same name. The intensely nationalistic Babylonians, on the other hand, never quite forgave Sargon for having rejected Babylon as a capital city in favor of Agade. For this reason, they would be loath to devise exploits for their Gilgamesh based upon the career of Sargon. It would be another matter, of course, to accept a ready-made adventure and to incorporate it within existing collections.

A question might be raised at this point. If the adventure of Gilgamesh in the Cedar mountain is of Assyrian origin, how does one explain its presence in ''Gilgamesh and the Land of the Living,'' a Sumerian text? It should brought to attention that despite its preservation in Sumerian, a language which became obsolete as a mode of oral communication in the late third millennium, ''Gilgamesh and the Land of the Living'' dates from the era of Hammurapi, By then, Sumerian was employed by priests and scribes much as Latin is used today in the Catholic church. I would like to hazard a guess which might be realized through stylistic evidence that ''Gilgamesh and the Land of the Living'' was a translation from the Semitic Akkadian into an ornate Sumerian.

To return to the old Babylonian poet. He seems to have introduced two elements into the collection which he inherited both from Sumer and Assyria. One of these, the transformation of Enkidu from the status of a passive servant to that of an active and often competitive companion, is probably the most inspired literary achievement in the annals of Mesopotamian creative thinking. In the Sumerian rendition Enkidu was conceived as a static servant whose every move depended upon the whim of his master. In the Babylonian version, however, Enkidu stands, at least at the outset, as Gilgamesh's opponent. . . .

The other theme introduced by the Semitic bard is the quest for immortality, or more precisely, for rejuvenation. This theme has been encountered tangentially in the Sumerian version, but this occurs precisely in the text which is suspected of being a rendering from the Semitic. No doubt, the important role which Shamash, the Sun-god, plays in the Babylonian renditions has something to do with inspiring this theme. As the god of Justice, a notion which included the apportioning of life, Shamash came to prominence among the Semites. His cult was particularly strong during the Old Babylonian era of *ca.* 1750 B.C.

The development of these two motifs, reinforcing each other, necessitated rearrangement of the available material and permitted the forging of a new pattern, that of a unified epic. Such a statement should, of course, be taken with a liberal dash of salt, for it treads upon tortuous territory: the origins of literary creativity. We can, however, stand on firmer ground when we consider the techniques employed by the poet to translate inspiration into the written word. In this paper, I would like to concentrate on one literary device, irony, and will attempt to demonstrate a subtlety on the part of the Semitic poet which might rank him with Homer, with slight exaggeration of course. (pp. 263–65)

Of irony's many qualities, I shall describe the Semitic poet's employment of two devices which have commonly been called ''dramatic irony'' and ''irony in the use of character.'' In some sense, dramatic irony is almost always playful, intellectual, and esoteric. Passages containing the ironic elements operate on two seemingly independent levels. On the one hand, the characters are shown by their utterances or deeds to be unaware of having fallen victims to a rush of events beyond their control. On the other hand, the audience, forewarned of subsequent developments by an omniscient author, evaluates differently the same passage. This discrepancy between the ultimate reality, as it is known to the audience, and the immediate situation, as it is understood by the characters, constitutes dramatic irony, well-known to us from the works of the Greek dramatists, of Shakespeare, and of Ibsen, among many others.

The *Gilgamesh* epic actually opens by offering a capsule summary, a sort of Miltonian argument, of the complete drama that is to unfold:

> Let me proclaim to the land (the feats) of him who
>     has seen the deep
> Of him who knows the seas, let me inform it fully
> He has (seen/visited) the. . . .
> The wise (one) who knows everything.
> Secret things he has seen, what is hidden to man
>     (he knows)
> And he brought tidings from before the Flood
> He also took the Long Journey, wearisome and
>     under difficulties
> All his experiences, he engraved in a stone stela.

The poet thus assures his listeners that he will be telling a ''true'' tale since its essence is derived from Gilgamesh's own inscription. He also reminds them that his hero will come back from a long journey, weary and worn, and lightly suggests it to have been an unsuccessful enterprise. Lest the audience be caught in a despairing mood, one which could inhibit its response to his story-telling, the Mesopotamian bard quickly adds praises of Gilgamesh's earthly, tangible achievements.

> Of ramparted Uruk, the wall he built
> Of hollowed Eanna, the pure sanctuary.
> Behold its outer wall, whose cornice is like copper
> Peer at its inner wall, which none can equal
> Seize upon the threshold, which is from old
> Draw near to Eanna, the dwelling of Ishtar,
> Which no future king, no man can equal.
> Go up and walk on the walls of Uruk,
> Inspect the substructure, examine the brickwork:
> Is not its core of baked brick?
> Did not the Seven (Sages) lay its foundations?

The above passage can be considered as the poet's editorial comment upon Gilgamesh's search for immortality. It is futile, he seems to argue, to be content with more than earthly accomplishments. When this notion is alluded to again, it comes at the end of the *epic,* after the long and fruitless odyssey is over. One cannot but admire the poet's cleverness in choosing a resigned Gilgamesh to utter the following:

> Go up, Urshanabi, walk up on the ramparts
>    of Uruk.
> Inspect the base terrace, examine its brickwork.
> (See) if its core is not of baked brick,
> And if the Seven Wise Ones laid not its
>    foundation!

Nor is the audience allowed a lapse of memory, for the poet repeatedly calls attention to Gilgamesh's eventual failure. Before every new venture, the hero is made to hear the truth about the success of his forthcoming enterprise. But the blinded and tragic protagonist fails to perceive it. In the first cluster of episodes, it is Enkidu who ironically is chosen to deliver the poet's messages. In two instances before the warriors' meeting with Humbaba, an encounter which could be considered as the prolegomenon to Enkidu's death, this brave companion has a series of premonitions. The first occurs immediately after Enkidu and Gilgamesh, appreciating each other's vigor: "kissed each other and formed a friendship." "My friend," says Gilgamesh, "why do your eyes fill with tears? (Why) is your heart ill, as bitterly you sigh?" "A cry, my friend," replies Enkidu, "chokes my throat. My arms are limp, and my strength has turned to weakness." As the two approach the lair of Humbaba, Enkidu has a presentiment once more: "Let us not go down into the heart of the forest," he implores Gilgamesh. "In opening the gate, my hand becomes limp."

But fate is not to be cheated, and the poet digs deeper into his bag of literary tricks, producing a fresh and sharper collection of ironical episodes. As the fateful confrontation with Humbaba draws even nearer, it is Gilgamesh's turn to be forewarned. In one remarkable statement intended to give courage to Enkidu, he is made to say: "Who, my friend, can scale heaven? Only the gods dwell forever with the Sun-god. As for mankind, numbered are its days; whatever they achieve is but wind. Even here you are afraid of death." It becomes Gilgamesh's tragedy that having enunciated the facts of mortal life, he did not perceive and learn from them. Moreover, Gilgamesh fails to heed significant warnings. Nocturnal messages were valued by all ancient civilizations as vehicles in which the gods counseled their creations. For this reason, Gilgamesh requested and was granted a series of three dreams. As it is conjectured by Oppenheim [in *The Interpretation of Dreams in the Ancient Near East* ], the first contains an admonition to leave the mountainous area of the Cedar-forest. In the second, a mountain collapses upon our hero, but miraculously he manages to escape injuries. In the third, the catastrophe is complete. With almost cynical irony, however, the poet assigns Enkidu the task of *favorably* interpreting these visions of obviously calamitous portent. Thus, an encounter with Humbaba which will bring great unhappiness to both the heroes is inexorably encouraged. Finally, when the monster evokes a response of mercy in the heart of Gilgamesh, the audience, by then thoroughly prepared, watches helplessly as Enkidu seals his own fate by counseling: "To the word which Huwawa (has spoken), hark not. Let not Huwawa (live)."

The examples offered above have all been chosen from one single, albeit major, episode. It can be demonstrated, however, that the Mesopotamian lyricist was able to invoke irony as one of many devices intended to bind his many tales into a single integrated cycle. This is done by carefully choosing the secondary characters and assigning each a task which heightens the contrast between reality and aspiration.

Except for Utnapishtim's wife, who originally may have played a larger role than the one she is assigned in Tablet Eleven, four females are prominent in the epic: two divinities, Ishtar and Ninsun, and two attendants of the gods, the hierodule and the divinized Siduri, barmaid to the immortals. Before we enter this topic, however, it might be of interest to say a few words concerning the characterization of Gilgamesh and Enkidu.

Departing radically from his Sumerian counterpart, the Semitic poet seems to have consciously attempted to fashion one personality who would combine the idiosyncrasies of his two major protagonists. At the outset, Gilgamesh is described as a king of unequaled potential and of boundless, though undirected, energy. He is haughty, spoiled, and egocentric. Once Enkidu is given what Oppenheim calls an *éducation sentimentale* —in it self a master touch of irony, for Enkidu's sexual excess is destined to end Gilgamesh's—he becomes gentle, experienced, calm, and concerned with ''justice.'' Not unlike the friendship which developed between Don Quixote and Sancho Panza, as the story unfolds we witness a rapprochement in temperament, a meeting of the minds between the two friends. So that, as Enkidu lies on his funerary couch, punished for acting with the impetuosity and hubris characteristic of Gilgamesh, the latter has been tamed to the point of embodying his friend's gentler spirit within his own. It is not accidental, I think, that Gilgamesh then recognizes . . . that his fate will henceforth be to roam over the steppe, precisely the region, foreign to the urbane Gilgamesh, where Enkidu was created. To be sure, the poet strews all sorts of hints that despite the apparent differences in their early behavior, Enkidu was conceived as *alter ego* to Gilgamesh. His creation in the hands of the goddess Aruru was to have been a *zikru,* a replica of Gilgamesh. Instead, she decided to fashion him in the image of the god Anu, perhaps to instill in him a divinity equivalent to, once the hierodule's instruction is completed, yet different from, Gilgamesh's. Exceedingly handsome and strong, Enkidu ''looks like Gilgamesh to a hair; though shorter in stature, he is more massive in frame.'' Repeatedly he is said to be Gilgamesh's equal. In his dreams, Gilgamesh encounters his ''double'' and responds to him not as a stranger, but as one who is uncannily familiar. Witness also the important events in Tablet Eleven. Gilgamesh had just been tested by Utnapishtim and his wife. He was to remain awake for six days and seven nights, a period which, incidentally, equals the length of Enkidu's consortings with the hierodule. But Gilgamesh fails, for ''sleep fans him like a whirlwind.'' It should not be doubted that sleep and ritual bathing were often considered to be *rites de passage,* transitions from one state to another. In this case Gilgamesh, upon his reawakening, was to undergo a transformation, one that duplicated wild Enkidu's metamorphosis toward civilization. To quote the epic:

> Utnapishtim (said to him,) to Urshanabi,
> the boatman:
> ''Urshanabi, (may) the qua(y) reject you, may the
> ferry landing refuse you forever!

> May you, who used to frequent its shore, be
> denied its shore.
> The man before whose face thou didst walk,
> whose body is covered with grime,
> The grace of whose body the pelts have hidden,
> Take him, Urshanabi, and bring him to the place
> of washing;
> Let him wash off his dirt in water like a
> clean (priest),
> Let him throw off his pelts and let the sea carry
> (them) away, that his body may come to
> look resplendent,
> Let the band around his head be replaced with
> a new one.
> Let the garment he wears be his best garment.
> Until he gets to his city,
> Until he finishes his journey,
> May (his) garment have no crease, but may it
> (always) be new.''

Lastly, just as the people of Uruk petition the gods for relief from Gilgamesh's rapaciousness, so do the hunters beg for respite from Enkidu's repeated interference with their trapping activities.

Characteristic of this earliest of epics, incidentally, we meet with the rudiments of all subsequent *Doppelgänger* narratives, very popular in western culture, in which two dramatized personalities are forged into one, ''two characters (are made) to complement each other both physically and psychologically and who together are projections of the crippled or struggling personalities of a third character with whom the author is primarily concerned.''

In interpreting the omina of Enkidu's arrival into Uruk, the divine Ninsun is chosen by the poet to fulfill an important function. In an unfortunately damaged section, it is she who solicitously binds Enkidu's fate to that of her son, Gilgamesh: '''Mighty Enkidu, you are not my womb's issue. I (have) herewith adopted you with the devotees of Gilgamesh, the priestesses, the votaries, and the cult women.' An *indu*-tag she placed round the neck of Enkidu.'' It is not without a certain amount of irony, I think, that this relationship is broken as a direct result of another goddess's ire. When, after killing the Bull of Heaven sent by Ishtar to punish Gilgamesh for his insolence, Enkidu flings the animal's right side toward the proud deity, he draws upon himself the brunt of celestial retribution. To be sure, this is not the only act of defiance in which Enkidu becomes involved. [Tablet VIII] specifically credits him with the killing of Humbaba. . . . In that version, Enkidu adds salt to the wound by foolishly taunting Enlil, Humbaba's protector. He who was created by the gods to control violence, please note, is now forsaken by them for glorying in it.

More pointed is the Mesopotamian poet's skillful use of the other two females. The role of the hierodule in civilizing Enkidu is well-known. In a sense, the harlot's instructions destroyed the innocence of the "noble savage" by presenting him with the realities of human life. It was through her unflinching devotion to duty that Enkidu was made to realize the amenities and the advantages that only a civilized man can extract out of existence. Faced with imminent death, Enkidu manages to gather enough strength with which to curse this woman who had led him away from the idyllic life of an uncivilized creature. But the Sun-god Shamash urges him to withdraw his powerful malediction, reminding him of the many benefits which were showered upon him by the ardors of the hierodule:

> Why, O Enkidu, [Shamash rhetorically asks] do
>      you curse the harlot
> Who made you eat food fit for divinity,
> And gave you to drink wine fit for royalty,
> Who clothed you with noble garments,
> And made you have fair Gilgamesh for a comrade?
> And has (not) now Gilgamesh, your bosom friend
> Made you lie on a noble couch?
> He has made you lie on a couch of honor,
> He placed you on the seat of ease, the seat
>      at the left,
> That the princes of the earth may kiss your feet.
> He will make Uruk's people weep over you (and)
>      the courtesans mourn for you,
> Will fill (the) people with woe over you.
> And when you are gone,
> He will invest his body with uncut hair,
> Will don a lion skin and roam over the steppe.

To eat, to drink, to be well clothed, and have lasting companionship were among the gifts that the gods gave to mankind. Beyond that nothing more can be obtained. How foolish of Gilgamesh to want more, the so-to-speak "existentialist" poet seems to say. When Gilgamesh appears, haggard and bedraggled, with "woe in his belly, his face (like) that of a way-farer from afar," he had plainly forsaken these pleasures which an assiduous hierodule, sent ironically enough by Gilgamesh himself, had taught Enkidu, his *alter ego*. Instead, Gilgamesh now sought rejuvenation. To bring Gilgamesh back to his reality, the poet elects another pragmatic personality, Siduri, barmaid of the gods. The following famous passage reminds the king of Uruk that eating, drinking, clothing, and companionship are the only achievable goals of man:

> Gilgamesh, for what purpose do you wander?
> You will not find the life for which you search.

> When the gods created mankind,
> Death for mankind they set aside,
> Retaining life in their own hands.
> You, Gilgamesh, let your belly be full
> Be happy day and night.
> Throw a party every day,
> Dance and play day and night!
> Let your garment be sparkling fresh.
> Your head be washed; bathe in water.
> Pay heed to the little one that holds on
>      to your hand
> Let your spouse delight in your bosom.
> For *this* is the task of mankind.

**Source:** Jack M. Sasson, "Some Literary Motifs in the Composition of the Gilgamesh Epic," *Studies in Philology,* Vol. LXIX, No. 3, July, 1972, pp. 259–79.

## Sources for Further Study

Dalley, Stephanie. *Myths from Mesopotamia: Creation, The Flood, and Others,* Oxford World Classics. Oxford: Oxford University Press, 1989.
    Includes two versions of the *Epic of Gilgamesh* as well as the Mesopotamian Creation Epic (the *Enuma Elish*) and other myths associated with Gilgamesh and ancient Mesopotamian civilization. The literary material follows the cuneiform closely. Excellent notes and scholarly annotations.

*Exploring Ancient World Cultures: An Introduction to Ancient World Cultures on the World-Wide Web,* March, 1997, http://eawc.evansville.edu
    Designed with the beginning college student in mind, the EAWC Homepage is the best place to start an online search for information on the ancient Near East. It offers links, essays, chronologies, history, literature, and teacher resources.

Ferry, David. *Gilgamesh: A New Rendering in English Verse,* New York: Farar, Straus and Giroux, 1992.
    A beautifully lyrical and evocative transformation of the *Epic* into verse couplets. Ferry follows the twelve tablet format and includes brief notes at the end of his translation. A haunting and poetic achievement informed by sound academic investigation.

Gardner, John, and Maie, Johnr. *Gilgamesh: Translated from the Sin-leqi-unninni Version,* New York: Alfred A. Knopf, 1984.
    A very readable rendering of the twelve tablets, with extensive notes and explanations for specific translation preferences. The introduction provides an interesting take on the *Epic,* though transposing the Greek concepts of "Apollonian" and "Dionysian" (via

Nietzsche) onto a Mesopotamian myth seems an unwarranted choice for understanding the dynamics of the story.

Gray, John. *Near Eastern Mythology,* Library of the World's Myths and Legends, New York: Peter Berdrick Books, 1982.
A handsomely illustrated coffee-table book covering the historical geography, religion, myths, and kingship of Mesopotamia, Canaan, and Israel.

Heidel, Alexander. *The Gilgamesh Epic and Old Testament Parallels,* 2d ed, Chicago: University of Chicago Press, 1949.
The most thorough examination of the relationship of the Mesopotamian materials to the Old Testament. Brings a religious point of view to the debate.

Joffe, Alexander. Review of *The Uruk World System: The Dynamics of Expansion of Early Mesopotamian Civilization,* by Guillermo Algaze. *Journal of World- Systems Research,* Vol. 1, Book Review 4, 1995. Reprint, *Journal of Field Archaeology,* Vol. 21, 1994, pp. 512- 16, http://csf.colorado.edu/wsystems/jwsr/vol1/v1_r4.htm
This technical article offers a thorough review of the current thinking concerning the rise, expansion, and fall of ancient Mesopotamian cities in general and Uruk in particular.

Jones, Charles E. *ABZU: Guide to Resources for the Study of the Ancient Near East Available on the Internet,* March 13, 1997, http://www-oi.uchicago.edu/OI/DEPT/RA/ABZU/ABZU.HTML
A comprehensive web site sponsored by the Research Archives of the Oriental Institute of the University of Chicago. Carries links to sources for the general reader and research specialist, including a regional and subject index and online journals, museums, and articles.

Katz, Solomon H., and Fritz Maytag. "Brewing an Ancient Beer," http://beer.tcm.hut.fi/SumerianBeer.html
Don't let the title fool you. The article, reprinted here from an unacknowledged source, is the latest in an ongoing academic discussion over whether ancient Mesopotamians first began to gather and domesticate grain for the production of bread or beer.

Kovaks, Maureen Gallery. *The Epic of Gilgamesh,* Stanford: Stanford University Press, 1989.
A faithful but very readable rendering of the Standard Version, following the structure of the original eleven cuneiform tablets. (Kovacks does not consider Tablet XII, The Death of Gilgamesh, to be part of the original version and so does not include it in her translation). Includes a fine, succinct introduction; helpful summaries introducing each tablet, and a useful glossary of key terms and names.

Kramer, Samuel Noah. *The Sumerians: Their History, Culture, and Character,* Chicago: University of Chicago Press, 1963.
Technical but readable. Kramer's introduction is still the standard introduction to Sumerian culture, though it is now somewhat dated.

Lloyd, Seton. *The Archaeology of Mesopotamia: From the Old Stone Age to the Persian Conquest,* London: Thames and Hudson, 1978.

A thorough, detailed, and interesting survey of the significant archaeological sites in the ancient Near East. Packed with illustrations and diagrams, it includes a significant section on Uruk, Gilgamesh's home city.

Oates, Joan. *Babylon,* rev. ed., London: Thames and Hudson, 1986.
Excellent comprehensive overview of Babylonian history and culture, including the *Epic of Gilgamesh.* Well illustrated and fully documented.

*Oriental Institute of Chicago WWW Page,* http://www-oi.uchicago.edu/OI/default.html
As this impressive homepage demonstrates, "The Oriental Institute is a museum and research organization devoted to the study of the ancient Near East. Founded in 1919 by James Henry Breasted, the Institute, part of the University of Chicago, is an internationally recognized pioneer in the archaeology, philology, and history of early Near Eastern civilizations." Check out especially the "Virtual Museum," with its variety of artifacts and artwork.

Pritchard, James B. *The Ancient Near East in Pictures, Relating to the Old Testament,* 2d ed. with supplement, Princeton: Princeton University Press, 1969.
A fascinating and informative photographic survey of the archaeological artifacts of ancient Near Eastern cultures. The book is organized topically: I. Peoples and Their Dress, II. Daily Life, III, Writing, IV. Scenes from History and Monuments, and so on. Viewing these photographs provides a reader with the best possible sense of the daily life and practices of these ancient peoples.

Renger, Johannes M. "Mesopotamian Epic Literature," in *Heroic Epic and Saga: An Introduction to the World's Great Folk Epics,* edited by Felix J. Oinas, pp. 27-48, Bloomington: Indiana University Press, 1978.
A general introduction to the epic literature of Mesopotamia, including the Lugulbanda and Gilgamesh cycles. Includes a succinct summary of literary techniques in the epics.

Sandars, N. K. *The Epic of Gilgamesh,* rev. ed., London: Penguin Books, 1972.
Rendering the *Epic* as a narrative, or in story form, Sandars has provided the most accessible and easily read translation. This edition also boasts a thorough introduction, though somewhat dated now, and glossary.

Sciafe, Ross and Suzanne Bonefas. *Diotima: Materials for the Study of Women in the Ancient World,* http://www.uky.edu/ArtsSciences/Classics/gender.html
Includes a searchable database and a good set of links to a variety of topics related to women and gender.

Siren, Christopher B. *The Assyro-Babylonian Mythology FAQ [Frequently Asked Questions], version 1.7html,* October 6, 1995, http://wilmot.unh.edu/~cbsiren/assyrbabyl-faq.html
Along with its companion, *Sumerian Mythology FAQ,* these FAQs provide a handy guide to the main aspects of ancient Mesopotamian mythology. Includes bibliography.

Siren, Christopher [B.]. *Sumerian Mythology (Version 1.8html),* October 6, 1996, http://wilmot.unh.edu/~cbsiren/sumer-faq.html

    Along with its companion, *Assyro-Babylonian Mythology FAQ,* these FAQs provide a handy guide to the main aspects of ancient Mesopotamian mythology. Includes a bibliography.

Thompson, R. Campbell. *The Epic of Gilgamesh: Text, Transliteration, and Notes,* Oxford: Clarendon Press, 1930.

    Designed for specialists, but is interesting to peruse for the transliterations of Sumerian, Babylonian, and Assyrian tablets. It also contains Thompson's own hand-copies of the individual cuneiform tablets.

# Iliad

## Homer
## c. 700 B.C.

For all practical purposes, Western literature begins with the *Iliad*. The *Epic of Gilgamesh*, while at least 1,000 years older, is neither as well-known nor as influential as Homer's work. We still use expressions like "Achilles' heel," "Trojan horse," or "the face that launched a thousand ships," all with roots in the *Iliad* or the mythic cycle on which it is based, nearly 3,000 years after the poem was written. And at least in terms of the number of copies to survive from antiquity, the poems of Homer are second only to the Bible in popularity.

Although "*Iliad*" means "the story of Ilion," or Troy, the poem has much more to say about Achilles and Hector than it does about Troy. As the first word of the Greek text suggests ("Rage! Goddess, sing the rage of Peleus's son Achilles"), this poem has a lot to do with anger. Honor, glory, and fate are also frequent themes.

Among the things for which the *Iliad* is most famous are its use of epithets, or formulaic phrases to describe an individual, an object, or even some events. Also noteworthy is the poem's masterful use of similes.

For more than 1,500 years the *Iliad* and the *Odyssey* set the standard by which epic poetry, if not all poetry of any kind, was judged. The epic form in poetry has not been widely practiced since the appearance of John Milton's *Paradise Lost* in 1667, but the story of the fall of Troy has remained a perennial favorite to the present day.

## Author Biography

Everything we know about Homer is either traditional, mythical, or some kind of an educated guess. Tradition tells us, probably following the *Odyssey* and one of the so-called "Homeric Hymns" from the middle of the seventh century BC, that Homer, like his own character Demodocus from the *Odyssey,* was a blind bard or singer of tales.

At least seven different places claimed that Homer was born on their soil in the ancient world. The two with the strongest claims are the island of Chios and the city of Smyrna (modern Izmir, in Turkey). Because he records many details of Ionian geography and seems to know less about other areas (like western Greece, where the *Odyssey* is set), and because the most common dialect in Homer's Greek is Ionic, most scholars now believe that Homer probably lived and worked in Ionia, the region along what is now the west coast of Turkey.

We can only guess at the time when Homer lived and wrote. Some ancient writers believed that Homer lived relatively close to the time of the events he described. The fifth-century historian Herodotus, on the other hand (*Histories,* II.53), said that Homer could not possibly have lived more than 400 years before his own time. The rediscovery of writing by the Greeks around 750 BC and the development, at about the same time, of some of the fighting techniques described in the *Iliad* have led scholars to assign Homer to the middle or late part of the eighth century BC.

Accurate dating of Homer's poems is impossible, but it is generally thought that the *Iliad* is older than the *Odyssey,* as that work displays some more "advanced" stylistic features. Both poems had to have been completed before the Peisistratid dynasty came to power in Athens in the sixth century BC, because it is known that a member of that family commissioned a "standard edition" of the poems. Also, during the sixth century BC, both the *Iliad* and the *Odyssey* were recited in full at the Great Panathenaia, a religious festival in honor of Athena, which was observed in Athens.

There have been any number of controversies about Homer since his time: beginning with contention over just exactly where and when he was born, lived, and died. Others have questioned whether Homer existed at all, and whether a poet named Homer actually "wrote" the poems attributed to him, or merely culled them from popular folklore.

The question of whether the same person produced both the *Iliad* and the *Odyssey* has also been debated. The English poet and critic Samuel Butler (1835-1902) suggested that the *Odyssey* was the work of a woman, but this view did not gain wide acceptance.

Most scholars, at least, agree that there was an epic poet named Homer, and that this poet was instrumental in producing the *Iliad* and *Odyssey* in their known forms.

## Plot Summary

### *The Background of the Story*

The goddess Eris (Discord) was not invited to the wedding of Peleus and Thetis (Achilles' parents), so in revenge she threw a golden apple inscribed "for the fairest" into the banquet hall, knowing it would cause trouble. All the goddesses present claimed it for themselves, but the choice came down to three—Aphrodite, Athena, and Hera. They asked Zeus to make the final decision, but he wisely refused.

Instead, Zeus sent them to Mount Ida, where the handsome youth Paris was tending his father's flocks. Priam had sent the prince away from Troy because of a prophecy that Paris would one day bring doom to the city. Each of the three goddesses offers Paris a bribe if he will name her the fairest: Hera promises to make him lord of Europe and Asia; Athena promises to make him a great military leader and let him rampage all over Greece; and Aphrodite promises that he will have the most beautiful woman in the world for his wife. Paris picks Aphrodite. From then on both Hera and Athena are dead-set against him, and against the Trojans in general.

The most beautiful woman in the world at the time is Helen, a daughter of Zeus and Leda. Helen is already married—to Menelaus, the king of Sparta. Helen's adoptive father Tyndareus had required all the men who wanted to marry her swear a solemn oath that they would all come to the assistance of Helen's eventual husband should he ever need their help.

Paris visits Menelaus in Sparta and abducts Helen, taking her back to Troy with him, seemingly with her active cooperation. Paris also takes a large part of Menelaus' fortune. This was a serious breach of the laws of hospitality, which held that guests and hosts) owed very specific obligations to each other. In particular, the male guest was obligated to respect the property and wife of his host as he would his own.

Menelaus, his brother Agamemnon, and all the rest of Helen's original suitors, invite others to join them on an expedition to Troy to recover Helen. An armada of some 1,200 ships eventually sails to Troy, where the Achaeans fight for years to take the city, and engage in skirmishes and plundering raids on nearby regions. The story opens in the tenth year of the war.

### Book 1: The Wrath of Achilles

Agamemnon offends Chryses, the priest of Apollo, by refusing to ransom back his daughter. Apollo sends a plague on the Achaeans in retribution. At a gathering of the whole army, Agamemnon agrees to give the girl back but demands another woman as compensation, and takes Briseis, Achilles' concubine.

Achilles is enraged, and pulls his whole army out of the war. In addition, he prays to his mother, the goddess Thetis, to beg Zeus to avenge his dishonor by supporting the Trojans against the Achaean forces. Zeus agrees, though not without angering his wife, Hera.

### Book 2: Agamemnon's Dream and the Catalogue of Ships

Zeus sends a false prophetic dream to Agamemnon, indicating that if he will rouse the army and march on Troy, he can capture the city that very night. As a test, Agamemnon calls another assembly and suggests instead that the whole army pull up its tents and sail back home.

This turns out to be a very bad idea. The troops rush away to get ready for the voyage home and their leaders have a very hard time restoring them to order. The army is eventually mobilized for war, and a catalogue of the Achaean and Trojan forces involved in the fight follows.

### Book 3: The Duel between Paris and Menelaus

In what is most likely a flashback episode, a truce is called so that Menelaus and Paris can meet in single combat, the winner to take Helen and all her treasures home with him. Solemn oaths are sworn by both sides to abide by the outcome of the duel. Helen watches the fight with King Priam from the walls of Troy, and points out the chief leaders of the opposing forces. Just as Menelaus is on the point of killing Paris, his protector, the goddess Aphrodite takes him safely out of the battle and back to his bedroom in Troy.

### Book 4: The Truce is Broken

Hera schemes with some of the other gods and goddesses to break the truce. Athena tricks Pandarus, an ally of the Trojans, into shooting an arrow at Menelaus, wounding him slightly. General fighting breaks out again.

### Book 5: The Aristeia

Helped by Athena, Diomedes sweeps across the battlefield, killing and wounding Trojans by the dozen. He even wounds the goddess Aphrodite when she tries to rescue her son Aeneas, and the war god Ares, when he tries to rally the Trojan forces. (Note: ''*aristeia*'' is a Greek word which means ''excellence'' and here refers to an episode in which a particular character demonstrates exceptional valor or merit.)

### Book 6: Hector Returns to Troy

While hacking his way through the Trojans, Diomedes meets Glaucus, the grandson of a man his own grandfather had hosted—which makes them ''guest-friends'' who cannot harm or fight against each other. Meanwhile, Hector has gone back to Troy to urge his mother to offer a sacrifice to Athena in an attempt to win back her favor for the Trojans. He then meets his wife and baby son on the wall of Troy before getting Paris and taking him back to the battle.

### Book 7: The Greeks Build a Wall

Hector and Paris return to the fighting, and Hector challenges one of the Achaeans to a duel. Ajax is chosen, but the outcome of the fight is indecisive. As night falls, arrangements are made for a truce to allow the dead on both sides to be collected and buried. During this truce, the Achaeans fortify their camp.

### Book 8: The Trojans Gain the Upper Hand

When the fighting resumes after the burial truce, Zeus forbids the other gods to interfere any further in the course of the war. He himself begins actively assisting the Trojans. Things go very badly for the Achaeans all day, and they retire behind their new fortifications for the night, while the Trojans camp out on the plain before them, to be ready for battle first thing the following morning.

### Book 9: The Embassy to Achilles

At the urging of several of his advisers, Agamemnon sends an embassy to Achilles and offers to give Briseis back, and promises greater rewards to come when Troy is finally conquered. Since Agamemnon has not apologized for taking Briseis, Achilles refuses to consider the offer, and instead vows to sail home with his army the next morning.

### Book 10: A Night Raid

Agamemnon spends a restless night, and eventually decides to send a spy into the Trojan camp to see what can be learned. Diomedes and Odysseus are chosen from among the volunteers. They capture a Trojan spy sent to reconnoiter their own camp and, based on information they get from him, the two men kill the newly arrived Thracian king Rhesus with some of his men and make off with a team of horses.

### Book 11: The Aristeia of Agamemnon

When fighting resumes the following morning, Agamemnon gets his day of glory, but eventually is wounded (as are many of the other leading fighters in his army). The Trojans push their opponents back to the wall of the camp, and Achilles sends his friend Patroclus to find out what is happening. Nestor meets Patroclus on this errand, and urges him to get Achilles to come back to the fighting or, failing that, to borrow Achilles' armor himself and masquerade as his friend in an attempt to trick the Trojans into giving the Achaeans some breathing room.

### Book 12: The Trojans Break Through

Before Patroclus can get back to Achilles's tent, the Trojans break through the fortification wall and head for the beached ships, intending to burn them and so prevent the Achaeans from returning home.

### Book 13: The Battle for the Ships

The fighting rages up and down the beach, and the Achaeans are barely able to keep the Trojans away from their ships. Zeus leaves Mount Ida temporarily, and Poseidon covertly assists the Achaeans. Ajax, with Poseidon's help, manages to halt Hector's advance.

### Book 14 : Hera Distracts Zeus

Hera schemes to distract Zeus while Poseidon helps the Achaean forces. She entices her husand into making love on the top of Mount Ida. As the two of them sleep after their lovemaking, Poseidon continues to help the Achaeans, who drive the Trojans back from the ships. In the fighting, Ajax stuns Hector but does not quite kill him.

### Book 15: The Achaeans at Bay

When Zeus wakes up and discovers what has been going on, he forces Poseidon out of the fighting. This swings the balance back toward the Trojans, who once more drive their opponents back to the ships and try to set fire to them.

### Book 16: Patroclus Fights and Dies

Patroclus finally gets back to Achilles, who lets his friend borrow his distinctive armor and his troops against the Trojans. Achilles warns him, however, not to pursue Hector or to get too close to the city itself. As Patroclus is putting on Achilles's armor, Hector sets fire to the first of the ships. When Patroclus and the Myrmidons enter the battle, the Trojans fall back and Patroclus has his *aristeia,* killing many Trojans, including Sarpedon, a son of Zeus himself.

Patroclus ignores Achilles's advice and pursues Hector and the Trojans all the way back to the walls of Troy. There he is confronted by Apollo, who stuns and disarms him. The Trojan Euphorbus wounds Patroclus, and Hector finishes him off, but not before Patroclus prophesies Hector's own impending death.

### Book 17: The Aristeia of Menelaus

Hector strips Achilles's armor from Patroclus's body. He tries to take the body as well, but the Achaeans fight him off, led by Menelaus. Helped by Ajax, Menelaus distinguishes himself in the fighting against Hector and Aeneas.

### Book 18: The Shield of Achilles

Achilles hears the news of Patroclus's death, and vows to revenge himself on Hector for the injury. His mother tells him that if he kills Hector, his own death will follow shortly, but Achilles insists he will have revenge. She asks the god Hephaestus to forge new armor for her son. Patroclus' body is recovered as Hephaestus makes a beautiful new suit of armor, including a richly worked shield, for Achilles.

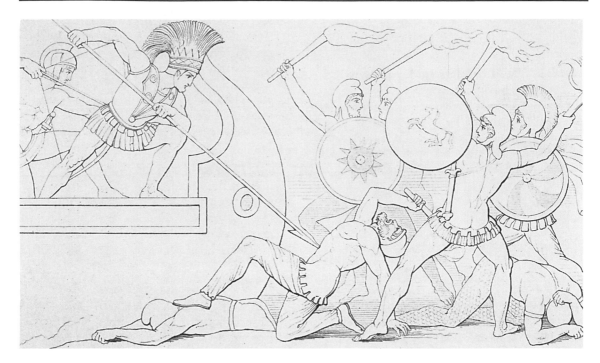

*Ajax defends the Greek ships against the Trojans.*

### Book 19: Achilles is Reconciled with Agamemnon

Prodded by Odysseus, Achilles agrees to a formal reconciliation with Agamemnon and accepts the gifts he is offered in recompense for Agamemnon's slight, but vows not to eat or drink until he has revenged Patroclus's death by killing Hector. He puts on his new armor, and his immortal horse Xanthus foretells his coming death.

### Book 20: The Gods Themselves Go to Battle

Zeus gives the gods permission to interfere in the fighting again, which they do with great enthusiasm. Achilles goes on a rampage against the Trojans, and only direct divine intervention saves anyone who is unlucky enough to turn up in his path.

### Book 21: Achilles and the River Scamander

Achilles continues to hack his way through the Trojan ranks. Eventually he kills so many that the river Scamander is clogged with corpses. The river god attempts to drown Achilles, but is balked by Hephaestus. Achilles eventually crosses the river and moves on toward Troy, where he is diverted by Apollo just long enough to allow the Trojans (except for Hector) to pull back behind the city walls.

### Book 22: The Death of Hector

Hector stands outside the gates, debating whether to stand and fight Achilles or to retreat within the city himself. As he ponders, Achilles approaches and begins to chase him around the city walls. After the third circuit of the city, Apollo withdraws his protection from Hector. Athena, taking the form of one of Hector's brothers, tricks him into fighting Achilles, who kills him. Still enraged, Achilles ties Hector's body to his chariot and drags it back to the Achaean camp, as Hector's family watches in horror from the walls of Troy.

### Book 23: The Funeral of Patroclus

Patroclus's ghost comes to Achilles at night and asks him for a speedy burial. The next day, his friend gives him a magnificent funeral, complete with memorial games, at which Achilles presides.

### Book 24: Hector's Body is Recovered and Buried

On the orders of Zeus and with the protection of Hermes, Priam makes his way to Achilles's camp at night to ransom back the body of his son. Achilles is moved to pity the old man and makes him comfortable after agreeing to accept the ransom he offers for Hector's body. Achilles guarantees the Trojans a suitable amount of time to prepare for and conduct Hector's funeral.

## Characters

### Achilles

Son of the mortal Peleus and the sea goddess Thetis, Achilles is the best warrior at Troy. He leads the *Myrmidons* (from the Greek word for "ant," as their ancestors were created by Zeus from ants after a plague had depopulated part of the kingdom of Achilles' grandfather, Aeacus).

His mother dipped the baby Achilles in the River Styx, which made him invulnerable. But she forgot to dip the heel by which she held him, which left one place where a weapon could injure him: hence an "Achilles' heel" is a weak or vulnerable spot.

Thetis knew that her son was destined either to go to Troy, where he would die gloriously as a young man, or to live a long (but dull) life ruling over his people at home. To keep him out of the army, Thetis sent Achilles away to another king's court dressed as a woman, but Odysseus tracked him down there and convinced him to join the army in spite of his mother's pleas. Knowing that his time is short, Achilles wants to make the most of it and is very sensitive to any suggestion that he is not the best, most respected man of his age—which leads to the conflict with Agamemnon that starts the poem.

Later Greek tradition held that Achilles and Patroclus were lovers as well as friends, not an uncommon practice in classical times. Bernard Knox suggests, in his introduction to Robert Fagles's translation of the *Iliad* (1990), that "the text gives no warrant" for this assertion, but other critics disagree. There are a number of instances in the poem where Achilles' words or actions indicate, though they do not necessarily prove the existence of, a level of attachment that is beyond mere friendship (e.g., XVIII.22 ff., XIX.4-5, XIX.319-21, and XXIII.144ff.).

Knox is correct, however, to note that Achilles is godlike in more than just appearance. For most of the poem, Achilles behaves more like one of the gods—petulant, self-absorbed, touchy, and well-nigh implacable when angry—than his fellow human beings. His words to Hector, just before he kills him, "to hack your flesh away and eat it raw" (XXII.347) recall Hera's attitude toward the Trojans, as described by Zeus, at the beginning of the poem (IV.35-36). It is only after Hector's death that Achilles becomes human again, a transformation that is completed when Priam comes to ransom Hector's body.

After killing Hector, Achilles and the Achaeans make headway against the Trojans once more. Achilles, however, does not live to see the city fall: he is killed by Paris (with the help of Apollo) shortly before the Achaeans resort to the "Trojan Horse" to gain access to the city by night.

### Achilleus

*See* Achilles

### Aeacides

*See* Achilles

### Aeneas

Son of Anchises and the goddess Aphrodite, Aeneas is a minor character in the *Iliad,* where he is portrayed as a fighter to be reckoned with (especially in Books 5 and 20), and at least once is described (VI.75f.) as Hector's equal in "both war and counsel," though apparently not everyone agreed with that assessment (see XIII.460).

Legend had it that Aeneas was the only member of the Trojan royal family to survive the sack of the city (see XX.302), and that he and his companions sailed westward. The Romans eventually claimed him as the ancestor of their race and the founder of their nation, as described by Vergil in the *Aeneid,* an epic poem in Latin.

### Agamemnon

Son of Atreus, brother of Menelaus, and king of Mycenae, Agamemnon is in overall command of the Achaean forces at Troy. His position is emphasized in the original Greek by the fact that the epithet *anax andrōn* ("lord of men"), which appears nearly 60 times in the *Iliad,* is for all intents and purposes used only in reference to Agamemnon (the five exceptions are all forced by the rules of the meter).

Homer portrays Agamemnon as a good fighter, a proud and passionate man, and a fair tactician, but

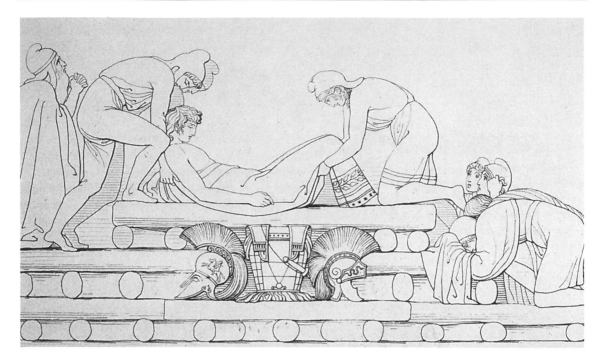

*The funeral of Hector.*

somewhat vacillating and relatively easily discouraged. He does seem to harbor at least a little resentment of the fact that, while he is in command, it is Achilles who gets most of the glory (just as Achilles seems to resent the fact that he does all the work, yet Agamemnon gets most of the material spoils of war).

In the Greek myths, Agamemnon seems a driven man: he sacrifices one of his own daughters to Artemis to ensure a favorable wind for the army on its way to Troy, he insults the best fighter in his army and refuses to be reconciled until his forces stand on the brink of disaster, and, at least in some traditions, on his return home from the war, he allows himself to be treated almost like one of the gods. These are all characteristics of what the Greeks called *hubris* (''arrogance,'' ''overweening pride'') or *Atē* ( what we might now call ''temporary insanity''), and they are Agamemnon's chief failings in life.

The Greeks explained these personality defects by appealing to the curse that was supposed to be on the house of Pelops (Agamemnon's grandfather), in retribution for a sacrilegious murder he committed while wooing his wife. The curse came home to rest on Agamemnon when he was murdered (according to Homer in the *Odyssey,* by Aegisthus, his cousin and the lover of Agamemnon's wife Clytemnestra;

according to Aeschylus in his play *Agamemnon,* by Clytemnestra herself) upon his return home from Troy. Agamemnon's young son Orestes, too young to go to Troy, eventually avenged his father's death by killing his mother and her lover, which forms the subject of the remaining two plays in Aeschylus' tragic cycle, the *Oresteia.*

### Aias
*See* Ajax

### Aineias
*See* Aeneas

### Ajax (Oilean, the Lesser)
When this character is in company with Ajax the Greater (Telamonian Ajax), Homer will sometimes refer to the two of them as ''Aiantes,'' the plural form in Greek of the name ''Ajax.'' As this expression, though perhaps confusing, is more graceful than ''the two Ajaxes,'' it is often used by translators.

Son of Oileus and leader of the Locrians at Troy. Shipwrecked on his way home after the war, he boasts of having escaped the sea in spite of the gods and is drowned by the sea god Poseidon.

# Media Adaptations

- There have been no films made that are directly based on the *Iliad*. There have been several films based wholly or in part on other aspects of the Troy legends, including Michael Cacoyannis' *The Trojan Women* in 1971 and *Iphigeneia* in 1977.

- In 1985, the British Broadcasting Corporation produced a television series, starring Michael Wood, entitled *In Search of the Trojan War*. The companion volume to this series was published by the BBC in 1986.

- Penguin Highbridge Audio put out an audiocassette version of Robert Fagles' translation of the *Iliad* in 1992 (six cassettes and a companion book). They also have a combined audio version of Fagles' translations of both the *Iliad* and the *Odyssey*. Harper Audio brought out a cassette version of Richmond Lattimore's translation, read by Anthony Quayle (1996). Norton offers a partial rendition of the *Iliad* in its Greek original, read by Stephen Daitz (1990).

- A number of films have distinctly Homeric qualities or make some reference to Homer and/or themes from his works. In the 1975 film *Monty Python and the Holy Grail*, for example, crusading knights plot to get inside a castle by concealing themselves within a gigantic wooden rabbit they construct and leave outside the castle walls (however, they forget to hide inside their "Trojan Rabbit"). In 1993's *Sommersby*, the Richard Gere character, an Odysseus-like figure who returns home from war after many years, actually reads the *Iliad* to his son. Gere's character can also be seen as something of a Hector figure, who

fights for his country (and eventually dies for it), even though he knows the cause is ultimately hopeless.

- The Perseus Project on the World Wide Web, administered by the Classics Department at Tufts University, is an excellent on-line resource for studying the classics or classical texts. The URL for the project's homepage is http://www.perseus.tufts.edu. Among the things you can find on this site are the original Greek (the Oxford Classical Texts version) and the Murray translation (from the Loeb Classical Library edition) of the *Iliad*, which you can find by selecting the "Texts Greek/English" button from the main site map, and then choosing either the "Ancient Greek texts" or the "English translations of Greek texts" link and selecting Homer as the author and the *Iliad* as the text. Many of the names in the translation have hypertext links (just click on the name and it will take you to the relevant information) to further information and sources relevant to that person, place, or concept. The Perseus material is also available (Macintosh format only, but a Windows version is in the works) on CD-ROM from Yale University Press.

- If you want to look for other WWW resources on the *Iliad* or other classics-related people, places, or things, a good place to start is with Alan Liu's "Voice of the Shuttle" classical studies page at http://humanitas.ucsb.edu/shuttle/classics.html. He has a broad collection of information and links to other sites relevant to the classics and classical literature.

## Ajax (Telamonian, the Greater)

When this character is in company with Ajax the Lesser Homer will sometimes refer to the two of them as "Aiantes," the plural form in Greek of the name "Ajax." As this expression, though perhaps confusing, is more graceful than "the two Ajaxes," it is often used by translators.

Son of Telamon and grandson of Aeacus (who was also grandfather of Achilles), Telemonian Ajax was king of Salamis, an island off the coast of Attica and not far from Athens that would later be the site of a major naval battle between the Greeks and Persians under Xerxes in 480 BC. One of the bravest and strongest fighters at Troy, he is nevertheless portrayed by Homer as somewhat obstinate and rather plodding, as if all he knew was fighting and nothing else.

It should be noted, though, that he does all his own fighting without divine aid. Diomedes, Achilles, Odysseus, and the others are all helped by one or another of the gods at some time in the poem: it is only Telemonian Ajax who muddles along (and rather well at that) on his own merits.

At the funeral games after Achilles's death, he and Odysseus competed for Achilles's armor and weapons. When they were awarded to Odysseus, Telemonian Ajax sulked and, in a fit of madness, slaughtered a flock of sheep in the belief that they were his enemies. When he discovers what he had done, he falls on his sword, unable to live with the shame. His death forms the subject of a tragedy by Sophocles.

### *Ajax the Lesser*

*See* Ajax (Oilean)

### *Akhilleus*

*See* Achilles

### *Alexandros*

*See* Paris

### *Andromache*

Daughter of Eetion and wife of Hector; mother of Astyanax (also called ''Scamandrius,'' his real name; ''Astyanax'' is a Greek word that means ''lord of the [lower] town,'' and is more a princely title than a name). After Hector's death, she marries the seer Helenus. When the city falls to the Achaeans, her son is killed and she is given as a prize to Achilles' son Neoptolemus.

### *Antenor*

One of the elders of Troy and a counselor of King Priam. He is perhaps best known in the *Iliad* for having fathered many sons who turn up throughout the poem.

### *Aphrodite*

Aphrodite is the Greek goddess of love. According to Homer, she is the daughter of Zeus and Dione; the poet Hesiod (who likely lived and wrote not long after Homer's time), however, claims that she sprang from the foam (*aphros* in Greek) of the sea, as seen in Sandro Botticelli's painting *The Birth of Venus* (circa 1485). She is married, though not faithful, to Hephaestus, god of fire and smithcraft. Among her many lovers was the god of war, Ares; another was the Trojan prince Anchises, the father of Aeneas. For this reason she favors the Trojans over the Achaeans in the Trojan war.

It could be said that Aphrodite is at least partially responsible for the war. Paris named her as the most beautiful of the goddesses, and the reward she promised him was the ''right'' to have the most beautiful woman in the world for his wife—Helen, who just happened to be married to another man. Menelaus was understandably upset when Paris ran off (or made off) with his wife, but such considerations did not apparently carry much weight with Aphrodite.

Nor should we expect them to. Aphrodite's main concern is the physical attraction, and the actions that result from it, between lover and beloved: this is the source of her power, and it is, as with all the gods in their respective spheres of influence, the thing she cares about most of all. Other concerns are secondary, if indeed they are noticed at all. This is why, after rescuing Paris from the duel with Menelaus in Book 3, she sends him off to bed with Helen, and also why she gives Helen a good scare when she questions the goddess' orders to go to her lover.

### *Apollo*

The son of Zeus and Leto, and twin brother of Artemis, Apollo is the god of archery, prophecy, music (especially the lyre, the stringed instrument that Achilles plays in Book 9), medicine, light (sometimes, though not in Homer, Apollo is identified with the sun), and youth. Plagues and other diseases, and sometimes a peaceful death in old age, were often explained as being the result of arrows shot by Apollo (for men), or by his sister Artemis (for women). Although he also worked with Poseidon at building the walls of Troy and was cheated out of his proper payment, he supports the Trojan side in the war.

### *Ares*

The son of Zeus and Hera, Ares is the god of war (or, more precisely, of warlike frenzy). He is more of a name in the *Iliad* than an actual character (as, for example, in the epithet "beloved of Ares"). When he actually does appear, however, Homer's characterization of him is quite negative. This attitude seems to have been fairly common in Greek mythology.

Ares is portrayed as a bully, someone who delights in causing trouble for the sheer enjoyment of watching what he stirs up, and more of a braggart than a man of deeds. He is not well-liked even among the gods, all of whom laugh at him when he is wounded by Diomedes in Book 5. Even his own parents seem to think poorly of him.

### Artemis

Daughter of Zeus and Leto, twin sister of Apollo, Artemis is a virgin goddess of the hunt, the moon, and, in some traditions, of childbirth and young things. With her brother, she supports the Trojan side. Plagues and other diseases, and sometimes a peaceful death in old age, were often explained as being the result of arrows shot by Artemis (for women), or by her brother Apollo (for men).

### Athena

The daughter of Zeus and Mētis, whom Zeus (following in the tradition of his own father, Cronus) swallowed when it was revealed that she would someday bear a son who would be lord of heaven and thus usurp Zeus' place. She was born, full-grown and in armor, from the head of Zeus after Hephaestus (or, in some traditions, Prometheus) split it open with an axe to relieve his headache.

Athena was revered as the patron goddess of Athens (where the temple known as the Parthenon was dedicated to her in her aspect as *Athena Polias,* protectress of the city), but also as a goddess of war, wisdom and cleverness (her mother's name means "Scheme" or "Trick"), and crafts, especially weaving and spinning. She exploits her position as Zeus's favorite daughter, and seems to be able to pacify him when no one else can. She favors the Achaean side in the war, and is especially devoted to Odysseus.

### Athene

See Athena

### Atreides

See Agamemnon

### Atrides

See Agamemnon

### Calchas

The son of Thestor, Calchas is a highly respected seer or prophet accompanying the Achaean forces. In addition to being the one to provoke Agamemnon by telling him it is his fault that Apollo is angry with the army, Calchas is said to have been the prophet who foretold the necessity of sacrificing Agamemnon's daughter, Iphigeneia, to Artemis in return for a fair wind on the way to Troy.

### Cassandra

Daughter of Priam and Hecuba, Apollo fell in love with her and gave her the gift of prophecy. When she rejected his advances, he gave her a companion "gift": even though her prophecies are always true, no one ever believes her. After the fall of Troy, she is taken as a slave and concubine by Agamemnon, and is killed with him on his return to Mycenae.

### Chryses

A priest of Apollo, he comes to Agamemnon seeking to ransom his daughter, taken in a raid on their city. When Agamemnon refuses to accept the offered ransom, Chryses prays to Apollo, who inflicts a plague on the army as a punishment. Once the girl is returned safely, he again prays to Apollo, who lifts the plague.

### Clytemnestra

Daughter of Tyndareus (who was also Helen's adoptive father) and unfaithful wife of Agamemnon. She takes a lover, Agamemnon's cousin and foster brother Aegisthus, during her husband's absence and with him plots to murder Agamemnon on his return from Troy. In some traditions she kills Agamemnon herself (by muffling him with a cloak or blanket in the bath and bludgeoning him with an axe), while in others she merely incites Aegisthus to do it for her (which is the tradition Homer follows in the *Odyssey*). She is eventually killed by her own son, Orestes, in vengeance for his father's death.

### Diomedes

Son of Tydeus and king of Tiryns and Argos, Diomedes is one of the principal fighters in Agamemnon's army, ranking second only to Achilles. He and Ajax the Greater bear the brunt of the fighting after Achilles withdraws to sulk in his camp. The bulk of the action in Books 5 and 6 centers on Diomedes.

Homer depicts Diomedes as an honorable man, though high-spirited and impetuous at times. Later tradition held that Aphrodite, in retribution for his having wounded her as she tried to shield her grandson Aeneas in battle, caused Diomedes' wife to be unfaithful to him while he was away at Troy. When he returned home and found out about her infidelity, he left home in disgust and was believed to have gone to Italy, where he founded several cities, died, and was eventually buried near the Apulian coast, in the so-called "Islands of Diomedes."

## Hades

In Homer, the name refers almost exclusively to a place and not a person. The name itself appears to be composed of the Greek words for "not" and "seeing," and so could be translated as "The Unseen" (place or person).

The place was believed to be beneath the ground. It is not so much a place of punishment, the equivalent of Hell, as it is a place of darkness in which the dead lead an existence that is quite literally a shadow of their former lives. Homer seems not to have been aware of the tradition that within Hades there was a brighter region of Hades (the Elysian Fields) for the souls of virtuous people, but he does mention Tartarus, the traditional place of punishment for particularly wicked persons.

The person Hades is mentioned only very rarely in Homer. Hades was the third son, with Zeus and Poseidon, of Cronus and Rhea. After Zeus had done away with their father, and the three brothers cast lots to divide up the world between them. Zeus got the sky, Poseidon got the sea, and Hades got the underworld.

## Hector

Son of Priam and Hecuba, husband of Andromache, and father of Scamandrius (also called Astyanax), prince of Troy and leader of the Trojan forces. As Achilles is for the Achaeans, so isHector the preeminent fighter on the Trojan side.

Hector is, if perhaps less dashing, a brighter and more human character thanAchilles for many read-

ers. He is staunchly devoted to his wife and son, his parents, and above all, to his city and his homeland. Unlike Achilles, Hector knows exactly what he is fighting for, and it is the very life of his city, his family, and his people. More importantly, he fights on for those things even though he knows, or at the very least suspects, that the cause is doomed.

Another difference between Hector and Achilles is that while Achilles is both described as, and acts like, the gods, Hector is very much a human being. Achilles is god-like in his rage and eventually in his fighting prowess, and only seems to recover his humanity at the very end of the poem, after Patroclus' death and especially after Priam comes to beg Hector's body from his killer. Hector, on the other hand, never loses his human qualities. He does occasionally become angry, but his rage is never as all-encompassing or as blinding as that of Achilles. In defeat no less than in victory, Hector is a man of honor and dignity. Even his implicit intention (XVII.125-127) to defile Patroclus' body, while perhaps offensive to our modern sensibilities, was no more than a standard practice (or at least a standard threat) in heroic warfare—quite unlike Achilles' eventual treatment of Hector's own body, which even the gods admit goes too far.

Hector may have the distinction of being the first great tragic figure in Western literature. He fights for a cause that he does not approve of and that he knows (though he rarely admits it) is doomed. All his successes are only temporary—the last great respite for the Trojans before their city is destroyed. Worse still, we know, as Hector does not, that he owes his success more to the will of Zeus in answer to the prayer of Achilles, than to his own efforts.

Nevertheless, in the face of all that he must endure, both in the present and anticipated in the future, Hector retains a quiet dignity and nobility of character that represents humanity at its best.

## Hecuba

Daughter of Dymas and wife of Priam, she is the mother of Hector, Paris, and Cassandra, among others. When Troy falls, she is given to Odysseus as a prize and has to watch as her daughter Polyxena is sacrificed at the tomb of Achilles. She is the central character in two surviving plays of Euripides (ca. 480 - 406 BC), the *Hecuba,* which is undated, and *The Trojan Women* (415 BC).

## Hekabe

*See* Hecuba

## Hektor

*See* Hector

## Helen

Daughter of Zeus and the human woman Leda, whom Zeus raped and impregnated while in the form of a swan. Every man in the Greek world (or so the myths suggest) wanted to marry Helen. Her foster father Tyndareus took the advice of Odysseus and had all her suitors swear a solemn oath to protect her even after her eventual marriage. And of course, after she married Menelaus, Paris abducts Helen. The Trojan War results when her husband and erstwhile suitors lay seige to Troy in order to recover her.

Helen is something of an enigma in Homer's poetry, and perhaps in Homer's mind as well. She seems to have gone along with Paris of her own free will, but perhaps under the compulsion of the goddess Aphrodite, who is known to fill mortals with uncontrollable lust in keeping with her nature. Yet she also seems both to regret her choice to accompany Paris back to Troy and the suffering that her choice to do so has visited on Troy and its people. Further, she seems happy to be reunited with Menelaus.

In keeping with her lineage as a daughter of Zeus, Helen has more in common with the goddesses Athena and Aphrodite than her human counterparts Andromache and Hecuba. It is difficult to imagine either of them standing up to a goddess, as Helen does to Aphrodite, for example. Nor does it seem likely that either woman would ever speak to a man in quite the biting words that Helen has for Paris after Aphrodite has rescued him from the duel with Menelaus.

## Hephaestus

Son of Zeus and Hera (or, according to Hesiod, of Hera alone, out of spite after Zeus given birth to Athena by himself), Hephaestus is the god of fire and the arts related to it, such as smithcraft. He is lame (in Homer, the result of being thrown off Olympus for taking Hera's side in a quarrel with

Zeus), and he is a source of amusement to the gods in addition to being their master craftsman. He makes thunderbolts for Zeus, houses and furniture for the other gods, and forges a new suit of armor for Achilles after Hector strips the old one from Patroclus's body.

## Hephaistos

*See* Hephaestus

## Hera

Daughter of Cronus and Rhea, sister of Zeus and also his wife, Hera is goddess of marriage and childbirth. She is known for her jealousy of Zeus and her intrigues against him and his many human mistresses and illegitimate children. In the *Iliad* Hera is a partisan of the Achaeans, both because their main cities are under her protection but also because she is angry at the Trojans because of Paris' decision to give the golden apple marked ''for the fairest'' to Aphrodite.

## Iris

Iris, the goddess of the rainbow and messenger of the gods, is the daughter of Thaumas and Electra, and married to Zephyrus, god of the west wind.

## Kalchas

*See* Calchas

## Kalkhas

*See* Calchas

## Kassandra

*See* Cassandra

## Klytaimestra

*See* Clytemnestra

## Menelaos

*See* Menelaus

## Menelaus

Son of Atreus and brother of Agamemnon, Menelaus is king of Sparta and the husband of

Helen. Menelaus could be described, with some accuracy, as the ''Mr. Average'' of the *Iliad*. One might have expected him to be the leader of the Achaean forces, not his brother Agamemnon—Helen was *his* wife, after all, and Sparta was at least roughly on a par with Mycenae in terms of wealth and power.

Yet Agamemnon has what Menelaus seems to lack: the ability to inspire people to follow him. Menelaus's fighting skills are only average, as Homer shows them to us. He is nowhere near the tactician his brother is, and certainly not on a level with Odysseus in that regard or the ability to hold an audience spellbound with his rhetoric. He does not even seem to be terribly bitter about having his wife spirited away from under his nose. Of course he is angry about the wrongs he suffers at Paris's hands, but even in his prayer to Zeus before he fights Paris, Menelaeus seems more annoyed that Paris has broken the rules of etiquette than outraged that a guest in his house has abducted his wife and has been living with her as her lover. Unlike his brother and many of the other Achaean kings, Menelaus enjoys a quick and safe return home after the war, with Helen and all his rightful possessions restored, and more besides from the spoils of Troy.

## Nestor

The only son of Neleus to survive, Nestor is the elderly king of Pylos, where it is said (I.250-52) that he has reigned already over two generations and is now ruling over the third. Nestor's role is that of the elder statesman and advisor. He does tend to be somewhat long-winded and given to telling stories about his remarkable feats in the old days, but his advice is almost always well-received, even though it sometimes has rather dire consequences (as, for example, when Patroclus takes his advice and borrows Achilles' armor).

After the fall of Troy, Nestor returns safely home to Pylos. He plays an important role in the *Odyssey* as well, where he serves as an advisor and host to Odysseus' son Telemachus.

## Odysseus

Son of Laertes and Anticleia, Odysseus is king of Ithaca in the western part of what is now Greece. Odysseus had been one of the suitors for Helen's hand in marriage, but decided his chances were not

good and married Penelope instead. It was his advice that caused Helen's stepfather Tyndareus to bind all her prospective suitors with an oath of mutual assistance if something should befall her eventual husband after the marriage.

Odysseus is renowned, in the *Iliad* and throughout literature and myth since, as a devious, clever man, better at dreaming up schemes and convincing people to go along with them, than as a slogger in the infantry or a fighter to be feared in individual combat. He is no slouch at warfare, it is simply not what he is best at. Agamemnon seems to rely on Odysseus to do most of his planning for him, and the trickier bits of negotiation on his behalf as well. Even the Trojans are somewhat in awe of his rhetorical skills: Antenor compares the words falling from Odysseus' lips to the flakes of snow in a winter blizzard (III.222), and suggests that his words make up for the deficiencies of his manner and appearance.

Yet for all his scheming, Odysseus is portrayed as a man of honor, somewhat cool and calculating, and boundlessly energetic. The night raid in Book 10, where Odysseus and Diomedes first promise to spare Dolon's life and then kill him anyway, then slaughter a dozen men in their sleep, seems quite out of character with the Odysseus presented elsewhere in the poem. This discrepancy of character has led some scholars to suspect that this book (or at least parts of it) may have been added later by another writer.

## Oilean

*See* Ajax

## Paris

Son of Priam and Hecuba and a prince of Troy, Paris was the subject of a prophecy which foretold that he would one day bring great troubles to the Trojans. In an attempt to avoid this prophecy (which, as usually happens in Greek mythology, only made certain that it came true), Priam sent Paris out of the city to tend some of his flocks on Mount Ida. There he was confronted by the goddesses Athena, Aphrodite, and Hera, who wanted him to judge which of them was most beautiful. Paris chose Aphrodite, who awarded him the right to take the most beautiful of all mortal women, Helen, for his wife.

There was, however, one small problem: she was already married to Menelaeus. In an age when women were thought of essentially as property, this was not an insurmountable obstacle. What made it worse was that Paris actually visited Menelaus's home in Sparta, incurring certain quasi-sacred obligations under the laws of hospitality—one of which was that he could not rob his host. But that is just what Paris does. While Helen seems to have come along of her own free will, Paris also loots Menelaus's storehouses, carrying off a number of unspecified ''treasures'' along with Helen.

Paris is not well-liked in the *Iliad:* his own father is ashamed of him, his eldest brother can hardly endure the sight of him (III.39ff.), and even Helen has some sharp words for him in the aftermath of his abortive duel with Menelaus. Paris is not known for his bravery in battle, and in fact is most talented as an archer—something the Greeks felt was a job for weaklings and cowards.

Yet Paris eventually brings down the great Achilles (with some help from the gods). In an ironic twist of fate, Paris himself is wounded by a poisoned arrow not long before the end of the war.

## Patroclus

Homer does not give much detail about Patroclus or his ancestry. His father was Menoetius, who had sailed with the hero Jason on the *Argo* during the quest for the Golden Fleece.

Homer's poem places both Patroclus and his father in the house of Peleus, as Nestor recalls his arrival with Odysseus on a ''recruiting'' mission in Book 11, to find ''the hero Menoetius inside, and you [Patroclus], Achilles beside you, and Peleus the aged horseman,'' all engaged in sacrificing an ox to Zeus. That same narrative suggests that Patroclus was sent to Troy at least in part as a check on Achilles' impetuosity, someone with a cooler head who could talk sense to the hero when no one else could.

From what we see of him in Homer, Patroclus is compassionate, caring, strong, brave, and level-headed: except when Zeus sends a ''huge blind fury'' (XVI.685-6) upon him, and he forgets Achilles' command not to pursue Hector, once he has driven the Trojans away from the Achaean ships. As a result of this fury, Patroclus is first disarmed and stripped of his armor by Apollo, wounded by Euphorbus' spear, and finally killed by Hector.

## Patroklos

*See* Patroclus

## Pelides

*See* Achilles

## Phoenix

Son of Amyntor, he quarrels with his father (and, in some versions of the story, was blinded by him, then cured by the centaur Chiron) and was taken in by Peleus, who made him king of the Dolopians. Phoenix helps raise Peleus's son Achilles, and eventually accompanies him to Troy. Phoenix dies on the way home and is buried by Neoptolemus.

## Phoinix

*See* Phoenix

## Poseidon

Son of Cronus and Rhea, and brother of Zeus and Hades, Poseidon is the god of the sea, earthquake, and horses. He is typically portrayed as a stately, older figure, though one capable of great passion and bluster (not unlike the storms at sea that were said to be caused by his anger).

Generally placid, when provoked he can be ruthless. Along with Apollo, he built the walls of Troy for King Laomedon. When Laomedon refused to pay them for their labors, Poseidon sent a sea monster to threaten the city. Laomedon promised his famous horses to the hero Heracles if he would kill the monster for him, but reneged on that promise as well, whereupon Heracles led an expedition against Troy and leveled it (an event that is referred to in passing in the *Iliad*). Still upset because of his treatment at the hands of an earlier Trojan king, Poseidon favors the Achaean side in the war.

## Priam

The son of Laomedon and husband of Hecuba, Priam is king of Troy at the time of the Achaean expedition against the city. He is often referred to, but appears rather infrequently in the poem.

When he does appear, however, Homer portrays him as a kindly older gentleman, courteous to everyone and trying to do his best despite his age and weakened condition. One might expect him to be bitter, but there is little indication of this in Homer's characterization. Indeed, he treats Helen, whom he could rightly be expected to despise, considering what she had brought upon him and his city, like a favorite daughter and refuses to let others maltreat her, at least in his presence.

There is something tragic in Priam's character as portrayed by Homer. He mourns for his dead children, and none more so than Hector, the greatest and apparently best-loved of all. Yet he never relinquishes his dignity, even when he finds himself in the unheard-of position of a guest in the home (however temporary) of the man who killed Hector, and whom he has to beg in order to recover Hector's body.

Priam knows, or at least suspects, that his city will eventually fall to the Achaeans, with their superior force. He refuses to dwell on that unpleasant fate, or allow it to cloud his judgment, however. One tradition held that he was killed by Achilles' son Neoptolemus during the sack of Troy. In William Shakespeare's play *Hamlet,* a traveling actor recites a dramatic scene in which Phyrrus kills Priam.

### Smintheus
*See* Apollo

### Thetis

A sea nymph and daughter of Neleus (whom Homer calls the "Old Man" of the sea). She was married to a mortal, which is somewhat unusual in Greek mythology, though not unheard-of.

There are differing stories of how she came to be married to Peleus. The first (and more common) version is that both Zeus and Poseidon were both in love with her, but stopped courting her when they learned of a prophecy to the effect that any son she bore would be greater than his father. She was then married off to Peleus at a grand banquet to which all the gods were invited except Discord.

The other version is that Thetis was raised by Hera and, out of love for her foster mother, refused to give in to Zeus's demands. Angered by her rejection, Zeus marries her to a mortal as punishment.

### Tritogeneia
*See* Athena

### Tydides
*See* Diomedes

### Ulysses
*See* Odysseus

### Zeus

The son of Cronus and Rhea, both brother and husband of Hera, brother of Poseidon and Hades, Zeus is the king of the gods and the god of sky, storm, and thunder. Homer says he is the eldest child of his parents, though his is a minority opinion: elsewhere Zeus is said to be the youngest child, who was hidden away by his mother before eventually overthrowing his father.

Scholars of ancient religion have long thought that Zeus represents a fusion of a multitude of local "head gods," which may explain the numerous children he is said to have fathered, and the equally numerous women (mortal and immortal alike) with whom he is said to have dallied. As with the other gods, Zeus is portrayed in the *Iliad* as, essentially, a larger-than-life human being, with augmented powers and knowledge but all of the passions, quirks, and shortcomings of any person. Zeus is, however, given a little more in the way of dignity and majesty than some of the other Homeric gods.

One characteristic of the other Homeric gods that Zeus does not share is caprice. While he grants some prayers and denies others, there is no sense that he is doing so merely on a whim. And while he will occasionally resort to threats of violence (as with Hera, for example), he seems generally to prefer to govern by rule of law and, to some degree, common consent among the other gods.

Richmond Lattimore, in the introduction to his translation of the *Iliad,* categorically states that Zeus can do as he pleases and is not subject to fate. On the other hand, Bernard Knox, in his introduction to the Fagles translation, says that the relationship between Zeus and fate "is a subtle one." A mere five lines into the poem, we are told that "the will of Zeus was moving toward fulfilment," suggesting that the whole course of the war was an act of Zeus's will: yet the discussion of Sarpedon's death in Book 16 seems to imply that Zeus *could* act in opposition to fate, but chooses not to in order to avoid the inevitable chaos that his action would cause. There is even some indication, as at XX.30 (where Zeus says of Achilles, ''I fear that he may raze the walls contrary to destiny''), that humans can sometimes act contrary to destiny. It may be that the correct answer is not whether Zeus is or is not subject to fate, but that he is in fact both.

# Themes

In the tenth year of the Trojan war, Agamemnon provokes Achilles into withdrawing from the fighting and asking his mother to get Zeus to give the Trojans an advantage until Agamemnon comes to his senses. As things look their bleakest for the Achaean forces, Achilles sends his friend Patroclus out with his army to keep the Trojans from completely overrunning the Achaean camp. Hector kills Patroclus, which causes Achilles to reconcile with Agamemnon and rejoin the fighting in order to revenge his friend's death by killing Hector.

## Anger and Hatred

As the first words of the Greek original suggests, anger—rage—is a very important theme in the *Iliad.* That specific term is only used in reference to three people: Achilles (five times), Apollo (three times), and Zeus (three times), and twice of the gods in general. Yet the emotion is widespread: the Trojans, for example, are angry with the Achaeans for making war on them; the Achaeans, in turn, are angry with the Trojans for harboring Paris and refusing to give Helen back to her rightful husband. Hera and Athena are angry at (or even hate) the Trojans generally, and Paris specifically, because he chose Aphrodite over them as the most beautiful even before the war began.

## Betrayal

Related to the themes of anger and hatred in the *Iliad* is the issue of betrayal. Achilles feels betrayed when Agamemnon belittles him in front of the whole army. Pandarus betrays the terms of the truce (and infuriates the Achaeans) by shooting and slightly wounding Menelaus in Book 3. Helen betrays her husband Menelaus by going off with Paris, and then betrays Paris by returning complacently to Menelaus

after the many years of terrible warfare. Paris betrays the sacred obligations of a guest toward a host when he took Helen away with him to Troy.

## Fate and Chance

The concept of fate, or destiny, is explicitly mentioned at least 40 times in the *Iliad.* It is used in such formulaic expressions as ''red death and strong fate seized his eyes.'' It gets its most notable and extended treatment, however, in Book 16 (lines 433 and following) when Zeus is pondering whether to save his son Sarpedon from his fated death at Patroclus's hands. It is also an important part of the ''subtext'' of the poem, the ''story behind the story'' or what can be read ''between the lines.''

It is not entirely certain just how fate works in Homer's thinking. Most of the time (as when Zeus balances ''two fateful portions of death'' in his scales, or when Achilles talks about the two different possible outcomes of his life in Book 9), it seems that a man's fate is set at birth and cannot be changed, even by the gods. In the Sarpedon story, however, Hera's words at XVI.444 and following seem to imply that Zeus *could* meddle with destiny, but that he chooses not to out of fear either of the ridicule of the other gods or the chaos that might result.

## Honor

Virtually everyone in the *Iliad* puts a very high value on the concept of honor. This is especially true of the gods, who get very upset if a mortal skimps on a sacrifice, or forgets it altogether, or—as in the case of Hera, Athena, and Aphrodite—if a mortal names one of them as possessing qualities in greater abundance than another. It is also true of the major heroes—Achilles and Agamemnon in particular. Indeed, Achilles considers a life of glory and everlasting honor that ends in battle at Troy preferable to a long, dull (at least in his opinion) life of respect at home.

## Love

Love is one of the subtler themes in the *Iliad,* but also one of the most powerful. In Chryses' actions at the opening of Book 1, or those of Hecuba and Priam in Books 22 and 24, we see eloquent testimony to the love of parents for their children. The tender scene between Hector and Andromache at the end of Book 6 is one of the most poignant

# Topics for Further Study

- What role do the gods play in the *Iliad?* Compare and contrast this role with the role of the divine in a contemporary religious tradition (your own or another that interests you).

- In his book *Homer: The Poet of the Iliad,* Mark Edwards writes: "From the very first lines, Homer will raise the origins of human suffering." What does Homer conclude about those origins? Contrast Homer's conclusions about "the origins of human suffering" with the precepts of modern psychology or anthropology.

- Consider the interaction between Glaucus and Diomedes that begins at line 119 of Book 6. Compare this story with the story of Baucis and Philemon in Ovid's *Metamorphoses* (Book 8, 619ff.), the story of Abraham at the oak of Mamre (Genesis 18:1-8), or the reception of Telemachus by Nestor (*Odyssey*, Book 3, 31ff.) or Menelaus (*Odyssey*, Book 4, 30ff.). What can you conclude about the proper relationship between hosts and guests from these stories? Does Diomedes treat his guest-friend fairly? How does Homer comment on their interaction?

- Pay careful attention to the treatment Homer gives the character of Helen. Do you think Helen really regrets leaving Menelaus, or is she making it up? How do you think Homer wanted his audience to look at Helen? What does the way in which her character is portrayed suggest to you about the role of women in Homeric society?

- Consider the following passage, taken from Peri-

cles' funeral oration for the Athenian dead in the first year of the Peloponnesian War (431-430 BC), as recorded by the historian Thucydides (*The Peloponnesian War*, Book II, chapters 42 and 43, adapted from the Crawley translation published in 1982 by the Modern Library): "For there is justice in the claim that steadfastness in his country's battles should be as a cloak to cover a man's other imperfections; for the good action has blotted out the bad, and his merit as a citizen more than outweighed his demerits as an individual. . . .These men, therefore, died in a manner befitting an Athenian. . . . The offering of their lives in a common enerprise gained for each of these men a fame that never grows old; instead of a tomb in which to lay their bones to rest, they gained the most noble of all shrines, in which their glory is placed, to be remembered on every occasion which calls for a commemoration of that glory, whether by word or action. For heroes have the whole earth for their tomb; and in lands far from their own, where the column with its epitaph declares it, there is enshrined in every breast an unwritten record, with no tablet to preserve it except that of the heart." Do you agree with Pericles that excellence in war (or other civic service) should "make up" for a person's shortcomings? Why or not? What do you think Pericles might have said about some of the Homeric heroes such as Hector, Achilles, Patroclus, or Agamemnon?

---

depictions of the love between husband and wife in Western literature, as well as one of the oldest. And no matter what other relationships there may have been between them, no one could fail to notice the loving friendship expressed by Achilles and Patroclus for one another.

Helen, while perhaps the obvious character to consider in this context, remains something of a

mystery. She certainly seems fond of Priam and at least those Trojans who do not hate or shun her. Her apparent love for both her lover Paris and her husband Menelaus has been seen as fickleness or caprice by some, but Homer and his audience would most likely have taken it to represent the workings of Aphrodite—who is, after all, the goddess of love and passion and thus stands for a power that frequently overwhelms rational thought and other, ''lesser'' considerations.

## Patriotism

Ironically, most of the patriotism that is found in the *Iliad* is on the part of the Trojans. It is a favorite rallying tactic of Hector's, as for example when he rebukes the seer Polydamas for predicting an eventual defeat for the Trojans and counseling a retreat with the words, ''Fight for your country— that is the best, the only omen!'' (XII.243, Fagles' translation). This is not to imply that Homer thought more of the Trojans than the Greeks, merely that the Greeks of Homer's day had only begun to develop a sense of themselves as a single nation—perhaps at least in part through Homer's own work, which describes, as Thucydides observed some centuries later, the first action taken in common by the Greek-speaking peoples.

## Peer Pressure (Shame)

Peer pressure is found virtually everywhere in the world of the *Iliad*. Consider, for example, the gambit used twice by Hera and once by Athena to get Zeus to do what they want: ''Do as you please . . .but none of the deathless gods will ever praise you'' (IV.29, XVI.443, and XXII.181). Menelaus' debate with himself as he tries to prevent the Trojans from making off with Patroclus' body at XVII.90ff. is in a similar vein, as is the fairly common tactic of ''encouraging'' a reluctant soldier by pointing out the potential consequences to his reputation of being found with a wound in the back. Even Helen pleads the need to avoid the ridicule of the Trojan women when she tells Aphrodite that she will not rush off to make love to Paris after Aphrodite has rescued him from the duel with Menelaus (III.406ff.).

## Revenge

Revenge is another theme which requires a little bit of reading between the lines. There are numerous places in the poem where one fighting man prepares or threatens to kill another to revenge another death, or an insult or offense. Achilles is fairly open about his desire for revenge on Agamemnon for his insults, and on Hector for having killed Patroclus.

Revenge also drives the hatred of Athena and Hera for the Trojans (they want revenge on Paris), and of Poseidon for the city and its inhabitants (he was cheated out of his proper payment for helping to build the city's walls).

# Style

Since it is the first work in its genre to have survived, the *Iliad* does not so much display the mechanics of epic poetry as *define* them. Epic poetry in the West was written in virtually the same form as the *Iliad* for at least 500 years, and the modifications that were later made tended to be minor.

## Meter

English meter involves patterns of stressed and unstressed syllables. Greek meter, on the other hand, involves patterns of long and short syllables in which, as a general rule, two short syllables equal one long syllable. Greek poetry does not rhyme, although it uses of alliteration and assonance (repeated use of the same or similar consonant patterns and vowel patterns, respectively).

The *Iliad* is written in dactylic hexameters, which is the ''standard'' form for epic poetry: in fact, this particular meter is sometimes referred to as ''epic meter'' or ''epic hexameter.'' *Hexameter* means that there are six elements, or ''feet,'' in each line; *dactylic* refers to the particular metrical pattern of each foot: in this case, the basic pattern is one long syllable followed by two short ones, although variations on that basic pattern are allowed. The final foot in each line, for example, is almost always a spondee (two long syllables, instead of one long and two short ones). Homer will sometimes vary the meter to suit the action being described, using more dactyls when things are moving quickly (horses galloping, for example), and more spondees when things are slow or sad (as, for example, at I.3, where ''strong souls by thousands'' are ''hurled down to Hades'').

## Simile

One of the techniques for which the *Iliad* is justifiably famous is its use of similes, or comparisons. Hardly a scene goes by that does not include at least one simile. Moreover, for a poem where most of the action takes place on the battlefield, most of the similes are drawn from peacetime and its occupations: the ranks of the armies are compared to rows of grain in a field, for example.

Homer's similes are drawn from commonplace, everyday objects and occurrences in the lives of his audience. Consider the following passage from Book 11, when the Trojans are driving Ajax back toward his own lines:

as when country-dwelling men and their dogs have driven a tawny lion away from the cattle pen. . . as when boys are driving a sluggish donkey past a cornfield and many sticks have been broken across his back, but he gets in anyway and mows down the deep grain. . . (XI.547-48; 557-59).

Two different similes are used to describe the same action, and both images would have been familiar and evocative to anyone with fields and flocks to tend.

### Foreshadowing

Foreshadowing, the practice of "hinting" at future developments in the plot either explicitly (in the form of prophecies, etc.) or implicitly, through indirect hints, is fairly common in the *Iliad*. It is not uncommon (and this is in line with Greek religious beliefs current at the time of Homer) for the dying to make some kind of a prophecy—usually (as, for example, at XXII.355-60 when the dying Hector foretells the death of Achilles), though not always, involving the impending death of the person responsible.

One example of a more subtle form of foreshadowing can be seen in the name of Achilles' home country, Phthia. This name is very similar to the Greek verb *phthiō*, which means "decay, wane, waste away, perish." In fact, the technical term for tuberculosis ("consumption," as it used to be known in English) was once *phthisis,* from this same verb. Achilles, who will die in the prime of his youth, comes from a place whose name might be translated "Deathville."

### Flashbacks

This technique, where a character in the present moment recalls an earlier event, is in its infancy in the *Iliad*. It is thought that the events in Book 3 represent an extended flashback, even though they hare not explicitly labeled as such. It is otherwise difficult to imagine how, after nine years of war, King Priam would be unable to recognize the chief leaders of the Achaean forces, and why no one had thought of having the two interested parties fight in single combat to decide the war's outcome.

### Ring Composition

Ring composition is a technique most often seen in poetry, where the writer "comes full circle," or "comes around" again to a particular theme, statement, or event at the end of a work (or significant segment of a work) that was featured at the beginning of the same work (or part of the

work). In the case of the *Iliad,* the poem starts with a ransom and a quarrel in Book I, continues with a figurative muster of the armed forces (Book II), followed by a duel (Book III). In Book XXII we have another duel, this time between Achilles and Hector, which is followed by a literal mustering of the armies for Patroclus's funeral games in Book XXIII. The poem ends in Book XXIV with the ransom of Hector's body from Achilles by Priam, thus "coming back around" again to the place where the action started.

## Historical Context

The context in which the Homeric poems were created is clouded by the fact that their creation is a process that spans several centuries. In a very real sense, the poems' historical and cultural background is rather like one of the archaeological sites from which we gather our information about the period: it is deep, it has many levels or layers, and over time things can get pushed up or down from their proper context. Consider, for example, the boars' tusk helmet Odysseus wears in Book 10: we find it depicted in art from the late Bronze Age, but it had long since disappeared from use or living memory by Homer's day in the Iron Age. Moving in the other direction, the cremation burials described in the poem were common in Homer's day, but extremely rare in the Bronze Age when the events he describes would have taken place.

### The Bronze Age

The Trojan War and its aftermath took place in the late Bronze Age, which began around 1550 BC. This is the date assigned to the wealthy burial sites found by Heinrich Schliemann in Grave Circle A at Mycenae in 1873. For this reason, the period is sometimes also called the Mycenaean era. This was a time of relative stability though not, of course, without its conflicts, wars, and raids. The dominant powers in the eastern Mediterranean were the Hittites in the central part of what is now Turkey, the Egyptians in what we now call the Middle East, and, apparently, the Mycenaean kings in Greece and the surrounding islands.

These three "great kings" all ruled over literate (at least to the extent of being able to keep records and official documents, even if they left us no "literature" to speak of), apparently complex, societies (complete with bureaucrats, if the Linear B

# Compare & Contrast

- **Late Bronze Age (the time of the Trojan War):** Burial is by inhumation. The bodies of the dead are laid to rest, often with grave goods and weapons, at least among the upper classes, in dug graves, stone-walled tombs (called "cist graves"), or *tholos* tombs built in the shape of a beehive, often under a hill.

  **Iron Age (Homer's own time):** The bodies of the dead are cremated and the remains are collected in an urn (often richly decorated), which is then buried in a specially dug pit. In the case of very important burials, a hill (or "tumulus") of earth or stone is raised above the grave, and the spot may further be marked with a column or other grave marker.

  **Late twentieth century:** The majority of burials are inhumation, though growing numbers of people choose cremation.

- **Late Bronze Age:** Writing is known, although mainly in cumbersome, syllabic forms such as Egyptian hieroglyphics, the Mycenaean Linear A and B scripts, or the Hittite/Akkadian cuneiform. Literacy is probably restricted to the highest levels of the aristocracy and a professional class of scribes, bureaucrats, diplomats, etc.

  **Iron Age:** Literacy, at least in the Greek-speaking world, is only beginning to be rediscovered, using a different alphabet, where each letter represents a particular sound and not an entire syllable. Literacy is still most likely restricted to the upper classes and some professionals, like rhapsodes and some artists.

  **Late twentieth century:** The majority of people are able to read and write well enough to conduct their own business affairs.

- **Late Bronze Age:** Trade, although extremely difficult and time-consuming, is fairly widespread. There is some evidence to suggest, for example, that the city of Mycenae was built where it stands because the location allowed its rulers to control several important trade routes and gain revenue from taxes they imposed on such trade.

  **Iron Age:** The scale of trade is reduced, now that the "great kings" are no longer around to secure the longer and more valuable trade routes, though goods are beginning to move more freely again.

  **Late twentieth century:** Trade is conducted on a woldwide scale, using mass transportation and instantaneous communications–means that were simply not possible in the ancient world.

- **Late Bronze Age:** Chariots are used as an integral part of the fighting force, often as a spearhead to break through the enemy's infantry or to shield one's own troops from those of the opponent. Infantry tactics are almost non-existent, with combat being almost exclusively of the individual, hand-to-hand variety described in the *Iliad.*

  **Iron Age:** Chariots, which are very expensive to build and maintain, are rare. Coordinated infantry tactics (called *hoplite* tactics), where groups of men fight and defend themselves in a structured formation (which Homer alludes to a few times in the *Iliad* ) are beginning to be developed.

  **Late twentieth century:** War today is carried out almost exclusively by trained professionals of both genders, in an almost complete contrast to the ancient methods of warfare. Tactics are coordinated, usually well behind the lines, to a degree unimaginable to Homer or his contemporaries. Where warriors in the ancient world often got close enough to learn the lineage of the men they fought and killed (or were killed by), modern soldiers may go through an entire war without ever seeing an opponent face-to-face.

tablets found at Pylos and elsewhere are any indication). They engaged in diplomacy with each other and with numerous smaller kingdoms on the edges of their territory that served as buffer zones between them and could be compelled to provide both military and economic support under the terms of the treaties that bound them to the particular kingdom with which they were allied. These secondary kingdoms were also prime targets for raids by other "great kings" and foreign invaders, especially those that were relatively distant from their protectors' centers of authority and military strong points.

Trade was flourishing, and, given the uncertainties of shipping and other means of transportation, together with a relatively low level of technological advancement (at least when considered by modern standards), quite surprisingly so. Distinctive Mycenaean pottery, whether as art pieces intended for display and ceremonial use, or purely for transporting trade goods like oil, grain, or perfume, is found all over the Mediterranean basin in staggering quantities throughout this period.

Military tactics were largely as we see them depicted in the *Iliad:* face-to-face combat between individuals or small groups of men, with little in the way of coordinated effort. It does seem, however, from wall paintings and other archaeological finds, that chariots were used for fighting ahead of the infantry, and not just for transporting people around the battlefield, as Homer describes their use.

The Trojan War, if it took place at all, came very near the end of this flourishing civilization. The Greeks, using generational calculations, set the date of the war at around 1184 BC; modern scholarship, based on archaeological evidence at Troy and other sites, puts it some 75 years earlier, around 1250 BC. But the traditional victors at Troy did not have very long to enjoy their victory.

## The Dark Age

For reasons that are not fully understood, this civilization begins to die out around 1220 BC with the mysterious destruction and subsequent abandonment of Pylos. That event ushers in a period of decline that lasts until roughly 1050 BC, when the Mycenaean civilization literally fades away into nothingness.

Whatever its causes, the disappearance of the Mycenaean civilization marked the start of about 250 years of very difficult times in Greece, aptly referred to as the Dark Age. This period has its end with the traditional date of the first Olympiad in 776

BC, very close to the time when we think Homer lived. Of this Dark Age we know almost nothing except what we can deduce from the period immediately following and the scanty evidence in the archaeological record.

Writing was lost, and with it, most trade seems to have disappeared except on a purely local or regional basis at best. Archaeologists working in this period report finding very little in the way of "luxury" goods like fancy pottery—when they can find anything at all. There may have been as much as a 75% decrease in population from Bronze Age levels.

## The Iron Age

Beginning around the 11th century BC, the Greeks began to use iron in place of bronze, to cremate their dead as opposed to burying them intact, and to establish colonies along the west coast of what is now Turkey. By Homer's day, roughly the middle of the eighth century BC, these trends were well-established and things were beginning to look up again.

Writing was just beginning to be rediscovered using a new alphabet borrowed from the Phoenicians, and foreign trade was improving: helped in no small part by the colonies along the Ionian coast which, while typically independent of their mother cities, nevertheless tended to remain on friendly terms with them. The population was again on the rise, which spurred another wave of colonization, this time chiefly toward the west (Sicily, parts of Italy, and the south of France).

At least on the Greek mainland, the era of kings was rapidly drawing to a close. By the beginning of the eighth century, the nobles had taken the reins of power from the kings almost everywhere and were ruling over family groups or tribes in what would come to be called the *polis,* or city-state.

Largely because of the decorations found on pottery from the period, this era has come to be known as the Geometric period, but increasing regularity was a feature of more than just the decorative arts. It was in this period that the beginnings of a Greek national identity come to the fore (prompting and/or prompted by the founding of the Olympic games and the dissemination of Homer's works, among other things). More coordinated military tactics were beginning to be used, the "*hoplite*" formation—a line of men with shields overlapping—alluded to by Homer at XII.105, XVI.210f.,

XVII.352f., and XX.361-2, which is shown on a wine bowl found at Veii and dating to around 650 BC.

Religious practices were also becoming more standardized at this juncture. While the Homeric heroes sometimes (as with the propitiatory sacrifice to Apollo in Book 1) go to specific places for religious observances, the majority seem to be family- or group-centered rituals that take place wherever the family or group may happen to be at the moment of the ritual, and archaeological evidence from the Bronze Age tends to confirm this view. Actual temples, like the one vaguely described in Book 6 when Hecuba goes to lay a robe on the knees of the statue of Athena, have not been identified in the archaeological record much before the ninth century BC, and become much more frequent thereafter.

After Homer's day, while the population, wealth, commerce, and industry of Greece were generally on the rise, the political pendulum swung back and forth from more aristocratic and democratic models to varying forms of one-man rule until just before the dawn of the Golden Age in the fifth century BC.

## Critical Overview

The critical reputation of the *Iliad* is perhaps best demonstrated by noting that it is generally regarded as the first work of true ''literature'' in Western culture. This is significant not only because the poem stands at the head of the list, as it were, but also because it had to beat out a fair amount of competition to achieve that status.

By the middle of the sixth century BC, around the same time as the Peisistratids in Athens ordered the first ''standard edition'' of Homer's works to be made, there were at least six other epic poems treating various parts of the Trojan War story. Most of these were fairly short, but the *Cypria,* which covered everything from the decision of the gods to cause the war through Agamemnon's quarrel with Achilles that begins Homer's work, was at least half as long as the *Iliad.* Unlike the *Iliad* and the *Odyssey,* however, none of the other poems in this ''epic cycle'' has survived except in fragmentary quotations in later authors. They simply could not measure up to Homer's standard.

Certainly by the beginning of the sixth century, and possibly late in the seventh, there was already a group of poet/performers calling themselves the *Homeridae* (''Sons of Homer''). This group may have been the forerunner of the *rhapsodes,* trained singers who, while they did apparently compose and improvise works of their own, were best known for performing Homer's poetry. At least on Plato's authority, the rhapsodes seem to have begun taking liberties with the poems (see *Ion* 530d), which may have led the Peisistratids to have the ''official'' text written down for the judges at the Great Panathenaia (a religious festival in honor of Athena held every four years), which included a contest for the rhapsodes which required them, presumably in shifts and over several days, to recite the whole of the *Iliad* and the *Odyssey.*

For most people, those public performances were probably their major form of exposure to Homer's work. For the educated class, however, knowing one's Homer quickly became the sign of culture and refinement. Homer is mentioned by name at least 600 times in surviving Greek literature, in texts that range from history to philosophy, religion, and even legal speeches. Aristotle holds him up not only as the ''supreme poet in the serious style'' (*Poetics* 1448b20), but also as the forerunner of both tragedy and comedy. Herodotus (*Histories* II.53) even credits Homer, along with his near contemporary Hesiod, with being the one who gave Greek religion its standard forms: the names, spheres and functions, descriptions and descent of the gods.

The one dissenting voice in the ancient world seems to have been that of Plato. Although he quotes Homer on more than one occasion, and even lampoons the rhapsodes and their ''beautification'' or embellishment of the standard text in his dialogue *Ion,* in the *Republic,* his lengthy discussion of the ideal state and the education of its leaders, Plato dismisses Homer as a mere ''imitator'' and excludes him (and poets generally) from his educational program (which was never implemented).

Homer was frequently imitated in the classical world, whether by the authors of the other poems in the epic cycle or lampooned as he was by Aristophanes in several of his plays (especially the *Birds* and the *Clouds*), yet his work was never equalled. Several Roman poets (chiefly Vergil, Ovid, and Lucretius) wrote epic works, and even used Homer's own epic hexameter line, but their works are not quite on the same level with Homer's originals.

Interest in Homer continued well into the Christian era, as evidenced by Macrobius' *Saturnalia* (dated to the early part of the fifth century AD), where educated Romans still know their Greek, and spend an evening discussing the relative merits of Homer's treatment of the Troy story in comparison with Vergil's. With the fall of Rome in AD 455, however, Homer and his works fell into disrepute for roughly one thousand years, until the scholars of the Renaissance "rediscovered" classical antiquity and learned to read Greek again. The *story* of Troy, however, remained popular throughout the period, and was widely known: there are accounts of the war in several languages, including Anglo-Saxon, Norman French, and English. It was from Caxton's *Recuyell of the Historyes of Troye* (circa 1475), not Homer's original work, that Shakespeare got his "facts" and details as he was writing *Troilus and Cressida* in 1602.

With the Renaissance came a revival of interest in Homer and his texts, which were first published in the modern era in Florence in 1488. This interest was further sparked in the 18th century when F. A. Wolf first proposed the "Homeric Question" (simply stated: "Who wrote what, and when?"), and again in the latter part of the 19th century and into the 20th with the excavations of Schliemann, Dörpfeld, and Blegen at Troy and Evans at Knossos, the work of Milman Parry and Adam Parry on the transmission of oral poetry like Homer's original sources, and the decipherment of Linear B in 1952 by Michael Ventris.

It is thought that Milton was significantly influenced by Homer in composing *Paradise Lost,* and he certainly provided inspiration for later poets such as Tennyson and Byron, though their works are narrower in scope and execution than Homer's. The *Iliad* continues to enjoy the critical acclaim and popular interest that have been associated with it throughout most of the two and a half millennia since it was first composed.

## Criticism

### Michael J. Spires

*In the following essay, Spires discusses some extra-literary concerns, including the historical and cultural importance of the* Iliad, *both in its own time and in the centuries that followed.*

In one sense, it is unjust to give Homer all the credit for the *Iliad,* since it is all but certain that he had at least some "help" in composing it. Whether he merely cobbled together shorter poems into one epic work, or whether he improvised the majority of the *Iliad* from a pre-existing repertoire of themes, epithets, and episodes, Homer had the benefit of several centuries' worth of material to draw upon in composing his own poem.

Looked at from another perspective, however, it is no less unjust to refuse Homer the credit for his work. Surely there were other artists, now lost in the distant past, on whom Homer drew for inspiration, technique, or source material. Yet it is his artistry that made the poem "sing," if you will. If we compare Homer to Ella Fitzgerald, for example (a metaphor which I owe to Michael Silk's commentary on the *Iliad*), no one would deny that some credit is due to the original author of the piece being "interpreted" or improvised upon, and some as well to the inventors and refiners of the art itself: yet it is indisputably Fitzgerald's artistry (or Homer's) that makes the piece something more than an exercise in musical theory or poetic technique.

While the Greeks would certainly have considered the poem an artistic creation, they saw more in it than merely great literature. For them, it contained elements of both history and religion as well. Herodotus and Thucydides both accept Homer as an historical source, to some degree, and archaeologists have found evidence of votive offerings and literal "hero-worship" at sites connected with the poem (Mycenae, for example, and at the tomb of Achilles even down to the days of Julius Caesar) that date back at least to the eighth century BC.

For centuries, Greek culture was saturated with the *Iliad.* The wealthy aristocracy were accustomed to hearing parts of the poem, or at least the Troy cycle, in private performances at dinner parties and other functions. By the time of the Golden Age in the fifth century BC, Homer was a standard part of the school curriculum and was widely quoted in later literature. At least in Athens the *Iliad* was recited, in full, every four years at the Great Panathenaia, giving everyone regular opportunities to experience the poem in performance.

In order to understand the original importance of the poem, it is vital to remember that the modern conception of "history" was first put forward by Herodotus in the middle of the fifth century BC, some three hundred years after Homer. Lacking a written historical record, the only route to immortality for the Greeks of Homer's day was either through the memory of the gods or of an artist: one could never be certain about the survival of one's family line in a world where disease, famine, and war were much more common than they are in ours. As Sarpedon says to Glaucus (XII.322-328, my translation):

> O my friend, if we could get through this war, live forever and be both ageless and immortal, I would neither myself fight in the front rank, nor command you to fight where men win glory: But now, seeing as the dooms of death stand all around in their thousands, which no mortal can either flee or escape, let us go on and grasp glory for ourselves, or yield it to others.

This is also the impetus behind the repeated invocations to the Muses scattered throughout the poem. (Especially revealing in this context is II.484-85, the beginning of the Catalogue of Ships: ''Tell me now, O Muses who have homes on Olympus: for you are goddesses, you are everywhere, and you know all things.'')

It is harder for us to get in touch with this mindset, living as we do in an age where all sorts of records and identifications follow us around for most of our lives, and, in many cases, well afterward. Yet we do still yearn to be remembered for something more than just having ''lived and moved and had our being'' here for a period of time, to borrow a phrase from Scripture.

That is enough to explain why the *Iliad* was important to the Greeks, in Homer's time and afterward. Why is it important to us, nearly three millennia later? Why do people still read this poem? Of course, because it is good literature: but what makes it not only good, but even popular?

The continued popularity of the poem is due to several factors. Chief among them are, first, the richness of its imagery, coupled with a certain sparseness of detail that allows the imagination of the reader (or, originally, the listener) to fill in the outlines left by the poet, thus inviting ''audience participation'' in the work, as it were; second, the balanced treatment it gives to both sides; and lastly, the excellent portrait of the human condition offered by the protagonists, Achilles and Hector.

The chief rule in poetry, as one of my teachers once described it, is ''show, don't tell''—and Homer is a master at this tactic. From the ubiquitous descriptive epithets up through the frequent similes and metaphors, to such masterful scenes as the bed of flowers put forth by the earth on Mount Ida when Hera seduces Zeus to draw his attention away from the war (XIV.345ff.), or the intricacies of Achilles'

new shield which occupies the latter half of Book 18, the *Iliad* is a richly woven tapestry of descriptive detail.

But like any good poet, Homer uses images that would have been familiar to his audience (though, as with those used by Jesus in his parables, they may be less so to us today), and he uses them to sketch a scene, no more. Consider, for example, that we have almost no description of Troy itself beyond the very general formulaic expressions ''well-built,'' and ''wide-wayed,'' and the detail that it contains a high place where there are temples to the gods. The rest is left to our imagination to supply.

It would have been very easy, in writing about the Trojan War, to play up or favor one side over the other (as later accounts did), but Homer opts for the middle road instead. More Trojans than Achaeans are killed, but in all other respects, the poet treats both sides equally. There is nobility and savagery on both sides: even the gods are fairly equally divided, if we hold Zeus and Ares to be fairly impartial, or at least alternatively favoring both sides. This keeps the poem from becoming a cheap bit of nationalistic propaganda, but it also says something, I think, about the nature of war itself: a supposition that is strengthened by the repeated use of peacetime imagery to describe the events of war. We are invited to consider that war afflicts both the victors and the vanquished, though in differing degrees, of course, and to remember all the good things in life that war destroys.

This balance is also found in Homer's treatment of the two protagonists, Achilles and Hector, who serve as both literal and metaphorical ''bookends'' to the poem. Achilles is the first person, and Hector the last, to be named in the poem, in the first and last lines, respectively. Achilles is mentioned by name 322 times, and Hector, 447 (probably because Achilles ''sits it out'' for the majority of the poem, while Hector continues to fight).

Achilles is better in war than Hector, but Hector clearly outshines Achilles in the activities of peace. Granted, we do not have an opportunity to see Achilles in the kind of peacetime activities like Hector's interlude with Andromache in Book 6, Achilles' main concern seems to be with war. Hector, on the other hand, is quite clearly a man of peace who had rather be doing anything but fighting: he fights because he must, and because it is

# What Do I Read Next?

- The *Odyssey* is the other epic poem credited to Homer, and was probably written some time after the *Iliad*. It describes the 10 years of Odysseus's wandering, trying to get home after the Trojan War has ended, and events in his absence from his home in Ithaca.

- Edith Hamilton's *Mythology* (Mentor, 1942) is an excellent (and fun) basic introduction to Greek and Roman mythology, and includes a section on the Trojan War. Her treatment of the Norse myths is a little sketchy, but nevertheless interesting and engaging.

- The *Aeneid* of Vergil (70-19 B.C.) is an epic poem in Latin that describes the wanderings of Aeneas and his group of Trojan and allied refugees following the fall of Troy. After many stops along the way (including a visit to the underworld), Aeneas and his people land in Italy and settle not far from the city that will eventually become Rome.

- The *Oresteia* is a cycle of three tragic plays (*Agamemnon, Choephori (The Libation-Bearers,)* and *Eumenides*) by Aeschylus (525-456 BC), produced in Athens in 458 BC. It describes the events surrounding the homecoming of Agamemnon at the end of the Trojan War, and subsequent troubles those events cause his household.

- Both Sophocles (496-406 BC) and Euripides (ca. 480-406 BC) also wrote tragedies that draw from the myths about the Trojan War. Excellent translations can be found in *The Complete Greek Tragedies*, edited by David Grene and Richmond Lattimore for the University of Chicago Press. Two of Sophocles' plays are relevant, and both

are contained in the second volume of his plays in the Grene/Lattimore series. They are the *Ajax*, whose date is uncertain, and the *Philoctetes*, produced in 409 BC.

- Euripides wrote at least seven plays that include characters or events from the Trojan War. Volume II of his plays in the Grene/Lattimore series contains both the *Helen* (412 BC) and the undated *Iphigeneia in Tauris*. Volume III contains *The Trojan Women* (415 BC) and two undated plays, *Andromache* and *Hecuba*. Volume IV has both the *Orestes* (408 BC) and the posthumously produced *Iphigeneia at Aulis* (405 BC, possibly containing some material by Euripides's son).

- For some modern fictional treatments of the Trojan War, see Marion Zimmer Bradley's 1987 novel *Firebrand,* which tells the story from the perspective of Cassandra, Priam's ill-fated prophetic daughter; and British author Rex Warner's 1996 book *Greeks and Trojans,* based mainly on the *Iliad*.

- Michael Wood's book *In Search of the Trojan War,* a 1986 companion volume to the 1985 BBC television series of the same name, is an excellent overview of the history (and some of the controversies and problems involved in our understanding of that history) behind the Trojan War as it has come down to us in Homer's work and elsewhere.

- David A. Traill's *Schliemann of Troy: Treasure and Deceit* (1995), is a recent critical biography of the German businessman/archaeologist who discovered and excavated the sites of Troy, Mycenae, and Tiryns, among others.

expected of him (see, for example, VI. 441-45 and 526-29).

At the beginning of the poem, Achilles is god-like in more than just the name. His rage is bound-

less, his fury is all-consuming: we see in him all the worst characteristics of humankind, all on a par with those of the divine characters of the poem. With Hector, we see the reverse: it is the exception for him to become enraged, and if anger does come upon him, it goes as quickly as it comes. He embodies all or most of the good qualities of humanity, and the better aspects of the gods.

It is in Hector's direction that Achilles moves throughout the course of the poem. He does not reach that goal until his rage has destroyed Hector, however: it may be that Homer was again making a moral point about the destructive tendencies of war in showing us how it destroys all that is good in us.

Yet Hector is not without flaws of his own. He rounds on Polydamas and refuses to heed his (usually sound) advice on several occasions (especially XII.231ff.). What is more, he and Achilles seem to share the same major flaw—an over-developed concern about what other people think of them—although it is expressed in different ways.

Achilles' need for the regard of others is explicit: he says repeatedly that he is concerned about his reputation, both while he is yet alive and in years to come after his death. He knows he will die whether or not he fights at Troy, but if he is denied his rightful honors, he seems to feel that he has lost everything, and all his efforts have been in vain. As he tells Odysseus (IX.315-22, my translation):

> I do not think that I will be persuaded by Agamemnon, the son of Atreus, nor by the rest of the Danaans, since there was no gratitude rendered for fighting on and on against [your] enemies, without end. The fate for one who hangs back and for one who fights well is the same, the coward and the brave man are held in a single honor: The man who has done much dies just the same as the man who has done nothing. Nor is there any advantage for me, now that my heart has suffered such pains, in forever holding out my life as bait in the fighting.

Homer depicts Hector's need for others' respect more sketchily than Achilles', but it *is* there. Feeling as he does about the cause of the war (see VI.280-85 and 325ff.), surely Hector could have refused to fight in it, or prevailed on his brother (directly or indirectly, through Priam) to give Helen and the looted treasures back. Why, then, does he fight on? Homer hints at the answer twice in Book 6, at the opening of Hector's speech to Andromache (441-45), and the close of his speech to Paris (526-29): he would be unable to hold up his head in Troy if he failed to fight, even in a war he felt to be unworthy.

In his portraits of Hector and Achilles, Homer shows us the best and the worst of humanity, set against the background of the war that eventually destroys them both. Neither one learns the lesson of self-respect in time to save himself: and that is the true tragedy of the *Iliad*.

**Source:** Michael J. Spires, for *Epics for Students,* Gale Research, 1997.

## Wallace Gray

*In the following excerpt, Gray looks in the* Iliad *for clues to Homer's attitude toward the epic hero and the Greek heroic code. Gray suggests that in the character of Achilles, Homer has created a new and different type of epic hero: one who breaks rules and promises, and even feels compassion for his enemies.*

The *Iliad* is not about the Trojan War; that war lasted ten years and the central actions of the poem occupy only a few weeks. War brutalizes men and women, wounds their bodies and minds, enslaves and kills them. This is Homer's message as he focuses on one hero, Achilleus, to demonstrate wrath's destruction of self and others. Achilleus' moral journey in the *Iliad* brings him face to face with his own humanity, leading him to a startling and essentially unheroic act of generosity toward his enemy. When he gives Priam the dead and mutilated body of Hektor, Achilleus stands for a few moments on the threshold of a different civilization, as Homer shows wrath dissolved through compassion, and human feeling overcoming the stringent heroic code of conformity.

A hero is one who willingly and eagerly confronts death, and three Greek words embody the heroic code: *áristos, areté,* and *aristeía. Áristos* is being the best at whatever is called for by the situation: in wartime, killing; in peacetime, husbandry; in seamanship, steering. To be known as the best requires *aristeía*—exploits which gain for the warrior the prestige of having comrades consider him possessed of *areté,* merit. *Areté* can only be bestowed by others, not by self. In the world of the *Iliad* what the world thinks of you is far more important than what you think of yourself. Indeed, it *is* what you think of yourself. Fame and glory, *kléos,* can only be achieved through action. This is why the withdrawal of Achilleus from the battle is such a devastating decision: without exploits he has no identity and can only sit in his shelter singing about fame and glory instead of achieving it. Achilleus is no longer *áristos,* the best of the Achaians, when Agamemnon succeeds in depriving him of Briseis. The girl, along with tripods, spears, and other parseus tells Achilleus of Agamemnon's offer of gifts if he will return to the battle. In response, Achilleus rejects the heroic code once again. We are all going to die, he says, both the brave and the weak, so it matters little whether you do a great deal or nothing. Look at me, how I've fought harder than anyone, and how I have nothing. And what was I fighting for, why are the Argives fighting the Trojans? For Helen? What is so special about Helen?

In a dramatic rejection of the heroic code, Achilleus questions the sexual cause of the war, finding it unworthy of dying for. He has alienated himself from the war and has had time to question the standards of his society. Returning to the battle only after the death of Patroklos, Achilleus slays Hektor and then mutilates the body. That behavior is properly heroic. But then, in another brave defection from the heroic code, Achilleus takes a stance of compassion toward his enemy: he gives the body of Hektor to Priam for proper burial, a rite that will not only ensure the eternal peace of a spirit Achilleus has reason to condemn to a restless eternity, but will also give the body a continuing temporal fame in a burial marker. Achilleus ceases his erasure of the identity of Hektor.

In this first great work of Western literature, Homer shows war destroying not only cities and civilizations but the souls of men. War turns men into things, objects without pity. What difference does it make? Achilleus asks. We are all going to die. And he plunges his sword through the neck of the naked and defenseless young son of Priam.

Hektor, prince and defender of the city of Troy, becomes for the reader a more complete human being than does Achilleus. The latter deals primarily with other warriors, whereas Hektor is seen responding to his mother, Hekuba, his sister-in-law, Helen, and his wife, Andromache. Hektor is revealed through these three women, and they reveal themselves, especially by their positions when, in Book 6, Hektor returns to the city for respite from the fighting. These scenes gain for Hektor a sympathetic response from us that might otherwise have been reserved solely for Achilleus.

Hektor's first encounter is with his mother (the present Queen of Troy); this woman does not bury herself deep within the palace, but, herself a fierce warrior who can cry out that she would like to eat the liver of Achilleus raw, she comes rushing to greet her son. However, her first words to Hektor are not of comfort but of reprimand: she demands to know what he is doing behind the city walls, away from the fighting. No mother to coddle her children,

she immediately commands Hektor to offer a libation of wine to Zeus for victory in battle, and only then does she suggest that Hektor may drink some of the wine himself. But only to restore his energy for battle. This stern Queen of Troy is equal to the Spartan enemies besieging the walls of her city. How different she is from Thetis; Achilleus' mother treats him like a little baby before his final battle with Hektor.

Hektor continues on to the palace of his brother, where he finds Paris and Helen (the former Queen of Sparta) in a most appropriate place, her bedroom. Paris is polishing his battle gear rather than fighting with it, and Helen is berating him, projecting the blame for the war on the gods, and referring to herself as a vile bitch. When she suggests that future poets will, as they indeed have done, make songs about her and perpetuate her fame, one wonders whether she really does resent her "misfortune." The lady protests at great length, and she responds to Hektor with much more tenderness and regard than she does to Paris. And Hektor, for all the ten years of suffering Helen has caused, treats her with the respect due a former Queen of Sparta. (To be fair to Helen, it must be remembered that women of this period had no more control over their fate than did those in the male-dominated Athenian "Golden Age.")

When Hektor goes searching for his wife (whom destiny will prevent from becoming Queen of Troy in the future), he finds her in a place that reveals her character as the wife of a prince who is slated to be the future King of Troy: she is standing on the city wall, from which she can watch the battle. There she reminds Hektor that Achilleus had killed her father as well as her seven brothers, and was responsible for the death of her mother. Hektor, then, she tells him, is both father, brother, mother, and husband to her. Indeed, when she loses Hektor to the sword of Achilleus, she loses everything in the world. Both she and Hektor know Achilleus is the greater warrior; they realize Hektor is going to die. He knows the city of Troy will perish and that Andromache and his son will be lost. Although he may at times deny it, Hektor returns to the battle knowing that he will die; this is his heroic grandeur. But, before he goes, he reaches out for his baby son, who, not recognizing his father in plumed helmet and battle gear, cries out in fear and terror. Homer shows that war is not just glorious action bringing fame and honor to the participants; it is also a mechanism turning men into creatures from whom even their children draw back in fright. There are neither good men nor bad men in the *Iliad;* this is the humanity of Homer, who, Hellenic himself, doesn't favor Hellenes over Trojans.

Homer is given credit for anthropomorphism, for providing the gods and goddesses with human traits. He endowed them with richly human characteristics, turning Ares into the blood-thirsty young god of war, Aphrodite into the "flighty" goddess of love, Hera into a jealous and conniving wife, and Athena and Apollo into grandiose, superhuman beings. To Homer's listeners, as well as to many in the following generations, these divine gods and goddesses constituted their religious beliefs, and their participation in the two Homeric poems was real—the gods controlled and directed the events. The modern reader, however, can choose among a variety of ways of reading the poem: the gods and goddesses are actually real and present; they are external symbols for the internal emotions, desires, and drives of men and women, of their good and bad luck; or, they are both at the same time.

In the first instance the reader can suspend his disbelief in ancient Hellenic religion and enter into the spirit of the times. In the second—the symbolic reading—the reader can consider that everything that happens to the heroes in the *Iliad* could have happened *without* the actions of the gods, since they are personifications of the fears and aspirations of the heroes. If a hero is suddenly filled with courage, or overcomes his opponent, or has good luck, or lets out a war cry that terrifies the enemy, then a god or goddess is given the credit. Even Apollo's stunning of Patroklos, and Athena's return of a spear to Achilleus—two occurrences often cited as indisputable evidence of divine intervention—can be considered as symbols for human actions.

However, in reading imaginative literature it is possible to have the best of both worlds: the imaginative reader need not consider the two readings mutually exclusive, need not choose between the actually divine and the symbolically divine. Indeed, this dual function is expressed by Diomedes when he is speaking about Achilleus' rejection of the embassy: "He will fight when the heart in his breast urges him, and the god arouses him." The single combat between Menelaos and Paris and its aftermath illustrate this dual role of the Olympians in Homer.

After ten years of battle it has been decided to resolve the conflict through single combat between Menelaos, Helen's first husband, and Paris, Helen's second husband. (This is one of a number of incidents in the poem which seem likely to have oc-

curred earlier in the war.) In the first moments of the contest Menelaos throws his spear at Paris and misses the body. He then grabs Paris by the helmet, spins him around until Paris falls, and begins to drag him away by the helmet. Aphrodite, however, the protectress of Paris, breaks the chin strap holding the helmet, and Menelaos strides on, carrying only the helmet. Thus, what was accident, a worn chin strap breaking and saving Paris, is attributed to the intervention of a goddess. Paris escapes through a cloud of dust, carried off by Aphrodite and deposited gently in the bed of Helen. The goddess is given credit for spiriting Paris away from the battle, whereas it could also be read as an act of apparent cowardice on his part. Aphrodite leads Helen to the bedroom—or perhaps she is led by her own lust. What happens next in that bed is a startling precursor of the link between sex and death in succeeding literature. Paris, turning to Helen, tells her he has never before felt such passion for her. Although this may be a formulaic statement always uttered at each instance of lovemaking in epic poetry of this period, it appears Homer is suggesting that the exciting stimuli of danger and imminent death have served to increase Paris' sexual excitement.

At this early stage of Greek civilization, the concept of *díkē,* justice, is inconsistent and rudimentary. Although the *Iliad* has been read by some as a poem about divine justice—Zeus' punishment of Troy in retribution for Paris' abduction of Helen—the gods and goddesses themselves are all too humanly fickle, wrathful, inconsistent, and ambiguous in their behavior for a reading of the poem as one concerned primarily with divine justice; the poet, after all, opens by telling the listener that his poem is about the "wrath of Achilleus."

*Díkē* in the *Iliad* consists of getting one's own fair share of war booty, food, or land—the share due a hero who risks his life. And the wrath of Achilleus is first stirred when he is deprived of part of his "fair portion," the captive Briseis. Among men, brute force determines justice: Agamemnon has more warriors than Achilleus and can thus have his way, and Achilleus can only resort to withdrawing from the war and thus causing vital losses to Agamemnon.

Divine justice seems to be based on favoritism and whim, and Judeo-Christian concepts of an all-knowing God must be set aside for a Zeus who seems not always to know the future. In order to determine which of two battling warriors will die, Zeus places their death portions on the scale; the heavier one will die that day. In spite of teaching at one point that the gods listen to those who obey them, the *Iliad* shows Zeus granting some prayers and denying others. Zeus has two urns, one of evils and one of blessings, and he mingles gifts from the two urns to be distributed to an individual without regard for merit. The definition of human life seems to be that it is always a mixture of both good and bad experiences for every human being, that those experiences are not always merited, and that all must die. Heroes who forget their human nature and begin to act like deathless gods are soon reminded of their mortality.

In the Homeric poems two kinds of *díkē* exist side by side; one for wartime and another for peacetime. In wartime a hero's experiences are usually the result of force or chance; in the city at peace on the shield of Achilleus, the poet presents a different concept of justice. When two men disagree, they go to arbitrators, elders of the city who listen to the men's cases as well as to the voice of the people; two talents of gold are given to the judge who speaks the best opinion. Homer portrays justice and love and dancing in the city at peace, but only destruction and death in the city at war. There is no arbitration in war, no peaceful solution, no restitution through the payment of a blood price, but only desecration by dogs and vultures. Deliberation and arbitration result in recompense for the killing of a man in the city at peace, whereas the victorious warrior on the battlefield always rejects the payment promised by the defeated warrior for his proper burial. In the *Odyssey,* Odysseus conquers the suitors through cunning rather than brute force, and his victory over them, as we shall see, is one that rights a civic injustice. In the two Homeric poems it appears that war is a time when justice is subject to irrational, arbitrary, and hasty determinations, and peace a time for reflection and rational deliberation.

Homer seldom relents in showing the brutality of war. Within a hundred lines at the beginning of Book 5, various fighters are struck in the back by a spear that drives on through the chest; pierced by a spear through the right shoulder; struck in the right buttock by a spear that plunges in under the bone and through the bladder; struck in the back of the head by a spear that drives on through the teeth and under the tongue until the spearhead sticks out through the warrior's mouth and he falls, gripping the spear between his teeth; struck by a spear that severs the arm, which then drops bleeding to the ground.

By using similes from experiences common to everyone at that time, Homer succeeds in making battle vivid to those in his audience who may never have been to war. He likens combat to lions attacking sheep, to the fury of thunderstorms, to lightning and raging forest fires: the comparisons are always to destructive elements or to violent animals. Heroes may achieve glory and fame on the battlefield, but war itself is brutal and degrading. On the point of death, a warrior pleads pitifully for mercy he knows is not forthcoming, while the hero stands crowing and vaunting over him, spearhead pointed at the sprawled warrior's chest.

Striking illustrations of Homer's technique of using familiar comparisons occur in Book 2. He first shows the visual aspects of war: the battle is like a raging forest fire running across mountaintops whose glorious bronze light dazzles all the way up to the heavens. He next compares the sounds of battle to flying geese and cranes, to the throated sound of swans and their wings as, when they are settling, meadows echo with their clashing swarms. The sound is also like horses' hooves thundering. Next he presents the kinetic movement, the impetus of thrusting armies, comparing them to swarming insects frantically buzzing around the milk pails in a sheepfold. The leaders of the armies are compared to goatherds separating and organizing goats, to the strongest ox of the herd, to a chief bull who stands out among the cattle. A touching comparison occurs when Apollo leads the Trojans in their destruction of the ramparts of the Achaians; Homer sings that they do this as easily as a little boy at the seashore amuses himself by trampling his carefully built sand towers with his feet.

Homer frequently employs what we would call a cinematic approach in dealing with large battles, photographing from a distance, then moving to the foreground, and only at the last showing a close-up of two specific warriors. At the beginning of the battle, . . . [in] Book 4, he gives an overview of two armies surging toward each other, and the comparison is to sea surf pounding in toward the shore, driven by the wind. The cries of the oncoming army sound from a distance, and the cries are compared to those of sheep waiting to be milked and yearning for their lambs. . . . [Later] the camera moves in closer to show still-unidentified men killing and being killed, and, Homer sings, blood running along the ground like rivers rushing down from mountain streams. The sound of armies clashing is like thunder. Having provided a long view followed by a move to the foreground, the poet is now ready for a close-up of a distinct individual: "Antilochos was first to kill a chief man of the Trojans."

One of the chief men of the Achaians is Patroklos, the dearly beloved friend of Achilleus. Patroklos is so youthful, so guileless, so saddened by the sufferings of others, that, given Achilleus' protective attitude toward him, it is necessary to remind ourselves that Patroklos is the older of the two: *he* has been sent along to protect *Achilleus*.

Patroklos initiates the final climactic scenes of the story. Moved by the sight of his wounded comrades, Patroklos—his name means glory to the fathers—pleads with Achilleus to allow him to reenter the fighting. Thus, clad in the armor of Achilleus, he goes forth only to be killed by Hektor. In an ironic foreshadowing of the final battle between Hektor and Achilleus, Patroklos, wearing the armor of Achilleus, is surrogate for that greater warrior. In larger terms, Achilleus experiences his own death, as well as that of his dear friend. "Die all," Achilleus shouts at a later point. And they *will* die all, including Achilleus, as he symbolically dies in the *Iliad* when he kills Hektor, a warrior clad in the armor of Achilleus that he stripped from Patroklos. Achilleus knows the prophecy that he is to die shortly after the death of Hektor; he thus embraces his own death when he kills Hektor, especially so since the armor makes that warrior another surrogate Achilleus. Like Patroklos, Achilleus also requires three instruments of death—in his case, Patroklos, Hektor, and finally, Paris—the actual killer.

Odysseus is a different breed of Iliadic warrior. The skill of the hero of Homer's second epic is not in brute force but in crafty strategies. Odysseus is intelligent and resourceful, descriptions not applied to other warriors. From the very beginning, in Book 2, he seems to take charge through speech and persuasion when decisions are to be made. And when Agamemnon finally gives in to the fact that he needs Achilleus, it is Odysseus who is put in charge of the embassy to persuade Achilleus to return. This embassy in Book 9 consists of the wily Odysseus, the older and respected Phoinix, and Ajax, that plain-spoken, tough, honest warrior. Each has his own approach to the unyielding Achilleus.

Odysseus speaks first, repeating the speech Agamemnon has delivered to him, promising numerous gifts to Achilleus if he will come to their aid. Odysseus cleverly omits the one part of Agamemnon's speech that would have much of-

fended Achilleus: Achilleus should yield to him because he is the kinglier of the two. Achilleus is unpersuaded; there is a standoff between the *mêtis*, cunning, of Odysseus and the *bíe*, might, of Achilleus. Both *mêtis* and *bíe* are needed to win the Trojan War. In the *Iliad* they are represented by the characters of Odysseus and Achilleus, whereas in the *Odyssey*, melded as they are into one hero, Hellenic awareness takes a sophisticated step forward in the realization that man needs to have both *mêtis* and *bíe* to be *áristos*, the best.

Phoinix next recounts a somewhat lengthy but pointed story about a warrior, Meleagros, who also withdrew from battle and, in spite of the failure of the army without him, refused the entreaties of mother, sisters, and friends to return to the fight. He succumbed only to the pleas of his wife, Kleopatra. Phoinix is being even more subtle than he perhaps realizes. He knows Patroklos is Achilleus' dearest friend, that only Patroklos could possibly persuade him, and he has chosen this particular story because the name Kleopatra is Patroklos in reverse, and he hopes the echo will set up some kind of emotional response in Achilleus. Kleopatra is the only one who is successful in persuading her husband, Meleagros, to put on his armor and return to the battle: Homer is here brilliantly foreshadowing Achilleus' return to the war because of Patroklos: the dead body of Patroklos becomes the ultimate persuasive force.

Finally, . . . the blunt Ajax speaks, and doesn't try to be psychologically clever or wily; he is incapable of either. He speaks directly: We're not getting anywhere with this stubborn and proud man, he is so hard that he doesn't even listen to his friends, and he is being selfish. This short, direct appeal succeeds more than the others—at least enough for Achilleus to promise to return to the battle should the Trojans fight their way up to the ships.

Achilleus is a new and different epic hero; he breaks rules, forswears sacred oaths, is moved by compassion for the enemy. The partially successful embassy to Achilleus is a stage in his development which reaches a climax in Priam's own embassy to Achilleus to plead for the mutilated body of his son.

The war and the world have come to a halt with the death of Hektor. Following the funeral games for Patroklos, Achilleus spends twelve days without sleep, alternately rolling in the dirt, weeping over the death of Patroklos, and tossing and throwing the body of Hektor in the dust as though it were some despoiled rag doll. Even the gods are upset by his behavior: Apollo complains that Achilleus doesn't even feel helpful shame about what he is doing, and that he has destroyed pity by tying Hektor's body to horses and dragging it around the tomb of Patroklos. Thetis, Achilleus' immortal mother, descends and urges him to return the body. Although this external appearance can be interpreted as the internal prompt-ings of Achilleus' spirit to give up his wrath, he does say that he will, for ransom, turn over the body. The emotional scene in which he offers Hektor's corpse to Priam shows that this action is for reasons other than ransom.

Within the walls of Troy, Priam prepares for his journey to Achilleus, much against the fears of Hekuba, who argues . . . that Achilleus cannot be trusted, will show no pity, and is an "eater of raw meat." Despite her warnings, Priam sets out on a strange, eerie, frightening journey past the great tomb of Ilos, alongside a river, and into the dark-ness. Zeus sends Hermes down to guide him, and even though Hermes appears to him as a young man, Priam is so frightened that his hair stands on end. Hermes questions him, asking why he is travel-ing through the immortal black night. Conducting him to the barricades protecting Achilleus' dwell-ing, Hermes casts sleep on the sentries.

All of the components of a fearful journey to Hades are here, as Priam travels past tombs and rivers through an immortal black night in which Hermes, who guides souls to Hades, casts sleep on watchdogs. This can only be a symbolic journey to Hades to visit Achilleus, who has truly become King of the Dead. And his dwelling is no ordinary battlefield shelter, but an imposing structure worthy of this symbolic King of Hades.

Priam enters alone, falls to the ground, clasps the knees and kisses the hands of Achilleus. Moved by the tears of the groaning father, the hero of the *Iliad* weeps at the thought of his own father's devastation had the body of Achilleus lain on a battlefield to be ravaged by wild dogs and vultures. As Priam and Achilleus shed tears of sadness and loss in recognition of their common human condi-tion, Achilleus, in a heroic thrust *through* the heroic code, agrees to return the body of Hektor, slayer of his dear friend and companion Patroklos. The days of wrath thus end with a compassionate human rather than heroic gesture.

**Source:** Wallace Gray, ''Homer: *Iliad*,'' in *Homer to Joyce*, Macmillan Publishing Co., 1985 , pp. 1–16.

## Jasper Griffin

*In the following excerpt, Griffin looks at the ways in which the* Iliad *deals with a past mythic age in which the gods involved themselves in the lives of godlike, heroic humans.*

With small exceptions, the serious poetry of Greece is concerned with the myths; and the subject of Greek mythology is the heroes. These are two obvious facts. Epic dealt with the ''deeds of gods and men,'' and so did the choral lyric, while even the personal lyric is full of mythical narratives and excursions. Tragedy, too, tended to restrict itself to the mythical period, although the *Capture of Miletus,* by Phrynichus, and the *Persians,* by Aeschylus, show that this was not actually a rule. The mythical period was quite a short one, two or three genera-tions about the time of the Theban and Trojan wars; the rest of the past, however vivid or striking in the memory, was felt to be different, and inappropriate for serious poetic treatment. Hence no tragedies about Pisistratus or Periander, the colonizing peri-od, or the Lelantine War.

There was something special about that time. Heroes, we read, were bigger and stronger than we are—a hero of Homer could pick up and throw a rock which ''nowadays two of the best men in a city could barely hoist on to a waggon''—but that is not the important thing. In that time gods intervened openly in human affairs, and it is their passionate concern and personal participation which marks heroic events as possessing significance. Aeschylus, brooding upon the morality of war and conquest, writes about King Agamemnon; Euripides, brood-ing upon the relation of the sexes, writes about Jason and Medea. An event like the murder of a husband by his wife, or a question like that of civil disobedience, is raised to the level at which it can be ''seen'' and taken seriously, when a poet writes of Clytemnestra or Antigone. In the epic, the divine presence and concern ensure that the story of Paris and Helen is a tragedy, not a mere spicy tale, and that the fall of Troy is not just one more disaster but an event of moral significance. The gods find noth-ing so enthralling as the spectacle of human heroism and suffering; their attention marks its importance, but equally their superiority marks its smallness in another perspective. The heroes were nearer to the gods than later men. ''Born of Zeus,'' ''nourished by Zeus,'' ''honoured by Zeus''; these are standard epithets for Homeric kings and princes, and not less interesting are ''loved by Zeus'' and ''god-like.''

"Like Zeus in counsel," "the equal of Ares," "a man equal to the gods," "god-like," "resembling the immortals," "divine," "with the appearance of a god," "honoured by his people like a god"—no reader of Homer needs to be told that these and other such epithets are among the commonest in the poems. Heroines, too, "have beauty from the goddesses" or "look like a goddess in face," and can be compared to Artemis or Aphrodite. A hero may be compared to several gods at once, as when Agamemnon is said to be "in eyes and head like Zeus who delights in thunder, in girdle like Ares, in chest like Poseidon." Priam says of his son Hector that "he was a god among men, and did not seem like the son of a mortal man but of a god." But these passages suggest complications, for Agamemnon is being led to disaster by Zeus, while Hector is dead, his body in the power of his ruthless enemy. What is it to be "god-like"?

There is one great difference between gods and men. Gods are deathless and ageless, while men are mortal. When Apollo thrusts Diomede back into the limits of his mortality, he shouts, "Reflect, son of Tydeus, and fall back; do not try to be the equal of the gods. Never is the race of immortal gods on a level with earthbound men." When Achilles is misled into attacking Apollo, the god says, "Son of Peleus, why do you pursue me, when you are a mortal and I a deathless god?" He declines to fight with Poseidon "for the sake of mortal men, wretched creatures, who one day flourish and another day are gone." The heroes who are "god-like" are subject to death, and we see them die. The epithets which belong to them as heroes contrast poignantly with their human fate. Sometimes the effect seems so light that it is not certain whether it is meant to be felt at all: as when in the boxing match the only challenger for the formidable Epeius is "Euryalus, that man equal to a god"—who is promptly knocked out and helped off by his friends, "with feet dragging, spitting out thick blood, with his head lolling to one side." Similarly light is the stress in a passage like that where Briseis tells the tragic story of her life: Achilles slew her husband and destroyed "the city of divine Mynes." The attentive listener is aware of a certain faint resonance, in the first case of irony, in the second of pathos.

More positively striking, perhaps, are such passages as those where old Nestor indulges himself in reminiscences of his great exploit in youth: "Would that I were young, as I was when I slew god-like Ereuthalion," and "Ereuthalion was their champion, a man the equal of gods . . . he was the biggest and strongest man I ever slew." Ereuthalion was a Goliath-figure whom nobody but the youthful Nestor dared to face; his great stature and terrifying power are dwelt upon by his slayer, who adds "He lay sprawling, far in both directions." He was like a god—but I slew him. The emphasis becomes, I think, clearly deliberate when we read of Paris, when he has gaily challenged any Achaean champion and Menelaus has appeared to fight him, that "When Paris, beautiful as a god, saw him appear, his spirit was dashed, and he slunk back into the ranks to avoid his fate. . . . So did he slip back into the body of the haughty Trojans, Paris as beautiful as a god, in fear of Atreus' son." For the poet makes it very clear that the beauty of Paris is what characterizes him, and is at variance with his lack of heroism: Hector at once rebukes him as "Evil Paris, great in beauty, woman-mad, seducer. . . ." and adds that "Your music and your gifts from Aphrodite, your hair and your beauty, would not help you when Menelaus brought you down in the dust."

But the poet can find deeper notes of pathos and significance in this way. When "the god-like Sarpedon" is dead, his body fought over by the two armies, "then not even a discerning man would have recognized god-like Sarpedon, for he was covered with weapons and blood and dirt, from his head right down to his feet." Zeus, his father, keeps his shining eyes fixed on the struggle over the body of his son, unrecognizable in blood and dirt; that is all that remains of the handsome warrior Sarpedon, who in life was like a god. The epithet helps to bring out the human pathos, and also to underline the contrast of the human, even at its greatest and most attractive, and the really divine. When Achilles has killed Hector, he starts a paean of triumph over his body: "We have won a great victory: we have slain the god-like Hector, whom the Trojans adored like a god in Troy." Here the epithet, and the idea of adoration by one's fellow citizens, become a triumphant taunt, in which what was largely left implicit in the boasts of Nestor is fully developed. It becomes pathetic explicitly when Hecuba laments her son: "You were my pride night and day, and you were the defender of all the men and women of Troy, who hailed you like a god. Alive, you were their great glory; but now death and fate have caught you." The greatness of his fall and her loss emerge in this touching claim.

In the light of these passages I think it is clear that we are also to see force in the epithet "god-like" when it is used in the context of Hector's body being dishonoured by Achilles. Thus the poet tells us that after Achilles' triumphant paean ''he wrought acts of humiliation on god-like Hector,'' piercing his ankles and dragging through the dust of his own country ''his head that before was comely.'' The immediate juxtaposition of ''god-like Hector'' and ''acts of humiliation'' enables the poet to bring out, without sentimentality, the pathos of the greatest possible fall for a man, from god-like stature to humiliation and helplessness. I find the same technique repeatedly in the last book of the *Iliad.* ''Achilles in his rage was abusing god-like Hector, and all the gods, looking on, felt pity for him.'' ''He has tied god-like Hector to his chariot, having robbed him of his life, and is dragging him round the tomb of his friend. That is not right or good for him; we gods may grow angry with him, for all his strength; for he is abusing dumb earth in his rage''— so says Apollo, and we see in the speech of the god the full nature of man, at once capable of being ''god-like'' and also doomed to be ''dumb earth.'' A last and rather different example: when Patroclus is called by Achilles to go on the mission which will lead to his return to battle and to his death, the poet, with unequalled economy and power, presents him in one line: ''He came out, the equal of Ares; and that was the beginning of his doom.'' His greatness and his fragility emphasize and reflect upon each other.

The love of the gods for men is not less capable of bearing a range of emotional overtones. That great gods ''loved'' great kings was an age-old part of the belief of Egypt and the kingdoms of the Levant. There it was a simple and unambiguous conception. The god would be on our side and would frustrate the knavish tricks of our enemies; our king was the special favourite of mighty forces, and rebellion against him was as wicked as war against him was futile. Such an idea is to be found in Homer, as when Odysseus warns the Achaeans not to provoke their king Agamemnon: ''Great is the anger of kings nourished by Zeus: their honours come from Zeus, and Zeus the Counsellor loves them.'' But the subject of the epic is not a simple and one-sided narration of ''our'' king's career of conquest, like an Assyrian or Egyptian historical inscription. Zeus honours Troy, he tells us himself, more than any other city under the starry heaven, and he loves Hector and his own son Sarpedon, on the Trojan side, no less than he loves Achilles and Patroclus, their slayers. And he loves Achilles, the opponent of Agamemnon, more than he loves the sceptred king himself, as Agamemnon is forced to learn.

Zeus loves Hector and Sarpedon, Patroclus and Achilles; but by the end of the *Iliad* three of the four are dead, and the fourth is to be slain very soon. He loves Troy, yet Troy will fall. He loves Agamemnon, but he sends a lying dream to him to deceive and defeat him. Odysseus, indeed, loved by Zeus and Athena, will survive, but that is the exception rather than the rule in the Homeric poems, and even he reproaches his patron goddess bitterly for her failure to protect him in his sufferings. Aphrodite claims that she has ''loved exceedingly'' the Helen whom she forces against her will into the shameless embrace of Paris:

> ''Do not provoke me, wretch, lest I be angry and forsake you, and hate you even as I have exceedingly loved you; between both sides, Trojans and Achaeans, I shall devise bitter suffering for you, and you will come to a miserable end.'' So she spoke, and Helen, daughter of Zeus, was afraid. She followed in silence, shielding her face with her shining robe, and none of the Trojan women saw her; the goddess led the way.

That is what it might be like to be loved by a god.

Even the greatest of the sons of Zeus, Heracles himself, ''who was the dearest of men to Zeus,'' did not for that escape suffering and disaster. Peleus, Hera tells us, was dear above all men to the immortal gods and all the gods attended his wedding to Thetis, but now he is alone and miserable, far away from his only son, who will never come home. Amphiaraus was ''loved exceedingly by aegis-bearing Zeus and by Apollo, with all kinds of love; yet he did not reach the threshold of old age, but died at Thebes by reason of a woman's gifts''— betrayed to death by his wife for a bribe. The poet of the *Odyssey* tells us with inimitable objectivity that the singer Demodocus was blind: ''the Muse loved him exceedingly, and she gave him both good and evil; she robbed him of his sight, but she gave him sweet singing.'' The ancients believed that Homer was a blind man, and that belief adds to the poignancy of his representation of another singer, his counterpart in his epic.

Zeus is a father to men, and Athena sometimes looks after a favourite ''like a mother''; Zeus is said to ''care for and pity'' Priam in his misery. It has often been emphasized that the gods of Homer love the strong and successful, not the weak and poor, but it is wrong to think that means a straightforward idealizing of successful power and force. The gods love great heroes, but that love does not protect them from defeat and death. The heroes who engross the attention of the poet of the *Iliad* are those who are doomed—Sarpedon, Patroclus, Hector, Achilles; they it is whom the gods love, and who will exchange their strength and brilliance for the cold and darkness of death. As they come nearer to that terrible transition, the shining eyes of Zeus are fixed on them all the more attentively; he loves them *because* they are doomed. They in their mortal blindness cannot know, as the god allows them temporary triumph, that in his long-term plan they must die; the victories of Hector and Patroclus, which show Zeus' love for them, are in that perspective only a stage in their planned defeat and death.

The hero who is most often compared with the gods is Achilles. But not only is he said to be "god-like," but also we observe in action how like the gods he is, and above all how like Zeus himself. He has sacked twenty-three cities in the Troad, he boasts, and he numbers "Sacker of Cities" among his formulaic titles: Zeus "has brought down the towers of many cities and will bring down many more." His quarrel with Agamemnon over his "honour" . . . is reflected in heaven when Poseidon resents the claim of Zeus to higher rank. Zeus rubs in his quelling of Hera's attempted mutiny by saying, "In the morning, if you wish, you will see the paramount son of Cronus destroy the Argive host yet more, ox-eyed Lady Hera." In the same words Achilles tells the envoys of Agamemnon that despite all their pleas he will go home: "Tomorrow . . . you will see, if you wish, and if you are interested, my ships sailing at dawn on the Hellespont." He possesses a special cup, from which no man drinks but himself, and libations are poured to no god but Zeus. He is urged to "be like the gods," whose prepotent power does not prevent them from relenting and giving way to suppliants, but his nature is god-like in a different sense. Patroclus, who knows him better than any other man, says "You know what he is like; he is terrible. He may well blame the innocent." We remember what Iris says that Zeus will do, if his will is crossed: "He will come to Olympus to cast us into confusion; he will seize in succession on the guilty and the innocent." The poet even creates a parallel between the bringing of the mourning figure of Thetis before the gods on Olympus and the appearance of the mourning Priam before Achilles. In both scenes the incomer emerges from the darkness, dressed in mourning, and finds the other in the light, sitting at ease and drinking; the gods press a wine-cup into Thetis' hand; Achilles insists that Priam eat and drink with him.

But above all it is in being irresponsible and arbitrary that kings resemble gods. Achilles, we have seen, is apt to blame the innocent. The conduct to be expected of a king is viewed in the same light, and with the same apprehension, in both epics. Calchas asks in advance for a guarantee of protection before he names Agamemnon as the cause of the plague, "for a king is too powerful when he is angry with a man of lower rank: even if he digests his wrath for a time, yet he keeps his anger in his heart thereafter, to pay him out." In the same way we hear of Zeus: "if the Olympian does not bring it to pass at once, he brings it out in the end, and men pay for it dearly." Penelope describes the normal kingly behaviour, to which Odysseus was such an exception: "This is the custom of god-like kings: one man he will hate, another he will love—but Odysseus never did violence at all to any man." The gods, in their superior power, can be arbitrary. Kings, placed on the pinnacle of mortal power, try to emulate them. Agamemnon tries to treat Achilles with mere force, as he tried with the suppliant Chryses. In both cases a greater force defeats him. Achilles is asked to be like the gods and yield; he might have replied that he emulated the gods at least as well in refusing to yield to prayer. We see in the *Iliad* Zeus accept the sacrifices but reject the prayer of the Achaeans for an early victory, reject the prayer of both sides for a negotiated peace, disregard the passionate prayer of Asius, and plan disaster for the Achaeans though they pour anxious libations to him all night long; and we see Athena reject the prayers of the women of Troy. The motives which impel the gods to intervene in human affairs are personal and arbitrary, all-too-human in fact. Men try to act in the same way and come to grief, for Achilles, god-like beyond any other hero and indulging his passionate and arbitrary will in rejecting prayers which he knows to be right, causes the death of Patroclus and wishes only to die himself. While he lives, the hero is god-like and loved by the gods. In his martial rage, the high point and essence of his existence, he is like a lion, a wild boar, a storm, a river in flood, a raging forest fire, a bright star from a dark cloud; his armour blazes like the sun, his eyes flash fire, his breast is filled with irresistible fury, his limbs are light and active. The mere sight of his onset and the sound of his great battle-cry are enough to fill enemy heroes with panic. Encouraged by gods, even "thrust on by the mighty hand of Zeus," he mows down opponents like a reaper in a cornfield, like a wind scattering the foam of the sea, like a great dolphin swallowing little fishes. Men fall and are crushed under his chariot wheels, and he drives on, his chariot rattling over them. He challenges his opponent to single combat with insults and exults over his body, so that the defeated must die with the taunts of the victor in his ears. He then aims to strip off his armour and abolish his identity by depriving him in death of burial, and leaving his corpse to be mauled by scavenging animals and birds.

''To be alive and to see the light of the sun'' is in the Homeric poems a regular phrase, along with ''while I have breath in my lungs and my knees are active.'' To die, conversely, is to ''leave the light of the sun'' and to ''go into the dark,'' or to have one's knees or limbs ''undone.'' The *Iliad* is full of detailed accounts of the moment of death of the warrior. The poet dislikes any account of men being gravely wounded but not dying; a wounded man either dies quickly or recovers and fights again. The incurable Philoctetes is left far from Troy, groaning on the island of Lemnos; the Achaean chieftains wounded in Book II are healed and will return to battle. This works with the removal of chance as a possible cause of a hero's death (no arrow at a venture can kill a Homeric hero as Ahab or Harold were killed), and the virtual suppression of trickery and treason, and the fact that, in the poem, prisoners are no longer taken, all suppliants being killed. The effect of all this stylization is to concentrate attention as exclusively as possible on the position of the hero, face to face with his destiny at the hands of another hero: either he must kill or be killed, dying a heroic death.

When a hero dies, dark night covers him, he is seized by hateful darkness; he is robbed of his sweet life, his soul rushes forth from the wound; it goes down to Hades bewailing its fate, leaving behind its youth and strength. The doom of death covers his eyes and nostrils, his armour rings upon him, he breathes out his life in the dust, hateful fate swallows him up, he gluts the god of war with his blood. Stabbed in the back, he lies in the dust, stretching out his hands to his friends; wounded in the bladder, he crouches breathing his last, and lies stretched out on the earth like a worm. With a spear driven through his eye he collapses, arms spread wide, and his killer cuts off and brandishes his head; he lies on his back in the dust, breathing his last, while all his guts pour from his wound to the earth; he dies bellowing with pain, clutching the bloody earth, or biting the cold bronze which has severed his tongue, or wounded between the navel and the genitals, ''where the wound is most painful for poor mortal men,'' writhing like a roped bull about the spear.

His eyes are knocked out and fall bloody before his feet in the dust; stabbed in the act of begging for his life, his liver slides out and his lap is filled with his blood; the spear is thrust into his mouth, splitting his white bones, and filling his eye sockets with blood which spouts at his mouth and nose; hit in the head, his blood and brains rush from the wound. Wounded in the arm and helpless, he awaits his slayer, seeing death before him; his prayer for life rejected, he crouches with arms spread out waiting for the death-stroke. After death his corpse may be driven over by chariots, his hands and head may be lopped off, all his enemies may surround his corpse and stab it at their leisure, his body may be thrown into the river and gnawed by fishes, or lie unrecognizable in the mêlée. His soul goes down to a dark and comfortless world, to a shadowy and senseless existence, for ever banished from the light and warmth and activity of this life.

That is what the hero faces every time he goes into battle. It is clear in Homer that the soldier would, in general, prefer not to fight. Not only do the Achaeans rush for the ships and home, the moment they see a chance, but the rank and file need constant and elaborate appeals and commands to keep them in the field, and even heroes have at times to reason themselves into a fighting mood, and at others to be rebuked by their superiors or their comrades. Women attempt to hold them back from the battlefield, as we see in Book 6, where Hecuba, Helen, and Andromache in turn try to detain Hector in the safe and comfortable women's realm, but the true hero, like Hector, must reject the temptation and go. We are not dealing with berserkers in the pages of Homer, whatever Mycenaean warriors may have been like in reality. Self-respect, respect for public opinion, the conscious determination to be a good man— these motives drive the hero to risk his life; and the crowning paradox of the hero, the idea of inevitable death itself. ''If we were to be ageless and immortal once we had survived this war,'' says Sarpedon to Glaucus, ''then I should not fight in the fore-front myself, nor should I be sending you into the battle where men win glory. But in fact countless dooms of death surround us, and no mortal man can escape or avoid them: so let us go, either to yield victory to another or to win it ourselves.'' If the hero were really god-like, if he were exempt, as the gods are, from age and death, then he would not be a hero at all. It is the pressure of mortality which imposes on men the compulsion to have virtues; the gods, exempt from that pressure, are, with perfect consistency, less ''virtuous'' than men. They do not need the supreme human virtue of courage, since even if they are wounded in battle they can be instantly cured; and since they make no sacrifice for each other, as Hector does for his wife and child and Odysseus for his, their marriages, too, seem lacking in the depth and truth of human marriage. We see no union on Olympus which has anything of the quality of those of Hector and of Odysseus.

Death is constantly present in the hero's thoughts. Hector knows that Troy will fall, and hopes only that he will be dead and buried first. Before his duel with Ajax he makes careful provision for the burial and memorial to be allotted to the man defeated. Achilles describes his life, fighting and ravaging the Troad, "constantly exposing my own life in battle," and in his speech to Lycaon he says "I too am subject to death and cruel fate: there will be a morning or an evening or a noonday, when someone will take my life in battle, hitting me with a spear or an arrow from the bow-string." No hero, not even the greatest, is spared the shameful experience of fear. Hector runs from Achilles; Ajax is put to flight, "trembling and looking at the crowd of men like a wild beast"; Achilles himself is alarmed by Agenor's spear, and later, reduced by the attack of the River Scamander to seeing a miserable death apparently unavoidable, he is told by Poseidon, "Do not tremble too much nor be afraid." We have seen that in some ways the fighting described by Homer is highly stylized, and that it omits some of the characteristic horrors of war. Yet the audience remains convinced that in fact the poet has done full justice to its nature, that its frightfulness has not been palliated or smoothed over. That effect is achieved, in great part, because the poet insists on presenting death in its full significance as the end, unsoftened by any posthumous consolation or reward; in depicting it dispassionately and fully in all its forms; and showing that even heroes fear and hate it. The hero is granted by the poet the single privilege of dying a hero's death, not a random or undignified one, but that death haunts his thoughts in life and gives his existence at once its limitations and its definition.

It is in accordance with this overriding interest in human life, in its quality as intense and glorious yet transitory, and its position poised between the eternal brightness of heaven and the unchanging darkness of the world of the dead, that the Homeric poems are interested in death far more than they are in fighting. Homeric duels are short; heroes do not hack away at each other, exhausting all their strength

and cunning, as do the heroes of Germanic epic or the knights of Malory. Recent work has emphasized the brevity and standardized character of these encounters. When a hero's time of doom has arrived, his strength is no use to him. The armour is struck from the shoulders of Patroclus by a god; Athena secretly gives back to Achilles the spear with which he has missed Hector, "and Hector, shepherd of the people, did not notice"—while as for his doomed opponent, when his death was foreshadowed by the Scales of Zeus, then "Phoebus Apollo abandoned him." In many killings the victim seems rather to wait passively for his death than to be killed fighting. The most powerful descriptions of death in battle are like that of Hector, recognizing that "the gods have called me to my death . . . now my destiny has caught me," and resolving to die fighting; Patroclus, disarmed and exposed helpless to death; Lycaon, arms outstretched, seeing death before him. Achilles, too, though the poem does not show his death, accepts and faces it; for this is what interests the poet very much, the sight of a hero succeeding in facing his own death. It is to produce and emphasize this situation that Homeric fighting is stylized as it is, when it might for instance have been developed much more as blow-by-blow accounts for the expert, interested in the technical details of fighting. The chariot race in Book 23 is treated much more in that manner. Walter Marg called the *Iliad* "the poem of death." I think it will be more appropriate to call it the poem of life and death: of the contrast and transition between the two. This is what the poet is concerned to emphasize, and on this he concentrates his energies and our gaze. It is part of the greatness of Achilles that he is able to contemplate and accept his own death more fully and more passionately than any other hero.

**Source:** Jasper Griffin, "Death and the God-Like Hero," in *Homer on Life and Death,* Clarendon Press, 1980, pp. 81–102.

## Sources for Further Study

Biers, William R. *The Archaeology of Greece: An Introduction.* Cornell University Press, 1980.

A good basic introduction to Greek archaeology. Many illustrations.

Camps, William A. *An Introduction to Homer.* Oxford University Press, 1980.

A solid introduction to Homer and his poetry, with ample citations from the texts of both poems.

Easterling, P. E., and Knox, B. M. W., editors, *The Cambridge History of Classical Literature,* Volume 1, Part 1, ''Early Greek Poetry.'' Cambridge University Press, 1989.
A brief, though somewhat technical, overview of the earliest Greek writers to have survived. This volume is the first in a series by Cambridge that covers the whole history of Greek literature through the Hellenistic period and into the empire.

Edwards, Mark W. *Homer: Poet of the Iliad.* Johns Hopkins University Press, 1987.
A fairly technical work, but a good literary analysis.

Hammond, N. G. L. *A History of Greece to 322 BC,* third edition. Oxford University Press, 1986.
The standard history of Greece before the time of Alexander. The print is small and the text fairly dense, but it remains a worthwhile resource to consult.

Harvey, Paul, compiler. *The Oxford Companion to Classical Literature.* Oxford University Press, 1984.
A very useful ready-reference tool for basic facts, names, and dates.

Herodotus. *The Persian Wars,* translated by George Rawlinson; introduction by Francis R. B. Godolphin. Modern Library, 1942.
Although not very recent, among the best translations of Herodotus. Although he was technically writing about the war between the Greeks and the Persians, as he is discussing the origins of the war Herodotus covers quite a lot of other ground, and offers some fascinating (and often fanciful) historical details, including several references to Homer and his works.

Homer. *The Iliad,* translated by Robert Fagles; introduction and notes by Bernard Knox. Viking, 1990.
One of the most recent and critically acclaimed translations of the *Iliad,* Fagles offers a rendition in blank verse that is somewhat more free than Lattimore's or Fitzgerald's translations, but without diluting the poetic character of the epic. Knox's introduction is well-written and very informative.

———. *Homeri Opera,* 3d edition, volumes 1 and 2, edited by David B. Monro and Thomas W. Allen. Oxford University Press, 1920.
The standard edition of the original Greek text.

———. *The Iliad of Homer,* translated by Richmond Lattimore. University of Chicago Press, 1961.
Lattimore's translation reproduces Homer's original line structure much better than any other verse translation known to me, yet without sacrificing either the

ease of reading or the flow of the translation. It remains my personal favorite.

———. *The Iliad,* translated by Robert Fitzgerald. Anchor, 1975.
A rather loose verse translation of the poem. Some readers may find Fitzgerald's direct transliteration of the Greek names confusing.

Knox, Bernard, editor. *The Norton Book of Classical Literature.* W.W. Norton, 1993.
More a book of selected passages from famous works of classical literature, it nevertheless contains some basic information about the authors and works it discusses.

Levi, Peter. *The Pelican History of Greek Literature.* Penguin, 1985.
A good basic reference for Greek literature generally, and one that does not require a knowledge of Greek.

Reynolds, L. D., and Wilson, N. G. *Scribes and Scholars: A Guide to the Transmission of Greek and Latin Literature,* 2nd edition. Oxford University Press, 1974.
A rather technical work dealing with books and the ''book trade'' in antiquity, and the process by which ancient texts have come down to us from the classical world.

Silk, Michael. *Homer: The Iliad* (Landmarks of World Literature series). Cambridge University Press, 1987.
A convenient, affordable, pocket-sized overview of the work and its author.

Solomon, Jon D. ''In the Wake of *Cleopatra:* The Ancient World in the Cinema Since 1963,'' *Classical Journal,* Vol. 91, no. 2, 1996, pp. 113-40.
A chronology with basic information on film and television productions which are based on or which mention works from classical antiquity.

Thucydides, *The Peloponnesian War,* translated by Richard Crawley; revised with an introduction by T. E. Wick. Modern Library, 1982.
One of the best translations of Thucydides into English, even given its age. Very readable.

Wood, Michael. *In Search of the Trojan War.* British Broadcasting Corporation, 1986.
The companion volume to the BBC series of the same name. Easy to read, lavishly illustrated, and Wood is careful to note when he is engaging in speculation and what the consensus of scholarly opinion may be on any given point.

# *Kalevala*

## Elias Lönnrot
## 1835

The *Kalevala* is Finland's national epic, drawn from a rich oral tradition with roots stretching back more than two millennia. Its compiler was Elias Lönnrot, a physician and folklorist who travelled throughout the Finnish-Russian borderlands recording the lyrics, ballads, charms, and epics sung by the rural people. From these poems (called runes) he assembled a coherent whole, a literary epic which fired the imaginations and the national consciousness of the Finnish people.

Steeped in magic, by turns dreamlike and dramatic, the *Kalevala* recounts the mythic history of the ancient Finns in a series of fifty poems. Its heroes are the sons of Kaleva: the wise shaman Vaïnämöinen, the skillful smith Ilmarinen, and the feisty warrior Lemminkäinen. Stories of their interactions with one another, the spirit world, the natural world, and with their northern neighbors, the tribe of Pohjola, unfold in the resonant, musical cadences of Finnish oral poetry.

The *Kalevala* became the foundation of Finnish cultural identity. Published in its final form in 1849, Lönnrot's epic immediately took its place alongside the Greek *Iliad* and *Odyssey,* the German *Nibelungenlied,* and the Norse *Eddas.* It established Finnish as a literary language and inspired a flowering of Finnish art and music, and also played a crucial role in the Finns' struggle for independence, giving them a heroic history and a focus for their national pride.

## Author Biography

Elias Lönnrot was born in the southern parish of Sammatti, Finland in 1802, the fourth of seven children in a poor tailor's family. In spite of his humble background, Lönnrot managed to attend the University of Turku, where he studied folklore and linguistics while supporting himself with various jobs. At Turku, Lönnrot became involved with the Finnish nationalist movement. He was strongly influenced by the ideas of Professor Henrik Gabriel Porthan, a historian who encouraged the study of folklore and believed that a nation's cultural identity must be rooted in the language and oral traditions of its ordinary folk.

Following the Turku fire of 1827, the University relocated to Helsinki, where Lönnrot continued his studies and earned his medical degree in 1832. From 1833 to 1853 Lönnrot worked as district physician and travelling health inspector in the remote northern town of Kajaani. Though he was the only doctor in this part of northeastern Finland, the job did not occupy his full time except during outbreaks of epidemic, giving Lönnrot time to pursue his study of Finnish language and folklore.

Between 1830 and 1850 he took several leaves of absence to travel to rural Finland, Ingria, Estonia, and eastern Karelia, meeting traditional singers and gathering folk poetry. During one of his research trips, he was struck by the idea of arranging these poems and fragments into a single, coherent epic narrative, writing in 1834:

> As I compared [the results of my collections on my fourth journey] to what I had seen before, I was seized by a desire to organize them into a single whole in order to make of the Finnish legends of the gods something similar to that of the *Edda,* the saga of the Icelanders. So I threw myself into the labors before me immediately and continued working for a number of weeks, actually months.

The result was *The Kalevala, or Old Karelian Songs from the Ancient Times of the Finnish People.* Published in 1835, it consisted of thirty-two runes (poems) totalling 12,978 lines. Lönnrot continued his field-work, and in 1840-41 he published the *Kanteletar,* a collection of ballads and lyric poetry intended as a companion to the *Kalevala.*

Lönnrot's work awakened the Finnish national consciousness and inspired others, most notably D. E. D. Europaeus and M. A. Castrén, to undertake their own poetry-collecting trips. The mass of oral material Lönnrot and others gathered during the

1830s and '40s caused Lönnrot to revise the *Kalevala,* and by 1849 he had finished a greatly expanded and modified version. Published under the title *New Kalevala* (and today known simply as the *Kalevala* ) it superseded the shorter 1835 edition.

Though he is remembered chiefly as the compiler of Finland's national epic, Lönnrot was also a pioneer of the Finnish Language Movement. He spent nearly forty years compiling the first Finnish-Swedish dictionary. He also founded the first Finnish language periodical, translated books on medicine and agriculture for use by non-specialists, and conducted linguistic field research with M. A. Castrén, the founder of the study of Finno-Ugric languages. In 1853 he succeeded Castrén as Professor of Finnish Language and Literature at University of Helsinki. He died in Sammatti in 1884.

## Plot Summary

### *Creation (poems 1-2)*

The world is young and empty, and the Air-daughter, weary of being alone, steps down into the ocean. Impregnated by the wind and sea, the Air-daughter/water-mother floats for seven centuries without giving birth. A sea-bird nests on her knee and lays seven eggs. When they begin to hatch, the water-mother jerks her knee, scattering the eggs into the water and smashing them to pieces. From the egg fragments are formed the earth and the heavens, the clouds and the stars, the moon and the sun. The water-mother shapes the shoreline and seabed. Finally she gives birth to Vaïnämöinen, who floats to shore.

Finding himself in a treeless land, Vaïnämöinen has the boy Sampsa Pellervoinen plant all kinds of trees. Only the oak refuses to sprout. A creature arises from the sea, burns a pile of hay, and sows the acorn again in the ashes. This time the oak grows so tall that its branches overshadow the whole earth, blocking out the sun and moon. Vaïnämöinen calls upon his mother, who sends a tiny sea-creature to cut down the oak with three strokes of his axe. Those who gather fragments of the fallen oak are blessed with magic, happiness, and love.

Now the sun and moon shine once more. Birds sing and berries ripen, but the barley does not grow. Vaïnämöinen cuts a great clearing in the forest but leaves one birch tree standing so that the birds will have a place to rest. The eagle, grateful for this kindness, strikes a fire to help Väinämöinen burn the clearing. Väinämöinen plants his barley in the ash-rich soil, prays to the earth and the clouds, and comes back a few days later to find that the barley has taken root.

## Aino (poems 3-5)

Väinämöinen's fame as a singer and wise man spreads to the Northland, arousing the envy of a young Lapp named Joukahainen. Heedless of his parents' warnings, Joukahainen sets off for Kalevala to challenge Väinämöinen. Väinämöinen easily defeats the young upstart, backing him into a swamp. As Joukahainen sinks up to his neck in the mire, he offers his sister Aino to Väinämöinen as a bride. Väinämöinen releases Joukahainen, who flees back north and tells his family the story. Though his mother is overjoyed at the prospect of having such a famous son-in-law, Aino is miserable.

Väinämöinen encounters Aino while she is out cutting leafy birch twigs to use as whisks in the sauna. When he asks her to be his wife, she tears off her jewelry and ribbons and runs home weeping. Her mother urges her to cheer up. Tearfully insisting that she does not want to be the wife of an old man, Aino runs off and loses her way in the woods. Finally she reaches the sea, where she goes for a swim and drowns. Her mother mourns.

Väinämöinen, also distraught at Aino's death, goes to the water to search for her body. He catches a strange fish and is about to cut it open when it leaps back into the water and reveals that it is Aino. He begs her to come back into the boat, but she refuses, leaving the old man disconsolate. Väinämöinen returns home, wondering aloud how he will get over his grief. His mother speaks from beneath the waves, advising him to travel northwards and woo the maidens of Pohjola.

## The Forging of the Sampo (poems 6-10)

Aino's resentful brother Joukahainen lies in wait with a crossbow and tries to shoot Väinämöinen, but the arrow hits Väinämöinen's horse instead. Väinämöinen falls into the water and is washed out to sea.

Väinämöinen drifts for many days. An eagle spots him and, remembering the birch tree that Väinämöinen spared, carries him to the shores of Pohjola. The Mistress of the Northland (Louhi) receives him well, but Väinämöinen is homesick for Kalevala. Louhi promises she will return him to his

*Title page of the 1835 edition of the "Old Kalevala."*

homeland and give him her daughter in marriage if he will forge a Sampo for her. Väinämöinen pledges he will send the master smith Ilmarinen to make the Sampo, and Louhi sends him home in her sleigh.

On his way, Väinämöinen meets Louhi's daughter and asks her into his sleigh. She assigns him several seemingly impossible tasks, which he performs without difficulty. The maiden then challenges him to carve a boat out of pieces of her spindle and launch it into the water without touching it. When Väinämöinen begins carving, his axe slips and cuts a deep gash in his knee. Unable to remember the charm for healing wounds made by iron, Väinämöinen limps away, bleeding heavily, and eventually finds an old man who can heal him. Väinämöinen sings about the origin of iron, and the old man weaves this information into a charm that stops the flow of blood.

Väinämöinen returns home and tries to convince Ilmarinen to go to Pohjola and forge a Sampo. When Ilmarinen refuses, Väinämöinen sings up a wind to carry the unwilling smith to Pohjola. Ilmarinen forges the Sampo, a bright metal mill that magically produces salt, money, and endless bins of grain for the people of the North. When he asks to marry Louhi's daughter, though, the maiden says she has too many tasks at home and cannot leave with him. Dejected, Ilmarinen sails back to Kalevala.

### Lemminkäinen's Adventures (poems 11-15)

The wanton young Lemminkäinen goes to woo the island maiden Kylliki, who has refused all suitors. He gets work as a herdsman on the island and manages to seduce all the other women living there. Kylliki is the only maiden he cannot charm, and he finally abducts her. Kylliki weeps, saying she does not want a husband who is forever going off to war. Lemminkäinen swears he will not go to war as long as Kylliki refrains from visiting the village.

When Kylliki forgets her oath and goes down to the village, Lemminkäinen deserts her in a rage and goes north to court the Maiden of Pohjola. His mother tries to stop him, and Lemminkäinen throws down his comb, saying that blood will run from it if he is killed. Arriving in Pohjola, Lemminkäinen sings his way past the guard dog and casts a spell over all the men except for one herdsman whom he sneeringly dismisses. Insulted, the herdsman runs off to the river Tuoni to prepare an ambush for Lemminkäinen.

Lemminkäinen demands one of Louhi's daughters, and Louhi assigns him several tasks to perform. He catches the Demon's Elk and bridles the Demon's foam-jawed horse, but when he goes to the river of Tuoni (Death) to shoot the swan, the herdsman kills him and throws him into the water, where Tuoni's son cuts him to pieces.

Lemminkäinen's mother and wife know he is dead when blood drips from the comb. His mother rushes to Pohjola, where Louhi tells her what has happened. Lemminkäinen's mother searches the river Tuoni for pieces of her son's body, which she reassembles and sings back to life with charms and ointments.

### Vaïnämöinen's Adventures (poems 16-17)

Vaïnämöinen builds a boat by chanting but cannot remember the three words for getting it into the water. His search for the words takes him to Tuonela, the land of the dead. Tuonela's inhabitants try to trap him there with nets, but he sings himself into a snake and slips away.

Vaïnämöinen goes to get the words from the sleeping giant Antero Vipunen. When Antero swallows him, Vaïnämöinen hammers at the inside of his stomach and refuses to leave until Antero relents and reveals all his magic songs.

### Courting the Maiden of Pohjola (poems 18-19)

Vaïnämöinen finishes building his boat and sails northward to court the maiden of Pohjola. On the way he passes Ilmarinen's sister Annikki, who rushes off to warn her brother of Vaïnämöinen's plans. Ilmarinen bathes and sets off for Pohjola on horseback. Seeing the two suitors approach, Louhi advises her daughter to choose Vaïnämöinen for his wisdom and wealth, but the maiden says she prefers Ilmarinen, the handsome forger of the Sampo.

Louhi tells Ilmarinen he can have her daughter only when he has plowed a field of vipers, captured Tuoni's bears and wolves, and caught the pike from Tuoni's river. Ilmarinen succeeds with the maiden's help, and Vaïnämöinen returns home, filled with regret that he never married in his youth.

### Ilmarinen's Wedding (poems 20-25)

Preparations are made for the great wedding feast in Pohjola: a giant ox is slaughtered, beer is brewed, and guests are invited, but Louhi warns her servant not to invite Lemminkäinen because of his reputation for picking fights. Wedding guests sing songs of celebration and praise as well as laments for the bride who must leave her home.

Bride and bridegroom journey to Ilmarinen's home. There is another feast at which Vaïnämöinen sings their praises. On his way home, Vaïnämöinen's sleigh breaks down, and he has to fetch a spike and a drill from Tuonela to repair it.

### Lemminkäinen's Second Journey to Pohjola (poems 26- 30)

Enraged at not being invited to the wedding, Lemminkäinen storms off towards Pohjola, disregarding his mother's warnings about the dooms that await him on the way. He chants his way past many perils, barges into the hall, and engages the Master of Pohjola in a contest of spells and of swords. Lemminkäinen slays the Master and flees from Louhi and her soldiers.

Lemminkäinen's mother directs him to an island where he can take refuge. True to form, he seduces all the women and eventually has to flee from the island men who want to kill him. He survives a shipwreck and swims home only to find that the armies of Pohjola have burnt his house down. Believing his mother to be dead, Lemminkäinen wanders off weeping, but he soon finds her hiding in the woods.

Lemminkäinen takes his old friend Tiera and sets out to fight against Pohjola. Louhi sends the Frost to freeze them, but Lemminkäinen banishes Frost with spells. Tiera and Lemminkäinen wander around wretchedly for a while before finally heading homeward.

## Kullervo (poems 31-36)

Untamo wages war on his brother Kalervo, slays his people, and takes his infant son Kullervo. Kullervo grows into a troublesome boy, and Untamo sells him to Ilmarinen as a slave. Ilmarinen's wife hides a stone in Kullervo's bread before sending him to watch the herd. The stone breaks Kullervo's knife, and in vengeance he sends bears and wolves disguised as cattle to kill Ilmarinen's wife.

Kullervo flees and learns that his family is still alive. He finds his parents, who tell him his sister was lost long ago. When Kullervo proves inept at most tasks, his father sends him to pay taxes. On his way home he meets and seduces a young woman who turns out to be his lost sister. She drowns herself in shame. Ever vengeful for the mistreatment he has suffered in his life, Kullervo destroys Untamo's farm before killing himself as well.

## Ilmarinen's Second Journey to Pohjola (poems 37-38)

Ilmarinen mourns his dead wife. After an ill-considered attempt to forge a new wife out of gold and silver, Ilmarinen returns to Pohjola to ask for Louhi's other daughter. When he is rejected, he abducts the maiden. She complains and insults him until he becomes angry and turns her into a seagull.

## The Theft of the Sampo (poems 39-42)

Ilmarinen tells Väinämöinen about the great prosperity Pohjola enjoys thanks to the Sampo. The two friends set out to retrieve the Sampo for Kalevala, and Lemminkäinen joins them. On the way, their boat becomes stuck on an enormous pike's back. They manage to kill the pike, and Väinämöinen makes a kantele (a harp) out of its bones. Many try to play it, but only Väinämöinen succeeds; his music is so beautiful and moving that all the creatures in the world come to listen. Tears roll down Väinämöinen's cheeks and turn into pearls when they hit the water.

When the three arrive in Pohjola, Louhi refuses to share the Sampo. Väinämöinen plays her soldiers to sleep with his kantele, and the three heroes steal the Sampo. Louhi awakes and sends a storm after their ship, causing the kantele to fall overboard.

## War Between Pohjola and Kalevala (poems 43-49)

Louhi pursues the heroes, and there is a great sea battle, during which the Sampo is broken. Defeated, Louhi returns to Pohjola with only the Sampo's lid; Väinämöinen gathers the other fragments and plants them joyfully.

Unable to find his pikebone kantele, Väinämöinen makes a new one of birch. Louhi curses Kalevala with plague, but Väinämöinen heals the people with charms and ointments. Louhi then sends a bear to destroy Kalevala's herds, but Väinämöinen kills the bear and there is a great feast, at which Väinämöinen sings songs sweet enough to bring down the sun and moon.

Louhi then captures the sun and moon, hiding them in a mountain and putting out the fires of Kalevala. Ukko (God) kindles fire for a new sun and moon. The fire falls to the ground, and Ilmarinen and Väinämöinen go to find it. They release the fire from a fish that has swallowed it, and it burns out of control, injuring Ilmarinen and destroying many lands before the heroes can subdue it. Ilmarinen uses it to forge a new sun and moon but cannot get them to shine. He journeys to Pohjola and compels Louhi to release the sun and moon.

## Marjatta (poem 50)

The virgin Marjatta swallows a lingonberry, which causes her to conceive and bear a son. After some dispute, the boy is baptized and declared King of Karelia. Väinämöinen departs from Kalevala, leaving behind his birch kantele and his songs and prophecying that he will return someday when the people need him.

## Characters

### Ahti of the Island
*See* Lemminkäinen

### Aino
The character of Aino is Lönnrot's own invention and addition to the *Kalevala.*. On one of his

# Media Adaptations

- The music of Finnish composer Jean Sibelius (1865-1957) has introduced countless non-Finns to the Kalevala. Sibelius visited Karelia in the 1890s and was enchanted by the rune singers. He based many of his orchestras on Kalevala poems. An appendix listing his works can be found in Keith Bosley's 1989 translation of the *Kalevala*. Recordings of Sibelius's music can be found in the classical music sections of most music stores.

- Though the Kalevala has inspired many Finnish film and television productions, most have not been translated for English-speaking audiences. The 1959 film *The Day the Earth Froze* is based on the Sampo cycle and Louhi's theft of the sun and moon (it is dubbed in English and available on videocassette from J & J Video, Whitedstone, NY). A rather campy movie, *The Day the Earth Froze* is porably more familiar to American

television viewers as episode #422 of *Mystery Science Theater 3000* (produced by Comedy Central; original air date January 16, 1993).

- *Pathfinder*, a critically acclaimed 1988 film from Lapland, is *not* based on the Finnish epic; nevertheless, it depicts a world similar in many ways to that of the *Kalevala*. It is the story of a young Laplander struggling to stop the the marauding Tchude tribesmen who destroyed his village. In the film, which is based on a twelfth-century Lapp legend, one can recognize many cultural elements familiar from the Kalevala: the shaman with his rituals, the sauna, the use of skis and crossbows, and small arctic villages where people subsist by hunting and fishing. Directed by Nils Gaup; in Saami (Lapp) with English subtitles; 88 minutes; distributed by Fox Lorber Video.

---

field trips to eastern Karelia, he heard a song about Anni, a reluctant bride who hangs herself in her wedding clothes rather than be married. Seizing on this motif, Lönnrot expanded on the basic story and created the character of Aino. She appears in Poems 3-5 as Joukahainen's sister, promised in marriage to Väinämöinen in exchange for Joukahainen's freedom. Unwilling to marry an old man, Aino runs away weeping. She drowns herself in the sea and is transformed into a fish. Väinämöinen catches her, but does not recognize her until she leaps out of the boat, reveals her identity, and swims away, never to be seen again. The Finnish composer Jean Sibelius (1865-1957) named his home ''Ainola'' after this character.

### Annikki

In Poem 12, Annikki is the name of Lemminkainen's sister, who tells him that his wife Kyllikki has broken her vow not to go into the village. In Poem 18, Annikki is the name of Ilmarinen's sister, who questions Väinämöinen on

his way to the Northland and then runs to tell her brother what the old man is up to. In general, the name Annikki seems to be associated with characters who are tattletales.

### Death's Daughter

*See* Tuonetar

### Demon

*See* Hiisi

### Devil

*See* Lempo

### ''Eternal Sage''

*See* Väinämöinen

### Far-Mind

*See* Lemminkäinen

---

### Flower of Saari
*See* Kyllikki

### Hiisi
Hiisi is foremost among the many evil spirits referred to in the Kalevala. He does not participate directly in the action of the epic, but his name is mentioned in Poems 4, 6, 14-17, 19-20, 23, 25, 32, 35, 45, and 47. When Lemminkainen first journeys to the Northland, Louhi has him capture Hiisi's Elk, a creature made of wood and grass and brought to life by magic.

### Ilmarinen
One of the three main figures in the Kalevala, Ilmarinen the smith is a great Finnish cultural hero, second only to Vaïnämöinen. Ilmarinen's name derives from the Finnish word *ilma,* meaning air, and the ancient Finns may have considered him a deity of the weather and elements. There is no trace of this divine identity in Lönnrot's epic, however, except for the mention that Ilmarinen once hammered out the sky and the stars themselves. Rather, he is depicted as the steadfast, skillful craftsman, forever laboring at his forge.

Ilmarinen's most famous feat is the creation of the Sampo, a mysterious mill that provides its owner with endless prosperity. Less successful are the gold and silver bride he forges to replace his dead wife and the new sun and moon he makes after Louhi steals the real ones: the bride is cold, and the sun and moon do not shine.

In many ways, Ilmarinen occupies the middle ground between wanton young Lemminkainen and celibate old Vaïnämöinen. Ilmarinen, who woos and marries Louhi's daughter, is the figure of a man in his prime, representing mature, married sexuality.

### Ilmarinen's wife
*See* Maiden of Pohjola

### Joukahainen
Joukahainen is the young upstart from the northern regions who foolishly challenges Vaïnämöinen to a singing match in Poem 3. His childish, second-hand verses are no match for the wise old man's vast knowledge. When Vaïnämöinen sings him into a swamp, Joukahainen saves his own skin by offering his sister Aino as a bride to the old man. After Aino drowns herself, Joukahainen bears a grudge towards Vaïnämöinen and tries to ambush and kill him (Poem 6). Not realizing that his arrow has missed Vaïnämöinen and hit his horse instead, the young Lapp boasts of the deed to his mother, who upbraids him for shooting at the great man.

### Jouko
*See* Joukahainen

### Jumala
*See* Ukko

### Ahtinen Kauko
*See* Lemminkäinen

### Kalervo
A Karelian fisherman and farmer, Kalervo is Untamo's brother and Kullervo's father. A longstanding and bitter feud between the brothers escalates until Untamo kills Kalervo and destroys his lands (Poem 31). Only Kalervo's wife, pregnant with Kullervo, is left alive. The name "Kalervo" is possibly a variant of "Kaleva."

### Kaleva
Kaleva, the patronymic ancestor of the Kalevala tribe, does not appear personally in the epic. Lönnrot speculated that "Kaleva was the very oldest Finnish champion. . . . He may be the person who first established himself permanently on the Finnish peninsula and whose clan spread into the hinterland."

"Kalevala" means "Kaleva's District," and its inhabitants, including Vaïnämöinen, Ilmarinen, and Lemminkäinen , are known as "Kaleva's sons." Kaleva's District seems to lie several days' journey south of Pohjola, along a sea or a bay.

### Kaukomieli
*See* Lemminkäinen

### Kauppi
Kauppi is the ski-maker who builds the skis that Lemminkäinen wears to track down the Demon's Elk in Poem 13.

### Kullervo
Kullervo, son of Kalervo and nephew of Untamo, is a tragic figure whose story unfolds in Poems 31-36. Mentally unbalanced after having been badly raised as an orphan on his uncle's farm, Kullervo is a bother and inconvenience for everybody to deal with. He is lazy, stupid, bitterly defiant, and unfit to do a young man's work; he makes a mess of

Untamo's farm, ruins the threshing, and kills a small child he was assigned to babysit. Finally Untamo rids himself of the troublesome youth by selling him to Ilmarinen as a serf.

For some reason, Ilmarinen's wife mistreats Kullervo, baking a stone into his bread before sending him off to watch the cattle herd. When Kullervo cuts into the bread, he breaks his knife on the stone and is thrown into a vengeful rage: the knife, he laments, was the only legacy he had from his dead father. Apparently Kullervo possesses enough magical powers to turn wolves and bears into cattle, which he sends to kill Ilmarinen's wife.

Kullervo then wanders off and finds that his parents are still alive, though his sister is lost. He rejoins the family but does not seem to fit in; once again, he botches all the chores assigned to him, until his father gives up and sends him far away on a tax-paying errand.

Murder and mishaps are followed by incest: Kullervo unwittingly sleeps with his own sister. Unable to live with the shame, the sister kills herself. Kullervo does not go into hiding; instead, he returns home and announces his intention of taking vengeance on Untamo. His mother laments his departure, but his fathers and siblings speak harshly to him, and he repudiates them in turn. He lays waste to Untamo's farm, then returns to the spot where he defiled his sister and kills himself with his own sword.

Kullervo is the embodiment of the poorly-raised and unloved child who grows into anti-social, inept, and vengeful man, bringing damage and death wherever he goes. Noting the predominance of guilt and death in Kullervo's tale, Juha Pentikäinen interprets it as "a Finnish tale of fate which dramatically relates the obvious fact that it is impossible to avoid death.... It presents life as tragic and incomprehensible." (*Kalevala Mythology*, p. 220.

### Kylli
*See* Kyllikki

### Kyllikki
Kyllikki is an aloof and beautiful maiden nicknamed the "Flower of the Island." Lemminkäinen woos her unsuccessfully and finally takes her by force. She and her new husband swear a mutual oath: he will not go off to war as long as she does not go gadding about the village. Her mother-in-law is

quite pleased with her, but the happy marriage does not last long. When Kyllikki breaks her promise and goes down to the village alone, Lemminkäinen deserts her in a rage, returning to his adventurous bachelor life.

### Lemminkäinen
Impetuous, young, handsome, and warlike, Lemminkäinen is one of the three main heroes of the *Kalevala*. He embodies the heroic, manly virtues of the Viking Age: courage, strength, fighting zeal, restlessness, and sexual appetite. He is always ready to avenge any affront to his honor. Though he is knowledgeable, it is fair to say he is not always wise; his headstrong and belligerent ways earn him a bad reputation and get him into trouble on more than one occasion. Twice he swears not to go to war, and both times he breaks his oath. He repeatedly ignores his mother's warnings and rushes off northwards on knightly quests. He is often injured and is eventually killed while pursuing his warlike activities.

Lemminkäinen is called "Wanton Loverboy" in Keith Bosley's translation of the *Kalevala,* and critic Michael Branch describes him as a "stone age Don Juan." Both epithets are appropriate, since his name is most likely derived from the word *lempi,* meaning erotic love. He seduces all the women of two separate islands and is unable to settle down for long with a wife before deserting her to woo someone else. However, there is more to Lemminkäinen's character than libido and aggression.

Lemminkäinen seems to possess great skill as a sorcerer. He may even be a shaman. On both his journeys to Pohjola, his knowledge of spells enables him to overcome dangers and avoid fatal traps. He sings Louhi's soldiers into a stupor and bests the Master of Pohjola in a contest of magic. In fact, apart from Väinämöinen, Lemminkäinen seems to be the most powerful magician in Lönnrot's epic.

The many facets of Lemminkäinen's nature may be explained by the fact that Lönnrot has combined several heroes from folk poetry into one composite character. Thus some of Lemminkäinen's adventures were originally associated with other legendary figures who do not appear in the *Kalevala.*

### Lempo
Lempo is an evil spirit who assists Hiisi.

### Lokka
Lokka is Ilmarinen's mother, who is mentioned in Poem 25 and called a "daughter of Kaleva."

## Louhi

Louhi is the Mistress of Pohjola (''Sariola''), the dark and cold land three days' journey north of Kalevala. Her tribe is apparently matriarchal, for though Louhi has a husband (killed by Lemminkäinen in Poem 27), she is clearly the leader of her people. She is a powerful sorceress, but her magic is not as strong as Väinämöinen's. At first, relations between her people and Väinämöinen's are fairly peaceful, and her daughter marries Ilmarinen in Poems 20-25. After the theft of the Sampo, though, Louhi becomes Kalevala's nemesis, sending plagues, beasts, and darkness in an ultimately unsuccessful effort to destroy the southern tribe.

Louhi is Finland's ''Witch of the North,'' a figure to frighten children in bedtime stories. Anselm Hollo and others suggest that the negative depiction of the Mistress of Pohjola is unfair, a literary consequence of men's struggle to dominate women at various times in history: ''it must be said that the *Kalevala* is, possibly due to the time of its collection and compilation, a remarkably patriarchal cycle of narrative poems . . . Louhi, the powerful and from our heroes' point of view 'vicious' Lady of the Northland, is Kali, the Great Mother, who is apt to devour feeble ambassadors. Her powerful and decisive presence in the epic as we have it now does seem to hark back to a time when a battle was waged between an ancient, shamanistic matriarchal culture and upstart bands of 'heroes'. . .'' (Hollo, ''The *Kalevala* through my years,'' 1985, p. 13).

## Loviatar

*See* Tuonetar

## Lyylikki

*See* Kauppi

## Osmo

*See* Kaleva

## Osmoinen

*See* Kaleva

## Maiden of Pohjola

The Maiden of Pohjola is Louhi's unnamed eldest daughter, famed for her beauty and courted by both Ilmarinen and Väinämöinen. She asserts her own will in the matter, choosing Ilmarinen against her mother's advice and secretly helping him to complete his three courtship tasks. She marries Ilmarinen in Poems 20-25 and journeys to his home, where she seems to undergo an strange personality shift. When we next meet her, it is as the spiteful mistress who bakes a stone into her slave Kullervo's bread before sending him out to herd the cattle. In vengeance, Kullervo sends bears and wolves back to Ilmarinen's farm disguised as cows. When Ilmarinen's wife goes to milk them, they tear her to pieces. Ilmarinen mourns her death.

## Mana

*See* Tuoni

## Marjatta

Marjatta appears in the final poem of the Kalevala. Her story parallels that of the Virgin Mary: she is the purest and most modest of all virgins, but when she eats a lingonberry and miraculously conceives a child, others revile her and refuse to let her into their saunas to give birth. Finally she finds a stable, where she delivers a son. He is crowned King of Karelia, causing Väinämöinen to depart from the earth.

## Master of Pohjola

The Master of Pohjola, Louhi's husband, appears only in Poem 27, when Lemminkäinen barges into his hall with belligerent words. The Master engages Lemminkäinen in a contest of sorcery but is unable to beat him. He then grabs a sword off the wall, and the two fight furiously until Lemminkäinen wins, cutting off the Master's head.

## Mielikki

Mielikki is Mistress of the Forest, Tapio's consort, mentioned in Poem 14.

## Mimerkki

*See* Mielikki

## Otso

*See* Otsonen

## Otsonen

Otso(nen), the ''forest's apple,'' is a euphemistic name for the bear, used by the people of Kalevala in Poem 46 because the word ''bear'' is ritually taboo.

## Pakkanen

Pakkanen is the personification of cold and winter.

## Sampsa Pellervoinen

Sampsa, whose surname means "of the fields," is the tiny boy who helps Vaïnämöinen sow trees all over the earth in Poem 2. Vaïnämöinen calls on him again in Poem 16, asking him to find an oak from which he can carve his boat. Sampsa travels all over the land speaking to various trees until he finds and an enormous oak in the far south. He cuts it down and brings it to Vaïnämöinen.

## Ahti Saarelainen

*See* Lemminkäinen

## Short-and-Squat

*See* Tuonetar

## Suvantolainen

*See* Vaïnämöinen

## Tapio

Tapio is the god of the forest; his realm is Tapiola. There is evidence that worship of Tapio and other forest spirits continued well into the Christian era: in 1828, Lönnrot journeyed to the home of a great Karelian hunter and singer named Kainulainen. He records that Kainulainen sang songs to the forest gods and goddesses and attributed his hunting success to their favor.

## Tellervo

Cattlemaid of Tapio and perhaps his daughter, Tellervo is one of the forest spirits. She is mentioned in Poems 14, 32, and 46.

## Tiera

Tiera appears in Poem 30 as Lemminkäinen's old friend and comrade-in-arms, whom Lemminkäinen enlists to help him attack Pohjola. Like Lemminkäinen, Tiera has a knight-errant personality; his lust for adventure and battle make domestic life unsatisfying for him, and he readily agrees to leave his new bride at home and accompany his friend.

The two warriors sail off impulsively towards Pohjola, but Louhi sends a frost to freeze them, and they lose their way. After wandering for a time in cold, unfamiliar lands, Tiera suggests that they are wasting their time and should call off their adventure before they both get killed. Lemminkäinen agrees, and the two friends return to their separate homes, having achieved nothing.

## Tuonetar

Mentioned in Poems 16, 23, and 45, Tuonetar meets Vaïnämöinen at the River of Death and tries to thwart his attampt to enter the underworld.

## Tuoni

Tuoni is the ruler of the underworld. His realm, called Tuonela or Manala, lies just across Tuoni's River. None but the dead may enter Tuonela, but Vaïnämöinen ventures there twice in search of knowledge and materials (Poems 16 and 25).

The idea that the dead, in order to reach the underworld, must cross a river or stream is a notion common to many mythologies. In Finnish myth, Death's Realm lies to the far north, near Pohjola. This proximity may explain why Louhi's courtship tasks often involve Tuoni's animals or his river.

## Tursas

Tursas is a benign water spirit who helps Vaïnämöinen with his sowing in Poem 2. Tursas should not be confused with the evil sea monster Turso.

## Turso

Turso is an evil sea monster sent by Louhi to retrieve the Sampo from the three heroes in Poem 42. Turso should not be confused with Tursas, a friendly water spirit.

## Ukko

Ukko, meaning "ancient one," is a pagan deity similar to the Norse thunder god Thor; *ukkonen* is the modern Finnish word for thunder. Eventually Ukko came to be equated with the Christian god (Jumala means "God"). In the Kalevala, Vaïnämöinen often prays to Ukko.

## Untamo

Untamo is Kalervo's estranged brother and Kullervo's uncle. Not much explanation is given for the fraternal strife between Untamo and Kalervo. In Poem 31, Untamo wages war on his brother and kills him. Only Kullervo's pregnant mother survives, and Untamo takes her back to his own home. When Kullervo is born, his uncle tries to make use of him around the farm, but since the boy does more harm than good, Untamo finally sells him to Ilmarinen as a serf (Poems 34-6). Later Kullervo returns to kill Untamo and destroy his farm.

## *Untamoinen*

*See* Untamo

## *Vaïnämöinen*

Vaïnämöinen is the central character of the *Kalevala*. He is born from the sea at the beginning of the world. In oral tradition he is often depicted as a god, but in the *Kalevala* he is a great shaman and singer, an "Eternal Sage" and prophet who prays to Ukko. Shamans are magician/priests able to achieve trance states in which they leave their bodies and travel in the spirit world, to see into the future, prophesy, and commune with the gods. Vaïnämöinen's visits to Antero Vipunen and Tuonela in search of knowledge can be read as the dream- or trance-journey of a shaman. More skilled in both music and magic than any other living human being, Vaïnämöinen outsings Louhi, Joukahainen, and even Death. Like the myth of the Greek singer Orpheus, Vaïnämöinen is able to enchant all hearers with his music and thus is able to escape from the underworld.

As a Finnish cultural hero, Vaïnämöinen is depicted as bringing both fire and agriculture to his people in their earliest history (Poems 4 and 48). He heals them of disease (Poem 45), and secures their prosperity by carefully collecting and planting the pieces of the broken Sampo (Poem 43). His birth is described in the opening poem, but he only appears in the narrative as an old man. On two occasions, his great age prevents him from winning a bride. Like King Arthur in British folktales, Vaïnämöinen is not lucky in love. The fate of such great men is to serve as a founding father of a whole nation, not to find personal happiness with a wife and family of his own. When Vaïnämöinen departs the earth to make way for Marjatta's son, he leaves his songs and his kantele behind as a gift to his tribe. Also like King Arthur, Vaïnämöinen predicts that someday he will return from "the land between earth and sky."

Vaïnämöinen, born of the sea or "water-mother," always prefers to travel by sea. He builds boats and makes a harp from fish-bones. His name is probably derived from the word *vaïnä*, meaning "slow-flowing river."

Vaïnämöinen is the only character in the *Kalevala* who experiences moral growth. In the first twenty poems, he is often depicted as an unsuccessful would-be suitor whose offers of love are continually rejected by young women. By Poem 25 he has become a more selfless character, devoting himself to the happiness of others. Though his attempts to win the love of the Maiden of Pohjola were rejected, he bears no grudge when his friend Ilmarinen wins her in marriage, and even sings at their wedding. When the Sampo breaks, he is wise enough to gather up the fragments, realising that even they will bring prosperity to the people. When Louhi tries to destroy the people of Kaleva in the second half of the epic, it is Vaïnämöinen who steps in again and again to save them.

## *Antero Vipunen*

Antero Vipunen is an ancient giant, a great shaman who now lies underground, more or less dead, with trees growing above him. In Poem 17, Vaïnämöinen visits the sleeping giant to obtain his knowledge. Vipunen revives enough to swallow Vaïnämöinen, in a scene reminiscent of the biblical story of Jonah and the whale. Vaïnämöinen hammers on Vipunen's innards until the giant finally reveals all his spells and releases him. Vipunen is a puzzling character: it is never clear, for instance, whether he is alive or dead, and whether his body is decomposed or intact. All we know is that he is a repository of ancient knowledge and magical songs. John Alphonso-Karkala, in *Transmission of Knowledge*, 1979, suggests that Antero Vipunen symbolizes the collective unconscious: "What the poet seems to suggest in the personification of the primeval character of Vipunen is that Vaïnämöinen, perhaps, goes to the cumulative fund of ancestral knowledge of the Finno-Ugric people, and in fact, searches deep in the collective unconscious of the race in the Jungian sense. This includes not only the living, but also those people who have ceased to exist, but whose experience, knowledge, visions, and wisdom continue to live among the surviving members of the race."

## Themes

The *Kalevala* is primarily the story of the relations—amicable at first but increasingly hostile—between the people of Kaleva and the northern tribe of Pohjola. Ilmarinen forges the Sampo for Louhi, Mistress of Pohjola, and weds her daughter. Later, when Louhi refuses to share the Sampo, Vaïnämöinen, Lemminkäinen, and Ilmarinen steal it, igniting a war between the Pohjola and Kaleva tribes. Interspersed with this central narrative are subplots recounting the exploits of Lemminkäinen and the tragedy of Kullervo.

# Topics for Further Study

- Various political factions have re-interpreted the *Kalevala* to suit their own ideological purposes. What elements of the *Kalevala* lend themselves to a political interpretation? How could both the political left and right use the same work of literature as a rallying point? Can the Finnish political parties' use of the *Kalevala* be compared to the Nazi propagandists' use of *Nibelungenlied* mythology during the 1930s and 40s? Do you know of analogous situations in other countries, where a work of imaginative literature has been pressed into the service of ideology? Is this an appropriate use of literature?

- The *Kalevala* was a source of ethnic pride for the Finns who were struggling for national independence and recognition. Later generations of Finns, however, used the *Kalevala* to advance the aggressive, militaristic cause of ''Greater Finland.'' Using examples from current world events, assess the benefits and the dangers of ethnic pride. You might consider the former Soviet republics, the Middle East, the United States, the former Yugoslavia, Serbia and Croatia, or Bosnia and Herzogovina. Is there a difference between ethnic pride and tribalism?

- Some critics have argued that the *Kalevala* is anti-feminist. Do you agree, or would you challenge this assessment? Support your argument with examples from the text.

- Lönnrot thought Finland's national soul lay with the oral traditions of the rural people, and he drew the material for the Finnish epic from these sources. A shared identity or myth is considered an important element in forming a sense of national pride and cohesion. There is no national epic of the United States, but North Americans do share some myths about their origins. If an American folklorist wanted to compile an American national epic, what elements might it draw

from? Consider the many shared national myths about the Pilgrim settlers and the Westward expansion, for example. Would these be necessary elements in a national epic of the United States? What other elements would be necessary?

- The book of poetry *Leaves of Grass* by the American poet Walt Whitman (1819-1892) has been interpreted as an attempt or first step toward an American epic. Can you find aspects of Whitman's work that seem to support or to disprove this idea?

- Compare and contrast the structure, content, themes, or characters of *Kalevala* to those of the *Iliad*, *Nibelungenlied*, or another of the world's major epics.

- What could an anthrolopogist infer about the material culture and daily life (diet, habits, clothing, etc.) of ancient Finns from reading *Kalevala* poetry?

- Lönnrot has been called the last great Finnish folk singer because he took elements from various songs and wove them together into a new form. In what way is his method similar to, or different from, that of today's folk singers and rap artists who build new songs out of samples? The band Negativland claims that copyright law is the death of folk music. ''True folk music, for instance, no longer exists. The original folk music process of actually incorporating previous melodies and lyrics as it evolved through time is no longer possible in modern societies, where melodies and lyrics are privately owned.'' (''Crosley Bendix on U.S. Copyright'' [http://www.negativland.com/crosley.html]) If Lönnrot were setting out to compile the *Kalevala* today, what would he have to do to avoid lawsuits from the performers who claim ownership of the songs they present?

## Magic and Ritual

Finnish poetry is steeped in magic. In the world of the *Kalevala,* knowledge of spells and skill in singing are prized above other qualities such as morality, valor, or strength. Scholars categorize the *Kalevala* as a "shamanistic" epic because its heroes are sorcerers and singers rather than kings and warriors. Almost every action in the poem is accomplished by incantation, even everyday activities like building a boat, brewing beer, or binding a wound.

Some critics complain that the charms and ceremonial songs are extraneous, and that they distract from the flow of the epic. However, spells and rituals pervade the *Kalevala* because they were a prominent feature of Finnish rural life.

Lönnrot's own written comments make clear that one of his chief aims was to create for Finnish posterity a sort of poetical museum of ancient Finno-Karelian peasant life, with its farmers, huntsmen, and fishermen, seafarers and sea-robbers, the latter possibly faint echoes from the Viking Age, also housewives, with social and material patterns looking back no doubt centuries—all reflecting a quickly passing way of life.

## Man and Nature

Many of the songs and rituals reflect human attempts to appease and control nature. The world of the *Kalevala* is marked by animism, the worship of nature spirits such as the forest god Tapio. Ilmarinen's wife chants spells to protect the cattle from wild beasts, Louhi conjures up a frost which Lemminkäinen subdues with spells, and Vaïnämöinen's people sing a ceremonial song to welcome and placate the bear that Vaïnämöinen has slain. Such rituals reflect the ancient Finns' daily struggle for survival in a harsh natural environment. For these people, the symbol of success and prosperity is the mythic Sampo, a magical mill which grinds out abundant food and wealth for the tribe that owns it.

## Order and Chaos

Another recurrent theme is the creation of order out of chaos. In the creation poem, the water-mother shapes the sea and shoreline out of broken eggs. Vaïnämöinen turns a wilderness into a barley field, and he repeatedly takes shattered fragments (of wood, of the magic mill the Sampo, for example) and makes them into something useful. Lemminkäinen's mother is even able to reassemble the pieces of her son's body and sing him back to life. In some ways, these actions parallel Lönnrot's own labors in creating a single coherent epic narrative out of scattered bits of folk poetry.

For Finns, the sauna is both a site and a symbol of this transition from chaos: "sauna bathing transforms situations of disorder to order—for example, it can change illness to health, drunkenness to sobriety, anger to calm, and weakness to strength" (Yvonne Lockwood, *Immigrant to Ethnic,* 1986). The sauna turns Ilmarinen from a soot-smeared laborer into a handsome suitor, and it delivers Marjatta from her labor pains.

## Life and Death

Finnish people believed that the line between life and death was a fine one. A person's death was not seen as an ending, but rather as a transitional between physical life and the other realm, the honored community of the dead.

This realm is Tuonela or Manala—the realm of the dead, across the river of Tuoni. It is similar to Hades, the underworld or world of the dead described in Greek mythology, even to its encompassing border of a river. In the *Kalevala,* Tuoni's daughter plays the role of the Greek Charon the ferryman, who will not allow the living to enter Death's realm. Finnish mythology about Tuonela originally resembled Greek myths, too, in describing it as the realm of the righteous and unrighteous dead alike. Under the influence of Christianity, Tuonela came to be depicted negatively, as a gloomy, hell-like place, to which only the evil dead are sent.

Because of the cyclical nature of life and death in the *Kalevala,* and traditional attitudes toward death in ancient Finnish culture generally, death is often a transformation rather than an ending. Vipunen, "dead these many years," sleeps underground and can still speak and sing to Vaïnämöinen. Aino drowns in the sea but returns as a fish. Lemminkäinen is not only murdered but dismembered and scattered in a river, but with the help of spells and ointments his mother is able to reassemble and revive him. The heroes themselves do not die: Vaïnämöinen has been alive since the beginning of the earth, and in the final poem he departs for another world "between earth and sky," promising to return someday.

Only in the Kullervo tragedy does a death have the air of grim finality; the many characters who die in the Kullervo cycle are neither transformed nor resurrected. Fate has made Kullervo a bringer of death. Ruin follows wherever he goes; he kills some people deliberately and others by accident, and in the end both he and his sister are driven to suicide by guilt.

### War and Peace

As opposed to most oral traditions that have contributed to national epic literature, the Karelian-Finnish runes primarily depict peaceful labor. The heroism of the battlefield is given little place in these works. In many cases, rivals or enemies try to defeat each other with songs rather than swords. The fight between Lemminkäinen and the master of Pohjola turns bloody only after a battle of spells ends inconclusively. Occasionally there is individual conflict: Väinämöinen and Lemminkäinen are each ambushed by a resentful enemy who tries to kill them, and Lemminkäinen starts a bitter blood-feud with Pohjola when he kills Louhi's husband. The major strife is the war that erupts between Pohjola and Kalevala after the theft of the Sampo.

### Good and Evil

By the end, the war between Pohjola and Kalevala can be seen as a struggle between good and evil. Even after the reason for the war—the Sampo—has been lost at sea, the witch Louhi remains bent on the total destruction of Väinämöinen's people. Her weapons are the terrors of primitive people: disease, ferocious animals, and the extinguishing of fire and sun. Pitted against Louhi's evil are the cultural heroes whose actions protect the people and enhance their lives. Väinämöinen and Ilmarinen have brought fire, agriculture, knowledge, technology, and medicine to the Finns, and in the end they save the tribe from the malevolent schemes of its enemies.

## Style

### Compilation

In 1835 Elias Lönnrot wrote, "Already while reading the songs previously collected, particularly those collected by Ganandre, I at least wondered whether one might not possibly find songs about Väinämöinen, Ilmarinen, and Lemminkäinen and other memorable forebears of ours until from these had been got longer accounts, too, just as we see that the Greeks [in the Homeric poems] and the Icelanders [in the *Poetic* or *Elder Edda*] and others got songs of their forebears. On his research trips, Lönnrot heard hundreds of individual short poems (a typical Finnish rune or epic song ranges from 50-400 lines and treats a single episode), which he judged to be imperfectly preserved. Bits had been forgotten, and in many cases Christian interpolations had replaced original names and themes. His wish was to take these distorted and corrupted poems and, by comparing as many variants as possible, attempt to reconstruct the truest versions.

In traditional Finnish rune-singing or chanting, two singers sat together with hands joined, while a third accompanies them on a kantele, a stringed musical instrument. The first singer sings one line, then the second responds, both of them swaying back in forth in rhythm with the music. During his researches, Lönnrot sat near the singers, copying down their words by hand.

Lönnrot did not compose the *Kalevala* from complete poems; in fact, researchers have determined that Lönnrot took no more than a few lines from each song variant. Contemporaries joked that he stitched these fragments together like a tailor (Lönnrot's father was a tailor). Others have compared him to a mosaic-maker. In fact, as Domenico Caparetti pointed out in 1891, Lönnrot's own technique was the same as that of the folk performers he was recording, but using pen and paper rather than voice or kantele to tell his stories.

### Plot Structure

Lönnrot imposed a thematic structure and coherence on the *Kalevala* to make it resemble existing works of epic literature. One plot device he introduced was the gradually mounting hostility between Pohjola and Kalevala. For the sake of unity, Lönnrot also substituted names and frequently combined several characters into one.

Lonnrot has been compared to the ancient Greeks who composed the Homeric epics; unlike the *Aeneid, Iliad,* and *Odyssey,* however, the *Kalevala* has an entirely earthly setting and a predominantly human cast of characters. Because Lönnrot was more concerned with human history than with the activities of the gods, he strengthened the historical, realistic elements in the poetry and reduced the Christian and mythological material.

### Formulas and Repetition

Although he recast the runes into an a single long work of literature, Lönnrot retained all the poetic characteristics of his oral material, including stock epithets and formulas, "oral fossils" which may date back as far as 2000 years. Formulas include frequently repeated phrases like the Iliad's "wine-dark sea" or the *Kalevala*'s "Steady old Väinämöinen, Eternal Sage." A typical feature of oral composition, formulas help singers remember the poems and retain the poetic metre of their singing.

Repetition—particularly threefold repetition— is also characteristic of Finnish oral poetry. The *Kalevala* is filled with triads: there are three heroes, embodying three qualities: the wise old singer Väinämöinen, the diligent craftsman Ilmarinen, and the reckless young lover Lemminkainen. Each in turn courts the Maiden of the North, and their courtship tasks are always grouped in threes. Kullervo attempts to seduce three maidens on his way home; Louhi tries three times to destroy Kalevala, and so on.

### Parallelism

Repetition in the *Kalevala* often takes the form of parallelism: a line or verse followed by another line that repeats the same thought in slightly different wording: "Bring a trump from beyond, from / the pole of heaven yonder / bring a honey-trump from heaven / a mead-trump from mother earth." (32: 117-20) Repetition of this type lends to the cadences and echoes that make *Kalevala* poetry unique and difficult to imitate.

Lönnrot also employs a parallelism of motifs, which gives the entire work a certain symmetry and resonance. The sun and moon are blotted out in both the second and the second-to-last poems; the oak fragments in Poem 2 parallel the Sampo fragments in Poem 43, and Väinämöinen's birth at the beginning of the epic is balanced with his departure from the world at the end. Rhetorical techniques such as these contribute to the thematic consistency and unity of Lönnrot's epic and keep it from being a disconnected aggregate of poems.

### Poetics

Finnish folk poetry consists of eight-syllable trochaic lines (a trochee is a two-syllable foot, with stress on the first syllable). It is unrhymed, and like most oral poetry, it relies heavily on alliteration, as can be seen in the opening lines:

Mieleni minun tekevi,
Aivoni ajattelevi
Lähteäni laulamahan,
Saa'ani sanelemahan,
Sukuvirttä suoltamahan,
Lajivirttä laulamahan

(Mastered by desire impulsive
By a mighty inward urging
I am ready now for singing
Ready to begin the chanting

*Vainamoinen plays his kantele of bone.*

Of our nation's ancient folk-song
Handed down from by-gone ages).

For more on the poetic devices used in the *Kalevala,* see Robert Austerlitz, "The Poetics of the *Kalevala,*" *Books from Finland,* Vol. 29, No. 1, 1985, pp. 44-47. For more on Lönnrot's method of composition, see Domenico Comparetti, "Concluions," in his *Traditional Poetry of the Finns,* translated by Isabella M. Anderton, Longmans, Green, and Co., 1898, pp. 327-59; reprinted in *Classical and Medieval Literature Criticism,* Vol. 6, Gale Research, pp. 219-227.

## Historical Context

The *Kalevala* was a part of a project of independence, providing the social mandate of the nationalist period in Finland's history (1809-1917).

### In Search of a National Identity

1809 marked a turning point in Finland's history. Following the Napoleonic wars of 1808-09, Finland was annexed to Russia as an autonomous Grand Duchy, a distinct political entity with its own

# Compare & Contrast

- *Kalevala* **Period (c. 500 B.C.-c. 1200 C.E.):** The Finns lived in a largely classless society organized by tribe. Tribes (like the Kaleva and Pohjola tribes depicted in the epic) consisted of people united by geography, culture, kinship bonds, and often a patronymic ancestor. There was frequent contact among tribes.

  **1800s:** In Lönnrot's day, Finland was ruled by a foreign power: the Swedes. Finnish society was split into two groups: an urban, educated class of people who spoke Swedish as their first language, and the rural majority, who still spoke Finnish.

  **Late twentieth century:** Finland is a modern, independent, industrialized European nation, whose population is united by a common language and culture. Its government is socialist.

- *Kalevala* **Period:** Independent tribes occasionally waged war on neighboring tribes, using sword and crossbow.

  **1800-1918:** The Napoleonic wars made Finland a pawn in the conflict between Russia and Sweden. While still a part of Sweden, Finland was left to defend itself against advancing Russian troops. Later, when Finland became part of Russia, young Finnish men were routinely conscripted to serve in the Russian army. Finland struggled for many decades to achieve independence, which was followed immediately by a civil war between rival political factions.

  **Late twentieth century:** Finland, a sovereign nation since 1917, is at peace.

- *Kalevala* **Period:** In a rural, agricultural economy, women worked alongside men. The *Kalevala* reflects a society in which a woman was judged not by her beauty or manners, but by how well she performed practical daily tasks such as baking bread, preparing the sauna, or working in the fields.

  **1906:** Finland became the first country to give its women full political rights, and nineteen women are elected to the Finnish parliament. Women had always worked in Finland, and with industrialization they moved into factory jobs (though at a lower wage than men).

  **Late twentieth century:** More than 70% of Finnish women hold full-time jobs, and women make up 60% of the workforce in Finland's public sector. The Finnish 1987 Equality Act banned sex discrimination in the workplace. In Finland, as in America, the average woman's salary is still lower than a man's, even though women under 40 are better educated than men in the same age group. In 1987 the Finnish Evangelical Lutheran Church began accepting women for the priesthood.

- **Before 1000:** The Finns were pagan, worshipping many gods and nature spirits and probably venerating dead ancestors as well. Spells and incantations were a part of daily life, used to ward off misfortune, protect cattle, make the crops grow, bless marriages, and appease the spirits of the natural world.

  **11th-13th centuries:** Byzantine-Russian Orthodox Christianity reached Finland from the east, while Roman Catholicism penetrated from the southwest, and many of the Finns' pagan rites became integrated into Christian worship. The Catholic saints took over the role of local guardian spirits, or *haltijat*, who watched over buildings, localities, and economic activities.

  **1800s:** Protestantism had replaced Catholicism in the sixteenth century, and most Finns were, like Lönnrot, devoutly Lutheran. Nevertheless, many of the ancient pagan rites persisted into the early twentieth century in rural Finland.

  **Late twentieth century:** Finland is Lutheran but largely secular.

governing body, subject to the czar's ultimate authority.

Finland had been ruled by Sweden for 600 years prior to the annexation, and the people of the central Turku region were so heavily assimilated into the dominant foreign culture that many of them thought of themselves as Swedes. Though over 85% of population continued to speak Finnish, Swedish had long been the official language of Finland's administration, education, and literature. Suddenly cut off from their Swedish affiliation, and having little in common with the new Russian rulers, the intelligentsia of Finland experienced something of an identity crisis.

Ethnic self-definition seemed to be based, at this point, on little more than a process of elimination. As a saying of the time went, "we are not Swedish; we can never become Russians; let us therefore be Finns." Educated Finns yearned for a national identity that would earn them respect and put them on the same footing as the other civilized nations of Europe; however, with no literature of their own, no history, and scarcely any knowledge of their country's language and traditions, they had no basis for such a national identity.

## Romanticism

A band of University of Turku scholars, inspired by Romanticism, was already engaged in a quest to reconstruct a Finnish national consciousness. A school of thought associated with the German scholar Johann Gottfried von Herder (1744-1803), Romanticism posited that culture is an organic unity that grows out of a people's interaction with their particular ecological surroundings. "Herder claimed that a people's character expressed itself in the form of folk poetry and other cultural systems, which thereby took on the aspect of a mirror of the national soul." (Friberg, p. 16) Thus Romanticism looked to the Folk—peasants living in the remote rural areas least touched by outside influences and modern developments—for the foundation of a national consciousness.

Herder's ideas echoed what Finnish professor Henrik Gabriel Porthan (1739-1804) had been teaching his students at the University of Turku. Believing that the essence of Finnishness was to be found in the oral traditions of the peasants, Porthan encouraged students to collect folklore in an attempt to recover the ancient cultural unity that had been dismembered and buried through the disruptions of history and foreign intervention. His teachings in-

spired a group of students to apply their linguistic and historical training to the project of cultural reclamation. One of these so-called "Turku Romanticists" was Elias Lönnrot, who would eventually compile the *Kalevala.*

Romantic nationalism had already begun to take hold among intellectual circles, but it was the uncertainty produced by the 1809 annexation that lent urgency to the scholarly quest for a Finnish national consciousness. "Following the establishment in 1809 of Finland as a Grand Duchy in the Russian Empire, Finnish interest in Herder's and Porthan's ideas grew in strength, and the cultivation of a national identity became a veritable duty for many educated Finns despite the fact that most of them scarcely understood Finnish at all." (Michael Branch, 1985)

## A National Epic

Ironically, when the first edition of the *Kalevala* was published in 1835, many Finns had to read it in Swedish translation. Nevertheless, they were aware of its importance and welcomed it for what it represented. At a stroke, Lönnrot's national epic gave Finns what they lacked: a rich and versatile literary language, an ancient and heroic past, and a link to the land. It provided an incentive to learn the Finnish language and fed the nationalist aspirations of "those who, fascinated as they were with the radiance and splendour of the ancient songs and ballads of our people, dared to believe in the talents of the Finnish nation, and who were bold enough to begin laying the foundations of an intellectually independent Finnish people." (236)

## Towards Independence

As one of the first books written in Finnish, the *Kalevala* gave the Finns a language not only worthy of literature, but also admired by foreigners, some of whom even attempted to imitate the meter of *Kalevala* poetry. To "a nation yearning for self-expression" (Karner, p. 160), the *Kalevala* provided the model for an emerging literature. Literary works in Finnish, previously censored, began to be produced, and many of them had a nationalistic flavor.

The *Kalevala* was a spur to the Finnish Language Movement and helped foster national unity and democracy. If the peasants held the keys to ethnic identity, then the elites would need to learn Finnish in order to share in that cultural heritage. Previously the social distinctions had been drawn along language lines; the upper and middle classes had become cut off from the peasants. The *Kalevala,* however, was something all Finns could share, including the rural people, who saw their own lives reflected in the poems. Thus the *Kalevala* bridged both language and class barriers and reversed the prejudice that had held the Finnish language to be inferior. As ''people of different social classes began to interact for the common goal of Finnish culture,'' liberal, democratic ideals of equality were also strengthened (Karner, p. 160).

During the middle years of the century, the Finnish Language Movement made significant strides, though it had to struggle against the pro-Swedish party, whose adherents claimed that the elite Swedish-speaking minority in central Finland constituted a separate nationality and that Swedes were racially superior to Finns. In 1858 the first secondary school to teach in Finnish opened. The *Kalevala* began to be taught in school, and in 1863 the czar was persuaded to elevate Finnish to equal status with Swedish as an official language of the Grand Duchy.

### Russification and Resistance

At first, the Russian authorities allowed and even encouraged Finland's budding nationalism, reasoning that it would weaken whatever remained of the Duchy's old ties to Sweden. In the 1890s, however, Czar Nicholas II reversed this policy of tolerance and instituted a program of Russification. His aim was the complete assimilation of all the provinces in the Russian empire, including Finland. With the February Manifesto of 1899, Russia usurped Finland's right to govern itself, declared Russian the official language of Finland, abolished the Finnish military, and made Finnish men subject to conscription into the Russian army.

The country was thrown into immediate turmoil. The *Kalevala* had helped generate European interest in Finland's independence, and the intellectuals of Europe showed their support for the nationalist cause with a petition to the Czar entitled ''Pro Finlandia.'' Paradoxically, however, the epic had alienated the Finnish church. The clergy considered the *Kalevala* pagan and attempted to squelch the widespread fascination with folk poetry and pre-Christian myths. Because the nationalists drew so much of their inspiration from the *Kalevala,* the church opposed them and backed the czar's Russification efforts.

However, the decades spent building ethnic solidarity had prepared Finns to face the crisis of Russification. The achievements of this period, including universal suffrage and opening of higher education to Finnish language speakers, paved the way for the resistance. There followed violence, anti-Russian demonstrations, and a general strike, as the struggle against assimilation continued through World War I.

On 6 December 1917, in the wake of Russia's Bolshevik revolution, the Finnish Parliament declared Finland independent, and one month later Lenin recognized the fledgling nation. Over the course of a century and with the help of the its national epic, the Finnish nation had both discovered and invented itself.

For more information of the *Kalevala*'s role in the Finnish independence movement, see Tracy X. Karner's article, ''Ideology and nationalism: the Finnish move to independence, 1809-1918,'' *Ethnic and Racial Studies,* Vol. 14, No. 2, April 1991, pp. 153-169. See also Eino Friberg's introduction to the *Kalevala* (1988) and Lauri Honko, ''The *Kalevala* Process,'' *Folklife Annual 1986,* pp. 66- 79.

## Critical Overview

### Foreign Reception

The *Kalevala* was translated into several languages soon after its initial publication and was hailed by European scholars as one of the world's great epics. A commentary by German linguist Jacob Grimm (of *Grimm's Fairy Tales*) had brought the *Kalevala* international recognition and prepared the way for its positive reception by other critics. Friedrich Max Müller, the influential German-born British philologist, said ''The *Kalevala* possesses merits not dissimilar from those of the *Iliad,* and will claim its place as the fifth national epic of the world, side by side with the Ionian songs, with the *Mahabharata,* and *Shanameh,* and the *Nibelunge*'' (quoted in *Public Opinion,* Sept. 15, 1888).

### Reception in Finland

The majority of Finnish-speaking people knew little of the *Kalevala* when it was first published. Ironically, many members of Finland's urban intelligentsia first read their national epic in M. A. Castrén's 1841 Swedish translation. They greeted the *Kalevala* with excitement and treated it as a source of ethnic pride. ''The thought that our remote people, although it had up till then made only small contributions to the common progress of human civilisation, had produced a folk-epic which could claim a prominent place in the literature of the world, awakened in the minds of the educated classes of our nation that faith in our future which was essential if we ever hoped to raise the Finns to the level of a civilised nation in the deepest sense of the word.''(E. N. Setälä )

Because it had such a decisive impact on the Finnish nationalist movement, the *Kalevala* was often treated with an uncritical reverence that hindered attempts to analyze it. Even today, some Finns regard the *Kalevala* as something of a sacred artifact: in a 1985 article celebrating the *Kalevala*, Paavo Haavikko proclaims ''The *Kalevala* is not for criticism. It is there to be admired.'' (''What has the *Kalevala* Given Me?'' *Books from Finland,* Vol. 29, No. 1, 1985, p. 65.)

### The Romantic View

Members of the Finnish Literature Society were of the opinion that Lönnrot had ''found the *Kalevala* in the forest''— that is, they thought the *Kalevala* was the collective masterpiece of the Finnish folk, rescued from oblivion and painstakingly restored to its ''original'' form by Lönnrot.

This Romantic view ignores Lönnrot's own artistic contribution to the *Kalevala*.Whatever his enthusiastic contemporaries would have liked to believe, he had not ''found'' a national epic lying magically intact in the backwoods of Karelia, nor did he claim to have reconstructed something that had existed in antiquity. Rather, he had chosen fragments from the huge, shapeless mass of oral poetry and turned them into a work of epic literature. As he wrote to a friend in 1848, ''I must explain to you that from the runes collected to date I could get at least seven volumes of *Kalevala*s, each unlike the other.'' (Lauri Honko, ''The *Kalevala* and Finnish Culture,'' p. 49) However, despite the fact that the 1849 *Kalevala* differed markedly from the earlier edition in both structure and content, the Romantic notion of a restored original persisted for some years.

### Backlash

One of the works to which the *Kalevala* had been compared was the Scottish *Ossiad* , a collection of supposedly ancient poems that had been useful in Scotland's national movement. In the 1880s, the discovery that the *Ossiad* was a modern fraud raised doubts about the *Kalevala*'s authenticity and led to charges of ''fakelore'' (John Alphonso-Karkala, ''Transformation,'' 1986). In order to refute C. G. Estlander's contention that Lönnrot had written the entire epic himself, scholars threw themselves into the study of the oral poetry on which it was based. They were able to prove that the *Kalevala,* like the *Iliad* or *Nibelungenlied,* was indeed compiled from genuine folk material, with only a few additional lines supplied by Lönnrot.

Some criticism was aimed at Lönnrot for his role in the composition. A. I. Arwidsson and C. A. Gottlund criticised him for blurring the poems together and distorting the original material. Many, beginning with Gottlund, have objected to the non-epic material in the *Kalevala:* ''He poured and stirred into the epic materials quite different in nature and of differing periods, mixing all manner of charms and conjurer's words into it, long incantations. . .and other ancient prattling, wedding verses, as well as additional superfluous verses'' (quoted in Juha Pentikainen, *Kalevala Mythology,* pp. 25- 6). However, the Italian scholar Domenico Comparetti recognized the value of this material: the charms ''tell of the life of the people and relate this to its religious past, its remembrances and ideals'' (quoted in Juha Pentikainen, *Kalevala Mythology* , p. 66). Charms were consistent with Lönnrot's purpose of preserving a record of Finnish rural life, and he deliberately added many more of them to the 1849 edition of the epic.

### Mythological vs. Historical Interpretations

Lönnrot himself took a historical view of folk poetry, believing that it preserved the deeds of ancestors who had lived during Finnish Viking Age, albeit filtered through centuries of poetic imagination. Nevertheless, Jacob Grimm's mythological interpretation of *Kalevala* poetry predominated among European Romantics. According to Grimm, ancient folktales should be read as myths rather than historical records, and Väinämöinen, Ilmarinen, and Lemminkäinen should be seen as gods. Many in Finland adopted this view that the the struggles in the *Kalevala* were symbolic or divine, because it seemed to put the *Kalevala* on a more equal footing with the Greek epics.

M. A. Castrén dismissed the controversy: ''For a mythologist, it is quite the same whether Pohjola or *Kalevala* existed in reality or not, and how they existed: he clarifies only what people thought about those places'' (quoted in Juha Pentikainen, *Kalevala*

*Mythology,* p. 9). For him, the poetry was significant not for its historical accuracy, but as an expression of what the ancient Finns thought about their surroundings and their experiences.

## Criticism

### *Deborah Jo Miller*

*In the following essay, Miller discusses the importance of the Finn's national epic to a sense of national pride and as an historical artifact.*

It is said that "the Finnish people through the *Kalevala* actually sang themselves into existence" (Eino Friberg, in *The Kalevala, Epic of the Finnish People,* 1988). What made this epic such a powerful unifying force during a period of national awakening? For the Finns, the *Kalevala* was more than simply a collection of fifty poems compiled by a country doctor in his spare time. It was "a portrayal of Finnish mythology," "the mythological dream of the Finnish people," and "a statement of the worldview of the Finnish people" (Juha Pentikäinen, "The Ancient Religion of the Finns"). Through *Kalevala* poetry, the Finns developed a language and a system of symbols for describing and envisioning their world.

### *A Portrayal of Finnish Mythology*

In the middle ages, the emerging nations of Europe used quasi- historical literature to forge national idenities. France's *Song of Roland* glorified Charlemagne and Frankish valor, while the Arthurian legends captured the English imagination. As paganism gave way to the universalizing force of Christianity, Icelandic poets rescued the Norse gods from oblivion, giving the Scandinavian people a link to their pre-Christian past and a source of ethnic cohesion. For these and other European countries, transferring oral mythology into writing was part of a process of self-definition.

Finland's legends, however, remained unrecorded into the nineteenth century. The church had attempted to banish the ancient Finnish demigods, shaman-heroes, and nature spirits, and centuries of cultural and political domination by Sweden had driven the legends even further to the periphery of the nation's cultural life. Preserved only in the songs of peasants, these myths were unknown to the outside world and familiar only in a vague and fragmentary way to most Finns; before Lönnrot set out to compile the folksongs into an epic, it was difficult to discover anything about what Vaïnämöinen, Ilmarinen, and the other figures from Finnish legend had meant to the Finnish people.

The Romantics had begun to suspect, though, that this scattered oral poetry was Finland's greatest cultural treasure. Eighteen years before the *Kalevala*'s first publication, K. A. Gottlund remarked, "If we wished to gather together the ancient folksongs and compile and order them into a systematic whole; whatever may become of them, an epic drama or what have you, it may bring to life a new *Homer, Ossiad,* or *Nibelungenlied;* and in its singular creative brilliance and glory, awakened to its sense of independence, the Finnish nation would receive both the admiration of its contemporaries as well as that of the generations to come." (K. A. Gottlund, *Swedish Literary News,* No. 25, 21 June 1817). Lönnrot's stated aim was more modest: "It is quite all right if [the songs] at least show that our forebears were not unenlightened in their intellectual efforts" (Preface to the *Kalevala,* in Magoun's 1963 translation).

In fact, both Lönnrot's hopes and Gottlund's grandiose predictions were fulfilled. The *Kalevala* showed the world that the Finns, far from being unenlightened or backward, had a long history of intellectual and artistic creativity. Lönnrot's epic drew international admiration and legitimized Finnish culture in the eyes of other Europeans. To have a national epic of world standing was a great source of pride to the Finns.

Perhaps even more significant was the effect *Kalevala* mythology had on Finns' capacity to express themselves. The *Kalevala* gave them a rich source of subject matter, themes, and characters; moreover, it was their own mythology. Within a few decades of its publication, the *Kalevala* began to be universally read and studied in schools; hence when one referred to "Vaïnämöinen" or "the Sampo," practically every Finn would understand the allusion and what it symbolized.

By 1860, artistic and literary works inspired by the *Kalevala* began to appear. Aleksis Kivi, for example, built his *Kullervo* tragedy on the *Kalevala*'s plot but deepened the characterization of the evil and malicious figure. By explaining Kullervo's violent rage as a result of his oppression and enslavement, Kivi magnified the political reality of his own day. Such artistic elaboration on *Kalevala* themes resonated with Finnish audiences and and helped foster dreams of independence.

# What Do I Read Next?

- Elias Lönnrot's *Kanteletar*, a collection of lyric poems and ballads, was published in 1840-41 as a companion work to the *Kalevala*. The poems in the *Kanteletar*, which come from the same oral sources Lönnrot used for his epic work, give a vivid and varied picture of daily life in rural Finland: there are laments and jokes; songs of courtship, marriage, and loss; tales of hunters, heroes, women, and children; and much more. Keith Bosley translated one hundred of the *Kanteletar* poems into English for Oxford University Press's *World's Classics* series, 1992.

- Lönnrot's *Old Kalevala* (1835) and *Proto-Kaleva* (c. 1835), along with excerpts from his 1927 university dissertation on Väinämöinen, have been translated into English by Francis Peabody Magoun, Jr., *The Old Kalevala and Certain Antecedents* (1969).

- The American poet Henry Wadsworth Longfellow (1807-1882) attempted to imitate the meter and spirit of the *Kalevala* in his narrative poem *The Song of Hiawatha* (1855), the tale of a wise and heroic leader of the Ojibway Indian tribe. Controversy surrounding *Hiawatha*—specifically, whether Longfellow had properly acknowledged the *Kalevala* as a source—brought the Finnish epic to many people's attention and and led to the first English translation of the *Kalevala*.

- Selections from Eino Leino's *Helkavirsia*, a collection of *Kalevala*-inspired poems written during the period of Russification at the turn of the century, have been translated by Keith Bosley under the title *Whitsongs* (Menard Press, London, 1978).

- Emil Petäjä, a Finnish-American author, wrote several science-fiction novels based on the *Kalevala* myths. Titles include *Stolen Sun* (1967) and *Star Mill* (1965).

- For information about Finland, consult the FINFO and Virtual Finland websites at http://www.vn.fi/vn/um/finfo/findeng.html and http://www.vn.fi/vn/um/index.html. The Ministry for Foreign Affairs of Finland produces these pages and keeps them up to date.

- *Two Voyagers Ohthere and Wulfstan at the Court of King Alfred* (Sessions of York, England, 1984) contains two ninth-century English merchants' accounts of their journeys to northern Norway and Finland. The logs, though brief, are packed with information and firsthand impressions. Explanatory essays accompany the primary sources.

- P. H. Sawyer's *Kings and Vikings* (London, 1982) is a 182-page survey of the Viking Age, with emphasis on Scandinavian society and its links to Western Europe.

- *Heroic Epic and Saga: An Introduction to the World's Great Folk Epics*, edited by Felix J. Oinas (1988) is a collection of fifteen articles on epic literature from the British Isles, Mesopotamia, India, Iran, Russia, Africa, and elsewhere. It also contains a brief and very useful introduction on oral tradition.

- Homer's *Iliad* (c. 800 B.C.) and the Scandinavian *Eddas* (9th-13th centuries C.E.) are works to which Lönnrot compared his *Kalevala*. The former is the epic of ancient Greece, and the latter are collections of Scandinavian poetry about Norse gods and heroes.

- The German *Nibelungenlied* and the Icelandic *Laxdaela Saga*, both written in the Middle Ages and available from Penguin Classics, provide interesting contrasts to the shamanistic world of the *Kalevala*.

- Wolfram von Eschenbach's *Parzival* (Penguin Classics), a thirteenth-century German chivalric romance, features a hero much like Lemminkäinen —powerful, yet rash and young. It tells of the quest for the Holy Grail, a mysterious object, somewhat analogous to the Sampo, which magically produces food and drink for its owners.

The period of Russification which began in the 1890s coincided with a period of great interest in folk romanticism as well as a flourishing age of Finnish art. The music of Jean Sibelius, the poetry of Eino Leino, and the writings of Juhani Aho were all inspired by *Kalevala* mythology. This creative activity was in part a form of resistance, an affirmation of the Finnish national identity in the face of a foreign power's attempts to erase it.

## The ''Mythological Dream'': Kalevala Symbolism

Nineteenth-century Finns looked at their ancient poetry and saw allegories for their current political situation. Thus the *Kalevala* mythology provided people of various backgrounds with a common frame of reference for describing their world and investing their own experiences with meaning.

Like all dreams, the ''mythological dream of the Finnish people'' expressed itself through the language of symbols. The oak that blotted out the sun might represent the shadow of foreign rule, and Pohjola could be equated with any enemy of the Finns. The reassembly and revival of Lemminkäinen could be read as a metaphor for Finnish culture itself, with the folklorists playing the part of Lemminkäinen's mother, singing the dispersed parts of a great whole back into life. Much of the literature of the day invoked Kullervo as the embodiment of social revolution. The *Kalevala* is full of such symbols, but the most potent of all is the Sampo, a mysterious object which could be interpreted in many ways depending on the needs of the teller of the tale.

An 1986 political poem by Eino Leino, for example, uses the Sampo as a symbol of the Finno-Ugric people's ancient renown— fragmented and buried, yet not completely lost:

> Beloved is a father's labored field, sweet the bread baked by a mother, stubborn a stranger's soil, bitter a stepmother's cake. Long our Finland ate barkbread, begged alms along the roads, gathered with its tears too many crumbs from others. But one day the begging will cease and the stranger's insult will end and Finland will stand tall and the people will raise their heads: Already Vaino's crop takes root and Kaleva's grain grows, and lack of bread is banished from the land and the longing for a stranger's crop! Thus the ramparts of the Finnish state will rise So the Finnish Sampo will be readied. The wave hath taken the Sampo and borne off the wondrous work of Ilmarinen and the renown of the Ugric tribes lies buried 'neath the skirts of night. But leaning on familiar strength we discover stars in the night and with love in our

eyes find bits of Ilmarinen's labor. (translated in Pentikäinen 1989: 223)

A Finnish audience would have recognized and appreciated Leino's poignant allusions to *Kalevala* Poems 23, 2, and 43. Such literary resonances allowed Finns to feel they were linked to the mythical time when Väinämöinen had buried pieces of the Sampo with a prayer for his people's future:

> Grant, Creator, vouchsafe, God grant that we may be lucky that we may live well always that we may die with honour in Finland the sweet in Karelia the fair! Keep us, steadfast Creator and guard us, fair God from the whims of men from the wiles of hags. . . Build an iron fence construct a stronghold of stone round my property on both sides of my people. . . that no foe may eat too much no enemy steal the wealth ever in this world not in a month of Sundays. (43: 401-434)

Eighteenth-century Finns could see themselves as the inheritors of Väinämöinen's blessing and prophecy.

## Worldview of the Finnish People

J. G. Linsén, the Chairman of the Finnish Literary Society, greeted the initial publication of the *Kalevala* by declaring ''Finland can now say to itself: 'I, too, have a history.' '' It was a poetic, fictionalized history, but it gave Finns something on which to model their expectations of the future. Reaching back to a time before Swedish domination began, the *Kalevala* depicted an idyllic epoch in Finnish history. The people of Kaleva are autonomous, noble, and prosperous; moreover, they are wiser and more resourceful than the northern enemies who try to destroy them. They have a deep knowledge of their natural environment and an amazing facility with the Finnish language, two things from which nineteenth-century Finnish intellectuals were largely cut off.

Though the *Kalevala* contains songs about the exploits of great men, Lönnrot deliberarely made it an epic about the daily life of an entire people. It is heroic but homey, concerned with such activities as preparing for a feast, brewing beer, heating the bath, taking a sauna, and tending to livestock. It depicts the rhythms of the tribe's life: courtship and marriage, childbirth, building and repair, injury and healing, planting and hunting, music and feasting. Thus the *Kalevala* linked Finns to the timeless customs of previous generations. The peasants saw their own lives reflected in the *Kalevala,* and elites saw the heritage they had misplaced. (The world of the *Kalevala* is in many ways a model for a more democratic society; it is free of aristocracy and hierarchy, and wealth is shared by the entire tribe.)

As anyone who has lived abroad knows, these simple, familiar things combine to create a sense of home, of a place where one belongs and which one is willing to defend. The sweetness of home and the unpleasantness of foreign lands are recurrent themes in the epic: brides weep in despair at leaving their own people; Väinämöinen sighs with homesickness when he is detained in Pohjola, and Kullervo epitomizes the wretched, wandering exile with no kin to claim him.

The idealized world of the *Kalevala* offered Finns a meaningful connection to their land, to their customs, and to one another in the face of an external enemy.

## The Kalevala After Independence

When their previously unregarded country suddenly attained world recognition, it was a source of pride for the Finns. Ethnic pride is a useful but potentially dangerous force; there is always the chance that it will be carried too far, mutating into national chauvinism and expansionist zeal. This happened in the 1920s, when a group of Finns nearly sang themselves into war. Finland's political right wing wished to expand the nation's borders to include eastern Karelia, still in Russian territory after the peace of 1920. They combed the *Kalevala* for metaphors to inspire and justify the dream of a Greater Finland. To them, the stealing back of the Sampo might represent the rescue of Karelia from "foreign" domination. The movement was brief and unsuccessful, but it illustrated the way national mythologies can be twisted into war propaganda. The appeal of the *Kalevala* endures long after Finland achieved its independence. Finnish children study the epic from the age of twelve to fourteen, and it provides the basis for behavior and activities at annual *Kalevala* festivals. Thus the *Kalevala* has become for today's Finns a cultural icon rather than a work of literature to be enjoyed; it is a focus of pride, a cherished relic of Finland's national awakening and coming of age. As such, it is perhaps valued most by Finnish emigrants to other lands, because it reminds them of who they are and whence they came.

According to Lauri Honko, "The powerful need for a national political self-consciousness was the greatest single factor in the *Kalevala*'s success." Perhaps this assessment is still true. Today, in a homogenized and shrinking world where one country is much like another, people's desire for ethnic affiliation and cultural pride seems stronger than ever. To some extent, national myths like the *Kalevala* still answer that need.

**Source:** Deborah Jo Miller, for *Epics for Students,* Gale Research, 1997.

## Felix J. Oinas

*The following discussion of the genesis, form, content, and national importance of the* Kalevala *is taken from a chapter on Balto-Finnish epic literature. The editors have included only those footnotes that apply to the excerpted material reprinted below.*

## The Technique of Compilation

Lönnrot's contemporaries . . . were of the opinion that Lönnrot had "found the epic in the forest," i.e., had restored the original form of the epic. That is, of course, only an illusion. In reality, in its structure the *Kalevala* was entirely Lönnrot's compilation. This compilation was based on the best and most complete variants of the songs that he had at his disposal, with the addition of verses from other variants and even from other songs. Research has revealed that Lönnrot did not take more than three or four consecutive lines from the same variant. Therefore, the majority of sequences of lines (verses) in the *Kalevala* never appeared this way in the oral tradition. This technique of compilation is unique in world literature. It has been pointed out half jokingly that Lönnrot, who in his youth worked for his father as a tailor's apprentice, made use of his tailoring skill while compiling the *Kalevala*.

The *Kalevala* reflects Lönnrot's ideas of the epic, his worldview, and his taste. Working with a definite artistic goal in mind, he chose from the vast material he had at his disposal the portions suitable for the epic and discarded those that were contradictory or violated the style. If it was necessary for the epic as a whole, he developed some seemingly insignificant details into important components of the work.[5] His editorial practices betray his tendency to reduce the Christian and legendary features, while strengthening both the heathen and the historical-realistic elements. He normalized the language, corrected the metrical defects, occasionally changed the names of persons and places, and created linking verses wherever necessary. The few hundred linking verses added by the compiler form less than five per cent of the epic, and even these are adaptations of verses used in folksongs.

The most important building materials for the creation of the *Kalevala* were the epic songs. Lönnrot had in his possession about thirty different epic songs, each of them in numerous variants. In addition, he used lyric songs, charms (incantations), wedding songs, laments, and proverbs. The charms were employed generously; about one-fifth of the whole epic is made up of charms. There are sections in the *Kalevala* which look more like collections of charms than parts of an epic, such as the curing of Väinämöinen's knee wound, the driving out of the cattle by Ilmarinen's wife, and Väinämöinen's trip to Antero Vipunen. Because of its richness in charms, the Italian scholar Domenico Comparetti called the *Kalevala* "the epic of charms."

. . . . .

The *Kalevala* was developed by Lönnrot into a broad panorama of the life of two tribes—the Kalevala and the Pohjola. The relations between them are shown both under peace-time conditions and in times of hostilities. The people of Pohjola are represented by the ruling family headed by Louhi. The heroes of Kalevala are not members of the same family, but they have close relations. Väinämöinen often calls Ilmarinen his brother, and he undertakes voyages together with him and Lemminkäinen. Kullervo is Ilmarinen's serf.

Only a few episodes in the *Kalevala* can be termed heroic. All of these reflect the Viking Age, when the heroic ideal of men was to surpass all others in strength and courage and win fame for posterity. This spirit appears in the fierce struggle of Väinämöinen and his companions with the forces of Pohjola in order to obtain the Sampo. We also find it in some folksongs about Lemminkäinen which were originally associated with other heroes. The last phase of Lemminkäinen's duel with the master of Pohjola in the *Kalevala* is modelled after the song of Kaukomieli (or Kauko or Kaukomoinen). Kaukomieli, during a drinking bout, kills Veitikkä (rascal) because he spilled beer on his mantle. This garment was the symbol of his stature as a warrior, since it had been gained "by blood." Following the feudal notion of honor, its soiling could be compensated for only with blood.

Lemminkäinen's abandonment of his young wife Kyllikki on the Island in the *Kalevala* is based on the "Ahti and Kyllikki Song," and is in the same spirit. For Ahti Saarelainen ("Ahti of the Island") the passion for sea adventures and battles is so strong that he hears even his boat complaining for not going to war. When Ahti's wife breaks her promise, he decides to leave her and set out to sea. His young companion Teuri (Tiera), who like Ahti

has just married, cannot contain his craving for battle and hastens along with him.

## *Kalevala as a Shamanistic Epic*

Except for these episodes, the *Kalevala* is not a heroic epic in the usual sense of this term, but can best be termed a shamanistic epic in which great deeds are accomplished, not by feats of arms, but by magical means—by the power of words and incantations. Thus it belongs to the peculiar arctic culture extending from Lapland to eastern Siberia and across the Bering Strait as far as Greenland. Its heroes are shamans and sorcerers who transcend the limits of the real world. Some of them are even demigods and culture heroes who participated in the creation or rendered great services to the people.

In Väinämöinen the Finns have the figure of an eternal sage, a great shaman, who in his capacity as the spiritual leader of his tribe possesses the deepest knowledge.[14] He undertakes a journey to the other world in search of knowledge and encounters deadly dangers on his way, as do the shamans of the arctic peoples in their "soul travels." For the same purpose he pays a visit to the dead shaman Antero Vipunen, whose body, during its long separation from the soul, has so badly rotted that the soul cannot return to it anymore. In the singing competition with Joukahainen, Väinämöinen sings his magic song so powerfully that his opponent sinks into the swamp and his horse and harness are transformed into different beings and things. In the song about his mastery at kantele playing, Väinämöinen reaches the stature of the ancient Orpheus; he enchants all the animals and birds of the forest, the fish of the sea, and the nature spirits. His music makes all those present, including the musician himself, shed tears. He builds a boat from a bit of distaff and creates a reef from pieces of flint and tinder-fungus on which Louhi's warship goes aground. Martti Haavio assumes that some of the songs of Väinämöinen may have been created at the latest in the ninth century in the coastal areas of western Finland, on the basis of legends about a great shaman who lived in Finland and enjoyed high esteem among the members of his tribe.

In his attempt to abolish darkness, Väinämöinen (together with his companion Ilmarinen) brings fire to the people and thereby acquires the dimensions of a demigod, a culture hero. . . . As culture heroes finally vanish, so Väinämöinen—after his young successor, the "King of Karelia," has emerged—disappears (according to numerous variants) into the mouth of the Maelstrom.[15] However, traces of him still appear in the elements where he once toiled, traces such as "Väinämöinen's scythe" (Orion) and "Väinämöinen's route" (a calm streak on the surface of rippling water) on the waters.[16]

Ilmarinen is also known in Finnish mythology as a culture hero, as the great smith who created the vault of the sky and furnished it with stars. A northern relative of Hephaestus, he succeeded in obtaining iron from crude ore in order to forge the Sampo. With Väinämöinen he obtained the first spark of fire which had fallen from the sky and entered the belly of a blue trout. Originally he may have been the ruler of the weather. The popularity enjoyed by Ilmarinen among the people caused him to be extended into numerous secondary roles.[17]

Lemminkäinen's figure in Finnish folklore is very complex and has caused widely differing interpretations. His shamanistic nature appears in a journey to the festivities in Päivölä (in the *Kalevala:* Pohjola), during which he overcomes three deadly perils, and also in his slithering unnoticed into the house in the shape of a snake. The singing competition between Lemminkäinen and the master of the house can be compared to that of Väinämöinen and Joukahainen. Both are contests of magic between two sorcerers in which the local sorcerer triumphs. As Martti Haavio recently demonstrated, the song of Lemminkäinen's journey evidently was created under the influence of the Russian bylina "Vavilo and the Troubadours," which in turn goes back to an ancient Egyptian story.[18]

Lemminkäinen's chivalric features, as mentioned above, are carried over from other figures. Due to a similarity between Lemminkäinen and Kaukomieli, Karelian singers had attributed some of Kaukomieli's adventures to Lemminkäinen and vice versa. Lönnrot, however, went still further in the *Kalevala:* he transferred the events connected with another Viking Age figure, Ahti Saarelainen, to Lemminkäinen and added the names of Ahti and Kauko or Kaukomieli as secondary names of Lemminkäinen.

Kullervo, Ilmarinen's vengeful serf-boy, applies witchcraft to turn wolves into cows and bears into cattle; these kill Ilmarinen's wife (the former maiden of Pohjola). Louhi, the mistress of Pohjola, is the personification of the powers of witchcraft, although in the use of magic she ultimately proves inferior to the Kalevala heroes.

. . . . .

The *Kalevala* as a work of art cannot escape criticism.[33] The action is thin in comparison with the great bulk of the epic, and some digressions that delay or interrupt the main course of events are rather tedious. In the eighth song, Väinämöinen wounds himself in the knee while building a boat. When we meet him again in the sixteenth song, he is still busy building it. The epic also suffers from repetitions. Väinämöinen goes to the realm of death twice, and he enchants people and animals twice with his kantele playing. Kullervo's demonstration of tremendous strength is also described twice. Väinämöinen and Lemminkäinen get into similar troubles at sea, and so forth.

The *Kalevala* is both a wooing and a war epic. However, there is much more wooing than fighting in it. There are seven or eight wooing stories, but only three or four descriptions of combat; the latter include the death of the master of Pohjola, the theft of the Sampo, the destruction of Untamo's farm, and Väinämöinen's last fights with Pohjola. The combats are described very briefly.

. . . . .

The Finns have no other work whose influence would have been as all-encompassing as that of the *Kalevala.* The *Kalevala* has enriched all areas of Finnish art, most notably in the paintings of Akseli Gallén-Kallela and sculpture of Väino Aaltonen, in Jean Sibelius' symphony *Kullervo,* and in musical compositions of Aarre Merikanto and Uuno Klami. In literature, numerous classical works owe their existence to the *Kalevala,* from Aleksis Kivi's drama *Kullervo* to Eino Leino's *Helkavirsiä.* A complete change in the literary language was effected by the *Kalevala:* under its influence, the awkward Finnish language gradually developed into a vehicle capable of expressing all the nuances of human thoughts and moods. Most importantly, however, the *Kalevala* awakened national ideas, interests, and aspirations. In the hard times of Finnish history at the turn of the century and during the 1930s and 40s, the *Kalevala* was an essential source of strength from which the people drew their faith for the future.[38]

[5] Vjajne [Väinö] Kaukonen, "Sozdanie èposa 'Kalevaly,'" in *Učenye zapiski Leningradskogo universiteta,* 314: *Finno-ugorskaja filologija* (Leningrad, 1962), p. 113.

[14] Martti Haavio, *Väinämöinen: Eternal Sage,* Folklore Fellows Communications, no. 144 (Helsinki: Suomalainen Tiedeakatemia, 1952).

[15] E. M. Meletinskij, *Proisxoždenie geroičeskogo èposa* (Moscow: Izdatel'stvo vostočnoj literatury, 1963), p. 137.

[16] Haavio, pp. 20 ff.

[17] Lauri Honko, ''Finnische Mythologie,'' in *Wörterbuch der Mythologie*, II: *Das alte Europa*, ed. H. W. Haussig (Stuttgart: E. Klett, n.d.), pp. 309–11.

[18] Martti Haavio, *Suomalainen mytologia* (Porvoo and Helsinki: Werner Söderström, 1967), pp. 238 ff.

[33] For a summary of these criticisms, see Collinder, ''The Kalevala and its Background,'' pp. 32–34.

[38] Martti Haavio, ''Das Kalevala—ein nationales Symbol,'' in *Finnland: Geschichte und Gegenwart* (Porvoo and Helsinki: Werner Söderström, 1961), pp. 234–35.

**Source:** Felix J. Oinas, ''The Balto-Finnish Epics,'' in *Heroic Epic and Saga: An Introduction to the World's Great Folk Epics*,'' Indiana University Press, 1978, pp. 286–309.

## Kenneth Rexroth

*In the following excerpt, Rexroth examines reasons that the* Kalevala *has endured as a work of literature that still has meaning for modern readers.*

Philosophical critics in the nineteenth century decided that a culture is most solidly based on a great epic which incorporates all the prime factors in the national or folk consciousness—or ''unconscious.'' There is a whole nest of very disputable assumptions hidden here. First, that Greek culture was solidly based. It was not. Its glory was in its dynamic equilibrium—which was short-lived. National consciousness does not come from the *Nibelungenlied* or *The Iliad*. It is an intellectual notion, born with the nation-state, which came to fruition with the State as an Armed People in the French Revolutionary Wars and degenerated into the idea of the ''folk unconscious'' in the long drawn-out struggle of the Germans for a national identity.

All national literatures today seek for epic foundations—the *Shāhnāma, The Knight in the Leopard Skin, Digenes Akritas*, the *Ramayana* and *Mahabharata*, the Serbian Ballads; even Dante's *Divine Comedy* has been forced into the service of the national consciousness. (The Italian national epic is in fact the operas of Verdi.) In many cases these constructions are purely synthetic, as manufactured for the purpose as ever was Virgil's *Aeneid* for Augustus, or Kallimachos' Serapis Cult for Ptolemy. Yet astonishingly, this does not necessarily invalidate them.

It would be easy to narrow the definition of a classic to the point where it applied only to literature that fulfilled such a role. Conversely, all literature that deserves the name of classic does, in a sense, define the consciousness of a particular people and yet is in extension a moment in the conscience of mankind. In the narrowest sense again, many synthetic epics, written as myths to shape the life of a people, have been successful and have been classics in the wider sense as well. The *Aeneid*, the *Kojiki* and *Nihongi*, the *Kalevala*, the history plays of Shakespeare, the *Shāh-nāma*, these are all synthetic myths, made by intellectuals, which succeeded. They did provide foundations for the structural relationships through which their peoples saw themselves. There is nothing really strange about this. The *Iliad* and *Odyssey* and even *The Epic of Gilgamesh* are literary products. The notion that they were grunted out by Folk sitting about a fire and munching bones was a hallucination of a few nineteenth-century German scholars.

If effect on his own people is a measure; if intensity, profundity, and duration of impact is a measure, the most successful of all was Elias Lonnrot. ''Who on earth was he?'' most people will say. He was a country doctor in the most remote country in Europe, a country that had never been a nation and would not become one for another century: the Grand Duchy of Finland. As with so many country doctors, his hobby was philology and folklore. Early in the last century he began collecting the folk songs and narrative ballads of the peasantry, especially in the most remote regions—along the borders of Lapland, and in the forests of Karelia. He became convinced that these songs were fragments of a connected epic narrative that had once been as coherent as the *Iliad*, or the *Nibelungenlied*.

In this assumption he has been proved wrong, but it does not matter. As he worked his folk materials into what he imagined the original must have been, he produced the most successful constructed myth in modern literature, and one of the most successful of all time. The *Kalevala* saturates Finnish life. Its deep, resonant evocation of the natural environment, the rich dark green or snow-white land of forests and lakes and pastures where herdsmen, hunters, and fishers go about their timeless ways; its strong matriarchal bias; its ironic acceptance of the tragic nature of life; its dry humor; its praise of intelligence and hospitality as prime virtues—all these elements go to sustain the unique Finnish character to this very day, and that amongst the most advanced sections of the intelligentsia as well as amongst the common people.

Yet most non-Finnish readers find the *Kalevala* puzzling and hard to read. In the first place, the trochaic meter, which is natural to Finnish, sounds artificial and monotonous when imitated by German and English translators. In *Hiawatha,* Longfellow deliberately imitated the *Kalevala* in meter, method, subject, and purpose. He took one of the first comprehensive collections of American Indian legends, itself distorted and Europeanized, and formed them into a connected narrative with many elements of the story borrowed from the *Kalevala.* He cast his American epic in the same eight-syllable trochaic lines and used the same repetitive devices and fixed epithets—none of them natural in English or American speech.

He hoped to write a poem that would connect white Americans with the earth beneath their feet through the Indian past, as the Greeks had been connected with groves and springs and mountains through their nymphs and satyrs and local deities. For two generations *Hiawatha* was taught in school and every American child could recite it, and the poem did play, feebly, something of the role Longfellow had hoped for it. Then it began to fail, and today most Americans, young or old, consider it comic, if they have ever heard of it. Yet the *Kalevala* is still successful amongst Finns who read Paul Eluard and Finns who read nothing. Why?

First, both Elias Lonnrot and his peasant informants were much better poets. Recited in the original language, the *Kalevala* has a gripping sonority and haunting cadences that make it quite unlike any other great poem in any language, and the repetitions and recurring epithets have a chime and echo very different from Longfellow's mechanical use of them. Longfellow's trochaics have the thump of doggerel and, since the meter is so unnatural in English, sound absurd. Lonnrot's meter swings; the rhythms are native to the language, and he continuously varies them; his trochees shift back and forth across the beat—swing, in other words. It is the difference between a heartbeat and a metronome.

The plot of *Hiawatha* is as clear as Longfellow could make it, far clearer than his sources—an incomparably more logical narrative than anything in the *Kalevala.* Modern research has proved that Lonnrot's sources were inchoate indeed, much of them not narrative at all. He reworked them into a most extraordinary pattern—not a story or series of tales, but a long-drawn-out dream sequence. The heroes of the *Kalevala* are not warriors or knights-errant; they are shamans—magicians, smiths, and dreamers—men of mystery and cunning. Their adventures are inconclusive, often seemingly pointless, and cryptically frustrating, and their connections are hidden underground.

The original Hiawatha was such a person too, but Longfellow exorcised him—took away his magic—and assimilated him to nineteenth-century rationalism. Lonnrot did the opposite. He awoke the night side of the nineteenth-century professional and middle-class mind, represented by himself, and connected it with the prehistoric culture of the subarctic medicine men which he found surviving amongst the Finnish peasantry.

No wonder Carl Jung was fascinated by the *Kalevala.* It is a kind of socially negotiable Jungian dream, full of archetypes and animuses and animas, totemic symbols of the soul; Methuselah figures; sacred, unobtainable maidens; impossible tasks and mystic beasts—all set in the forests, lakes, and waterfalls of primeval Finland. All its tales seem to be moving toward an unknowable end—the ultimate integration of the integral person—just like the dreams of Jungian patients under analysis.

Yet the *Kalevala* is far more than any psychoanalytic text. Its heroes struggle in dreams, but they simultaneously live wide awake in the Finnish land, in conflict with a hard but beautiful environment. They are undivided beings, in a real world. In our modern destructive world civilization, Finland stands out as enjoying a high level of ecological success. The Finns cope with their setting of living nature far better than do the Russians or Americans. This talent is reflected in and reinforced by the *Kalevala,* certainly the most ecological of epics. In the poem, as in Finnish life, there survives that ecological life philosophy without which no subarctic people could endure. Like the Lapps or Eskimos, they must cooperate with nature or perish. They are still there. So the *Kalevala* succeeds and endures because it expresses not just a national consciousness, but the consciousness of the kinship of a race of men with all living creatures about them. Maybe it was put together by a country doctor five generations ago, but it is the opposite of a synthetic epic: it is a synthesis of nature, man, time, and place.

**Source:** Kenneth Rexroth, "The *Kalevala*," in *Classics Revisited,* New Directions, 1968, pp. 24–8.

### Francis Peabody Magoun, Jr.

*In the following excerpt, Magoun notes ways that the* Kalevala *is significantly different from most national epics, and proposes that first-time readers of this work abandon the usual approach of a straight-through reading and instead read different sections or story cycles almost at random. He identifies several sections that stand well on their own and repay such an approach.*

Again and again the *Kalevala* has been described as the national heroic epic of the Finnish people, a description which, at least outside Finland, has tended to do the work a certain disservice by raising expectations that the reader is not likely to find fulfilled, regardless of what else he may find that is richly rewarding at a poetical, folkloristic, or ethnographic level. Any talk about a national heroic epic is bound to evoke thoughts of the Greek *Iliad* and *Odyssey,* the Old French *Chanson de Roland,* or the Middle High German *Nibelungenlied,* all of which possess a more or less unified and continuously moving plot with actors who are wealthy aristocratic warriors performing deeds of valor and displaying great personal resourcefulness and initiative, often, too, on a rather large stage. The *Kalevala* is really nothing like these. It is essentially a conflation and concatenation of a considerable number and variety of traditional songs, narrative, lyric, and magic, sung by unlettered singers, male and female, living to a great extent in northern Karelia in the general vicinity of Archangel.

. . . . .

Lönnrot's title *Kalevala* is a name rare in the singing tradition; it describes a completely legendary region of no great extent, and is rendered here "the Kaleva District." The personal name Kaleva upon which the local name is based refers to a shadowy background figure of ancient Finnish poetic legend, mentioned in connection with assumed descendants and with a few nature or field names. The action, like that of the Icelandic family sagas, is played on a relatively small stage, centering on the Kaleva District and North Farm. . . . The actors are in effect Finno-Karelian peasants of some indefinite time in the past who rely largely on the practice of magic to carry out their roles. Appearing at a time when there was little or no truly bellelettristic Finnish literature, the *Kalevala* unquestionably—and most understandably—became a source of great satisfaction and pride to the national consciousness then fast developing among the Finns, who had been growing restive under their Russian masters. To some extent the *Kalevala* thus became a rallying point for these feelings, and permitted and in a measure justified such exultant statements as "Finland can [now] say for itself: I, too, have a history!" (*Suomi voi sanoa itselleen: minullakin on historia!*).

Lönnrot's own comments in his prefaces . . . make clear that one of his chief aims was to create for Finnish posterity a sort of poetical museum of ancient Finno-Karelian peasant life, with its farmers, huntsmen and fishermen, seafarers and sea-robbers, the latter possibly faint echoes from the Viking Age, also housewives, with social and material patterns looking back no doubt centuries—all reflecting a way of life that was, like the songs themselves, already in Lönnrot's day destined for great changes if not outright extinction. Thus, from Lönnrot's point of view the many sequences of magic charms and wedding lays, at times highly disruptive to the main narrative, are for what they tell of peasant beliefs and domestic life quite as significant as the narrative songs about the Big Three—Väinämöinen, Ilmarinen, and Lemminkäinen.

Owing to the special character of its compilation or concatenation, the *Kalevala* possesses no particular unity of style apart from the general diction of the Karelian singers and the indispensable ubiquitous traditional formulas. . . . Comprising miscellaneous materials collected over many years from many singers from all over Karelia and some bordering regions, these poems range in style and tone from the lyrically tragical, as in Poem 4, to almost sheer horseplay, as in Poem 3; some are poems of warfare, while a number consist of magic incantations and magic charms. Among the most interesting, though perhaps superficially pedestrian, are the so-called "Wedding Lays" (Poems 21–25), with their keen, detailed observations on the daily life of the Karelian peasant. All call for quite varied styles in any English rendering.

The digests at the beginnings of the poems are Lönnrot's and were written in prose. Lönnrot is also the artless composer of Poem 1, lines 1–110, and Poem 50, lines 513–620; both these passages are pure flights of Lönnrot's fancy, and, despite a semblance of autobiography, bear no relation to the author's life.

In reading a new poem or a sequence of poems it is normal to begin at the beginning and read straight ahead, but in the case of the *Kalevala* this natural procedure has little to recommend it, since in a general way the present order of the poems is quite arbitrary, differing considerably, for example, from that of Lönnrot's 1835 *Old Kalevala.* Instead of starting with Poem 1 and reading through to the end, the reader is likely to derive greater satisfaction by beginning with some single story cycle—say, the Lemminkäinen stories (Poem 11 and following); though not in sequence, these can easily be picked out from the table of contents. One might then pass on to the Ilmarinen stories and to those dealing with Kullervo. The Väinämöinen poems form a somewhat miscellaneous group, and Väinämöinen keeps appearing here and there in a large number of poems dealing primarily with the other principals.

The many magic charms, inserted here and there, can usually be skipped on a first reading of the poem or poems in which they occur, though some of the shorter are entirely appropriate in their contexts and do not appreciably obstruct the flow of the narrative. Some of the more extensive charms and series of charms—for example, the Milk and Cattle Charms of Poem 32 and the Bear Charms of Poem 46—can be enjoyed when read out of context.

. . . . .

There are surely many possible approaches to a first reading of the *Kalevala,* and the remarks in the preceding paragraphs should be taken only as the suggestion of one person, proffered in the hope of making a first acquaintance with this remarkable work a greater pleasure and more meaningful than the head-on approach.

**Source:** Francis Peabody Magoun,, Jr., in an foreword to *The Kalevala; or, Poems of the Kalevala District,* edited by Elias Lonrott, translated by Francis Peabody Magoun, Jr., Harvard University Press, 1963 , pp. xiii–xxiv.

## Sources for Further Study

Aaltonen, Hilkka (compiler). *Books in English on Finland: A Bibliographical List of Publications Concerning Finland until 1960, Including Finnish Literature in English Translation* . Turku University Library, Turku, 1964.
    An exhaustive, unannotated bibliography on Finland. Now out of date, but some parts may still be useful.

Alfonso-Karkala, John B. ''Transmission of Knowledge by Antero Vipunen to Väinämöinen in Kalevala and by Sukra to Kacha in *Mahabharata,*'' in *Proceedings of the 7th Congress of the International Comparative Literature Association, Vol. 2, Comparative Literature Today: Theory and Practice* , edited by Eva Kushner and Roman Struc, Kunst and Wissen, Erich Bieber, 1979, pp. 619-23.
    Alfonso-Karkala examines the symbolism of Väinämöinen's quest to obtain three magic words and suggests a Jungian interpretation of the figure of Antero Vipunen.

Bako, Elemer (compiler). *Elias Lönnrot and his Kalevala: A Selective Annotated Bibliography with an Introduction to the National Epic of Finland.* Second Edition. Library of Congress, Washington, DC, 1985.
    Published to commemorate the 150th anniversary of the *Kalevala,* this twenty-nine-page bibliography is broken down by topic.

*Books from Finland,* Vol. 29, No. 1, 1985.
    *Books from Finland* is a quarterly journal on Finnish literature. The first issue of 1985, subtitled ''*Kalevala 1935-1985,*'' is entirely devoted to the *Kalevala.* It contains numerous articles and essays, beautiful illustrations, and suggestions for further reading.

Bosley, Keith (translator). *The Kalevala.* World's Classics Series, Oxford University Press, Oxford, 1989.
    Bosley's 1989 edition is the most recent English translation of the *Kalevala* and is readily available in paperback. In his introduction, Bosley discusses the *Kalevala*'s literary and historical context, summarizes the plot, and explains certain episodes and relationships found in the poem.

Bradunas, Elena. ''The Kalevala: An Introduction,'' *Folklife Center News,* October-December, 1984. Reprinted in *Folklife Annual,* 1986, pp. 64-65.
    A two-page introduction to the *Kalevala* written in honor of the epic's 150th anniversary.

Branch, Michael. ''Kalevala: from myth to symbol,'' *Books from Finland,* Vol. 19, No. 1, 1985, pp. 1 8. Reprinted on the FINFO website [http://www.vn.fi/vn/um/finfo/english/kalevala.html].
    An excellent and easily accessible general introduction to the *Kalevala.*

Crawford, John Martin. *The Kalevala, The Epic Poem of Finland.* 2 volumes. John A. Berry & Company, New York, 1888.
    The first complete translation of the *Kalevala* into English, Crawford's verse edition includes a still-useful preface on the myths, language, and culture of Finland.

DuBois, Thomas. *Finnish Folk Poetry and the Kalevala.* New Perspectives in Folklore Series, Vol. 1. Garland Publishing, New York and London, 1995.
    A study of the folk poetry and oral traditions that lie behind and beyond Lönnrot's epic. This is a scholarly work, containing a great deal of sophisticated literary analysis and detailed discussion of particular poems.

''Elias Lönnrot,'' in *Ninteenth-Century Literature Criticism,* Vol. 53, pp. 304-341. Gale Research, Detroit, MI.

Contains biographical information on Lönnrot, an excerpt from his Preface to the *Old Kalevala,* a wide-ranging collection of reprinted modern criticism, some photographs, and an annotated bibliography.

FINFO: The Finland Information Pages [http://www.vn.fi/vn/um/finfo/findeng.html]
FINFO is part of the Virtual Finland Website [http://www.vn.fi/vn/um/index.html]. It is produced by the Ministry for Foreign Affairs of Finland (Department for Press and Culture, Information Service Unit) and contains a wealth of information on all aspects of Finland, past and present.

*The Finnish Literature Forum* [http://www.kaapeli.fi/flf/]
An internet magazine publishing Finnish fiction, essays, interviews, poetry, and reviews, all in English translation.

Friberg, Eino (translator). *The Kalevala, Epic of the Finnish People.* Otava Publishing Company Ltd., Keuruu, Finland, 1988.
Recent verse translation of the *Kalevala,* with dozens of full-page color illustrations and three introductory essays on the epic's historical significance, structure, and translation.

Hollo, Anselm. "The Kalevala through my years," *Books from Finland,* Vol. 19, No. 1, 1985, pp. 12-15.
A personal and half-humorous reflection on what it was like to grow up with the *Kalevala.*

Honko, Lauri, editor. *Religion, Myth, and Folklore in the World's Epics.* Religion and Society Series, Number 30. Mouton de Gruyter, Berlin and New York, 1990.
A collection of articles on epics from around the world. Many of the articles focus on the *Kalevala* as epic literature, comparing it to epics from other countries such as Germany and China.

———. "The Kalevala and Finnish Culture," in Ralph J. Jalkanen (ed.), *The Finns in North America: A Social Symposium.* Michigan State University Press, Hancock, Michigan, 1969, pp. 46-52.
In this concise encyclopedia entry, Honko traces the *Kalevala*'s impact on nineteenth-century Finland's national life and literature.

———. "The Kalevala Process," *Folklife Annual,* 1986, pp. 66-79.
Here and elsewhere, Honko argues that the *Kalevala* is not merely an individual work, but a poetic evolution which began long before the runes were recorded and continues as each generation re-interprets Finland's folk poetry to suit its own needs and purposes. The article is illustrated with paintings depicting scenes from the *Kalevala* (courtesy of the Finnish embassy) and contains maps of Finland showing Lönnrot's seven field trips.

Johnson, Aili Kolemainen (translator). *Kalevala: A Prose Translation from the Finnish.* The Book Concern, Hancock, Michigan, 1950.
A prose translation of the *Kalevala,* followed by brief notes and a glossary.

"Kalevala," in *Classical and Medieval Literature Criticism,* Vol. 6, pp. 206-288. Gale Research, Detroit, MI.

Contains an introduction to the *Kalevala,* reprinted excerpts of criticism by various authors from 1835 to 1989, some photographs, and an annotated bibliography.

Karner, Tracy X. "Ideology and nationalism: the Finnish move to independence, 1809-1918." *Ethnic and Racial Studies,* Vol. 14, No. 2, April 1991. Pages 152-169.
A detailed socio-historical study of the *Kalevala*'s role in Finland's emergence as an nation.

Kirby, W. F. (translator). *Kalevala the Land of Heroes.* 2 vols. Everyman Series, London, 1907.
One of the better verse translations, preserving the trochaic meter of the Finnish original. Each poem is preceded by a brief synopsis.

Lehtonen, Juhani U. "Finnish Folklore." Written for the Ministry of Foreign Affairs of Finland and published by FINFO [http://www.vn.fi/vn/um/finfo/english/folkleng.html]. May 1993.
A brief reflection on the way Finnish folklore has preserved the memory of rural life and old traditions in the modern age.

Lockwood, Yvonne Hiipakka. "Immigrant to Ethnic: Symbols of Identity Among Finnish-Americans," *Folklife Annual,* 1986, pp. 92-107.
Lockwood discusses some of the symbols that give Finnish-Americans a sense of cultural identity: the sauna, Finnish food, the festival of Saint Urho, and the *Kalevala.*

Magoun, Jr., Francis Peabody (translator). *The Kalevala or Poems of the Kaleva District.* Harvard University Press, Cambridge, Massachussetts, 1963.
Magoun supplements his prose translation with useful appendices, including Lönnrot's own introductions to the 1835 and 1849 editions of the *Kalevala* and a few scholarly essays on the epic.

———. (translator). *The Old Kalevala and Certain Antecedents.* Harvard University Press, Cambridge, Massachussetts, 1969.
The so-called *Old Kalevala* (published in 1835) and the unpublished *Proto-Kalevala* represent earlier stages in Lönnrot's work and provide an interesting comparison to the more familiar 1849 version, which we call simply the *Kalevala* but which was known in its time as the *New Kalevala.* The book also includes part of Lönnrot's 1927 dissertation on Väinämöinen, photographs of his manuscripts, and a map of his travels.

———. "Materials for the Study of the Kalevala," in Ralph J. Jalkanen (editor), *The Finns in North America: A Social Symposium.* Michigan State University Press, Hancock, Michigan, 1969, pages 24-45.
Contains a brief biography of Elias Lönnrot, an overview of the *Kalevala*'s composition and publication, and notes for further research on its cultural significance.

Manninen, Merja. "The Status of Women in Finland." Written for the Ministry of Foreign Affairs of Finland and published by FINFO [http://www.vn.fi/vn/um/finfo/english/naiseng.html], 1996.

Surveys the history of women's rights in Finland from the beginning of this century to the 1990s.

Oinas, Felix J. "The Balto-Finnic Epic," in *Heroic Epic and Saga: An Introduction to the World's Great Folk Epics,* edited by Felix J. Oinas, pp. 286-309. Indiana University Press, Bloomington, IN, 1978.

Oinas examines the *Kalevala* as a shamanistic epic, discussing its themes and form, the stages of its composition, and the milieu out of which it sprang. He then summarizes Estonia's national epic, the *Kalevipoeg*

————. *Studies in Finnic Folklore: Homage to the Kalevala.* Finnish Literature Society, Bloomington Indiana, 1985.

Oinas's aim is to introduce English-speaking countries to the rich tradition of Finnish, Estonian, Karelian, and Ingrian folklore. The book contains fourteen separate articles, which survey various aspects of Finnic and Finno-Baltic poetry and provide a literary context for the *Kalevala.*

Pentikäinen, Juha Y. "The Ancient Religion of the Finns." Written for the Finnish Ministry of Foreign Affairs of Finland and published by FINFO [http://www.vn.fi/vn/um/finfo/english/muinueng.html], n.d.

Pentikäinen traces the history of Finnish settlement and examines the ancient traditions, rites, and beliefs of the Finns' ancestors.

————. *Kalevala Mythology.* Translated and edited by Ritva Poom. Folklore Studies in Translation Series, Indiana University Press, Bloomington, Indiana, 1989.

A clearly written, comprehensive study of the *Kalevala,* this book provides English-speakers with an excellent introduction to most aspects of Lönnrot's epic. Includes maps, appendices, chronologies, bibliography, and photographs.

Puranen, Rauni (compiler). *The Kalevala Abroad: Translations and Foreign-language Adaptations of the Kalevala.* Suomalaisen Kirjallisuudenseura, Helsinki, 1985.

An indexed list of foreign-language versions of the *Kalevala* up to 1985. The list covers thirty-three languages, from Armenian to Yiddish.

Sawin, Patricia E. "Lönnrot's Brainchildren: The Representation of Women in the Kalevala." *Journal of Folklore Research,* Vol. 25, No. 3, 1988. Pages 187-217.

Sawin argues that Lönnrot deliberately inserted negative depictions of women into the *Kalevala* to further a nationalistic and patriarchal agenda. Men are the heroes of the epic whereas female characters are either self-sacrificing or evil.

Screen, J. E. O. *Finland.* World Bibliographical Series, Vol. 31. Clio Press, Oxford and Santa Barbara, 1981.

An annotated list of sources on Finland up to 1981, broken down by topic, with some emphasis on history and art.

Timonen, Senni. "Lönnrot and His Singers," *Books from Finland,* Vol. 9, No. 1, 1985, pp. 24-29.

Timonen examines specific folk-singers' contributions to Lönnrot's epic, noting that the individuals who gave Lönnrot his raw material and inspiration are sometimes overlooked.

Wilson, William A. "The Kalevala and Finnish Politics," *Journal of the Folklore Institute,* Vol 12, No. 2-3, 1975, pp. 131-55.

Williams examines how, in the earlier part of this century, Finland's political left and right wings both tried to re-interpret the *Kalevala* to suit their own idelogical agendas.

# Mahabharata

## Anonymous (attributed to Vyasa)

## c. 400 B.C.-400 A.D.

The *Mahabharata* is the great national epic poem of India (offically known as "Bharat"). Comprising one hundred thousand stanzas of verse divided into eighteen books, or *parvas,* the poem is the largest single literary work in existence. Originally composed in the ancient language of Sanskrit sometime between 400 BC and 400 AD, it is set in a legendary era thought to correspond to the period of Indian culture and history in approximately the tenth century BC. Its main subject is a bloody feud between two branches of the ruling family of the northern Indian kingdom of Kurujangala, the Pandavas and the Kauravas. Their conflict culminates in an epic eighteen-day battle and the annihilation of nearly all those involved in the war, except the victors, the five Pandava brothers—Yudhishthira, Bhima, Arjuna, Nakula, and Sahadeva—and a handful of others.

The poem's theme focuses on the Hindu concept of *dharma,* or sacred duty. In essence, the epic story represents an extended exploration of the responsibilities set forth by the code of *dharma.* In addition to recounting a heroic tale, the *Mahabharata* contains a collection of writings on a broad spectrum of human learning, including ethics, law, philosophy, history, geography, genealogy, and religion. It also features a number of legends, moral stories, and local tales all woven into an elaborate narrative.

In the rest of the world, the poem is largely recognized for several of these exotic tales and for the *Bhagavad Gita,* which encapsulates many of the basic tenets of Hinduism. In India, the *Mahabharata* is considered one of the finest works on Hindu culture, and is widely read and studied. In addition, it continues to provide inspiration to new generations of Indian writers and artists, and is perceived as the nation's most valued classical work of literature. The encyclopedic character and cultural importance of the *Mahabharata* are characterized in this statement from the work: "That which is found in these pages may be found elsewhere, but what is not in these pages exists nowhere."

## Author Biography

Most scholars agree that the *Mahabharata* was not written by a single individual. Instead multiple authors compiled it over the course of several centuries. According to mythic tradition, however, the *rishi* (sage) Vyasa—who is also a character in the *Mahabharata*—wrote the work. In Sanskrit, the name Vyasa means "collector," "compiler," or "arranger." Thus, Vyasa represents the countless individuals who put together the various tales, stories, histories, legends, and treatises that are known collectively as the *Mahabharata.* A legendary figure occupying a prominent position in ancient Sanskrit literature, Vyasa is said to have composed the eighteen *puranas,* or "ancient tales," and to have written the four *Vedas,* the sacred texts of the Hindu religion. Also according to myth, he is supposed to have written more than 3 million stanzas of the epic poem, the majority of which were for the entertainment and enlightenment of the gods, while only one hundred thousand of the stanzas were to be repeated among human beings as the *Mahabharata..* The legend of Vyasa's creation of the poem is this: The great seer Vyasa wanted to write down the story of his people, the Bharata (an ancient Aryan tribe whose name has became synonymous with India). While meditating on how he would give the work to his disciples, the elephant-headed god of writers, Ganesha, appeared. The deity offered to write down Vyasa's story on the one condition that the wise man never stop telling his tale. If he did, the god would disappear, never to return. Vyasa weighed Ganesha's proposal and agreed to it, providing that he could stop if ever Ganesha failed to understand something he had said. The agreement was made, and thus, so the legend goes, the *Mahabharata* is filled with many digressions and complexities because of Vyasa's need to confuse and bewilder his scribe.

## Plot Summary

### *Adi-Parva, First Book: The Origins of the Families*

The story opens as Sauti, a storyteller returning from the snake sacrifice of King Janamejaya, approaches several wise men, or *rishis,* in the forest of Naimisha. He relates to them the *Mahabharata* as he has heard it from Vaisampayana, a disciple of the poet Vyasa. Sauti begins by recounting the death of King Parikshit of the Bharatas at the hands of Takshaka, a *Naga,* or snake-man. King Janamejaya, Parikshit's son and successor, had held the snake sacrifice in order to avenge the death of his father, but the ceremony was stopped by the intervention of the learned *Naga,* Astika. Sauti then recounts the origins of the Bharatas (also known as the Kurus), a race descended from the great King Bharata of Kurujangala.

Sauti quotes the story as told by Vaisampayana at the sacrifice. Vaisampayana describes the origins of Santanu, a descendent of Bharata loved by Ganga, the goddess of the Ganges river. She and King Santanu have a child called Bhishma. Later Santanu falls in love with Satyavati, a beautiful woman born from a fish. Long ago Satyavati had given birth to the poet Vyasa, but now she agrees to marry Santanu on the condition that her future son by Santanu would become king. Santanu tells his son Bhishma of this wish, and Bhishma forsakes his right to the throne. The two then marry, and Satyavati bears two sons, Chitrangada and Vichitravirya. Chitrangada, the elder, becomes king after Santanu retires to the forest. But the new king is killed in battle before he can produce an heir and the young Vichitravirya takes his place. Bhishma, in an attempt to continue the royal line, abducts three princesses from a neighboring kingdom. Two of them, Ambika and Ambalika, agree to marry Vichitravirya, while the third, Amba, departs to be with her true love. But the young king dies of consumption before siring any children, so Bhishma asks his half-brother Vyasa to father children by Vichitravirya's wives.

When Vyasa approaches Ambika she closes her eyes, and thus her son Dhritarashtra is born blind. When her sister Ambalika sees Vyasa she turns pale with fright and her son, Pandu (meaning ''pale''), is born with very light skin. Although Dhritarashtra is older, Bhishma makes Pandu king because his brother cannot see. Pandu marries Princess Kunti, who chooses him at her *svayamvara*, the ceremony of self-choice. Pandu also takes a second wife, Madri. He reigns as king of Kurujangala, living in the city of Hastinapura for several years and then retires to the Himalayas with Kunti and Madri. One day while out hunting, Pandu shoots a deer that curses him, foretelling that he will die while making love to one of his wives. The formerly sexually insatible Pandu avoids sexual contact with his wives, and encourages them to bear him sons from unions with the gods. His wife Kunti summons Dharma, the god of justice, who fathers Yudhishthira. Then she gives birth to Bhima by Vayu, the god of the wind, and Arjuna by Indra, the king of the gods. Madri also uses Kunti's mantra, evoking the gods called the Aswins, who give her twin sons, Nakula and Sahadeva. Meanwhile, Dhritarashtra has become king and marries Gandhari, who choses to live with her eyes blindfolded when she learns that her husband is blind. As Vyasa had prophesied, Gandhari gives birth to one hundred sons and one daughter— all of whom come from a single ball of flesh that lies in her womb for two years. Called the Kauravas, the eldest son is Duryodhana, the second boy is Duhsasana, while the sole daughter is called Duhsala.

Several years later, Pandu gives in to desire and embraces Madri. He dies instantly, according to the prophecy, as does Madri, from fear. Pandu's sons, known as the five Pandavas, return with Pandu's widow Kunti to Hastinapura. They are welcomed by King Dhritarashtra, and raised with his own sons. All are instructed in the military arts by the tutors Kripa and Drona, as is Drona's son Aswatthaman. The Bharata princes excel at warfare, but Drona's star pupil is Arjuna. Adept with a bow, Arjuna's skills are unparalleled, until one day an even greater warrior arrives. This is Karna. The son of Kunti and Surya (the sun god), Karna was born with golden armor attached to his skin. But Kunti, young and unmarried, set her son adrift on a river to be found and raised by suitable parents. He was adopted by Adhiratha, a charioteer. None of the Pandavas realize that Karna is their brother, and the armored warrior bests them all in martial feats. Kripa, however, questions Karna's presence, noting that he is not a prince. Duryodhana is impressed with Karna— and more importantly, he has been looking for a warrior who could defeat Arjuna. Duryodhana and Karna become friends, but according to traditions of obligation, Karna is indebted to Duryodhana for his

kingship and hence owes the prince a great favor. Led into battle by Drona, the Pandavas attack the nearby kingdom ruled by Drupada, and Drona seizes one half of the king's lands.

The Pandavas return to Hastinapura and Yudhishthira becomes heir to the throne of Kurujangala. Jealous and fearing the loss of his future throne, Duryodhana hatches a plot to destroy the five and acquire the kingdom for himself. While his cousins and Kunti are visiting the town of Varanavata, they are to stay in a special house constructed by one of Duryodhana's henchmen which he plans to have burned. Before the Pandavas leave, however, Vidura warns Yudhishthira of the planned trap. Bhima plans an escape route by digging a tunnel under the house through which they escape. Kunti and the five Pandavas are thought to have perished in the flames. They actually flee into the forest.

While traveling in the wilderness, Bhima happens upon Hidimba, the beautiful sister of a *Rakshasa*, or forest-demon. Hidimba-asur. Bhima falls in love with her and kills her brother as the fiend is about to kill the Pandavas and Kunti. Hidimba bears Bhima a son, Ghatotkacha, ''the pot-headed.'' The five brothers, disguised as *Brahmans* (religious men), and their mother continue to wander through the forest. Bhima slays another *Rakshasa*, Vaka, saving the people in the village of Ekachakra. Hearing of the upcoming *svayamvara* of King Drupada's daughter, Draupadi, the Pandavas set out for his kingdom. Arjuna, still in disguise, succeeds in the king's test of skill with a bow, and wins the beautiful Draupadi as his wife. Fulfilling a prophecy, Draupadi marries not just Arjun but all five of the brothers. Dhritarashtra hears that the Pandavas are alive and consults his advisors. Bhishma, Drona, and Vidura suggest that the kingdom be divided. Yudhishthira becomes king and the Pandavas construct the splendid city of Indraprastha.

Yudhisthira's rule at Indraprastha is peaceful for more than a decade. Meanwhile Arjuna leaves his brother's kingdom for twelve years. He visits the wise and mighty Krishna in the city of Dwaraka. There he falls in love with Subhadra, Krishna's sister, and embarks on several adventures.

### Sabha-Parva, ''Assembly Book'': The Game of Dice

Back in Hastinapura, Duryodhana is still powerfully jealous of five Padavas and their growing power and wealth. He consults his uncle, Sakuni, asking him how he might defeat the Pandavas. Sakuni points out that Yudhishthira has a weakness for gambling, and if challenged to play at dice will not decline. Duryodhana invites the Pandavas to Hastinapura, and offers the challenge, which Yudhishthira accepts, playing against the cunning Sakuni in place of Duryodhana. But Sakuni cheats at the game, and soon the Kauravas win Yudhishthira's wealth and kingdom, and also his four brothers, their wife Draupadi, and Yudhishthira himself.

The Kauravas have Draupadi brought forcibly before them. She is in traditional monthly seclusion, so it is especially offensive that her privacy is thus violated. Compounding the insult to her honor, Duhsasana humiliates her and attempts to strip off her clothing. Bhima, enraged by this treatment of his wife, vows that he will kill Duhsasana and drink his blood. King Dhritarashtra rebukes his sons for their behavior and offers to grant Draupadi any wish to make up for the wrong done to her. She asks the Yudhishthira and his brothers, whose freedom has been forfeited in the dice game, be set free. The king does this. As the Pandavas and their wife turn to leave, the Kauravas, hoping to thwart their future vengeance, suggest a final gambling match. The losers of this final throw of the dice must spend twelve years in forest exile, and a thirteenth year living in disguise in a foreign kingdom. The Pandavas agree; but Sakuni cheats again and they lose.

## Vana-Parva, "Forest Book": Exile in the Forest

The five Pandavas—Yudhishthira, Bhima, Arjuna, Nakula, and Sahadeva—and their wife Draupadi depart for the Kamyaka forest. While there, under the advice of Vyasa, Arjuna leaves the others and goes in search of weapons to aid them when they return and seek to avenge themselves against the Kauravas. He encounters Shiva, god of destruction, who gives him a weapon called Pasupata. Later, Arjuna's father, Indra, appears and takes his son up to heaven. There Arjuna meets a heavenly dancer, or *Apsara,* named Urvasi. Because Arjuna resists her amorous advances, she curses him so that he must spend one year of his life as a eunuch.

Back in the forest, Yudhishthira meets the *rishi* Vrihadaswa. The seer relates the story of Nala and Damayanti to comfort the grief-stricken king. Soon Arjuna returns from Indra's heaven. He recounts his adventures to his brothers and Draupadi. Meanwhile, Duryodhana and Sakuni plan an expedition to the forest, hoping to taunt their exiled cousins.

*The gods observe Krishna and Arjuna.*

While there, the Kauravas engage the army of the powerful Chitraratha, king of the Gandharvas, who imprisons them. Arjuna, armed with magical weapons, arrives and frees his cousin. Duryodhana, shamed by this turn of events, seeks to starve himself in the forest instead of returning, humiliated, to Hastinapura. Rebuking his hastiness, however, his brother Duhsasana dissuades him. Later, Jayadratha, king of Sindhu sees Draupadi in the forest and instantly falls in love with her. He abducts her while the Pandavas are away hunting. When they return, the brothers track down Draupadi and Jayadratha. Yudhishthira decides to spare the unscrupulous king's life and lets him go. Soon another *rishi,* called Markandeya, appears. He relates the tale of the princess Savitri to the Pandavas.

Elsewhere, Indra endeavors to win Karna's armor from him. Though warned by his father of this plot, Karna allows Indra, disguised as a Brahman, to remove his natural protection. In exchange he asks that the god give him a powerful dart. Guaranteed to kill any enemy, the weapon may be used only once. Back in the forest, Nakula happens upon a magical lake. Though forbidden to drink the water by an unseen voice, he disobeys and falls dead. Sahadeva, Arjuna, and Bhima follow and do the same; all are killed. Lastly Yudhishthira walks to the lake. Seeing the dead bodies of his brothers, he hears the same warning. Then the voice asks him to answer its questions. Yudhishthira does this satisfactorily, and the voice reveals itself to be his father, Dharma. The god of justice, finding Yudhishthira truly worthy, then brings his brothers back to life.

### *Virata-Parva, ''Book of Virata'': The Thirteenth Year of Exile*

During their final year of exile the Pandavas travel to the city of Matsya in the kingdom of King Virata. Each takes a disguise. Yudhishthira becomes Kanka, a Brahman and dice-player. Bhima takes the name of Vallabha, claiming to be a cook formerly in the service of King Yudhishthira. Draupadi assumes the identity of Sairindhri, a serving-maid in the employment of Virata's queen. Sahadeva calls himself Tantripala, a cowherd and talented astrologer. Nakula disguises himself as Granthika, a horse-keeper. Arjuna invokes Urvasi's curse, becoming the eunuch Vrihannala, the singing and dancing instructor of Virata's daughter. One day toward the end of the last year of exile Kichaka, Virata's general, happens to see Draupadi. Enthralled by her beauty, he desires her as his wife. Draupadi refuses, but Kichaka will not yield. She asks for Bhima's aid, and he kills the general, crushing him to death. Back in Hastinapura, Duryodhana hears of Kichaka's demise and launches an invasion against Virata's kingdom. Arjuna, with the assistance of Virata's son, Uttara, as his charioteer and armed with his magical Gandiva bow, defeats the attacking Kauravas. Soon after, at the end of the thirteenth year, the Pandavas disclose their true identities. King Virata offers his daughter to Arjuna in marriage. Arjuna accepts the princess as a fitting wife for his son, Abhimanyu.

### *Udyoga-Parva, ''Effort Book'': The Preparations for War*

Eager for the return to his kingdom, Yudhishthira asks Krishna to travel to Hastinapura and secure Indraprastha from the Kauravas. Overriding the opinions of Dhritarashtra's other advisors, Duryodhana refuses to give away half of Kurujangala and war soon appears inevitable. Arjuna and Duryodhana both travel to Dwaraka to seek Krishna's aid in the upcoming hostilities. Krishna offers a choice, himself—as an advisor, not a warrior—or ten thousand of his Yadava troops. Arjuna selects

Krishna, while Duryodhana is pleased with the soldiers, despite the fact that he was not allowed to choose first. Both princes depart, and back in Kurujangala further preparations for battle are made. At a grand assembly, Krishna, the avatar or physical manifestation of the mighty god Vishnu, reveals his divine form. Undaunted, the Kauravas continue to marshal their forces for war. Bhishma, forced to lead their army as a general, reveals that he will not fight against Sikhandin, a warrior of the Pandava forces. According to legend, Sikhandin's soul was reincarnated from the princess Amba, who is fated to be the cause of Bhishma's destruction.

### *Bhishma Parva, ''Book of Bhishma'': The Battle Under Bhishma's Command*

In order that he might relate the events of the battle to Dhritarashtra, Vyasa grants Sanjaya the power of heavenly sight, allowing him to see all things. On the first day, the armies gather on the vast Kurukshetra plain. Arjuna, viewing the assembled warriors—including his cousins, uncles, and grandfather—hesitates, unwilling to fight his kin. To dismiss his fears Krishna sings The *Bhagavad Gita,* or Song of the Lord. In it, Krishna assures Arjuna that all souls are immortal, and that death is only a temporary state between incarnations. Strengthened by these words, Arjuna prepares to engage his foes. Before the conflict, however, Yudhishthira removes his armor and puts down his weapons. He moves toward Bhishma and asks his permission to fight. Yudhishthira does the same to Drona, Kripa, and Salya. For nine days the Kauravas and Pandavas wage war. Each day both forces align themselves in different formations and clash; many die in the carnage. Each night the warriors retire to their camps, while *Rakshasas* and ghouls feast on the decaying bodies of the slain. In the evening of the ninth day of battle, the five Pandavas and Krishna travel to Bhishma's tent and ask him how he will die. They learn that he will not fight the warrior who was once a woman, Sikhandin. The following day Sikhandin, with the help of Arjuna, shoots Bhishma with his arrows. Soon, the general is pierced by Pandava arrows. Bhishma remains alive, however, and waits for the appropriate time of his death.

### *Drona Parva, ''Book of Drona'': Drona's Command and Death*

Drona accepts Duryodhana's invitation to become the new general of the Kaurava army and vows to take Yudhishthira alive, thereby ending the war. In order to accomplish this goal, Arjuna must be lured away from his eldest brother; a task to be undertaken by Susarman and the five brothers of Trigartas. On the day of battle, Arjuna defeats the warriors from Trigarta and thwarts Drona's plan. Elsewhere Arjuna's son, Abhimanyu, cut off from the main Pandava force by King Jayadratha, is slain by Duhsasana. That night Arjuna vows his revenge on Jayadratha. This he does the following day—despite the intervention of Karna—and Jayadratha lies dead. The battle continues into the night as Bhima's demon son, Ghatotkacha, draws his power from the darkness and fights for the Pandavas. But Karna intercedes, ending Ghatotkacha's destruction of the Kaurava forces by slaying him with his magical dart.

On the twelfth day of battle, Krishna devises a ploy to eliminate Drona. Bhima kills an elephant called Aswatthaman—the same name as Drona's son—and cries, ''Aswatthaman is dead.'' Drona asks the usually honest Yudhishthira if this is true. The Pandava prince carries on with the lie in order to win the war. Overcome with despair, Drona ceases to fight. Dhrishtadyumna, seeing he is undefended, ends Drona's life, but Aswatthaman, still alive, is hungry for revenge. He uses the weapon of Narayana, which will kill all of those who do not immediately drop their weapons and turn their thoughts from war. Before the Pandavas are killed, the wise Krishna informs them of this defense and the warriors survive, preventing Aswatthaman's vengeance.

### Karna Parva, ''Book of Karna'': Karna's Command and Death

Following the death of Drona, Karna takes command of the Kaurava army. During that day of battle, Duhsasana attacks Bhima. Initially wounding him, Bhima retaliates by hurling his mace at the attacker. The Pandava prince then tears open Duhsasana's chest and drinks his blood—as he swore he would—thereby avenging the humiliation of Draupadi. Later, Karna and Arjuna battle. When Karna's chariot wheel sinks into the earth he calls to Arjuna to stay his arrows until he might raise it. He claims that to kill him in such an undefended position would be cowardly. Arjuna refuses to listen and beheads the mighty warrior.

### Salya Parva, ''Book of Salya'': The Defeat of Salya and Duryodhana

With Karna gone, Salya takes command of Duryodhana's army. Bhima first engages the king

*Bhisma on the bed of arrows.*

of the Madras, but the conflict ends in a stalemate. Then Yudhishthira, usually mild rather than savage, pursues Salya. Flanked by his brothers, Nakula and Sahadeva, the eldest Pandava kills Salya and defeats his warriors. Duryodhana, seeing virtually his entire army destroyed, flees into the forest and seeks refuge at the bottom of a lake. Turning the water solid by means of a magical spell, Duryodhana stays hidden until the three remaining Kaurava warriors, Kripa, Aswatthaman, and Kritavarman arrive. They urge Duryodhana to defeat Yudhishthira or die in battle. Some nearby hunters hear this conversation and inform the Pandavas of their cousin's whereabouts. Yudhishthira then arrives at the lake and challenges Duryodhana to fight any of the five Pandavas with the weapon of his choice. If he wins he will be king. According to his choice, Duryodhana and Bhima battle with maces. The conflict continues and Bhima realizes that to win he must fight a deceiver with deception. He breaks Duryodhana's thighs with his mace, outraging Balarama as he watches the match. Krishna's brother calls Bhima an unfair fighter for attacking below the waist, and leaves for Dwaraka. Still, Bhima is victorious, though Duryodhana upbraids him for his treachery. Later the eldest son of Dhritarashtra sends a message, making Aswatthaman his new general.

### Sauptika-Parva, ''Sleeping Book'': The Destruction of the Pandava Army at Night

Aswatthaman, with the aid of a powerful weapon from Shiva, enters the Pandava camp and slays Dhrishtadyumna, Sikhadin, and the rest of the Pandava force in their sleep. Only the seven Pandavas not at the camp—the five brothers, Krishna, and Satyaki—survive the slaughter. When the seven catch up to Aswatthaman, he attempts to use the Brahmasira weapon, an implement of war so powerful that it is capable of destroying the entire world. Arjuna counteracts it with is own Brahma weapon, then withdraws it. But Aswatthaman is unable to stop his attack, and unintentionally redirects it toward the womb of Abhimanyu's wife, Uttarah, killing her unborn child. Krishna, however, restores the baby's life.

### Stri-Parva, ''Eleventh Book'': The Lament of the Wives

The widows of the Kaurava and Pandava warriors, along with Dhritarashtra and Gandhari, visit the battlefield to mourn and number the dead. Meanwhile, Yuyutsu and Sanjaya build pyres and perform funeral rites.

### Shanti Parva, ''Book of Consolation'': Bhishma's Discourse

A grieving Yudhishthira speaks to Bhishma, who tells him the ways of kings, the origins of all things, and the duties of humankind.

### Anusasana Parva, ''Book of Precepts'': The End of Bhishma's Discourse and his Death

Bhishma continues to tell Yudhishthira of the duties of kings, of the gods, and of the nature of life in this world. He then bids his friends goodbye and his soul ascends to heaven.

### Aswamedha-Parva, ''Fourteenth Book'': Yudhishthira's Horse Sacrifice

Yudhisthira sacrifices a horse in order to purify the sins of the combatants in this war.

### Asramavasika-Parva, ''Hermitage Book'': Dhritarashtra's Retirement

Dhritarashtra officially grants the kingdom of Kurujangala to Yudhishthira and departs for the forest, accompanied by Gandhari and Kunti. Vyasa and the Pandavas travel to their hermitage, and the *rishi* raises the souls of all the fallen warriors from the Ganges river so that the dead might visit the living for one night. Several years after the visit, the Pandavas hear news that Dhritarashtra and the two queens have been killed in a great forest fire.

### Mausala-Parva, ''Book of the Clubs'': The Death of Krishna and the Yadavas

Thirty-six years after the end of the great battle, evil portents prophesy the destruction of Dwaraka—Krishna's city—in a mighty flood. Another curse tells of Krishna, incensed by an argument, picking up a handful of grass, which then became a club, and killing all of his people, the Yadavas. When Arjuna arrives to investigate, he finds that these stories are true and that Balarama and Krishna have died. Arjuna's former companion, Krishna, lies slain by an arrow that pierced his foot—the only vulnerable portion of his body—when a hunter mistook him for a deer.

### Mahaprasthanika-Parva, ''The Book of the Great Journey'': The Five Pandavas Ascend Mount Meru

Hearing of the Yadava's destruction, Yudhishthira forsakes his throne and makes Parikshit, Arjuna's grandson, king. Yudhishthira, his four brothers, Draupadi, and his dog walk north on their way to Mount Meru, the entranceway to Indra's heaven. First Draupadi, then Sahadeva, then Nakula, then Arjuna, and finally Bhima, all fall dead. Indra appears in his chariot to escort Yudhishthira to heaven, but demands that he leave his dog behind. Yudhishthira refuses to abandon the devoted animal. Instantly the dog transforms into Dharma, god of righteousness, praises his son, and the former king ascends to heaven.

### Swargarohana-Parva, ''Book of the Ascent to Heaven'': The Five Brothers and Draupadi Arrive in Heaven

Yudhishthira finds Duryodhana in heaven. He is there because he obeyed the *dharma* of the warrior and died on the battlefield. Yudhishthira asks to see his brothers and wife and is informed that they are in hell, serving penance for their sins. Soon cleansed, they join Yudhishthira. At this point Janamejaya's ceremony of the snake sacrifice ends, thus closing Vaisampayana's narrative. Soon after, Sauti finishes his retelling of the *Mahabharata.*

## Characters

### Abhimanyu

Arjuna's son by Subhadra, Abhimanyu is killed in the great war by Duhsasana after his chariot is cut off from the main Pandava force by King Jayadratha. He fathers one son, Parikshit, by his wife Uttarah.

### Adhiratha

A charioteer from the kingdom of Anga, Adhiratha adopts and raises Karna after finding him floating in the Ganges river.

### Amba

The eldest princess of Banaras, Amba is abducted by Bhishma along with her sisters Ambika and Ambalika to serve as wives for Vichitravirya. She refuses, and instead flees west to be with her true love, the King of Salwa. She later throws herself into a flaming pyre in order to be reincarnated as Sikhandin.

### Ambalika

The second of Vichitravirya's wives, Ambalika is impregnated by the poet Vyasa. Frightened by Vyasa's appearance, she turns pale, and gives birth to a pale-skinned son whom she names Pandu, meaning "white," "pale," or "pale yellow."

### Ambika

Though married to Vichitravirya, Ambika's son Dhritarashtra is fathered by the poet Vyasa. She reacts to Vyasa's frightful appearance by closing her eyes, and her son Dhritarashtra is born blind.

### Arjuna

Son of Kunti by the god Indra, Arjuna is, next to Karna, the greatest warrior in the poem and one of the five heroes of the *Mahabharata*. Trained by the military expert Drona from a young age, this Pandava prince is skilled in archery, able to string and release dozens of arrows with deadly accuracy in mere seconds. A gallant warrior, Arjuna is called Vijaya, or "victor" and Dhanamjaya, or "winner of wealth." Although an unconquerable fighter at the start of the great battle, Arjuna experiences an intense feeling of self-doubt and loses his resolution to fight when he sees his kinsmen lined up against him. His courage is restored by Krishna, who sings to him the *Bhagavad Gita*, or the "Song of the Lord." With these words the divine Krishna convinces Arjuna that death is merely an illusion, that souls are

# Media Adaptations

- The *Mahabharata* was adapted as a full-length stage play by Jean-Claude Carrière and premiered in Avignon, France in 1985. Peter Brook's English translation of Carrière's play toured in 1987-88 with an international cast. Brook later directed a five-and-a-half-hour film version of the *Mahabharata*, televised worldwide in 1989; available on videocassette from The Parabola Video Library.

immortal and return, reincarnated, to the earth after a period in heaven.

Arjuna's exploits include his journey to Indra's heaven—where his father, the king of the gods, advises him—and his discovery of magical weapons to aid the Pandavas in the war against the Kauravas. He also draws King Drupada's bow at Draupadi's *svayamvara,* or ceremony of self-choice, winning her as wife for himself and his brothers. He defends the town of Matsya from the attacking forces of Duryodhana, and slays Karna during the climactic moment of the great war. Near the end of the poem, he ascends to heaven with his brothers and wife, after a brief time of spiritual cleansing in hell.

### Astika

The learned son of a *Naga* and a hermit, Astika asks King Janamejaya to stop the snake sacrifice on behalf of his people.

### Aswatthaman

Son of Drona, Aswatthaman is a mighty warrior who fights with the Kaurava army. After the death of his father during the war, Aswatthaman gives way to an almost uncontrollable anger and thirst for revenge. He employs the magical weapon of Narayana, which is capable of killing the entire Pandava army. Krishna counteracts its force, however, by telling the Pandavas to drop their weapons and turn their thoughts from war, rendering them immune to its power. After the Narayana fails, Aswatthaman is demoralized and believes the Kauravas will lose. Following their defeat, he unleashes an incredible weapon, taught to him by his father. Called the Brahmasira, it even has the power to destroy the world. Stopped by Arjuna with the help of Krishna, Aswatthaman nevertheless cannot fully control the weapon and launches it into the womb of Uttarah, killing her unborn son Abhimanyu (though Krishna later restores the child's life). Aswatthaman was born with a blue jewel affixed to the middle of his forehead, which he relinquishes to Arjuna after his final defeat.

## The Aswins

Twin gods known as "the harbingers of dawn," the Aswins father Nakula and Sahadeva by Madri, Pandu's second wife.

## Balarama

Krishna's brother, Balarama teaches the art of mace warfare to both Bhima and Duryodhana. He is appalled when Bhima fights unfairly by striking Duryodhana below the navel with his mace. At his death a huge snake with a thousand heads comes out of his mouth.

## Bharata

A legendary king called Chakravarti or "Universal Emperor," Bharata gives his name to the people that are the subject of the *Mahabharata*.

## Bhima

Son of Kunti by Vayu and one of the five Pandava princes, Bhima possesses incredible strength. He is a rash, impulsive warrior who often fights with a huge mace, standing in sharp contrast to his elder brother, Yudhishthira, who embodies nobility, patience, and wise judgment. Among his epithets are "Bhimaparakrama," or "he who has a terrible valor." Representing unchecked power, Bhima is the source of incredible carnage throughout the *Mahabharata*. He kills countless *Rakshasas,* Kaurava soldiers, even armored elephants. His violence often has a higher purpose, however. He consistently defends the honor of his wife, Draupadi, although his measures are typically extreme. Bhima crushes Kichaka to death when the general pursues his wife. He vows revenge against Duhsasana for his affront to Draupadi by publicly disrobing her. Some interpretations of Bhima's character find that he goes too far when he kills Duhsasana and drinks his blood as he swore to; however, other

commentators note that in so doing, Bhima was avenging a terrible wrong and fulfilling a vow he had sworn to carry out. Bhima exemplifies heedless but well-intentioned action, and after expiating his sins in hell, he ascends to heaven.

## Bhishma

Although Bhishma fathers no children of his own, he is more than any other figure in the *Mahabharata* the patriarch of the Bharata people. His name means "awe-inspiring," and this son of Santanu and the goddess Ganga is an emblem of the wise warrior. Renouncing his right to the throne, he agrees to remain celibate so that his father might marry Satyavati. Instead of ruling, Bhishma seeks to strengthen his race through wise action. In exchange for giving up his future rights to kingship, Santanu grants him a blessing, that he will never die until he so chooses. During the great war, Bhishma is selected by Duryodhana as the first general of the Kaurava army. His skill as a military commander is unparalleled, and he leads his forces to many early victories. Bhishma, however, will not fight Sikhandin, who was born a woman but later changed sex. After nine days of battle the Pandavas learn this fact and send Sikhandin against Bhishma. Bhishma is not immediately killed by Sikhandin. After the hostilities have ended, Bhishma speaks to King Yudhishthira, counseling him on ethics, law, morality, kingship, and philosophy. After he has finished, his soul departs for heaven.

## Chitrangada

Santanu's eldest son by Satyavati, Chitrangada dies in battle before marrying or producing a son.

## Chitraratha

Chitraratha is king of the Gandharvas, powerful supernatural creatures who are the heavenly musicians. A friend of Arjuna, he imprisons Duryodhana and his entourage in an iron net until Arjuna arrives and frees them.

## Chitrasena

*See* Chitraratha

## Danvir-Karna

*See* Karna

## Dharma

God of justice, truth, and righteousness, Dharma fathers Yudhishthira and tests his son's worthiness on several occasions in the *Mahabharata*. Dharma disguises his true identity while on earth, taking the form of a crane or a dog. It is in the form of a dog that he accompanies his son Yudhishthira on his final journey before his death; Yudhishthira proves his righteousness one last time through his kindness to his animal companion over the difficult journey.

## Dhrishtadyumna

Dhrishtadyumna is the son of King Drupada, brother of Draupadi, and the general of the Pandava army. Born with armor and a sword from a fire Drupada built for the god Shiva, Dhrishtadyumna fights valiantly in the great war, but shamefully slays Drona while his opponent kneels, unarmed. This act is one of revenge for his father's death, but is considered cowardly according to the dharma of war. As a form of poetic justice, Dhrishtadyumna is likewise killed unheroically, as he sleeps in his tent, by Aswatthaman.

## Dhritarashtra

King of Kurujangala for most of the *Mahabharata*, Dhritarashtra's name means "he who supports the kingdom." This is somewhat ironic, however, considering that he lacks the will to stop the great war, though by his own admission he possesses the strength to do so. Dhritarashtra is the eldest grandson of Santanu. Blind from birth, he ascends to the throne after the abdication of his younger brother Pandu. He marries Gandhari, who bears him one hundred sons, the Kauravas, who are the antagonists of the poem and represent the forces of evil and chaos. Dhritarashtra's primary failing is not malice, however, it is, appropriately, blindness—his inability to see clearly the events that are unfolding and to stop them. Dhritarashtra does exhibit kindness on occasion, though it sometimes has detrimental effects. He offers aid to Draupadi after the game of dice in which Yudhishthira loses her, as well as his kingdom, his brothers, and himself. She asks that her husbands be set free, and he grants this wish. Unfortunately, this action opens the way for the future revenge of the Pandavas. Following the war, Dhritarashtra laments the destruction of his sons and steps down from his throne.

## Draupadi

Daughter of King Drupada of Panchala, Draupadi marries all five of the Pandava princes. Born of a fire that Drupada built in honor of Shiva, Draupadi is brave, pure, noble, and beautiful. Her strength of character is equal to that of her five husbands, and from her comes the most resolute feminine perspective in the *Mahabharata*. Because of her great beauty, Draupadi is frequently abused or abducted by men who desire her. Thus, she must constantly be protected by her husbands from such individuals as King Jayadratha, General Kichaka, and Prince Duhsasana. Despite these continual assaults on her character and person, however, Draupadi maintains her poise, balance, and dignity throughout the poem.

## Drona

A Brahman and military man, Drona teaches the Bharata princes the art of warfare. His star pupil is Arjuna, whom he teaches—along with his own son, Aswatthaman—the most deadly techniques of war. His name means "bucket." According to the story of his birth, Drona was conceived when his father saw a heavenly *Apsara* and his seed fell into a bowl of water. A respected figure in the Kuru court, Drona acts as an advisor to Dhritarashtra and serves as general of the Kaurava army after the elimination of Bhishma. A formidable warrior and commander who obeys the rules and codes of martial conflict, Drona slays King Drupada during the great battle. When he hears the untruth that his son is dead he throws down his weapons in anguish and is slain by the king's son, Dhrishtadyumna.

## Drupada

Drupada is king of Panchala. Motivated by revenge for Drona's attack on, and occupation of, his kingdom, Drupada fights on behalf of the Pandavas during the great war. In a dream King Drupada hears Shiva tell him that he will be given a son and a daughter, born of fire. He builds this fire in honor of the god, and from the flames step Dhrishtadyumna and Draupadi. During the war, Drupada is slain by Drona, but his death is avenged by his son.

## Duhsala

Duhsala is the sole daughter of Dhritarashtra and Gandhari.

## Duhsasana

The second son of Dhritarashtra, Duhsasana forcefully attempts to publicly disrobe Draupadi after she is lost to the Kauravas in a game of dice. Cunning, evil, and fearless in battle, Duhsasana often taunts his opponents. His remarks and actions earn him the disdain of the Pandavas, especially Bhima, who vows to avenge his insult to Draupadi by drinking his blood. When Duhsasana attacks Bhima during the great war, Bhima fulfills this promise and slays the Kaurava prince.

## Duryodhana

Eldest son of Dhritarashtra, Prince Duryodhana plays the role of chief antagonist in the *Mahabharata*. His name means "difficult to conquer," and his intelligence, determination, strength, and military skill make him a worthy opponent, equal to any of the five Pandavas. A wicked, powerful man, Duryodhana often scorns good advice. Ruled by ambition, his primary motivation is a lust for power, leading to his absolute refusal to split the kingdom of Kurujangala with his cousin Yudhishthira, and prompting the great war that is the subject of the poem.

Highly opportunistic, Duryodhana seizes a chance for conquest whenever possible. He attacks King Virata's kingdom when he hears that General Kichaka has been killed—though his plans are thwarted by Arjuna. When the tide of battle turns, Duryodhana flees rather than fight and perhaps die with honor. Duryodhana is sometimes called "suryodhana," or "good fighter." While he frequently employs deception to defeat his enemies, in his final battle with Bhima, Duryodhana fights fairly and it is the Pandava prince who cheats by striking him in the thighs. Although driven by malice and pride, Duryodhana behaves generously on occasion—but usually with an ulterior motive. For example, Duryodhana disregards Karna's apparently low birth and lack of rank to make him king of Anga—but this is primarily so that Karna will he in his debt.

## Gandhari

Queen and wife of Dhritarashtra, Gandhari is the former princess of Gandhara. When she learns that her future husband is blind, she blindfolds herself and never removes the veil from her eyes. Her pregnancy by Dhritarashtra lasts for two years. She expels a ball of flesh from her womb. Vyasa orders that the ball be separated into one hundred and one portions, and each piece placed in a jar. Eventually Duryodhana, Duhsasana, ninety-eight more sons, and one daughter emerge from the jars. During the great battle, Gandhari observes that victory will be on the side of dharma, meaning that the Pandavas will win the war.

## Ganesha

Son of the gods Shiva and Devi, Ganesha is the elephant-headed god of writers and merchants. He appears, summoned by the great god Brahma, to record Vyasa's poem, the *Mahabharata*. .

## Ganga

Known as the goddess of the river, Ganga is the divine manifestation of the Ganges river, which flows through north-central and eastern India, emptying into the Indian Ocean. In heaven, eight Vasu gods (attendants of Indra) are cursed to be born on earth. They request that Ganga be their mother, and she agrees. King Santanu falls in love with Ganga while she is on earth and asks her to be his queen. She accepts on the condition that he promise never to ask who she is or to question her actions. He does this for seven years. Each year for seven years she bears a son (each with a cursed Vasu soul) and drowns him in the Ganges. On the eighth year, after the birth of the final child, Santanu stops her from killing the boy. Ganga then reveals her identity and leaves Santanu with his son, Bhishma.

## Ghatotkacha

Ghatotkacha is a powerful demon born to Bhima and Hidimba. His name means "pot-headed" because his head was said to be shaped like a water pot. Although he never leaves the forest where he was born, Ghatotkacha takes part in the great war on the side of the Pandavas. Initially causing great destruction and striking fear in the hearts of the entire Kaurava army, Ghatotkacha's attacks are stopped by Karna, who kills him with a magical dart.

## Hanuman

Endowed with incredible strength and the ability to speak, Hanuman is a magical monkey who plays a significant part in the epic poem, the *Ramayana*. He also appears briefly in the *Mahabharata*: Bhima encounters Hanuman on his travels through the Kamyaka forest. Hanuman imparts some of his vast wisdom to the Pandava prince.

## Hidimba

Hidimba is a *Rakshasa*, or forest-demon.

## Hidimba-asur

Hidimba-asur is a *Rakshasa*, or forest demon. She and her brothers ambush the five Pandavas and their wife Draupadi. Eventually she and Bhima fall in love and have a son, Ghatotkacha.

## Indra

The king of the gods and of thunder and rain, Indra rules in heaven. He fathers the hero Arjuna. Later Indra assists his son by disguising himself as a Brahman and requesting Karna's natural armor as a boon, thus rendering Karna no longer invincible in war. Indra also transports Arjuna to heaven for twelve years, and advises him on a variety of matters.

## Janamejaya

Great-grandson of Arjuna, King Janamejaya rules Kurujangala as the story opens. In order to avenge the death of his father, Parikshit, at the hands of a *Naga* (snake-man), Janamejaya holds a snake sacrifice, during which the *Mahabharata* is recited by Vaisampayana.

## Jayadratha

The king of Sindhu, Jayadratha carries off Draupadi while the five Pandavas are away hunting in the Kamyaka forest. Though Arjuna, Bhima, and Yudhishthira track him down, they spare his life. During the war, however, Jayadratha once again invokes Arjuna's wrath by outmaneuvering his son, Abhimanyu, indirectly causing the young warrior's death. Bold and resourceful, Jayadratha represents one of the Pandavas most troublesome foes. He is motivated by a desire for personal gain, rather than hatred or vengeance.

## Kali

Kali is the god of misfortune. In the famous tale of King Nala, Kali inhabits Nala's body in an attempt to thwart the king's love for Damayanti and gain the beautiful princess for himself.

## Karna

Karna, "the archer-king," is son of Surya, god of the sun, and Kunti. A magnificent warrior, Karna is born with natural armor attached to his skin, making him nearly invincible in battle. Because she is unmarried when she gives birth to him, Kunti sends him adrift on a river, hoping that he will be found by worthy parents. He is adopted and raised by Adhiratha, a charioteer, and travels to the imperial capital of Hastinapura when he grows up. Duryodhana, who has been looking for a warrior skilled enough to defeat his enemy Arjuna, makes Karna king of Anga. Thus, Karna fights on the side of the Kauravas against his own half-brothers, the Pandavas, in the great war.

Karna is a tragic figure in the *Mahabharata*. He remains true to his *dharma,* or sacred duty as a warrior, even when it causes him great personal sorrow to do so. Once he swears to fight his brothers, he never rescinds his vow. He also deeply regrets the fact that his mother will not acknowledge him publically as another of her sons. When the god Indra, Arjuna's father, requests his armor, Karna gives it to him, even though he knows this will put him at a great disadvantage on the battlefield. In return for this sacrifice, Karna asks for a weapon of incredible power, a magical dart that will assure the destruction of any enemy, but may be used only once. The Pandavas force the use of this weapon against early, so that it will no longer be a threat to the Pandavas. Without his armor or secret weapon, Karna cannot overpower Arjuna when the two meet in battle, and Arjuna defeats him

## Kichaka

Virata's general, Kichaka sees Draupadi disguised as a serving maid and attempts to win her for his wife. Though Draupadi refuses him and attempts to warn him of the vengeance of her husbands, Kichaka is resolute in his passions and refuses to give up. Unlike Jayadratha, who in a similar situation sees his life spared by the restraint of Yudhishthira, Kichaka faces Bhima and is killed for his presumptuousness. Pompous and vain, Kichaka is nevertheless a respected general whose death prompts Duryodhana to launch an invasion of Virata's kingdom.

## Kripa

Found on a doorstep as a child by a Kuru soldier, Kripa rises to a position of immense respect in the court of Dhritarashtra. He serves as war tutor of the Bharata princes and advisor to the king. His name means "compassion," and though he follows the dharma of the warrior, Kripa practices restraint in his decisions and remains alive (one of only three Kauravas to do so) at the end of the war.

## Kripacharya

*See* Kripa

## Kripi

Kripa's twin sister. Found as a child with her brother by a Kuru soldier, Kripi later marries Drona.

## Krishna

The earthly manifestation of the Hindu god Vishnu (the Preserver), Krishna is chief of the

Yadavas, a race hailing from the ancient city of Dwaraka in western India. A physical incarnation, or avatar, of the god in mortal form, Krishna is the binding force and spiritual center of the *Mahabharata.* His name means ''dark,'' and Krishna is usually represented as having dark blue skin. Though mortal in the poem, he is able to reveal his divine form to those around him. Possessing the wisdom of the all-pervasive Vishnu who is said to ''repose in truth, truth in him,'' Krishna is infallible. During the great war, however, he refuses to fight on either side. Instead he offers himself, unarmed, or ten thousand of his Yadava warriors. Arjuna chooses the former, while Duryodhana happily takes the latter.

Krishna is sometimes called Krishna Vyasa Dvaipayana and credited with composing the *Mahabharata,* yet in the poem he is Arjuna's friend and charioteer, a character separate from the poet and seer Vyasa. As Arjuna's companion, Krishna is present throughout the work, though he makes his divine presence known most effectively when he sings the Song of the Lord, the *Bhagavad Gita.* Krishna's song serves to dispel Arjuna's doubts about the war. Krishna imparts his wisdom to the warrior and destroys his fear, informing him that death is an illusion, a moment of passage between one existence and the next. Krishna tells Arjuna that he must fight with detachment, without desire, according to the dictates of *dharma,* his sacred duty. Krishna dies long after the end of the great war. Accidentally shot in the foot (the only place where he is not invulnerable) by a deer hunter, he dies unheroically.

### Kritavarman

A Yadava warrior, Kritavarman fights for the Kauravas under Krishna's orders. He is one of the three surviving members of the defeated Kaurava army.

### Kunti

Kunti is the first wife of King Pandu. Known for her hospitality, Kunti welcomes the hermit Durvasas into her palace. In return the ascetic rewards her with a powerful mantra that allows her to summon any god to sire a son with her. Prior to her marriage with Pandu, she tests the spell by calling Surya, god of the sun, who impregnates her with her son Karna. Being without a husband, she blesses the child and sends him adrift on a river. Later, after her marriage and discovery that Pandu cannot have children of his own, she calls down the gods Dharma, Vayu, and Indra. Each of them father

a son with her. These three—Yudhishthira, Bhima, and Arjuna—are the heroes of the *Mahabharata.*

### Kuru

A legendary king, Kuru gives his name to the Bharata people.

### Madri

Second wife of Pandu and daughter of the king of Madras, Madri uses Kunti's mantra to summon the fleet-footed gods, the Aswins. From them she bears the fourth and five Pandava brothers, the twins Nakula and Sahadeva.

### Markandeya

A sage, or *rishi,* Markandeya recites the tale of ''Savitri'' to comfort Yudhishthira after the abduction of Draupadi by King Jayadratha. (*See* Savitri.)

### Nakula

Twin brother of Sahadeva. The twins are the sons of Pandu's second wife Madri by the Aswins, gods called the ''harbingers of dawn.'' A mighty warrior, fleet of foot, Nakula accompanies his brothers throughout the *Mahabharata,* although both twins play a secondary role to the sons of Kunti: Yudhishthira, Bhima, and Arjuna.

### Nala

King Nala is the protagonist of ''Nala and Damayanti,'' a tale told to Yudhishthira by Vrihadaswa. According to the story, the god Kali, jealous of King Nala and his love for Damayanti, possesses the king's body. Kali then forces him to lose his kingdom in a game of dice and to desert his love. Eventually, Nala breaks free from Kali's hold on him and recovers both his throne and Damayanti. This tale parallels that of Yudhishthira's situation, and its happy ending foreshadows the similar resolution of the epic plot.

### Pandu

Grandson of Santanu and primogenitor in name of the Pandavas, Pandu is crowned king of Kurujangala because his elder brother, Dhritarashtra, was born blind. His name means ''white, ''yellow-white,'' or ''pale,'' denoting the nature of his physical complexion.

Pandu is sexually insatiable until he is told that his next act of physical love with his wives, Kunti and Madri, will certainly kill him. He is nevertheless regarded as the father of Arjuna, Yudhishthira, Bhima, Nakula, and Sahadeva—all of whom are born from unions between his wives and various gods. After the birth of his five sons, Pandu gives in to temptation, carnally embraces his wife Madri, and dies in her arms.

## Parikshit

Son of Abhimanyu and Uttarah, and grandson of Arjuna, Parikshit succeeds Yudhishthira as king of Kurujangala following the former's abdication and departure for the holy Mount Meru. After ruling peacefully for sixty years, Parikshit, in a fit of rage over his unsuccessful hunting, shoots an innocent *Naga*. The snake-man then curses the king to die in one week. Despite efforts to alter his fate, Parikshit is poisoned and killed by the *Naga* prince Takshaka.

## Parikshita

*See* Parikshit

## Sahadeva

Twin brother of Nakula. The twins are the sons of Pandu's second wife Madri by the Aswins, gods called the ''harbingers of dawn.'' A mighty warrior, fleet of foot, Sahadeva accompanies his brothers throughout the *Mahabharata,* although both twins play a secondary role to the sons of Kunti: Yudhishthira, Bhima, and Arjuna.

## Sakuni

Uncle of the Kaurava princes, Sakuni cheats at dice to help them win Yudhishthira's kingdom of Indraprastha. He later falls in the great battle, slain by Nakula and Sahadeva. A sly and largely evil figure, Sakuni serves as a contrast to such men as Kripa and Vidura, who represent wisdom, restraint, and forthrightness.

## Salya

King of the Madras, Salya fights with the Kauravas and leads their army after Karna's death. While his generalship is superb, Salya is slain by the inspired warcraft of Yudhishthira.

## Sanjaya

Dhritarashtra's charioteer, Sanjaya reports the events of the great war to his king after Vyasa blesses him with heavenly sight and magical protection in battle.

## Santanu

King of Kurujangala, Santanu is grandfather of Dhritarashtra and Pandu. The patriarch of the Bharatas, he falls in love with Ganga and then Satyavati, producing sons by both; though of them only Bhishma takes part in the main action of the poem. Santanu leaves his throne to Pandu in his old age and retires to the forest to die.

## Satyaki

A Yadava who fights for the Pandavas, Satyaki is one of seven warriors from the Pandava army—the others being the five brothers and Krishna—to survive the great battle.

## Satyavati

Wife of Santanu, Satyavati was born of royalty, but lived her early life as a fisherwoman who sometimes ferried travelers across the Yamuna river. According to legend, her father was King Uparichara of Chedi. One day while dreaming of his queen, his seed fell on a leaf. Carried by a hawk, the leaf eventually fell in the river and was swallowed by a fish. Inside the fish's belly the girl grew until she was rescued by a fisherman who adopted her. Though beautiful, she smelled of fish until Parashara, a minstrel, happened upon her. Convincing her to make love to him, Parashara removed the odor of fish and replaced it with that of flowers. Later, Satyavati gave birth to the poet Vyasa, the ostensible author of the *Mahabharata.* Still later, King Santanu sees Satyavati and, captivated by her beauty and scent, he makes her his queen. He promises her that their son will be the future king of Kurujangala.

## Sauti

The name Sauti means ''bard'' or ''storyteller.'' Sauti quotes Vaisampayana's recitation of the

*Mahabharata* to a group of sages, or *rishis,* at the opening of the poem.

### Savitri

Savitri is the main character of a tale of the same name recounted by Markandeya to Yudhishthira. After falling in love with and marrying Satyavan, Savitri learns that her husband has only one year to live. As the time of his death approaches, she waits by his side and sees Yama, the god of death arrive to take Satyavan's soul. He catches the soul in his noose and begins to walk off. Savitri follows the god and begs him to restore her husband's life. He refuses, offering to grant any other wish, but she is steadfast. Finally, Yama suggests that he return Satyavan's soul in exchange for half of Savitri's remaining days. She agrees and the two live together happily for 400 years.

### Shakuni

*See* Sakuni

### Shiva

Called "the Destroyer," Shiva is a deity of stature equal to Vishnu, the Preserver, and Brahma, the Creator. In the course of the *Mahabharata,* Shiva provides a powerful weapon to Arjuna for his use in the war against the Kauravas.

### Sikhandin

A warrior in the Pandava army, Sikhandin is responsible for Bhishma's death in battle. His soul was reincarnated from that of the princess Amba and Sikhandin was originally born a woman. He later exchanges sexes with a *Rakshasa* in order to fight in the great war.

### Subhadra

Krishna's sister, Subhadra marries Arjuna and bears him the son Abhimanyu.

### Surya

God of the sun, Surya fathers Karna and warns his son that Indra will ask for his natural armor. In exchange, the sun god tells him that he must demand a mighty weapon of war, which Karna does.

### Susarman

King of Trigarta (The Land of the Three Castles), Susarman leads an attack on Arjuna to lure him away from Yudhishthira during the great war. Though valiant, he and his kinsmen are slaughtered by the mighty Pandava bowman.

### Takshaka

Prince of the *Nagas,* a race of snake-men, Takshaka kills King Parikshit to avenge the murder of an innocent *Naga.* He takes the form of a small copper beetle in order to achieve entry to Parikshit's guarded dwelling and commit the act.

### Urvasi

A beautiful heavenly dancer called an *Apsara,* Urvasi curses Arjuna to live for one year as a eunuch after he rejects her offers of love.

### Uttara

King Virata's son, Uttara—along with Arjuna—repels Duryodhana's invasion of Matsya. Later, Uttara and Virata's forces fight for the Pandavas in the great war.

### Uttarah

King Virata's daughter, Uttarah marries Abhimanyu and gives birth to Parikshit.

### Vaisampayana

Sage and disciple of Vyasa, Vaisampayana recites the *Mahabharata* at the snake sacrifice of King Janamejaya.

### Vaka

The *Rakshasa* called Vaka terrorizes the town of Ekachakra by eating a cartload of food and one human sacrifice each year until Bhima slays the demon.

### Vayu

God of the wind, Vayu fathers the mighty Pandava prince Bhima.

### Vichitravirya

Second son of King Santanu, Vichitravirya has two wives, Ambika and Ambalika—secured for him by Bhishma. He dies of consumption at a young age, however, before producing an heir. Vichitravirya's ironic name means ''colorful virility.''

## Vidura

Sage and uncle-advisor of both the Pandavas and the Kauranas. Vidura is the son of Vyasa and Shudra, a slave girl. He is representative of honor and wisdom in the poem. Duty-bound to serve his king and country, his first allegience is to the Dhritrashtra and his sons.

## Virata

King of Matsya, Virata admits the disguised Pandavas and Draupadi into his court during their thirteenth year of exile. After they defend his kingdom from the attacking forces of Duryodhana, Virata offers his daughter Uttarah and support in the great battle with the Kauravas.

## Vrihadaswa

A *rishi,* or sage, Vrihadaswa tells the tale of Nala and Damayanti to Yudhishthira. (*See* Nala.)

## Vyasa

The poet attributed with composing the *Mahabharata,* Vyasa's name means ''arranger'' or ''compiler''—thus appropriate to his role in creating the encyclopedic poem. Vyasa also appears in the work as the son of Satyavati from a union prior to her marriage with King Santanu. His father was the *rishi* Parashara, and like him Vyasa is a powerful sage and seer. His powers include the ability to prophesy the future—he knows, for example that Queen Gandhari will bear one hundred sons—as well as greater magics. He also grants Dhritarashtra's charioteer, Sanjaya, with the ability to see all the events of the great battle, day and night, and with divine protection so that he might report the war to his king. In addition to his role as a man of knowledge, Vyasa fathers the kings Pandu and Dhritarashtra by the former wives of his half-brother, Vichitravirya. Vyasa's frightening appearance, his ''ugliness, grim visage, foul body, terrible odor,'' as Joseph Campbell quotes in his *The Masks of God: Oriental Mythology,* 1962, upsets the two women, Ambika and Ambalika. The first closes her eyes and produces the blind Dhritarashtra, the second turns pale, producing the light-skinned Pandu.

## Yama

The god of the dead, Yama appears in Markandeya's tale of Savitri. (*See* Savitri.)

## Yudhishthira

Son of Pandu's first wife Kunti by Dharma (the god of justice), Yudhishthira is the oldest of the five Pandava brother and destined to be king of Kurujangala. Noble and aloof, he is the foremost example of the Hindu warrior who follows the precepts of *dharma,* or sacred duty. Seldom perturbed, Yudhishthira is courageous, strong, prudent, and patient. His name means ''firm in battle,'' a quality which he displays near the end of the great war, as he forsakes his otherwise tranquil exterior and savagely attacks the Kaurava general, Salya. He also demonstrates his courage and propriety by dropping his weapons and armor prior to the battle, and asking the permission of Bhishma, Drona, and Kripa to fight them.

Yudhishthira's most notable trait, apart from his detachment, are his taste for gambling and inability to refuse a challenge. (This last is related to his code of conduct as a warrior, and therefore is not regarded as a flaw). Duryodhana and Sakuni exploit these qualities of Yudhishthira's character by inviting him to take part in a game of dice. Yudhishthira agrees and, due to their cheating, loses first his kingdom of Indraprastha, then—because he will not stop gambling even though he is losing—goes on to lose his brothers, their shared wife Draupadi, and himself; thus setting the stage for the great battle.

After the war, Yudhishthira, now king, feels a great responsibility for the near total destruction of his people. He performs a horse sacrifice to absolve the sins of all those who took part in the hostilities. After many years of rule he abdicates his throne to Arjuna's grandson, Parikshit, and sets out northward towards Mount Meru, ''the world mountain,'' with his brothers and Draupadi. On the way all but Yudhishthira fall dead. He survives the journey to the mountain, never forsaking his faithful dog—Dharma in disguise. Later he is joined by his companions in heaven.

## Yuyutsu

Son of Dhritarashtra and a slave girl, Yuyutsu defects from the Kaurava to the Pandava army moments before the great battle begins.

# Themes

## *Dharma: Responsibility and Sacred Duty*

Despite its size and complexity, the *Mahabharata* explores one over-arching theme predominantly: the observance of one's sacred duty, called dharma. All other thematic issues in the work relate to the question of dharma obeyed or ignored. The characters who satisfy the dictates of dharma are eventually rewarded, while those who consciously refuse to obey their dharma are inevitably punished. According to Hindu law, each individual has a special place in society and must behave in strict accordance to the requirements of that position, called caste. In the *Mahabharata,* all the important characters belong to the Kshatriya or warrior caste. Individuals such as Yudhishthira, Arjuna, Bhima, and Duryodhana must obey the dharma of warriors. They must be courageous, honorable, and respectful of their opponents. They must never take unfair advantage; for example, attacking an unarmed or unprepared enemy. Duryodhana, for example, fights fairly against Bhima, who wrongly strikes him "below the belt" in their combat. At the end of the narrative, we see that Duryodhana, despite his often evil and unkind actions, gains admittance to heaven because he always adhered to the code or dharma of the warrior.

More than any other figure in the *Mahabharata,* Yudhishthira represents the proper observance of dharma. This is underscored at the end of the narrative, when he will not abandon the faithful dog who accompanied him on his final journey. It is revealed to the reader that this dog is the god Dharma in disguise, testing his son's worthiness one last time. Thus symbolically Yudhishthira is shown refusing to forsake his dharma and therefore demonstrating that he is deserving to enter into heaven at his death. Likewise, most of his actions throughout the poem are those of a man committed to engaging in right behavior as a king and a warrior. When he does fail to live up to these high ideals—as, for example, when he continues gambling until he has lost his wealth and kingdom as well as his wife and his own and his brothers' freedom—he suffers greatly and pays a high price.

In additional to depictions of the importance of dharma embodied in specific characters, the *Mahabharata* contains passages that teach specific lessons about social and spiritual responsibility. Bhishma's speeches to Yudhishthira focus on the dharma of good leadership and effective ruling. Ultimately, the *Mahabharata* observes that existence and happiness depend less on courage and destiny than on an understanding and acceptance of the rules and responsibilities of dharma.

## *Virtue and Truth*

The concepts of virtue and truth are closely related to that of dharma. The *Mahabharata* includes the story of a great, epoch-spanning and empire-establishing war, and so often stresses the virtues of bravery, honesty, and nobility that form the basis of Kshatriya dharma, the code of warriors in ancient India. The narrative also shows many instances of individuals violating various codes of conduct. Sakuni, for instance, cheats in order to defeat his guests, thus violating codes meant to govern rules of hospitality and of fairness. This event stands as a telltale sign to original hearers and readers of this epic that Sakuni and his family are destined to be defeated in the coming war.

Truth and truthfulness are also prominent in the *Mahabharata.* Krishna, an incarnation of the god of truth Vishnu, reveals many important truths to the moral characters. Most importantly, he sings the *Bhagavad Gita* to Arjuna before the great battle begins, revealing to the reluctant fighter the essential truths about the illusory nature of death and the cyclical nature of life. By itself the *Bhagavad Gita* is a sacred Hindu test; in the plot of the *Mahabharata* it has both sacred and secular functions, serving to fill Arjuna with the confidence and conviction of divine truth so that he may pursue his dharma. His destiny is to fight for the Pandavas and to defeat the Kauravas.

## *Order and Disorder, Good and Evil*

On a symbolic level, the *Mahabharata* tells an ancient story of a mythic, primal conflict between opposing forces of light and darkness. Pandu, the pale, and his sons the Pandavas, represent order and goodness in opposition to the blind Dhritarashtra, his son Duryodhana, and the Kauravas, who represent darkness and disorder. As an allegory, then, the poems shows the classic conflict between the forces of good and evil. In the end, of course, the forces of good triumph, aided by the god Vishnu, who comes

# Topics for Further Study

- Who writes history? Much of Indian history prior to the entrance of Muslims into the region in the 11th century exists only in literary form, as stories and tales. Examine the *Mahabharata* as a historical document. What does it tells use about the time in which it was set and the person, or persons, who wrote it? You might, for instance, compare aspects of classical India with parallel features of Europe during the middle ages. What does it mean to interpret history through a work of literature?

- Religion and society: Investigate the similarities and differences between Hinduism, as it is presented in the *Mahabharata,* and Buddhism, another great world religion with its source in India. Compare the ways in which Hinduism structures society and salvation through the caste system and the critique that Buddhism offers of this system.

- What is a hero? The *Mahabharata* contains many examples of the Hindu hero, especially in the character of Yudhishthira. Outline his characteristics and then compare them to the qualities of an epic hero from the western tradition, such as Odysseus from Homer's *Odyssey,* or Achilles from his *Iliad.* What makes these heroes ''eastern'' or ''western'' in character? What qualities to they share? Do the same with Bhima, Arjuna, or Duryodhana.

---

to earth as Krishna to ensure the ultimate triumph of good. But in the process of winning, the Pandavas themselves are nearly destroyed. They also find themselves using deception and dishonorable tactics to defeat their opponents. This fact has often been seen as an indication that assessments of absolute good and absolute evil are difficult to make; further, that sometimes a rightful end can only be reached through unrighteous means.

In the *Mahabharata,* the desired and rightful end is for a lasting peace. Yet to attain this goal, the Pandavas and Kauravas must engage in the great war. Many are killed horribly on both sides. The people suffer and their nation is impoverished as the two groups fight. The symbolic goal, however, is the defeat of evil and the restoration of order.

### Hinduism—The Flesh versus the Spirit

Perhaps the most important transcendent or spiritual theme of the *Mahabharata* is primarily embodied in the *Bhagavad Gita,* and entails the basic teachings of Hinduism. In particular, this section of the poem transmits information about reincarnation and the possibility of ascension into heaven. As Krishna explains in his song to Arjuna, death is not the end of life. Human souls are immortal and are reincarnated through a process called samsara, or transmigration. Further, according to the concept of karma, those who have lived their lives in proper accordance with their dharma will be rewarded in each subsequent life. The final step in the life cycle is that of nirvana: both karma and samsara are transcended. The soul that attains nirvana moves beyond desire and individual consciousness to a pure, enlightened state, freed from the cycle of reincarnation. To accept this endless cycle of purification is to see that physical life and death on earth are only a small part of the true cycle of human existence.

## Style

### Narrative Technique—Frame Stories

The complex structure of the *Mahabharata* exists in part due to its shape as a series of stories

*Indra welcomes Yudhisthira to heaven.*

and narratives nested one within another. It opens with the first of two frame stories, which act as introductions, leading the reader toward the heart of the poem, the epic story of the great battle between the Pandavas and the Kauravas. The reader first encounters the tale of Sauti, a bard or storyteller, who recounts what he has heard of the *Mahabharata* to several listeners in the forest. Sauti quotes the sage Vaisampayana, who has learned the poem from his master, Vyasa, the author of the work. Vaisampayana's tale thus comprises the second frame story. He recites most of the *Mahabharata* at the snake sacrifice of King Janamejaya. Within the main plot of the poem several more sages, or *rishis,* such as Markandeya and Vrihadaswa, recount legends, folktales, or popular stories that illustrate a moral or theme somehow relevant to the main plot. Occasionally Sauti surfaces within the narrative to make an observation, as does Vaisampayana, but these intrusions are generally brief. Overall, this structure allows for the many breaks in narrative flow and chronology, repeated accounts of events from different points of view, and lengthy digressions that mark this massive poem.

### Sanskrit Literature and Versification

The *Mahabharata* represents one of the finest examples of classical Sanskrit poetry. Like Latin, classical Sanskrit is no longer a living, spoken language though a modern form of the language is a curricular requirement in many schools. The language of the work also differs somewhat from the Vedic tongue, a precursor of Sanskrit in which several holy texts of Hinduism, including the sacred *Vedas* and the *Upanishads,* were written. The subject of much scholarly study and several translations, the *Mahabharata,* while often referred to as an epic, is more specifically a *purana,* or "ancient tale" in verse. Originally written as one extended poem, the work eventually grew as more scenes, stories, and other material—including writings on ethics, law, philosophy, history, and religion—were added. The basic unit of the poem is the epic *sloka,* two verse lines with alternating stressed and unstressed syllables. Other meters are also employed throughout, all of which adhere to the strict and formal rules of poetics that typify classical Sanskrit verse.

### Language and Style

Several stylistic elements of the *Mahabharata* indicate that the poem was once repeated verbally as part of an oral tradition rather than written down. These include: repeated words and phrases, the use of clichés, and some stereotypical descriptions, such as those found in the many battle scenes in the poem. Overall, however, the language of the work is said to be simple and restrained. In many cases the narrative downplays the more grisly elements of war. Yet much of the *Mahabharata*'s imagery is also vivid and highly evocative. Metaphors and similes—comparisons designed to describe one thing by invoking another—are common in the text, and are especially used to portray the superhuman qualities and feats of the poem's heroes. Exaggeration is also used in typical mythic fashion to underscore the grandeur and scope of the events being described. Arjuna, for example, can unleash dozens of arrows in a second, and during the war these the arrows launched by all the combatants can block out the sun.

Much of the story is delivered in dialogue—conversation—or individual speeches. Sometimes a character's thoughts are rendered in soliloquy, as if spoken even though no one else is present. Additionally, the poet employs the classic epic device of foreshadowing, by mentioning or alluding to future events before they occur. Thus, Gandhari observes that the Pandavas will win the war, because *dharma* is on their side, long before the battle has ended. Finally, many characters are depicted with epithets, symbolic names that describe some significant or interesting characteristic, or have allegorical names. Duryodhana's name, for instance, means "hard to conquer."

## Historical Context

Scholars locate the historical setting of the *Mahabharata* in a vast area of northern India sometime around 1000 BC. The poem features the classical Indo-Aryan civilization—a culture that represents a mix of two groups: the indigenous Indus valley peoples and the Aryans. The latter group invaded the Indus region and subsequently assimilated elements of the Indus society as part of their own.

### Indus Valley Civilization

Archealogical evidence has uncovered a somewhat mysterious Bronze Age culture that existed along the Indus river in what is today Pakistan, a nation situated to the immediate west of modern India. Contemporary with the ancient Mesopotamian and Egyptian civilizations, the Indus Valley culture thrived between about 2500 and 1500 BC. Largely agricultural, the Indus peoples seem to have had a relatively complex society and advanced material culture. They lived in mud-brick dwellings, produced art and pottery, lived under a loosely democratic form of government, and offered women a equitable status in relation to that of men. Other aspects of their social organization remain a mystery to archaeologists, though they worshipped and sacrificed to many gods, including Indra and Agni, both of whom appear in the *Mahabharata*. Their belief system also seems to have been an early form of the Vedic religion. Its precepts were later organized and written down by the Aryans as the *Vedas,* the early sacred texts of the Hindu religion.

### Aryan Culture

By around 1500 BC the warlike Aryans (a northern tribe whose name means "noble" in San-

skrit) had begun to invade the Indus valley, subjugating and later assimilating many of the indigenous peoples they found there. With their skills in iron metallurgy, the Aryans brought the Indian subcontinent under their rule and created a highly advanced civilization along the valleys of the Ganges and Yamuna rivers, the geographical location of the *Mahabharata.* In contrast to the Indus peoples, the Aryans were militaristic, with a strongly patriarchal, or male-dominated, society. Their culture was organized along a strict hierarchy that eventually developed into the caste system—a social design in which priests and warriors occupied positions of authority and power. By the 5th century BC, the Aryan civilization in India had become an advanced feudal aristocracy, made up of several constituent states. Kingship and court life had grown increasingly important. Meanwhile, stable institutions, professional occupations, a trade economy, and a rich tradition of Sanskrit literature had developed.

### The Caste System

The rigid system of social hierarchy developed by the Aryans was based on hereditary class divisions called castes. Justified by religious and cultural means, the caste system has become a recognizable part of Hindu culture that survives today, though in a very different form. Within the Aryan system, individuals were classified into four *varnas,* or "classes." At the top of the hierarchy were the Brahmans or priests. Though lacking political power, the Brahmans had created the system, and therefore placed themselves in positions of respect above the rest of society. They performed sacrifices and other religious ceremonies, and relied on the generosity of the lower castes for their economic survival. They were also teachers, instructing younger members of the Kshatriya or warrior class in particular, as Drona and Kripacharya do in the *Mahabharata.* Brahmans often appear in the *Mahabharata* as hermits or ascetics, individuals who have sacrificed material wealth and human desires in order to attain religious enlightenment. The Brahmans were typically the source of great awe and respect in classical Indian civilization. Below the Brahmans in the caste system were the Kshatriyas, or warriors. These individuals made up the ruling class of Aryan society. Including kings, princes, and the remainder of the social aristocracy, nearly all of the significant individuals in the *Mahabharata* are members of the Kshatriya caste. Beneath the warriors were the Vaisyas, merchants, farmers and other non-aristocratic individuals. Still further below the Vaisyas were the Sudhras. Laborers and servants to the

# Compare & Contrast

- **1000 BC (the period in which the *Mahabharata* is set):** Three thousand years ago the region which is today known as India was ruled by feudal kings and princes, people upon whom figures such as Yudhishthira, Duryodhana, Virata, and Salya were based. The princes often battled one another for land, prestige, or wealth, and governed according to a system much like that of Medieval Europe.

  **Late twentieth century:** India is made up of several states. It is a federal, secular republic, not unlike the United States of America, and in fact is the largest democracy in the world. Important figures and institutions in the Indian government include the president, prime minister, and two houses of parliament.

- **1000 BC:** The caste system, a strict hereditary organization of social classes, defined classical Indian society. Warriors ruled and offered gifts and reverence to priests, or Brahmans. Most Indians engaged in agriculture as farmers; slavery was prevalent and these individuals served the higher social classes.

  **Late twentieth century:** Slavery has been outlawed in India for more than a century and a half. The caste system still exists to a degree, but social mobility has become a reality. India is a still-developing country, but the growth of capitalism has been tremendous in the twentieth century. India is a modern, industrializing nation.

- **1000 BC:** Classical Indian society was highly patriarchal, or male-dominated; women played a subordinate role in most aspects of life. Like Draupadi, Gandhari, and Kunti, they were wives and mothers first. At this time a women's value resided primarily in her ability to produce sons, her subservience to her husband, and her personal beauty.

**Today:** Educational opportunities and democracy have greatly increased the status of and standard of living for women in India. Although women still occupy a secondary role in many areas of society, restrictions on them are beginning to loosen. Between 1966 and 1977, and again from 1980 to 1984 a woman, Indira Gandhi, governed India as prime minister. Many avenues of employment, however, are still very difficult for women to enter.

- **1000 BC:** The practice of polygamy, several wives for one husband, was common, especially among men of great wealth and power. Polyandry, several husbands for one wife, like that of Draupadi and the five Pandavas, was quite rare. This example in the *Mahabharata,* therefore, should not be interpreted as the norm in classical Indian society.

  **Late twentieth century:** The practices of polygamy and polyandry are virtually unknown in modern India.

- **1000 BC:** War between tribes or kingdoms was a common fact of everyday life. Warriors were among the most esteemed members of society.

  **Late twentiety century:** Armed conflict involves modern India as it does the rest of the world. The reasons for these conflicts are varied, but many hostilities derive from religious differences or territorial disputes. Since the late 1940s, India and the Muslim nation of Pakistan have struggled over a disputed area of land in the Kashmir region; antagonism between the countries persists. In 1974 India surprised many of its neighbors and the world community when it tested an atomic bomb.

---

higher classes, the Sudhras also included slaves. Outside the system were the Untouchables. These

individuals were considered without caste. This group included social exiles, religious outcasts, and

Dravidians (the aboriginal inhabitants of India). The caste system required that individuals never marry outside their caste. Likewise, many occupations were unavailable to members of a particular caste. Sometimes the restrictions of caste could be overcome, however. Prince Duryodhana, for example, makes Karna—whom he believes is the son of a charioteer—the King of Anga. In the context of the story, however, this is intended to demonstrate the temporal power of the prince rather than the possibility of moving to a higher caste, which did not in fact exist. Individuals were caste-bound throughout their lives—although a good person could look forward to being reborn as a member of a higher caste.

## Hinduism

Out of the tradition of the Vedic religion that flourished in the Indus river valley came the major world religion called Hinduism. The term "hindu" comes from the word "sindu," or river—specifically the Indus river. Those who practiced the religion, which today is prominent in India, parts of Africa and southeast Asia, and other parts of the world, worship a large number, or pantheon, of gods. Among the most popular are Shiva and Vishnu, both of whom appear in the *Mahabharata*—Vishnu as an earthly manifestation of Krishna. The sacred texts of Hinduism include the four *Vedas* and the *Upanishads,* a collection of ancient wisdom and ethical writings. Among the other great Hindu texts are several non-sacred, or secular works. These include the eighteen *puranas* or "ancient tales," the most important of which are the *Mahabharata,* specifically the section of Krishna's speech to Arjuna knows as the *Bhagavad Gita,* and the *Ramayana.* Dramatized in these works are the key ideas of Hinduism. To begin with, the religion teaches a cyclic conception of the universe. Over vast periods of time the universe is created and destroyed, endlessly. Likewise, human life flows in cycles. The human soul, according to Hindu doctrine, is immortal and might experience countless lifetimes on earth. This process is called *samsara,* which means reincarnation or transmigration of the soul. The form that the soul will take in succeeding lifetimes is ruled by the dictates of *karma. Karma,* sometimes characterized as "the fatality of the act" is, simply put, the workings of a cosmic law of retribution. According to *karma,* good actions in this lifetime will be rewarded in the next, and evil deeds will be punished. Those who are predominately good might be reincarnated into a higher caste, those who are evil might be born into a lower one, or even as a

lower form of life, such as an animal. Heaven, in this system, still exists but only as a temporary stage where souls wait before being reborn. Eventually an end to the cycles of death and rebirth might be achieved, however, if one can attain *moksa,* or release from worldly desires and learn to no longer differentiate between the individual soul (*atman*) and the universal soul (*Brahman*).

## Critical Overview

Although not exclusively a religious work, the *Mahabharata* is considered by many to be the fifth of the *Vedas*—the other four are sacred texts of Hinduism designed to teach proper moral and ethical conduct. It has a prominent position in Indian literature and enjoys great religious and cultural significance for many Hindus. Critical interpretations of the work, particularly from European and American commentators, have varied. Philo M. Buck, in *The Golden Thread* (1931), called it "chiefly a celebration of war ... its ideal, the princely warrior, and emperor." Other commentators suggest that the work is not so one-sided. They point out that the work contains expressions of regret for the violence and destruction of armed conflict. Further, some critics point out that while the great battle is the climax of the *Mahabharata*, it is only a small part of a vast, multipart narrative. For its Indian audience, the sacred text the *Bhagavad Gita,* sung by Krishna to Arjuna before the war, holds much greater significance that the details of the battle itself. In fact, the war is generally interpreted more as a metaphysical struggle between good and evil than as the actual physical encounter of two armies.

### Synthetic versus Analytic

The two main lines of critical thought concerning the *Mahabharata* have focused on whether this massive poem is artistically unified and coherent or riddled with inconsistencies that invalidate any possible coherence. The first group is known as the synthetic camp. Common among Indian scholars, the synthetic stance contends that the *Mahabharata* is thematically unified and presents a clear statement on the effects of proper adherence to the rules of personal and sacred duty (*dharma*), and the negative results of abusing dharmic responsibilities. Many non-Indian critics, however, approach the poem analytically, examining its constituent parts without perceiving any such unity. This is termed the analytic approach. Moriz Winternitz, in *A History of Indian Literature* (1926), for example, calls the *Mahabharata* ''not one poetic production at all, but rather a whole literature.'' He also describes the work a ''monstrosity,'' full of repeated and slightly changed material. Winternitz and other analytic critics argue that because of its growth over the years and the addition of sometime irrelevant tales, legends, local myths, and didactic (or lesson-teaching) material, the *Mahabharata* is self-contradictory rather than unified.

## Formal Criticism

Stylistic criticism of the *Mahabharata* largely reflects the division between synthetic and analytic critics. The analytics have concentrated on what they see as flaws in the poem, including inconsistencies in the text, its loose structure, and occasional repetitiveness. According to the synthetics, however, many of these traits can be explained by the fact that the *Mahabharata* existed for centuries as part of an oral tradition. Not written down, but repeated by poets and sages for the entertainment and spiritual enlightenment of their listeners, the poem inevitably changed greatly over time. As new scenes and stories were added or retold, they were sometimes altered slightly by different speakers. In addition, oral literature commonly relies on stock phrases that appear over and over again. The synthetics argue that overall the simplicity and purity of the Sanskrit language shines through in the *Mahabharata*. They praise the work for its poetic beauty.

## Myth and Symbolism

Mythological interpretations have occupied a significant portion of modern criticism of the *Mahabharata*. Reflections on good and evil in the work, however, have been superseded by more complex readings aimed at discovering the meaning of the poem in relation to the cultural conditions found in India during the era between the Aryan conquest of the Indian subcontinent and prior to the advent of Buddhism there. Thus, the simple conflict between the powers of light and darkness is significant, but only part of the mythological picture of the poem. Other critics have examined the nature of the Hindu gods as literary figures and in comparison to western mythological systems, such as those of the ancient Greeks or medieval Scandinavians. Georges Dumézil, for instance, has employed as system of comparative mythology to describe similarities between the destruction of the great battle in the *Mahabharata* and the Norse myth of *Ragnorak,* or the end of the world. Joseph Campbell has outlined the poem's relation to other mythological systems and evaluated the symbolic conflict between truth and ignorance in the work. In addition to these comparative approaches, most scholars agree that the *Mahabharata* is primarily a collection and synthesis of hundreds of years of Hindu thought and spirituality.

## Literary Influence

The importance of the *Mahabharata* (and its companion piece, the *Ramayana* ) is almost unparalleled by that of any other literary work in India and elsewhere in Asia where Hinduism predominates. Likewise, as the highest form of the *purana,* or ''ancient tale,'' it is considered a work of art of the first magnitude, as well as an enlightening treatise on ethics, morality, and human behavior. In other parts of the world, in particular Europe and America, its influence has been much more diffuse. Some of its constituent stories, such as those of Nala and Savitri, are known, but the narrative as a whole has been somewhat neglected. Prose translations and abridgments of the poem, including the readable rendition of the poem in English by William Buck, have increased its accessibility to other cultures than that of its origin. Many commentators see the *Mahabharata* as a valuable historical and sociological document concerning Indian life in the period around 1000 BC. Thus, the poem has helped scholars to trace the impact of Aryan culture—with its social hierarchy and new philosophical ideas—on the indigenous peoples of the Indus river valley three thousand years ago, and to outline the development of Hindu thought in the centuries since.

# Criticism

## Sean McCready

*In the following essay, McCready discusses the role of* dharma, *sacred duty, on the characters in the poem, focusing primarily on the five Pandavas and also on Bhishma.*

The *Mahabharata* holds a place of special veneration in Indian society. An ancient tale, thousands of years old, it inspires poets, writers, and artists across the globe. Its creator is unknown, except as the

# What Do I Read Next?

- The hero of Virgil's *Aeneid,* the Trojan warrior Aeneas, departs from the Trojan War and wanders for seven years in the Mediterranean region because it has been foretold that he and what remain of his people are destined to found a great nation in Italy. He stays briefly in the North African city of Carthage, but his abruptly ended love affair with Queen Dido eventually leads to her suicide. Later, Aeneas travels to Italy where he defeats King Turnus and establishes a settlement along the Tiber River that eventually grows into the city of Rome. The *Aeneid* is a mythological glorification of the early Roman Empire and of Octavian, the emperor known as Augustus.

- A Irish epic tale from the first century BC, *The Cattle Raid of Cooley* describes an attack by Queen Mebd of Connacht on the kingdom of Ulster in order to steal its prized Brown Bull. Part of the Ulster cycle of legends, it features the Gaelic hero Cuchulain, a youth of great strength whose body and face contort horribly as he enters a rage before each battle. Alone, Cuchulain destroys Mebd's army, defeating one warrior per day until killed by her treachery.

- Achilles, the hero of Homer's epic poem the *Iliad,* refuses to fight for King Agamemnon and the invading Greeks at Troy. Without his strength the war will be lost, and so Achilles's friend Patroclus borrows his armor and shield and joins the battle, but is soon killed by the Trojan hero Hector. Overcome with grief and anger at his friend's death, Achilles and his men, the Myrmidons, join the attack, killing Hector, and bringing victory to the Greeks.

- Thomas Malory's *Le Morte d'Arthur* (1485, *The Death of Arthur*) describes the adventures of Arthur, legendary king of the Britons. Of mysterious birth, Arthur becomes king after receiving the magical sword, Excalibur, from the super-

natural figure of The Lady in the Lake. He later builds a mighty castle and attracts the greatest knights from France and the British Isles to his round table at Camelot. With the help of these warriors and the wizard Merlin, Arthur battles the evil sorceress Morgan Le Fay and his own upstart nephew, Sir Mordred.

- Niccolò Machiavelli's *The Prince* (1532) examines the means by which a ruler might consolidate and expand power. Recommending the use of cunning and even treachery, Machiavelli portrays rulership as a science that place kings above ordinary ethical considerations.

- The second great classical Indian epic poem is the *Ramayana.* Probably composed in about the third century BC, it details the life of Rama, the seventh incarnation of the god Vishnu. Attributed to the sage Valmiki—also a character in the poem—the *Ramayana* recounts Prince Rama's exile from the kingdom of Ayodhya and his rescue of his wife Sita from the demon Ravana. With the help of Hanuman and his army of monkeys, Rama saves Sita, kills the demon, and returns to his home.

- The poem "Song of Myself" from nineteenth-century American poet Walt Whitman's 1855 collection *Leaves of Grass* celebrates the symbolic unity of all people and places.

- Written during approximately the same period as the *Mahabharata,* the *Upanishads* contain philosophical meditations on the Hindu conceptions of reality, reincarnation, and Brahman—the universal soul.

- The 1989 novel *The Great Indian Novel,* by Shashi Tharoor, is a funny and entertaining retelling of the basic *Mahabharata* story, drawing events and characters from twentieth-century Indian life.

mythic figure of Vyasa, a poet and seer who appears in the verses he is supposed to have written. Likely the poem was authored by countless writers who grafted its many tales and moral stories onto the skeleton of this epic tale of the five Pandavas, five brothers. Foremost among these brothers is Yudhishthira, the eldest. He was born to be a king. A pillar of morality, intelligence, restraint, and confidence, he possesses a small weakness, his love of fortune. He is a gambler at heart, or else he longs to test his luck at the throw of the dice in order to escape from the walls of sacred duty that surround him. Yudhishthira is the model Hindu hero. He encapsulates the tenets of this great religion, and is so well-versed in them that they have become part of his soul—a soul that is immortal, destined to eternal joy in Indra's heaven. Still, Yudhishthira has a price to pay. He must lead his brothers in battle. He must fight the great war of the Bharatas, the *Mahabharata.*

Fortunately this Hindu king has his four brothers and their shared wife to accompany him. Bhima, a mighty warrior indeed with the strength of a dozen men or more, is a man of passions, yet faithful and steadfast. Bhima may be easily moved to revenge, but he always has a good justification for his actions. But when his rage is enflamed it is not easily quenched. He has a thirst for blood, a substance he spills more often than any other man, good or evil, in the poem. Arjuna, Yudhishthira's next brother, ultimately proves himself a warrior without equal. He possesses a skill with a bow so great that his foes tremble in his presence. Yet there exists a match for Arjuna, a mysterious soul named Karna. Karna is a brother of Yudhishthira and Arjuna, though they do not know it.

Karna suffers from the fact that his mother will not acknowledge him as her son and the half-brother of the Pandavas. Without such public acknowledgment, Karna has no choice but to honor his obligation to fight the Pandavas on the side of the Kauravas when asked to do so by the prince Duryodhana.

The twins Nakula and Sahadeva appear as reflections of their oldest brother. Without saying or doing as much as either Arjuna or Bhima, they exemplify the same restraint and quiet power that will one day restore Yudhishthira to the throne. And, finally, the wife of all five brothers, Draupadi. She is woman personified. Strong, noble, and beautiful, she matches each of her husbands in intelli-

gence, will, and respect for the sacredness of right action. She knows the ways of *dharma.*

For *dharma,* one's sacred duty, is truly the subject of the *Mahabharata.* Called a monstrosity by some critics because of its sheer size, the national epic of India nevertheless has a consistency of vision. Employing the numerous voices of varied storytellers, sages, priests, demons, and heroes, the poem describes the Hindu ideal of sacred duty. Similar ideas can be found in western philosophy. Plato's conception of the ideal state in *The Republic* placed each individual in his or her specific place in society, each with duties and responsibilities that assure happiness for everyone. The Greek philosopher also elaborated an idea of the transmigration of the soul, reincarnation or samsara. The ancient Indians knew of the existence of the Greeks, and quite possibly Plato and his predecessors received their ideas from the east without bothering to give credit for these acquisitions—as philosophers rarely do. The Indians, however, much more than the Greeks, seem to have had their vision fixed on preparations for the next world. Happiness in this life is an important good, but the *Mahabharata* calls to mind more important struggles of cosmic significance. The poem details an imbalance between the forces of chaos and order. Thus, the mighty god Vishnu, the Preserver, has once again appeared.

Hindu legend includes nine manifestations of Vishnu on earth, eight of which have occured by the time in which the *Mahabharata* is set (the incarnation as Krishna is in fact the eighth; the ninth has not yet appeared). Many of these are contained in the ancient stories, or *puranas,* attributed to the prolific poet Vyasa. In each instance the god has appeared to restore the careful balance of harmony and dissonance in the world. The *Mahabharata* represents the eighth and final visit of Vishnu. He takes the form of Krishna. Chief of the Yadavas, Krishna hails from western India, but is well known along the Ganges river in Kurujangala where the dispute between the Kauravas and the Pandavas takes place and escalates into a great cleansing war. Krishna represents wisdom and the true path of *dharma.* Therefore he does not engage in battle himself, but he makes his presence known. He drives Arjuna's chariot, and spurs the Pandava prince to fight, even though he will slaughter his kinsmen: Duryodhana, Karna, and many others. Krishna speaks the sacred words of Hindu law, reciting the *Bhagavad Gita,* a work known worldwide as the central text of Hindu doctrine. Scholars, likewise, have noted his affinities with Jesus Christ from the western religious tradition. He epitomizes truth, giving it a human form, and provides the *Mahabharata* with a spiritual center.

Still, the *Mahabharata* is a poem about human suffering and war. It requires a link between the spiritual and the worldly. It needs an individual that focuses the qualities of human sacrifice, follows the most difficult path of *dharma,* and explains the proper way to achieve success in this world and the next. This man is Bhishma. The celibate warrior, Bhishma renounces his birthright to the throne of Kurujangala in order that his father might satisfy his desire for a woman. He cannot die, except by his own choosing, and therefore is above the world of the flesh and indifferent to many of the baser motivations of human beings. He represents the observance of *dharma* on an almost superhuman level, without fear for his neglect of worldly pleasures. His spreads his wisdom even after he should be dead. Lying on a bed of arrows each of which pierces his body, Bhishma recites the ancient knowledge of rulership to Yudhishthira, thereby preparing the Pandava to be king. The irony, of course, is that the Bhishma might have made a greater king than any of the other men who sit on the throne of Kurujangala during the course of the poem. And, had he presided over Kurujangala in place of the weak-willed Dhritarashtra, the great war might never have been fought. All of this because his father wanted another woman.

Bhishma's total renunciation of desire and near flawlessness make him more a symbol than a real person. Tradition, however, requires internal struggle of the epic hero. Thus, Bhishma cannot provide the heroic center of the work. Vyasa reserved this role for Yudhishthira, Bhima, Arjuna, Nakula, Sahadeva, and Draupadi—a hero split into six important, if unequal, sections. As commentators have noted, these individuals represent the human in all of its capacities: thought, action, wisdom, mind, body, emotion, and will. Each of these characters contains these aspects of human nature mixed in different proportions. Bhima represents violent power and strength, Arjuna symbolizes skill and grace. Yet Bhima's strength sometimes becomes savagery, as when he drinks Duhsasana's blood. Likewise Arjuna doubts himself when called to fight his kinsmen in the great war. Yudhishthira, who combines the superb qualities of his brothers with wisdom and restraint, also suffers from very real defects. When gambling with Sakuni and

Duryodhana he loses everything that he owns. He even stakes his wife after he has already lost himself. The remainder of the *Mahabharata* can be interpreted as Yudhishthira's effort to regain what he has squandered, a process that results in incredible destruction. Yudhishthira has obeyed his *dharma* as a warrior in accepting the challenge of Duryodhana, but betrays the *dharma* of a king by allowing his kingdom to be lost in a game of dice. What truly has been lost is order, sacrificed to the randomness of dice rolls. Yudhishthira has forsaken the wisdom of order so that he might engage in a game of chance. In so doing he—a symbol of order—unleashes great chaos into the world. As Yudhishthira, the epic center of this immense poem, learns of his mistakes and conquers them, the wisdom of the *Mahabharata* unfolds.

**Source:** Sean McCready, for *Epics for Students,* Gale Research, 1997.

### Arun Kumar Mookerjee

*In the following excerpt, Mookerjee describes the* Mahabharata *as a record of the cultural life of India to the close of the Vedic-Aryan age, circa 1500–500 B.C., focusing specifically on the spiritual concept of dharma.*

The *Mahābhārata* is a *jayagrantha,* as is said in the *mangalācarana* (salutation to God before undertaking any task) as well as in the *Ādi Parva. Jaya* is a technical term for the whole of the eighteen *Purāna*(s), *Rāmāyana, Visnudharmaśāstra*(s), *Śivadharmaśāstra*(s), and the *Mahābhārata* (the "fifth Veda") composed by Vedavyasa Krsnadvaipāyana. Vaiśampāyana, a disciple of Vedavyāsa, recited the one hundred thousand verses of the *Mahābhārata* at Taksasīlā (now Taxila in Rawalpindi district, Pakistan) in the presence of King Janmejaya, great grandson of Arjuna. Without the episodic and didactic diversions, the story of the *Mahābhārata* extends to twenty-four thousand verses. A shortened form comprising one hundred and fifty verses was also written. Sauti Ugraśravā, a bard by profession, retold it in Naimisāranya (now Nimsar in Sitapur district of Uttar Pradesh) before the ascetics there who wanted to hear this "great history and great *śāstra*" in one book. Vedavyāsa says that the *Mahābhārata* "principally" records the rise of the Kuru dynasty, Gāndhārī's righteousness, Vidura's wisdom, and Kuntī's patience, Krsna's glory, the Pāndava(s)' adherence to Truth, and Duryodhana and his companions' ill treatment toward them. It was composed around an epic war that destroyed the Kuru dynasty.

[The] *Mahābhārata* is a document of the life and ideas of the people of India up to the turn of an epoch.

It gives us the picture of a highly complex society compared to that of the Vedas and *Rāmāyana.* Undoubtedly the *Mahābhārata* is guided by the *Manu Smrti* (canonical laws laid down by Manu), by the common and particular duties of the four *varna*(s) (Brahmin, Ksatriya, Vaiśya, and Śūdra) prescribed by it. Yet the society of the *Mahābhārata* appears to be very liberal. Drona and Aśvatthāmā were Brahmins turned Ksatriya(s). Yudhisthira tells his curse-stricken forefather Nahusat hat it has become difficult to decide the *varna* because of cross-marriages. A Brahmin must be truthful, benevolent, forgiving, honest, amiable, strictly religious, and kind. One who lacks these qualities is not a Brahmin. A Śūdra having these qualities is a Brahmin. Vidura was born of a Śūdra mother and neither in marriage nor in *varna* was ever given the status of Brahmin or Ksatriya or Vaiśya; and Dharmavyādha the hunter was born of Śūdra parents and yet was engaged in his traditional profession. Yet Vidura was not only a most pious man, an unstained character in the gallery of characters in the *Mahābhārata,* but he was held in high esteem by all—except, of course, Duryodhana, and was believed to be the God Dharma born as a man, on account of a curse given by an ascetic. And Kauśika the Brahmin took lessons in *dharma* from Dharmavyādha (*Vana Parva*).

Performing the duties of the station of life one belongs to by *trivarga* (*dharma, artha, kāma*) and ultimately attaining worthiness by *niskāma-karma* (duty for the sake of duty) or by *sa . nyāsa* (renunciation) man could attain *paramagati,* that is, salvation. It was by this faith and philosophy that the culture and society of the *Mahābhārata* flourished. Through all the vicissitudes of historical events the *Mahābhārata* carried this message of the good life, a life of duty as prescribed in the sacred books, and expressed a faith in human capability to achieve the greatest value in life. For over and above the differences in *varna,* profession, social placement, etc., it is the ethical being of man that stands supreme. The *Mahābhārata* is not a tragic record of the futility of man's life and purpose, a record of the holocaust of a fratricidal war. At the passing of the Vedic age, it liberalized the Brahmanic religion, disciplined life

and society by laying down prescriptions in the form of *rājadharma,* that is, a king's duties as well as the duties of a common householder, *moksadharma,* etc. The novelty of *Mahābhārata* is that all these duties of particular stations of life have not been made ends in themselves but subordinate to a concept of *dharma* . While the Vedas became the prerogative of the Brahmins and were thus closed to the larger section of the people, the *Mahābhārata* came as the fifth Veda surpassing the *Upanisad*(s) and four Vedas in scope and size and encompassing all their teachings. Bringing together for the people both the archaic and the historical material, it has given every Indian his cultural and historical identity. As *dharmaśāstra* it has revealed to man his duties and purpose in life. The epic war that it depicts may be regarded as a saga. In ferocity, suffering, and heroism, it was unrivaled. Only ten persons, seven on the Pāndava side and three on the Kaurava side survived. Magnificent heroes fought and fell on both sides. But what made all the difference was neither fate nor heroism but adherence to *dharma.* Gāndhārī said before the war that irrespective of advantages and disadvantages the balance of *dharma* was in favor of the Pāndava(s). The *Mahābhārata* is much more than a narration of an epic war. Throughout the ages it has taught a philosophy of life and practice. It has been a source of innumerable poetic creations in all ages, (*Abhijñāna Śākuntalam* of Kālīdāsa is only one example).

In a general way *dharma* means prescriptions, the observance of which keeps human beings from falling from the station of life or from their own true selves. This is what Krsna says in the *Mahābhārata.* Adherence to *dharma* protects men from evils created by men. This Sanskrit word, *dharma,*can be derived from the root *r* with *dhana* and *mak* as prefix and suffix respectively. It also is derived from the root *dhr* with *man* as suffix. In the *Mahābhārata* it has been used in both the senses. By the first, *dharma* is a means to attain *dhana,* that is, value, both material and spiritual. By the second derivation it means that which preserves creation and protects it from harm and bestows good. In a very important sense *dharma* is the law of both human and nonhuman existence, the *rta* in the *RgVeda.* The prescriptions define *dharma* in the human situation, for man's material and spiritual good. *Dharma* has two ways, one prescribes actions leading to the achievement of *artha* (the economic good) and *kāma* (the hedonistic good). It is *sakāmadharma,* that is, observance of *dharma* with desire for *artha* and *kāma*. *Dharma* with *artha* and *kāma* is called the *trivarga* and is prescribed for a householder. By *artha* is meant riches, might, skill, family, health, fame, and enjoyable objects. *Kāma* is enjoyment itself; it is desire for pleasure. To achieve *artha* and *kāma* by means other than the prescribed *dharma* is to commit a wrong—that is, sin. To acquire them in the prescribed way is good—that is, merit. *Dharma* in its other way is *niskāma*, that is, without a desire of anything for one's own. *Sakāmadharma* earns the performer merit to enjoy earthly and heavenly pleasures as long as the merit lasts. *Niskāma dharma* brings the performer salvation and breaks the chain of life and death. Thus it is said in the Vedas that we shall perform sacrifices (*yajña*) and drink *soma* to enjoy heaven; this is the practice of *sakāmadharma*. The heavenly pleasures will wear out in time for one to reenter the cycle of life and death.

Regarding the relative merit of *dharma, artha, kāma*, and *moksa*, there is a dialogue among Vidura and five Pāndava(s). Yudhisthira opened the dialogue by saying that with *dharma, artha,* and *kāma* is carried out our daily life. Of these three, which is superior to which? To this Vidura said that learning, asceticism and meditation (*tapasyā*), forgiveness, simplicity, kindness, truthfulness, and restraint are the elements of *dharma*. Taken severally, *dharma* is the highest value. *Artha* is subservient to *dharma*. *Kāma*, taken by itself, is inferior to the other two. Then Arjuna said that *artha* is the principal value because it is the aid to *karma*, pursuits of life like farming, trade, dairy, industry, etc. With *artha* one can achieve enjoyable objects in life, can perform the prescriptions of *dharma* in a better way. Also the motivation to acquire *artha* is very strong in man. Nakula and Sahadeva said that *dharma* and *artha* should go together. Man must adhere to *dharma* and earn *artha* without transgressing *dharma*. It will then be like nectar mixed with honey. With *dharma-artha* one should go for enjoyments of life. Bhīmasena's answer was a notable one. He said *kāma* or desire is the driving force of life. It is by desire for the pleasures of heaven that great sages are motivated and are engaged in religious performances, austerity, etc. It is by desire that the trader, the farmer, artists, and artisans are engaged in their respective professions. *Kāma* is the essence even in all our prescribed behaviors and our efforts at earning riches, fame, etc. *Dharma* and *artha,* that is, prescripts and riches, are useless without *kāma*. But it is best to pursue the *trivarga*, the "triple" value, that is, *dharma-artha-kāma*. To pursue only one of

them is worst, two only better. Thus, Bhīmasena is advocating *sakāmadharma,* though taken severally *kāma* is the best of the three values. An intriguing point in this discourse is that he is looking for a driving principle in our behavior of all kinds. This principle, he says, is *kāma,* desire or love for happiness and enjoyment, but at the same time he does not want to override *dharma,* that is, prescription.

Yudhsthira spoke last. *Moksa* is the highest value, he said. One should do the duties of his station of life without any self-seeking. This is practicing *dharma* with indifference to sin or merit, riches or poverty, pleasure or pain. Such is *niskāma dharma,* which alone can break the cycle of life and death, supersede merit and sin, and lead to salvation in the absolute (*moksa, brahmaprāpti*). Bhīsma also told them that *moksa* is the highest value for man (*parama purusārtha*). Quoting ancient tales, he told them that both pain and pleasure are transitory, one following the other in a causal cycle driven by persisting desire. Of the two—happiness gained by effort driven by desire and happiness gained by forsaking desire—the latter is preferable because it frees man from the cycle of pleasure and pain. Bhīsma said that once King Yayāti, one of the great forefathers of the Kurus, asked the sage Bodhya how he acquired the wisdom that gave him a quietude such that nothing could disturb him. Sage Bodhya replied that he learned from the tale of Pingalā the prostitute that hopes of desire brought pain and frustration; from the tale of the heron that killing for one's own pleasure invited antagonism from others; from the snake that there was no compulsion about building a home and that a mendicant should live without one; from the bee that an ascetic need not bother about food for living and that he could collect alms from the householders; from the tale of the arrow maker that if he did his job with necessary attention and devotion nothing could distract him, not even the presence of a king; from the tale of the maiden who threw away the extra bracelets because they were resounding too much that if one wanted to avoid disturbance one could get away from it by leaving the company. The teaching is that one can take to the *niskāma dharma* of *sa . nyāsa* (renunciation) and practice *yoga,* or one may take to the *niskāma dharma* of a *grhī* (householder, family man) that Vidura practiced. For others, it should be *trivarga, dharma-artha-kāma.* Bhīsma's instructions to Yudhisthira and others covered both.

The supreme teaching of the *Mahābhārata* is *dharma* in the sense of both *sakāma* and *niskāma dharma.* It taught King Yudhisthira how to become an ideal ruler. The fundamental point in these instructions was that a king was bound by law (*dharma,* prescriptions), and his commands were only rules of law. As a matter of *dharma,* a king must look to the welfare of his subjects, secure the kingdom from external attack, keep men to their stations of duty, decide carefully on war and peace, maintain a well-trained army and efficient police and intelligence services. If necessary, the king shall take to a scorched-earth policy in the face of an enemy attack. So long as one remains a king he should follow the *trivarga* guided by *dharma,* not by *kāma* as Bhīmasena had said, like an ideal householder. Then Bhīsma talked about the personal qualities that a king should have, like earning riches without cruelty, being brave without being a braggart, etc., and the qualities that a king must not have, such as showing charity to the greedy, trusting a man of ill will, indulgence in sex, etc. The king shall also be a shrewd ruler and shall put up a show as is necessary like actors. Pretension of friendship with a strong enemy and at the same time preparing secretly for war at an opportune moment against him was a valuable piece of advice that Bhīsma gave Yudhisthira as a matter of *dharma.* Bhīsma also gave such advice as abjuration of anger, adherence to truth, proper distribution of wealth and earning, forgiveness, having children by one's own wife, purity of thought and action, nonviolence, simplicity, and care for the dependents—the ninefold *dharma.* During the war Krsna told Arjuna that nonviolence (not to injure others) is a great *dharma* and that telling a lie is preferable to violence. In the same place he says that there is nothing greater than truth. In this context, Krsna's reply to Sanjaya, Dhrtarāstra's envoy to Yudhisthira just before the war broke out, is quite interesting.

Sanjaya, trying to dissuade Yudhisthira from war in the name of *dharma,* said that one who takes *dharma* as superior to *kāma* and *artha* is great. Desire for *artha* binds one to sorrow. Therefore, Yudhisthira, the champion of *dharma,* had better live by begging than killing such men as Drona, Asvatthāmā, Krpa, Salya, Vikarna, Duryodhana, Karna. War is evil, desire is a blemish on the pious soul. That war has no necessary connection with virtue or vice, but that war is unmitigated evil is evident from the fact that a senseless fellow or a sinner may win wealth by war while the sensible and virtuous may lose. Why should, therefore, Yudhisthira wage a war and leave the path of *dharma?* He must not be led by ill-advising minis-

ters. They are really his detractors in his journey to *moksa,* the highest *dharma.* To this Krsna replied that no one could abandon his station of duty. One must act, and act according to the injunctions, prescriptions of *dharma.* Knowledge for the sake of knowledge is really empty; it must guide action. The whole universe is in activity without respite, nothing is at rest. Indra is the king of gods because he is untiring in his care and concern for them and sticks to truth and *dharma,* looking to others before looking into his own happiness. Brhaspati is the supreme guru because he practices perfect reticence and rectitude. Yudhisthira is a Ksatriya and had his duties already prescribed. Along with study of scriptures and performances of religious rites he was engaged even more with arms. A Ksatriya living a good life of a householder would attain the merit of heaven if he fell in battle. Yudhisthira, called by the duty of his station in life, was going to war. He must get back his kingdom. As for *moksa,* he would attain it ultimately by pursuit of *niskāma dharma* and learning the scriptures and thereby living a holy life. No one could therefore accuse him of any deviation.

On his return Sanjaya told Dhrtarāstra that Yudhisthira, a perfect follower of *dharma* and well versed in scriptures and generous as a man, only wanted to get back the part of the kingdom that Dhrtarāstra had given him (although the entire Kuru kingdom legitimately belonged to him). To escape from one's station, that is, to neglect the duties that define a station of life in this creation, is a fall from one's true being. Arjuna was goaded to pick up arms again and fight by the Lord Krsna when the warrior became stricken by the thought of the Doom looming large and the thought of killing the near and dear ones. After the war Yudhisthira, in a melancholy mood, wanted to abandon his kingdom and take to a forest life. Bhīsma, Vyāsa, Krsna, and others consoling him in his sorrow nevertheless reminded him of his duties as a king. Krsna even told him that he, the *Dharmarāja* (Yudhisthira) was becoming too occupied with his personal sorrow and bereavements. (It reminds one of Rāma's deciding to abandon his beloved queen Sītā. Rāmachandra could very well abdicate the throne and live with Sītā like a common man, but Rāmachandra the king could not leave his place of duty on account of personal love and sorrow.) Only by fulfilling the obligations of his immediate station in life can man take the next step to his journey to salvation. Till the realization of *moksadharma,* man has to act and enjoy or suffer the fruits of his own acts. Charity, religious devotion, knowledge of the Vedas, composure, compassion, nonviolence, etc., help life flourish in *dharma* and help preserve the creation. Action negates action and thus man ultimately goes beyond pleasure and sorrow, friendship and enmity, sense of loss and gain, etc., and becomes indifferent to the vicissitudes of life, leading to self-realization and *moksa*. In this context one may remember what Yudhisthira himself had once told Draupadī during their hard days in the forest—that he did his duties without any expectation of return, observed charity, and performed religious rites because he should and that he did the duties of a householder by the prescriptions and by the ways shown by the virtuous. This he said when Draupadī complained, like an unbeliever in a moment of sorrow and distress, that *dharma* was not protecting one who would rather forsake her along with the brothers than deviate from the path of *dharma* . Then he told Draupadī that he himself caused the sorrow to them by his own acts. He had very well detected the fraud of Śakuni but lost his composure and was led to irrational acts by his anger, something that he should not have done.

It may appear paradoxical that the concept of *dharma* in the *Mahābhārata* teaches nonviolence yet does not consider war an evil, teaches truth along with deception, and so on. Critics of the ethics of the *Mahābhārata* have called it dubious and its great character Machiavellian. For did not Sanatsujāta, one of the twelve great teachers of *dharma,* say that an act of sin is a necessity where one must commit it for the sake of *dharma* itself? Does it not appear then that *dharma* and sin might go together? Instances can be multiplied. The incident of Drona's killing is often pointedly referred to. After the fall of Bhīsma, Drona was made the supreme commander and threatened to destroy the Pāndava army. To contain or rather eliminate him, a course of deception was devised and adopted at the insistence of Krsna. It was known beforehand that Drona could be killed only if he would involuntarily give up his arms at the loss of one dearest to him. Next to Arjuna, the dearest to this great guru was his son Aśvatthāmā. Bhīmasena, simple-minded as he was, killed the giant elephant of the same name which King Bhagadatta rode and started shouting that Aśvartthāmā was dead. Drona did not believe him, for he knew that his son was an invincible warrior like Arjuna. He asked Yudhisthira, the *Dharmarājā,* the champion of *dharma,* if it were true. Yudhisthira would not tell a lie, but Krsna pleaded with him. Reluctantly, Yudhisthira told the lie that Aśvatthāmā was dead. In grief Drona left

arms and armor and sat down with a will to die (*prāyopavesana*) a ritual suicide. Being thus vulnerable, he was killed.

One may also point to the four accusations made by Gāndhāri. It may be recalled that each day of the eighteen-day war when Duryodhana came to ask for the blessings of his mother he was told that victory would be on the side of *dharma.* Before the war broke out she gave her last warning that, other things being equal, the balance of *dharma* was on the side of the Pāndava(s). Therefore her accusations bore weight. She said that Bhīmasena, encouraged by Krsna, hit Duryodhana below the belt to kill him and win; that Arjuna without any warning cut off the right arm of King Bhurisravā engaged in fighting Sātyaki (the great Yadu warrior); that Sātyaki killed the incapacitated Bhurisravā when the latter had abandoned arms and sat down with a will to die; and that Krsna was indifferent to the fate of the Kuru dynasty (Pāndava(s) and sons of Dhrtarāstra are all Kurus) in this self-annihilating war, even though he and he alone could stop it, if necessary, by force. Gāndhārī cursed him that he would be instrumental in a similar destruction of his own people, the Yadus. Incidentally, the same accusation was made against Krsna by sage Uttanka. Yet the epic war of *Mahābhārata* was said to be a war for the sake of *dharma,* and the Pāndava(s) deservedly won it. How can we explain that in spite of her grief over the death of her sons and the massive destruction on both sides and the four very legitimate accusations, Gāndhārī had no doubt that the Pāndava(s) had won a war of *dharma?*

This great concept of *dharma* delineated in the *Mahābhārata* deserves indeed more careful attention than a passing remark. *Dharma* and rules of morality are different, and they may or may not go together. Violation of a moral rule does not necessarily imply a deviation from *dharma,* though there is a necessity the other way. *Dharma* commands absolute obligation, whereas the rules of morality are contingent on their situation of application. In a case where violation of rule is also a violation of *dharma* and calls for punishment, it is retributive in nature: the suffering clears the guilt to bring back the person to the path of *dharma.* When it is said that truth is the locus of *dharma,* this Truth does not mean the same thing as truth-telling. Bhīsma tells Yudhisthira that Truth is the highest *dharma,* and it has thirteen elements—impartiality, control of the senses, absence of avarice, forgiveness, modesty, endurance, freedom from envy, generosity, contemplation, simplicity, patience, kindness, and nonviolence. Upon these rests *dharma.* Moral rules are related to merit and sin, *dharma* with *moksa,* that is, salvation. Some of the moral rules are, in fact, rules of *dharma.* As specific laws they replace the general ones in specific cases.

Krsna says that the Vedic prescriptions are the main source of *dharma.* But one may have to decide about *dharma* in a given case not covered by the Vedic injunctions. Here one must decide starting from the premise that *dharma* makes possible the rise and prosperity of the people, ameliorates sufferings, and ultimately leads to *moksa.* Bhīsma says that the injunctions of the Vedas, the *smrti* (canonical scriptures), and ways of the pious men (*śistācāra* ) show the path of *dharma.* In case of doubt, these three again shall be the means of right decision. For the common people, of course, the ways of the pious and virtuous men are the best. The hunter's sermon to Kauśika the Brahmin, retold to Yudhisthira by Mārkandeya elucidates the meaning of *śistācāra* (way of the pious men). Performance of religious rites (*yajña*), charity, meditation, reading scriptures, and behavior in accordance with truth are the marks of piety. The pious abjures pleasure, anger, deceit, greed, crookedness and remain contented in the way of *dharma.* The essence of the Vedas is the element of truth; the essence of truth is control of the senses; the essence of the control of sense is the sacrifice of self-interest. All these three are eminently characteristic of pious men.

**Source:** Arun Kumar Mookerjee, ''Dharma as the Goal: The Mahabharata,'' in *Hindu Spirituality: Vedas through Vendanta,* edited by Krishna Sivaraman, Crossroad, 1989, pp. 127–47.

## *B. A. van Nooten*

*In the following excerpt from an introduction to William Buck's prose retelling of the* Mahabharata, *van Nooten outlines the story told in the epic work, provides some historical background to the period portrayed in this epic, and discusses the systems of morality, eschatology (a branch of theology), and philosophy that underlies and informs the action.*

The *Mahabharata* is the story of a dynastic struggle, culminating in an awesome battle between two branches of a single Indian ruling family. The account of the fight between the Kurus and the Pandavas for the fertile and wealthy land at the confluence of the Yamuna and Ganges rivers near Delhi is enhanced by peripheral stories that provide a social, moral, and cosmological background to the climactic battle.

We do not know exactly when the battle took place. The *Mahabharata* (pronounced with the stress on the third syllable: mahabhárata) was composed over a period of some four hundred years, between the second century B.C. and the second century A.D., and already at that time the battle was a legendary event, preserved in the folk tales and martial records of the ruling tribes. The Indian calendar places its date at 3102 B.C., the beginning of the Age of Misfortune, the Kaliyuga, but more objective evidence, though scanty and inferential, points to a date closer to 1400 B.C.

At that time Aryan tribes had just begun to settle in India after their invasion from the Iranian highlands. The land from western Pakistan east to Bihar and south not farther than the Dekkhan was occupied by Aryan tribes whose names are often mentioned in records much older than the *Mahabharata.* The tribal communities varied in size and were each governed by the ''prominent families'' (*mahakulas*) from among which one nobleman was consecrated king. The kings quarreled and engaged in intertribal warfare as a matter of course, their conflicts were sometimes prolonged affairs, sometimes little more than cattle raids.

It is in this context that the Bharata war took place. The Kurus were an ancient tribe who had long been rulers of the area in the upper reaches of the Yamuna River. The Pandus, or Pandavas, were a newly emergent clan living in Indraprastha, some sixty miles southwest of the Kuru capital, Hastinapura. According to the *Mahabharata,* the new aristocrats were invited to the court of the ancient noble house of Kuru to engage in a gambling contest. There they were tricked first out of their kingdom and then into a promise not to retaliate for twelve years. In the thirteenth year they took refuge at the court of the Matsyas, where they allied themselves with the Kurus' eastern and southern neighbors, the Pancalas. Together in a vast host they marched up to Hastinapura, where they were met on Kuruksetra, the plain of the Kurus. Here the Kurus and their allies were defeated.

In bare outline that is the story of which the bard sings. But the composer of the *Mahabharata* has portrayed the actions of the warriors in both a heroic and a moral context, and it should be understood as a re-enactment of a cosmic moral confrontation, not simply as an account of a battle. Unlike our Western historical philosophy, which looks for external causes—such as famine, population pressure, drought—to explain the phenomena of war and conquest, the epic bard views the events of the war as prompted by observances and violations of the laws of morality. The basic principle of cosmic or individual existence is dharma. It is the doctrine of the religious and ethical rights and duties of each individual, and refers generally to duty ordained by religion, but may also mean simply virtue, or right conduct. Every human being is expected to live according to his dharma. Violation of dharma results in disaster.

Hindu society was classed into four castes, each with its own dharma. The power of the state rested with the *Ksatriyas:* kings, princes, free warriors and their wives and daughters. Their dharma was to protect their dependents, rule justly, speak the truth, and fight wars. The priest caste was not socially organized in churches or temples, but consisted of individual *Brahmans* in control of religion. Among their other duties, they officiated at great sacrifices to maintain the order of the world and accomplish desired goals. They were also in control of education, could read and write, and taught history according to their outlook on life. The *Mahabharata* in its final form was largely the work of a Brahman composer, so we find in the peripheral stories an emphasis on the power and glory of the Brahman caste, although in the main story of the epic there is not one powerful Brahmin. The *Vaisyas,* of whom we hear little in the *Mahabharata,* were merchants, townspeople, and farmers, and constituted the mass of the people.

The three upper castes were twice-born: once from their mothers and once from their investitures with the sacred thread. The lowest caste, the *Sudras,* did menial work and served other castes. They were Aryans, however, and their women were accessible to higher-caste men: Vyasa was the offspring of a ksatriya and a sudra, and so was Vidura. Outside the caste system were the ''scheduled castes,'' the tribal people of the mountains, such as the Kiratas, as well as the Persians and the Bactrian Greeks.

Besides their caste dharma, people had a personal dharma to observe, which varied with one's age and occupation. So we find a teacher-student dharma, a husband-wife dharma, the dharma of an ascetic, and so on. One's relation to the gods was also determined by dharma. The lawbooks specify the various kinds of dharma in detail, and this classifications and laws still govern Indian society.

The Hindu system of eschatology is often expounded in the *Mahabharata.* In brief, it is the doctrine of the cycle of rebirths (*samsara* ), the doctrine of the moral law (dharma), which is more powerful than even the gods. The moral law sustains and favors those creatures that abide by it, while thwarting those that trespass. Its instrument is *karma,* the inexorable law that spans this life and the afterdeath, working from one lifetime to another, rewarding the just and making the evil suffer. In this Hindu universe those in harmony with dharma ultimately reach a state in which rebirth is not necessary any more. If, however, the forces of evil are too strong, the moral law reasserts itself and often uses forceful means to restore harmony where it has been lost. To accomplish that, often a being of a higher order, a god, who in his usual manifestation has no physical body, takes birth among the people and becomes an *avatara,* a ''descent'' of his own power on earth. Often the physical manifestation is not aware of his divine antecedents, but discovers them in the course of his life on earth. Therefore an avatara has many human qualities, including some that by our own standards would be less than divine: hostility, vengefulness, and an overweening sense of self-importance. These qualities are necessary for him to confront confidently the forces of evil, the *asuras,* who have taken flesh also and appear as bitter enemies committed to a battle to the end.

The emphasis on morality in the *Mahabharata* brings with it considerations of the nature of the divine. There are many gods; the Indian pantheon is overwhelming in its diversity and vagueness. At the highest level of creation are the gods (*devas*), who are in continual conflict with the demonic forces, the asuras. Among the gods, Visnu, Siva, and Indra are especially important. Visnu is mainly manifest through his incarnation as Krisna. He is a supreme god worthy of love and devotion. Siva is also a supreme god, but represents the ascetic side of Indian religion. He dwells on a mountain, dresses in a tiger skin, and wears a characteristic emblem, the trident, still carried by Indian mendicants. The third eye in the middle of Siva's forehead scorches his enemies. Indra is in name the king of the gods, but in fact his importance had declined by the time of the *Mahabharata,* although he remained a principle god. In the *Mahabharata* he is the god of rain and father of Arjuna, a Pandava.

Less powerful are the elemental gods of fire (Agni), wind (Vayu), water (Varuna), sun (Surya), and moon (Soma). Kama is the god of love. Unlike the gods in Western mythologies, the prominent Indian gods are difficult to characterize. Although they are assigned obvious functions as powers, their spheres of power and their characteristics overlap because they are ultimately all manifestations of the universal principle, Brahman, the universal soul or being to which individual souls will be reunited after the illusion of time and space has been conquered.

At a lower level, still divine but progressively less lofty, are the hosts of the Gandharvas, Apsarases, Siddhas, Yaksas, and Raksasas. The first three classes are usually benevolent to mankind. Gandharvas play heavenly music to which the nymphs, the Apsarases, dance. Indra also uses the Apsarases to seduce ambitious ascetics who, by their severe selfcastigation, have accumulated so much spiritual power that it becomes a threat to Indra's supremacy; as a result of seduction the anchorite loses his power. Yaksas are sprites, dryads, and naiads. Raksasas are malevolent demons who prowl around the sacrificial altars or in other ways disturb human beings.

Humans look at the gods as powers to be appeased or controlled, with the exception of Visnu, who is simply adored, Gods often interact with humans, marry them, give them weapons, invoke their assistance or aid them. At times gods interact with men through the intermediary of wise old men, sages whose advice was obeyed by prudent warriors who would not violate the will of the gods in order to avoid incurring the sage's curse. Upon his death, the ancient hero expects to go to Indra's heaven, where there is feasting and rejoicing.

Rivers and other landscape features are personified and function as both divine or semi-divine beings and as natural phenomena. In the *Mahabharata* gods communicate with men, animals talk and are sometimes real animals, sometimes human beings or gods. The story often moves into an idealized land where heroic feats, deeds of valour and physical strength are regarded with awe and fear. These incidents foster a sense of marvel in the reader: we are transported into an idyllic world where illusion and reality cannot be separated.

The *Mahabharata* should be understood as a moral and philosophical tale as well as an historical one. Only in this way can we appreciate the significance of the *Bhagavadgita,* the Song of the Lord, which is part of the *Mahabharata,* but which is usually excerpted and read as an independent religious work. In India, the *Mahabharata* as a whole has been regarded for centuries as a religious work, to awesome battles and gruesome deaths as tragic yet natural events in human experience, these are just a

few of the features that have found response in the hearts of millions of Asian people.

**Source:** B. A. van Nooten, in an introduction to *Mahabharata ,* by William Buck, University of California Press, 1973, pp. xiii–xxiii.

# Sources for Further Study

Buck, Philo M. ''Kama, Karma, and Nirvana,'' in *The Golden Thread,* The Macmillan Company, 1931, pp. 186-211.
Investigates the cultural and religious backgrounds of the *Mahabharata.*

Buck, William, reteller. *Mahabharata,* University of California Press, 1973, 417 p.
A highly readable prose adaptation and abridgment of the epic poem. Although Buck makes some minor adjustments and interpolations in the story, his translation is vivid and compelling.

Campbell, Joseph. ''The Indian Golden Age,'' in *The Masks of God: Oriental Mythology,* 1962. Reprint by Penguin Books, 1976, pp. 321-70.
Discusses the nature of Vyasa, the mythical author of the *Mahabharata,* and the symbolic conflict between the forces of light and darkness in the work.

Murdoch, John. *The Mahabharata: An English Abridgment with Introduction, Notes, and Review,* 1898. Reprint by Asian Educational Services, 1987, 160 p.
Offers comprehensive prose outlines of both the story and secondary material within the *Mahabharata.* Additionally includes background historical and cultural information, as well as critical commentary on the work.

Stone, Charles. ''Historical Suggestions in the Ancient Hindu Epic, the *Mahabharata,''* *Transactions of the Royal Historical Society,* Vol. II, 1885. Reprint by Kraus Reprint, 1971, pp. 272-92.
Overview of the historical contexts surrounding the composition of *Mahabharata.*

Sukthankar, V. S. *On the Meaning of the Mahabharata,* The Asiatic Society of Bombay, 1957, 146 p.
Interprets the *Mahabharata* on three levels: the mundane, the ethical, and the transcendental.

Tharoor, Shashi. *The Great Indian Novel,* Arcade Publishing, 1989.
Modern retelling of the *Mahabharata* with a cast of characters and events drawn from twentieth-century Indian political and cultural life.

Van Buitenen, J. A. B. Introduction to *The Mahabharata: The Books of the Beginning, Vol. I,* edited and translated by J. A. B. van Buitenen, The University of Chicago Press, 1973, pp. xiii-xlviii.
Analyzes the narrative structure of the *Mahabharata* as an intricate, but cohesive whole.

Van Nooten, Barend A. *The Mahabharata,* Twayne Publishers, Inc., 1971, 153 p.

Full-length study of the *Mahabharata,* including chapters on its narrative structure, language, influence, and critical history.

———. ''The Sanskrit Epics,'' in *Heroic Epic and Saga: An Introduction to the World's Great Folk Epics,* edited by Felix J. Oinas, Indiana University Press, 1978, pp. 49-75.
Examines the narrative structure and language of the *Mahabharata* and another great Indian epic, the *Ramayana.*

Winternitz, Moriz. ''The Popular Epics and the Puranas,'' in his *A History of Indian Literature, Vol. I,* translated by S. Ketkar, revised edition, 1926. Reprint by University of Calcutta, 1962, pp. 273- 416.

Surveys the range of stories and legends as well as non-fictional matter included in the text of the *Mahabharata.*

Wolpert, Stanley. ''North Indian Conquest and Unification (ca. 1000-450 BC),'' in his *A New History of India,* third edition, Oxford University Press, 1989, pp. 37-54.
Explores the period of Indian history, culture, and philosophy reflected in the *Mahabharata.*

Zaehner, R. C. Introduction to *Hinduism,* second edition, Oxford University Press, 1966, pp. 1- 13.
Zaehner provides an overview of Hinduism and notes its relation to the *Mahabharata.*

# Nibelungenlied

## Anonymous

## c. 1200

The *Nibelungenlied* is a German epic poem which was written sometime around 1200, probably in what is today Austria. The title means "Song of the Nibelungs." "Nibelungen" is the plural of "Nibelung," which refers to a dynasty which is conquered by the hero or protagonist of the epic, the dragon-slayer Siegfried. The word "lied" means "lay," which is a Germanic word for a song, poem, or lyric. The poem exists in more than thirty manuscripts, but three main versions represent the story as we know it. For the purposes of study, many modern editions are translated in prose rather than rhymed poetic form to be more accessible to students.

Reasons why the *Nibelungenlied* has enjoyed such a wide readership for so many centuries include: much is known about the historical context of the poem as well as about the literary sources it drew on, including mythology and legend. The story is one of heroes, romance, courtly manners, deception, and revenge. It has been enjoyed by many readers for its literary techniques and for its adventurous qualities and complex characters as well.

The *Nibelungenlied* combines elements of many different historical, legendary, and mythological tales. The legend of the Nibelungs arose from the historical destruction of the Burgundian kingdom on the Rhine River by Etzel's army of Huns (later identified in legend with the army of Attila the Hun) around the year 437. Many other characters in the *Nibelungenlied* have some historical basis as well.

Gunther was King of Burgundy, and Dietrich is thought to be based on Theodoric the Ostrogoth, who was King of Italy in 493. The events in the poem, however, were altered and combined with other legends when the story was first written down for a medieval audience around 1200.

The *Nibelungenlied* and the legends it was based on existed in oral form long before it was ever written down. A version of the *Nibelungenlied* was first translated into modern German in 1757 under the title of *Kriemhild's Revenge.* Many more versions followed, but no English translation appeared until 1814. The first complete English prose version appeared in 1848. There have been many more, in both prose and verse form.

The *Nibelungenlied,* as an epic, celebrates the achievements, adventures, and battles of several heroic figures. It also encompasses elements of the romance genre as well, and includes tales of knights, courtly behavior, and chivalry. The *Nibelungenlied* draws on history, mythology, and legend for its details. It encompasses themes such as heroism, feudalism, justice and revenge, honor, loyalty, deception, dreams, and the importance of ''keeping up appearances.''

The ''meaning'' of the *Nibelungenlied* is difficult to determine. It does not have a clearly-defined moral message for the reader. However, it raises important questions about the nature of loyalty, honor, and what constitutes tragedy. It also attracts study and commentary purely on the basis of its accomplished literary features, such as its structure, character development, and the use of foreshadowing. The *Nibelungelied* poet combined disparate material and stories into a comprehensive whole that captures modern readers no less than audiences of eight hundred years ago.

## Author Biography

The author of the *Nibelungenlied* is not known. The author is thought to have been male, possibly an Austrian from the Danube region, either a minstrel poet (a travelling poet or one associated with a court), a knight, or a clergyman associated with court life. Some critics express doubt that the author was a knight, primarily because the epic does not contain convincing or extensive details about military skill and technique, despite the numerous battle scenes. Critics believe that the ''final'' version of the poem was written by only one author because of its consistency in tone, language, and action. It was conventional at the time not to sign literary works. In fact, many written work that survive from the Middle Ages (the years 500 through 1500, approximately) are anonymous.

## Plot Summary

### Chapter 1

The *Nibelungenlied* opens with an exhortation to the reader to expect a tale of brave knights and furious battles. The main site of the action is the land of the Burgundians, which is ruled by the three brothers Gunther, Gernot, and Giselher. They have a beautiful sister, Kriemhild, and live in the city of Worms (pronounced ''Voorms'') on the Rhine River. Their mother is called Uote, and their deceased father was named Dancrat.

We also learn in this chapter that Kriemhild dreamed that a falcon she had raised was attacked and torn to pieces by two eagles. Her mother Uote suggests that the falcon in the dream is a noble man that Kriemhild loves who will be torn away from her. Kriemhild says that rather than risk such a loss, she will never marry. The narrator ends the chapter by warning that the dream foretells a great tragedy which will befall the Burgundians.

### Chapter 2

We are introduced to another city, Xanten in the Netherlands, where the royal family of King Siegmund, his wife Sieglind, and their son Siegfried live and rule. Siegfried is described as handsome, brave, honorable, and an expert knight. Siegmund holds a lavish feast and festival honoring the knighting of his son and a host of other young warriors. The description of the festival, and of Siegmund's generous gifts of money, jewels, and clothing, is elaborate and detailed.

### Chapter 3

Siegfried hears of the beauty of the Burgundian princess Kriemhild, and decides to win her hand in marriage. His father and mother are not happy to hear this at first, for Kriemhild's brothers are reputed to be fearsome warriors. Siegmund himself does not relish the possibility of war with the Burgundians if they oppose the Xanten prince's suit, but he will not be deterred.

*Siegfried and the dragon, from an 1841 illustration.*

Siegfried and his knights travel to Worms. The Burgundian knight Hagen recognizes Siegfried, and shares what he knows about the Xanten prince's reputation: Siegfried is known to have slain the two Nibelung princes (''Nibelung'' here is the name of a dynasty or powerful, long-established family) and to have won their great treasure, including a magic cloak which makes the wearer invisible. Siegfried also once killed a dragon and bathed in its blood. As a result, he cannot be harmed by weapons. Therefore, says Hagen, Siegfried must be welcomed as a special guest.

Siegfried is greeted hospitably, and offers words of great flattery to Gunther and his men. However, his words contain a veiled threat: he indicates that he wishes to possess all that the Burgundians now have! Siegfried challenges Gunther to a battle, proposing that the loser give up his kingdom to the winner. Gernot and Hagen object that Siegfried has challenged Gunther without provocation. Gernot intervenes and convinces the two that little honor is to be gained from such an endeavor. A war is barely averted.

Gernot now officially welcomes Siegfried with true courtesy and offers him the full hospitality of Worms, provided he behave honorably. Siegfried does not reveal his true reason for visiting Worms until much later. Siegfried and his men are given the best accommodations, and proceed to take part in many social events, ncluding sporting contests, war games, and hunting. Siegfried outshines all the participants in each and every endeavor.

Siegfried does not see Kriemhild, who is kept in seclusion, but he cherishes his thoughts of her. He does not know that she is watching from her window as he competes against the knights of her own kingdom, and is falling in love with him. Siegfried lives with the Burgundians for a year without ever seeing her.

## *Chapter 4*

Gunther and the Burgundians receive more surprise visitors—envoys from King Liudegast of Denmark and his brother King Liudeger of Saxony. The Burgundians are informed that the kings intended to invade Burgundy in twelve weeks. When told of the impending invasion, Siegfried pledges his aid, and Gunther accepts the offer. The envoys are informed that forces have been gathered and that the Burgundians are ready to receive the invaders.

When the envoys arrive home and tell King Liudegast that Siegfried of the Netherlands has allied with the Burgundians, he and King Liudeger summon over 40,000 troops. Meanwhile, Gunther gathers his own forces. Siegfried asks Gunther to remain behind at Worms so that he might fight the battle. The Burgundians, led by Siegfried, ride through Hesse toward Saxony, destroying enemy towns and villages along the way.

When the main forces meet in battle, Siegfried captures both King Liudegast and King Liudeger. The Burgundians also take many other Saxon prisoners, and bring the wounded back to Worms to be cared for. Most of the Danes return to Denmark, defeated. Gunther rides out to meet the returning army, and learns of the Burgundian victory. Everyone is welcomed; even the prisoners are received like honored guests. King Liudeger promises to remain with his captured troops until they are given leave to return home. Gunther dismisses the troops of warrior-vassals who had gathered to fight for Burgundy along with Siegfried, asking them to return in six weeks for a great feasts. Gunther asks Siegfried to remain in Worms, and Siegfried agrees because of his secret love for Kriemhild.

### Chapter 5

The promised festivities are underway. The narrator tells us that Gunther has noticed Siegfried's secret devotion to Kriemhild, and arranged for Kriemhild and their mother Uote to join the celebration. Gunther introduces Kriemhild and Siegfried, and the narrator dwells at length on their immediate attraction to one another.

The Danes return home after asking for a pledge of peace between themselves and the Burgundians. Gunther agrees. Siegfried again plans to leave, but young Giselher asks him to remain at Worms. Again, Siegfried does so in hopes of winning Kriemhild's hand.

### Chapter 6

Gunther, having heard of many beautiful maidens in other lands, decides to win one for his wife. One particular queen, Brunhild of Iceland, is very famous for her great physical strength and beauty. Her suitors are expected to engage in three tests of strength agains her in order to win her hand. Those who do not outmatch her lose their heads. Gunther is determined to win Brunhild, and Siegfried agrees to help him in his quest if in exchange he is permitted to marry Kriemhild. Gunther agrees.

### Chapter 7

The Burgundians arrive at Brunhild's kingdom. Siegfried pretends to be Gunther's vassal, or liegeman (a servant or subordinate to a noble person) and speaks on his behalf, praising his lord and explaining that they have come so that Gunther might win Brunhild as his wife. Brunhild explains the tests which he must undergo to win her: Gunther must "cast the weight" (a heavy boulder which twelve men can barely lift); perform a leap (a type of long-jump); and throw a javelin (a long spear). Gunther accepts the challenge.

As Gunther takes part in each event, Siegfried secretly helps him while wearing his magic cloak of invisibility. Together they defeat Brunhild, who grudgingly accepts Gunther as her husband and king, and joins her kingdom to his. A feast and games follow, and Siegfried leaves to visit the land of the Nibelungs, which he earlier conquered.

### Chapter 8

When Siegfried arrives at the land of the Nibelungs, of whose great treasure and lands he is

*An 1883 depiction of Siegfried slaying the dragon.*

lord, he is challenged by the gatekeeper and a fight ensues. Siegfried wins and binds his attacker; news of the event spreads quickly. Alberich, the dwarf from whom Siegfried had taken the magic cloak, arrives and attacks Siegfried, whom he has not recognized. Siegfried wins again, and ties up Alberich. Realizing who his captor is, Alberich is relieved, and welcomes him.

When the Nibelungs arrive at Iceland, Brunhild is surprised, but welcomes them. The Burgundians prepare to return to Worms with Brunhild as queen.

### Chapter 9

On their journey home, Siegfried is asked to travel ahead to tell of the good news so that all might be ready to welcome Gunther's new bride. Gifts are prepared for Brunhild, and when Gunther and his company arrive a ceremonious entourage is ready to welcome them.

### Chapter 10

Kriemhild, Uote and all the king's vassals are standing by to greet those arriving. Brunhild is welcomed by Kriemhild with special attention, and the two queens at first seem destined to be friends. A wedding party is held, with games and a wonderful feast. Siegfried reminds Gunther of his oath to allow him to marry Kriemhild, and Gunther happily complies. Gunther tells Kriemhild of his wish, she gladly accepts, and the two are married at once. Brunhild is surprised that Gunther intends to let his sister marry Siegfried, since she believes what he told her in her own country: that Siegfried is only a vassal of the prince, and therefore not really an appropriate husband for a princess.

When Gunther and Brunhild retire for their wedding night, Gunther learns that Brunhild intends to remain a virgin. When he attempts to embrace her, she becomes enraged. She uses her great physical strength to tie him up and hang him from a hook on the wall, where she leaves him until morning, taking him down just before attendants enter the room the next morning, in order to spare him the embarrassment of the whole court finding out that he was overpowered by his new wife.

The next morning Gunther tells Siegfried of the humiliation he suffered. Siegfried, whose own wedding night had been quite enjoyable, offers to use his magic cloak again to help Gunther consummate his marriage, promising that he will not take advantage of the situation for his own sexual pleasure. That night, when Brunhild again resists Gunther's advances, the invisible Siegfried intervenes. He violently fights with and subdues Brunhild, holding her helpless on the bed for Gunther. Siegfried takes a girdle (a belt or any garment that encircles the waist) of silk and a golden ring from Brunhild before he returns to his own chamber, where Kriemhild waits. She is suspicious about where he has been, but he avoids her questions. He gives her the silken belt and the ring, but does not tell her where he got them. Meanwhile, Brunhild realized that with her virginity she has lost her physical strength as well, and is now no more powerful that any other woman.

This episode can be offensive to a late twentieth-century reader. However, according to the traditions of the era in which the *Nibelungenlied* was written, it was considered seriously wrong—perverse and unwomanly—of Brunhild to refuse to consummate her marriage with Gunther. As disturbing as it is to a modern sensibility, Gunther's virtual rape of his new bride was viewed as his right and as the logical next step after she refused to submit to him. As later events show, however, the involvement of his friend Siegfried is questionable, even within the context of the times.

## Chapter 11

Siegfried and Kriemhild prepare to return to the Netherlands, but not before Gunther, Giselher, and Gernot arrange to grant them the lands that are part of Kriemhild's inheritance. (Brunhild is not present at this exchange, and scholars have suggested that is perhaps because she would then have realized that Siegfried is certainly not Gunther's vassal.) They are welcomed at Siegfried's home with open arms, and King Siegmund crowns Siegfried as king on the spot. The narrator skims quickly over the next several months, telling the reader only that Siegfried and Kriemhild have a son whom they name Gunther after his uncle. In the meantime, Brunhild gives birth to a son as well, whom she and Gunther name Siegfried.

## Chapter 12

Brunhild has been wondering why so much time has passed since Siegfried rendered his "lord" Gunther any tribute (money paid regularly by a vassal to a lord, usually in exchange for the use of land and military protection). She keeps her thoughts to herself, however, and asks Gunther to invite Siegfried and Kriemhild for a visit. Gunther initially objects, claiming it is too far for them to travel. Brunhild reminds Gunther of Siegfried's obligations as a royal vassal (Gunther does not contradict her) and says that she wishes to see Kriemhild again. When the invitation reaches them, Kriemhild is anxious to visit her homeland. Siegfried accepts the invitation, but brings along his father and many warriors.

## Chapters 13 and 14

Siegfried and Kriemhild arrive in Burgundy. A great feast is held and war games are played. Tension develops between Brunhild and Kriemhild. Each boasts of the bravery and honor of her respective husband. Brunhild objects to Kriemhild's boast. Kriemhild does not at first understand Brunhild's objection, because she does not realize that Brunhild still believes that Siegfried is Gunther's vassal. When Brunhild explains herself, Kriemhild denies it, and states that the true nature of Siegfried and Gunther's relationship is one of equals. The argument becomes quite heated as both claim higher status than the other. When Brunhild tries to prevent Kriemhild from entering a cathedral ahead of her, saying that her own higher status means that she should enter first, Brunhild angrily tells her that she is no better than a paramour, or mistress, and that Siegfried and not her own husband was the first to be intimate with her. The narrative never indicates either that Siegfried had sexual contact with Brunhild or that either Siegfried or Gunther ever told Kriemhild how Siegfried used his magic cloak to help Gunther subdue Brunhild. However she came by the knowledge, Kriemhild does produce, as proof, the golden ring that Siegfried took from Brunhild.

Brunhild demands to know the truth from Gunther. Siegfried denies having compromised Brunhild's honor and even publicly criticizes his own wife Kriemhild for saying such things. Gunther accepts Siegfried's word and is prepared to forget the matter. Hagen, however, promises Brunhild that he will punish Siegfried for her public humiliation (although nothing has been proven), and he and his knights plot Siegfried's death. Gunther tries to prevent the plot, but finally agrees to take part in Hagen's plan. The narrator concludes Chapter 14 by deploring the fact that events have started that will end in the deaths of many men because of "the wrangling of two women."

## Chapter 15

Kriemhild asks Hagen to protect her husband, not knowing that it is he who has sworn to avenge his liege lady's honor by causing Siegfried's death. She also calmly admits that Siegfried beat her for publicly humiliating Brunhild. Hagen asks Kriemhild how he should protect him, that is, where Siegfried's weak spot is. She tells him that Siegfried has one tender part on his body, between his shoulder blades. As the narrator tells us, she thinks she is saving her husband's life, but in fact she is inadvertently giving Hagen the means to kills him.

## Chapter 16

The knights prepare to go hunting. Kriemhild is deeply troubled, apparently because of her indiscretion to Hagen. She describes to Siegfried a dream she had the night before, in which two boars chase her husband through a field of blood-colored flowers. Siegfried promises he will return from the day's hunt. Kriemhild describes a second dream, in which two mountains fall upon and kill Siegfried. He does not take her concerns seriously.

The narrator describes the hunt in great detail (hunting is an important and noble sport in the Middle Ages). Siegfried kills many beasts in a great show of bravery and skill. Then Siegfried and a few of the company, including Hagen and Gunther, stop

to rest. As Siegfried drinks from a stream, Hagen throws Siegfried's own spear at him, aiming for the cross that Kriemhild stitched onto his tunic in hopes that it would impart holy protection. The weapon passes through Siegfried's body. Still alive and maddened with rage and pain, Siegfried reaches for his weapons, but Hagen has removed them from where they lay. Able to lay hands only on his shield, he uses the last of his strength to strike one mighty blow against Hagen that shatters the shield. Siegfried collapses in a bed of flowers (reminiscent of Kriemhild's dream) and speaks, deriding Hagen and his company for their dishonor. At his words, Gunther regrets his action. The chapter closes on the image of blood-drenched flowers.

## Chapter 17

The hunting party returns and, in a deed of "pride and grisly vengeance," Hagen has Siegfried's corpse placed outside Kriemhild's door so that she will find him on her way to matins (morning church services). A servant finds the body the next morning, but cannot recognize it. Only Kriemhild sees who it is, and collapses with grief. Her grief is compounded by her guilt for having told Hagen how to "protect" Siegfried. Suspecting that Brunhild and Hagen are responsible, she swears vengeance. Word spreads of Siegfried's death, and Siegmund is especially grief-stricken. He goes immediately to Kriemhild and they both mourn. The Nibelung warriors arm themselves, and, now with Siegmund, are determined to seek out Siegfried's killer. Kriemhild convinces them all to wait until there is proof.

At the funeral, Gunther and Hagen join the mourners. Kriemhild challenges them both to approach Siegfried's body. There is a belief at this time that the wounds on the corpse of a murder victim would bleed in the presence of the killer, and this happens when Hagen approaches Siegfried's body. Gunther and Hagen both protest Hagen's innocence, but Kriemhild does not believe them.

## Chapter 18

Kriemhild decides to remain at Worms with her brothers as Siegmund returns to the Netherlands. Kriemhild confers the raising of her son to his grandparents at Xanten. Kriemhild, although she will remain with her own people, will not retain her position as a queen. She and Brunhild remain unreconciled.

*Kriemhild discovers Siegfried's body. Drawing by Josef Hegenbarth, 1923.*

## Chapter 19

Kriemhild remains at Worms for three and a half years without ever speaking to Gunther or Hagen. She is still convinced of Hagen's guilt, primarily because she told him of Siegfried's weak spot. Hagen, meanwhile, plots to bring the treasure of the Nibelungs, now Kriemhild's, to Worms. Gunther sends his brothers to speak to her and beg her to see Gunther. She finally agrees, and once they are reconciled, she agrees to send for the treasure. Eight thousand men are sent to fetch it. Against the wishes of the kings, however, Hagen has the treasure secretly sunk in the Rhine river so that few know its whereabouts.

## Chapter 20

Meanwhile, in Hungary, Helche, the wife of King Etzel of the Huns, has died, and he wishes to take another bride. He has heard of Kriemhild's beauty and sends his trusted vassal, Rudiger of Pochlarn, to win her hand on his behalf. Rudiger arrives at Worms with five hundred warriors and secures an audience with the kings. Rudiger tells Gunther the purpose of his visit and is promised an answer within three days. Gunther is willing to let Kriemhild decide whether to marry Etzel, but Hagen discourages him, fearing that Kriemhild will use Etzel's forces to exact vengeance on the Burgundians for Siegfried's death.

Kriemhild is determined not to accept Etzel's offer until Rudiger swears an oath promising to avenge any wrongs she suffers. She decides to accept Etzel's offer.

## Chapter 21

Kriemhild and her company travel through Bavaria to Passau, where she encounters Bishop Pilgrim, her uncle. They pass on to Rudiger's lands where they remain for a short time. There Kriemhild meets Rudiger's wife Gotelind and her daughter. Thence they travel through Austria, and the narrator comments that in this land Christians and pagans live side by side (Etzel is a pagan). The company stays at the fortress of Traisenmauer for four days and then journeys to Etzel's court.

## Chapter 22

On their way through Austria, Kriemhild sees many strange customs being followed and meets many knights and Kings of the various principalities of the land. They all owe loyalty to King Etzel and are eager to meet their new queen. When she meets Etzel she is greeted courteously. Jousts and festivities follow. Etzel and Kriemhild, along with a great company, then ride on to Vienna where more festivities occur in honor of Kriemhild's arrival. They are married in Vienna and the festivities continue for seventeen days. Kriemhild, however, continues to grieve for Siegfried. Then they leave Vienna for Hungary, where Kriemhild is welcomed at the court by royal princesses, especially Herrat, the former Queen Helche's niece, who is betrothed to a lord named Dietrich.

## Chapter 23

In her seventh year of marriage to Etzel, Kriemhild has a son whom she names Ortlieb. She is by now loved, respected and even feared by the Hungarian people. She still plots revenge against Hagen. One night she has a dream of walking with her brother Giselher, and the narrator implies that everyone at Giselher's court would soon know much suffering.

Kriemhild asks Etzel to invite her countrymen to visit them. He dispatches two minstrels, Swemmel and Werbel, to invite them to the summer festival. Kriemhild speaks to the envoys separately and asks them to pretend that she sorrows no longer for Siegfried, and bears no ill feeling for his loss. Thus, she wishes to see all of her brothers, and Hagen as well. The messengers do not know of Hagen's role in Siegfried's death, and so are oblivious to her alternate motives for luring Hagen to Hungary.

## Chapter 24

Werbel and Swemmel stop in Pochlarn on their way to Worms and visit Rudiger and Gotelind, who send their own greetings to the court in Worms. They are welcomed with open arms after Hagen recognizes them. They deliver the invitation and are promised an answer within the week. Meanwhile, Gunther deliberates whether to visit Hungary. Hagen is vehemently opposed to the journey, and openly cites his own murder of Kriemhild's husband as the reason that all of their lives will be in danger if they visit her. Gunther, however, assumes that Kriemhild's anger has passed. Gunther suggests to Hagen that, since he is conscience of his guilt, he should remain behind—implying that Hagen is not brave enough to face Kriemhild and her new vassals (Gunther says nothing about his own passive role in Siegfried's death). Hagen accepts the challenge and decides to go along, but insists that they go armed.

## Chapter 25

As the Burgundians prepare to travel to Hungary, Uote has a dream that all the birds in Burgundy had died. She takes this to be a prophecy of doom and warns her sons not to go, but they disregard her. The Burgundians travel toward Hungary, and on the twelfth day reach the Danube River. Hagen encounters water sprites or faeries bathing in the river, and steals their clothes, returning them in exchange for their word that the trip will be undertaken in safety. However, after Hagen returns their clothes, they tell him that, in fact, great danger awaits them in Hungary, and that they are all doomed to die.

Then, Hagen fights and kills a boatman who refuses to ferry the men across the river. Once everyone has safely crossed the Danube, Hagen destroys the ferry, claiming that it is to prevent any cowards in the group from returning home.

## Chapter 26

When they arrive on the other side of the river, Hagen tells the others of the prophecy he received from the faeries. He also admits to having killed the ferryman, warning that the ferryman's lord, Gelphrat will probably have heard of the death of the ferryman and seek revenge. Shortly, the Burgundians are approached by Gelphrat and his brother Else and their men. Gelphrat is slain by Dancwart and the rest of his men flee. The Burgundians continue on. They reach Rudiger's residence where they can rest.

## Chapter 27

Rudiger welcomes his guests with great honor, especially Hagen, whom he had met before. His wife, Lady Gotelind, and their daughter also offer welcome. The (unnamed) daughter becomes the object of much admiration, and before the Burgundians leave, she is betrothed to Giselher. Several days later the Burgundians set out for Etzel's court, laden with gifts from Rudiger, who accompanies them on the last leg of their journey.

## Chapter 28

The Burgundians arrive in Hungary and are greeted by Hildebrand and Wolfhart, two brave knights of Amelungland and vassals of Dietrich, Lord of Verona. They warn the Burgundians that Kriemhild still mourns the death of Siegfried. Undaunted, the Burgundians ride on to the court.

Kriemhild welcomes the visitors, but does not withhold her anger from Hagen, and immediately asks where he has hidden her treasure, that of the Nibelungs to which she was entitled after Siegfried's death. Hagen claims that her brothers ordered it sunk in the Rhine River.

## Chapter 29

Kriemhild weeps and is asked by Etzel's warriors why she is upset. She explains that she wants Siegfried's death avenged, and will pay dearly for it. Sixty men swear to kill Hagen, but she insists that they gather more forces and so they do. However, the knights then back away from their promise, afraid of Hagen and Volker.

Gunther and his brothers and men then enter the court of Etzel and are welcomed by the King, who is ignorant of the threat the man poses.

## Chapter 30

At the end of the evening, Gunther and his men ask leave to retire, but as they leave the hall, they are surrounded by a jostling crowd. This enfuriates Volker, and tensions run high between the two groups of knights. The Burgundians are shown to a large hall where beds are set up. Hagen and Volker stand guard outside the room as the others sleep.

## Chapter 31

After morning mass, festivities commence, with games and mock battles. One of these is the ''bohort'', a pageantry sport played on horseback with shields and lances. Rudiger, noticing the angry mood of many of Gunther's men, recommends that the bohort be canceled, but it continues anyway. Volker enters the game. When he charges, his lance kills one of the Huns (ostensibly by accident). Everyone jumps for their swords, but Etzel arrives to settle the matter. He rules that the death was an accident.

Kriemhild, meanwhile, again asks her vassals for help in avenging Siegfried. Despite being angered by the recent death, they are wary of attacking the Burgundians. So she begs lord Bloedelin to help her, but he, too, is unwilling until Kriemhild promises him much wealth and land, as well as the young woman Herrat, already promised to Dietrich as bride. Then he agrees.

## Chapter 32

Bloedelin attacks the Burgundians. Entering the hall where Dancwart and his men are eating, he challenges him. Dancwart immediately cuts off Bloedelin's head and a mighty battle ensues. The Burgundians drive the Huns from the building, but only after many losses on both sides. Dancwart endeavors to fight his way out to tell his brother Hagen of the attempted massacre.

## Chapter 33

Dancwart enters the hall where Hagen is dining with Etzel and Kriemhild. Dancwart calls on his brother for assistance, saying that Lord Bloedelin and his men have massacred many of the Burgundians. Between them then prevent the pursuing Huns from entering and barricade the room, then stand guard at the stairs. Then Hagen steps forth and decapitates Kriemhild and Etzel's son, Ortlieb; his head falls into Kriemhild's lap. A battle erupts, Huns against Burgundians. Kriemhild begs Dietrich to help her and Etzel escape, and he does so. Rudiger of Pochlarn is also permitted to leave with his men, for the Burgundians' fight is not with them.

## Chapter 34

The Burgundians kill or seriously wound all of the Huns in the hall. They clear the hall by throwing the dead and dying alike down a flight of stairs, and many more of the wounded die because of this rough handling. Hagen and Volker address King Etzel, who is standing with a crowd outside. They taunt and insult him and his queen Kriemhild. She is incensed, and calls on her men to kill Hagen, promising great wealth in return.

## Chapter 35

Iring of Denmark now calls for his weapons, determined to fulfill his queen's wishes. He engages the Burgundians in battle. Giselher strikes him down, but he is only stunned. They think him dead, however, so when he leaps to his feet it surprises them. He runs toward Hagen and manages to wound him and then retreat back to the crowd gathered outside. Kriemhild is delighted when she hears of the events. Iring is now determined to try again, and reenters the hall. Hagen is enraged and wounds Iring on the spot (with a spear shaft through his head).

## Chapter 36

Kriemhild and Etzel send twenty thousand men into battle, but the Huns are again unsuccessful. Etzel is by now unwilling to let any of the Burgundians live. Things have gone too far.

Giselher addresses his sister, asking for mercy, but she refuses. Her heart is devoid of mercy. She says, however, that if they will hand over Hagen as prisoner, she will consider letting her brothers live; but Gernot and the others refuse to break faith with their friend. Kriemhild then orders the Huns to set fire to the hall. As the heat rises, those trapped inside even drink the blood of the slain to quench their thirst. They decide to enter the gathering hall of the palace and remain silent so that the Huns will think they have perished. But the Huns attack at daybreak, spurred on by loyalty for their king, and Kriemhild's promise of wealth. The narrator tells us that twelve hundred men attacked, but all were killed.

## *Chapter 37*

Rudiger is now called upon to lend a hand to the Huns, but is reluctant since he has pledged friendship (and betrothed his daughter) to the Burgundians. He struggles with the decision to engage his new friends in battle, but is chastised by Etzel for his disloyalty on the other side. Etzel and Kriemhild are both upset by his decision not to fight. Kriemhild reminds him of his oath of allegiance to her. But he is tormented by his role in bringing the Burgundians to Etzel's court, only to see them attacked, and cannot decide what to put first — feudal obligation or a vow of friendship and kinship.

Both Kriemhild and Etzel kneel before Rudiger, who is tormented by the decision he must make. There is essentially no right choice for him. Whatever his decision, he will be betraying one of his oaths. He even offers to exile himself to avoid making the decision. But Etzel's entreaties convince him, unwillingly, to engage the Burgundians in battle.

When Giselher and the others see Rudiger and his men approach, they think help is on the way, but soon realize that their friend is here to fight them. The Burgundian kings try to dissuade him from his intention. Rudiger even gives Hagen his shield, as Hagen's was destroyed. Emotions run high, and the knights weep at the evil turn of events that pits friends against friends. They engage in battle, and Rugider and Gernot kill each other. All of Rudiger's men are slain.

## *Chapter 38*

An emissary is sent by Dietrich of Verona to the Huns to inquire as to the state of affairs. Dietrich next sends Hildebrand, his Master-at-Arms, to the Burgundians for more information. When Volker sees Hildebrand and his knights approaching he assumes they will attack, but they are addressed by Hildebrand instead. Hildebrand asks whether it is true that they have slain Rudiger, in which case Dietrich will never be able to forgive them. Hagen confirms the report.

Hildebrand asks for Rudiger's body, but is told that they must fight for it. Hildebrand and his men engage them (contrary to Dietrich's orders). Wolfhart goads the Burgundians into battle and many of Hildebrand's men lose their lives. Hildebrand kills Volker after the latter kills Dietrich's nephew Sigestap. Hagen is devastated by Volker's death. Dancwart is also killed by Helpfrich, a vassal of Dietrich. Wolfhart (nephew of Hildebrand) and Giselher slay each other. Finally, all of Dietrich's men are killed except Hildebrand. He and Hagen fight and Hildebrand flees from the hall, wounded. Only Hagen and Gunther are left alive.

Dietrich is angry with Hildebrand for engaging in battle with the Burgundians, since he had only been sent to talk to them. Dietrich, saddened by the confirmation of Rudiger's death, is determined to fight the Burgundians himself, but is shocked to hear that he has no warriors left. Without his men, he has no way to serve Etzel as vassal, or to protect himself.

## *Chapter 39*

Dietrich and Hildebrand return to the hall where Hagen and Gunther wait. Dietrich offers to protect the Burgundians if they surrender themselves to him, but his offer is refused. Hagen claims that to surrender themselves would mean disgrace. Hagen insults Hildebrand for having fled the battle earlier, which provokes Dietrich. Dietrich and Hagen fight and Dietrich captures and binds Hagen, bringing him to Queen Kriemhild. Kriemhild has Hagen locked in the dungeon.

Dietrich returns to fight Gunther, whom he defeats and brings, bound, to Kriemhild. Kriemhild imprisons her brother as well, and keeps the two prisoners separate. She has Gunther killed and brings his head to Hagen. She then kills Hagen with her first husband Siegfried's sword in the presence of Etzel, Dietrich and Hildebrand. Hildebrand, however, will not allow her to go unpunished for killing such a great warrior. Despite the harm that Hagen has inflicted, Hildebrand swears to avenge his death, and kills Kriemhild. Even Etzel mourns the death of Hagen. ''The King's high festival had ended in sorrow, as joy must ever turn to sorrow in the end.''

# Characters

## *Alberich*

The dwarf who was the Lord Treasurer of the Nibelung dynasty. When Siegfried conquered the Nibelung brothers, he took his magic cloak of

# Media Adaptations

- *Die Nibelungen* was made into a two-part black-and-white silent movie in 1924. It was produced in Germany, and directed by Fritz Lang. It is now available on Laser Disc (Disc Format CLV) as well as on 16mm film. The two parts are "Siegfried's Death" and "Kriemhild's Revenge." The movie elaborates on the tales of Siegfried's youth, and is quite faithful to the story of the *Nibelungenlied.*

- German composer Richard Wagner turned the story of the Nibelungs into the four operas of *Der Ring des Nibelungen (The Ring of the Nibelungs).* Separately, the four operas are: *Das Rheingold* *(The Rhinegold), Die Walkure (The Valkyries), Siegfried* and *Gotterdamerung (The Twilight of the Gods).* He drew from both the *Nibelungenlied* and on the Norse Eddas to compose his plots. Many versions of the operas are available on CD, video, and laser disk.

- J. R. R. Tolkien's *Lord of the Rings,* a fantasy tale that focuses on the early accomplishments of Siegfried the dragon-slayer, is available in a 1978 animated film. It was directed by Ralph Bakshi, and produced by Republic Pictures. It is available on video.

---

invisibility and made Alberich Lord Treasurer of the Nibelung treasure.

### Aldrian

Hagen and Dancwart's father.

### Amelung

This is the name of Dietrich's dynasty. It applies to his vassals as well.

### Astolt

One of the lords of Melk.

### Attila the Hun

*See* Etzel

### Balmung

The name of Siegfried's sword. In heroic legends, swords were often given names. After Siegfried's death, Hagen steals Balmung. When Hagen is captured at the end of the epic, Kriemhild uses the sword to kill Hagen.

### Bloedelin

Etzel's brother. Dancwart kills him in battle in Chapter 32.

### Brunhild

The Queen of Iceland, a beautiful maiden of almost superhuman strength. Gunther, king of the Burgundians, travels to Iceland to win her hand in marriage. He must perform certain acts of strength and skill in order to marry the Queen. His friend Siegfried helps him perform these tasks while wearing the magic cloak of invisibility, so it appears as if Gunther is acting alone. Siegfried also help Gunther subdue Brunhild and possess her sexually after they are married (again hidden in the magic cloak), which bring about the loss of her extraordinary strength. Brunhild is not aware of Siegfried's role until she is taunted about it by Kriemhild. The argument that follows between the two women results in Siegfried's death and in the downfall of the Burgundians.

### Dancrat

Deceased father of Gunther, Giselher, and Gernot, kings of the Burgundians, and the husband of Uote.

### Dancwart

Hagen's younger brother and also a vassal of the Burgundian kings. He kills Gelphrat in chapter 8 and often aids his brother. He is challenged by

Bloedelin in Chapter 32, and killed. This is the beginning of the final confrontation between the Huns and the Burgundians. Dancwart is killed by Helpfrich, Dietrich's vassal, in Chapter 38.

## Dietrich

Lord of the Amelung dynasty. He is engaged to Herrat and lives in exile at Etzel's court. When the Burgundians come to visit Kriemhild in Chapter 28, he tells the kings that she still mourns her dead husband Sicgfricd, and warns them that their visit may not be a pleasant one. He is also an old acquaintance of Hagen and greatly respected by all the Huns. He helps Kriemhild and Etzel escape when fighting breaks out between the Huns and Burgundians, and is finally responsible for the capture of Hagen and Gunther.

## Eckewart

A military governor for the Burgundians. He brings Kriemhild to Hungary to marry Eztel. In Chapter 26 he is discovered on Rudiger's frontier. The narrator does not tell us how he came to be separated from Kriemhild's household. His character may have been conflated with another historical figure.

## Else

Brother of Gelpfrat and Lord of the Marches on the Bavarian bank of the Danube River. He flees Hagen's men in Chapter 26 after Dancwart kills his brother.

## Etzel

King of the Huns in Hungary. Marries Kriemhild after his wife Helche dies.

## Gelphrat

Military governor of Bavaria and brother of Else. Gelpfrat attacks Hagen and his men after Hagen kills his ferryman. Gelpfrat is in turn killed by Dancwart in Chapter 26.

## Gerbart

One of Dietrich's vassals

## Gere

A military governor and kinsman of the Burgundian kings. In Chapter 12, after the marriage of Siegfried and Kriemhild, he travels back to the Netherlands to invite them to visit the Burgundians.

## Gernot

Brother of Gunther, Giselher, and Kriemhild. Second-oldest of the brothers, he is killed by Rudiger in Chapter 37.

## Giselher

The youngest brother of Gunther, Gernot, and Kriemhild. He is betrothed to Rudiger's daughter in Chapter 27, but is killed by Wolfhart in Chapter 38.

## Gotelind

Wife of Rudiger, military governor and Etzel's vassal. Her daughter is betrothed to Giselher.

## Gunther

Eldest king of Burgundy; brother of Gernot, Giselher and Kriemhild; son of Dancrat and Uote. He wins the hand of Brunhild in marriage with the help of Siegfried. He is then complicit in the death of Siegfried, and dies by order of Kriemhild in Hungary. Before he dies, he and Hagen defend themselves in Etzel's hall, and are responsible for killing many Huns. Gunther's character is problematic, as many critics have considered him to be weak and ineffectual.

## Gunther

Son of Siegfried and Kriemhild. He is born and grows up in the Netherlands, Siegfried's kingdom.

## Hadeburg

The name of the water-faerie in the Danube river who warns Hagen that the journey to Hungary will end in disaster.

## Hagen

Brother of Dancwart, eldest son of Aldrian, and chief vassal of the Burgundian kings. Also called the Lord of Troneck. He was once a hostage at Etzel's court. He is responsible for Siegfried's death and is the object of Kriemhild's revenge-plot. He discourages the Burgundian kings form travelling to Hungary upon Kriemhild's invitation, but is not heeded. Then he is warned by water-faeries that the journey will end in tragedy. Kriemhild kills him with Siegfried's sword in Hungary.

## Hawart

A Danish prince who lives in exile at Etzel's court and is overlord of Iring. He is killed by Hagen in Hungary.

### Helche

Etzel's first queen. She is already dead when Etzel enters the narrative.

### Helmnot

One of Dietrich's vassals.

### Helpfrich

One of Dietrich's vassals. He kills Dancwart, Hagen's brother, in Chapter 38.

### Herrat

Niece of Helche, Etzel's first wife. She is betrothed to Dietrich. Her father is Nantwin.

### Hildebrand

Vassal and Master-at-Arms of Dietrich of the Amelungs. He is also Wolfhart's uncle. He and Dietrich are the last to fight with Hagen and Gunther before the Burgundians are captured. He executes Kriemhild in the last Chapter.

### Hornboge

One of Etzel's vassals.

### Hunold

Lord Chamberlain of Burgundy.

### Iring

Vassal of Hawart, a Danish prince living in exile at Etzel's court. Iring is killed by Hagen in Chapter 35 when he tries to fulfill Queen Kriemhild's wishes.

### Irnfried

Also referred to as the Landgrave of Thuringia. He lives at Etzel's court, in exile. He is killed by Volker.

### Kriemhild

Princess of Burgundy, sister of Gunther, Giselher, and Gernot, and daughter of Uote and Dancrat. She is sought in marriage by the renowned warrior Siegfried, who remains in the Burgundin court for a year in the hope of meeting her. Kriemhild and Siegfried marry after Siegfried helps her brother Gunther to win the hand of the Icelandic queen Brunhild.

The main action of the *Nibelungenlied*—the violence between the Burgundians and Huns— is started by the bad feelings that arise when Kriemhild and Brunhild argue, first over whose husband is the greater, and then over Siegfried's role in Brunhild's marriage to Gunther. After Siegfried's death Kriemhild marries Etzel of Hungary (Attila the Hun), always planning her revenge on her brother's wife and liegemen for Siegfried's death. She has a son (Gunther) by Siegfried, and another son (Ortlieb) by Etzel. She kills Hagen with Siegfried's sword in Chapter 39 and is subsequently killed by Hildebrand.

### Liudegast

King of Denmark, brother of Liudeger. He declares war on Burgundy and is captured by Siegfried.

### Liudeger

King of Saxony and brother of Liudegast. He is captured with his brother while at war with the Burgundians.

### Margrave

A title given to a military governor of a border province. It is roughly equivalent to a British marquess. The wife of a margrave is called a margravine.

### Nantwin

Father of Herrat, who is betrothed to Dietrich. He is also a vassal of Etzel.

### Nibelung

The name given to the lords of Nibelungland, Kings Schilbung and Nibelung, to whom was bequeathed the treasure of the Nibelungs by their father, King Nibelung. The term also describes the members of the dynasty of Nibelung and their followers. Later in the poem, the term is used to describe the Nibelung followers who became Siegfried's vassals when he conquered their lords. When Kriemhild went to live with Etzel, the Nibelungs did not accompany her, and so the term is sometimes used as an alternative name for the Burgundians after her departure.

### Nuodung

A kinsman of Gotelind, wife of Rudiger. He does not appear in this story except by implication.

He is said to have died earlier, and his shield is given to Hagen when he visits Rudiger. Nuodung's betrothed is later promised to Bloedelin by Kriemhild to lure him into battle with Hagen.

## Ortlieb

Kriemhild's son by Etzel. He is around six years old when he is killed by Hagen, and plays a very minor role in the story.

## Ortwin

Hagen's nephew, Lord High Stewart of Burgundy and Lord of Metz.

## Bishop Pilgrim

Bishop of Passau and Uote's brother. He is the uncle of Kriemhild, Gunther, Giselher, and Gernot, all of whom stop to visit on their respective ways to Hungary.

## Ramung

One of Etzel's vassals and Duke of Wallachia.

## Ritschart

One of Dietrich's vassals.

## Rudiger

A vassal of Etzel, margrave and lord of Pochlarn and husband to Gotelind. He travels to Burgundy to ask for Kriemhild's hand in marriage on behalf of Etzel of Hungary. He betrothes his daughter to Giselher but in Chapter 37 is slain by Gernot, whom he kills at the same time. He is a heroic figure who must in the end decide whether to acknowledge his feudal oath of loyalty to Kriemhild, or his oath of friendship and kinship to the Burgundians.

## Rumold

Vassal of the Burgundians and Lord of the Kitchen in Burgundy. Gunther appoints him regent to look after the kingdom when the kings leave for Hungary.

## Schilbung

One of the Lords of Nibelungland, son of Nibelung (also the name of his brother). He is killed by Siegfried, who takes over his lands and treasure.

## Schrutan

One of Etzel's vassals.

## Siegfried

Son of Siegmund and Sieglind, and lord of the Netherlands, Norway and Nieblungland. He marries Kriemhild, princess of Burgundy, and helps King Gunther to win Queen Brunhild's hand in marriage. He is later killed by Hagen. Kriemhild's avenging of his death forms the majority of the story. The name Siegfried is also given to King Gunther's son by Queen Brunhild.

## Sieglind

Queen of the Netherlands, wife of King Siegmund, and mother of Siegfried. This is also the name given to the water-faerie that prophecies the fall of the Burgundians to Hagen.

## Siegmund

King of the Netherlands, husband of Sieglind and father of Siegfried. He visits the Burgundian kingdom with his son and Queen Kriemhild after they are married, and then returns to the Netherlands after Siegfried is killed.

## Sindold

A vassal of the Burgundians and Cup-bearer of Burgundy.

## Swemmel

Etzel's minstrel. He travels to Burgundy with Werbel to invite Kriemhild's kinsmen to visit for the summer festival.

## Theoderic the Great
*See* Dietrich

## Uote

Widowed Queen of Burgundy, mother of Gunther, Giselher, Gernot and Kriemhild. She is sister to Bishop Pilgrim of Passau. She is the one who interprets Kriemhild's dream at the beginning of the story, and tries to warn her sons not to travel to Hungary after she has a dream that indicates the journey will end in tragedy.

## Volker

A vassal of the Burgundians, lord of Alzei. He is Hagen's chosen comrade in arms and stands guard with Hagen to protect the Burgundian warriors at Etzel's court. He is also referred to as "The Minstrel" or "The Fiddler" for his musical ability. He is killed by Hildebrand in Chapter 38.

### Waske

The name given to Iring's sword.

### Werbel

Etzel's minstrel. He travels with Swemmel to Burgundy to invite Kriemhild's kinsmen to Hungary for the summer festival.

### Wichart

One of Dietrich's vassals.

### Wolfbrand

One of Dietrich's vassals.

### Wolfhart

Nephew of Hildebrand, and Dietrich's vassal. He goads Hagen and the Burgundians into a fight in Chapter 38, wherein he and Giselher kill each other.

### Wolfwin

One of Dietrich's vassals.

## Themes

The *Nibelungenlied* is a heroic epic which tells the story of the knight Siegfried's marriage to Kriemhild and his subsequent death at the hands of Kriemhild's kinsman, Hagen. In the second part of the story, Kriemhild marries Etzel, king of the Huns. She uses her new position to exact revenge on Hagen for her husband's death; her own brothers and many more of her kinsmen die in the process.

### Chivalry

Chivalry was a code of behavior which evolved in the Middle Ages. It is associated with the tradition of mounted knights in armor, lord and ladies, feasts, jousts, and war games. In fact, "knights" arose from the development of new military techniques. The behavior of a knight both on the battlefield and in everyday life was expected to follow a certain set of rules— a moral, social and religious code of conduct. The notion of chivalry encouraged knights to foster the virtues of courage, honor, and service to their lord or kinsmen. Part of this code prescribed respectful treatment of women, who had few legal rights in the Middle Ages. For instance, in the *Nibelungenlied,* Siegfried's respectful treatment of Kriemhild and their closely-regulated courtship followed the code of chivalry. Chivalry is also associated with class, noble rank, and social standing as well as expertise on the battlefield. For instance, when the kings Liudeger and Liudegast surrender in battle, they and their men are brought back to Worms. There, they are not treated like prisoners of war, but as guests. The wounded knights receive care and medical treatment, and the others are housed and fed. This treatment adheres to the chivalric code.

### Clothing and Appearances

For the characters in the *Nibelungenlied* appearances and first impressions are very important. One way this concern is manifested is through clothing and personal adornment. Clothing, in fact, sends certain messages that, within the courtly culture depicted, can be easily read. When Siegfried first decides to visit Worms to seek Kriemhild's hand in marriage, much effort is put into describing his attire and that of his companions. When they arrive at Worms in Chapter 3, the narrator tells us that they are assumed to be "either princes or princes' envoys, judging by their handsome chargers and splendid clothes." Nobility, honorable status, good breeding, and class are judged by appearance. Gift of fine clothes can also be a way to honor a guest. It is also interesting to note that as the story progresses, less time is spent discussing splendid garments, and more on fine armor and weapons, keeping with the tone of the story.

### Courtly Love

Courtly love is as much a literary convention as it was a behavioral code. Courtly love represented the relationship between a suitor and his lady, and sometime, between a courtier or leigeman and the wife, sister, or daughter, of the lord whom he served. This does not mean that extramarital affairs were a part of courtly love. Such relationships were confined to the suitor's pledges of devotion and service. Sometimes such relationships between rela-

# Topics for Further Study

- What type of warfare was practiced in the Middle Ages? How did it differ from the warfare practiced by the soldiers of the Roman Empire?

- Explore the development of knighthood and the code of chivalry. This includes the growth of jousts and tournaments, new developments in armor, and the traditions of courtly love. Give examples of how the*Nibelungenlied* poet presents these issues.

- Explore the development of feudalism as a sociopolitical structure in the Middle Ages. How is feudalism manifested in the *Nibelungenlied*?

- What personal, social, cultural, and political roles do women play in the social setting presented in the *Nibelungenlied?* Compare their roles with women's roles in the late twentieth century.

- Compare and contrast the characters of Brunhild and Kriemhild. Are they more alike or different?

- The narrator of the epic states explicitly several times (for example, at the close of Chapter 14), that the bloodshed in the second part of the *Nibelungenlied* is the result of pettiness on the part of the two queens. Compare and contrast the reasons for strife between the Burgundians and Huns in the *Nibelungenlied* with that between the Greeks and Trojans in the *Iliad,* between the kingdoms of Malinke and Sossa in *Sundiata,* or between any two modern nations that have gone to war. Is the cause of warfare in the *Nibelungenlied* any more or less valid than in your other example? Are some wars started for justifiable and others for unjustifiable reasons?

- What are the qualities of a ''hero'' by twentieth-century standards? Compare this to the concept of hero in the the *Nibelungenlied.* Then compare the ''heroic'' roles of Hagen and Rudiger. Are they both heroes? How do they compare to what constitutes a modern hero? Use evidence from the text.

- What are the qualities and characteristics of a good leader? In view of those qualities, is Gunther a good leader? How does he compare with Etzel of Hungary? Use evidence from the text.

---

tive social equals would develop and lead to marriage. Other times, the suitor would plead for his lady's love in vain. This behavior was conventional. The suitor always treated his lady with respect and admiration, sometimes even adoration. An examples of courtly love in the *Nibelungenlied* is Siegfried's unspoken devotion to Kriemhild and then his respectful wooing of her through Gunther over more than a year. Similarly, the vassals and knights of Etzel's army pledge themselves to avenging Kriemhild's honor because she is married to their lord.

## Deception

The *Nibelungenlied* is as much a story of political and social disintegration as it is about heroes and revenge. By the end of the story, the Burgundian rulers are all dead, and many of Etzel's own vassals have been killed as well. Essentially, two kingdoms have been destroyed. The roots of this disintegration are a series of deceptions in which many characters participate. The theme of deception is problematic, since some of the instances of deception can also be seen as examples of courage, bravery, or skill. When Siegfried helps Gunther win Brunhild by taking part in the sporting events under the cover of his magic cloak, he is contributing to a marriage based on a false premise—Gunther's superior strength and skill. Then, when Siegfried subdues Brunhild after the wedding, he essentially ''tames'' her for Gunther. Hagen, too, is deceitful. He engages in the decepion of Siegfried's death, and Gunther himself is complicit in the deed. Many scholars justify Hagen's actions by maintaining that he acts according to his feudal obligations. His queen, Brunhild, is insulted and publicly humiliat-

*Kriemhild delivers Gunther's head to the imprisoned Hagen in an 1805 illustration.*

ed, and it is his duty to avenge the wrongs done to her. Nevertheless, the planning that goes into Siegfried's death, including determining his "weak spot," was deceitful.

### Dreams and Prophecies

Dreams and prophecies occur at various points throughout the story, and add to the constant element of foreshadowing that the narrator uses. Subsequent events of the story then represent the events of the dreams, either directly or indirectly. At the very beginning of the *Nibelungenlied,* Kriemhild has a dream which portends her marriage to Siegfried and his death. Other dreams occur at important transition points in the story. Kriemhild has two dreams before Siegfried's hunting trip that seem to foretell his death. Later, Kriemhild dreams of her brother Giselher before she invites her kinsmen to visit her in Hungary. Shortly thereafter, her mother, Uote, dreams that all the birds in Burgundy are dead, and takes it to mean that her sons should not journey to Hungary, which of course turns out to be true as they all perish there.

The *Nibelungenleid* poet uses prophecy in other ways. Hagen is warned by the Danube water-

faeries that the Burgundians' trip to Hungary will end in destruction. Such "foretellings," the type of imagery used, and the way that dreams are then represented in the subsequent actions of the story constitute an important element of the poet's use of foreshadowing.

### Feudalism

The *Nibelungenlied* is set at a time when feudal obligations represented the socio-political foundation of society. Feudalism prevailed in Europe from about the ninth to the thirteenth centuries. It was an interdependant relationship of "lord" and "vassal" established through an oath of loyalty. The lords (for instance, Gunther and Etzel) owned the land in their respective kingdoms, but they allowed "vassals" to live on the land, and to engage in farming, hunting, fishing, trade, and other forms of livelihood. Vassalage does not imply mere servitude or peasantry: vassals were often of noble blood and—and is often the case with characters in the *Nibelungenlied*—included high-ranking and influential men. In exchange for military and political protection for his family and property, vassal paid tithes, or yearly sums of money, to their lord, and were pledged to military service when needed. The relationship of lord and vassal which causes much of the tragedy in the *Nibelungenlied.* In Chapter 14, Brunhild criticizes Siegfried for not performing his financial obligations as a "vassal." She had been told that Siegfried was Gunther's vassal, or "liegeman"; and so she believes that Kriemhild, being of lesser social status, should not enter the cathedral before her. Kriemhild objects, and claims that she is a "free noblewoman," that is, the wife of a lord, not a vassal. This argument instigates the events which will lead to the death of Siegfried and then of many Burgundians.

### The status of women

During the Middle Ages women did not enjoy great freedom, security, or legal protection. They could not inherit land, and husbands commonly controlled household wealth. The code of chivalry encouraged the respectful treatment of a small strata of women of the upper classes and nobility, but did nothing to grant them autonomy or personal power. Even Kriemhild, the wife of a king, has difficulty persuading the vassals who owe her husband allegiance to fight for her honor. Women of the upper classes were expected to marry and bear children; their marriages were often arranged by their families for social or political purposes. Entering a convent was another of the limited choices available to women of the upper classes. The vast majority of women performed hard physical labor, either as workers or simply in running a household, for their entire lives. Most were not educated beyond practical training in weaving, spinning, and cooking; women of the nobility were taught to play musical instruments and to dance.

### The Hero

Heroism in the Middle Ages was somewhat different from what we imagine it to be today. In the Middle Ages, heroism represented brave or exemplary actions, but not necessarily actions that were looked upon approvingly by the audience. A person's heroism is defined largely by how that individual comes to terms with fate. This often entails making difficult decisions. Sometimes one has no favorable alternatives from which to choose. For instance, Hagen is sometimes considered a moral villain, but must also be recognized as a hero like Siegfried, despite the differences in their characters. A "hero" was recognized as such not by the individual himself, but by the other members of his society. Heroism is also associated with wealth and class status. Heroism in the *Nibelungenlied* encompass not only brave deeds on the battlefield, but other feats which represent strength of character, such as Siegfried's willingness to help Gunther win Brunhild's hand in marriage and his expertise in the hunting scene. Deeds such as this create an image of a character for whom status is reliant on noble characteristics such as honor, bravery, and justice. Even Kriemhild is heroic in her unwavering loyalty toward Siegfried. By the force of her will, she seeks revenge for his death, and even though the final result is death and destruction for many, she does not waver from her purpose; this is seen as essentially heroic. Rudiger, represents yet a different type of hero. He is distinguished from the others by his deeply moral character, his gentility, and his tragic inner struggle at the end, when he must decide between his feudal oath to Etzel and his vow of friendship and kinship to the Burgundians.

### Hospitality and Gift-giving

The giving of gifts and the granting of hospitality to guests and friends are very important and interrelated elements in the *Nibelungenlied*. The granting of hospitality was integral to the establishment of bonds of loyalty and trust among equals. In

*Kriemhild slays Hagen and falls to Hildebrand's sword.*

an age in which visitors to one's kingdom might be friends or enemies intent on war, it was important to ensure that one's identity, reputation, and intent be clearly know. Thus when Siegfried first arrives at Worms, word of his exploits has preceded him; when he challenges Gunther for his kingdom to show his strength and noble heritage, there are a few tense moments before a bond of friendship is established. This friendship is based on an agreement of peace, loyalty and honor. Gunther extends hospitality to his guest to show him honor. To give gifts represents the bestowing of honor, and is also part of the bond of friendship.

### Romance Genre

Romance as a literary genre treats topics which are similar to those treated in the "epic" genre. First, it must be rememberd that "romance" here is referring to a literary genre which arose in the Middle Ages, not to modern conventions of flowers and chocolates! "Romance" in the Middle Ages was perhaps equivalent to the historical romance novel today, but with complex plots, and highly developed and often "tragic" or "lovesick" characters. Romance is, in this sense, motivated by the plot development and the characters. Romance and epic both used set "conventions". Conventions were, and still are, literary devices or forms which both author and reader understand to be fitting to a certain type of literature. Thus in a "romance", the knight fighting dragons, engaged in battles or travelling on a perilous journey would be doing so not for the glory of the deed alone, but in order to win the favor of his beloved lady. Thus even Siegfried's generous offer to fight the Saxons and the Danes arises less from a desire to show Gunther his prowess in battle than to convince Gunther that he is a suitable husband for Kriemhild. In turn, Kriemhild, hearing of Siegfried's victory, falls even deeper in love with him. This is one of the conventions of romance.

## Style

### Nibelungenlied as Epic

The *Nibelungenlied* draws on two important literary traditions, that of the epic, and that of the romance. As an epic, it celebrates the adventures and achievements of several noble, admirable people. It draws on history, mythology, and legend for its details, and the story is largely advanced through action. The *Nibelungenlied* also employs elements drawn from the literary romance: the quests of knights, chivalry, and complicated love relationships worked out over time. The romance genre is largely driven by plot or character, as are the romantic sections of the *Nibelungenlied.* In fact, this work is often regarded as one of the first examples of a new, hybrid form of literature, encompassing elements of both epic and romance. It has also been suggested that the *Nibelungenlied* also draws on a type of story associated with the romance genre known as the "bridal-quest." This literary model encompasses several typical episodes: the report of a distant and eligible princess; a man moved to woo and win her in marriage; her initial resistance to him; commonly, a series of tasks each potential bridegroom must undertake; and finally, a triumphant bridal journey ending in a wedding. These events—which are familiar to many readers through the traditions of nineteenth-century folk and fairy tales—are played out in the relationships between both Siegfried and Kriemhild and of Gunther and Brunhild.

### Point of View

The *Nibelungenlied* is told from the point of view of an omniscient, or "all-knowing" narrator.

The narrator is aware of all the events as they unfold, and also those that are about to occur. To portray a unified story to the reader, the narrative unfolds with little personal commentary and employs repetitive or stock phrases: the character of Volker, for example, is often referred to as "the valiant minstrel" in order to recall both his valor and his role as a musician to the reader. Since the basic *Nibelungenlied* story was well known long before it was ever written down, the narrator trusts that the audience knows what is going to happen. This is a commonplace of medieval literature and of epic stories, which drew from existing bodies of shared cultural knowledge.

### Foreshadowing

In the literary technique of foreshadowing, events that are to come later in the narrative are "foreshadowed" or hinted at in advance. Foreshadowing occurs throughout the *Nibelungenlied,* for example, through the interpretations that Uote offers of her own dream and that her daughter, the prophecy of the water faeries to Hagen, and the narrator's frequent interpolations that doom is about to befall certain characters or that terrible things will result from whatever has just happened. This type of foreshadowing adds both structural unity and interest to the story: it ensures a steady tragic tone while it keeps the reader wondering, not exactly what will happen next, but how the inevitable tragic events will play themselves out.

### Structure

The *Nibelungenlied* partakes of a twofold structure. The story is divided into two sections: the first encompassing Kriemhild's marriage to Siegfried and his subsequent death (chapters 1-19); the second covering Kriemhild's marriage to Etzel and her quest to revenge Siegfried's death (chapters 20-39). The second part builds upon and fulfills the events of the first (a type of structural foreshadowing). There is also an internal symmetry corresponding to these two parts. For instance, both parts begin with a bride-quest and a marriage, and end with death. In keeping with the literary technique of building on and expanding on events, the first part ends with the death of a single individual, while the second part concludes with depictions of massive loss of life on both sides of a great conflict between peoples. Gift-giving, invitations to visit, arrivals, leave-taking, and battles are represented in both parts as well. In another example of building on what has come before in the narrative, the battles depicted in part one are largely the mock fights of pageants and war games, while the fighting that concludes the epic is deadly earnest.

# Historical Context

## *Socio-historical Context of the Nibelungenlied*

While the version of the *Nibelungenlied* known to twentieth-century readers was written around 1200, it deals loosely with historical and legendary events which occurred or were first recounted several hundred years before. The Huns (Etzel's people in the *Nibelungenlied*) were originally a nomadic tribe from Asia. They invaded Europe around 360. They eventually settled most of their kingdom in what is now Hungary. Attila (Etzel in the *Nibelungenlied*) became king of the Huns in 433. In Latin legends he was given the nickname of "Scourge of the Gods" for his cruelty, and this is the image that has survived most widely regarding Attila. However, in the Germanic legends, he is portrayed as hospitable and fair.

The kingdom at Worms is believed to have been founded in the year 406 by the Burgundians, a Germanic people. They were conquered by the Huns under Attila in a battle in which the entire Burgundian royal family was killed. After this, what remained of the Burgundians settled in the area of France known today as Burgundy. It was after this that the names of Gunther, Giselher, and Gernot appear in their records.

The character of Dietrich of Verona is based on the historical figure of Theodoric, king of the Ostrogoths from around the year 475. As ruler of Italy from 493 he implemented legal, social, and economic reforms. He appears in the *Nibelungenlied* as Dietrich of Verona because of his historical connection to Italy.

Legends about the mythical dragon-slayer Siegfried somehow came to be associated with the tale of the overthrow of the Burgundian kingdom by the Huns. The same stories about a dragon- killing knight or warrior named Siegfried also appears in the Icelandic epic tales (called "Eddas"). These northern versions of the story differ somewhat from the Germanic versions, although they are thought to have originated from common sources. The source stories were popular throughout the regions that are now Iceland, Denmark, Norway and England.

Critical to an understanding of what motivates the characters in the *Nibelungenlied* is an understanding of the bonds of feudalism, family, and friendship. In Germanic culture of the twelfth and thirteenth centuries, these issues were of compelling importance. The loyalty bond of a vassal to a lord, the bonds of blood kinship and of friendship, and the bond between husband and wife are all crucial; many conflicts in the text arise when a character is torn between conflicting demands of these varied obligations. For instance, Hagen feels honor-bound as a vassal of Brunhild's husband Gunther to defend Brunhild's honor by killing Siegfried, but since Siegfried is Kriemhild's husband and Kriemhild is Gunther's sister, he is also violating an implied bond not to hurt her. Kriemhild, in turn, betrays her husband Etzel by using him as a pawn to draw the Burgundians to their slaughter in Hungary. Rudiger is torn between his sworn loyalty to his lord, Etzel, and his bond of friendship and kinship with the Burgundians.

Such brutal behavior is rarely offset by the sometimes-explicit reminders that these events take place in a Christian culture, bound by the rules of Christian conduct. Christianity began to spread throughout Europe in the early Middle Ages. The historical figure of Dietrich (Theodoric) was a Christian, although he belonged to an alternative, heretical sect of Christianity known as Arianism. Attila remained a pagan, but we are not certain how soon the Burgundian tribes were converted. The prevalence of Christian culture in the *Nibelungenlied* was probably the invention of the anonymous author, who was writing in the twelfth or thirteenth century, when western Europe had become almost entirely Christian. These two worlds—pagan and Christian—collide in the *Nibelungenlied* when Kriemhild, a Christian, marries Etzel, a pagan. Christian beliefs in the story are, however, given only scant treatment. There is less tension between pagan and Christian beliefs than there is within the Christian culture of the Burgundians regarding the conflicting demands of feudal obligations and self-interest.

# Critical Overview

The *Nibelungenlied* was one of the most popular poems of its age, and is probably the best-known

# Compare & Contrast

- **Middle Ages:** During the Middle Ages, laws and punishments varied from country to country, sometimes even from city to city. The type of justice and the punishments inflicted in the Middle Ages often "fit" the crime in very literal ways.

  **Late twentieth century:** Modern legal systems eschew "eye for an eye" retributive justice. The legal systems of most nations purport to be fair and objective, with rehabilitation being a primary goal.

- **Middle Ages:** Vengeance—revenge for a wrong done—is seen as an equitable form of justice.

- **Late twentieth century:** Justice is commonly interpreted as punishment for the guilty and preservation of the innocent. Revenge is not supposed to be a reason for seeking justice.

- **Middle Ages:** Kingship was hereditary. Rulers in the Middle Ages had almost unlimited power and control over their subjects.

  **Late twentieth century:** Most monarchs are primarily figureheads who live under the same laws and enjoy the same rights as all citizens.

---

Germanic poem from the Middle Ages. Most literary analysis of the poem began after 1800, and soon Germany embraced the poem as a work of nationalism, often comparing it with Homer's *Iliad.* Essentially, commentary on the *Nibelungenlied* falls into three categories: the study of source-texts; socio-historical studies; and literary interpretations.

Much of the critical work on the *Nibelungenlied* since the eighteenth century has been done in German, but English scholarship has appeared as well. Some twentieth-century scholars have analyzed the sources of the poem, concentrating on the author's blend of historical fact, myth, and legend. Other scholars have done more literary analyses of the work, concentrating on characterization, theme and structure. According to T. M. Anderssons's *A Preface to the Nibelungenlied,* critical work in Germany on the *Nibelungenlied* from about 1902 to 1941 focused on the context of the early legends which preceded it, dealing primarily in comparisons between the known version *Nibelungenlied* and earlier versions. This critical approach is in keeping with the German to establish the *Nibelungenlied's* historical significance as a national epic.

After World War II, focus shifted to a more global European context, including historical studies on French historical works and courtly literature. This focus looked at the possible influences on the *Nibelungenlied* of works such as the *Chanson de Roland (Song of Roland)* (written around 1100) and other heroic tales. The historical context of medieval Germany was also explored to widen this context. Also, explorations of the "courtly" and "chivalric" elements in the work began to appear.

After about 1950, literary approaches dealing with the structure of the poem itself became popular. Such studies, according to Andersson:

> assume that the structure is coherent and meaningful, thus departing from an earlier view that the poet recast an inherited story, making piecemeal modifications without strict regard for the overall plan of the poem and without necessarily imputing a consistent meaning to the whole.

It is also Andersson's argument that the first half of the *Nibelungenlied* was modelled after the second part, and not vice versa.

In recent years, critical commentary has addressed qustions concerning the internal structure of the poem, its characterization, and coherence of plot. Scholarly discussions include the nature of Kriemhild's character development (from innocent bride to avenging queen), Gunther's perceived weaknesses as a king and suitor, and Hagen's guilt or innocence in the context of his role as Gunther and Brunhild's vassal.

Francis G. Gentry's article in *Monatshefte* (see Sources for Further Study) defends Hagen's actions in killing Siegfried, claiming that as Gunther's chief vassal, his "one concern is to uphold and preserve the honor and integrity of his lord, regardless of the consequences." Not all readers would agree. Rudiger's difficult choice of whether to fight the Burgundians is also defended by Gentry, who suggests that "by entering the battle he is only doing that which is required of him under law, the defense of his lord." However, Gentry also acknowledges the difficulty of Rudiger's decision, and the impossibility of making it with a clear conscience. Rudiger ultimately chooses his feudal obligation over his moral obligation. As Rudiger says in Chapter 37 of the *Nibelungenlied*, "Whichever course I leave in order to follow the other, I shall have acted basely and infamously." Nevertheless, the choice must be made.

Gunther's character is problematic as well, and has variously been described as both strong and weak. His acquiescence to Siegfried's superior abilities in winning Brunhild is, according to most scholars, a mark against him. Lynn Thelen's article in *Monatshefte* (see Bibliography) suggests that Gunther, "is upon closer inspection revealed to be a weak and impotent ruler who must rely on the strength of others and stoop to deceit in order to preserve his realm and to realize his desires."

Scholarship on the *Nibelungenlied* has reflected the difficulties faced when trying to reconcile the various motives, intentions, and reactions of its characters, and of trying to account for the many "loose ends" left in the text. For instance, after Siegfried's death, Brunhild almost disappears from the story. Kriemhild's actions after her husband's death (chosing to remain in the court that harbors her husband's killers; agreeing to marry Etzel without being sure that this will help her avenge herself on the killers), are also puzzling to many readers. Hagen's role (with respect to leadership, authority, and power) comes to supercede that of Gunther in the second part of the story. These issues have been and will probably continue to be extensively debated by critics and students studying *The Nibelungenlied*.

## Criticism

### *Laurelle LeVert*

*In the following essay, LeVert surveys both critical and popular reception of the German national epic and addresses questions of genre.*

The *Nibelungenlied* is a work which has elicited both critical acclaim and literary frustration. W. A. Mueller in *The Nibelungenlied Today* suggests that the *Nibelungenlied* "reflected the Germanic concepts of strife, misfortune, death as fate . . . which he must meet with courage and defiance to triumph over them." These issues do pervade the story, as does the characters' abilities to deal effectively with them. Many heroic deeds are performed in the name of honor. Friends even kill friends in the name of honor. But is the *Nibelungenlied* a story which celebrates honor and heroic deeds? As an epic, yes, it is. But the question deserves a more complex answer.

As an epic which encompasses strong elements of the romance genre, the *Nibelungenlied* has sometimes been accused of trying to be neither, and yet both. However, several factors must be taken into account before readers can make such a judgment. First, the elements treated in both genres are largely similar. They both deal with the adventures of knights and ladies, fierce battles, and a code of honorable conduct which pervades the lives of everyone. The difference between epic and romance is in *how* the author treats the elements at hand. It is perhaps due to a combination of these two approaches that the *Nibelungenlied* at times seems unable to decide what it wants to be, or what it wants to say. The epic genre was more concerned with the deeds of knights and noblemen, with "heroic" issues of nobility of spirit, fortitude of character, and physical displays of strength. These are all discussed in a very "grandiose" style. The deeds are performed in battle, on perilous journeys, while fighting dragons and monsters, and always with extensive commentary and long speeches by the characters or narrator himself.

In addition to the *Nibelungenlied's* merging of the literary genres of both epic and romance, the tale attempts to develop its characters into a tragic framework which complements both genres. A tragic figure is one whose misfortunes arise not out of an evil personality, and not necessarily out of a character flaw. Rather, tragedy often strikes "good" characters who make some tragic error in judgment. If

# What Do I Read Next?

- The story of *Beowulf*, written around the tenth century (though the actual poem is thought to be several hundred years older), tells the story of the heroic Beowulf, who slays monsters and dragons. It is full of brave feats and skilled swordplay on the part of its hero.

- *The Epic of Gilgamesh* is a creation epic written in ancient Sumeria around 3000 BC. It tells the story of King Gilgamesh, who befriends the wild man Enkidu. Together they accomplish many great things, including the defeat of fearsome rampaging animals. After Enkidu's death Gilgamesh embarks alone on a journey at the end of which he discovers, and then loses, the secret of eternal life.

- Gregory of Tours' *History of the Franks* is a rich source of information about the history and society of the geographic region which is today France. His book provides interesting insights into the political, social, and military workings of medieval European society such as that portrayed in the *Nibelungenlied*.

- J .R. R. Tolkien's *The Lord of the Rings* is a modern fantasy tale written in 1954. Tolkien's sources for his story include the *Poetic Edda* and the legend of Siegfried the dragon-slayer. In the tale (divided into three volumes), a variation on events in the *Nibelungenlied* occurs. After Siegfried wins the Nibelung treasure, he wakes the beautiful ''Sigrfrida the Valkyrie'' from a magical sleep and woos her for King Gunnar (Gunther). Later, Gunnar and Hogni (Hagen) kill Siegfried for the Nibelung treasure.

- The *Poetic Edda* is a collection of mythological and heroic stories from Iceland, recorded around 1270. Many of the stories draw from the same folk tales and legents as the *Nibelungenlied*, providing a Norse perspective against which to compare the Germanic point of view of the *Nibelungenlied*.

---

this is a suitable working definition, then the reader must ask what error in judgment instigates the final tragedy of the *Nibelungenlied*.

Many scholars suggest that Kriemhild is the protagonist who sets the tragic consequences in motion. The evolution of Kriemhild's character in the *Nibelungenlied* is certainly the force which wreaks havoc at the end of the story, and indeed, throughout. Perhaps she herself is the tragic ''flaw''. She certainly evolves, or perhaps devolves, from innocent child-bride to avenging queen. This is an example of how epic and romance merge, and perhaps conflict. Kriemhild's motives are perhaps in keeping with an ''epic'' character. She does, after all, seek vengeance for a murdered husband. Nonetheless, Kriemhild's ''just vengeance'' is not an ideology that all the characters agree with. Here there are inconsistencies in the literary text itself. For instance, when Siegfried's corpse begins to bleed at Hagen's approach, why do Siegfried's Nibelungs not immediately seek the justice that Kriemhild had promised earlier would be theirs? Why does not Kriemhild herself not give the order to attack? Perhaps because the story would have to stop right here and now! But perhaps it is because Kriemhild's development has just begun.

Does Kriemhild utterly lose her feminine, ''romantic'' image? It would seem so. Indeed, Kriemhild could perhaps be seen as a character who evolves from a ''romantic'' to an ''epic'' character. This evolution is seen throughout the *Nibelungenlied* . Even the narrator's objective tone cannot omit the constant, tragic foreshadowing which follows Kriemhild throughout the story. She never stops mourning Siegfried's death, and her grief grows into bitterness, vengeance, and a truly epic bloodlust. Charles Moorman, in his article on ''The *Nibelungenlied* '' suggests that Kriemhild develops ''from obstinate maiden to charming bride to grief-stricken widow to revengeful devil.'' W. A. Mueller in *The Nibelungenlied Today* has suggested that the author of this story subscribes to a "tragic view of life." This causes the characters to initiate their "own sorrows in spite of the potentials of greatness, happiness, and innocence." This certainly describes Kriemhild's results. But can she be "judged" according to modern standards for her actions? This is a question that readers must determine for themselves.

Whatever Kriemhild's persona represents, it seems clear that the event of Siegfried's death is the catalyst which spurs all further action. Thus two questions arise. First, what led to Siegfried's death in the first place? Next, what events led to the subsequent downfall of the Burgundian dynasty? With respect to the first question, the reader must ask what event "triggered" the murder. Was it Siegfried's initial decision to help Gunther win Brunhild? His pride and arrogance in taking the girdle and ring from Brunhild? Or his foolishness in giving them to Kriemhild, who used them to goad Brunhild? Moreover, what role does Brunhild really play in the *Nibelungenlied*? Is she a pawn used to further the action? The question can be raised, but perhaps not sufficiently answered. What is clear, however, is that Kriemhild's evolution in character is a unifying force in the story.

Now for the second question. What led to the downfall of the Burgundian dynasty? Before attempting to answer (and there is not necessarily a "correct" answer to this question either), it must be remember that, by killing Siegfried, Hagen was technically only fulfilling his feudal oath of loyalty to Brunhild. He could not have known the tragedy which would ensue. Or could he? Nevertheless, his actions instigate what amounts to an international incident. But is Hagen "responsible" in the modern sense? Moreover, what role does Etzel ultimately play in the tragedy which ensues? Is he used as a pawn as well? Let us first consider the events which followed Siegfried's death.

The events at Siegfried's funeral were enough to plant the seeds of vengeance in Kriemhild, seeds which grew into a plan of all-encompassing devastation. But several questions arise with regards to the unfolding story. First, why does Gunther himself not acknowledge the portent of Siegfried's bleeding corpse? It is perhaps because he himself was complicit in the death of Siegfried, the very man who won Brunhild for the king. If Gunther at this point were to agree with Kriemhild that Hagen was the murderer, would he not open himself to similar charges for his own involvement? Hagen himself is an enigma. He on the one hand does not at first admit the deed; nor does he deny it. In fact, he is silent on the matter. It is Gunther who speaks in Hagen's defense. But is Gunther's authority so absolute that his word goes unquestioned? It has not seemed so thus far. These are all loose ends, questions and puzzles which scholars have for centuries tried to reconcile.

Perhaps the tragic events merely provide a forum in which the author can explore the issue of heroism. W. A. Mueller in *The Nibelungenlied Today* believes that although some of the "heroes" in the story epitomize "the concept of heroic death as glory and fulfillment, the poet does not dwell upon the triumph which they voice; instead, we are reminded of the tragic aspects of their death and of the sorrow of their surviving friends and king." It is true that death and destruction are paramount in the story. Charles Moorman in his article on "The *Nibelungenlied*" believes that there are *no* heros in the *Nibelungenlied*. Moorman suggests that even though a character like Hagen may represent the ideals of chivalry, integrity and loyalty, the ideals are reduced to "barbarous cruelty." The same might be said for Kriemhild, Hagen's only equal in the story. Moorman suggests that "like integrity in Kriemhild, fidelity in Hagen breeds barbarity rather than heroic valor."

Gunther himself has come under much critical fire. Lynn Thalen has suggested that Siegfried's wooing of Kriemhild serves as a foil for Gunther's wooing of Brunhild. She suggests that by "juxtaposing Siegfried's valorous feats with Gunther's anxious inactivity, the author effects a devastating portrayal of the Burgundian king." This is indeed a scathing commentary on Gunther, but not an uncommon one. The reader might find it disturbing that the king and leader of a conquering dynasty should be portrayed as weak and ineffectual; unless, of course, the author's purpose is to highlight the deeds and personalities of Siegfried and Hagen, which he does. Thus the issue of "heroism" arises again. Lynn Thalen further criticizes Gunther for his weak nature in the scenes where he welcomes guests: "Gunther is challenged and each time he responds in awed silence, necessitating the quick wits of others to preserve his honor." These are not the actions of a hero, nor a "leader" in either the medieval nor the modern sense.

And what of Rudiger's moral struggle at the end? How does one reconcile the two conflicting worlds he has found himself between? Rudiger in many senses represents the best of both worlds. He is an exemplary feudal vassal and a loyal and trustworthy friend. These two ideals should not have to conflict, and yet they do.

So what is the reader left with? A "testament of despair" as Charles Moorman suggests? A mixed bag of history, legend, myth with only tragic threads to connect it all? What is the "message" of the *Nibelungenlige,* or does it have one? In reading a text which admits so many contradictions and critical disagreement, each reader is placed in his or her own critical position. Nonetheless, perhaps the merging of two genres, epic and romance, both raises and answers all of the above questions. It should not be necessary for the author to "choose" between writing an epic and writing a romance. Nor should it be necessary for Rudiger to "choose" between feudal bonds and friendship. With this in mind, the reader should try to reconcile the merging of two literary ideals, romance and epic, and try to determine how and why they work together in this tragic story.

**Source:** Laurelle LeVert, for *Epics for Students,* Gale Research, 1997.

## A. T. Hatto

*In the following essay, Hatto offers reasoned speculations about the anonymous author of* The Nibelungenlied.

Nothing is known about the poet beyond what we learn from his work. It was evidently a convention that the authors of heroic poems, which were written in a more traditional and popular style than the fashionable romances of the knights, should remain anonymous. No author of a heroic poem names himself during the earlier history of medieval German poetry. On the evidence of the *Nibelungenlied* alone we can only guess at the poet's status, and there is no agreed guess.

Some think that the poet may have been a ministerialis, or 'unfree' knight bound to the service of a lord, that is a man of the same status as his great contemporaries Hartmann von Aue and Wolfram von Eschenbach. Others think of him as a menial cleric with a turn for poetry in his mother tongue. Yet others take him to be a superior sort of 'minstrel', a type of poet that whether in fact or theory, belonged to the nondescript class of wayfarers or strolling entertainers, somewhat suspect, because rootless, plebeians. Yet there are well-authenticated instances of 'minstrels' who were not only members of the households of lords lay or spiritual, but also sometimes settled owners of fiefs, well-to-do, valued men capable of discharging a variety of useful offices for their masters. These guesses virtually exhaust the possibilities, for it is unthinkable that the *Nibelungenlied* was the work of a secular lord, an ecclesiastic, a monk, a merchant, or a peasant.

Despite forthright and even ill-tempered assertions that our poet must have been a knight, the evidence for this claim is weak. Interest in courtly customs, ceremonies, and dress is of course not decisive, since courtly patrons at this time will have expected it. Our poet's sensitive outlook may have matured below the salt. A man of humbler origins than a ministerialis could have had ample opportunity of conversing with his betters as Haydn and others would in a later age, had he been as gifted. But if, against probability, he was indeed a ministerialis, we may be thankful that he kept any enthusiasm he had for the new French fashions of chivalry within such reasonable bounds, since he might easily have ruined his theme. There is, however, a powerful argument, hitherto overlooked, why the poet is unlikely to have been a knight of any sort. It applies to his idea of a hunt. No nobleman who wished to be accepted as such by his fellows would have concocted so absurd a sequence of events as those narrated in Chapter 16, for no student of the hunt can take them seriously. It is quite the flimsiest affair of the chase among all the more respectable narratives of the German Middle Ages. This is at one with the remarkable fact that in an epic in which there is so much fighting there is not a single military technicality such as one finds in other heroic epics like the *Iliad* and the *Song of Roland,* or even in contemporary Arthurian narratives like *Parzival.*

Perhaps the best reason for thinking of the poet as a cleric is that he could cope with over two thousand quatrains on parchment. Yet there are grounds for believing that non-clerical poets could do the same — competition was growing keen in the field of literary entertainment. This would justify us in thinking of the poet as 'semi-clerical', if we like, that is as having enjoyed some schooling. Another reason for thinking him a cleric might be him assumed connexion with the Bishop's City of Passau. Yet the very bishop in whom many would see his chief patron, Wolfger, later Patriarch of Aquilea, generously supported lay poets, the most famous of whom was Walther von der Vogelweide. But if the poet was in fact a cleric, which of course does not necessarily mean a priest, he had a remarkable capacity for thrusting ecclesiastical considerations aside and abandoning himself to the ethos of his subject-matter, which, as we have seen, is far from Christian. We have reviewed the argument that the *Nibelungenlied* may be a sermon on the Fall of Pride, and found that if it is, it is a very unclerical sermon. The most clerical touches in the whole epic, perhaps, are two instances in which the poet praises natural at the expense of counterfeit complexions (pp. 83, 206), and a passage in which he dwells, with much tolerant humour and even complacency, on the long-drawn-out greetings of the ladies (p. 83). This is all, and it amounts to very little. On the other hand, God, the Devil, Church, and the mass are mere narrative conveniences to this poet, or they are part of the normal social background. The warning in Chapter 31 should be heeded, for surely we know where we stand when a man of Hagen's stamp, having dragged a chaplain from the sacred utensils of his mobile altar and thrown him into the Danube without provocation, reminds the Burgundians to confess their sins. Nor is there a note of zeal or disapproval when he tells of Christian living cheek by jowl with pagan at Etzel's Court. If the poet was indeed a cleric he doffed his cassock and folded it neatly away before taking up his quill. He would have been the most facile cleric in medieval German literature, had he in fact been a priest. Much has been said above on his astonishing lack of candour in attributing motives for the deeds he narrates.

We are left with the least hazardous surmise, that the author of the *Nibelungenlied* was a lay poet of plebeian status who had acquired the art of letters at a school and then considerable personal culture in the household of a lord. Are there any positive arguments in favour of this conception?

There is the general argument that heroic poetry in German during this period was purveyed by the miscellaneous and not easily definable 'minstrel' class, and we shall see that what can be reconstructed of our poet's main sources was strongly marked by the 'minstrel' style, which he adopts and refines. There is in the narrative of our poem some very special pleading on behalf of superior minstrels, in part inherited and retained from a minstrel predecessor, in part our poet's contribution. King Etzel sends a leading vassal, the Margrave Rüdiger, to Burgundy to sue for the hand of Kriemhild, yet to invite her royal brothers to Hungary he dispatches the minstrels Werbel and Swemmel, highly favoured men within their own class, but very small fry beside Rüdiger. One might be tempted to explain

this away by arguing that minstrels were the accepted go-betweens, secret agents, and tools for dirty work of their day, and that this pair were appropriately chosen to lure the Burgundians to their doom (for which, incidentally, one of them paid with his hand) (p.243). But however this may have been in the poet's source, as he tells the story they were chosen for their mission not by Kriemhild but by Etzel, and in good faith. Another explanation offered is that the Burgundians might have harboured less suspicion towards on invitation conveyed by men of so peaceful a profession. In real life they are unthinkable as royal ambassadors for such an occasion, and it is best to ascribe them to the wistful and perhaps ironic imaginings of a poet on the fringe of high society. And here, no doubt, is the point: what gifts were lavished on Werbel and Swemmel, going and coming on their embassy!. It is both amusing and touching to see in what princely fashion these minstrels — already worth a thousand marks each from the takings at Kriemhild's wedding — live for the brief space of their royal mission. The same theme of largesse is touched on with a rather personal show of impersonality when Kriemhild rewards the messenger for his news of the Saxon war: 'Such gifts encourage one to tell such news to great ladies.' And then there is the enigmatic figure of Volker, Hagen's comrade-in-arms. We know for sure that the poet inherited Volker from his source for the second part of his poem, and there are some grounds for believing that Volker may have been of minstrel status in it. Our poet, however, presents Volker as a nobleman who brings thirty of his own vassals to the wars, and he gives him prominence in battle. Volker nevertheless retains his viol and his title of 'Fiddler' and 'Minstrel' as a sobriquet, and he plays the army to sleep. He is further distinguished by being made to sing to Lady Gotelind to his own accompaniment, earning the favour of a rich reward. Thus the poet by implication thrice advances the claims to honour of 'minstrels': in diplomacy, at court before the ladies, and on the field of battle. It is hard to imagine either a poor knight or a menial cleric doing this for his professional rivals.

The safest guess is, then, that the strange genius who wrote the *Nibelungenlied* was a semi-clerical poet by profession, technically of the order of *vagi* or wayfarers, though probably sedentary for much of his life.

**Source:** A. T. Hatto, in an Appendix to *The Nibelungenlied*, translated by A. T. Hatto, Penguin, 1969 , pp. 354–57.

## D. G. Mowatt

*In the following essay, Mowatt talks about both the literary merits of* The Nibelungenlied *and its role as the German national epic.*

The *Nibelungenlied* has on occasion been compared to the *Iliad.* The fact that Germans have been impelled to make, and foreigners disposed to deride, such a comparison, is revealing in itself, for it shows the veneration both works have suffered. Assessment of their literary merit has been geographically conditioned, with Homer belonging to western civilization as a whole, and the *Nibelungenlied* for the most part only to Germany. But in both cases scholars have painstakingly erected a barrier between heritage and inheritors. The occasional whiff of vanished glory that came over has been made to serve the literary and political establishment. The interesting circumstance that both works deal with events and customs that must have appeared exotic, if not bizarre, to their authors, is not emphasized. The suggestion that the virtues of our Achaean or Germanic ancestors could have been held up to bardic ridicule is discouraged. And yet they obviously are. Agamemnon, as Robert Graves points out in the introduction to his recent translation, *The Anger of Achilles* (1959), is completely out of his depth throughout most of the *Iliad.*

What poet, after all, would wish to identify himself with a bloodthirsty, conceited and obstinate king, who is not successful even by his own standards, and eventually comes to a sticky end? And the career of King Gunther in the *Nibelungenlied* is no more exemplary. Like Agamemnon, he is killed in ignominious circumstances, by a woman. Admittedly she is only his sister. But his wife shows little respect for his kingly person either: she removes him from their conjugal bed on the first night, and hangs him on a convenient nail till morning. It seems that the whole concept of royal infallibility was at least questionable in the eyes of these two poets.

The *Nibelungenlied* goes further in this direction than Homer, and the efforts of its scholarly guardians not to notice the fact have been correspondingly stronger. Unfortunately, the increase in narrative detachment seems to have involved a deterioration in traditional clichés, so that the recitals of bloody deeds and barbaric splendours are even more perfunctory in the *Nibelungenlied* than in the *Iliad.* Stripped of its irony, the *Nibelungenlied* is tedious in the extreme, and can only be taken seriously by someone in desperate need of a heroic past. The blond Germanic beast marching bravely towards his fate is not to everyone's taste. Nor, for that matter, is the hidebound medieval court, obsessed with power and protocol. As long as these two elements were kept isolated, and regarded with bovine earnestness, the *Nibelungenlied* was guaranteed a cool reception by most people, and in most ages. It was offered, and rejected, as a work extolling two self-contradictory orthodoxies, neither of which is very interesting in itself. Luckily, however, orthodoxies are seldom sacred in literature and the *Nibelungenlied* is no exception to this rule. Positions are certainly taken up in the work, but they clash, sometimes comically, sometimes tragically, and very little is left of any of them at the end. The particular pretensions chosen for undermining were historically conditioned. Instead of Trafalgar, the sanctity of the home and the royal family, for instance, they had their heroic past, the sanctity of woman and an ideal of courtly behaviour. Instead of the hydrogen bomb, or sex, they had mythical figures like Sifrid and Brünnhilde on which to focus their hopes and fears.

Much work has been devoted to finding out something about the author, and the literary tradition in which he worked. . . . The yield is meagre: he was an unknown poet, probably of knightly (i.e. unexceptionable) status, writing at the turn of the twelfth and thirteenth centuries. He was probably Austrian, and may have worked for a certain Bishop of Passau. He must have known earlier versions of parts (perhaps the whole) of the material he was using, because variations on the same characters and situations are found scattered throughout Scandinavian and German literature. Any attempt to achieve greater precision on this score must be speculative. All the Scandinavian sources are later than the *Nibelungenlied,* although parts of them must be based on much earlier material. . . . In Germany there is the *Hildebrandslied* (written down at Fulda in the nineth century), which treats the story of Dietrich, Hildebrand and his son in archaic and highly idiosyncratic language. It is possible that the *Nibelungenlied* poet was familiar with a version of this poem, but if so he made no use of it. The Walther story referred to by Hildebrand in stanza 2344 is similarly unexploited, apart from this one mention.

The truth is there are no immediate sources; and those who need something to compare with the finished product have been reduced to reconstructing earlier versions for themselves. The process is circular, and the result unverifiable. . . . It seems reasonably certain that there were in existence a number of short episodic lays clustering round such figures as Sifrid, Brünnhilde, Dietrich, Hagen and Kriemhilde; and perhaps an extended narrative treating the downfall of the Burgundians. Nothing is established for these works beyond the bare probability of their existence.

The ultimate sources of the *Nibelungenlied* are much easier to discern. They are: legend (from a heroic past in the fourth to sixth centuries), chivalry (an orthodoxy from the twelfth and thirteenth centuries) and myth. The wars and great migrations following the advent of the Huns in eastern Europe threw up legendary heroes like Theoderic (Dietrich) of Verona, Hildebrand, Hagen and Gundaharius (Gunther), King of the Burgundians. Some of these men actually existed, as Theodoric, who ruled over Italy from 493 to 526, and Gundaharius, whose kingdom by the Rhine was in fact destroyed by the Huns (though not under Attila) in 435. Others, like Hildebrand, are just prototypes of the Germanic fighting hero. These figures carry their legendary past with them, and their social unit is the family or tribe, As might be expected from their origins, there is often something of the landless knight or exile about them, especially when heroic exploits are involved. But the details of their dress, speech, eating and courting habits, public rituals and, in the case of Rüdeger at least, of their moral preoccupations, are taken from medieval courtly society. These details constitute the second, or chivalric, element. The third, or mythological, element is embodied in figures like Sifrid, Brünnhilde and Alberich the dwarf, who stand out as belonging to no society at all, as being in some way subhuman or superhuman.

So much for the ingredients. The mixture seems to have gone down well, to judge from the number of manuscripts which have survived, and it is not difficult to see why. Past greatness, present pretensions and the possibility of rejuvenation (or destruction) from outside—this is a combination which must exercise a perpetual fascination for all self-conscious societies. It is true that an expansive community may believe for short periods that sophistication is an irreversible process; but recent history has shown how easily the most complex network of relationships can be reduced to primitive posturing, given the right circumstances. And this is exactly what happens in the *Nibelungenlied,* where a highly developed society reverts under strain.

We are shown, first of all, the court at Worms. It is presided over by the brothers Gunther, Gernot and Giselher, and actually run by Hagen. Everyone knows his place, and there are set procedures for every situation. They are, on the whole, a tedious and complacent company. Their sister Kriemhilde is outwardly an exemplary Burgundian lady, but she shows signs of being self-willed about her emotional life (stanza 17), and has an ominous future foretold for her (stanza 14).

The court at Santen is much the same. As at Worms, the homogeneity extends to the names Sigebert and Sigelinde, but their son Sifrid is even more of a misfit than Gunther's sister. Not only is his name wrong (just as Kriemhilde refuses to alliterate with her brothers), but he has a rather unorthodox past. As we later learn from Hagen, he is invulnerable, has slain a dragon and owns a magic treasure.

The court at Isenstein, by contrast, is dominated by a single remarkable woman, determined to rely on her own strength until the right man arrives. Her demands are quite simple: he must be the best (i.e. the strongest and bravest) man available. This is not perhaps so very different from the standard applied at Worms, where the king is by definition endowed with both these qualities. But the really anti-social thing about Brünnhilde is that she insists on putting royal pretensions to the test, and killing all the mighty monarchs who fail. She is a challenge to people like Gunther to justify their title. Of course Gunther himself is no fool, and would never dream of exposing himself to such a blast of reality; but the arrival of Sifrid opens up new possibilities. Here, suddenly, is a man who equates kingship with conquest (stanzas 108 ff.), just like Brünnhilde, and who is eminently capable of meeting the challenge. Moreover he wants to marry Gunther's sister, and is prepared to go to any lengths to do so. Presented with this happy circumstance, it is an easy matter for the practised diplomat to manipulate Sifrid into satisfying all Brünnhilde's demands incognito, leaving all the credit, and the tangible prize, to Gunther. There is the rather intimate question of the bed, but after that has been solved and hushed up the glory of Burgundy seems assured.

The thing which destroys the foundations, if not at first the complacency of Worms, is the tension between inflated appearance and mean reality. The qualities in Sifrid and Brünnhilde that eventually uncover this tension are precisely those which the Burgundians have tried to use for their own aggrandizement. Brünnhilde is too honest and uncompromising to accept the official version of Sifrid's status, and once again she insists on putting appearances to the test. The quarrel between the two queens and the ritual murder of Sifrid are the result. Sifrid's own crime is simply to behave in character. He is quite willing to let the Burgundians use his strength, but he makes no attempt to disguise his superiority. He is quite blandly indifferent to all the jealousies, rules and compromises which hold the society together. He is not interested in money (stanzas 558, 694–5), status (stanza 386), face-saving ceremony (stanzas 748–9) or political etiquette (stanzas 314–15). And, worst of all, he seems to have forgotten all about the sanctity of women as soon as he married Kriemhilde (stanzas 858, 894). Such innocence is in itself provocative. His one vulnerable spot is known only to Kriemhilde, and she, like a good Burgundian, betrays it to Hagen.

With Sifrid dead, and his treasure hastily dumped in the Rhine, it is left to Kriemhilde and Hagen to fight it out. In the process, the whole way of life at Burgundy is inexorably deflated and destroyed. The last magnificent tournament ends in a brutal killing; the elaborate political speeches are reduced to childish defiance; the subtly interlocking loyalties and prohibitions to blind tribal solidarity; the splendid feasting and drinking to the final macabre meal of blood, with corpses for benches. The mighty king is trussed up, and slaughtered by his sister. The crown of courtly womanhood is carved up by Dietrich's retainer.

Loyalty and good faith, made for security, are turned to destruction, so that allegiance to either side is the equivalent of a death sentence. Neutrality, on the other hand, is impossible, as even Dietrich discovers. He does, it is true, survive, but stripped of all the relationships which he and Hildebrand had built up round themselves (stanza 2319). Rüdeger, a much weaker and more dependent character, is pathetically caught in a dilemma of his own making. His hospitality and his readiness to oblige a lady, both excellent social qualities, have tied him equally to the Burgundians and to Kriemhilde. Obsessive generosity, designed to win lifelong friends, provides the instrument of his death. The bonds that once held society together now destroy it. At Etzel's court everyone is an exile.

**Source:** D. G. Mowatt, in an introduction to *The Nibelungenlied,* translated by D. G. Mowatt, Dent, 1962, pp. v–x.

### Arthur E. Huston and Patricia McCoy

*In the following excerpt, the critics explore some possible source material for this epic. They commend the work's blending of historical fact with mythic elements, and maintain that it was probably written by a single author.*

The *Nibelungenlied,* like the *Beowulf,* is a poem embodying materials drawn from Germanic history, mythology, and legend, a story of "old, unhappy, far-off things, and battles long ago." ... It contains the story of Siegfried, dragon-slayer and winner of the treasure of the Nibelungs; his courtship of Kriemhild, sister of Gunther, King of the Burgundians, and their marriage; his winning of Brunhild, by a trick, for Gunther; the feud between Brunhild and Kriemhild; the murder of Siegfried by Gunther's vassal, Hagen; the marriage of Kriemhild to Etzel, King of the Huns, and Etzel's invitation to the Burgundians; the death of Gunther and Hagen in Etzel's hall; and finally, the death of Kriemhild.

We recognize parts of this story from our knowledge of its most recent version, that found in Wagner's operas called the *Ring of the Nibelungs.* We notice, also, that Wagner's version is in many respects quite different from that of the *Nibelungenlied.* Wagner saw the story as one in which the most important personages were Siegfried and Brunhild, and, like many Germans of his time, he thought of them as figures drawn from the Germanic pantheon: a culture-hero, almost a demigod, and a Valkyr, a battle-maiden, the chooser of the slain destined for Valhalla. In order to attain his artistic objective, he wrote two operas, *Das Rheingold* and *Die Walküre,* which tell of the events preceding the story of Siegfried and the rival queens found in the *Nibelungenlied.* In the central opera, *Siegfried,* he tells the story of the dragon-slaying and the winning of the hoard, and includes an event scarcely glanced at in the *Nibelungenlied,* the betrothal of Siegfried and Brunhild. And in the final opera of the cycle *Die Götterdämmerung (The Twilight of the Gods),* he tells of the murder of Siegfried and the self-immolation of Brunhild on his funeral pyre, this last incident also not found in the *Nibelungenlied.*

Wagner's version, also, makes much more use of Germanic mythology than does the *Nibelungenlied.* The Middle High German poem, written in a thoroughly Christian atmosphere, could not well bring in Wotan, the principal deity of the Germanic pantheon; but Wagner's presentation of the story demanded the presence of these gods. For such materials he went to the versions of the story current in medieval Scandinavia, preserved in the Eddas, and, most completely, in the thirteenth-century Icelandic *Volsungasaga.*

The *Volsungasaga* tells a story very like that found in the *Nibelungenlied,* but it contains also other elements not found in the Germanic poem, especially the story of the birth of Siegfried (called Sigurd in the Norse), and the events which took place after the death of Gunther (Gunnar) and Hagen (Hogni). Although it was written down some two hundred years after the *Nibelungenlied,* it was not in the least influenced by that poem; rather, it is another version of the same story, drawn from the same source.

And here we must repeat what we said earlier, that the *Nibelungenlied* is a poem embodying elements drawn from Germanic mythology, legend, and history. In the *Nibelungenlied,* it is true, the mythological elements are of the slightest, if indeed, strictly speaking, they exist at all. Folklore material is there in plenty: the slaying of the dragon, for instance, and the *Tarnkappe,* the hood of invisibility, are matters met with in many fairy tales. Basically, however, the story is legend founded on history.

The historical fact underlying the legends, found widely throughout the Germanic-speaking areas, is the destruction of the Burgundian capital at Worms, in 437, by the Huns, whose king was Attila. We recognize that this must be the same name as Etzel, found in the *Nibelungenlied,* and Atli, in the *Volsungasaga.* The Burgundian princes, was we know from an early document called the "Law of the Burgundians," were named Gibica, Gundahari, and Gislahari. and these must be the same names as Gibich, father of Gunther, Gernot and Giselher. The treacherous invitation of Etzel at his wife's prompting, and his killing of Gunther and Hagen, must be a legendary reflection of the defeat of the Burgundians, for people do not celebrate their defeats in their stories; rather, they adapt history to legend in order to explain their defeats. Modern examples of this phenomenon are not lacking.

The adaptation of history to legend is the prerogative of the epic poet, who need have no concern with fact as such. Theodoric of Verona, or Dietrich von Bern, another famous German legendary and historical figure, died in 526; yet the *Nibelungenlied*-poet has him present at the death of Kriemhild, which must have been nearly a century earlier. Probably the poet was not in the least aware that he was mixing up his centuries, for he was a poet, not a historian, and, just as Wagner was to do many

centuries later, he used whatever material he had as his artistic necessities demanded.

The Germanic values of the *Nibelungenlied* still prevail, beneath the courtly façade. Gunther is a medieval prince, adept in political intrigue; but it is not difficult to see in him, as in King Siegfried, the earlier "bestower-of-rings" and "shield-of-knights." This courtliness, however, owes something to the expanding influences of French models. None of the earlier Germanic stories takes any great interest in romantic love; and love between man and woman is one of the primary forces of the *Nibelungenlied.* In this the epic is the product of its time, the late Middle Ages; for romantic love was not earlier a source of the question of loyalties.

The *Nibelungenlied*-poet could have found easy scope for lyricism in the magical background of the poem. The ring and girdle of Brunhild, the winning of the Hoard, the awakening of Brunhild within the circle of fire—these episodes, and many more, could have carried him from his artistic purpose. Fortunately, these temptations were not victorious; perhaps, if they had prevailed, the *Nibelungenlied* would be only another interesting lay of medieval Germany. As in other poetry of epic stature, however, the mythological tradition behind the creation of the work is either told in episodic, narrative fashion, or implied. In the *Nibelungenlied,* most of this material is implied. It is very difficult to trace the mechanical techniques by which the effect is accomplished. Why does Brunhild tower over Kriemhild, in spite of their mutual ownership of the magical objects of power, and the greater number of lines which are given to Kriemhild and her revenge? Why, without a single explicit line of proof, does Hagen tower above Gunther, worthy to be the nemesis of Siegfried and the last of the men of Nibelung to die in battle? Even without any knowledge of the Eddas or the *Volsungasaga,* any perceptive reader can feel their stature.

Keeping the mystic elements in the background, the poet of the *Nibelungenlied* saves his lyric power for more human and personal topics, as does Dante in the episode of Paolo and Francesca in the *Divine Comedy.* The German poet's description of Siegfried's first meeting with Kriemhild is scarcely to be rivaled:

> Even as the full moon stands before the stars, so pure in her radiance that all clouds must run away before her, so did she stand in beauty among her ladies.

For Dante's Francesca, "the greatest pain of all is remembrance of past happiness in present woe";

for Kriemhild, "all pleasure, no matter how sweet, must at last turn to pain." But, whether the emphasis be upon fate or upon the Christian eternity, the sweetest passages in both epics are those of human love.

Scholarly search for the author of the *Nibelungenlied* has, to date, been inconclusive. A bishop of the late tenth century—Pilgrim of Passau—had created most of the main incidents of the story, as his own version of popular legend; he is accepted as a main source for the poem. A Minnesinger known as "*Der Kurenberger*" is known to have written at least fifteen detached stanzas in the same metre. Yet, although the "folk-epic" theory of the nineteenth century has long been in disrepute, no valid scholarship has established the identity of the poet. The uniformity of style, as well as the method of incorporating myth, points to a single author. Karl Lachmann, the Germanic scholar, has found at least twenty lays of ancient origin which seem to form a part of the poem; his research, although of the "folk-epic" school, has indicated to many modern critics the probability of individual authorship; it is unlikely, they argue, that these vastly rich background sources could have been coordinated in such a manner by a "folk-author." Furthermore, his nineteen "twelfth-century additions" would appear to indicate a uniformity too great for a "folk epic." It is, in fact, unlikely that any poem of epic stature could have been other than individual in authorship. An epic cannot have "the quality of growth, rather than of authorship," although centuries of growth may lie behind it.

Some critics believe that the *Nibelungenlied* was, in its earliest form, meant to be sung rather than read. Its verse-form, a four-line strophe, instead of the couplet-form of the later romantic epics, seems to corroborate this theory. There can be little doubt that the early lays of which it is formed were sung in courtly circles. But the music of the German epic is not the music of the Minnesinger; there is now little question that it was meant to be read. There were, as we have seen, many versions of the story available, but this does not mean that it grew by itself from the songs of minstrels. The story of the fall of the Burgundian kingdom must have inspired many poets, even as the absorption of the Geats led to the creation of the semi-mythological Beowulf. But, as the *Beowulf* is now accepted as the creation of an individual, so must the *Nibelungenlied* have been a unification of many poetic tales by one author. Its simplicity and uniformity of diction, its classical richness, so well disciplined, seem ample testimony, combined with the usual linguistic and literary tests, of its single authorship. But it is very pleasant to think of the poem as recited to the sound of harps. Its meter, with the marked caesura, the measured half-line of three feet, with the last half-line of each strophe extended to four feet, seems admirably suited to such presentation. However, the careful artistic variation of accent indicates that it was meant to be read.

**Source:** Arthur E. Hutson and Patricia McCoy, "Nibelungenlied," in *Epics of the Western World*, J. B. Lippencott Company, 1954, pp. 297–336.

## Sources for Further Study

Andersson, Theodore M. *A Preface to the Nibelungenlied.* Stanford University Press, 1987.
> Andersson discusses the *Nibelungenlied* in the context of the development of epic poetry, focusing on the rise of the romance genre and the ways that the *Nibelungenlied* participates in both genres. He provides extensive bibliographic entries for each of his chapters, and deals with the sources, literary context, and critical history of the *Nibelungenlied.*

Boggs, Roy A. "The Popular Image of Brunhilde," in *The Roles and Images of Women in the Middle Ages and Renaissance,* edited by Douglas Radcliff-Umstead. University of Pittsburgh Press, 1975.
> Boggs discusses the various interpretations of Brunhilde's role in the *Nibelungenlied* and in other works. She is primarily seen as the "noble but betrayed queen of Iceland," but her character does appear and take other roles in some Scandinavian epics such as the *Volsunga Saga* and the *Poetic Edda.*

Gentry, Francis G.. "Hagen and the Problem of Individuality in the Nibelungenlied." *Monatshefte,* Vol. 68, 1976, pp. 5-12.
> Gentry attempts to determine the attitudes of the anonymous author of the *Nibelungenlied* toward the legal and moral demands of feudalism made on characters in the work.

Hatto, A. T. Foreword to *The Nibelungenlied,* translated by A. T. Hatto, Penguin Books, 1969.
> Brief introduction to the work and its place in world epic literature. This useful edition also includes "An Introduction to a Second Reading," "A Note on the Translation," and appendices consisting of essays on "The Status of the Poet," "The Manuscript Tradition, Bishop Wolfger of Passau, and the Homeland of the Last Poet," "The Date of the Poem," "The Genesis of the Poem," "The Geography of the Poem," and "A Glossary of the Characters' Names."

Haymes, Edward R. *The Nibelungenlied: History and Interpretation.* University of Illinois Press, 1986.
> Discusses the relevance of medieval literature to a modern audience, and discusses the genesis of oral

and written culture in the Middle Ages. He deals with the structural and thematic issues presented in the *Nibelungenlied.*

Haymes, Edward R. and Susann T. Samples. *Heroic Legends of the North: An Introduction to the Nibelung and Dietrich Cycles.* Garland Publishing, Inc., 1996.
    Haymes and Samples provide a comprehensive historical look at the sources from which the *Nibelungenlied* drew. They discuss the history and development of heroic poetry and epic, and the legends of the germanic peoples. This text also deals with the evolution of heroic legends from oral transmission to written literature.

Mowatt, D. G. In an introduction to ''The Nibelungenlied,'' translated by D .G. Mowatt, Dent, 1962, pp. v-x.
    Mowatt discusses the *Nibelungenlied's* role as a historical national epic of Germany.

Mueller, Werner A. *The Nibelungenlied Today: Its Substance, Essence, and Significance.* AMS Press Inc., 1966.
    Mueller discusses some of the dominant themes in the *Nibelungenlied,* such as honor, loyalty, gentility, and the role of family and social relationships and oaths.

Thelen, Lynn D. ''The Internal Source and Function of King Gunther's Bridal Quest.'' *Monatshefte,* Vol. 76 (1984): pp. 143-155.
    Thelen suggests that Gunther's wooing of Brunhild is problematic in the story of the *Nibelungenlied,* and provides the reader with reason to doubt Gunther's strength as a leader. She suggests that the bridal games in which Siegfried takes part on Gunther's behalf serve to entertain the reader, to further characterize Gunther, and to ''underscore the theme of real versus claimed power.''

# Odyssey

## Homer

## c. 700 B.C.

For all practical purposes, the *Odyssey* is the "sequel" to the earlist well–known surviving work in Western literature, the *Iliad*. (The *Epic of Gilgamesh*, while at least 1,000 years older, is neither as well-known nor as influential as Homer's work.) Unlike many sequels in the present era, however, the *Odyssey* actually seems to be an improvement, in some respects, on the original, and stands quite well as an independent work.

*Odysseia*—the poem's name in Greek since Herodotus called it that in the fifth century BC—means simply "the story of Odysseus." The word "odyssey" that derives from this name has come to mean any significant and difficult journey. Although the poem is technically about one particular man's journey, as Horace observed in his first *Satire,* "*mutato nomine, fabula de te narratur,*" "just change the name and the story could be told about you."

If we were to call the *Iliad* the world's first adventure story, the *Odyssey* could be called its first opera: certainly some of the plot twists along the way would be at home in that extravagant genre. In the context of Odysseus's voyages and troubles, the poem touches on a number of significant topics such as loyalty, heroism, creativity, and order. Where the *Iliad* is noteworthy for its similes and epithets, the *Odyssey* is justly famous for its use of symbolism and for the pace and variety of its action.

For more than 1,500 years the *Iliad* and the *Odyssey* set the standard by which epic poetry, if not all poetry of any kind, was judged. The epic form in poetry has not been widely practiced since the appearance of John Milton's *Paradise Lost* in 1667, but the story of Odysseus's wanderings has remained a perennial favorite to the present day.

## Author Biography

Everything we know about Homer is either traditional, mythical, or based upon educated guesswork. Tradition tells us, probably following the *Odyssey* and one of the so-called "Homeric Hymns" from the middle of the seventh century BC, that Homer, like his own character Demodocus, was a blind bard or singer of tales.

At least seven different places claimed that Homer was born on their soil in the ancient world. The two with the strongest claims are the island of Chios and the city of Smyrna (modern Izmir, in Turkey). The consensus of opinion is that Homer probably lived and worked in Ionia, the region along what is now the west coast of Turkey. This conclusion is based on several ancient traditions about Homer and his origins, and also on clues in his works, chiefly the preponderance of Ionic dialect in the poems and the sketchy knowledge of the geography of western Greece displayed in the *Odyssey* (the overland chariot journey from Pylos to Sparta at the end of Book 3 would have been physically impossible, and Homer's description of Ithaca is so vague that some scholars have suggested he did not mean the island that currently bears the name), in contrast to the vivid depictions of Troy and its environs in the *Iliad*.

We can only guess at the time when Homer lived and wrote. Some ancient traditions suggested that Homer lived relatively close to the time of the events he described. The fifth-century historian Herodotus, on the other hand (*Histories,* II.53), said that Homer could not possibly have lived more than 400 years before his own time. The rediscovery of writing by the Greeks around 750 BC and the development, at about the same time, of some of the fighting techniques described in the *Iliad* have led scholars to assign Homer to the middle or late part of the eighth century BC.

Accurate dating of Homer's poems is impossible, but it is generally thought that the *Iliad* is older than the *Odyssey,* as that work displays some more "advanced" stylistic features. Both poems had to have been completed before the Peisistratid dynasty came to power in Athens in the sixth century BC, because it is known that a member of that family commissioned a "standard edition" of the poems. Also during the sixth century BC, both the *Iliad* and the *Odyssey* were recited in full at the Great Panathenaia, a religious festival in honor of Athena which was observed in Athens every four years.

There have been any number of controversies about Homer since his time, beginning with the contention over just exactly where and when he was born, lived, and died. Others have questioned whether Homer existed at all, and whether a poet named Homer actually "wrote" the poems attributed to him or merely culled them from popular folklore. The question of whether the same person produced both the *Iliad* and the *Odyssey* has also been debated. English poet and critic Samuel Butler (1835-1902) suggested that the *Odyssey* was the work of a woman, but this view did not gain wide acceptance.

Most scholars at least agree that there was an epic poet called Homer, and that he played the primary part in producing the *Iliad* and *Odyssey* in their known forms.

## Plot Summary

### *The Background to the Story*

After ten years, the Trojan War is over and the Achaeans head for home—with varying results. Some, like Nestor, come home quickly to find things pretty much as they left them. Others, like Agamemnon, arrive home to find things considerably changed. Still others, like Menelaus, wander for a time but eventually return home safely and little the worse for wear.

Odysseus, on the other hand, has been having no end of trouble getting home. As the story opens, we find ourselves in the tenth year since the end of the war, a full 20 years since Odysseus first left his home and wife Penelope to sail off for Troy with the rest of the Achaean forces.

### *Book 1: Athena Inspires Telemachus*

In a council of the gods, Athena asks her father Zeus why Odysseus is still stuck on Calypso's island ten years after the end of the war. Zeus responds that Poseidon is angry at Odysseus for having blinded his son, Polyphemus. But since Poseidon is temporarily absent, Zeus gives Athena permission to begin arrangements for Odysseus's return. Athena goes to Ithaca in disguise and inspires Odysseus's son Telemachus to go in search of news of his father. Heartened by her words, Telemachus announces his intention to sail to the mainland.

## Book 2: Telemachus Sails to Pylos

Telemachus calls an assembly and asks for assistance in getting to the mainland. His independent attitude does not sit well with his mother Penelope's suitors, who oppose him in the assembly so that he does not receive the aid he sought. After making secret preparations, Telemachus and the disguised Athena depart for Pylos that same evening.

## Book 3: Nestor Tells What He Knows

Telemachus and Athena arrive in Pylos, to find Nestor and his family offering sacrifice to Poseidon. After joining in the ritual, Telemachus introduces himself to Nestor and explains his purpose in coming. Nestor has heard news of the returns of both Menelaus and Agamemnon, which he relates to Telemachus, but has had no news of Odysseus since all of the Achaeans left Troy ten years previously. Nestor sends Telemachus, accompanied by one of his own sons, Pisistratus, to visit Menelaus in Sparta.

## Book 4: In the Home of Menelaus and Helen

Telemachus and Pisistratus arrive at Menelaus's home during a celebration, and are warmly entertained by Menelaus and Helen. Menelaus tells a long story of his adventures on the way home from Troy, including news that he got from Proteus in Egypt that Odysseus was alive on Calypso's island. Meanwhile, back in Ithaca, the suitors learn of Telemachus's secret departure and are not pleased. They plot to ambush and kill him on his way home. Penelope also learns of her son's departure.

## Book 5: Odysseus Sets Sail for Home—and is Shipwrecked

At another council of the gods, Zeus orders Hermes to go to Calypso and tell her to let Odysseus leave for Ithaca. Calypso is unhappy, but obeys the order. She offers Odysseus a chance to become immortal and to live with her forever; which he declines. Odysseus builds a raft with tools and materials she provides, and sails off. Poseidon comes back from feasting with the Ethiopians and wrecks the raft in a storm. Odysseus, with the help of a sea goddess, is washed safely ashore in the land of the Phaeacians.

## Book 6: Nausicaa Encounters a Stranger

The Phaeacian Princess Nausicaa finds the shipwrecked Odysseus asleep behind a bush. Odysseus asks Nausicaa for help. She gives him some clothing to wear and sends him into town to find the palace of her father, Alcinous.

## Book 7: Odysseus and the King of Phaeacia

Odysseus arrives at the palace and begs the assistance of King Alcinous and Queen Arete. He gives an edited version of his "adventures" to date, but does not disclose his identity. He deftly turns aside Alcinous's suggestion that he should remain in Phaeacia and marry Nausicaa.

## Book 8: The Phaeacians Entertain Odysseus

The Phaeacians treat Odysseus to a day of feasting, song, and athletic events. When Odysseus begins weeping during Demodocus's tale of the Trojan War, Alcinous cuts the banquet short. At dinner that evening, Odysseus speaks highly of Demodocus's skill and offers him a prime cut of his own portion. When Demodocus sings the story of the Trojan Horse, Odysseus begins crying again, and Alcinous asks Odysseus who he is and why stories about Troy make him cry.

## Book 9: Odysseus Tells His Story–Polyphemus and the Cyclopes

Odysseus reveals his identity and tells his story, beginning with his departure from Troy with 12 ships. He sacks Ismarus in Thrace, is blown off course to the land of the Lotus-Eaters, and eventually reaches the island of the Cyclopes, one-eyed giants who are sons of the sea god Poseidon.

Odysseus and the crew of his ship go to investigate this island and end up imprisoned in Polyphemus's cave. The giant finds the intruders and eats several of them for dinner. After a similar breakfast, he takes his flocks of sheep and goats to graze, leaving Odysseus and his remaining men penned in the cave. Upon Polyphemus's return, they manage to get the giant drunk and blind him. The next day they escape from his cave hiding under the

*Map of the Aegean region.*

bellies of his sheep and goats. Odysseus unwisely reveals his true name, and Polyphemus asks his father Poseidon to avenge his injury.

### Book 10: Odysseus Tells His Story–At the Islands of Aeolus and Circe

Odysseus and his surviving crewmen now sail to the island of Aeolus, king of the winds. Aeolus gives Odysseus a bag containing all the winds that would blow him off his homeward course. They sail away and come close enough to Ithaca to see the watch-fires, when Odysseus falls asleep at the helm and his crew, thinking the bag contains a hoard of

gold, untie it and release the captive winds—which blow them right back to Aeolus's island.

Aeolus refuses to help them again, saying that they are obviously cursed by the gods.

Odysseus and his crew set sail once more and eventually reach the land of the Laestrygonians, who destroy all but one of his ships. The survivors sail to Circe's island, where most of them are promptly turned into pigs by this enchantress. Odysseus, forewarned by Hermes, avoids Circe's trap and frees his men. They remain with Circe for a year before Odysseus's men ask to leave. Circe tells

Odysseus that he must first visit the underworld and consult with the shade of the prophet Tiresias on how best to get home.

## Book 11: Odysseus Tells His Story–In the House of the Dead

Obeying Circe's instructions, Odysseus and his men sail to the underworld, where they make sacrifices to Hades and Persephone, and consult Tiresias. When Tiresias retires, the shades of Odysseus's mother and several of his comrades at Troy appear, including those of Achilles and Agamemnon. Odysseus also witnesses the punishment of several notorious offenders against the gods.

## Book 12: Odysseus Tells His Story— The Sun-God's Cattle

Upon his return from the underworld, Odysseus receives sailing instructions from Circe: how to avoid the lure of the Sirens, how to get past the monster Scylla and the whirlpool Charybdis, and above all, not to harm the cattle of the sun-god on the island of Thrinacia. Cast upon Thrinacia by a fierce storm and out of provisions, Odysseus's men disobey him and slaughter some of the cattle. The sun god complains to Zeus, who destroys the ship with a thunderbolt. Only Odysseus survives, and he drifts to Calypso's island by hanging on to floating wreckage. This ends Odysseus's story as told to the Phaeacians

## Book 13: Return to Ithaca and the Stone Ship

The Phaeacians return Odysseus and all his treasures to his home of Ithaca while he himself is deep asleep. Athena, in disguise, meets Odysseus and he tries to trick her, without success, with a false story about himself. She reveals her identity and tells him how much she cares for him, and together they plot a stratagem for dealing with Penelope's suitors. After stowing Odysseus's treasure safely in a cave, Athena disguises Odysseus as an ancient beggar and sends him on his way. Poseidon, angry that the Phaeacians have helped Odysseus get back to Ithaca, turns their ship into a huge stone, visible to onlookers on shore and rooted to the sea-bottom.

## Book 14: The Loyal Swineherd

Odysseus makes his way to the dwelling of Eumaeus, a swineherd who has remained loyal to his long-absent employer. Odysseus, still in disguise, entertains Eumaeus with some ''lying tales'' about himself.

## Book 15: Telemachus Heads for Home

Telemachus takes his leave of Helen and Menelaus. Telemachus offers passage to the seer Theoclymenus, who is fleeing vengeance for a kinsman's death. Back in Ithaca, Eumaeus tells Odysseus the story of his life. Telemachus evades the suitors' ambush and sends Theoclymenus home with a friend, as he intends to visit Eumaeus in the country before returning to the palace and the suitors.

## Book 16: Father and Son Reunited

Telemachus goes to Eumaeus's hut, where Odysseus reveals himself to his son and impresses on him the need for secrecy and deception if they are to overcome the suitors. Meanwhile, the ship the suitors had sent out to ambush Telemachus returns, and the suitors try, without success, to come up with an alternative plan to get rid of him.

## Book 17: A Beggar at the Gate

Telemachus returns to the palace and speaks with his mother. Eumaeus brings Odysseus to the palace. On the way they encounter the goatherd Melanthius, an ally of the suitors, who insults Odysseus. As Odysseus enters the palace, an old hunting dog recognizes him and dies on the spot. Most of the suitors treat Odysseus with at least grudging respect, but Antinous throws a footstool at him. Penelope asks Eumaeus to arrange a meeting with her disguised husband.

## Book 18: The Two Beggar-Kings

Odysseus is insulted by Irus, a professional beggar whom the suitors favor. The two men fight, much to the amusement of the suitors, and Odysseus quickly subdues Irus. Penelope comes to the hall to extract presents from the suitors and to announce her intention of remarrying. Odysseus is insulted by the maid Melantho and Eurymachus, one of the leading suitors, who throws another footstool at him.

## Book 19: Penelope Interrogates her Guest

Odysseus and his son take all the weapons from the great hall, assisted by Athena. Melantho again insults Odysseus. Penelope speaks to her disguised husband, who claims to know Odysseus and tells her that he is nearby and will be home quickly. She does not believe him, but orders his old nurse, Eurycleia, to wash him. The nurse recognizes Odysseus by a scar he received as a young man and is sworn to secrecy. Penelope details the trial of the bow, by which she will choose her new husband on the following day.

## Book 20: Things Begin to Look Bad for the Suitors

Odysseus lies awake plotting revenge until Athena puts him to sleep. On the next day, the loyal oxherd Philoetius arrives at the palace, where Odysseus is again insulted by one of the suitors, Ctesippus, who throws an ox-foot at him. The suitors all laugh at this, which Theoclymenus interprets as a sign that they are all marked for death.

## Book 21: The Great Bow of Odysseus

Penelope fetches Odysseus's hunting bow and announces the test: she will marry the man who can string the bow and shoot an arrow through the rings on twelve axe-heads set in a line in the ground. Odysseus reveals himself to his two loyal servants and enlists their help in getting revenge on the suitors. None of the suitors is able to string the bow. Telemachus is on the point of succeeding when Odysseus stops him. Telemachus, by prearrangement with his father, sends his mother from the hall and gives the bow to Odysseus, who strings it and shoots an arrow through the axes.

## Book 22: The Death of the Suitors

With his next arrow, Odysseus shoots Antinous and announces his true identity to the rest of the suitors. Odysseus, Telemachus, Philoetius, and Eumaeus, assisted by a disguised Athena, kill all the suitors. When all the suitors are dead, the disloyal maids are hanged and Melanthius is punished. The loyal servants begin to clean the palace after the slaughter.

## Book 23: The Reunion

Old Eurycleia wakes Penelope with the news that her husband has returned and destroyed the suitors. Penelope refuses to believe it. When he answers her trick question about their marriage bed, she accepts him as her husband and they retire to bed after making plans to deal with the relatives of the suitors whom Odysseus has just killed. Before they sleep, Odysseus tells his wife his true story.

## Book 24: Peace at Last

The shades of the suitors arrive in Hades, and tell Agamemnon and Achilles of Odysseus's triumphant revenge on them for their destruction of his estate. Odysseus goes to meet his aged father Laertes in the country and, after telling him another "lying tale," reveals himself to his father. The suitors' relatives arrive at that point, seeking vengeance for the deaths of their kinsmen. Athena and Zeus intervene in the fighting that ensues and, after a few of the suitors' relatives are killed, Athena makes peace.

# Characters

## Achilles

Son of the mortal man Peleus and the sea goddess Thetis, Achilles is the best warrior at the siege of Troy. Odysseus encounters his shade (spirit) in the underworld in Book 11 while waiting for the seer Tiresias to tell him how he is to return home after being delayed for ten years.

## Achilleus

*See* Achilles

## Aeacides

*See* Achilles

## Aeolus

The son of Hippotas, Homer describes him as "beloved of the immortal gods" (X.2) and relates that Zeus put him in charge of the winds, letting him "hold them still or start them up at his pleasure" (X.22). He and his family (six sons married to six daughters) live on Aeolia, a floating island. After listening to Odysseus's tales of Troy, he agrees to help and makes Odysseus a present of a bag containing all the adverse winds that could blow him off his proper course home. Unfortunately, Odysseus's men untie the knot, thinking they will find gold in the bag; the winds blow them back to Aeolia. Aeolus casts them out, saying he has no desire to help anyone who is so obviously cursed by the gods.

## Agamemnon

Son of Atreus, brother of Menelaus, and King of Mycenae, Agamemnon commands the Achaean forces at Troy. Odysseus encounters his shade in the underworld. Agamemnon tells him about what he (Agamemnon) found waiting for him when *he* returned home after the war, and he cautions Odysseus to be careful until he is sure of his wife's loyalty.

## Aias

*See* Ajax

# Media Adaptations

- There have been several film and television productions based wholly or in part on the *Odyssey*, beginning in 1954 with the Dino De Laurentiis production of *Ulisse* (released in English as *Ulysses* in the same year), directed by Mario Camerini and starring Kirk Douglas as Ulysses and Anthony Quinn as Antinoos. In 1963, Pietro Francisi directed the film *Ercole sfida Sansone*, released in 1965 in the United States as *Hercules, Samson, and Ulysses*. A 1967 British production of *Ulysses*, based on the 1922 James Joyce novel which was itself based in part on the *Odyssey*, starred Martin Dempsey and Barbara Jefford. Radiotelevisione Italiana (RTI) produced a television version of the poem in 1969, directed by Mario Bara and Franco Rossi. NBC television produced a two-part miniseries of the epic in May of 1997, starring Armand Assante, Isabella Rosselini, Vanessa Williams, and Irene Pappas.

- The British rock band Cream, made up of Eric Clapton, Jack Bruce, and Ginger Baker, recorded the song "Tales of Brave Ulysses" on their second album, *Disraeli Gears,* in 1967. The song includes characters, themes, and motifs from the epic.

- There is at least a symbolic link between Homer's poem and the classic 1968 MGM production *2001: A Space Odyssey*, directed by Stanley Kubrick and starring Keir Dullea, beginning with the title of the movie. Kubrick's film, although based on a 1950 novel by Arthur C. Clarke, does seem to ask at least some of the same questions about human nature and its meaning as Homer does in the *Odyssey*.

- Elements from the *Odyssey* have received at least two (widely separated) operatic treatments. The first was in 1641 when Claudio Monteverdi (1567-1643) composed *Il Ritorno d'Ulisse in Patria* ("The Return of Ulysses"), treating Odysseus's return to Ithaca after his wanderings. The second is Richard Strauss's (1864-1949) *Die ägyptische Helena* in 1928, with a libretto by the Austrian poet Hugo von Hofmannsthal based on the account of Helen's visit to Egypt in Book 4 of the *Odyssey*.

- Princeton University is host to a World Wide Web site entitled "The Odysseus Page" (http://www.princeton.edu/~cdmoen/). The site discusses the various encounters Odysseus experiences in his wanderings, and includes quotes from the *Odyssey*, links to images of some of the places and things mentioned in the poem, and some brief commentary. The Perseus Project at Tufts University (http://www.perseus.tufts.edu/), which is also available on CD-ROM for Mac from Yale University Press with a Windows version in the works, offers both the original Greek text and the Loeb Classical Library translation in English (which is, unfortunately, written in a highly artificial style and not recommended for use except as a reference), together with background information on many of the characters and places in the poem. Alan Liu's "Voice of the Shuttle" classical studies page (http://humanitas.ucsb.edu/shuttle/classics.html) is a good place to start looking for information and links to other sites relevant to the classics and classical literature.

- Audio cassette versions of the *Odyssey* are available from Dove Audio (1996), Penguin Highbridge Audio (two versions, both dated 1996: the Fagles translation, narrated by Sir Ian McKellen, and Allen Mandelbaum's translation), and Harper Audio (1996, the Lattimore translation, narrated by Anthony Quayle).

### Ajax (Oilean, the Lesser)

Son of Oileus and leader of the Locrians at Troy. Shipwrecked on his way home after the war, he boasts of having escaped the sea in spite of the gods—and is subsequently drowned by Poseidon. Odysseus encounters his shade in the underworld in Book 11.

### Ajax (Telamonian, the Greater)

Son of Telamon and grandson of Aeacus (who was also grandfather of Achilles), Ajax was one of the bravest and strongest fighters at Troy. At the funeral games after Achilles's death, he and Odysseus competed for Achilles's armor and weapons. When they were awarded to Odysseus, Ajax sulked and, in a fit of madness, slaughtered a flock of sheep in the belief that they were his enemies. When he discovered what he had done, he killed himself, unable to live with the shame. Odysseus encounters the shade of Ajax in the underworld, and even apologizes for the outcome of their contest at Achilles's funeral games. Ajax, angry with Odysseus even after death, refuses to speak to the man he believes had unfairly beaten him in life.

### Ajax the Greater

*See* Ajax (Telamonian)

### Ajax the Lesser

*See* Ajax (Oilean)

### Akhilleus

*See* Achilles

### Alcinous

Son of Nausithous, husband of Arete and father of Nausicaa and Laodamas, Alcinous (the name means "sharp-witted" or "brave-witted") is king of Phaeacia and a grandson of Poseidon. Homer depicts him as a kind, generous, and noble man, eager to help the stranger and put him at ease (e.g., VIII.94-5, 532-34). He even suggests that Odysseus should stay in Phaeacia and marry his daughter.

### Antinoos

*See* Antinous

### Antinous

Son of Eupithes, Antinous's name literally means "anti-mind" and could be translated as "Mindless." He is one of the boldest and most ambitious (not to say obnoxious) of the suitors for Penelope's hand. He wants to supplant Telemachus as the next ruler of Ithaca (I.384ff.). It is his idea to attempt to ambush Telemachus on his way home from the mainland, and he proposes killing Telemachus outright at least three different times (XVI.383, XX.271-74, and XXII.49-53). He is the first man Odysseus kills in Book 22.

### Aphrodite

Aphrodite is the Greek goddess of love (the equivalent of the Roman Venus). According to Homer, she is the daughter of Zeus and Dione; the poet Hesiod (who likely lived and wrote not long after Homer's time), however, claims that she sprang from the foam (*aphros* in Greek) of the sea, as seen in Botticelli's painting *The Birth of Venus* (circa 1485). She is married, though not faithful, to Hephaestus, god of fire and smithcraft. Among her many lovers was the god of war, Ares. Aphrodite appears in the *Odyssey* only by "reputation," so to speak, when Demodocus sings the story of how her husband conspired to trap her in bed with her lover Ares and expose the two of them to the ridicule of the gods (VIII.266-366).

### Apollo

The son of Zeus and Leto, and twin brother of Artemis, Apollo is the god of archery, prophecy, music, medicine, light, and youth. (Sometimes, though not in Homer, Apollo is identified with the sun). As we frequently see in the *Odyssey* (e.g., III.279, IV.341, VI.162, etc.), plagues and other diseases, and sometimes a peaceful death in old age, were often explained as being the result of "gentle arrows" shot by Apollo (for men), or by his sister Artemis (for women).

### Arete

Niece and wife of Alcinous and mother of Nausicaa, Arete is queen of the Phaeacians. Her name means "Virtue" or "Excellence" in Greek. Athena tells Odysseus that Alcinous honors Arete "as no other woman on earth" is honored (VII.67).

### Artemis

Daughter of Zeus and Leto, twin sister of Apollo, Artemis is the virgin goddess of the hunt, the moon, and, in some traditions, of childbirth and the young. As we frequently see in the *Odyssey* (e.g., IV.122, V.123, VI.102, etc.), plagues and other diseases, and sometimes a peaceful death in old age, were often explained as being the result of "gentle arrows" shot by Artemis (for women), or by her brother Apollo (for men).

## Athena

The daughter of Zeus and Mētis. Zeus (following in the tradition of his own father, Cronus) swallowed her at birth when it was revealed that she would someday bear a son who would be lord of heaven (and thus take Zeus's place). She was born, fully grown and in armor, from the head of Zeus after Hephaestus (or, in some traditions, Prometheus) split it open with an axe to relieve his headache.

Athena was revered as the patron goddess of Athens (where the temple known as the Parthenon was technically dedicated to her in her aspect as *Athena Polias,* protectress of the city), but also as a goddess of war, wisdom and cleverness, and crafts, especially weaving and spinning. She describes herself in the *Odyssey* as being "famous among all the gods for scheming and clever tricks" (XIII.299).

Athena does not behave in the same way as most of the other gods in the *Odyssey:* she is closely involved with both Odysseus and Telemachus all through the poem, whereas the other gods (with the exception of Poseidon) are more remote and rarely intervene in the affairs of mortals. Indeed, the account of Athena's interaction with Odysseus, where he finally reaches Ithaca in Book 13, reads more like an encounter between old friends or cherished family members than between a mortal and a god. Homer may have intended such closeness to underscore Odysseus's heroic status: the gods only assist those who are worthy, and even then they tend to be somewhat distant. For Athena to treat Odysseus so familiarly indicates his superior status even among heroes.

## Athene

*See* Athena

## Atreides

*See* Agamemnon

## Atrides

*See* Agamemnon

## Calypso

Daughter of Atlas, who holds the world upon his shoulders, Calypso (whose name is related to the Greek verb "to hide" and which might therefore be translated as "Concealer") is a goddess who lives on the island of Ogygia. She falls in love with Odysseus during the seven years he lives on her island (I.15, IX.30), and proposes to make him immortal (V.136, 209): not a gift usually given lightly.

She says as much to Hermes in Book 5 when he comes to tell her of Zeus's decision that she must let Odysseus go. She is not happy with Zeus's decision, but she abides by it. She again offers to make Odysseus immortal. When he turns her down, she provides him with the materials and tools he needs to make a raft. When it is completed, she sends a favorable wind at his back that almost gets him home—until Poseidon catches sight of him.

## Circe

Daughter of Helios (the sun-god) and Perse, and sister of Aeetes, the king of Colchis who plagued Jason and the Argonauts. A minor goddess who "speaks with the speech of mortals," she is also a powerful enchantress.

Her "specialty" lies in turning men into pigs (in Homer; pseudo-Apollodorus also mentions wolves, donkeys, and lions; this may be reflected in the reference to wolves and lions at X.212) by means of potions and spells. Yet once she recognizes Odysseus, and swears an oath not to harm him, she becomes the most charming of hostesses, so much so that Odysseus and his men remain with her an entire year before the crew asks Odysseus if it is not time to head for home.

Apollodorus also records the tradition that Circe bore a son, Telegonus, to Odysseus during his stay on the island. Homer merely notes (IX.32) that she wanted Odysseus to remain as her husband.

## Ctesippus

A suitor from the island of Same whom Homer describes (XX.287) as "a man well-versed in villainy," though he does not specify exactly what Ctesippus has done to earn that nickname. His name literally means "Horse-Getter," so we might conclude that he was, literally, a horse-thief.

Ctesippus insults Odysseus and throws an ox-hoof at him when he goes around the hall begging on the day the suitors are killed. Odysseus ducks the missile, and Telemachus orders Ctesippus to leave the stranger alone or suffer the consequences. Ctesippus is later killed by the oxherd Philoetius (XXII.285).

## Demodocus

The blind bard, or poet, of the Phaeacian court. Traditionally, Demodocus has been taken as representing Homer, but not all scholars accept this idea.

## Demodokos

*See* Demodocus

## Eumaeus

Son of Ctesius, who was king of two cities on the island of Syria (not to be confused with the Middle Eastern country of the same name), Eumaeus was kidnaped at a young age by one of his father's serving women and taken by Phoenician traders, who sold him as a slave to Laertes, Odysseus's father. Odysseus's mother, Anticleia, raised him together with her own daughter, and then sent him to the country when the daughter was married (XV.366ff.). His name might mean something like "one who seeks the good." Eumaeus seems quite content with his lot in life. He remains loyal to his absent master and does his best to protect the property entrusted to his care from the depradations of the suitors. He grieves for the loss of Odysseus (XIV.40-44, etc.) no less than for his lost home and family, and when Telemachus returns from his overseas journey, Eumaeus greets him as if he were his own son (XVI.14-22).

It should be noted in passing that the sort of slavery described in the Homeric poems, while it had some aspects in common with the variety later practiced in Europe and America, is also different from the later practice in several significant respects. Chief among them is the fact that in Homer, the slave is often as much a part of the household as the son of the house, with a place within it and defined rights and privileges: Eumaeus, for example, was raised together with his masters' daughter and is both permitted and sufficiently wealthy to have a slave of his own (XIV.449-52).

## Eumaios

*See* Eumaeus

## Eurycleia

The daughter of Ops, Eurycleia is a long-time servant of Odysseus' family. Odysseus' father Laertes bought her in her youth for 20 oxen (not an insignificant price, especially for an island king with relatively little land for cattle). She was Odysseus' nurse, and then Telemachus', and in her old age she now attends Penelope.

As with Eumaeus, although Eurycleia is a slave in the household of Odysseus and his family, there is every indication that she is loved and repected just as much as any of the "regular" members of the household. It is she whom Thelemachus tells of his plans to travel to Pylos and Sparta (II.348ff.), not Penelope, and also she who comforts Penelope when the latter learns her son has been away all this time. Laertes, in his day, is said to have "favored her as much as his own devoted wife" (I.432).

It should be noted in passing that the sort of slavery described in the Homeric poems, while it has some aspects in common with the variety later practiced in Europe and America (i.e., use of slaves for sexual relief, chattel ownership of one human being by another, and, to some extent, the power of life and death over one's slaves), it is also different from the later practice in several significant respects. Chief among them is the fact that in Homer, the slave is often as much a part of the household as the son of the house, with a place in it and defined rights and privileges: Euryclcia, for example, is the one to insist that Odysseus' grandfather be the one to name the new baby, and has a few suggestions of her own on that point (XIX.401ff).

## Eurylochos

*See* Eurylochus

## Eurylochus

A companion of Odysseus, Eurylochos is the one who ties Odysseus to the mast to keep him from responding—fatally—to the song of the Sirens, and it is he who leads the first group of men to Circe's palace, then has to report that they have not come back out, and begs Odysseus not to make him go back (X.266-69). Eurylochos eventually turns on Odysseus and refuses to obey him on Thrinacia, where he urges the rest of the men to slaughter the sun-god's cattle (XII.339ff.).

## Eurylokhos

*See* Eurylochus

## Eurymachos

*See* Eurymachus

## Eurymachus

Son of Polybus, Eurymachus is described as the "leading candidate" for Penelope's hand (XV.17-18). His name means "wide-fighting."

Eurymachus is shown to be arrogant, disrespectful, hypocritical, cowardly, and abusive. He is the second of the suitors to die by Odysseus's hand. Odysseus's words to him, after Eurymachus offers to make good on the damages the suitors have done to his household in his absence, are virtually the same as Achilles's words in response to Agamemnon's offer of a ransom for Briseis in Book 9 of the *Iliad.*

### Eurymakhos
See Eurymachus

### Helen

Daughter of Zeus and Leda, the most beautiful woman of her time. Wife of Menelaus, Helen went, apparently willingly, with Paris to Troy: the resulting war formed the background for Homer's other epic poem, the *Iliad.*

Even in the *Iliad,* Helen was something of an enigma: a status that is still hers in the *Odyssey.* She herself tells the story of how she recognized Odysseus on a scouting mission in Troy (IV.244ff.) and announces that by that time, "my heart had already turned toward going home" (IV.260). Yet scarcely 20 lines further on, Menelaus tells of how she came by night to the Trojan Horse, accompanied by one of Priam's sons, and walked around it, calling out to the men hiding inside by name, and imitating the voice of each man's wife (IV.274-79).

One might have expected Menelaus to be angry with Helen for running off to Troy, and she with him for having dragged her back. Instead, Homer treats us to a portrait of marital bliss: Helen and Menelaus are to all appearances deeply in love with one another, and quite happy to be back in Sparta among their people and their possessions. Helen is regal and somewhat mysterious, apparently as much an advisor to Menelaus as a wife. She is understanding and compassionate as well, as evidenced by her putting soothing drugs into the wine being served around the hall as everyone is on the verge of breaking down and crying for their lost relatives (IV.220ff.).

### Kalypso
See Calypso

### Kirke
See Circe

### Ktesippos
See Ctesippus

### Laertes

Son of Arcesius (and thus a grandson of Zeus), husband of Anticleia, and father of Odysseus. Laertes was one of those (along with Menoetius, father of Patroclus; Peleus, father of Achilles; and Telamon, father of Ajax the Greater) who sailed with Jason on the Argo in the quest for the Golden Fleece, according to pseudo-Apollodorus (*Library,* 1.97).

By the time the *Odyssey* begins, however, Laertes is old and worn by care and grief. His wife has died, his son has been absent for 20 years, first at the Trojan War and then on his wanderings on his way home from it. He has retired to a country estate, where he lives more like one of the servants than the owner (XI.187-96).

This behavior has puzzled scholars and readers for many years. Presumably, in the absence of his son and at least until Telemachus is old enough to take over, Laertes would have acted as Odysseus's regent in Ithaca, maintaining order and seeing to the safety of both the people in general and of Odysseus's household in particular. Details are sketchy in the *Odyssey,* but we do know that the suitors have only relatively recently arrived on the scene (within three or four years, according to II.89-90) and, while we do not know precisely when she died, that Anticleia's death was especially hard on Laertes. We may conjecture that Laertes did in fact act in Odysseus's place for most of the time he is absent, but subsequently retired to the country on the death of his wife, when the burdens of rule became too great. This retirement, of course, is also a necessary dramatic device: without it, there would be no explanation for the suitors' presence, much less their audacity, and thus no framework either for demonstrating the excellence of Telemachus and his fitness to succeed his father, or for anything more dramatic for Odysseus's homecoming than a simple announcement of his arrival.

### Melanthios
See Melanthius

### Melanthius

Son of Dolius, Melanthius is Odysseus's goatherd. During his master's long absence, Melanthius has become friendly with the suitors of Odysseus's wife Penelope. He insults Odysseus as Eumaeus is bringing him into town, and again on the morning of the day that Odysseus kills the suitors. He attempts to bring armor from the storeroom for the suitors once Odysseus has revealed himself, but is caught in the act by Eumaeus and imprisoned there until the end of the fighting. He is severely mutilated (and presumably dies of his wounds, though Homer is not explicit on this point) by Telemachus, Eumaeus, and Philoetius.

## Menelaos

*See* Menelaus

## Menelaus

Son of Atreus and brother of Agamemnon, Menelaus is king of Sparta and the husband of Helen. While Menelaus was extraordinarily unassuming in the *Iliad,* in the *Odyssey* he shines as an example of the happy husband and father, the good ruler, and the perfect host, who is outraged at the suggestion (IV.31-36) that he should send Telemachus and Pisistratus away, even though they have arrived in the middle of a double wedding.

One might have expected him to be bitter at Helen's betrayal, but we see no evidence of this in the *Odyssey:* quite the contrary, he seems overjoyed to have her back at home. He has his share of adventures on the way home from Troy, but unlike his older and more powerful brother Agamemnon, in whose shadow he stands throughout the *Iliad,* Menelaus returned home to a peaceful kingdom with a loving wife at his side.

Menelaus is happy to see Telemachus, who he says reminds him very much of his father Odysseus (IV.148-50), and to help him in whatever way he can. (He even offers to take the boy around central Greece, collecting gifts, an offer which Telemachus refuses, as he does several of Menelaus's own gifts, which he says he is incapable of caring for on Ithaca.) Homer tells us that because he is the husband of Helen, who is herself a daughter of Zeus, he is destined after death to be taken by the gods to the Elysian Fields.

## Nausicaa

Daughter of Alcinous and Arete, Nausicaa is a Phaeacian princess. The night before Odysseus is discovered in the bushes, she dreams of her marriage: and after Athena makes him look more regal, she seems to think that Odysseus would make a suitable husband (VI.239-45): a sentiment her father echoes (VII.311-16). Her name, as with many of the Phaeacian characters, is related to the Greek word for "ship," *naus.*

Initially shy when confronted with a naked stranger, she quickly recovers her poise and remembers the rules about dealing with strangers and guests. She puts Odysseus at his ease, gives him clothing, and directions on how to find the palace and how to proceed when he is admitted. Samuel Butler suggested in *The Authoress of the Odyssey* that Nausicaa was either herself the author of the *Odyssey* or intended to represent the author of the poem, but this theory has met with almost universal skepticism.

## Nausikaa

*See* Nausicaa

## Nestor

The only surviving son of Neleus to survive, Nestor is the elderly king of Pylos, where it is said (III.245) that he has reigned over "three generations of men." As in the *Iliad,* Nestor's role is that of the elder statesman and advisor. He is longwinded and prone to telling stories about his remarkable feats in the old days (which Telemachus tries diplomatically to avoid having to listen to on his return to Ithaca at XV.200), but his advice is almost always sound, and his help is essential to Telemachus's mission.

## Odysseus

Son of Laertes and Anticleia, husband of Penelope, father of Telemachus, and absent King of Ithaca. In the *Iliad,* Odysseus was a first-rank character of the second rank: important, but clearly secondary to the likes of Agamemnon, Achilles, Hector, and Ajax. He was still known for guile, tact, and diplomacy more than for courage, and there seemed to be something at least mildly sinister about his talents.

In the *Odyssey,* however, we are given an opportunity to see Odysseus at the center of the stage, doing what he does best—getting out of difficult situations as easily as he seems to get into them—but in a much different light. Whereas in the *Iliad,* Odysseus was always trying to get someone else to do what he wanted, or what some third party wanted (e.g., the embassy to Achilles), now we see him using his wits just to stay alive, and in situations where it is quite clear that he needs every scrap of guile, intelligence, and endurance he can muster. He acts as he does because he has no choice: circumstances or the gods repeatedly force his hand.

We also see the more human side of Odysseus: his ability to inspire affection and respect in others (Penelope, Calypso, the Phaeacians, Eumaeus, etc.), his strength (even though he might not have been able to stand up to Hector in battle, he is the only one of 110 people who try to string his bow that manages to do so, and he breaks Irus's jaw with one punch), and his love for his wife and family.

Some have argued that too much of the "human" side of Odysseus shines through, that he is nothing more than a grasping, greedy, selfish, disreputable man who simply bides his time, does as little as possible to help anyone else, and always makes sure he takes care of Number One first. The seeds of this view, which stretches all the way back to the tragedian Euripides (c. 480-406 BC), are definitely present in Homer (especially in the episode with the Laestrygonians in Book 10). Nevertheless, it is not a view that Homer would be likely to accept.

Others, beginning with Dante (who puts Odysseus in Hell for wanting to know too much) and continuing through Alfred, Lord Tennyson, have seen in Odysseus the eternal wanderer, not content to rest too long in any one place, and always seeking to learn new things. Again, there are some hints of this interpretation in Homer, but no more than that.

For Homer, Odysseus is a loyal husband, loving father, and a true hero who wants nothing more than to return to his home and his loved ones. To achieve this goal he even turns down an easy chance at immortality: not a gift which is frequently given to begin with, and not usually without a great deal of hardship in the bargain.

### Oilean
See Ajax the Lesser

### Pelides
See Achilles

### Penelope
Daughter of Icarius, wife of Odysseus, and mother of Telemachus. Commentators have noted that Penelope is a woman in conflict: should she await the return of her long-missing husband, or remarry? Should she remain in the house she shared

with Odysseus, or move on? Is she still wife, or widow?

Penelope has a rough time of it throughout most of the *Odyssey*. She cherishes memories of the past she shared with her long-absent husband. But there is nothing grim, nothing suggestive of denial, in her relationship to the past.

Penelope is not indecisive and she does not live in the past. She is an intelligent woman (as both the episode of Laertes's shroud and the trial with Odysseus's bow demonstrate). She wants to wait to consider remarriage until she is sure that her son Telemachus can stand on his own without her support.

Fidelity to her husband, devotion to her son, care for the household, and resourcefulness on a par with Odysseus's own, especially where any of the foregoing are concerned: these are the characteristics of Homer's Penelope. She is a realist: she knows there is almost no hope that Odysseus will come back after an absence of twenty years, but she will not deny that last little bit of hope its chance, which sets her apart from the suitors and the faithless servants. Her test of Odysseus's identity by mentioning their marriage bed proves that she is the equal of the master of schemes himself.

### Philoetius
A longtime servant of Odysseus, Philoetius manages the herds for the household. He has remained loyal to his absent master, who he hopes will return, but thinks it unlikely.

### Philoitios
See Philoetius

### Polyphemos
See Polyphemus

### Polyphemus
A son of Poseidon and a Cyclops, a one-eyed giant. He lives on an island which is usually thought to be Sicily. He is presented as a member of a lawless race that does not acknowledge the gods, but which also lives in an area that provides for all their needs without effort on their part.

Polyphemus, in Homer, is depicted as a particularly savage giant, who eats human beings raw and washes them down with either milk or wine. He briefly captures Odysseus and his men; they get him drunk and blind him, after which they escape from his cave by clinging to the bellies of his sheep and goats. The blinded giant counts his livestock by feeling their backs, but is unaware of the escaping men sneaking out under the animals. Polyphemus asks his father Poseidon for revenge against Odysseus, which he gets.

### Poseidon

Son of Cronus and Rhea, and brother of Zeus and Hades, Poseidon is the god of the sea, earthquakes, and horses. He is typically portrayed as a stately, older figure, though one capable of great passion and bluster (not unlike the storms at sea that were said to be caused by his anger).

In both the *Iliad* (where he is still furious with the Trojans because of a slight a generation in the past) and the *Odyssey* (where Odysseus languishes for years because of an injury to one of Poseidon's sons), Poseidon is stubborn and prone to holding a grudge, but not entirely unreasonable. When he is all set to bury the island of Scheria under a mountain in retribution for the assistance the Phaeacians gave to Odysseus in getting home, he gives way to Zeus's persuasion and "contents" himself with turning their ship into stone as it sails back into the Phaeacian harbor.

### Teiresias

*See* Tiresias

### Telamonian

*See* Ajax the Greater

### Telemachos

*See* Telemachus

### Telemachus

Son of Odysseus and Penelope, Telemachus is only a baby when Odysseus left for Troy (IV.112). He grows to manhood in a land beset by civic disorder (II.26-27) and a household that has lately become the object of a concerted effort to drive it into poverty or at the very least to reassign control to someone other than its rightful heir.

As we see him early in the poem, Telemachus is rather shy and diffident. He has no memories of his resourceful father to use as a model, and no strong male figure to look up to or to show him the ways of a ruler. Yet under Athena's guidance, Telemachus begins to grow in confidence and something approaching wisdom, until at the very end of the poem we find him all but the equal of his father, even to

the point of nearly stringing Odysseus's great bow (XXI.125-30), until his father signals him not to.

As with Odysseus, the very fact that Athena acts as his champion demonstrates his worth: had he not been worth, the goddess would have had disregarded him. Nor is his new-found eloquence, poise, and grace entirely Athena's doing: she helps him to discover the qualities that have long lain dormant in him, lacking the proper atmosphere in which to grow and flourish.

### Tiresias

A famous prophet from the Greek city of Thebes, the son of Everes and the nymph Chariclo. Homer's near-contemporary Hesiod tells the story of how Tiresias was changed from a man into a woman after separating a pair of snakes he found mating in the woods, and eventually was changed back into a man when he again separated the same pair of snakes. He was blinded either because he took Zeus's side in an argument and Hera wanted revenge, or—in a different tradition—because he beheld Athena in the nude.

Tiresias is already in residence in the underworld at the time of the epic. He is the only person in the underworld who has any degree of current knowledge about the world above: everyone else knows only what has happened up to the time of his death, unless news can be obtained from a new arrival. Tiresias is also a prominent character in the Theban plays of Sophocles (496-406 BC), particularly the *Antigone* (441 BC) and *Oedipus the King*.

### Tritogeneia

*See* Athena

### Zeus

Son of Cronus and Rhea, brother and husband of Hera, brother of Poseidon and Hades, Zeus is god of the sky, of the clouds, of storms and thunder, and the ruler of the other gods. Zeus in the *Odyssey* is much more in the background than was Zeus in the *Iliad*. In the present poem, Zeus is more of a cosmic enforcer of the customs, a keeper of the peace among the gods (and sometimes among mortals, as in XXIV.482-86), and a benevolent observer than the direct participant he was in Homer's previous work.

His hand seems to rest more securely on the reins of power in the *Odyssey* as well. Whereas in the *Iliad* the other gods frequently challenged his decisions and stood up to him in council until he tactfully reminded them of his superior power, in the *Odyssey,* his directives are obeyed without hesitation or threats, and no one even seems to consider opposing him.

## Themes

### Creativity, Imagination, and Deception

You might say that "Creativity" or "Imagination" is Odysseus's stock-in-trade. In fact, he is not mentioned by name for the first 20 lines of the poem: the first word used to describe Odysseus, at the end of the very first line of the poem, is *polutropon,* which literally means "of many twists." We might say "shifty" these days, except that Homer does not appear to mean anything negative by the word, merely descriptive—Odysseus *is* rather a twisty-turny sort of fellow: he has to be, just in order to survive.

It should be no surprise, then, to discover that Odysseus is beloved of Athena, who is the goddess of creativity and imagination. She and Odysseus have much in common, as she remarks in Book 13 (XIII.296-99), including a joy in "weaving schemes" (XIII.386).

A large part of Odysseus's creative energy is channeled into deceiving the people around him. In fact, Athena gives Odysseus what is either a left-handed compliment or a mild reproach in Book 13 when she says:

> Wily-minded wretch, never weary of tricks, you wouldn't even dream, not even in your own native land, of giving up your wily ways, or the telling of the clever tales that are dear to you from the very root of your being (XIII.293-95).

Yet it is important to remember that Odysseus only tells such "clever" (or "thieving"–the Greek word used can have both meanings) tales because he needs to: he waits until he is certain of their motives to tell the Phaeacians his true identity, but he does so when pressed. Only when he must remain anonymous to stay alive or to further some ultimate purpose does he continue a deception beyond the first moment when it could be dropped.

### Heroism

Odysseus is a legitimate hero: his reputation from the *Iliad* is enough to establish that, quite apart from the close relationship he has with Athena and, to a lesser degree, with Hermes. The gods only help those who are worthy, after all: none of the gods lifts a finger to help the suitors, for example, who get what they deserve (II.281-84, XX.394).

Yet how are we to explain the very un-heroic (if not actually anti-heroic) things Odysseus does in this poem? None of the heroes in the *Iliad,* for example, would likely have endured the kind of insults and abuses that Odysseus takes from the suitors, or even have considered concealing his identity, even to further a noble goal such as the destruction of those very suitors. Should readers therefore assume that Odysseus is not a hero after all? Or—can Odysseus be seen as an entirely new kind of hero?

The heroes of the *Iliad* were locked into an almost ritual pattern of behavior that is suited to war and the battlefield. Odysseus has his place in that heroic environment as well, but in the *Odyssey,* Homer gives us a glimpse of what it means to be a hero *off* the battlefield as well as on it. Odysseus is facing circumstances that are enormously different from those he had to contend with during the war, and he responds to them in an appropriately heroic fashion. Homer is broadening the definition of what it means to be a hero.

### Human Condition

"What does it mean to be human?" This may be the single most important theme in the *Odyssey.* The poem gives us every kind of example of humanity—good, bad, young, old, individuals and groups, the living and even the dead. Each is an integral part of the story of Odysseus—which is in turn our own story, as we try to discover the answer to that question for ourselves.

There are two incidents in the poem that highlight the importance of this theme for Homer. One is Odysseus's refusal of Calypso's offer to make him immortal (V.215-24). The other is Achilles's reply when Odysseus attemps to console him in the underworld:

> "I'd rather be a field-hand, bound in service to another man, with no land of my own, and not much to live on, than to lord it over all the insubstantial dead" (XI.489-91).

To be human, Homer implies, and to be alive, is to matter, to be important. The dead in the underworld, like the gods on Olympus, may have a kind of existence, but it is ultimately one that is empty.

# Topics for Further Study

- In the "lying speech" to his wife in Book 19, Odysseus says to Penelope (speaking of himself in the third person): "Odysseus would have been home long ago, but he felt in his spirit that it would be better to go all about the world collecting possessions." Consider carefully Odysseus's character, as portrayed by Homer in the poem so far. Do you think he was motivated only by greed? Why or why not? The Greek word *chrēmata,* which can be translated as "possessions," can mean money or other valuables: but its literal meaning is "things that are useful or needful." What sorts of "useful" or "needful" things does Odysseus collect on his wanderings?

- What are the values of a hero (for example, Achilles, Hector, or any of the other major characters in the *Iliad* )? How do they compare with the values of Odysseus in the *Odyssey*? What sorts of differences do you find, and which set of values do you think are more likely to produce a harmonious, ordered society? Why? How do those values compare to the ones that prevail in our day and age?

- How are the gods portrayed in the *Odyssey?* What differences (or similarities) do you find between this depiction and the one found in the *Iliad?*

- Read Alfred, Lord Tennyson's poems *The Lotos-Eaters* and *Ulysses.* Do you think the sentiments expressed in the latter poem were intended as an answer to those expressed in the former? Why or why not? Does the portrait Tennyson has painted of Odysseus match Homer's? In what way(s)?

## Love and Loyalty

Love and loyalty are two very important parts of the human condition, and also two important themes running through the *Odyssey.* The loyalty of Eumaeus, Eurycleia, and Philoetius, for example, stands in direct contrast to the behavior of Melantho, Melanthius, and the suitors, for which they are eventually punished. Helen and Menelaus are clearly in love, and there can be little doubt that Odysseus and Penelope feel much the same way, despite Odysseus's philanderings on his way home and Penelope's testing of her husband when he finally reveals his true identity.

Love in the *Odyssey* is neither a tempestuous passion (as it sometimes seems to be in the *Iliad,* at least where Helen and Paris are concerned) nor a "deathless romance" as it would become in the lays of the Middle Ages. Love in the *Odyssey* is much quieter: but, as the saying goes, "still waters run deep." Odysseus and Penelope may not have a grand passion any longer, but the love they do have is clearly one of the most important things in each of their worlds: it is what pulls Odysseus home (V.215ff., IX.29-34), and what keeps Penelope hoping for his return, and plotting to put off the suitors as long as possible.

## Order and Disorder

From the very beginning of the poem, we have indications that there is supposed to be an order to life, and that those who ignore or threaten that order will be punished for it (I.32ff.). The main component of that ordered system that we find in the *Odyssey* is *xenia,* the laws of hospitality. In a world without regular places for travelers to lodge, and where neither police nor other international law-enforcement bodies are known, refusing shelter to a traveler or taking advantage of a guest under one's roof (or, as with the suitors, one's host) constitutes a serious breakdown in the moral and civic order of the world. Hence the laws of hospitality are raised to the level of a religious duty, and to violate those laws merits the ultimate punishment (XX.394).

But there are other indications of disorder in the poem as well. We are told at the beginning of Book 2, for example, that the assembly on Ithaca has not met since Odysseus left for Troy (II.25-27). This breakdown in civil order may have been a contributing factor in the ability of the suitors to flout the laws of *xenia* for almost four years: surely if there had been any kind of a regularly functioning government in Odysseus's absence, it would have put an end to their depradations, and Odysseus would not have had to slaughter more than a hundred people on his return home. The implication seems pretty clearly to be that the rules matter in the Homeric world, and that even small violations of those rules can have disastrous consequences.

# Style

Since it is one of the first works in its genre to have survived, the *Odyssey* does not so much display the mechanics of epic poetry as help to define them. For at least 500 years after it was written, only minor modifications were made to the epic form as we see it in the *Odyssey*.

## General Technique

In general, the *Odyssey* is more technically advanced than the *Iliad*. The flashbacks that seemed so awkward in the earlier poem are handled much more subtly, for example; the action jumps seamlessly from one place to another even in the middle of a book and is itself much more lively than the formalized battle scenes in the *Iliad*.

## Meter

English meter involves patterns of stressed and unstressed syllables. Greek meter, on the other hand, involves patterns of long and short syllables where, as a general rule, two short syllables equal one long syllable. Greek poetry does not rhyme, either, although it does make use of alliteration and assonance (repeated use of the same or similar consonant patterns and vowel patterns, respectively).

The *Odyssey* is written in dactylic hexameters, which is the "standard" form for epic poetry: in fact, this particular meter is sometimes referred to as "epic meter" or "epic hexameter." *Hexameter* means that there are six elements, or "feet," in each line; *dactylic* refers to the particular metrical pattern of each foot: in this case, the basic pattern is one long syllable followed by two shorts, although variations on that basic pattern are allowed. The

final foot in each line, for example, is almost always a spondee (two long syllables, instead of one long and two shorts). The meter is sometimes varied to suit the action being described, using more dactyls when things are moving quickly (horses galloping, for example), and more spondees when things are slow or sad.

## Similes

The similes that were such common features of the *Iliad* are used much more sparingly in the *Odyssey*, which makes them all the more striking when they do appear. Often this seems to underscore the importance of a particular passage, as at the beginning of Book 20, where the following two similes are used of Odysseus, plotting the downfall of the scheming maids and the suitors, respectively, within 15 lines:

> The heart inside him growled low with rage, as a bitch mounting over her weak, defenseless puppies growls, facing a stranger, bristling for a showdown—so he growled from his depths, hackles rising at their outrage. (XX.13-16, Fagles)

> . . . But he himself kept tossing, turning, intent as a cook before some white-hot blazing fire who rolls his sizzling sausage back and forth, packed with fat and blood—keen to broil it quickly, tossing, turning it, this way, that way—so he cast about. . . . (XX.24-26, Fagles)

## Foreshadowing

Foreshadowing, the practice of "hinting" at future developments in the plot either explicitly (in the form of prophecies, etc.) or implicitly, is fairly common in the *Odyssey*. It is seen most commonly in the form of the frequent "wishes" or prayers that the gods will punish the suitors for their insolence (which of course they do), and especially in Book 11, when Odysseus recounts his trip into the underworld to consult the shade of Tiresias.

Another example is the eventual destruction of the suitors in Books 21 and 22. Their doom is explicitly foretold by at least one prophet (Theoclymenus, at XX.350-57). It is also hinted at by several omens and portents. For example, the suitors are killed on a feast day of Apollo: who is, among other things, the god of archery. Furthermore, when Odysseus eventually strings his bow it gives off a "sound like the voice of a swallow"

(XXI.411): a bird which, as Homer's audience knew well, both migrates and always returns to its previous nest.

### Symbolism

Homer makes very heavy use of symbolism throughout the *Odyssey*. For example, the olive trees under which Odysseus falls asleep in Book 5, and under which he and Athena thrash out their plan of action in Book 13, are symbolic of Athena, the goddess of wisdom, craft, weaving (hence the expression at XIII.386, ''weave a scheme''), and war. Most of the names encountered in Books 6-12 are symbolic as well: ''Alcinous'' means ''sharp-witted'' or ''brave-witted,'' while his queen, Arete, has a name that means ''virtue.'' The Phaeacians's names are, almost without exception, connected in some way with the sea or with sailing, and the nymph Calypso's name is closely related to the Greek verb meaning ''to hide'' or ''conceal.'' There has been some speculation that the name ''Odysseus'' may be related to another Greek verb meaning ''to cause pain'' (or, in the middle or passive voice, ''to suffer pain'').

There are also two masterful symbolic plays on words in the Greek original which unfortunately do not reproduce well in English. The first is in Book 9 when Odysseus and his men are blinding Polyphemus. Odysseus has told the Cyclops that his name is ''Nobody,'' *Outis* in Greek, from the words for ''no'' and ''someone.'' When it follows ''if,'' as when Polyphemus's neighbors respond to his cries, the Greek negative changes from *ou* to *mē: ou tis* then becomes *mē tis* which, though it still means ''no one,'' sounds exactly like the Greek word for ''scheme'' or ''plot,'' part of the epithet *polumētis,* ''of many schemes,'' often applied to Odysseus.

The other play on words occurs whenever Penelope mentions Troy (XIX.260, 597, and XXIII.19). Since she herself says that the city's name is ''unmentionable,'' whenever she has to mention it she combines its alternative name, ''Ilion,'' with the word for ''evil,'' making, in Greek, the word *Kakoilion,* ''Eviltroy'' or, as Fagles renders it, ''Destroy.''

## Historical Context

The context in which the Homeric poems were created is clouded by the fact that their creation is a process that spans several centuries. In a very real sense, the poems' historical and cultural background is rather like one of the archaeological sites from which we gather our information about the period: it is deep, it has many levels or layers, and over time things can get pushed up or down from their proper context. Consider, for example, that the cremation burial of Elpenor described in XII.11-15 would have been common practice in Homer's day, but extremely rare in the Bronze Age when the events he describes would have taken place.

### The Bronze Age

The Trojan War and its aftermath took place in the late Bronze Age, which began around 1550 BC, the date of the very wealthy burials found by Heinrich Schliemann in Grave Circle A at Mycenae in 1873. For this reason, the period is sometimes also called the Mycenaean era. This was a time of relative stability though not, of course, without its conflicts, wars, and raids. The dominant powers in the eastern Mediterranean were the Hittites in the central part of what is now Turkey, the Egyptians in what we now call the Middle East, and, apparently, the Mycenaean kings in Greece and the surrounding islands.

These three ''great kings'' all ruled over literate (at least to the extent of being able to keep records and official documents, even if they left us no ''literature'' to speak of), apparently complex, societies (complete with bureaucrats, if the Linear B tablets found at Pylos and elsewhere are any indication). They engaged in diplomacy with each other and with numerous smaller kingdoms on the edges of their territory that served as buffer zones between them and could be compelled to provide both military and economic support under the terms of the treaties that bound them to the particular kingdom with which they were allied. These secondary kingdoms were also prime targets for raids by other ''great kings'' and foreign invaders, especially those that were relatively distant from their protectors' centers of authority and military strong points.

Trade was flourishing, and, given the uncertainties of shipping and other means of transportation, together with a relatively low level of technological advancement (at least when considered by modern standards), quite surprisingly so. Distinctive Mycenaean pottery, whether as art pieces intended for display and ceremonial use, or purely for transporting trade goods like oil, grain, or perfume,

# Compare & Contrast

- **Late Bronze Age (the time of the *Odyssey*):** Government consists of a few "great kings" (those of Egypt, the Hittite empire, and, the kings of Mycenae, among others) who control very large areas of territory, either directly or by alliance in loose confederations, at least some of which were explicitly spelled out in treaties. Raids and looting are fairly common, especially at the edges of these kingdoms, far away from the central authority.

  **Iron Age:** Monarchy is still practiced in places, but it has been widely replaced by aristocratic or oligarchic societies based on family or clan groupings. The development of what would eventually be called the *polis*, or city-state, is well under way. Inter-"national" cooperation is beginning to be re-established after the isolation of the Dark Age.

  **Late twentieth century:** Many different types of government are practiced, though various kinds of democracy are more common than monarchy these days. There are still, however, a relatively small number of "superpower" or highly influential nations. Cooperation is practiced to a very high degree (e.g., the United Nations), although with some occasional hitches.

- **Late Bronze Age:** Writing is known, although mainly in cumbersome, syllabic forms such as Egyptian hieroglyphics, the Mycenaean Linear A and B scripts, or the Hittite/Akkadian cuneiform. Literacy is probably restricted to the highest levels of the aristocracy and a professional class of scribes, bureaucrats, diplomats, etc.

  **Iron Age:** Literacy, at least in the Greek-speaking world, is only beginning to be rediscovered, using a different alphabet, where each letter represents a particular sound and not an entire syllable. Literacy is still most likely restricted to the upper classes and some professionals, like rhapsodes and some artists.

  **Late twentieth century:** The vast majority of people are at least able to read and write well enough to conduct their own business affairs.

- **Late Bronze Age:** Religious observances take place mainly in family or group gatherings. There may be a place set aside for a cultic figure or idol, but sites specifically set aside for formal, public worship are rare and difficult to identify, if they existed at all.

  **Iron Age:** Family observances are still practiced, especially with regard to reverencing the graves of one's ancestors, but formal cultic centers are beginning to be established and playing a more important role as religious practices crystallize.

  **Late twentieth century:** Religious practices vary from country to country and from one religion to another, though most of the major world religions do have certain specific places set aside for formal public worship which are identified as such and not used for other purposes. Many believers may also have at least some objects of religious devotion or practice in their homes.

---

is found all over the Mediterranean basin in staggering quantities throughout this period.

The Trojan War, if it took place at all, came very near the end of this flourishing civilization. The Greeks, using generational calculations, set the date of the war at around 1184 BC; modern scholarship, based on archaeological evidence at Troy and other sites, puts it some 75 years earlier, around 1250 BC. But the traditional victors at Troy did not have very long to enjoy their victory.

### The Dark Age

For reasons we do not really yet understand, this civilization begins to die out around 1220 BC with the mysterious destruction and subsequent abandonment of Pylos. That event ushers in a period of decline that lasts until roughly 1050 BC, when the Mycenaean civilization literally fades away into nothingness. Some echoes of this troubled period seem to be preserved in the *Odyssey* where, for example, the first question asked of a stranger is almost always along the lines of ''Are you a pirate?'' The social unrest, migrations of peoples, and foreign invasions that seem to have characterized the end of the Mycenaean civilization may also have served as a model for the troubled homecomings of some of the Homeric heroes that are recounted in the poem.

Whatever its causes, the disappearance of the Mycenaean civilization marked the start of about 250 years of very difficult times in Greece: aptly referred to as the Dark Age. This period has its end with the traditional date of the first Olympiad in 776 BC, very close to the time when we think Homer lived. Of this Dark Age we know almost nothing except what we can deduce from the period immediately following and the scanty evidence in the archaeological record.

Writing was lost, and with it, most trade seems to have disappeared except on a purely local or regional basis at best. Archaeologists working in this period report finding very little in the way of ''luxury'' goods like fancy pottery—when they can find anything at all. Biers (1980) suggests that there may have been as much as a 75% decrease in population from Bronze Age levels.

### The Iron Age

Beginning around the 11th century BC, the Greeks began to use iron in place of bronze, to cremate their dead as opposed to burying them intact, and to establish colonies along the west coast of what is now Turkey. By Homer's day, roughly the middle of the eighth century BC, these trends were well-established and things were beginning to look up again.

Writing was just beginning to be rediscovered using a new alphabet borrowed from the Phoenicians, and foreign trade was improving, helped in no small part by the colonies along the Ionian coast which, while typically independent of their mother cities, nevertheless tended to remain on friendly terms with them. The population was again on the rise, which spurred another wave of colonization, this time chiefly toward the west (Sicily, parts of Italy, and the south of France).

At least on the Greek mainland, the era of kings was rapidly drawing to a close. By the beginning of the eighth century, the nobles had taken the reins of power from the kings almost everywhere and were ruling over family groups or tribes in what would come to be called the *polis,* or city-state.

Largely because of the decorations found on pottery from the period, this era has come to be known as the Geometric period, but increasing regularity was a feature of more than just the decorative arts. It was in this period that the beginnings of a Greek national identity come to the fore (prompting and/or prompted by the founding of the Olympic games and the dissemination of Homer's works, among other things). There is also evidence that more coordinated military tactics were beginning to be used.

Religious practices, if not beliefs, also seem to have begun a process of standardization at this juncture. While the Homeric heroes sometimes go to specific places for religious observances (e.g., the ''shady groves'' sacred to Apollo mentioned in Book 20), the majority seem to be family- or group-centered rituals that take place wherever the family or group may happen to be at the moment of the ritual, and archaeological evidence from the Bronze Age tends to confirm this view. Formal altars, like the one at the fountain described in Book 17, are known from the Bronze Age, but temples, buildings specifically set aside for formal public worship, have not been identified in the archaeological record much before the ninth century BC, and become much more frequent thereafter.

After Homer's day, while the population, wealth, commerce, and industry of Greece were generally on the rise, the political pendulum swung back and forth from more aristocratic and democratic models to varying forms of one-man rule until just before the dawn of the Golden Age in the fifth century BC.

## Critical Overview

The critical reputation of the *Odyssey* is perhaps best demonstrated by noting that it is generally regarded as one of the first works of true ''literature'' in Western culture. This is significant not only because the poem stands near the head of the list, as it were, but also because it had to beat out a fair amount of competition to achieve that status.

By the middle of the sixth century BC, around the same time as the Peisistratids in Athens ordered the first "standard edition" of Homer's works to be made, there were at least six other epic poems treating various parts of the Trojan War story. Most of these were fairly short, but the *Cypria,* which covered everything from the decision of the gods to cause the war through Agamemnon's quarrel with Achilles that begins Homer's work, was at least half as long as the *Iliad.* Unlike the *Iliad* and the *Odyssey,* however, none of the other poems in this "epic cycle" has survived except in fragmentary quotations in the works of later authors. They simply could not measure up to Homer's standard.

Certainly by the beginning of the sixth century, and possibly late in the seventh, there was already a group of poet/performers calling themselves the *Homeridae* ("Sons of Homer"). This group may have been the forerunner of the *rhapsodes,* trained singers who, while they did apparently compose and improvise works of their own, were best known for performing Homer's poetry. At least on Plato's authority, the rhapsodes seem to have begun taking liberties with the poems (see *Ion* 530d), which may have led the Peisistratids to have the "official" text written down for the judges at the Great Panathenaia (a religious festival in honor of Athena held every four years), which included a contest for the rhapsodes which required them, presumably in shifts and over several days, to recite the whole of the *Iliad* and the *Odyssey.*

For most people, those public performances were probably their major form of exposure to Homer's work. For the educated class, however, knowing one's Homer quickly became the sign of culture and refinement. Homer is mentioned by name at least 600 times in surviving Greek literature, in texts that range from history to philosophy, religion, and even legal speeches. Aristotle holds him up not only as the "supreme poet in the serious style" (*Poetics* 1448b20), but also as the forerunner of both tragedy and comedy. Herodotus (*Histories* II.53) even credits Homer, along with his near–contemporary Hesiod, with being the one who gave Greek religion its standard forms: the names, spheres and functions, descriptions, and descent of the gods.

The one dissenting voice in the ancient world seems to have been that of Plato. Although he quotes Homer on more than one occasion, and even lampoons the rhapsodes and their "beautification" or embellishment of the standard text in his dialogue *Ion,* in the *Republic,* his lengthy discussion of the ideal state and the education of its leaders, Plato dismisses Homer as a mere "imitator" and excludes him (and poets generally) from his educational program (which was never implemented).

Homer was frequently imitated in the classical world, whether by the authors of the other poems in the epic cycle, or lampooned as he was by Aristophanes in several of his plays (expecially the *Birds* and the *Clouds*), yet his work was never equalled. Roman literature in particular owes a great deal to Homer, and to the *Odyssey* in particular: later authors dated the beginnings of their national literature to a translation of the *Odyssey* into Latin made by the slave Livius Andronicus around 220 BC, and the great Roman national epic the *Aeneid* not only uses Homer's epic hexameter line, it consciously imitates themes and events from both the *Iliad* and the *Odyssey.*

Interest in Homer continued well into the Christian era, as evidenced by Macrobius's *Saturnalia* (dated to the early part of the fifth century AD), where educated Romans still know their Greek, and spend an evening discussing the relative merits of Homer's treatment of the Troy story in comparison with that of Virgil. With the fall of Rome in AD 455, however, Homer and his works fell into disrepute for roughly a thousand years, until the scholars of the Renaissance "rediscovered" classical antiquity and learned to read Greek again.

During that time, the story of Odysseus received somewhat less attention than did the story of the Trojan War, but never entirely died out. With the Renaissance came a revival of interest in Homer and his texts, which were first published in the modern era in Florence in 1488. The French moralist François de Fénelon (1651-1715) turned the story of Telemachus into a Christian fable with his 1699 publication of *Les Aventures de Télémaque* (incidentally one of Heinrich Schliemann's favorite books), and the Spanish poet Pedro Calderón (1600-1681) did the same with the story of Odysseus and Circe.

Interest in Homer and his works was revived in the eighteenth century when F. A. Wolf first proposed the "Homeric Question" (succinctly stated: "Who wrote what, and when?"). Johann Wolfgang von Goethe (1749-1832) started, but did not finish, a romantic tragedy about Odysseus and Nausicaa. It is thought that Milton was significantly influenced by Homer in composing *Paradise Lost,* and he certainly provided inspiration for later poets such as Tennyson and Byron, though their works are narrower in scope and execution than Homer's. As the recent mass-market printing of Fagles's translation suggests, the *Odyssey* continues to enjoy the critical acclaim and popular interest that have been associated with it throughout most of the two and a half millennia since it was first composed.

# Criticism

## *Michael J. Spires*

*In the following essay, Spires focuses on the human element and scale of the* Odyssey *as an important reason for its continued popularity.*

As Peter Jones remarks in his 1991 introduction to E. V. Rieu's translation of the poem, ''The *Odyssey*—the return of Odysseus from Troy to reclaim his threatened home on Ithaca—is a superb *story,* rich in character, adventure and incident . . . and making the household, rather than the battlefield, the centre of its world'' (p. xi). That, I think, goes a long way toward explaining its perennial appeal, even some 3,000 years after it was written.

That is not to say that the *Iliad,* Homer's other epic poem, is not also a superb story: just a different kind of story. If Homer's works were operas, the *Iliad* would be something out of Wagner: rather heavy, highly formalized, and full of deep meaning—along with some really great singing and special effects. The *Odyssey,* on the other hand, would be something like Mozart's *The Marriage of Figaro:* it has a definite moral message, but that message is conveyed through humorous means, on a human scale, with plenty of mistaken identities and other plot twists—and again, some really great singing and special effects. Or, to put it in somewhat more modern terms, the *Iliad* is more like Cecil B. DeMille's treatment of *The Ten Commandments,* while the *Odyssey* has a bit more in common with George Lucas's *Star Wars* films.

Jones also suggests (p. xxxii) that Homer has adapted Odysseus's adventures in Books 9-12 from the myths surrounding Jason and the voyage of the Argo (which were themselves made into a short epic poem by Apollonius of Rhodes in the third century BC). While there are certainly characters in Homer that also appear in those myths (chiefly the parents of the Homeric heroes, but Circe is also the sister of the king who proves so troublesome to Jason and his companions), and certain of the episodes do bear a resemblance to those attributed to the company of

the Argo, it seems to me that ''adapted'' is perhaps too strong a word: and it must be emphasized that Homer would have had excellent reasons for including such material in the first place, if that is what he did.

To begin with, heroism is usually set against the background of a great war or major battle. Having already used that setting in the *Iliad,* Homer must now turn to the other traditional setting for heroes and heroism, the long and difficult journey: there was simply no other ''vocabulary'' for heroic behavior available for him to use.

Related to that problem is one of what we might call ''credentials.'' Tradition had it that Odysseus's father was one of those who sailed with Jason on the Argo: enough to establish Odysseus as a potential hero, but not to prove him a hero in his own right. (The same sort of thing happens to Telemachus in the *Odyssey:* merely being the son of his father is enough to put him in line to inherit Odysseus's estates and authority, but if he is going to hold on to that inheritance, he must earn the respect of others and demonstrate his ability and fitness to succeed his illustrious father.)

Given that Odysseus was much more skilled at stratagems, ambushes, and tactics than at simple hack-and-bash fighting (at least given the way Homer depicted him in the *Iliad* ), the best way to establish Odysseus's ''credentials'' as a hero would be for him to do the same sorts of things his father Laertes had done in his younger days, as those are the sorts of things that heroes *do* when they are not ''lucky'' enough to have a war in which to prove their merits.

Unlike the *Iliad,* the *Odyssey* is concerned more with the individual than the group, and with individuals who are much more down-to-earth than those we find in the earlier poem. Most of us will never be a Hector, keeping an invading force at bay all by ourselves, or an Achilles, single-handedly responsible for the continued success of our comrades-in-arms. But we might measure up to a Penelope, a Telemachus, or even an Odysseus, at least in spirit and understanding: there may not have been enchantresses, magic potions, and interfering gods to contend with, but at least until the middle of the 20th century there were still new places and new peoples to discover and to explore, much as Odysseus did on his wanderings. Our eyes are now beginning to turn outward into the reaches of space, but the spirit of Odysseus is no less comfortable there than it was here on earth: it can scarcely have been by

# What Do I Read Next?

- The *Iliad* is the other epic poem written by Homer, and it tells some of the events of the Trojan War which take place before the opening of the *Odyssey*. The best translations into English are those of Lattimore (Harper & Row, 1967) and Fagles (Viking, 1996).

- Alfred, Lord Tennyson's poem *Ulysses* takes a look at Odysseus in later life and is generally regarded as one of the better examples of English Romantic verse. He also wrote *The Lotos-Eaters*, focusing on a specific incident from Book 9 of the *Odyssey*.

- Nikos Kazantzakis (author of, among other works, *The Last Temptation of Christ*) wrote his *Odyssey* in 1938. In this work, Odysseus is presented as a dissatisfied and wandering man who leaves home, kidnaps Helen, and travels all across the known world—part of the way on an iceberg.

- Perhaps the best-known related work in English is James Joyce's 1922 novel *Ulysses,* which was very nearly banned in the United States when it was originally published. Joyce's work depicts scenes and events from everyday life in the dramatic framework of the *Odyssey*. For example, the Circe episode from Homer's work is portrayed as an extended romp in a brothel.

- For a factual look at the life of Heinrich Schliemann, the German businessman/ archaeologist who first excavated Troy, Mycenae, and several other Homeric sites (including several on the island of Ithaca), David A. Traill's *Schliemann of Troy: Treasure and Deceit* (St. Martin's Press, 1995) is a commendable critical biography.

---

accident that the command module of the ill-fated Apollo XIII mission was christened the *Odyssey*.

As Jasper Griffin points out in his discussion of the "after-life" of the *Odyssey* (1987, p. 99), the popularity of the Homeric poems is something of an anomaly: most epic works are popular for a time, then fade away into obscurity, only to be read by scholars and specialists. One of the things that makes the *Odyssey* so enjoyable to read is that it is full of people that we can relate to, unlike so many of the traditional stories handed down over the centuries. There is a little bit of Odysseus, of Penelope, of Telemachus, of Eumaeus (and, to be honest, probably some of the suitors as well) in each of us. These are people we relate to: people we might conceivably meet in real life, on the street, in our homes, at school, where we work, etc.

H. D. F. Kitto is right to say (p. 288) that Longinus's criticism of the *Odyssey* tells us more about Longinus than it does about either Homer or his work. Longinus was looking for things in the

*Odyssey* that simply were not there: and for very good reasons. While it has obvious connections with the *Iliad,* and was almost certainly written or composed after that poem, it is important to look at the *Odyssey* as a work in its own right. It is incorrect to call it an "epilogue" to the *Iliad,* as if it were merely an afterthought, something to tie up a few of the loose ends Homer leaves hanging at the end of the earlier tale.

It is also important to look at the *Odyssey* as a work of its time. There is much in the poem that we can relate to, but at least a few things that do not sit well with most modern readers. Slavery, for example, is something that everyone in the poem (and in Homer's own time) took for granted. Although it may disgust us, it should be noted that the slaves in the *Odyssey,* especially Eumaeus and Eurycleia, are well-fed, prosperous (Eumaeus even has a slave of his own: see XIV.449- 453), and treated more like a member of the household itself than a servant in it. Laertes is said to have honored Eurycleia no less than his own wife (I.432-33), and Anticleia raises

*Recreation of the city of Troy.*

Eumaeus with her own daughter and, when the daughter is married off, she gives him gifts and sends him to a country estate (XV.361-70).

There is also the question of the suitors' destruction. The wholesale slaughter of 108 men simply because they thought to pay court to an available woman, even given that they were rude and disrespectful, seems a bit much to our modern sensibilities. No one in Homer's audience would have given this a second thought: something that could also be said, at least in parts of the world, even well into the modern era. As Homer is careful to point out from the very beginning of the poem, the suitors bring their destruction down on themselves and could easily have avoided it if they had paid attention to the warnings they were given (e.g., II.160-70, XX.350-57).

To understand that attitude, it is important to remember, first of all, that the obligations of a host to a guest and vice-versa were considered sacred duties, enforced by Zeus in his aspect as god of strangers. Ancient mythology is full of allusions to the fate of those who maltreat their guests, from the story of Baucis and Philemon in Ovid's *Metamorphoses* right back to the destruction of the Cities of the Plain in the Hebrew Scriptures. Secondly, in Homer's Greece, the ability of a family or a household to survive is directly linked to its being able to feed itself. By consuming the resources of the household, the suitors are threatening nothing less than the survival of Odysseus's family. On top of that disruption of the social order, the suitors are also plotting to kill both Telemachus (IV.843) and Odysseus, if they can manage it (II.244-51). Where we have police forces and law courts, in Homer's day personal vengeance and family retribution were the only means for redressing wrongs. Eventually the Greeks would come to see that this system had its own problems, and to lay the groundwork for our modern legal system, but that day was several centuries after Homer's time.

Any suggestion that the *Odyssey* is the production of a mind in decline is not worthy of serious consideration. Just consider the intricacy of the plot, the masterful choice of both setting and the point of dramatic "time" at which Homer begins the story, the way he manipulates his chronology so the major characters can tell *their* stories of what has taken place during the 20 years of Odysseus's absence without being dull or anti-climactic, the extensive use of foreshadowing and symbolism, etc. It was quite likely for reasons of this kind that Aristotle described Homer as the "supreme poet in the serious style" (*Poetics* 1448b20).

Aristotle also ascribed to Homer the origins of Athenian tragedy and comedy, and it is probable that he had the *Odyssey* specifically in mind when he made that claim. There is little question that both Achilles and Hector are quasi-tragic figures in the *Iliad*, but it is in the *Odyssey* that the norms of tragedy as Aristotle would later describe them in his *Poetics* can best be seen. We have the noble man, temporarily brought low by misfortune and, at least to some degree, by his own character, together with some rather ignoble types who enjoy early prosperity but eventually reap their just rewards. There is even a double change of circumstances: from good to bad for the suitors, from bad to good for Odysseus. Justice and order prevail in the end, Odysseus is safely restored to home, kingdom, and family—and along the way we are treated to some fantastic stories and comic episodes that Aristophanes in all his glory would have been happy to use.

Peter Levi accurately sums up the *Odyssey*'s merits and attractions when he says:

> What is refreshing in the *Odyssey* is its expression of simple and vigorous human appetites. What is more deeply satisfying in it is deeply entangled in the miseries and dangers of the long story, the sadness of Odysseus and the terrible momentum of his home-coming, lit, as it were, by the lightning-strokes of Zeus. One would be justified, perhaps, in reading this long poem only for its surface brilliance and variety. But at a deeper level the satisfaction of the *Odyssey* is hard to disentangle from the recurring motifs and images that are mirrors of its meaning. Men are foolish, strangers are dangerous, the anger of the sea is obscure and implacable, Zeus is hard (*Pelican History of Greek Literature,* 1985, p. 42).

**Source:** Michael J. Spires, for *Epics for Students,* Gale Research, 1997.

### Peter V. Jones

*In the following excerpt, Jones offers a general overview of the* Odyssey, *encouraging the modern reader to explore this work in order to discover its "enduring hold on our imagination."*

The *Odyssey* is the second work of Western literature (the *Iliad* is the first). The ancient world agreed almost unanimously that both epics were the work of Homer. The *Odyssey*—the return of Odysseus from Troy to reclaim his threatened home on Ithaca—is a superb *story,* rich in character, adventure and incident, reconciling reality with fantasy, the heroic with the humble, the intimate with the divine, and making the household, rather than the battle-field, the centre of its world. . . .

What stands out . . . is the brilliant ingenuity with which Homer has engineered situations in which accounts of Odysseus' adventures and of developments on Ithaca in his absence can be plausibly given—not merely the great flashback of [Books] 9–12, but a host of smaller, highly significant, moments. And the more one thinks about it, the more difficult it becomes to envisage an *Odyssey* which *did* follow a purely temporal sequence. . . . Consider an *Odyssey* which started in [Book] 1 with Odysseus leaving Troy. First, the adventures which the poet has put into Odysseus' mouth as a flashback in [Books] 9–12 would have to be narrated as a third-person narrative. ('First Odysseus went to X and then he went to Y', etc.) Consequently they would lose much of their excitement as a personal reminiscence, and of their significance as an extended exercise in heroic self-revelation. Second, once the hero had returned, it would be impossible to give the intensive treatment to Penelope, Telemachus, the suitors and the effect of Odysseus' prolonged absence on the household that the poet achieves in his chosen version. One would not know what the hero was returning *to,* and why his return was so urgently needed. We would lose the rich and subtle characterization of, and interaction between, the people in Ithaca to which he returns. . . .

Seen in this light, Homer's decision to target the epic on the moment of Odysseus' return is a master-stroke. Far from losing perspective on the previous twenty years, the reader is endowed with a far sharper and more telling focus on it, because the events of the intervening years are selected by, and told through the mouths of, the characters themselves. What those twenty years *mean to them* is of far greater significance to the plot than simply 'what happened during Odysseus' absence'.

This rich interaction of past and present is one of the great glories of the *Odyssey,* and is an important component of the narrative's power and pathos. . . . The past [gives] the key to the present, as it does so often in the *Odyssey.* In an epic of return and recognition, how could it not? When Argus recognizes Odysseus, we go back to Odysseus' hunting days (17.291–317); when Eurycleia does, we go back to his naming ceremony (19.392–466); when Laertes does, we go back to the young Odysseus in his father's garden (24.336–44). . . .

There was no law that forced the poet to stick to material within the traditional story. It is, for example, clear that the poet has introduced all sorts of non-Odyssean material into the *Odyssey.* The Ares-

Aphrodite story . . . is obviously one. Calypso is probably an invention to allow time for Telemachus to grow up. . . . Sometimes the joins in such material show. For example, the tales which Odysseus tells in [Books] 9–12 were almost certainly adapted from the Jason/Argonaut saga (Circe, the Wandering Rocks, the Sirens and Scylla and Charybdis were all probably Argonautic adventures before they became Odyssean ones too; cf. 12.70). The result is that in an epic where Poseidon is the main antagonist, Odysseus' men are finally destroyed by the sun-god. Again, consider the effect of the bow-contest upon the narrative. Athene is Odysseus' great patron, but the bow is Apollo's instrument: consequently, it is not until Odysseus has used up the arrows (22.116–25) that Athene enters the fray (22.205–6). . . .

In the *Iliad,* divine intervention is commonplace. Gods appear either as themselves or in disguise (usually the former) and are ever-present, helping their favourites and hindering their enemies. In the *Odyssey,* their presence is far less noticeable, and with the possible exception of 15.1–9, they appear only in disguise. Zeus himself remains on the whole apart from the action, and when he does intervene, he is a quite unIliadic god of human justice. Observe how Homer sets out the ethical programme of the *Odyssey* in the opening book: Odysseus' men brought their own death upon themselves by eating the cattle of the sun-god (1.7–9), and Aegisthus did likewise by ignoring divine warnings, killing Agamemnon and marrying Clytaemnestra (1.32–43). In other words, the gods are concerned about the justice of human behaviour in a way in which they are not in the *Iliad.* What, therefore, will be the consequences for the suitors of *their* behaviour in Odysseus' household? The moral lesson is firmly drawn at their slaughter (22.35–41, 23.63–7).

But there is one god with a high profile in the *Odyssey*—Odysseus' patron, Athene. She stands by her favourite and guides his steps almost continually, and the teasing encounter they enjoy at 13.221 ff. is unique in Homer for the closeness of the relationship it depicts between god and mortal. It is tempting to say that Athene's continuing presence diminishes the stature of Odysseus. But it is important to emphasize that in Homer the gods help only those who are worthy of it. Athene's patronage does not diminish but enhances Odysseus' status as a hero. Her willingness to help his son Telemachus is a similar index of *his* value. . . .

This hero [Odysseus] needs more than martial skills if he is to survive, return home and restore his house to what it used to be. His cunning is evinced in many different episodes. . . . Restraint and endurance, deception and disguise: these Odyssean characteristics are shared, of course, by Athene, and willingly embraced by Telemachus when he is reunited with his father in [Book] 16. In the prevailing atmosphere of ignorance of the true nature of things in which characters wallow from the very beginning of the *Odyssey* . . . such characteristics help to generate a text dominated by irony, pathos, despair and joyously happy surprise (especially in the recognition scenes).

Odysseus, down the ages, has been a man of many parts. But the text of our *Odyssey* invites us to admire its multifariousness: it is the secret of its enduring hold on our imagination. Howard Clarke summarizes those qualities which make our *Odyssey* what it is:

> The *Odyssey* is broad and inclusive: it is an *epic* poem, not in the *Iliad's* way, with men and nations massed in the first conflict of East and West, but epic in its comprehension of all conditions of men—good and bad, young and old, dead and alive—and all qualities of life—subhuman, human and superhuman, perilous and prosperous, familiar and fabulous. The Greek critic Longinus described it as an 'ethical' poem, a word that Cicero later explained (*Orator* 37, 128) by a definition that could well be applied to the *Odyssey*— 'adapted to men's natures, their habits and every fashion of their life'.

**Source:** Peter V. Jones, ''Introduction,'' in *The Odyssey,* by Homer, translated by E. V. Rieu, Penguin Classics, 1991, pp. xi–lii.

## Jasper Griffin

*In the following excerpt, Griffin offers a wide-ranging appraisal of the structure and themes of the Odyssey.*

The conception of starting the poem with Odysseus offstage for the first four books was a bold one. Not only did it involve technical difficulties in handling and uniting two strands of narrative, it also risked the first appearance of the hero being an anti-climax. In the first four books Odysseus is constantly mentioned: he is in everyone's thoughts. On Ithaca life has been in a kind of limbo for twenty years, with no public assemblies since Odysseus left. Old Nestor, a well-informed man, thinks constantly of Odysseus but has not set eyes on him for ten years. A long journey brings us to Sparta, where Menelaus tells us that long ago and far away he was told by a god that Odysseus was held on an island by a nymph, without a ship. From that tremendous climax of remoteness the hero must somehow return.

The decision that the *Odyssey* should be set ten years after the fall of Troy—the figure strongly recalling the ten years of war at Troy which have elapsed before the *Iliad*—meant that most of Odysseus' adventures would have to be told retrospectively. It would be highly anti-climactic to narrate all that after the killing of the Suitors and the dissipating of tension, so a place needed to be found where the stories could be unpacked at leisure. . . .

The Phaeacians provide the setting for the tales. They are men, but remote from ordinary humanity and close to the gods: they serve as a transition between the fantasy world of the tales and the human world of Ithaca. The poet is explicit about their early history and also about the reason why there are no marvellous Phaeacian ships to bring home shipwrecked mariners nowadays: that may suggest that they are largely the poet's own creation. . . .

The adventures are in themselves timeless and placeless, belonging to Sinbad the Sailor as much as to Odysseus. Somehow they have become attached to the name of one of the heroes who fought at Troy, in a definite historical context. An effort has been made to arrange them in a coherent and morally intelligible order, especially in terms of obedience to the gods and resolute endurance. Apart from their intrinsic interest, they are needed in order to keep the Odysseus of Books Thirteen to Twenty-One, who does very little that is heroic, accepts humiliations, and at moments looks like a real beggar than a hero, in our minds as a man of truly great deeds. . . .

The whole poem is pervaded and held together by a very explicit theory of justice and of divine behaviour. . . . Zeus is ultimately responsible for the protection of the helpless, beggars and suppliants and good kings in distress. All that happens in the *Odyssey* is, as far as possible, made to illustrate that conception. Sinners are, in the end, punished; the final triumph of Odysseus is a triumph for goodness over evil. . . .

All serious poetry of early Greece involves the gods. The presence of the divine agents, visibly at work in what happens, enables the poet to show the meaning of events and the nature of the world. . . . But the divine cast-list [in the *Odyssey* ] is considerably less extensive, with a number of the great gods of the *Iliad* barely appearing, such as Hera, Apollo, Artemis, and Hephaestus, and no more lively scenes of divine dissension. Poseidon does not want Odysseus to get home, and so the subject is simply not raised among the gods until a day comes when he is away (Book One); and when Odysseus says to Athena that he was not aware of any help from her on his perilous journey, she replies that she did not want to fight with Poseidon her uncle. . . .

Fewer gods, then, appear, and they do not behave in the old turbulent manner. The frivolity of the gods, indeed, is now concentrated in the story which Demodocus sings to the Phaeacians:. . . again with Ares and Aphrodite in an undignified role . . . .[The] tale is a variation on the central theme of the *Odyssey,* a wife's chastity menaced in the absence of her husband. On earth that ends in tragedy, whether she yields like the guilty wife of Agamemnon or resists like the virtuous Penelope; in heaven there is temporary embarrassment, laughter, and the adulterous pair go off to their separate cult centres and resume their existence of splendour. . . . But the gods draw the same moral from this story as men draw from the destruction of the Suitors: ''Ill deeds come to no good'' (8.329). . . .

The *Odyssey* is . . . a poem of wide interests and sympathies. Animals, servants, exotic foreigners, craftsmen, beggars, women: all are objects of its curiosity. It is no good to be a modest vagrant (17.577); it is better to beg in the town than in the country (17.18); outdoor servants like to talk face to face with the mistress and hear her news, and have a meal, and go off with a present (15.376-8). Such humble truths interest the poet of the *Odyssey* . . . .

In the *Odyssey* the individual stands against the group, Odysseus against his insubordinate sailors, Telemachus and Penelope and Odysseus in turn against the Suitors. When Odysseus is alone among the Phaeacians we see the same pattern, though with less hostility: the isolated individual with no resource but his wits, confronting a self-confident and homogeneous mass. It is not an accident that the Suitors remain so little individualised.

Not only is it now one against many: in this world the hero must contend not only with his equals but also with turbulent inferiors. Odysseus' sailors are mutinous, and they find a ring-leader in Odysseus' kinsman Eurylochus (10.429ff., 12.278ff), apart from their disastrous action, caused by jealousy, of opening the bag of the winds (10.34–55) . . . .[In his false tales,] Odysseus may claim to be the illegitimate son of a wealthy man, exluded from inheriting by his legitimate brothers at the old man's death (14.199–215), or even a man who was in bad odour with a great chief because he insisted on leading his own contingent rather than subordinating himself, who was consequently treated unfairly in the division of booty, and who avenged himself by killing the chief's son . . .(13.256–68). These stories of Odysseus are close to real life and the events of the stormy archaic period; there is little high-flown heroism about them. . . .

In such a world loyalty is a treasured quality. Some of Odysseus' servants are faithful, and they are rewarded. Others are disloyal. The maidservants are hanged, Melanthius the goatherd comes to a sticky end. The fidelity of Odysseus' wife is crucial to the story, and the contrast between her and the disloyal wife of Agamemnon is repeatedly emphasised. . . .

The plot of the *Odyssey* [creates] a tension between two types of heroism: the dashing Iliadic fighter like Achilles, pitted against other heroes in equal battle, and the wily opponent of giants and witches, who must use guile against overwhelming force and impossible odds. Achilles chooses a glorious death at Troy rather than long life without fame, but Odysseus will die in his bed, a very gentle death in sleek old age. To reach that goal he must show himself a survivor, prepared to beg, to use guile, to accept humiliations, to conceal his feelings. . . .

In all these ways, the attitude to property, to food, to telling the truth, Odysseus stands closer to the common attitudes of men. He is brave and he has fought well in battle, but he is more at home in night expeditions, ambushes, stratagems. He finds himself in situations in which Achilles cannot be imagined: you simply cannot be Achilles in the cave of a Cyclops. The heroism of Achilles represents the highest flight of the heroic which early Greece could imagine, living for glory and accepting death. Odysseus is not just less heroic than that; he also has human attachments of a sort which Achilles does not. . . .

Odysseus is forced to learn the power of self-control, to keep silent and not go in for easy heroism. He fails once, early in his adventures, at the end of the ordeal with the Cyclops. Having kept his nerve and his self-possession, remembered to give a false name instead of his real one, remembered that it will not do to attack the sleeping monster and kill him with his sword—that would be heroic, but they would all be doomed without the power to roll away the mighty stone—and having kept his men

up to the mark in the act of blinding the monster, he yields to a temptation of heroism in revealing his own name as a shout of triumph. That was a disastrous mistake, and we do not see him repeat it. In his own house he endures in silence, accepts insults without immediate response, and bides his time, even watching Penelope weep while appearing unmoved (19.209ff). . . .

The power to conceal one's feelings is important in a world full of treachery and hostility. But for those who, in such a world, show themselves worthy to be trusted, the response is warmly emotional. . . . At last the ice can melt, as it does again in the meeting and embrace between husband and wife in [Book 23]. Fidelity is rewarded, and the guard finally can be lowered. Still there lie perils ahead, but the ultimate outcome will be happy, with gods benevolent and love restored in the family and prosperity among their people. . . . From the narration of suffering we are to draw serenity: the gods devise disasters, Odysseus is told, that there may be song among men (8.579), and to listen to that sad song gives delight. Listen and learn, Penelope was told: the gods bring unhappiness on many others besides you (1.353–5). In the end Odysseus and Penelope have learned that hard lesson. Life is full of unhappiness, but that is what is transmuted into song. They achieve harmony with that process and learn, as we are to learn, the lesson of the *Odyssey*.

**Source:** Jasper Griffin, in *Homer: The Odyssey,* Cambridge University Press, 1987, pp. 47–98.

## Sources for Further Study

Biers, William R. *The Archaeology of Greece: An Introduction.* Cornell University Press, 1980.
    A good basic introduction to Greek archaeology. Many illustrations.

Camps, William A. *An Introduction to Homer.* Oxford University Press, 1980.
    A good overview of Homer and his work, not too technical, and with notes on important points in both poems.

Easterling, P. E., and Knox, B. M. W., editors, *The Cambridge History of Classical Literature,* Volume 1, Part 1, "Early Greek Poetry." Cambridge University Press, 1989.
    A brief, though somewhat technical, overview of the earliest Greek writers to have survived. This volume is the first in a series by Cambridge that covers the whole history of Greek literature through the Hellenistic period and into the empire.

Griffin, Jasper. *Homer: The Odyssey* (Landmarks of World Literature series). Cambridge University Press, 1987.
A convenient, affordable, pocket-sized overview of the work and its author.

Hammond, N. G. L. *A History of Greece to 322 BC,* 3d edition. Oxford University Press, 1986.
The "standard" history of Greece before the time of Alexander. The print is small and the text fairly dense, but it remains a worthwhile resource to consult.

Harvey, Paul, ed. *The Oxford Companion to Classical Literature.* Oxford University Press, 1984.
A very useful ready-reference tool for basic facts, names, and dates.

Herodotus, *The Persian Wars,* translated by George Rawlinson; introduction by Francis R. B. Godolphin. Modern Library, 1942.
Although not very recent, among the best translations of Herodotus. Although he was technically writing about the war between the Greeks and the Persians, as he is discussing the origins of the war Herodotus covers quite a lot of other ground, and offers some fascinating (and often fanciful) historical details, including several references to Homer and his works.

Homer. *The Odyssey of Homer,* translated by Richmond Lattimore. Harper & Row, 1967.
Lattimore's translation reproduces Homer's original line structure much better than any other verse translation, yet without sacrificing either the ease of reading or the flow of the translation.

———. *The Odyssey of Homer,* 2nd edition, edited, with general and grammatical introduction, commentary, and indexes, by W. B. Stanford. Macmillan, 1974.
A very good edition, with technical commentary, of the Greek original.

———. *The Odyssey,* translated by Robert Fitzgerald. Anchor, 1963, reissued in 1990 by Vintage Books.
A rather loose verse translation of the poem. Some readers may find Fitzgerald's direct transliteration of the Greek names confusing.

———. *The Odyssey,* translated by Robert Fagles; introduction and notes by Bernard Knox. Viking, 1996.
Perhaps the most recent and certainly one of the more critically acclaimed translations of the *Odyssey,* Fagles offers a rendition in blank verse that is somewhat more free than Lattimore's or Fitzgerald's translations, but without diluting the poetic character of the epic. Knox's introduction is well written and very informative.

*Homeri Opera,* Vols. III and IV, 2nd ed., edited by Thomas W. Allen. Oxford University Press, 1919.
The standard edition of the original Greek text.

Internet Movie Database, The. (http://us.imdb.com)
An exhaustive listing of movie and television productions from the 1890s to the present, with extensive search capabilities.

Jones, Peter V. "Introduction," in *The Odyssey,* translated by E. V. Rieu. Penguin Classics, 1946, 1991.
A good, broad-based introduction to the poem that does not require a knowledge of Greek. An excellent resource for finding textual references to various people and places named in the poem, and a good bibliography of further reading material.

Knox, Bernard, editor. *The Norton Book of Classical Literature.* W. W. Norton, 1993.
More a book of selected passages from famous works of classical literature, it nevertheless contains some basic information about the authors and works it discusses.

Levi, Peter. *The Pelican History of Greek Literature.* Penguin, 1985.
A good basic reference for Greek literature generally, and one that does not require a knowledge of Greek.

Perseus Project, The. (http://www.perseus.tufts.edu/).
An extensive online reference source for primary and secondary source materials in both Greek and English, standard reference works, etc. Invaluable for tracing down references to characters in secondary sources, and much quicker for determining the frequency of word usage, etc.

Reynolds, L. D., and Wilson, N. G. *Scribes and Scholars: A Guide to the Transmission of Greek and Latin Literature,* 2nd edition. Oxford University Press, 1974.
A rather technical work dealing with books and the "book trade" in antiquity, and the process by which ancient texts have come down to us from the classical world.

Solomon, Jon D. "In the Wake of *Cleopatra:* The Ancient World in the Cinema Since 1963," *Classical Journal,* Vol. 91, no. 2, 1996, pp. 113-40.
A chronology with basic information on film and television productions which are based on or which mention works from classical antiquity.

Thucydides, *The Peloponnesian War,* translated by Richard Crawley; revised with an introduction by T. E. Wick. Modern Library, 1982.
One of the best translations of Thucydides into English, even given its age. Very readable.

# *Omeros*

## Derek Walcott
## 1990

Publication of *Omeros* in 1990 signaled a milestone in the already remarkable career of Derek Walcott. This is not only because the author, who was born on the small Caribbean island of St. Lucia, went on to win the 1992 Nobel Prize for literature, but because his poem subtly undermines the very genre out of which it emerges.

Since Walcott himself voices reservations about the ''heroic'' dimensions of *Omeros* it is understandable that critics who are guided by textbook definitions have been reluctant to grant epic status to the poem. On one hand, Walcott's characters are unassuming peasants who fight no monumental battles; his persona/narrator is allowed no Olympic trappings; and on the other hand, the requisite narrative flow is occasionally disrupted by the poem's lyrical exuberance. Nevertheless, *Omeros* is not a literary parody. The title itself pays homage to Greek origins, deriving from the pronunciation of Homer's name. Walcott's poem has the length, the geographic scope, and enough recognizable variations on traditional epic ingredients to ensure comparison with the standard masterpieces.

Indeed, the essence of Walcott's contribution to the epic genre resides in the insights afforded by that comparison. Walcott revisits the canonical works of Homer, Virgil, Dante, Milton, Walt Whitman, James Joyce, and Hart Crane because they epitomize the ideals of Western civilization. Much as Walcott admires these predecessors, he also notes that the

first four reflect a world of hegemonic domination or colonialism, dividing humanity into conqueror and conquered, or marginalized ''other.'' Walcott's perspective is that of an artist who grew up in a neglected colony; he therefore asserts that the disenfranchised citizens of the world deserve their own validation. Whitman's *Leaves of Grass,* Joyce's *Ulysses* and Hart Crane's *The Bridge,* initiate the movement toward recognition of the common man. *Omeros* does nothing less than offer an alternative to the terms of classical heroism.

## Author Biography

From his earliest verse written at the age of eighteen, Walcott has drawn material from his own experience. The autobiographical aspect of *Omeros* becomes unavoidable, given the frequency with which he explicitly interjects his own persona. Furthermore, the primary subject of this poem is his native St. Lucian heritage: the rich Creole culture of his transplanted countrymen, the unfulfilled legacy of his father who died prematurely, and the all-embracing sea.

Derek and his twin brother Roderick were born to Warwick (a civil servant) and Alix Walcott (headmistress of a Methodist school) in the capital city of Castries on 23 January 1930. When the twins were about a year old, their artistically gifted father died suddenly, willing them his desire to capture the beauty of the island in the few poems and watercolors he left. Derek showed an early interest in both media. He took painting lessons from his father's friend Harold Simmons; and with a loan from his mother, privately published his first collection of verse, *25 Poems,* which he sold on the streets of Castries.

After completing his secondary schooling at St. Mary's College under English and Irish Catholic teachers, Walcott accepted a Colonial Development Scholarship to earn his baccalaureate degree from the University of the West Indies in Jamaica in 1953. He taught briefly in Grenada and Jamaica before winning a Rockefeller fellowship to study theater in New York under Jose Quintero and Stuart Vaughan in 1958. The months he spent in New York were beneficial in two ways. First, they introduced him, through the examples of Bertolt Brecht's epic theater and the films of Akira Kurosawa, to the stylized technique of classical oriental drama. Second, the experience convinced him that New York was unreceptive to black actors and unsuitable for the kind of West Indian theater he was determined to create.

Disenchanted with prospects in the United States and armed with a new determination to succeed in the Caribbean, Walcott cut short his Rockefeller grant and settled in Port of Spain, Trinidad, in 1959. There he began writing an arts review column for the *Trinidad Guardian* while he gathered around him a group of amateur actors, dancers, musicians and stage technicians. From this highly experimental, modest beginning in the basement of a local hotel, eventually emerged the Trinidad Theatre Workshop, an institution viewed by many as the first truly professional West Indian theatrical company. The Workshop gained regional and international acclaim over the years, even winning an Obie award for Walcott's *Dream on Monkey Mountain* in 1970. After seventeen years of mutually rewarding collaboration, personal and artistic differences led Walcott to resign from the Workshop in 1976.

After a few unsettled years of writing and mounting occasional productions as he traveled among the islands of the West Indies, Walcott began accepting a series of lectureships and visiting professorships in the United States. He taught at New York University, Columbia, Harvard, Rutgers, Yale and finally Boston University, where he remained from 1981 until he was awarded the Nobel Prize for literature in 1992. Throughout this period Walcott divided his residence between the United States and various Caribbean locations. In 1993 he decided to leave Boston and build a home at Cap Estate on the northern tip of St. Lucia. Based once again on the island that has always been the center of his universe, Walcott travels frequently to different parts of the world.

## Plot Summary

### *Overview*

One of the initial challenges in reading *Omeros* is the complexity of its multi-layered plot. The meaning of the epic builds on events that are straightforward within themselves (simple fishermen Achille and Hector fight over Helen, a woman they both desire). Walcott expands these basic facts so that Helen comes to personify an island nation historically coveted by European powers. While his narrative does move toward an end, Walcott is essentially interested in the journey itself. As a matter of fact, the nearer he comes to the final resolution, the more he focuses on the act of writing. Given his conscious emphasis on the text of the poem as one of his subjects, his epic becomes self-reflexive.

*Omeros* is a story of homecoming comprised of seven books recounting a circular journey that ends where it begins. Books one and two introduce St. Lucia, key sets of characters and initiate the basic conflicts. Books three, four and five retrace the triangular trade route that once linked Europe, Africa and the Americas. Books six and seven return to St. Lucia where the wandering author and his uprooted countrymen are eventually reconciled to their Creole identity.

## Book One

The primary fous of the first book is a group of indigenous fishermen and their friends in Gros Ilet village. Philoctete entertains a group of tourists willing to pay to hear local lore and to photograph the gruesome scar on his shin. Philoctete's tale, like that of his Greek namesake Philoctetes, goes back to the cause of his old wound and his quest for a cure. We learn that two of Philoctete's companions, Achille and Hector, have ended their friendship fighting over Helen, while Helen herself has broken with Achille, the man she loves, and out of spite has moved in with Hector. Pregnant by one of these rivals and out of work, she is, like her counterpart Helen of Troy, caught between two jealous contenders. Rounding out the central cast of peasants are the old blind sailor, Omeros, also known as "Seven Seas," and Ma Kilman, proprietress of the No Pain Cafe. Omeros in different manifestations serves as a wise seer, an interested commentator on the fate of others, and ultimately as the incarnation of the Greek epic poet Homer himself. Ma Kilman serves as a medicine woman, interested in a folk cure for Philoctete's suffering.

Another equally important set of characters includes the author himself, whose character moves in and out of the story to recount his own journey toward self-realization. On a social level comparable with the author's persona is the white, expatriate couple Major Dennis Plunkett and his wife Maud Plunkett. As Walcott puts it in one of his earliest incursions into the plot, each of his characters is wounded in one way or another because "affliction

is one theme of this work" and he goes on to admit candidly that "every 'I'" including the narrator's own "is a fiction."

Achille, Hector, Walcott, and Plunkett all seek to possess Helen. Walcott makes her, as personification of St. Lucia, the object of his epic. Alienated as Dennis and Maud are on their adopted island, their deepest regret is that they have no heir. To occupy his mind, it occurs to the Major that Helen and her neglected people deserve to have their story recorded. To Plunkett's allusive imagination, correspondences between the Trojan war and the protracted Anglo-French battle to dominate St. Lucia, the Helen of the West Indies, are too close to be merely coincidental. As these two writers undertake their projects, Achille agonizes over Helen's defection to Hector, while Hector suspects that Helen still loves Achille.

Book one concludes with an episode that may be seen as a reversal of Major Plunkett's longing for a son. Walcott has always regretted not having a father. In the final scene, the ghost of Warwick Walcott materializes to encourage his son to complete his unfinished work. He urges his son to honor their nameless ancestors, all the overlooked Helens, the female colliers who marched like black ants down to visiting steamers—"to give those feet a voice."

## Book Two

The second book centers on two major events, each affecting one of the groups of characters already introduced. The first event involves a 1782 sea battle that ensured British sovereignty over St. Lucia. Leading up to his retelling of the Battle of the Saints, Walcott takes us back to meet a young midshipman on a spy mission for British Admiral Rodney in a distant Dutch port two hundred years earlier. Next he brings us across the Atlantic to witness Rodney's simultaneous preparations for the defense of St. Lucia. Rodney singles out one of the slaves struggling to transport a cannon up the coastal bluffs for recognition. These two new figures fill ancestral blanks for Major Plunkett and Achille: the ill-fated young midshipman entrusted with the Dutch mission is named Plunkett. When Dennis discovers his surname among dusty island archives, he claims the son he has always wanted. The slave, Afolabe, whom Rodney distinguished with the Greek name "Achilles," is an ancestor of Achille. These preliminaries out of the way, Walcott interposes a flashback to the Battle of the Saints and Midshipman Plunkett's untimely death. At the moment that the French ship *Ville de Paris* broadsides Plunkett's vessel *Marlborough,* the midshipman accidentally falls on his own unsheathed sword.

The second of the pivotal episodes of this book involves a political campaign sweeping the newly independent island. Philoctete and Hector join Maljo's fledgling United Love Party. Maljo points to lame Philoctete as a symbol of the infirm status of the nation. Hector, who has given up the sea to convey passengers around the island in his van, the Comet, provides transportation. Maljo's get-out-the-vote extravaganza is rained out; and after defeat, the candidate retreats to Florida to work the citrus harvest. The point of this interlude is to note that the transition from imperial rule to self-government has not improved the life of the average citizen. As Major Plunkett observes, local politicians have not helped Philoctete and have not affected the price Ma Kilman pays for fuel. Hector's remaking himself into a taxi driver has been equally ineffectual. Closing book two, Achille puts out to sea, where the sun induces hallucinatory visions. As Achille's fantasy begins, he sees past generations of drowned men rising to the surface. These remnants of the Middle Passage conjure up vestiges of his enslaved forefathers. As his fishing boat, the pirogue named *In God We Troust* heads toward his lost African home, Achille considers for the first time the question of his identity.

### Book Three

The actual time span covered in book three is approximately twenty-four hours, but in his trance, Achille retraces the middle passage back over centuries and vast distances to his ancestral African village. There he encounters his grandsire Afolabe, who instructs him in his forgotten tribal identity. In the primitive dances, rituals, tools, and musical instruments, Achille recognizes the origins of St. Lucian customs and devices. Together Afolabe and the village griot, or storyteller, rectify the historic amnesia of the African diaspora. Dream turns to nightmare, however, as Achille is forced to stand by helplessly as tribal enemies raid his village for slaves.

Meanwhile, *In God We Troust* does not return at dusk with the rest of the pirogues. Philoctete and Helen wait anxiously until the next day for Achille. Back in St. Lucia, he acquires a new interest in the common fates of dispossessed Native Americans

and Africans in the New World. Bob Marley's song "Buffalo Soldier" heard on the radio subtly broadens Achille's perspective, and at the same time offers a foretaste of the setting for the fourth book.

### Book Four

Time and space are once again divided in the fourth book. It includes scenes set in present-day New England, where Walcott suffers over the failure of his marriage, and a visit to the Dakota Indian territories in the 1890s. There, the Oglala Lakota Sioux are reacting to the genocidal policies of white men by joining the Ghost Dance, a millenarian religous movement of Plains tribes. Participation in the Ghost Dance alarmed officials monitoring activities on the reservations and led to the the massacre of more than three hundred families camped along Wounded Knee Creek on the Pine Ridge reservation in South Dakota on December 29, 1890. The dominant point of view for this sequence of events is that of the historical figure Catherine Weldon. Weldon, a wealthy white woman from New York, resembles the Plunketts of Walcott's main narrative in that she is both emblematic of her race and at the same time has voluntarily broken with her own race and class in order to identify with people who have been deprived of their place in history. In a scene mirroring the aftermath of the slave raid in Afolabe's village, Weldon stands, helpless as Achille had been, listening to the shaman Seven Seas recite the litany of an Indian village wiped out by cavalrymen.

Inevitably, Walcott identifies with Weldon. As she watches the blanketing snow eradicate traces of disappearing Native Americans, he watches the snow wipe out familiar landmarks around his Boston townhouse. While he contemplates the breach of man-made treaties—government documents to wedding vows—the ghost of Warwick Walcott reappears to instruct him that his odyssey, like all journeys, is circular. Before Walcott can go back to his tropical island, however, his father urges him to experience the metropolitan capitals of the Old World that have ingrained their influence into his colonial culture.

### Book Five

Europe has always been more than just the seat of imperial domination to Walcott: his ancestry include a mixture of Dutch and English forebears in his grandparents' generation. When he crosses the

Atlantic this time, he selects four destinations that hold special significance. First is Lisbon, Portugal, early patron of the African slave trade, and once so powerful that (in 1493) Pope Alexander VI allotted it half the unexplored world. Second is London, England, the colonial administrator and source of the language Walcott has treasured since birth. Third is Dublin, Ireland, the island immortalized by Walcott's childhood idol, James Joyce, and Maud Plunkett's native country. The fourth destination is the Aegean islands, the birthplace of Western culture. From his examination of the grand monuments of the past, Walcott concludes that he prefers "not statues, but the bird in the statue's hair." In other words, although he continues to be influenced by the established literary canon, he wishes to draw material from the life around him, just as did Homer and Joyce.

## Book Six

By the sixth book, Walcott has made his return to St. Lucia and it remains for him to gather the strands of his converging plots. After depicting the wreck of the Comet in which Hector is killed, Walcott is guided to the site by a talkative taxi driver. Next, Ma Kilman follows a trail of ants into the mountains and retrieves the homeopathic African herb that finally cures Philoctete's open wound. As Philoctete is cleansed, Walcott catalogs the terms of his healing. His flesh and spirit are restored as his racial shame is washed away and he reclaims his lost name.

In the same vein, Walcott exorcizes the flaw in his love of St. Lucia. His artistic preservation of local color does no justice to the integrity of living people. Soon afterward, Major Plunkett achieves a similar change of heart. His epiphany dawns shortly after his wife Maud's death from cancer. Walcott sums up their mutual conversion when he denounces the grandiose classical trappings in their homage to Helen: "Why not see Helen as the sun saw her, with no Homeric shadow?"

Nearing the end of *Omeros,* Walcott's announced theme of affliction gradually yields to the theme of reconciliation. Not only is every "I" a fictional construct, but each is easily interchangeable. Walcott invests his father in Plunkett, his mother in Maud, and he sees himself as a Telemachus launching his own odyssey in search of his missing Odysseus. The father/son variations proliferate. History may have shaped the present, but nothing prevents the individual from adjusting the perception of present and future options. At Maud's funeral, Helen informs Achille that she is coming home. As this sixth book concludes, Achille helps Helen understand the insights of his African dream: the costumes, dances, and rituals celebrating Boxing Day (the day following Christmas) have roots that descend through Western customs into African origins. In their Creole practice, they now inform St. Lucian identity.

## Book Seven

The Protean Omeros materializes as an animated statue in the seventh book to assure Walcott that a living woman "smells better than the world's libraries"; therefore, he should concentrate on what he sees around him. Walcott resolves to emulate the sea that absorbs history and to appreciate the privilege of knowing "a fresh people." Helen is no longer the object of an agenda for Walcott or Major Plunkett. The Major accepts Maud's death, and learns to work among rather than oversee his employees. Achille, who will never read anything Walcott writes, is depicted returning from a day of fishing, and the final line of the epic notes that "the sea was still going on."

## Characters

### Achille

The primary protagonist among the villagers of Gros Ilot in St. Lucia, Achille (pronounced A-sheel) is a fisherman deeply in love with the local beauty, Helen. Because he and his friend Hector both love Helen, they become arch-rivals, as did their Homeric namesakes three thousand years earlier. Afflicted with the rootlessness that often results from living under colonialism, Achille not only needs to win Helen, he also must discover his personal and racial roots in order to confirm his rightful place in St. Lucia. The event that gives his life ultimate meaning is a sunstroke-induced trance that transports him through time and space to his ancestral river village in Africa. There he meets his distant grandsire Afolabe, who teaches him his name and the forgotten ceremonies that restore the racial memory taken from his predecessors by the Middle Passage. When he reawakens the following day, he must still face all his old problems, but he has acquired a new appreciation for the transplanted

*Painting of Achille's fishing pirogue "In God We Troust" by Jared Hamner*

customs, rituals, and ceremonies that survived in St. Lucia's Creole culture. After his estranged friend Hector dies, he acknowledges their brotherly bond and is reconciled with Helen.

Unlike Homer's superhuman Achilles (son of the sea nymph Thetis and King Peleus), Achille represents the unacknowledged type of earthy protagonist Walcott described to D. J. R. Bruckner in an interview (see Sources for Further Study). Looking at the people of the Caribbean who come from distant lands and who have been neglected by history, Walcott is inspired to capture their names,

lineaments, and features in painting or words. He insists to Bruckner that a classically derived slave name such as Achille or Hector is not simply a metaphor lightly given: "It is something you watch becoming itself, and you have to have the patience to find out what it is." In *Omeros* it is significant that Achille misspells the name of his pirogue "In God We Troust." Not only does this replicate the name of an actual canoe Walcott saw in St. Lucia, but it reflects the simple, unadorned humanity Walcott wishes to celebrate. When his mistake is challenged, Achille declares "Leave it! Is God' spelling and mine." Near the end of *Omeros,* Walcott admits that despite his determination to give voice to these remarkable figures, Achille will never read the epic to which he is so central.

### Achilles

*See* Afolabe

### Afolabe

In the dream taking Achille centuries back to his African origins, Afolabe appears as his distant grandsire. Afolabe challenges Achille to reclaim his African name, believing that the person who forgets who he is lacks the substance to cast his own shadow. Under Afolabe's instruction, the amnesia caused by the Middle Passage and generations of slavery is eliminated. Achille is surprised to see that elements of African tribal customs survive in familiar St. Lucian rituals.

While Achille watches helplessly, Afolabe and most of his village are abducted by a band of marauding Africans who sell their captives to slave runners on the coast. As it turns out, the story of Afolabe in the third book fills in the background for an episode leading up to the Battle of the Saints already recounted in the second book. When Afolabe appeared in that earlier account, he and other slaves were preparing the British defenses against an anticipated French invasion of St. Lucia. At that point, Admiral Rodney changed Afolabe's name to Achilles. This episode now acquires added significance, as it appears that Walcott intends Afolabe to represent his own African blood.

### Antigone

The Greek sculptress who instructs Walcott in the proper pronunciation of Omeros (Homer's name) is given the pseudonym "Antigone." She appears briefly as Walcott's lover in her Boston studio in book one. She disappears almost at once because she has grown tired of America and wants to return to her native islands. Nevertheless, the encounter resonates throughout *Omeros*. The pronunciation of *Omeros* leads to Walcott's explication of the Antillean patois for the name: *O* expands from the throat of utterance to "the conch-shell's invocation" to all the other ovular openings in the poem; *mer* means "both mother and sea"; *os* evokes gray bone and the surf lacing the island's shore.

Frequently, Walcott's allusions to statuary, recall this character's sculptures. When he takes to the lonely streets of Boston toward the end of the fifth book, he wanders vainly attempting to relocate her dusty, marble-strewn studio. The statue of Omeros that emerges from the sea to guide him through his St. Lucian inferno in book seven is one of the last vestiges of her influence.

### Christine

Christine is Ma Kilman's niece, a country girl who comes to work in the No Pain Cafe at the end of *Omeros*. For her Gros Ilet is an amazing city and she is said to be like a new Helen.

### Chrysostom

Chrysostom is one of the fishermen who gather with Achille and others on the shore before beginning work each day.

### Circe

*See* Helen

### F. Didier

Convinced that there is no significant difference between the two major parties that are polarizing the island in attempting to win the general elections, this character, known as Maljo, creates his alternative United Love party. Maljo runs an ineffective, American-style, grass-roots campaign, driving the streets, shouting through an unreliable megaphone about Greek and Trojan parties fighting over Helen. When Maljo is defeated, he leaves for Florida to work the citrus harvests.

### Hector

Achille's friend turned rival, Hector manages to take Helen home with him early in *Omeros,* but he suffers from knowing that he has not won her heart. Hector's downfall is the result of his turning away from the calling of the sea to become a taxi driver. His van named the Comet, decorated with flames on the outside and leopard-skin upholstery within, symbolizes the island's cultural ambiguity.

# Media Adaptations

- Excerpts from Walcott's *Omeros*, *The Odyssey* and *Collected Poems* are read by the author on a Caedmon audiotape, recorded November 18, 1993, copyrighted 1994; available from HarperCollins Publishers.

- Walcott reads excerpts from *Omeros* and discusses the epic in a 1991 taped interview with Rebekah Presson, released as "Derek Walcott" in the *New Letters on the Air: Contemporary Writers on Radio* series; available from the University of Missouri, Kansas City.

The leopard motif harks back to an Africa that no longer exists, while the blazing comet suggests an alluring future driven by tourism and corporate exploitation far beyond local control. Once he abandons the sea, Hector is never at peace, and he can find no security in Helen. In the sixth book, reckless driving takes him over a cliff to his death. Despite Hector's treachery in life, Achille mourns an irreplaceable friend. Hector appears in the inferno section of the seventh book, a soul in the purgatory of his own choosing.

### Helen

From the beginning, it is necessary that Helen be perceived as an exceptional woman because she is pivotal to the action of the epic on four levels. First, she is the cause of the conflict between Achille and Hector, just as conflict between Paris and Menelaus in the *Odyssey* over her namesake, Helen of Troy, was the cause of the Trojan war. Second, Walcott, as a participating narrator, is inspired to immortalize her in *Omeros*. Third, the character of Dennis Plunkett undertakes to base a history of St. Lucia on her. Fourth, she embodies and symbolized the island of St. Lucia itself, since the island has been fought over so many times by France and England that it has earned the epithet "Helen of the West Indies." In spite of all the Homeric paraphernalia surrounding her, Walcott insists on her existence as a real person. As he explained to J. P. White (see Sources for Further Study), Helen is based on a woman he saw in a transport van he described in the poem "The Light of the World."

Helen is called Penelope as she awaits impatiently for Achille's return from the prolonged dream of Africa; Achille once refers to her as Circe when he feels unworthy to approach her sexually; and when the Major responds to the full power of her charm, he compares her to other memorable women of the past: Helen of Troy, Judith, and Susanna from the Apocrypha. The woman carrying all this metaphorical weight in *Omeros* is out of work and unsure whether the father of her unborn child is Hector or Achille. She had been a maid to the Plunketts until they fired her when her proud assurance made them feel like intruders in their own home. Then there is the question of the low-backed yellow dress that Helen may have stolen or that may have been given to her by Maud Plunkett. Walcott leaves the issue ambiguous through most of the poem.

Hector's untimely death in book six leaves Helen to Achille. Both Walcott and Major Plunkett abandon their desire for Helen when both men realize that by regarding her as an idealized object, they are repeating the shameful pattern of hundreds of years of imperial domination. Many of the ambiguities surrounding Walcott's reliance on classical allusions are resolved when, in the text, he and Plunkett recognize Helen's right to be herself, untainted by the various meanings that they have tried to heap on her.

### James Joyce

When Walcott stops in Dublin on his tour of Europe, he pays homage to James Joyce. As he stands on the embankment of the Liffey River one evening, he imagines Joyce's Anna Livia (from *Finnegans Wake*) scurrying by. Then he conjures up the image of Joyce (with his notoriously poor eyesight) as a "one-eyed Ulysses" gazing seaward after a departing ship.

Walcott's attachment to Joyce may be traced back to his school days at St. Mary's College. Walcott recalls in an autobiographical essay in *London Magazine,* 1965, his schoolboy identification with Joyce's character Stephen Dedalus. In a later interview with J. P. White (see Sources for Further Study), he disucsses the epic qualities of Joyce's *Ulysses* and of Joyce's reflective, rather than heroically active, protagonist Leopold Bloom.

### Ma Kilman

Ma Kilman is the repository of African animism that has been adopted into St. Lucia's Catholicism through generations of obeah-women (practitioners of sorcery and magic with roots in African traditions). She has lost the memory of herbs, potions, and spells, but when she sheds the uncomfortable garments of civilization, she finally reestablishes contact with the homeopathic fruit of the earth. It is she who follows a trail of ants into the mountains to unearth the foul plant shaped like the anchor that gave Philoctete his incurable wound. From that plant she concocts the steaming bath that drains all the poison from Philoctete and makes him whole again. Her No Pain Cafe is the village gathering place. A skeptical but grieving Dennis Plunkett seeks her out there in order to contact his deceased wife. When he asks Ma Kilman if she sees her in heaven, she responds simply "Yes. If heaven is a green place." Knowing his wife's attachment to Ireland, the Emerald Isle, Dennis is understandably moved: "That moment bound him for good to another race." Ma Kilman serves as an earth-mother figure, healing men and linking them with the natural environment.

### Lawrence

The waiter having difficulty making his way among customers on the beach when both Walcott and the Plunketts observe Helen's first appearance in *Omeros* is sarcastically called "Lawrence of St. Lucia." He is no Lawrence of Arabia. Near the end of the epic Walcott mentions his name once again as an example of the "wounded race" who laugh uncomprehendingly when an exasperated Achille curses a group of intrusive tourists.

### Maljo

*See* F. Didier

### St. Omere

*See* Omeros

### Omeros

The title character is an ageless blind man who has settled in St. Lucia after sailing the oceans of the world. Omeros, like both the island's sightless patron St. Lucia and the Greek Homer, possesses the gift of inner vision. Omeros is a citizen of the earth, not limited to citizenship of a single place and time. For most of the story Omeros is a trusted counselor among the villagers of Gros Ilet, but Walcott takes him through a series of reincarnations.

In book three, he joins Afolabe as a tribal griot in Achille's African dream. In book four he reappears as a Sioux shaman. Walcott encounters him in Trafalgar Square in London while on his own odyssey, clutching a worn manuscript of his odyssey—testimony to the fact that Homer, Omeros, and Walcott are engaged in the same enterprise. This particular incarnation reinforces Walcott's explicit statement in an interview with Robert Brown and Cheryl Johnson (see Sources for Further Study) that his poem has nothing to do with the renowned Homer of classical tradition. While he may exploit affinities with Homer's legacy, his purpose is to do for his own island nation what the itinerant wanderer Homer did for the emerging people of his Mediterranean.

The earthy Omeros of Walcott's conception steps forward to advise the Caribbean poet that "a girl smells better than the world's libraries," but a greater cause for an epic is "the love of your own people." The walking statue of Omeros then acts in the capacity of Dante's Virgil, who escorted the poet through Hell, escorting Walcott through a hellish region of the city of Soufriere. The experience introduces Walcott to the mercantile exploiters and selfish poets being punished for violations of the island's natural resources. Because Omeros embodies the wisdom of the ages, he is in a position to sum up the narrative strands of the epic. In his capacity as advisor to Walcott, he refines the terms of the duty imposed by Warwick Walcott. When he is last seen, sitting among the customers of Ma Kilman's No Pain Cafe, he hums quietly to himself the song of "the river griot, the Sioux shaman," and he predicts that, like Philoctete, "all shall be healed."

## Pancreas

Pancreas is one of the fishermen who gather with Achille and others on the shore before beginning work each day.

## Penelope

*See* Helen

## Philo

*See* Philoctete

## Philoctete

In conformity with the role of his classical namesake, Philoctetes, Philoctete serves as an integral mediator. He tries to convince Achille and Hector that they are brothers in the bond of the sea

and should not be estranged from each other. When budding political parties in his newly independent nation threaten to divide the population against itself, he regrets the fact that people do not love St. Lucia as a whole. Furthermore, he bears a terrible shin that allegorically implies all the afflictions plaguing his countrymen. He sets the example of patience under duress, the kind of fortitude that has allowed the progeny of slavery to endure and thrive.

As Philoctetes is cut off by the offensiveness of his wound in the Greek myth, Philoctete is too debilitated to participate fully in village activities throughout most of the poem. Just as the Greeks were dependent on the reclamation of Philoctetes before they could defeat the Trojans in the *Iliad,* the villagers of Gros Ilet do not begin to overcome their colonial malaise until Philoctete is restored to health. When Ma Kilman effects Philoctete's cure in book six, Walcott catalogues the larger psychological virtues of his restoration. As the mind-forged chains of his inferiority drop away in the herbal bath, the residue of tribal shame dissolves; his muscles respond naturally to the bow and oar of his warrior ancestors; he accepts both the lost past and his new name and language until he stands a new Adam in Eden. The moment is pivotal for the self-reflexive emphasis of the rest of the epic. In the scene immediately following Philoctete's healing, Walcott announces the revelation that he has been harboring the wrong kind of love for St. Lucia. He and others must follow the example of Achille and Philoctete in shedding any prejudices that stand between themselves and the island as it really exists.

## Philosophe

*See* Philoctete

## Placide

Placide is one of the fishermen who gather with Achille and others on the shore before beginning work each day.

## Major Dennis Plunkett

Expatriate Dennis Plunkett, a retired British Major, settled in St. Lucia with his wife Maud shortly after World War II. He sustained a head wound in the War and Maud nursed him back to health. As Walcott informs the reader in one of his earliest authorial intrusions, the Major's injury is in keeping with the central theme of affliction that runs throughout the epic. At first glance, this white, landowning couple seems out of place among the predominantly black islanders. Their presence may be justified on at least two counts. First, they represent the centuries-old European entanglements in St. Lucian affairs. Second, Walcott's identification of the Plunketts with his own parents recognizes the European blood in his own veins.

The deepest regret in Dennis Plunkett's life is that he and his wife never had a son. Although the Major busies himself with the duties of raising swine, his interest in historical research fills an emptiness in his life. As it turns out, that avocation eventually provides him with a substitute son. The initial impetus is provided by none other than Helen herself. Plunkett had to fire Helen as a maid due to her imposing proprietorial attitude, but he becomes obsessed with the desire to give her a written history. For him, it is a shame that St. Lucia and her population are always marginalized or omitted from the sanctioned History texts (always capitalized) of the imperial nations. Given Plunkett's allusive imagination and the coincidence of such local names as Achille, Hector, Helen and Philoctete, his design quickly assumes classical overtones. His historical record seizes upon the actual Battle of the Saints as a latter-day confrontation between Greeks and Trojans over a Caribbean Helen. Adding to the Major's enthusiasm, his research into the Battle of the Saints leads him to the name of a Midshipman Plunkett who died serving under the famous British Admiral Rodney. Centuries stand between this father-son connection, but it supplies Dennis Plunkett with the physical link he needs to authenticate his island birthright.

The Major's literal function gradually achieves a deeper significance as he comes to appreciate Helen as a real woman, and not just as the object of his historical manipulation. In this respect his character contributes to the self-reflexive aspect of the text. When he realizes that Helen needs no inscription to give her life meaning, he abandons the project to which he had been so devoted that it "had cost him a son and a wife." The Major continues to heal and to grow after his wife's death from cancer, turning to Ma Kilman's powers as a medium to communicate with his wife's spirit, and learning to relate to his workmen by their individual names.

### Maud Plunkett

The wife of Dennis Plunkett longs for the music and the seasonal changes of her native Ireland. Much as she would like to see her homeland once again, Plunkett will not spare the money for passage. Maud is a static character, the steady anchor to her husband's often quixotic energy. Plunkett refers to her as his "crown," his "queen."

Although she is a secondary character, her influence can be traced in an ever widening circle. While Dennis devotes himself to salvaging a place for Helen in the history of declining empire, he feels guilty for abandoning his wife emotionally. Maud occupies her lonely hours apart from her husband sewing a tapestry with all the birds of the archipelago, complete with Latin name tags, thus functioning as Dennis's Penelope (the wife of Ulysses, who spun by day and unraveled her spinning by night all the time her husband was away). The yellow, low-backed dress that becomes Helen's signature garment is "borrowed" from Maud without permission. Incidentally, Maud's death brings about a sequence of communal bonding. At her funeral Walcott notes the "charity of soul, more piercing than Helen's beauty" revealed in Achille's sympathetic tears. Just outside the church, Helen informs Achille that she is coming back to him. In the ensuing weeks, Major Plunkett seeks out Ma Kilman to ease his grief and he learns to work among his laborers without being patronizing.

### Midshipman Plunkett

Young Midshipman Plunkett serves two primary functions in *Omeros*. In an historical flashback, he is the man Admiral Rodney entrusts with a spy mission to Dutch ports to gather information on the enemies of England. Unfortunately he dies later by accidentally falling on his own sword after his ship is breached in the Battle of the Saints. His second, more important, role is to lie dormant for two hundred years before his name is rediscovered, allowing him to become the surrogate son of Major Dennis Plunkett. The Major uses the midshipman imaginatively to link his ancestry with his adopted St. Lucia. It does not matter that the young man passed away centuries before Dennis was born; the event allows him to take pride in the actions of a namesake who died honorably in defense of the Helen of the West Indies.

### Admiral Rodney

Commander of the British fleet stationed in Gros Ilet Bay in the eighteenth century, Admiral George Rodney defeated the French fleet under the Count de Grasse on April 12, 1782. The Battle of the Saints, named for the small group of Les Saintes islands, is famous in naval history because Rodney's bold "breaking of the line" maneuver established precedent for future naval engagements and his victory solidified the British position in peace negotiations with France.

In *Omeros,* Admiral Rodney dispatches Midshipman Plunkett to spy on the Dutch in book two. He is also responsible for changing the African name of Achille's ancestor from Afolabe to Achilles.

### La Sorciere

*See* Ma Kilman

### Seven Seas

*See* Omeros

### Professor Static

*See* F. Didier

### Statics

*See* F. Didier

### Theophile

Theophile is one of the fishermen who gather with Achille and others on the shore before beginning work each day.

### Alix Walcott

Alix Walcott, the aged mother of Derek Walcott, appears only once in *Omeros,* but Walcott makes the comment that she is incorporated into his portrayal of Maud Plunkett. The character of Derek Walcott visits her at the nursing home where she is cared for.

The domestic scene in which Walcott meets Alix is a respite from the constantly shifting narrative. The poet must prompt his mother, who struggles to remember the names of her loved ones. She finally recalls ''Derek, Roddy, and Pam,'' the children she bore Warwick. The scene reconfirms Walcott's roots in the island before he must be off again, pursuing a calling that takes him away from the source of his inspiration.

### Derek Walcott

Walcott introduces his own persona into *Omeros* and joins in the action on two primary levels. He

expresses his own fascination with Helen, enters into dialogue, and is often a participant among groups of characters. In addition, he candidly discusses autobiographical details and discloses the underlying structure of *Omeros* as he is engaged in the writing process. Despite the apparent transparency of motive, however, it would be a grave error to conclude that the Walcott who appears in *Omeros* is identical to the Walcott who is the author of the text. He expects readers to give him great latitude for poetic license.

The self-reflexive style of the poem depends on the author's freedom to shift perspectives and enter any of the other characters he chooses. His loss of his father, his failed marriages, his schizophrenia are embedded in the afflictions of Achille, Hector, Philoctete, and Dennis Plunkett. He states that in one scene he looks at Maud Plunkett through her husband's eyes. Attending her funeral, he contemplates the irony of his mourning the death of a creation of his own imagination and admits that ''the fiction of her life needed a good ending.'' Then he takes the self-reflection one step farther. Referring to the interchangeableness of his ''phantoms'' Walcott predicts that readers who suspend their disbelief will themselves become phantoms of the characters with whom they identify.

Elusive as he makes himself, Walcott carries a significant portion of the narrative in his own right. Beginning in book four, he takes the reader with him as he moves to Boston, looks back at the Indian territories through his reading of Catherine Weldon, and tours Europe at the urging of his father's ghost. In Lisbon, he compares the Old World port and its equestrian monuments of conquest with his New World counterpart of colonial ruins and a past ''better forgotten than fixed in stony regret.'' In London, he catches sight of Omeros in the guise of an old bargeman clutching a ragged manuscript. In Maud Plunkett's native country of Ireland, thinking of James Joyce's *Finnegan's Wake,* he recognizes Anna Livia: ''Muse of our age's Omeros.'' Then, having visited the fabled cities of his father's dreams, he completes the circle and finally returns to St. Lucia in the sixth book. There, under the tutelage of the animated statue of Homer/Omeros in the seventh book, Walcott reaches the same accommodation that Dennis Plunkett has achieved with Helen. Given the choice between the Aegean and the Caribbean Helens, he prefers the living woman rather than the classical image. Art has its compensations, but only St. Lucia's ''green simplicities'' prove sufficient to maintain his inspiration.

### Warwick Walcott

The father of Derek Walcott, Warwick Walcott was an influence on his son's artistic ambitions. This accounts for the two pivotal appearances of Warwick's ghost in *Omeros,* and for the father/son relationships that proliferate throughout the epic as well. Warwick appears first at the end of book one to focus Derek's attention on events of the past and present in the city of his birth. Warning against foreign distractions, Warwick notes the example of the local barber whose loyalties to the Seventh Day Adventists and Marcus Garvey leave him suspended between two Messiahs, representing phantom religious and African paradises. Prominent among the books on the barber's shelf is the multi-volume *World's Great Classics* a collection rife with icons treasured by Major Plunkett, Walcott, and his father. Warwick's second object lesson is more positive. He reminds his son of the unrecognized generations of mothers and grandmothers who labored their lives away hauling coal up the gangplanks of transient steamers in the deep-water harbor of Castries. Then he performs the role of Virgil's Anchises, who dictated Aeneas's inherited duty to him. Warwick argues that, whereas their ancestors used the implement of their feet, Derek must use his pen ''to give those feet a voice.''

Warwick materializes a second time at the conclusion of the fourth book, catching his son in a period of depression over his broken marriage and life in Boston. At this juncture, Warwick advises his son to follow the example of the sea-swift and complete his odyssey by circling back home. Because Warwick knows his son still needs to achieve a more balanced grasp of Western influences, he instructs him to walk the streets of the European cities immortalized in *The World's Great Classics* before he returns to St. Lucia. Well before Derek Walcott finds within himself the right kind of love for his homeland, Warwick pronounces their common goal: ''to cherish our island for its green simplicities.'' Only Warwick's untimely death prevented his doing more toward this end. Walcott introduces him into his text in order to establish the hereditary continuity of his epic task in *Omeros.*

### Catherine Weldon

The actual Catherine Weldon was a widow from New York whose commitment to the cause of

Native Americans led her to the Indian territories of the Dakotas in the 1890s. Walcott's treatment of her as a fictional creation seems to be faithful to the historical and biographical accounts that are available. Weldon became private secretary to Sitting Bull during the time that the Ghost Dance movement was making its way through the plains tribes, creating uneasiness among white settlers and frontier military units. The Ghost Dance offered the Sioux the false promise both the vanishing buffalo herds and past generations of native American warriors would return. They also believed that the magic shirts worn during the dance rituals would render their wearers invulnerable to bullets. White frontiersmen feared the unifying, rallying force of the movement and used the unrest it caused as an excuse for the Wounded Knee Creek massacre of 1890.

Perhaps the most consistent criticism of *Omeros* questions the inclusion of non-Caribbean segments in what is supposed to be a West Indian epic. Critic Robert Bensen has observed that Walcott is more concerned with the person of Catherine Weldon than simply with the time and place she appears in actual history. Weldon is another of Walcott's composite characters, embodying at different times Major Plunkett, Helen, Achille, and Walcott himself. Like Dennis Plunkett, she is an outsider attempting to carveout a place in an adopted society. She is as emblematic and unfathomable as Helen, poised between two worlds. In a mirror image of Achille watching the decimation of his African village, Weldon is relegated to standing by helplessly as Omeros in the persona of a Sioux shaman bemoans the destruction of his village. Weldon servest, as does Dennis Plunkett, to lend a vulnerable human face to the oppressor's side of the imperial equation.

# Themes

### Hegemony and Identity

On several levels, *Omeros* presents the strategies by which human beings survive and assert their integrity in spite of the restraints of overwhelming hegemonic forces. Walcott's peasant fishermen of Gros Ilet suffer neglect and shame due to the fact that imperial power has deprived them of their ancestral culture. Expatriate residents of St. Lucia Dennis Plunkett and Maud Plunkett must learn to accommodate themselves to existence in a colony that has been relegated to the margins of history. In a reversal of the standard paternalistic relationship between metropolis and colony, Walcott introduces several father-son combinations that are liberating and mutually beneficial. Last, the author uses vestiges of the epic literary tradition to assert a basis for self-esteem, even heroism, among his dispossessed people, while he simultaneously challenges the very artistic form through which he makes his assertion.

## *Affliction, Deprivation, and Self-Esteem*

Walcott mentions early in *Omeros* that ''affliction is one theme of this work.'' Philoctete already has the seemingly incurable wound on his shin, and Major Dennis Plunkett has sustained his head injury. Walcott makes it clear, however, that this theme operates on a figurative level as well. Philoctete, for example, traces the persistence of his open sore to the chains shackling his enslaved grandfathers. The Major is tormented by his feelings that, like the history and people of his adopted colonial home, unfairly pushed to the margins of history, his own name and fame will die with him because he has no heir. Achille's afflictions include both the pain in his heart over his loss of Helen and the amnesia he suffers in having been cut off from his cultural roots. Recognizing the dimensions of such wounds, it follows that the cures must be necessarily complex. Philoctete is restored to health when Ma Kilman rediscovers an herb and the homeopathic remedies of her ancient African grandmothers. In order to regain his soul, Achille must be transported in a dream back to the African village from which his ancestors were taken into slavery hundreds of years earlier. Later, when he has grown to accept his identity as a transplanted man of the New World, Helen returns and he can begin the process of helping her to understand the African roots that now draw nourishment from St. Lucian soil. The Major gradually learns to feel whole and to make for himself a place. Helen figures prominently in his quest in the role he has imposed on her as the personification of the island of St. Lucia. Dennis Plunkett decides to rectify history's negligence toward Helen and her people by dedicating himself to writing her history. His subsequent research into the Battle of the Saints fortuitously provides the name

# Topics for Further Study

- Dennis Plunkett, a British expatriate, feels a sense of greater belonging to his adopted community of St. Lucia after he discovers that a possible ancestor of his died in its defense. Identify and write about an actual historical case of a member of another race or culture dying or risking death in the defense of a land, people, or cause not his or her own.

- As American leaders discovered in the years following the revolution of 1776, the requirements of achieving true independence extend far beyond a declaration, a war, and the formation of a national government. There are challenges of cultural, economic, psychological, and social independence as well. Conduct research into the post-revolutionary period of the United States. Compare the obstacles that had to be overcome with those faced more recently by a nation such as St. Lucia, newly emerged from colonialism since World War II.

- Although sophisticated forms of art may seem to be detached from the real world, Walcott recognizes that art can serve as a valuable means of human expression. Investigate some of the folk arts, crafts, dance, music, or rituals of Africans or native Americans. Determine ways that these media help people to identify and define themselves as a culture.

of Midshipman Plunkett as his putative. The young man may have died in the conflict, but the crucial value of the Major's discovery is that it gives him a blood tie to St. Lucia. Later, after his wife dies, his attachment to the local people is eternally confirmed as Ma Kilman helps him to feel even closer to Maud than he did when she was alive.

## *Colonialism and Independence*

One of the unfortunate legacies of colonial domination is that subject peoples are prone to value themselves and their colony according to the standards of their subjugators. In *Omeros*, Walcott registers this fact in terms of psychological, sociological, political, and cultural effects. This is the underlying reason he begins his epic by deliberately calling for classical comparisons, and it launches his odyssey to North America and Europe in books four and five. The gesture, however, leaves him open to charges of imitation. This unavoidable influence is also what prompts Major Plunkett to champion Helen's cause by attempting to match Eurocentric history. Achille's journey to Africa gives him back his name and establishes justifiable pride in his origins, but his most valuable insight is that Africa is not his home. His ancestors "crossed, they survived. There is the epical splendour. . .the grace born from subtraction." Philoctete's involvement in Maljo's abortive political campaign underscore's the internecine strife that threatens a newly independent nation experimenting with democracy. Self- determination all too obviously does not guarantee cultural independence. One of the most insidious vestiges of neo-colonialism has become tourism. The natural beauty of tropical havens attracts so many leisure transients that national economies become vulnerable to foreign priorities. Reacting to the changes being wrought in St. Lucia by modernizing entrepreneurs, Walcott's persona begins to suspect his own relationship with the island. Near the end of the poem, the influx of tourists and corporate interests drives Achille and Philoctete to undertake a voyage in search of an unspoiled island where they could begin anew. Eventually they recognize that they must return and defend their integrity in the midst of a society that remains under duress.

### Art and Reality

One of the pervasive themes that begins early and grows to paramount importance in the last two books centers on Walcott's self-reflexive point of view in *Omeros*. Walcott names his poem after Homer, the wandering poet who initiated the epic tradition, and he incorporates elements of the genre in order to sustain expectations. Since his intention is to validate a corner of the world that past generations have considered unimportant, he must ultimately negate expected terms of heroism and advance a new perspective. He creates room to maneuver when he first insists that every "I" is a fiction. This allows him to invest some aspect of his own persona in one after another of his characters. Such candor also disrupts the artifice of his text and allows the reader to feel more immediately privy to his intentions. He and Major Plunkett start out

together in asserting their West Indian Helen's right to the coincidental Greek and Trojan parallels. But both of them come to understand that by molding Helen into the object of their imaginative designs, they do an injustice to the actual woman, who has a right to be no more nor less than just herself. In keeping with every imperial conqueror before them, they were exploiting a resource for their own gain. Gradually *Omeros* begins to dismantle the artistic structure to advance the reality that is its inspiration. After having been impressed by the monuments dedicated to European conquistadors in the fifth book, Walcott expresses a preference not for the statues, "but for the bird in the statue's hair." He advances another step when in the next book he comes to realize that as an artist he is guilty of wanting to preserve the quaint world of the poor in his imagery. He concludes that "Art is History's nostalgia," sacrificing the real for his idealized creation. He then risks interrogation of his own reason for writing about Achille, who would never care to read his own story. His answer, typically metaphorical, is twofold. First, the illiterate sea, which never reads the epics of mankind is still its own "epic where every line was erased / yet freshly written in sheets of exploding surf." Second, Achille's race, like living coral that builds on itself, "a quiet culture / is branching from the white ribs of each ancestor." Finally he speaks through Major Plunkett when he decides to let Helen be herself, the reality on which the sun shines naturally, for "she was not a cause or a cloud, only a name / for a local wonder."

Form serves function in *Omeros* as forces of hegemonic power, deprivation, colonial neglect, and paternalistic literary influences come under the scrutiny of an artist from the third world, who records his people's struggle to establish their identity, self-esteem and independence even while he questions his own artistic processes.

## Style

### Epic Features

Although *Omeros* superficially resembles canonical epics in many ways, Walcott purposely deviates from the genre in order to broaden the scope of this traditionally heroic form. The lengthy though not consistently elevated poetic language is often more lyrical than purely narrative. There is no attempt to appear objective and the protagonists range from the poet himself to simple peasants who are the opposite of demigods engaged in great battles. Walcott depends on frequent allusions to and parallels with Homer, Virgil, Dante, and others, but his goal is to validate simple men and women whose very survival possesses unexpectedly heroic dimensions.

## Point of View

Because Walcott makes his own persona one of the protagonists, his perspective is always at hand. Under other circumstances this might undermine the individuality of other characters; however, in this case, Walcott uses a self-reflexive technique, candidly insisting that each narrative ''I'' is a fiction, including his own. This is a crucial point, considering that one of his purposes is to dramatize the fact that all accounts of events, whether in an epic poem or a ''factual'' history, are selective narratives. The controlling ''I'' determines what is central and what is relegated to the margins. Walcott is present in his characters, and from that vantage point he is able to comment on roles played within the text.

## Setting

The main action takes place in postcolonial St. Lucia, North America, and some major European capitals. Historically, the West Indies have been indelibly shaped by the influx of alien races and cultures; therefore, the story telescopes backward in time to introduce past events that have impacted the present. In a vision, Achille is transported three hundred years into the past to recover forgotten African rituals and witness tribesmen being captured by members of their own race for sale into slavery. Other episodes include the Battle of the Saints from 1782 and incidents from the 1890s in the American frontier. The story follows Walcott himself as he travels from St. Lucia to Boston, to Europe, and back to the Caribbean. Since all the events have psychological repercussions for various characters, much of the action is internal, as each resolvse personal problems.

## Allusions

From the very beginning, *Omeros* depends on the reader picking up on numerous allusions to classical literary epics. The title refers to Homer, and many of the characters' names echo leading figures from the *Iliad* and *Odyssey*. In addition, as Major Plunkett pursues his historical research, he finds parallels between the Trojan war and the

Battle of the Saints. Aside from the classical and historical allusions, Walcott also makes reference to more recent authors, painters, and sculptors as he explores the manner by which he and other artists translate their reality into art.

## Imagery

Walcott makes extensive use of sensory perception throughout *Omeros*. The pronunciation of Omeros' name is replicated in the ''O'' sound of the blown conch shell. The blind Omeros perceives his environment by ear. Walcott and his fishermen characters relate to the sea as mother, ''mer'' in their patois, and her surf writes and erases her message all along the shoreline of their island. Birds proliferate on Maud Plunkett's tapestry and the sea-swift becomes a focal point for several characters, both literally and figuratively. Philoctete's existence is almost defined by his painful wound. Helen's beauty, her proud bearing, and her signature yellow dress turn heads wherever she appears. Aside from these standard appeals to the senses, Walcott's self-reflexive text draws attention to itself. He mentions his thought of a Crow horseman taking shape as he inscribes it in book four; then in the fifth book falling snow and the whiteness of the physical page itself become conflated with ''the obliteration / of nouns fading into echoes, the alphabet / of scribbling branches.''

## Symbolism

The ubiquitous sea is not only the element surrounding Walcott's island, connecting it with distant continents and serving as the source of the fishermen's sustenance. It also symbolizes the historical amnesia afflicting St. Lucia's native population. Generations of African emigrants have forgotten their roots, just as each wave line left on the shore is erased by its successor. Time and again these ancestors are seen as a line of worker ants, toiling anonymously under unfair burdens. The sea-swift in flight makes the sign of the cross against the sky; it leads Achille's pirogue on his African odyssey. The ghost of Warwick Walcott cites the swift's habitual flight pattern, seaward and back, as the model his son must trace back to St. Lucia. Wounds within each character symbolize the afflictions attendant upon slavery, colonialism, and metropolitan subjugation. Ma Kilman's homeopathic cure of Philoctete serves as baptism into a new life, freeing him to remember the past without being its victim. The journey motifs—whether in dreams to Africa or to Soufriere's Malebolge; whether they are the poet's personal sojourns to the United States and Europe; whether to connect the present with Greece, the Battle of the Saints, or the American Dakotas—all represent the diverse paths leading to wholeness for Walcott's protagonists.

### Prosody

The basic poetic structure of *Omeros* is occasionally off-rhymed terza rima stanzas. The rhyme scheme often interlocks, as is expected of terza rima, but Walcott ranges from exact to many forms of off-rhyme. On rare occasions, there are couplets and tetrameter passages. Walcott had descrived his meter as "roughly hexametrical"; the "roughly" needs emphasis. The numbers of loose iambic feet vary to the extent that the stanzas often approximates free verse.

## Historical Context

### Helen of the West Indies

The setting of *Omeros* ranges from the past to the present in the Caribbean, Africa, North America and Europe, but the constant center is Walcott's native island of St. Lucia. St. Lucia is the second largest of the Windward group of the Lesser Antilles. Small and insignificant as it may appear among so many islands, it has a remarkably colorful history. The population in 1990 was 151,00, comprised of 90.3% African descent, 5.5% mixed, 3.2% East Indian, 0.8% European. Early attempts at European settlement were undertaken in the sixteenth century. Largely because of its strategic location and its fine harbors, St. Lucia rapidly became a pawn in Europe's imperial expansion. The island was passed between England and France fourteen times before it was finally ceded to England by the Treaty of Paris in 1814. As a result of the martial and legal contention, St. Lucia has been called the Gibraltar of the Caribbean and the Helen of the West Indies. Agricultural products have been the main source of revenue—first sugar, then bananas. Until the advent of petroleum fueled ships in the late 1920s locally mined coal was important in the economy.

Despite the fact that the official language has been English since 1842, a majority of the population continues to speak a French patois and 90% are Roman Catholic. This is the milieu in which Derek

Walcott, an educated, middle-class, artistically gifted member of a Methodist family, grew to adulthood. Contending with white grandfathers and black grandmothers on both sides of his family and the premature death of his father when he was only an infant, Walcott struggled to find himself with few established guidelines. As he expressed it in his autobiographical poem *Another Life,* 1972, "The dream / of reason had produced its monster; / a prodigy of the wrong age and colour." As a student, he was impressed with the poetry of Guadeloupe born Saint-John Perse (pseudonym of Alexis Saint-Leger Leger), but his own early verse and drama reflect the British colonial educational influences of the metaphysical poets and of Milton, Dylan Thomas, Eliot, Johm Millington Synge and Joyce. Later he adds traces of Hemingway, Kipling, Conrad, then writers who have become personal friends, Robert Lowell, Joseph Brodsky, and Seamus Heaney. Regardless of the number of Western masters he may have assimilated, Walcott remains constant in his determination to draw from the most immediate subject matter of his life, the confluence of disparate cultures in the West Indies.

### The Middle Passage

One inevitable pole of Walcott's heritage is Africa. For this reason, he felt it necessary to send Achille back three hundred years, across the Middle Passage on a dream quest to eliminate the amnesia and the shame inflicted by the history of Western subjugation. Treated as merchandise and dispersed without regard to family ties, or place of origin, forced to give up their religions, customs, and given Western names, slaves could retain and pass down only fragments of their African identity. Walcott treats Achille's indoctrination as instinctive or racial memory. In the primitive dress, instruments, and rituals, he detects traces of ancient African practices he only partially understands in St. Lucian society. When he has Achille observe one African tribe abduct members of another to be sold into slavery, Walcott dramatizes the fact that man's inhumanity to man knows no racial boundaries. Walcott is careful not to imply that Achille's knowledge of tribal life makes him somehow become African. It is important to him that Achille simply reclaim this part of his past and incorporate it into his authentic identity as a West Indian, an integral member of a Creole culture. Toward the end of *Omeros* he is thus enabled to teach Helen the deeper meaning of Boxing Day masquerades that predate their Christmas associations.

# Compare & Contrast

- **1600s-1820:** The African slave trade along the Middle Passage brought approximately 6,777,000 slaves into Brazil and the West Indies by 1820. During the same time, immigration brought approximately 964,000 Caucasians into the region. This created an ethnic imbalance, with an 88% majority population of African descent. By 1820 in North America, 550,000 Africans were imported among a Caucasian population of 651,000, making blacks an ethnic minority of 46%. In the third book of *Omeros,* Walcott has Achille retrace three hundred years of history to reaffirm his African origins.

  **1833-1865:** British Parliament abolished slavery in its West Indian colonies in 1833. President Lincoln's Emancipation Proclamation abolished slavery in the United States in 1863 and the Thirteenth Amendment to the Constitution guaranteed freedom at the close of the Civil War in 1865.

  **Late twentieth century:** St. Lucia has a population of approximately 151,000, with a majority of African descent (90.3%), racially mixed (5.5%), East Indian (3.2%), Caucasian (.8%). With a population of 22 million, the ethnic distribution of the United States is more varied: Native American .8%, Asian-Pacific 2.9%, Hispanic 9%, African-American 12%, non-Hispanic Caucasian 71.3%. Books four and five of *Omeros* recount Walcott's reaction to racially divided Boston.

- **1776-1814:** The English colonies in North America fight to win their independence in 1776. This corresponds with the height of conflict between the French and Great Britain for disputed possessions in the Americas. In *Omeros* the Battle of the Saints is central to Major Plunkett's historical research. France finally ceded St. Lucia to England in the 1814 Treaty of Paris.

  **1941-1979:** In 1941, after the Japanese attack on Pearl Harbor, the United States joins the British Commonwealth and her allies against the Axis powers in World War II. In *Omeros* Major Plunkett frequently recalls his participation in Montgomery's North African campaign during World War II. The Plunketts' retirement to St. Lucia after the war makes them a part of the post-war independence movement. The time period includes the short-lived experiment with the West Indian Federation (1958-1967) and St. Lucian independence on February 22, 1979.

  **Late twentieth century:** The United States has a tricameral government with an elected president as chief executive. St. Lucia owes allegiance to the British regent, who is represented by a governor general, but is governed by an elected parliament, led by the prime minister. In the second book of *Omeros,* Walcott recounts an election campaign pitting the St. Lucia Labour Party against the United Workers Party.

- **1780-1870:** Historically, the St. Lucian economy has depended on agriculture. By 1780 there were already nearly fifty sugar plantations. This labor-intensive crop that fueled the rapid influx of slave labor in the West Indies.

  **1870-1930:** During the late 1800s, natural coal deposits in St. Lucia became a significant source of income. This industry is recognized by the ghost of Warwick Walcott in the first book of *Omeros* when he draws attention to the female colliers loading steamers in Castries Harbor. By the 1940s, income from coal production declined due to the replacement of steam power with petroleum-fueled shipping. In 1923, bananas were introduced into the local economy and eventually replaced sugar as the main source of agricultural income.

  **Late twentieth century:** While agriculture remains the primary source of St. Lucia's international income, efforts are being made to diversify crops (67% banana production), to encourage tourism and industry into the 1990s. Tourism is the second largest sector of the economy, bringing in millions of dollars each year. As Walcott indicates in *Omeros,* there are considerable misgivings about the commercialization of property, handicrafts, and local customs for the entertainment of foreign visitors.

### The Battle of the Saints

At the other pole of Walcott's existence is his European heritage. This aspect of Caribbean history is largely devoted to Major Plunkett and his discovery of Midshipman Plunkett: men from separate centuries whose lives intersect after some two hundred years over a famous maritime battles between England and France. Walcott's treatment of the Battle of the Saints does not emphasize European glory. Walcott and his character Dennis Plunkett are interested in this momentous battle for more domestic reasons. Together they see it as evidence of St. Lucia's intrinsic value, not as a European prize, but for its claim on them as individuals.

### Independence

For modern emancipated citizens of the country, such as Philoctete, Hector, and Maljo, the current battle to possess Helen centers on their social and political custodianship. Walcott witnessed the abortive experiment of the West Indian Federation from 1956 until its collapse in 1962. The failure of the Federation disappointed Walcott because he saw it as an opportunity to integrate and combine the resources of smaller islands into a more effective, stronger unit. In the aftermath of the Federation, St. Lucia became an independent state within the British Commonwealth on February 22, 1979. Although the Federation does not figure directly in *Omeros,* the shortsightedness and destructive political infighting that destroyed the Federation are embodied in the epic's national election scene. It is tempting to see in the acronyms of the two parties Maljo wishes to oppose (LP and WWPP) the Progressive Labour Party and the United Workers Party. The parallel is especially interesting since Walcott mentions a candidate named Compton and the Honorable John Compton of the United Workers Party actually won the bitterly contested election of May 1982.

### North and South

The shadow of North America looms large over the Caribbean basin and Walcott's professional life, and is included in his West Indian epic. Since Walcott is a participant in the poem and he insists that as a West Indian he is a citizen of the Americas, his sojourn in the United States is as much a part of his extended landscape as is Africa. Once again he telescopes history, this time to dramatize the irony of a postcolonial United States that nearly wiped out one race and enslaved another. Rather than focus on the genocidal policies that threaten to annihilate the Crow and Sioux, Walcott concentrates on the historical figure of Catherine Weldon, who lost a son and suffered the ostracism of her own race in order to support the Native American cause. Walcott gives a human face to sympathetic members of the white oppressor class, such as Weldon and the Plunketts, and in alluding to the many Western authors and artists in the Euro-American section of his epic, but he is not attempting to mitigate the overwhelming evil of imperial domination and slavery; rather, he is attempting to come to grips with both the black and white polarities of his personal existence. The essential thrust of *Omeros* is reconciliation, redemption, and the empowerment of Creole West Indian consciousness.

## Critical Overview

Since *Omeros* is a book of epic proportions written primarily in English by a black poet from a small Caribbean islands, its very existence is fraught with political complications. Walcott is an assimilator who does not hesitate to exploit every facet of his polyglot experience, whether his choices offend Afro-Caribbean purists or humanist liberals. Too little time has passed since publication of *Omeros* in 1990 for critical opinion to have settled definitively; however, certain aspects of the work often come under scrutiny in the commentary that has appeared. In spite of Walcott's argument to *New York Times* columnist D. J. R. Bruckner that he was not writing a "conundrum for scholars," it is impossible for commentators to ignore explicit epic references and parallels. To their credit, most of them quickly delve beneath the surface to focus on Walcott's creative deviation from the formula. Rei Terada's book *Derek Walcott's Poetry: American Mimicry,* for example, stresses the complexity and sophistication of Walcott's manipulation of Homeric and other Western paradigms. Her chapter on *Omeros* pursues the idea that Walcott subtly disguises the representational nature of his own fictional characters by comparing them with their classical Greek archetypes. As a result, his "realistic" characters are more immediately vivified in contrast with the "art" they imitate. John Lucas, reviewing for the *New Statesman and Society,* argues that Walcott's exploitation of the masters presents no constriction. Classical analogies aside, Lucas contends that "the glory of *Omeros* is in the manner of its telling, in Walcott's masterly twining of the narrative threads, and also in the poem's seemingly inexhaustible linguistic riches.

Regarding the prosody and scope of *Omeros* the verdict is divided. Among those who suggest that Walcott is too ambitious, that he may have overwritten, or spread this West Indian poem too thinly in attempting to incorporate North America and Europe are Christopher Bakken in *The Georgia Review,* Christopher Benfey in *The New Republic,* Brad Leithauser in *The New Yorker,* David Mason in *The Hudson Review* and Sean O'Brien in *The Times Literary Supplement.* Regardless of his reservations, Leithauser echos Lucas in praising Walcott's linguistic virtuosity. Impressed by the range and variety of Walcott's rhyme schemes, Leithauser offers *Omeros* as "a rhyme casebook" because Walcott has "a sure, prepossessing vocabulary, a deft and ludic wit, . . . an intricately calibrated ear. . . . wonderful analogical talents." St. Lucia-born scholar Pat Ismond, in her *Caribbean Contact* review, goes so far as to assert that Walcott's poem is "informed by a lyric" rather than an epic muse. Furthermore, writing from her perspective within the Caribbean, she disagrees with those metropolitan critics who find Walcott's excursions beyond the West Indies to be problematic. She appreciates the larger New World nexus of colonial reality. In confronting North America's unconscionable treatment of Native tribesmen, Ismond contends that Walcott "makes a truly revolutionary gesture," positing the heart of America in the Dakota plains rather than embracing the stereotypical image of Pilgrims in New England. Equally sensitive to the impetus behind Walcott's looking beyond the Caribbean, Geert Lernout argues in *Kunapipi* that it is the poet's dual vision that makes *Omeros* a "powerful achievement": "Walcott presents the two sides, the benevolent colonialism of the minor officials of the empire on the one hand and the descendants of slaves on the other."

The polarities noted by Lernout are obviously also the sources of Walcott's personal and cultural heritage. The African episode in *Omeros* fits so seamlessly as to go unremarked by most critics. Creole by birth as well as by experience and education, his roots are nurtured by European as well as African sources. Lernout mentions in passing that Walcott and James Joyce accomplish similarly patriotic objectives for their respective island nations. Writing for the *Southern Review,* Sidney Burris insists that in rhetoric, humor, structure and style, Joyce's *Ulysses* is likely "to emerge as the most generous sponsor of *Omeros.*" In addition to Hom-

er and Joyce, critics are finding a growing number of informative parallels with other Western models. At least three recent articles that seize upon Helen as the thematic center of *Omeros* make the case for Walcott's contribution to and extension of time-honored prototypes. According to Charlotte McClure in *Studies in the Literary Imagination,* Walcott's female protagonist assumes an identity of her own after 2500 years of varied treatment. Comparing the Helens of Hart Crane and Hilda Doolittle with Walcott's creation, McClure concludes that without the benefit of female support within her patriarchal society, the Caribbean Helen achieves autonomy, ultimately breaking free of Homeric and Sophoclean associations. In *World Literature Today,* Julia Minkler draws upon Shakespeare's *Tempest* to discuss Helen among her St. Lucian Calibans, Prospero, Miranda Ariel and Sycorax. Minkler finds Walcott's Helen "not only Caliban's physiognomically complementary mate but the pivotal force of creation and procreation as well." Then, contributing to a collection entitled *Robinson Crusoe: Myths and Metamorphoses,* Paula Burnett locates Walcott's new Helen within the rich Crusoe-Friday myth that itself grows out of the Ulysses legend. Due to their healing power, "moral courage, endurance, compassion, and knowledge of the human condition," Helen and Ma Kilman are primary forces in Walcott's narrative of the "handover of white power to black, in the name of a multiracial and multicultural future in which the wounds of history stay healed."

From some of the claims represented among these critics, it is apparent that Walcott's *Omeros* is expected to be capable of sustaining a weighty philosophical and aesthetic burden. Even before Walcott's receipt of the Nobel Prize in 1992, *Omeros* began attracting more and more serious scholarly attention. Among the books on the poem that will inevitably be making their appearance is Robert Hamner's *An Epic of the Dispossessed: Derek Walcott's Omeros,* scheduled for publication in 1997.

## Criticism

### Robert D. Hamner

*In the following essay, "The Aleatory Muse of Omeros," Hamner surveys ways that Walcott's*

# What Do I Read Next?

- Austin Clarke's *Growing up Stupid under the Union Jack,* 1980, is a humorous account of a youngster's attempts to cope with the contradictions of colonial society in Barbados.

- Nobel Laureate Seamus Heaney's play *The Cure at Troy: a Version of Sophocles' ''Philoctetes,''* 1991, focuses on the Greek character Philoctetes (who appears as Philoctete in *Omeros*). Heaney and Walcott are friends who have drawn from the same classical sources in these works.

- George Lamming's novel *In the Castle of My Skin,* 1954, recounts an aspiring artist's experiences of village life in Barbados, similar in many ways to Walcott's Gros Ilet village in St. Lucia.

- Rex Alan Smith's *Moon of Popping Trees,* 1981, is the book alluded to but not named in *Omeros,* from which Walcott reads about Catherine Weldon and the Sioux Ghost Dance.

- Irish writer James Joyce's *Finnegans Wake* is a complex, allusive, humorous landmark stream-of-consciousness novel recounting H. C. Earwicker's odyssey through one night in Dublin.

- Walcott's *Collected Poems 1948-1984,* 1986, reprints several poems with classical allusions and themes that show up again in *Omeros,* including the mini-epic ''The Schooner *Flight*'' from *The Star-Apple Kingdom* and the whole of the highly autobiographical *Another Life*.

- Walcott's play *The Odyssey,* 1993, is a somewhat more straightforward West Indian adaptation of Homer's epic account of Odysseus' difficult journey back to Ithaca after the victory at Troy.

---

*work both adheres to and diverges from classic epic traditions.*

Most critics and reviewers recognize the obvious epic dimensions of *Omeros* and wisely proceed to Walcott's deviations from the traditional formula. At this point some conventional approaches begin to note perceived weaknesses. One common objection, voiced by David Mason in *The Hudson Review* and Sean O'Brien in *The Times Literary Supplement,* is that Walcott errs in attempting to include Euro-American material in what is ostensibly a West Indian epic. Another complaint, offered by Christopher Bakken in *The Georgia Review,* is that rhetoric occasionally threatens to overwhelm the narrative impetus. One answer to both these concerns is that *Omeros* is to a significant extent the offspring of chance, fortune, the coincidental roll of dice, Walcott's aleatory muse. At least this is a stratagem, an authorial ploy that allows Walcott to exploit the ambient space between the vital people

who are his immediate subject and the aesthetic distance required to depict their lives artistically.

Chance and coincidence are sufficiently important to Walcott that he makes them explicit in minor details and within the thinking processes of major characters. In her *American Mimicry,* for example, Rei Terada comments on 1) Walcott's paying attention to spelling errors; 2) both Walcott's and English expatriate Major Plunkett's fascination with one-to-one correspondences between Aegean and Caribbean events; and 3) coincidental details mentioned by Warwick Walcott that link him with Shakespeare and *Hamlet*. Certainly, Achille accidentally gets ''trust'' wrong in naming his canoe *In God We Troust,* Major Plunkett misspells the Arawak word ''Iounalo,'' and a sign is misprinted ''HEWANNORRA.'' Clearly, Walcott in his own persona and Major Plunkett expend much of their energy in the poem pursuing a well-intentioned, nonetheless misguided, quest to immortalize their West Indian Helen in emulation of Homer's white paradigm. This eclectic blend of misprision and fancied correspondence in *Omeros,* however, goes much deeper than these overt manifestations. Indeed it pervades the subtext and Walcott's aesthetic technique. Since Walcott makes himself a participant within *Omeros,* the circumstances of his birth serve as one antecedent accident. As he describes his predicament in *Another Life,* "reason had produced its monster: / a prodigy of the wrong age and color." Even his obscure island happened to be so desirable to France and England that he grew up being taught St. Lucia was the "Helen of the West Indies."

An impressionable Walcott absorbed such incidental correspondences until he eventually realized their potential not only as subject for analogy, but also for the recognition latent within any accident or mistake. Shortly before undertaking the writing of *Omeros,* Walcott explained at a literary conference the lesson he learned when he mistyped the word "love" in his manuscript where he intended to say "life." It immediately occurred to him that this slip of the finger registered a truth he had not previously conceptualized. He records his conclusion later in "Caligula's Horse" for *Kunapipi:* "That is one part of the poetic process, accident as illumination, error as truth, typographical mistakes as revelation." As a matter of fact, early in the second chapter of *Omeros* Walcott candidly informs readers that his very title grows out of a simple mistake. When he speaks of Homer to his lover, a Greek sculptress, she informs him that the authentic pronunciation of the name is "Omeros." Title in hand, with all its connotations, Walcott undertakes the conversion of Aegean rudiments into a Caribbean narrative. This epic of the dispossessed centers on a Creole island that has dropped between the lines of history. Since St. Lucia and her people have been lost or marginalized in the record of European conquest, Walcott may be said to have "found" them and himself as subject matter. Already at hand are black countrymen named after figures from classical myth and legend, educated under a system of hierarchical Western values. The precursor of Helen, he explains in a *Green Mountains Review* interview with J. P. White, is the woman he happened to encounter on a local transport bus. Portraying this incident in "The Light of the World" from *The Arkansas Testament,* Walcott introduces this remarkable ebony rival to Delacroix's *Liberty Leading the People,* a van like Hector's Comet, the Halcyon Hotel where Helen will be employed at the close of *Omeros,* and he registers his desire to give something to these people he has abandoned in pursuit of art.

Thus it would be appropriate to categorize the contents of *Omeros* as "found art." At least that is the impression Walcott cultivates in having Helen first appear as a mirage before his persona. When his eye happens upon this feline beauty in madras head-tie and yellow dress, the narrator can only pronounce, "And all the rest followed." From one unexpected vision, all the other characters, themes, and plot lines cohere in Helen both as a person and as the embodiment of St. Lucia. Initially, she may serve as a cause just as her Greek namesake does in the *Iliad;* however, in the modern setting no demigods are found working their will on a grand scale. Instead, Walcott consistently presents a sequence of events wherein ordinary humans must feel their way tentatively, reacting to shifts in fortune, whose most well-intentioned plans may turn out to be misguided. Of the four major questing figures, only Achille and Ma Kilman achieve untainted goals. In each case, they succeed not through personal assertion but by allowing an external power to reveal missing knowledge. The overriding difference is that Ma Kilman responds to instinct and follows a trail of ants in locating the African herb that cures Philoctete's physical and spiritual affliction. Achille, in turn, succumbs to a sunstroke-induced trance to regain the African heritage that had been wrested from his people by the Middle Passage. For Dennis Plunkett, "all the rest" begins with his commitment to giving Helen the history she has been denied, making her the object of the Battle of the Saints. Apparently, even Helen's possession of the butterfly-colored frock that serves as the standard for that famous battle comes into her possession due to misunderstanding. Whether she imagined Maud Plunkett intended it for her or she stole it, there is the accomplished fact. Equally determined to exonerate Helen, Walcott undertakes her artistic representation through the Westernized paraphernalia of *Omeros.*

Before these men realize the colonial paternalism inherent in their agendas for Helen, the stations of their quests afford fruitful insights. Pursuing his research, the Major happens upon a surrogate for the son he and Maud were unable to conceive. Although young Midshipman Plunkett died over 200 years ago, by accidentally falling on his own sword during the Battle of the Saints, the Major's discovery of his name in the annals of the military engagement is sufficient to confirm his blood-ties to his adopted country. His luck in finding the name unexpectedly and his obsession with fortunate parallels, however, only affirm the European framework of his historical account. After his wife's untimely death, he becomes more thoroughly integrated into authentic island society when he calls on Ma Kilman's powers as an obeah-woman to establish communication with Maud in the afterlife. Humbled by personal loss and realizing that he had been inadvertently imposing his will on Helen's story, he at last concedes that she is "not a cause . . . only a name / for a local wonder."

Walcott's sojourn carries him away from the island to North America and Europe in books four and five—the portions of the epic that some critics see as the least artistically defensible. The fact that Walcott's own professional life necessitated foreign residence is insufficient alone to justify the material of these two books. An equally autobiographical yet more compelling motive may be found in the "accident" of his being born of mixed blood. Not only has he sung this theme since adolescence, but it is as integral a component of his existence, as it is of all Creoles, regardless of whether they wish to acknowledge the disparate sides of their ancestry. Walcott's "all the rest" encompasses this broader context. When he needs an alter ego to share the pain of a broken marriage and growing disenchantment with the American Dream, an unlikely figure jumps from the pages of a book he is reading, Rex Smith's *Moon of Popping Trees.* As Walcott explains, "Catherine Weldon arose in high relief / . . . making a fiction of my own loss." Prompted by the ghost of his father, he traces the roots of colonialism to the decadent seats of European empire. In the Old World, he learns to prefer the birds perched on the commemorative statues to the monuments themselves. That lesson is reiterated when he returns to St. Lucia and the image of Homer himself counsels that, "A girl smells better than the world's libraries." In addition, this talking statue of authority argues that as powerful as love for a woman may be, "the love of your own people is / greater." Acting in Virgil's capacity as guide to Dante in *The Inferno,,* the statue removes Walcott's remaining illusions by taking him through St. Lucia's inferno near Soufriere. After thisecorrective experience, Walcott reaches an epiphany similar to that of Dennis Plunkett: "The sea was my privilege. / And a fresh people."

Although Walcott draws many literary figures into *Omeros,* it is imperative to note one other crucial influence on the epic. Walcott, who is a painter as well as a poet and playwright, has always sketched scenes for his poetry and drama. This is important because he plans to publish in a separate book the ink and watercolor illustrations he has prepared for *Omeros,* and also for his technical affinities with two out of the many graphic artists he cites directly. The lucky coincidence of Winslow Homer's surname, in itself, merely fits into the litany of correspondences. However, when Walcott chances upon Homer's *The Gulf Stream* he is forced into a singular recognition. Homer's realistic depiction of a lone Negro sailor adrift in a dismasted skiff between voracious sharks and an oblivious sailboat on the horizon leads to his exclamation, "Achille! My main man, my nigger! /. . . forever, between our island / and the coast of Guinea." Combined in that electric moment are two painters, two Homers, and two representatives of a race suspended precariously between the Old and New Worlds. The second painter deserving special notice is equally instructive, but for an entirely different reason. Walcott's allusion to Marcel Duchamp's *Large Glass* should elicit the heart of Dadaist "aleatory," "chance" or "found art" theory. It is this anti-art technique that underlies Walcott's non-linear plotting of *Omeros.* Whereas Duchamp declares a "ready-made" urinal to be an art object, Walcott proclaims the artistic validity of St. Lucia's readily available but disregarded population. Furthermore, when Walcott mentions the accidental cracks in Duchamp's *Large Glass,* he draws from this artist's celebration of the creative value of mishaps. Speaking to Katherine Kuh in *The Artist's Voice,* Duchamp explains his random dropping of three lengths of thread onto painted strips of canvas to form his iconoclastic *3 Standard Stoppages:* "The idea of letting a piece of thread fall on a canvas was accidental, but from this accident came a carefully planned work. Most important was the accepting and recognizing of this accidental stimulation."

Neither Duchamp's nor Walcott's manipulation of chance and ready-made objects can be taken as purely haphazard. Their material is carefully selected, yet each choice is cast as random enough to maximize a sense of spontaneity—creativity arising from the mundane. Walcott's characters may seem diminished when compared with the glorious warriors of the *Iliad,* the *Odyssey* and the *Aeneid,* but as he demonstrates, they possess a dimension of heroism all their own. *Omeros* has room for good-hearted Dennis Plunkett whose putative son inadvertently anchors the Major's life in St. Lucia by his accidental death. It is also about Walcott, Achille and the other descendants of Afolabe and the female colliers whose menial labor fueled the economy of an empire. Walcott's contribution is to demonstrate that, although they did not set out to conquer anyone, were not able to return to their native land, and did not found a marbled Rome, "they crossed, they survived. There is the Epical splendour."

**Source:** Robert D. Hamner, for *Epics for Students,* Gale Research, 1997

## Julia A. Minkler

*In the following essay, Minkler proposes that in many ways, Walcott's* Omeros *retells Homer's version of the story of Helen of Troy — but with Helen a victorious rather than victimized figure. Minkler also offers comparisons with* The Tempest, *by William Shakespeare—a play that, similarly to Walcott's work, features an island setting and a much-desired central female character.*

*But she'd last forever, Helen.*[1]

In book 1 of *The Histories* Herodotus implies that Helen of Sparta (alias Helen of Troy) was lewd and unchaste (an opinion shared by other fifth-century men of letters as well), "for," he says, "it is obvious that no young woman *allows* herself to be abducted if she does not *wish* to be."[2] Herodotus also mentions another version of the abduction story (a version, however, of which he himself seems quite skeptical), according to which Helen did not really go to Troy but ended up in Egypt, where she spent some time at the court of King Proteus.[3] Finally, according to Euripides in *Helen,* Hera, "angry that she was not given the prize," gave Priam's son "a breathing image out of the sky's air"[4] so that Paris would hold a "vanity" (i.e., a shadow) instead of the real woman.

Certainly, Helen's legend has endured numerous interpretations from many cultures, from classical mythology to the present, or, as Derek Walcott says in *Omeros,* his most extensive poetic work, "Smoke wrote the same story / since the dawn of time" (2.23.2). Caribbean culture is no exception. Resonant of the Homeric story yet at the same time successfully adapted to the specificity of the region's *tempora* and *mores,* the Helen theme is multifariously present in Caribbean literature and folklore. From the popular Jamaican song "Helena,"[5] to Stanley French's play *The Rape of Fair Helen,*[6] to Walcott's *Omeros* and his recent stage adaptation of the *Odyssey,*[7] Helen's myth and "nature" are now seen under a new, inter/metacultural perspective.

Specifically in *Omeros* the St. Lucian poet, critic, and playwright Walcott treats Helen in an idiosyncratic narrative of Caribbean aspiration and inspiration. His version of Helen deviates considerably from the original matrix. For him, Helen's story is no longer the account of her abduction by Paris and her exile in Troy but rather that of her growth as a woman after the war. What is more, Paris himself is no longer accounted for in the text except through a pun implied by the name of the sunken battleship *Ville de Paris* ("City of Paris," "Vile Paris").

This new Antillean Helen should not be seen as a victim but rather as the axis about which the entire "horned island" (1.7.2) and its elemental men rotate: Achille, a dignified version of Menelaus; Hector, Paris's counterpart and, like Paris, a man of duplicitous nature; Philoctete, a low-key character suffering from an incurable leg wound; the Vagrant Poet, a version of divine Homer himself; and Dennis Plunkett, the softhearted colonizer of a town "he had come to love" (2.22.3). In brief, Walcott changes the original story, in which the male captor victimizes his female captive, into a story of seduction—this time, however, it is a seduction of the male by the female.

Finally, and above all, Walcott turns the original story into an account of textual rebirth for both male and female. This new story, "Not his, but her story," takes over immediately after the war, "Not theirs, but Helen's war" (1.5.3). Unlike the white Helen, who has died long ago "In that pause / that divides the smoke with a sword" (1.6.2), this Helen of the West Indies (7.62.1) seems happily settled down in a revived postwar Troy, which she now tenderly but possessively calls *her* village (1.5.3); for, in her new Antillean transformation, as one sees it unfold in and out of *Omeros,* Helen symbolizes as well as personifies the island itself, which is likewise called Helen (2.19.1, 2.19.3).

In addition to being resonant of the Homeric story, however, Walcott's *Omeros* is also reminiscent of yet another work, Shakespeare's *Tempest.*[8] Not only does it share with the latter such characteristics as an island setting and a storm as catalyst, but it also relates to *The Tempest* on the basis of the psychological and/or symbolic proximities of its main characters, save one. In particular, both Achille and Hector, the local fishermen antiheroes of the poem, partly identify with Caliban, the "abhorred slave," the "savage," and the "thing most brutish" of Shakespeare's play. At times Philoctete, who "anoint[s] the mouth of his sore" (1.3.2), thus "feeding" his wound, also identifies with Caliban, who, in *The Tempest,* is bound by Prospero to "feed" the island's gaping "wound," its furnace. Omeros, the omniscient, omnipresent, yet invisible Poet, and his local visible reduction, Seven Seas, the island's blind griot and seer (3.28.1), resemble Prospero, the island's master poet, sage, and magus. The Vagrant Poet-Narrator (and at times Walcott himself) often evokes an echo of Ariel, Prospero's bewildered captive. Eager to disentangle himself from Homer's intellectual web (thus opting for a Caribbean identity that is no longer uncritically dependent on a cultural subordination to the West and its tradition), he gradually succeeds in freeing himself and his island from *the* poet's enchanted but fatal grasp. Ma Kil[l]man, the owner of the No Pain Café, an Obeah figure who ultimately cures Philoctete's gangrenous wound, represents the domesticated version of Sycorax, Caliban's absent mother. Last but not least, Maud Plunkett, obsessed with her never-ending (and Penelope-like) quilt-making, stitching birds "into her green silk / with sibylline steadiness" (7.62.2), becomes a more mature, toned-down Miranda.

Helen, on the other hand, who in the poem personifies the concretized version of a long-awaited Caribbean identity, resists comparison and belongs to no one. Throughout the narrative she functions independently of the other characters' fates, as she alone stands and acts outside that narrative. At the same time, and of all the other characters in *Omeros,* she is the one to determine the narrative's progressions and its crucial outcome as well. Already divergent from her Greek counterpart, Walcott's Helen does not on first impression seem to parallel any of the characters from *The Tempest,* yet in a unique way she does.

In "Beyond Miranda's Meanings: Un/silencing the 'Demonic Ground' of 'Caliban's Woman'" Sylvia Wynter analyzes the adverse relation of "sameness" and "difference" that unifies yet differentiates Caribbean womanists from white feminists. Wynter brilliantly suggests that we see the silenced Caribbean and black American woman as the long-anticipated mate of Caliban, so pronouncedly absent from *The Tempest.*[9] Addressing previously posed questions on the absence of Caliban's legitimate father and the "silent presence of a mother not yet fully understood,"[10] Wynter now poses the significant question on the absence

of Caliban's Woman, i.e. "of Caliban's physiognomically complementary mate" (SW, 360). Characteristically, Wynter says:

> Nowhere in Shakespeare's play . . . does Caliban's mate appear as an alternative sexual-erotic model of desire. . . . Rather there, on the New World island, as the only woman, Miranda . . . is canonized as the "rational" object of desire; as the potential genitrix of a superior mode of human "life," that of "good natures." (SW, 360)

According to Wynter (as well as to Maryse Condé, whom Wynter quotes), Caliban is reduced to a labor machine. His nondesire for his own mate, a woman like him, as well as his nonneed for the procreation of his own "kind," constitutes the founding function of the social pyramid of a global order, "put in place following upon the 1492 arrival of Columbus in the Caribbean" (SW, 360). The absence of Caliban's endogenous desire for his kind of woman and instead the soldering of his nevertheless-existing sexual desires onto Miranda (SW, 361), the woman he absolutely *cannot* have, polarize Caliban's unconscious. Thus he is now displaced from the state of a "brutish slave" to that of a frustrated and almost schizohrenic being. In Wynter's view, Caliban's Woman, seen as the harbinger of a new era of consciousness in the Caribbean, would/could have helped (if allowed into existence) to reinstate Caliban's human status, otherwise subhuman.

At this point, further elaboration on the concept of Caliban's Woman is necessary. In her essay Wynter seems primarily concerned with the political rather than literary dimensions of this concept. For her, the Caribbean womanist—whether a member of the intelligentsia, a middle-class housewife, or a member of the working class—is at last becoming an indispensable factor of Caribbean sociopolitical and cultural reality; and although Wynter too reckons Caliban as a symbol of the Caribbean people in general, from the beginning of their enslavement to their present status of economic subordination to the West, she seems particularly disturbed not so much by the fact of *his misrepresentation* (Caliban now personifying Caribbean males) as by the total *lack of representation* of Caliban's Woman, because of racial and patriarchal domination. In other words, Wynter's concerns as a womanist pertain to the fact that women's marginalization in the Caribbean is colonization twice removed: first by colonial Prosperos and second by colonized Calibans and their repressed desires and needs. Still, one should keep in mind that Wynter's essay is after all *the* concluding statement of a selection of essays written by women who write, or write about, literature and who address not only political but literary questions as well. What is more, the fact that in this same essay Wynter calls Caliban's Woman "demonic" (SW, 364)—a notion that in my view is diametrically opposed to Walcott's "Adamic" notion —brings to the surface literary connotations equally implied by this very concept.

Walcott states in "The Muse of History," an essay written in the early seventies, that although amnesia—and especially amnesia of the literary European past—is the "true history" of the Caribbean, "The great *poets* of the New World, from Whitman to Neruda, reject this sense of history. *Their* vision of *man* in the New World is Adamic."[11] By mentioning Whitman and Neruda, and also Borges, Césaire, Saint-John Perse, and other New World (American, Latin American, or Caribbean) poets, vis-à-vis the Adamic element, Walcott unquestionably relates this image not to political or politicized issues but directly to literature and literary concerns. In addition, Walcott also looks at Caliban from a purely literary angle, openly distancing himself from those New World, militant poets who see Caliban's *mastery* of the *master's* language not as victory but as self-deceit (3–4), thus reducing it to a language that, as Shakespeare put it, taught Caliban only how to curse. Referring to the Adamic man of letters (who is newly "made" but not ignorant of the world) and his second Eden, Walcott says:

> The great poetry of the New World does not pretend to such innocence [i.e., molded after the myth of the noble savage], its vision is not naïve. Rather, like its fruits, its savor is a mixture of the acid and the sweet, the apples of its second Eden have the tartness of experience. (5)

As a matter of fact, Walcott's Adamic concept obviates female intervention. Like the biblical Adam, this New World Adam is "made" directly by his "god," without female interference or any other connection, for that matter. As described in *Omeros,* in the New World "each man was a nation / in himself, without mother, father, brother" (3.28.1). In this "second Eden with its golden apple" (2.18.2), all "men are born makers, with the original simplicity / in every maker since Adam. This is prehistory" (3.28.2).

Going back at this point to Wynter's demonic image, I suggest we see the term *demonic* as the antonym of *Adamic.* I likewise suggest we see the term as far removed from the current Christian connotation as possible. *Demonic* derives from the Greek word *daimon,* meaning god- or goddesslike, a link between gods and humans, and good or bad spirit. In this particular context (i.e., as a good spirit) a demon, especially a female demon, can virtually relate to the spirit (or force) of inspiration, creativity, or to a faculty pertaining to the mind or soul of the individual involved, very much in the sense of the Socratic *daimon*—namely, his conscience. (It is worth mentioning that, in Greek, words such as *inspiration, creativity,* and *conscience* are all feminine.) In this sense, Wynter's "demonic Woman" could represent the second stage of growth for Caliban's Woman, a stage of cultural (since pertaining to creativity) rather than solely political self-consciousness and maturation. Thus, in her demonic stage, Caliban's Woman is no longer looked at as just a Muse—i.e., the inspirational force behind *male* creativity (a stereotypical male contrivance)—but rather creativity *herself,* especially creativity of the mind, for her and for women to follow. As such, Caliban's Woman is viewed as the female creative force that propagates, procreates, and builds upon her own mental capabilities, without man's or "god's" intervention.

. . . . .

> . . . her beauty is what no man can claim any more than this bay. Her beauty stands apart in a golden dress, its beaches wreathed with her name.

(7.57.3)

In my view, Walcott's Helen in *Omeros* is the well-balanced conflation of Wynter's demonic model and Caliban's Woman. She is not only Caliban's physiognomically complementary mate but the pivotal force of creation and procreation as well. As the personification of Caliban's Woman, this new and promising Helen is now pregnant, "carrying Hector's child" (6.49.3). In her saffron dress, stolen from Maud, Helen meanders enigmatically from man to man "with the leisure of a panther" (7.64.2), yet her eyes "never betrayed horned Menelaus / or netted Agamemnon in their irises" (7.64.2). She, "Black maid or black mail," is everywhere, yet her presence is "oblique but magnetic" (2.18.2). She could be everybody's, yet, in her remote stillness (7.64.2) and Sphinx-like evasiveness, she belongs to nobody. In her case even the term "Caliban's Woman" becomes a misstatement, since it no longer describes Walcott's Helen accurately, a woman with a glossy but nevertheless substantial personality. It is a fact that in *Omeros* Caliban has at last been blessed with a woman of his "kind," but it is also a fact that he has not, under any circumstances, been able to claim this woman as his own. Rather, it is Helen who *owns* him and men like him.

In an unexpected turn of events, the island's men have become Helen's men instead—Helen's Calibans, so to speak. Her radiance and exuberance push them to extremes. Achille feels "like a dog that is left / to nose the scraps of her footsteps" (1.7.1). Hector, *un homme fou* (1.3.1), is determined to fight an enraged Achille (7.59.3), his former friend and companion, "for a tin and Helen" (6.46.1), later to lose his life unfairly and ingloriously. And Major Dennis Plunkett, the colonizer with the heart of gold—himself a Caliban—is "fixed by her glance" (2.18.1), fatally lost in her "seduction of quicksand" (6.53.1). Even Philoctete, who is beyond caring about women, has suddenly become her "footman" (2.20.2). Knowing "It was her burden [the woman's and the island's] he bore," he now wonders:

> Why couldn't they love the place, same way,
>     together,
> the way he always loved her, even with his sore?
> Love Helenlike a wife in good and bad weather,
> in sickness and health, its beauty in being poor?
> The way the leaves loved her, not like a
>     pink leaflet
> printed with slogans of black people fighting war?

(2.20.2)

From now on, Helen has become an aphorism: Helen, the woman, is no man's prey, no warrior's spoil; Helen, the *island, is* no man's *land.* Finally, as the personification of the demonic woman mustering creativity and wisdom, Helen has bewildered two more of the island's Calibans, the last ones to fall into her nets: Omeros, the divine poet himself; and the Vagrant Poet, the most complex of the poem's Caliban-like characters.

According to the Vagrant Poet, Omeros, who is both his nigger and his captain (3.30.2)—in a word, his exorcism (7.59.1)—personifies creativity, knowledge, and enchantment. Introduced to him by a Greek girl exiled in America, Omeros also personifies the experience of a past trying to grow roots anew inside the New World poet, a past that does "what the past always does: suffer and stare" (1.2.3). What is more, for the Vagrant Poet, Omeros is a vision, the sibylline voice of divine wisdom, and the ever-living discourse with that past. He says "Omeros,"

> and *O* was the conch-shell's invocation, *mer* was
> both mother and sea in our Antillean patois,
> *os,* a grey bone, and the white surf as it crashes
> and spreads its sibilant collar on a lace shore.

(1.2.3)

As the source of knowledge (a Prospero figure in the Shakespearean sense as well), Omeros is also portrayed as a snake, thus evoking Eden's serpent.

> I saw white-eyed Omeros motionless. He must
> be deaf too, I thought, as well as blind,
>     since his head
> never turned, and then he lifted the dry rattle
> in one hand, and it was the same sound I
>     had heard
> in Cody's circus, the snake hiss before battle.

(5.43.2)

Both a serpent- and a godlike figure (a trickster/seer),[12] this Caribbean-construed[13] Omeros feels no anger for having shown Woman how to partake of God's knowledge. On the contrary, himself a symbol of wisdom, he allows Helen to savor the fruit of that wisdom unconditionally, in an act of divine communion. In addition to the yellow dress, Helen also steals a bracelet from Maud (the bracelet of knowledge) but is caught in the act by Dennis Plunkett, who, bewitched by her spell, lets her take it.

> . . . he was fixed by her glance
> in the armoire's full-length mirror, where,
>     one long arm,
> its fist closed like a snake's head, slipped through
>     a bracelet
> from Maud's jewel-box, and, with eyes calm
>     as Circe,
> simply continued, and her smile said,
>     "You will let
> me try this," which he did. He stood at the mercy
> of that beaked, black arm, which with serpen-
>     tine leisure
> replaced the bangle. . . .
> The bracelet coiled like a snake. He heard
>     it hissing:
> Her housebound slavery could be your salvation.

(2.18.1-2)

Viewed as *the* poet's embrace with her in disguise,[14] this serpentine bracelet underlines Helen's spiritual communion with the absolute ideal of knowledge.

Last of all, the Vagrant Poet—Walcott's Adamic man par excellence—entrusts Helen with the secrets of his mystical,[15] metaphysical,[16] and poetic[17] experience, an experience that derives not only from Homer and the classical tradition but also from Shakespeare and the perpetuation of that tradition. During a metaphorical descent into the depths of his soul in pursuit of knowledge and spiritual fertility, the New World poet of *Omeros* visits with the phantom of his Father/father,[18] who in turn unveils to his initiate son the secrets of their patrilineal heritage. He says to him: "I was raised in this obscure Caribbean port, / where my bastard father christened me for his shire: / Warwick. The Bard's county. But never felt part / of the foreign machinery known as Literature. / I preferred verse to fame, but I wrote with the heart / of an amateur. It's that Will you inherit" (1.12.1). Later on in the poem the Vagrant Poet also meets with the phantom of his mother,[19] who too feels compelled to emphasize her son's origins: "'You are my son.' / 'Warwick's son,' she said. / 'Nature's gentleman'" (3.32.1).

Once the spiritual journey to his personal past is completed, the Vagrant Poet undertakes a series of journeys to a communal past via Africa, Europe, and North America over a considerably long but discontinuous span of time. It is during these voyages that he begins to have particular doubts about the nature of his Adamic identity and decides to set sail for maternal roots. And, although he will later admit "I had nowhere to go but home. Yet I was lost" (4.33.2), he finally, deliberately and unconditionally, surrenders to Helen: the mother figure of Africa, the earth goddess of Greece, the Nereid of the "other" archipelago. He ponders:

> "If this place is hers, did that empty horizon
> once flash its broadsides with their inaudible rays
> in her honour? Was that immense enterprise
> on the baize tables of empires for one who carries
> cheap sandals on a hooked finger with the Pitons
> for breasts? Were both hemispheres the
>             split breadfruit
> of her African ass, her sea the fluted chitons
> of a Greek frieze?" (7.62.2)

And in response to his own psychological qualms, he adds:

> "You were never in Troy, and, between
>             two Helens,
> yours is here and alive;. . .
> . . .These Helens are different creatures,
> one marble, one ebony. . . .
> but each draws an elbow slowly over her face
> and offers the gift of her sculptured nakedness,
> parting her mouth."

Still later he exclaims, "What a fine local woman!" (7.64.2). The Vagrant Poet is home at last! "I sang our wide country, the Caribbean Sea,"[20] he says. Let "the deep hymn / of the Caribbean continue my epilogue" (7.64.2). As for Helen, her cycle come to a closure, she now passes the torch of her "demonic" nature to a new Helen (7.63.1), Christine, Ma Kilman's niece. Thus the *Helenic*— and no longer Hellenic— character of Walcott's story has created a literary intercultural continuum, which, like the sea, will be going on forever (7.64.3).

Almost two decades ago, in "The Muse of History," emphasizing the New World poet's Adamic idiosyncrasy, Walcott wrote: "I needed to become omnivorous about the art and literature of Europe to understand my own world. I write 'my own world' because I had no doubt that it was mine, that it was given to me, by god, not by history, with my gift."[21] Contrasting his ideology to the militant beliefs of the "new prophets of bitterness" in the Caribbean, he also wrote: "I say to the ancestor who sold me, and to the ancestor who bought me, I have no father, I want no such father, although I can understand you, black ghost, white ghost."[22]

In *Omeros,* through the persona of the Vagrant Poet (often seen as Walcott's own alter ego), Walcott's Adamic theory seems revised. The poet no longer considers his mythopoeic gift divinely sent but rather realized and propagated through a female demon: the demon of imagination—or, as Walcott calls it in "The Muse of History," the "memory of imagination in literature" (25). In *Omeros,* however, this spirit is no longer an abstraction. On the contrary, it is conveyed by the intellectual, spiritual, and physical powers of a "real" woman, Helen, who also identifies with that New World woman Wynter calls "demonic" and constitutes the companion of the New World man. This new woman (of whatever class, status, or occupation) has taught her "Caliban" the way of belonging anew. She has taught him the way of belonging not to a person but to a present that draws its energy from the past, a past that, although no longer Adamic (i.e., god-sent and male-propagated), nevertheless musters the divine and, at the same time, *fe*/male characteristics of life.

*Notes*

[1] Derek Walcott, *Omeros,* New York, Farrar Straus Giroux, 1990. "Omeros" is the Greek form of "Homer." In the epigraph here Walcott refers to an Ideal—i.e., the eternal and universal "Helen" rather than the mythological figure of Homer's epics. Subsequent citations are followed by parentheses indicating book, chapter, and section number.

[2] Herodotus, *The Histories,* Aubrey de Selincourt, tr., London, Penguin, 1983, book 1, p. 42 (emphases added).

[3] Ibid., book 2, pp. 170–74.

[4] Euripides, *Helen,* in *Euripides II,* Richard Lattimore, tr., Chicago, University of Chicago Press, 1969.

[5] "Helena," *Jamaican Folk Singers, vol. 3, Encore!, n.d.*

[6] Stanley French, *The Rape of Fair Helen,* Barbados, Carib Printers, 1983. French is a contemporary Caribbean playwright from St. Lucia, West Indies.

[7] For a review of the production of Walcott's *Odyssey* at The Other Place in Stratford-upon-Avon, England (Summer 1992), see Oliver Taplin, "Hustling Homer," *Times Literary Supplement,* 17 July 1992, p. 19. Taplin calls the production a "feat of poetry" and a "meta-heroic folk-tale." As far as Helen is concerned, and although the central female character here is Penelope, any connection with the Helen theme should be made by juxtaposition of flighty, untamed Helen to domesticated Penelope, the faithful wife par excellence for the Greeks.

[8] William Shakespeare, *The Tempest,* Robert Langbaum, ed., New York, New American Library, 1964. As in *Omeros,* links between Homer and Shakespeare are also apparent in Walcott's *Odyssey.* Taplin characterizes Shakespeare's tragedy *Troilus and Cressida* as the "forerunner in English" of Walcott's play adaptation, although, unlike the latter, which is based on Homer's *Odyssey, Troilus and Cressida* is based (among other sources) on the *Iliad.* For a textual interpretation of Helen in *Troilus and Cressida,* see Mihoko Suzuki's *Metamorphoses of Helen: Authority, Difference and the Epic,* Ithaca, N.Y., Cornell University Press, 1989, pp. 210–57.

[9] Sylvia Wynter, "Beyond Miranda's Meanings: Un/silencing the 'Demonic Ground' of Caliban's 'Woman,'" in *Out of the Kumbla: Caribbean Women in Literature,* Carole Boyle Davis & Elaine Savory Fido, eds., Trenton, N.J., Africa World Press, 1990, p. 363. Subsequent citations use the abbreviation SW.

[10] For an exhaustive analysis of the figure of Caliban's mother, see Lemuel Johnson, "Whatever Happened to Caliban's Mother? Or, The Problem with Othello's," in *Shakespeare and Cultural Traditions,* Fifth World Shakespeare Congress, Tokyo, August 1991.

[11] Derek Walcott, "The Muse of History: An Essay," in *Is Massa Day Dead? Black Moods in the Caribbean,* Orde Coombs, ed., New York, Anchor, 1974, pp. 2–3 (emphasis added).

[12] The spider/trickster Anancy (or Anansi) is an important figure of Caribbean and African folklore. For a different, creative retelling of Anancy, see Andrew Salkey's *Anancy's Score* (London, Bogle-L'Ouverture, 1973) and *Anancy, Traveller* (London, Bogle-L'Ouverture, 1992). In particular, Salkey's Anancy is the conflation of a lovable trickster and a clairvoyant sage.

[13] In an interview following *Omeros*'s publication, Walcott called Homer a great Caribbean artist. For excerpts of that interview and a review of *Omeros,* see D. J. R. Bruckner, "A Poem in Homage to an Unwanted Man," *New York Times,* 9 October 1990, pp. C13, C17.

[14] The spiritual union/embrace of Omeros (disguised as a bracelet) with Helen is reminiscent of the various metamorphoses of Zeus and his sexual embraces with mortal women.

[15] Pertaining to a *mystes,* in Greek "the initiate to a mystery or cult."

[16] Pertaining to the epic hero's *katubatic* venture. According to the conventions of the epic, the hero, although still alive, undergoes a *katabasis*— i.e., a descent into Hades—in pursuit of knowledge and/or fertility.

[17] Pertaining to creation in general, from the word *poiētēs,* Greek for "creator," "composer," "maker."

[18] In this episode the Vagrant Poet follows the example of Vergil's Aeneas (*Aeneid,* book 6), who descends into the underworld to consult with the soul of his dead father Anchises about the founding and destiny of Rome.

[19] This scene is reminiscent of Odysseus' descent into Hades to consult with Teiresias about his future (*Odyssey,* 11, "Nekyia"). While in Hades, Odysseus runs across the soul of his dead mother Anticleia, who informs him about the fates of his loved ones (wife, son, and father) after his departure for Troy.

[20] For a personification of Caribbea (the Caribbean Sea), see Andrew Salkey's epic poem *Jamaica* (London, Hutchison, 1973).

[21] Walcott, "The Muse of History," p. 26.

[22] Ibid., p. 27.

**Source:** Julia A. Minkler, "Helen's Calibans: A Study of Gender Hierarchy in Derek Walcott's *Omeros,*" *World Literature Today,* Vol. 67, No. 2, Spring, 1993, 272–76.

## Brad Leithauser

*In the following excerpt, Leithauser considers Walcott's epic poem as a recovered history of 400 years of the Antillean islands, most of which has passed without being recorded. He also discusses the links between* Omeros *and the* Iliad *and* Odyssey *of Homer. Leithauser also discusses Walcott's style and prominent themes in the work.*

In one of the first glimpses we have of Helen, the heroine of Derek Walcott's book-length poem *Omeros,* she walks barefoot along a beach on her native Antillean island of St. Lucia, singing a Beatles song. The tune is "Yesterday," and the line she focusses on strikes a note of understated wistfulness: "Yesterday, all my troubles seemed so far away." Helen is reflecting upon the upheavals of romance— as well she might, for she, in her surpassing beauty, is a heart-breaker. An "ebony girl" in a "lemon frock," she has recently been fired from her job as a servant to a pair of British expatriates, Dennis and Maud Plunkett. Dennis, a retired major who has taken up the disciplining of a new sort of troops— he has become a pig farmer—is silently mad about her. So are, silently or vociferously, most of the other men on the island, including a pair of fishermen whose rivalrous designs threaten to unravel the community's uneasy workaday calm.

Some forty pages farther along, we learn that the young woman's troubles were never "far away," as Walcott resurrects "Helens from an earlier time," whose lives were indentured to an inhumane colonialism. He vividly summons those forebears of hers who, working for pittances under the scorching Caribbean sun, once carried staggering loads of anthracite down from the hills to the holds of imperial freighters:

> Hell was built on those hills. In that coun-
> try of coal
> without fire, that inferno the same colour
> as their skins and shadows, every labouring soul
> climbed with her hundredweight basket, eve-
> ry load for
> one copper penny, balanced erect on their necks
> that were tight as the liner's hawsers from
> the weight.
> The carriers were women, not the fair, gentler sex.

As she sings, Helen is ruefully conscious of an unwanted burden: she is pregnant and does not know who the father is. But she bears, simultaneously and unwittingly, a greater burden still. She, like all the dark-skinned islanders, carries the weight of a history of generations of cruelty and chicanery, most of which has passed away unchronicled and unrighted. Through Helen, and Helen's precursors, Walcott ventures back more than four hundred years, to that "yesterday" when the first African slaves were transported to the Caribbean.

Yet his backward-looking muse does not halt there. He equates the Caribbean and the Mediterranean—both belonging to a "sea without time"— and thereby likens his Helen to Homer's, and his squabbling fishermen to the warring Greeks and Trojans. The whole of *Omeros* (the title is Homer's name in Greek) is anchored to *The Iliad* and, in a lesser degree, *The Odyssey*. Only a page after Helen strolls the beach, Walcott forges a litany of yesterday's, and St. Lucia dissolves into the fields of Troy:

> And yesterday these shallows were the Scamander,
> and armed shadows leapt from the horse, and
>      the bronze nuts
> were helmets, Agamemnon was the commander
> of weed-bearded captains; yesterday, the
>      black fleet
> anchored there in the swift's road. . . .

Implicit in the undertaking of this colossal poem are a number of presuppositions, among them a root belief in the sustaining continuities of history. The links between ancient Greece and the modern Caribbean are regarded as genuine and artistically negotiable. No matter that the Greeks were empire builders and the Antilleans are portrayed as the pawns of new empire-makers, the multinational corporations. Both peoples are seafarers, and Walcott makes much of the notion that to a marine community the daily nudge and drain of the tides overrides more recent life rhythms. His characters may watch American TV programs or dance to reggae music or hot-rod down the streets, but all such trappings of modern life vanish before the larger reality of the "ocean's voice." Similarly, Walcott confederates the two cultures on the basis of their pagan convictions; they are alike in inhabiting islands flush with ghosts and natural spirits. "Omeros" opens in a state of what might be called vegetal panic: jungle trees are quaking in fear as islanders hack their way toward them in search of trunks that might make seaworthy canoes. Finally, Walcott assumes that his dark-skinned islanders cultivate a spoken language of sufficient beauty, punch, and dexterity to render it suitable for the elevated dignities of an epic poem. Needless to say, there is in this assumption a touch of the antiquated. The broad consensus among English-language poets is that the eclogue is no longer viable. The conventions that deemed it plausible for the common man, in the guise of shepherd or fisherman, to declaim in elaborately patterned verse died some time ago, perhaps when the last of Frost's rugged New Englanders traded in his Vermont sheep farm for a rent-with-option-to-buy condo in Sarasota. Fortunately, news of the form's demise has not yet reached Walcott, who presents his fishermen, taxi-drivers, domestics, and barkeeps as natural poets. To be sure, he has fun with their linguistic uncertainties—their solecisms and malaprops and misspellings. But make no mistake: he is singing a song of praise to the mettle and resilience of a tongue that has wandered far from those shores where the King's English is spoken.

It becomes evident after only a couple of pages that Walcott in "Omeros" has set himself a pair of sizable tasks, one a matter of content and the other of technique. As regards the former, he must have recognized from the outset the grave risk that the parallels between Homer's Greeks and Walcott's Antilleans would, in the long haul, grow artificial and contrived. (It is a danger he has chosen to confront head on, going as far as to name the two fishermen who battle over Helen's affections Achille and Hector.) In terms of technique, Walcott has likewise deliberately courted our eventual fatigue, by deciding to work in three-line stanzas whose rhymes evoke Dante's terza rima. In English, as opposed to rhyme-rich Italian, the rhymed tercet has proved to be of scant utility over the centuries, its currency typically restricted to the short lyric. A potential reader is therefore entitled to hesitate before embarking on an epic poem set in the modern Caribbean which draws heavily for subject upon Homer and for music upon Dante. But these are reservations likely to fade straightaway in the presence of Walcott's sure-handed stanzas. The welcome truth is that in *Omeros,* his ninth full-length book of verse, Walcott has overcome a number of seeming insurmountables. Even those readers who, like me, have admired much in his previous work may well find *Omeros* an inspiring and enlivening surprise.

Although Homer lends his name to its title and many details to its plot, *Omeros* is hardly a mere retelling or updating of *The Iliad* or *The Odyssey.* *Omeros* moves on a wide diversity of tides and currents, and the bulk of the book is devoted to incidents and meditations that have an exiguous link, at best, to Homer's epics. Its narrative encompasses a nineteenth-century woman pioneer on the Great Plains; an eighteenth-century midshipman ancestor of Dennis Plunkett's; an aborted Antillean political campaign; a sunken treasure; a hallucinatory pilgrimage to Africa; a faith healer; and a con-

temporary poet—not so much a persona of the author as the author himself—who ponders modern urban life in Boston and Toronto. In dreams, in memory, sometimes in the flesh, Walcott's characters venture onto at least four continents and across at least four centuries.

Generally, what unites these far-flung souls and objects is the sea (or its agonizing absence, as when Major Plunkett relives the campaign against Rommel in the Sahara). In Greek mythology, it was of course a body of water—the navigable Styx—that conjoined the living and the dead, and Walcott has solid precedents for supposing that an epic poet should feel at liberty to travel by means of the mind's waterways from one end of creation to the other. Still, there are moments when, in aspiring to be all things to all people, *Omeros* winds up chugging like an overburdened motorboat. The Great Plains sections, in particular, seem not only narratively peripheral but thematically superfluous. They feel didactic, as though composed chiefly to highlight our nation's betrayal of the Indian. But do they—one must finally ask—add anything noteworthy? Hasn't the issue of the Old World's pillage of the New already been broached, unignorably, by Walcott's decision to center the poem on impoverished Antilleans? One recalls the lesson that, half a century ago, the Irish poet Patrick Kavanagh encapsulated in his sonnet "Epic," in which Homer's ghost materializes in order to point out that *The Iliad* was fabricated from nothing but a "local row." Even for the epic writer, Kavanagh reminds us, largeness needn't begin large; the trick is not in the scale of the tale but in the skill of the telling.

*Omeros* is most moving, significantly, when it stays close to home. The extended interludes in which the poet converses with the ghost of his father are indelibly drawn: spooky and graceful and loving and wrenchingly sad. Although the poet is, implicitly, an eminent man (he's the author, after all, of the brilliant feat of learning that is *Omeros*), and the father in his life-time was, explicitly, a gifted man whose career was hamstrung by poverty and race prejudice, the place of honor throughout the meeting belongs to the father. He is at once taskmaster, supporter, and counsellor. It is from him that we learn of those earlier Helens who slaved under hundredweights of anthracite, and he is the one who—playing upon the multiple meanings of "feet"—tautens the cords that bind the poet's burden to the poet's craft. He reveals to his son a method of fusing form and content:

Kneel to your load, then balance your stag-
      gering feet
and walk up that coal ladder as they do in time,
one bare foot after the next in ancestral rhyme.
Because Rhyme remains the parentheses of palms
shielding a candle's tongue, it is the language's
desire to enclose the loved world in its arms;
or heft a coal-basket; only by its stages
like those groaning women will you achieve
      that height
whose wooden planks in couplets lift your pages
higher than those hills of infernal anthracite.

And yet as rich a character as the poet's father becomes, Major Plunkett may be a still more considerable artistic achievement, in part because he begins so unpromisingly. When we first see him, in his "khaki shirt and capacious shorts," he is wiping the froth of a Guinness from his "pensioned moustache." He looks, in brief, like an all too easy stereotype and target—the English-colonial "hanger-on"—and the reader naturally worries that Walcott's rage will get the better of him. But quickly, as the lineaments of Plunkett's life come clear—his bewilderment over Britain's geopolitical decline, his flair for puns, his unfulfilled dream of a freewheeling trip around the world, his taciturn grief in the face of his wife's illness—he takes on subtler pigments and finer shadings. Indeed, the tragedy that eventually sinks him, as he careens into a stunned widowerhood, is the book's most fully realized bereavement. We feel for him. And that a man who appeared destined to provide the poem with its villain instead becomes a stirring, weighty figure testifies to the deep sympathies that inform *Omeros*. It's a bighearted book.

AS a prosodic form, the rhymed tercet is no workhorse; it's nearer to a carrier pigeon. It offers only four self-contained rhyme schemes (AAx, AxA, xAA, AAA), as opposed to the fourteen available to the quatrain. Little wonder, then, its relative unemployment among English-language poets; and no surprise that Walcott, having accepted the challenge of fitting so straitened a form to so vast a project, has resorted to a great deal of cross-stanzaic rhyming. He rhymes with broad flexibility, though he frequently, feintingly suggests that he plans to proceed otherwise. Time and again (by my estimate, there are more than a hundred such examples), he opens a new section as though he were going to adopt terza rima. The initial stanza's first and third lines will rhyme, as will its second line and the first line of the next stanza. But then—almost invariably after four lines—he snaps the pattern and begins rhyming catch-as-catch-can. (Why he has chosen this particular juncture as his breaking point,

and has stuck to it so faithfully, remains something of a conundrum—one of many formalistic puzzles woven into *Omeros*. I was similarly mystified by his decision, in an otherwise uneventful passage deep in the middle of the poem, to run twenty-four "L" rhymes in twenty-seven lines: vertical / skull / smell / swell / idle / sail / middle / supple / gunwale / skill, and so on. As you would expect, the music shifts from lilting to leaden—but you're never sure why Walcott has brought the change about.)

Minute scrutiny of this sort might seem finicky but for the matchless variety and inventiveness of Walcott's rhymes; the care he has manifestly lavished upon them solicits our closest attention. In any poem of this length you would expect to find a range of rhyme types, if only because the customary prototype—exact rhyme—can become constraining or monotonous over time. But Walcott extends himself far beyond all foreseen deviations. A teacher of versification might well employ *Omeros* as a rhyme casebook. Here, in addition to exact masculine and feminine rhymes, one encounters triple rhymes (gentility / humility) and visual rhymes (plough / enough) and pararhymes or rim rhymes (often coming in strings: nose / canoes / noise) and anagrammatic rhymes (organ / groan) and apocopated rhymes (river / deliverer) and macaronic rhymes (come / *homme,* glory / *mori*) and light rhymes (sea / money) and rime riche (piss / precipice, Raj / mirage) and hosts of intricate couplings—each bearing its own distinctive acoustical qualities—for which, so far as I know, no terms have been coined except that grabbag designation "off rhyme." (How would one classify, for example, the not quite rime-riche pairings of pier / happier or captains / capstans? Or a blend of visual rhyme and rime riche, like fishpot / depot? Or a hybrid of light rhyme and rim rhyme like egret / great? Or the sort of rhyme—a favorite of Walcott's—in which one word, orthographically speaking, envelopes another, as in brows / burrows or rows / arrows or acre / massacre?)

Perhaps the most striking feature in his rhyming is his ready use of outlandish pairings of a sort usually reserved for light verse. When he rhymes "panther" with "and her" or "altar" with "halt. Her" or "Florida" with "worried her" or "hunter" with "front of her," we are closer to W. S. Gilbert or Ogden Nash than to Milton or Spenser. We are perched right at the teetering edge of parody—which is where he wants us. *Omeros* is no sendup of epic traditions—it is no *Rape of the Lock*

—but Walcott is keenly attuned to the humble, farcical aspects of his island world, as when his hero Achille, with a touching combination of faith and ignorance, christens his boat In God We Troust.

*Omeros* is a poem of elusive metres. Robert Frost once observed that there are ''virtually but two'' metres in English—strict iambic and loose iambic. *Omeros* initially looks like an example of the latter, with interspersings of a tighter iambic line. But elsewhere the lines are loosened to a point where the iambic beat disappears, with the result that any systematic attempt to read the poem metrically —with that easy sense of place, that fluid but constant awareness of where you stand within the line, which is the hallmark of solidly metred poetry— must end in frustration. There are simply too many uncertain feet, extra stresses, ambiguous emphases, and so forth, for comfortable processing. Perhaps Walcott would have us take another approach? So many of the lines contain twelve syllables that one is tempted to conclude that he has forgone conventional metrics in favor of purely syllabic verse. However, the uncertainties that attend syllabic count in English, and the reader's difficulties in comprehending such a long syllabic line, make this interpretation problematic. The cadences are powerfully rhythmic, to be sure, and one may decide that Walcott has ''captured the music of the sea,'' or something of the sort, and let the matter drop there—but the lack of an orthodox metre is in fact a crucial, individuating trait. Rhyme— which could not help playing a signal role in *Omeros,* given Walcott's ingenuity with it—becomes preëminent in the absence of a clearly felt metre. Rhyme-based rather than metre-based, *Omeros* is a nonesuch among long poems.

One might go as far as to call it rhyme-driven. Over and over, rhymes are what hold the tumbling, pell-mell stanzas together, and since so many of the rhymes are unorthodox and recherche the poem's structure is forever on the verge of being lost. Even more than most verse, *Omeros* demands to be read aloud. When the prosodic underpinnings of a poem consist of rhymes like, say, ''coffee'' and—some twenty syllables later—''of the,'' you probably can't depend on your eye alone to catch the buried order that balances the hurly-burly; for this, you probably need actual, spoken echoes lingering in the air. (Here and there, one might describe the poem as rhyme-driven in another sense, for Walcott occasionally allows his appetite for choice rhymes to bend his phrasings or sentence structures. But

even in such instances the sheer oddity of his music often diverts the reader from any impression of strained or forced rhyming.) Although one can conceive of a somewhat altered *Omeros* whose faint ghost of an iambic-pentameter line has been expunged and whose metre is purely free, an *Omeros* without rhyme is unthinkable. It would be a different beast altogether.

Writers on English-language prosody generally contend that metre is a fundamental and rhyme a secondary or ornamental tool. But this view, while sound in the main, may distort those unusual poetic imaginations—in our century one thinks immediately of Charlotte Mew and Louis MacNeice and, especially, John Crowe Ransom— for whom metre is often expendable but rhyme remains essential. (Like *Omeros,* Ransom's œuvre is imaginable without metre but Ransom wouldn't be Ransom without rhyme.) Such poets usually are demons for brevity. It has been left to Walcott to demonstrate a means by which rhyme —the ''invention of a barbarous age,'' according to Milton—might support a Miltonic macrocosm.

Douglas Wakiihuri, the winner of [1990's] New York City Marathon, remarked after the race that real fatigue hadn't set in until Mile 20, some three-quarters of the way. Among marathoners, Mile 20 traditionally represents the point of greatest pain and trial and despair, and it is tempting to postulate that among the epic poets—the marathoners of the versifying world—a similar testing ground arrives at about the three-quarters mark. In any case, I had reached approximately that point in my reading of this more-than-three-hundred-page poem when either my own or the poet's energies flagged a little. Somewhere toward the close of *Omeros* the reader sees that its various branches are never going to wind up belonging to a single trunk; and with the knowledge that the poem will remain a thing of disparate parts comes the realization that one can in fairness formulate piecemeal judgments— can conclude, perhaps, that the passages dealing with Plunkett's ancestor could use some trimming, or that Hector's character needs to be clarified. Late in the poem, too, one may weary somewhat of Walcott's penchant for the sweepingly abstract— for big, summational declarations about the nature of time or history or love. Every poetic virtue contains its hazards, obviously, and Walcott's characteristic eagerness to don a sage's getup and utter vatic grandiosities carries the risk that he may at times stumble on his robes, or his beard may slip a bit.

But they're apt to be momentary lapses, these stumblings or slippages, since Walcott wields all kinds of strengths that can bolster a sagging passage in a twinkling. He has a sure, prepossessing vocabulary, a deft and ludic wit (''she was an adamant Eve''), an intricately calibrated ear. He's a man of wonderful analogical talents, especially when he fixes his eye on the natural world. He gives the reader roosters that really crow (''their cries screeching like red chalk / drawing hills on a board''), jellyfish that truly float (''tasselled palanquins of Portuguese man-o'-wars / bobbed like Asian potentates''), swifts that genuinely fly (''this frail dancer / leaping the breakers, this dart of the meridian''). And he's better than wonderful—he's little short of miraculous— when he stirs up some weather. The hurricane he brews in an early chapter is so splendidly overmastering that a reader is left feeling dazed, windblown, waterlogged. If to read *Omeros* is to sign on for a substantial voyage during which small doubts are constantly raised and quelled, raised and quelled—well, what long poem of our time can be read without misgivings or objections? Who doesn't find elements to quarrel with or quibble about in John Berryman's ''The Dream Songs'' or James Merrill's ''The Changing Light at Sandover''? And who, even so, is any the less grateful to their makers?

So bright and immediate are many of Walcott's local virtues that one can lose sight of the lowering darkness of *Omeros*. Not until I'd set the book down, the journey completed, did it become clear what an unbroken line of woes it enfolds. Maud Plunkett is not the only one whose life ends sadly: Hector dies in an accident; the midshipman falls in combat while still a boy. And, year by year, political corruption cankers the island's soul, pollution threatens its beauty. There is a loud call of anguish at the center of *Omeros*, but the book is something more— something better—than a simple cry from the heart. It's a complex cry from the heart, for Walcott has succeeded in filtering all sorts of titanic sorrows through a limpid and ferocious intellect.

**Source:** Brad Leithauser, ''Ancestral Rhyme,'' *The New Yorker,* 11 February, 1991, pp. 91–5.

## Sources for Further Study

Bakken, Christopher. Review in *The Georgia Review,* Vol. 45, No. 2, Summer 1991, pp. 403-06.

Notes that although Walcott tends to tell rather than show, his epic of the people who are usually excluded from the narrative of history ''demands a revision of our world view.''

Benfey, Christopher. ''Coming Home,'' *The New Republic,* Vol. 203, October, 1990, pp. 36-9.
    Concludes that *Omeros* shows great ambition but lacks the ''surefootedness and verve'' of Walcott's best poetry.

Bensen, Robert. ''Catherine Weldon in *Omeros* and 'The Ghost Dance','' *Verse,* Vol. 22, No. 2, Summer 1994, pp. 119-25.
    Offers a thorough analysis of the role of Weldon in Walcott's *Omeros.*

Brown, Robert, and Cheryl Johnson. ''An Interview with Derek Walcott,'' *The Cream City Review,* Vol. 14, No. 2, Winter, 1990, pp. 209-23.
    Walcott expresses thoughts on the composition of *Omeros.* He sees similarities in between ancient Greeks and modern West Indians.

Bruckner, D. J. R. ''A Poem in Homage to an Unwanted Man,'' *New York Times,* October 9, 1990, pp. 13, 17.
    In an interview with Bruckner, Walcott discusses influences on *Omeros,* and his reservations about calling the poem an epic.

Burnett, Paula. ''The Ulyssean Crusoe and the Quest for Redemption in J. M. Coetzee's *Foe* and Derek Walcott's *Omeros,''* in *Robinson Crusoe: Myth and Metamorphoses,* edited by Lieve Spaas and Brian Stimpson, St. Martin's Press, 1996, pp. 239-55.
    Compares and contracts the two works cited, singling out for analysis Helen's unifying role in *Omeros* and Walcott's portrayal of women generally as figures of healing and redemption.

Hamner, Robert D. *Derek Walcott.* Rev. ed. Twayne, 1993.
    Examines Walcott's career through his receipt of the Nobel Prize in 1992.

Ismond, Patricia. ''Walcott's *Omeros:* A Complex, Ambitious Work,'' *Caribbean Contact,* Vol. 18, No. 5, March-April, 1991, pp. 10-11.
    Overview and analysis of the work and its influences.

Lernout, Geert. ''Derek Walcott's *Omeros:* The Isle Full of Voices,'' *Kunapipi,* Vol. 14, 1992, pp. 90-104.
    Interprets *Omeros* as a ''counter-narrative'' critical rather than imitative of Western traditions.

Lucas, John. ''The Sea, The Sea,'' *New Statesman and Society,* Vol. 3, October 5, 1990, p. 36.
    Commends the linguistic richness of *Omeros.*

Mason, David. Review of *Omeros* in *The Hudson Review,* Vol. 44, No. 3, Autumn 1991, pp. 513-15.
    Contents that Walcott's introduction of material extraneous to the central Caribbean setting weakens the narrative.

McClure, Charlotte S. ''Helen of the 'West Indies': History or Poetry of a Caribbean Realm,'' *Studies in the Literary Imagination,* Vol. 26, No. 2, Fall, 1993, pp. 7- 20.

Considers the character of Helen a fresh conception of her Greek counterpart because of the Carribean background against which Walcott portrays her.

O'Brien, Sean. "In Terms of the Ocean." *Times Literary Supplement,* Vol. 4563, September 14-22, 1990, pp. 977-78.
Review contending that the narrative fails to hold reader interest in the North American and European sections.

Ramazani, Jahan. "The Wound of History: Walcott's *Omeros* and the Postcolonial Poetics of Affliction." *PMLA* 112, No. 3, May, 1997, pp. 405-18.
Discusses *Omeros* as a repudiation of postcolonial writing as a "literature of victimization" through examination of wound and affliction imagery in the work.

Terada, Rei. "*Omeros,*" in her *Derek Walcott's Poetry: American Mimicry,* Northeastern University Press, 1992, pp. 183-227.
Examines Walcott's utilization of the Homeric literary model.

White, J. P. "An Interview with Derek Walcott." *Green Mountains Review,* New Series, Vol. 4, No. 1, Spring-Summer, 1990, pp. 14-37.
In this wide-ranging interview, Walcott discusses the difficulties of progressing from a slave mentality to authentic freedom. After commenting on the epic aspects of *Moby Dick, Ulysses,* and Walt Whitman's poetry, he states his desire to capture, in *Omeros,* "the names of things and people in their own context."

# Paradise Lost

## John Milton
## 1667

*Paradise Lost,* one of the greatest poems in the English language, was first published in 1667. Milton had long cherished the ambition to write the definitive English epic, to do for the English language what Homer and Virgil had done for Greek and Latin, and what Dante had done for Italian. He had originally planned to base his epic on the Arthurian legends, which were the foundational myths for English nationalism, but later turned his attention to more universal questions. He decided to focus on the foundational myth of humanity itself, the Genesis account of creation and fall. It was an ambitious project, for Milton was determined to attempt ''things unattempted yet in Prose or Rhyme,'' and his success is indicated by the esteem in which the poem is held to this day.

Milton's epic poem received mixed reactions in the seventeenth century, and, over the years, has continued to arouse both praise and blame. Yet, its admirers have always been more numerous that its detractors. The poem has influenced many authors and artists, from John Dryden to William Blake, Mary Shelley to Philip K. Dick, C. S. Lewis to Gene Roddenberry. Aside from the sheer beauty of its language and the power of its characterization, the subject matter of the poem has continued to absorb readers of every generation. Milton does not hesitate to ask the most difficult of questions: If the world was created by a good, just, and loving God, why is there little evidence of goodness and justice in the world? What does it mean for humankind to

be created in the image of that God, and how does humanity endure in a fallen world? It is this aspect of the poem which will continue to enthral readers, as they continue to ask the same difficult questions and turn for answers to Milton's exploration of one of the foundational myths of Western culture.

## Author Biography

John Milton was born in London on December 9, 1608, the son of a prosperous Puritan family. His father, a musician, encouraged him to pursue an excellent education, hiring private tutors and enroling him in St. Paul's school (c. 1620).

The first stage of Milton's literary career began in 1625, when he entered Christ's College, Cambridge, where he studied until 1632. He seems not to have been very popular with his fellow students or his professors, and on one occasion he was "sent down" for a fight with a tutor, but was allowed to return. Milton seems to have spent the years between 1632 (when he completed his Master's degree) and 1637 in private study at his father's country home near Windsor. Following this, he travelled in France and Italy (1638-1639), and many of the descriptions in *Paradise Lost* (such as the description of Hell) reflect things which he saw on these travels. Poems from this period include "Prolusions," "On the Morning of Christ's Nativity" (1629), "Comus" (1634), and "Lycidas" (1639), a poem based on the death of a fellow student, Edward King.

The second stage of Milton's career began in 1640, when he returned to England to teach his nephews. This stage of Milton's life was marked by controversy and civil unrest in England. In 1642 civil war broke out between the Puritan Roundheads and the Royalist supporters of Charles I. Milton was involved in many of the religious and political controversies of his day, and many of his prose works (both in English and Latin) date from the years between 1641 and 1660. His devotion to the principles of Oliver Cromwell's Commonwealth (as well as many of the themes and motifs which would later dominate *Paradise Lost*) are evident in the many pamphlets he penned during this period.

In 1642 Milton married Mary Powell, but the marriage was a failure and she seems to have left him within months of the wedding, not to return until 1645. His two daughters, Anne and Mary, were born after their reconciliation.

In 1649 Charles I was executed and Cromwell's Commonwealth seemed secure. In March of that year, Milton was appointed Secretary in Foreign Tongues to the Council of State (a kind of foreign-affairs minister). Charles I's death was highly controversial both in England and Europe, and in October Milton published *Eikonoklastes,* in which he defended Cromwell's actions. In 1651, responding to further European criticism of Cromwell's regime, he published his first *Defensio pro populo Anglicano (The Defence of the People of England)* . The year 1651 also saw the birth of his only son, John.

The following year was one of tragedy for Milton. Within days of the birth of his third daughter, Deborah, his wife died, and a month later his son John also died. To compound the tragedy, his eyesight, weak since 1644, failed completely and he became totally blind. One can only imagine how devastating this must have been for a poet whose work is as dominated by vivid visual imagery as is Milton's.

In 1656, Milton married his second wife, Katherine Woodcock, who died less than two years later. Over the next few years, Milton published a number of tracts which reflect his deep concern for church government and the abuses therein.

Following the Restoration in 1660, Milton was placed for a time under house arrest, but was released within six months. This begins the third and final stage of Milton's literary career. Retired from public life, in 1663 he married his third wife, Elizabeth Minshul, and in 1667, he published the first edition of *Paradise Lost* in ten books. Although much of the material subsequent to the fall is missing from this edition, the concern to "justify the ways of God to man" is evident, as is Milton's conviction that, despite the fall of the Commonwealth and the Restoration of the monarchy, political justice can be achieved in this world. Between 1670 and 1673 he published several of his greatest works, including *Paradise Regained* and *Samson Agonistes.* Only months before his death, he published *Paradise Lost, A Poem in Twelve Books,* the complete edition of his epic. He died on November 8, 1674, and was buried in St. Giles, Cripplegate, London.

## Plot Summary

### Book I

Book I introduces the main subject matter of the poem: the creation, fall, and redemption of the world and humankind. Milton invokes the aid of the muse and the Holy Spirit as he sets out to perform ''Things unattempted yet in Prose or Rhyme,'' and, through the medium of the epic, to ''justify the ways of God to men.'' In true epic style, Milton begins his story in mid-action (*in medias res*), after the great battle in Heaven and the fall of the rebel angels. The poem thus introduces its readers first to Satan, the cause of the fall of humankind, at the moment following his own first fall into Hell. Satan and his angels are described lying on a lake of fire in a place where flames cast no light, but only ''darkness visible.'' Satan is the first to rise and, using his great spear as a walking stick, limps to the shore. He then awakens his legions, addressing them in a stirring speech and rousing them to action. He informs them of his hope of regaining Heaven and of the rumor of a new world to be created which they might yet make their own, if heaven be closed to them. He determines to call a full council and sets his host to work to build a suitable palace from which to rule Hell. The result of their efforts is Pandemonium, the palace of Satan, and there the angels of Hell enter to begin their council.

### Book II

Book II recounts the council of the demons and their deliberations concerning whether to attempt further battle in order to regain Heaven. Satan invites his minions to speak freely, and Moloch opens the debate, urging open war. Belial, who represents sloth, responds, arguing that battle against a foe who has so decisively defeated them is futile, and proposing that the demons take their ease in Hell and make the best of it. Mammon follows, counselling that they build a new kingdom in Hell and there rule supreme. Beelzebub, Satan's right-hand man, concludes, returning to the suggestion made by Satan in Book I, that they seek out the truth of a rumor about a new world and another creature to be created by God. If the rumor is true, he submits, they should then attempt to seduce God's new creature, Man, and rule on earth if they cannot regain Heaven. The demons applaud this suggestion and Satan undertakes the dangerous task of searching out this new world. While the rest of the devils (in true epic style) play epic games to vent their grief and occupy themselves in the absence of their

*John Milton.*

leader, Satan sets out alone. He travels to the gates of Hell, which he finds closed and guarded by Sin (his daughter) and Death (the son of their incestuous union). Satan persuades them to open the gates by offering the world to Sin to rule with him, and humankind to Death. He then makes the arduous journey through Chaos to the new world which he seeks.

### Book III

Book III moves the action to Heaven, where God, sitting on his throne, sees Satan flying towards the world. God tells his Son of Satan's diabolical plan to seduce humankind, foretelling Satan's success and simultaneously clearing himself of blame. He contends that humankind was created free and able to withstand temptation, yet outlines his purpose of allowing humankind grace, since they will fall, not out of malice, as Satan did, but deceived. This grace, however, cannot be achieved unless divine justice is satisfied, and the Son freely offers himself as a ransom for this purpose. God then ordains the Incarnation, and all the hosts of heavenly angels praise and adore the Son. Meanwhile, Satan has reached the world's outermost sphere, where he finds a place called the Limbo of Vanity. He moves up to the Gate of Heaven and passes from there to the Orb of the Sun, where he encounters

Uriel, the regent of that orb. He changes himself into the shape of a lesser angel and approaches Uriel, professing a great desire to behold the new creation and the human creature placed therein. Uriel, deceived by his disguise, directs him to the newly created world.

## Book IV

Book IV returns to the quest of Satan who, as he approaches the Paradise of Eden, is beset by doubt, fear, envy, and despair. His confidence soon returns however, and, confirmed in his evil purpose, he journeys on to Paradise. The reader's first view of Paradise is thus seen through Satan's eyes. The Garden and Satan's first sight of its inhabitants are described as he sits in the shape of a cormorant on the Tree of Life (the highest tree in the Garden) and looks around him. Overhearing a conversation between Adam and Eve, Satan learns that they are forbidden to eat fruit from the Tree of Knowledge, on pain of death. This provides Satan with a plan for their destruction. Meanwhile Uriel, observing Satan's earlier struggle with himself, has seen through his disguise. He warns Gabriel, the guardian of the Gate of Paradise, that trouble is afoot, and Gabriel promises to find Satan by morning. Evening descends, and Adam and Eve retire to their rest after performing their evening worship. Gabriel appoints two angels to watch over Adam and Eve's bower, where they discover Satan (in the form of a toad) whispering into Eve's ear and tempting her in a dream. They bring him to Gabriel, who questions him. Satan answers scornfully and seems ready to resist, but at a sign from Heaven he decides to flee instead.

## Book V

Morning arrives and Eve tells Adam of her troubling dream. Disturbed, he comforts her, and they proceed to their morning worship. In order to deprive them of any excuse for transgression, God sends Raphael to remind Adam of his freedom and the necessity for obedience, and to warn him of Satan's plan. As Adam and Raphael enjoy a meal of choice fruits prepared by Eve, Raphael tells Adam of Satan's rebellion and how he incited all the angel Legions of the North to join him, with the sole exception of Abdiel, a seraph who had tried to dissuade him and, failing, had forsaken him.

## Book VI

In Book VI Raphael continues the story of Satan's revolt in Heaven, which was prompted by his envy of the Son. Raphael relates how Michael and Gabriel fought against Satan for two days. On the first day, Satan is routed, but under the cover of night convenes a council and invents some ''devilish Engines,'' including gunpowder, which his armies introduce on the second day. These cause considerable disorder amongst Michael and his angels, but they manage to overwhelm the forces of Satan by pulling up mountains. The battle is not yet won, however, and on the third day God sends his Son (the Messiah) into the fray. The Son drives into the midst of the enemy force with his chariot and thunder, pursuing them to the wall of Heaven, through which they leap down with horror and confusion into the Deep (a place which has been prepared for their punishment). The Messiah then returns in triumph to his Father.

## Book VII

At Adam's request, Raphael continues his tale with the story of the creation of the world. He explains that, after the expulsion of Satan and his angels from Heaven, God wishes to repopulate Heaven. Rather than create more angels, God decides to create another world and other creatures to dwell in it. He therefore sends his Son with attendant angels to perform the work of Creation, which the Son accomplishes in six days. The angels celebrate creation with hymns, and return with the Son to Heaven.

## Book VIII

Raphael's tale being ended, Adam seeks to satisfy his thirst for knowledge and inquires about the movements of the heavenly bodies. Raphael, while conceding that Heaven is a veritable book in which Adam can read the wondrous works of God, admonishes Adam concerning the limitations of knowledge and advises him to seek out knowledge which is more worthwhile. Adam agrees, and, in his turn, tells Raphael all that he can remember since his own creation: his being placed in Paradise, his talk with God, his first meeting and marriage with Eve. After a discussion of Adam's relationship with Eve, Raphael departs with a final warning.

## Book IX

Satan returns to Eden by night as a mist, and enters into the sleeping serpent. In the morning Adam and Eve go out to their labor in the garden. Eve suggests that they would work more efficiently apart, but Adam expresses concern that the enemy of which they have been warned might harm her if he found her alone. Eve does not wish to be thought weak, and insists on working apart, and Adam gives in to her. Satan, in the form of the serpent, finding her alone, is momentarily struck dumb by her beauty. He proceeds to flatter her, praising her beauty and charm. Eve wonders at his ability to speak, and he explains that he attained both speech and reason by eating the fruit of a certain tree. Eve asks to be shown the tree, but when she finds that it is the Tree of Knowledge she asserts that eating of its fruit is forbidden. The serpent, after many arguments, persuades her to eat. Pleased with the taste, she debates whether or not to take the fruit to Adam, but eventually decides to do so and repeats the arguments by which she was persuaded to eat. Adam is not deceived, but seeing that she is lost, resolves to perish with her because he loves her too much to live without her. He eats the fruit, and the consequences are dire. Their first response is lust, followed by shame. After covering themselves, they begin to argue and to blame each other.

## Book X

The angels who are guarding Paradise return to Heaven, to be absolved by God of any responsibility for the fall of Adam and Eve, which they could not have prevented. God then sends the Son to judge Adam and Eve. Sin and Death, who have been waiting by the gates of Hell, are aware of Satan's success and decide to follow Satan up to the world. In order to make the journey easier, they pave a bridge over Chaos, from Hell to the world. Satan, meanwhile, returns to Hell and boasts of his success to the assembly of his angels in Pandemonium. Instead of applause, however, his tale is received with a "universal hiss," as he and his angels are transformed into serpents, according to the judgement pronounced upon him in Paradise by the Son. Deluded by a mirage of the forbidden tree, they devour the fruit, only to find themselves chewing on dust and ashes. Sin and Death having arrived in the world, God foretells their final defeat at the hands of the Son, but in the meantime commands certain alterations to take place in the heavens. Adam and Eve lament their fallen condition and Eve tries to comfort Adam. He at first refuses her consolation, but eventually he is appeased and they reconcile. She suggests several violent ways of evading the Curse pronounced upon them and their offspring, but he resists and counsels hope, reminding her of the promise that revenge against the serpent would

be given through her offspring. They seek peace with God through repentance and supplication.

## Book XI

Hearing the prayers of Adam and Eve, the Son intercedes with God on their behalf. God accepts their prayers, but decrees that they can no longer live in Paradise and sends Michael with a band of cherubim to cast them out. Adam sees Michael coming and goes out to greet him. Upon hearing that they must leave, Eve laments and Adam pleads, but eventually they submit. Before removing them from Eden, however, Michael takes Adam up to a high hill and reveals to him in a vision all that will happen until the Flood of Noah's age.

## Book XII

Michael continues his story of things to come, moving from the Flood to Abraham and then to Christ. He explains that Christ will be the Seed of the Woman who was promised to Adam and Eve at their fall, and that his Incarnation, Death, Resurrection, and Ascension will inaugurate the salvation of humankind. Michael then describes the Age of the Church until the Second Coming of Christ. Adam is comforted by these revelations and returns to Eve, who has been sleeping. She wakes from gentle dreams, refreshed and composed. Michael takes them by the hand and leads them out of Paradise, setting a fiery sword and cherubim to guard the gates. Adam and Eve pause for a moment, looking back and shedding some "natural tears" at the loss of Paradise. The reader's last view of Adam and Eve is, however, a hopeful one as they dry their tears and walk away, hand in hand, the whole world before them and Providence as their guide.

# Characters

## Abdiel

Abdiel is a seraph who, though originally one of Lucifer's legions in Heaven, remains faithful to God. He attempts to persuade Satan and his rebel angels to abandon their revolt and, failing, abandons them. He symbolizes true fidelity.

## Adam

Adam is the first created human being and the true "hero" of *Paradise Lost*. The reader's first

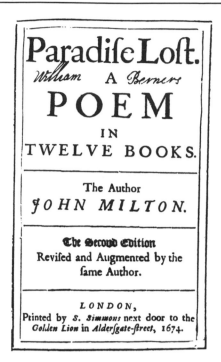

*Title page of the second edition of "Paradise Lost."*

view of Adam is, significantly, seen through the eyes of Satan as he perches like a cormorant on the Tree of Life (ironically planning Adam's death). The distinction between Adam and Eve, the only humans in the garden, and the other living creatures, the animals, heightens our perception of their uniqueness as beings created in the image of God. They are "of far nobler shape erect and tall, / Godlike erect, with native Honor clad" and "In naked Majesty seem'd Lords of all" (IV.287-290). The image of God in humankind is associated with wisdom, truth, holiness, freedom, and authority. These things characterize *both* Adam and Eve in their unfallen state.

The reader is not left to assume, however, that Adam and Eve are equal. In fact, Milton hastens to assure us that they are "Not equal, as their sex not equal seem'd" (IV.296). Adam is formed for contemplation and valour; Eve for softness and grace. It is Adam who is truly the image of God; Eve is the image of Adam, from whose side she is created. They are created, "He for God only, she for God in him" (IV.299), and it is this distinction which is both their strength and their downfall. Adam is characterized by reason and free will, created for absolute rule and authority; he must not only obey God, but must inspire obedience in Eve. If Eve's fall

results from a failure to obey God's commandment, it is equally a failure to heed Adam. Adam's fault lies in the failure to use his superior reason to convince Eve to stay by his side and in his failure to exercise his inborn authority, to enforce obedience when she will not offer it freely.

If Adam's fall is in large part due to a failure in reason and authority, however, it is also due to an excess of another characteristic to which the reader is introduced early: love. Adam and Eve are presented as a couple, a "happy pair" living in perfect conjugal bliss. Their mutual love and respect are obvious, and fan Satan's already-active jealousy. Once again, their strength becomes their downfall. Adam, being superior in reason and wisdom, is not deceived by the serpent, as Eve is. However, he eats of the fruit because he loves Eve, and would rather die with her than live without her. While commendable in itself, his action indicates a further failure of authority: Eve falls because Adam has failed to rule *her;* Adam falls because he fails to rule *himself.*

## The Arch-Enemy
*See* Satan

## Beelzebub

Beelzebub is the chief of the devils, Satan's "second-in-command." He is the first devil to awaken from his stupor on the fiery lake and is thus the audience for Satan's opening speech (I.84-124). Beelzebub, like Satan/Lucifer, is associated with light—or rather, lost light, for Satan's address to Beelzebub is the first indication of how far indeed they have fallen, and how much they have changed. It is thus appropriate that Beelzebub, the first to join in Satan's plans for rebellion in Heaven, is the first to respond to his exhortations in Hell. Beelzebub's name, in Hebrew, means "lord of the flies," and he is an appropriate commander of the demons who, like flies, swarm into Pandemonium for the council.

At the council of devils (Book II), Beelzebub, like Satan, is content to wait until the others have had their say. (See also Moloch, Belial, and Mammon.) As the final (and strongest) speaker, when he does speak, his grave manner, majestic face, and stately words present an effective contrast to Moloch's reckless despair, Belial's hollow and slothful vice, and Mammon's greed. A true statesman and loyal second-in-command, he presents not his own strategy, but Satan's, promoting the subtle plan

# Media Adaptations

- *Paradise Lost* has never been adapted as a film or play. However, it is discussed in the video *Milton and 17th-Century Poetry* (Films for the Humanities and Sciences, Princeton N.J.).

- The story of the garden of Eden is included in the film *The Bible—In the Beginning* (1966), directed by John Huston and produced by Dino DeLaurentis, starring Ulla Bergryd as Eve and Michael Parks as Adam.

- The devil's work is presented in four periods, one of which is the temptation of Adam and Eve in Eden, in Luigi Maggi's film *Satan—or the Drama of Humanity* (1912).

- There is a reference to *Paradise Lost* in the 1967 *Star Trek* episode "Space Seed." Ricardo Montalban portrays Kahn (who resurfaces in the movie *Star Trek II: The Wrath of Kahn*), a eugenically enhanced human who flees earth after leading an unsuccessful revolt of "supermen" like himself. Having taken him aboard the *Enterprise,* Kirk offers Kahn and his "rebel angels" the choice of exile on an untamed and uninhabited planet or returning to earth to face trial. Kahn chooses exile, referring to Satan's statement that it is "Better to reign in hell, than serve in heav'n." This is consistent with the theme explored in other *Star Trek* episodes, such as "The Apple," "Return of the Archons," and "This Side of Paradise"—that if there is a paradise, unredeemed humanity does not belong there.

- *Paradise Lost* is an important source for Mary Shelley's novel *Frankenstein*, which explores the themes of forbidden knowledge and the proper relationship between creator and creature. *Frankenstein* has been adapted as a film several times. A recent adaptation, by Francis Ford Coppola (Tri Star Pictures, 1994), stars Robert DeNiro and Kenneth Branagh and is available on video.

- *Frankenstein* and its presentation of *Paradise Lost* is also a source for Philip K. Dick's novel *Do Androids Dream of Electric Sheep?* (1968), which was adapted into a popular movie in Ridley Scott's *Blade Runner* (The Ladd Company, 1982), starring Harrison Ford, Rutger Hauer, and Sean Young. It is also available on video.

---

of taking revenge against God by seducing or destroying humankind.

### Belial

Belial is the fallen angel who speaks second at the council of devils in Book II. In keeping with his faint-hearted counsel of "ignoble ease and peaceful sloth" (II.226), he is the last to rise from the burning lake. Because Belial is not the name of a pagan god, but an abstract noun meaning "wickedness," he represents vice in general and is associated with atheism. In Book II, he is described as outwardly dignified, but false and hollow, speaking persuasive words which disguise his inner weakness and vice. He argues that it is useless to pursue a war they cannot win, and admonishes that Hell is not the worst fate that could befall them. In essence, his is a counsel of craven fear: he wishes to avoid war in order to avoid worse punishment, and clings to the hope that if they do not give God further cause for alarm, in time God's anger may abate and the fires of hell will lessen.

### Death

Death, Satan's son, is literally conceived in Sin, as he is born of Satan's incestuous union with his daughter, Sin. True to his parentage, Death becomes the father of all sins, as he rapes his mother, Sin, almost at the moment of his birth. Guilty of rape and incest, he would also be guilty of matricide, but for the fact that Sin's demise would also be his own. As it is, he and Sin continue in an uneasy co-existence, characterized by hatred and pain. Death is described as a crowned but shapeless terror, before whom even Hell trembles, and who dares to threaten even Satan with his fatal dart.

### Eve

Eve, the mother of humankind, is presented as an ambiguous character. On the one hand, she is, like Adam, created in the image of God, noble, virtuous, and above all, beautiful. On the other hand, she is the first to fall because from the beginning it is obvious that she is not equal to Adam. Outwardly, she is less obviously the image of God; even her beauty is "dishevelled" and "wanton," indicating the natural wildness which she will be unable to tame. In character, too, she is inferior, weaker in reason and authority, uninterested in Adam and Raphael's intellectual conversation. Eve is characterised by the sensual, by wilfulness, and by appetite.

Being weaker in reason, Eve is easier prey for Satan. Satan uses Eve's innate characteristics, playing upon her desire while appealing to her pride, which has been wounded by Adam's suggestion that alone she will be unable to resist their adversary. Determined not to seem weaker, Eve leaves herself open to Satan, who preys upon her weaknesses. He flatters her, suggesting that *she* is the true ruler; not only "Queen" of all, but a "goddess among gods." He arouses her curiosity (not a desire for knowledge, which she does not have) by extolling the virtues of the fruit which has given him the power of speech, and finally convinces her by the use of persuasive arguments which *sound* reasonable to her inferior reason. Deceived, she eats and falls.

In many ways, though she is presented in a condescending manner before the fall, Eve's true strength is seen only after the fall. Unlike Adam, she sins because she is deceived, and once she faces the truth of her folly she is able to move on. Adam, fully aware of both the nature and the consequences of his action, sins for love, and repudiates that love immediately. Their conjugal bliss deteriorates first into lustful sexuality, and then into vicious recrimination. If Eve initiates the fall, however, she also initiates redemption. The first to sin, she is also the first to attempt reconciliation, going to Adam with soft words in an effort to mend their quarrel. While her first suggestion (self-destruction) is neither rational nor practical, she does rouse Adam out of his bitterness, and inspires him to formulate the more appropriate plan of prayer and repentance, and to take that crucial first step towards reconciliation with God through reconciliation with Eve.

Fittingly, the final speech in the poem is spoken by Eve, and is a message of consolation and hope. As the temptation which led to her fall was begun in an evil dream whispered in her ear by Satan, the hope for the redemption of humankind comes to her in a dream. Knowing that she will bear the Promised Seed who will restore humankind, she is willing to leave Eden and take her place in the world at Adam's side. The love which prompted Adam to prefer death with Eve to life without her now becomes the source of Eve's strength, as Adam becomes her paradise on earth: "In me is no delay; with thee to go, / Is to stay here; without thee here to stay / Is to go hence unwilling; thou to me / Art all things under Heav'n, all places thou. . ." (XII.615-168).

### Gabriel

Gabriel is the angel who is second in rank only to Michael, and who, with Michael, leads the faithful angels in their first two days of battle against Satan and his rebels. After the creation of the world, Gabriel is given the task of guarding the gate of Paradise. It is Gabriel whom Uriel warns of the danger which threatens Adam and Eve, Gabriel who sets two angels to watch over Adam and Eve as they sleep, and Gabriel to whom those angels bring Satan when they discover him at Eve's ear, tempting her in a dream.

### God

God is the Creator and Ruler of all, including Heaven, Hell, the angels (fallen and unfallen), earth, and humankind. He is all-knowing and all-powerful, and nothing occurs without his foreknowledge and consent. Although he is the causal force behind the poem and the events described in it, he takes remarkably little action in the poem, relegating most action either to the Son or to his angels. His primary function is to create, and to explain his purposes to the Son, who then acts on them. Opposite to Satan in every way, he is good, true, and, above all, just. However, neither God nor His Son are as compelling as the character of Satan as presented by Milton, appearing bland by comparison.

### The Infernal Serpent
*See* Satan

## Lucifer

*See* Satan

## Mammon

Mammon is the third devil to speak at the council in Book II. In Book I, Mammon is described as the least of the fallen angels. Like Belial, he is not a god, but the personification of an abstract concept, covetous wealth or greed. His mind is always on gold and riches: it is he who leads the ransacking of Hell for material to gild Pandemonium, and it is he who inspires men to "rifle the bowels of their mother earth / For treasures better hid" (I.687-88). True to his name and character, he suggests that they seek out the hidden gems and gold which lurk beneath the desert soil of Hell, and build a new realm there. He, too, argues against war, on the grounds that unless they overpower God altogether (which he concedes is impossible), they will simply return to servitude in Heaven, an eternity spent in worshipping one whom they hate (which he argues is unacceptable). Rather, he suggests that they prefer the "hard liberty" of Hell to the "easy yoke of servile pomp" which will be their lot in Heaven, and make the most of what Hell can offer.

## Messiah

*See* The Son

## Michael

Michael is the chief of the angels in Heaven and leads the army of loyal angels against Satan and his minions in the War in Heaven. Michael wields a mighty sword, with which he strikes Lucifer, shearing his right side and causing him to feel pain for the first time. It is Michael who is sent to cast Adam and Eve out of Paradise and seal the gates with a fiery sword after the Fall; but in spite of his seeming austerity, he is also kind as he fulfills his commission to reveal the future of humankind to Adam, thus offering hope and consolation.

## Moloch

Moloch, the fallen angel who speaks first at the council of devils in Book II, is also the fallen angel described first in the list of Satan's legions in Book I, as they rise from the burning lake and stand before their leader and his second-in-command, Beelzebub. Milton identifies the fallen angels with the idols and pagan deities of the ancient world, and thus gives them the "new names" by which they are known to the "sons of Eve," whom they corrupt. Described in Book I as "Moloch, horrid king, besmeared with blood / Of human sacrifice, and parents' tears" (I.391-2), Moloch was a sun god to whom children were offered as burnt sacrifices. It is fitting, then, that as "the strongest and fiercest spirit / That fought in Heaven, now fiercer by despair" (II.44-45), Moloch fears neither God nor Hell, and counsels open war. He argues that nothing could be worse than the "pain of unextinguishable fire" (II.88) to which they have been condemned. Being, therefore, without hope, they have nothing to lose. If they cannot attain victory, he implies, at least they can have revenge.

## Mulciber

Mulciber is the fallen angel who designs Pandemonium, Satan's palace and the setting for the council of devils. Milton relates in Book I that Mulciber also designed many of the beautiful palaces in heaven, merging him with the mythical figure Vulcan, who, according to Homer, was tossed out of heaven by Jove amidst much laughter (*Iliad* I). Milton "corrects" Homer's "error" as a corrupt version of the true story of the fall of the angels, which he here recounts.

## Raphael

Raphael is the angel who acts as God's messenger to Adam, warning him of the danger which threatens him and reminding him of his duty of obedience. Raphael also fills in the gaps created by the epic style, which begins the poem *in medias res,* or in the middle. He tells Adam of the revolt of Satan and the War in Heaven, and of the Creation of the World. In turn, he is the audience for Adam's recounting of his memories since his first awakening, and of the creation of Eve. Raphael ends his long discussion with Adam by reminding Adam that he was created with both the freedom to choose and the ability to choose wisely, and by repeating his warning about the danger presented by Satan.

## Satan

Satan, whose name means "enemy" or "adversary" in Hebrew, is the first character to whom the reader is introduced, and the most complex. The leader of the fallen angels, Satan was known as "Lucifer" (Latin, "lightbearer") before he initiated a rebellion against God and was cast out of Heaven. It has been suggested that Satan is the true "epic hero" of the piece, largely because of his epic language and heroic energy. However, as Robert M.

Adams and George M. Logan point out in their introduction to the poem in *The Norton Anthology of English Literature,* it is "energy in a bad cause," even if it is heroically exercised. Satan is characterized in Book I by pride, by the refusal to accept defeat, and by the conviction that it is "Better to reign in Hell, than serve in Heav'n" (I.263). Even here, of course, the careful reader will discern his envy, his false ambition and his self-deception, as he characterizes God as a tyrant and plots his revenge. Yet his speech is stirring, and the reader can see the valiant leader who was able to draw one third of heaven with him in rebellion as he rouses his troops to action and embraces his new home, declaring that "the mind is its own place, and in itself / can make a Heaven of Hell, a Hell of Heaven" (I.254-5).

Milton's portrayal of Satan is honest and reflects an important truth: evil is powerful because it is attractive, and this is part of its danger. It is this attraction which will ultimately cause the downfall of Eve, as well as of Satan and his minions. This surface attraction, however, hides a deeper weakness, based on flawed character and self-deception. Satan maintains that, as an angel, however fallen, he cannot change or fail, yet from the beginning of the poem, it is obvious that he *has* changed and, ultimately, he *will* fail. As the poem progresses, Satan appears less compelling, shifting from the heroic warrior to a vulture, a cormorant, a toad, and finally a snake. As his form shifts, so too does his character, and the reader sees his ambition tainted by envy and hatred. His speech to Eve is characterised by sibilant "s" sounds, simulating the hissing of the serpent into whose form he has voluntarily entered and into which he will be involuntarily transformed in Book X as, returning in "triumph" to Hell, he is defeated by the curse pronounced upon him as judgement for his sins.

### Sin

Sin is Satan's daughter who, along with Death (the product of her incestuous union with Satan), guards the gates of Hell. Satan, Sin, and Death together thus form an unholy parody of the Trinity. In a curious combination of Edmund Spenser's Duessa (from *The Fairie Queene*) and the Questing Beast (from Arthurian myth), Sin is described as a woman to the waist, and a serpent from the waist down, with hellhounds about her middle who bark and howl from within her womb. (These hellhounds represent her other "children," sins, which are

conceived when her son, Death, rapes her.) Paralleled to Athena, who sprang full grown from the head of Zeus, Sin literally sprang from Satan's head when he first conceived the idea of rebellion against God, and thus is the realization or personification of his "original" sin. Like Duessa (and like Satan), she combines beauty with grotesque ugliness, illustrating both the attraction and the repulsiveness of sin and evil. Satan is attracted to her in a parody of Adam's love for Eve, becoming enamoured with his "perfect image" which he perceives in her. Ironically, however, when he encounters her at the gates of Hell, he recognizes neither her nor the son he has never seen (but whom he should know), indicating how far they both have fallen.

### The Son

The Son of God is the character closest to God, in whom God confides. It is the Son's exaltation as king of the angels which arouses Lucifer's envy and provokes his revolt. The Son leads the final battle in which the rebellion is ended, and as a result of which the rebel angels are cast out of Heaven. He volunteers to die for the sin of Adam and Eve (Book III) and intercedes with God on their behalf, before being sent to pronounce God's final judgement upon them (Book X). He is not yet named Jesus, which is the name he takes during his earthly existence when he sets out to fulfil the vow taken in heaven to repair the harm done in Eden by Satan, and to redeem Adam, Eve, and their descendants.

### Uriel

The faithful and radiant archangel of the sun, Uriel is one of the seven spirits who stand in the sight of God's throne. Deceived by Satan, who disguises himself as a young cherub, Uriel directs him to Paradise, thus both enabling and foreshadowing the deception of Eve, though on a higher plane. Unlike Eve, however, Uriel's deception is not associated with either disobedience or fall, and Milton makes it clear that Uriel's failure to discern Satan's hypocrisy is not only sanctioned but willed by God. Later, Uriel recognizes Satan as the latter debates with himself on the borders of Paradise. Uriel immediately glides to Gabriel on a sunbeam and warns him of the danger that threatens God's newest creatures.

### Vulcan
*See* Mulciber

# Themes

*Paradise Lost* is essentially the story of two parallel falls; the fall of Lucifer and his rebel angels, and the fall of humankind. The poem thus relates the story of the revolt of the rebel angels in Heaven, and their subsequent banishment to Hell, and the story of the creation of the world, the temptation and disobedience of Adam and Eve, and their subsequent banishment from Eden.

## Justice

Milton's stated purpose is "to justify the ways of God to man," and he does so by placing responsibility for the fall squarely on the shoulders of the first human pair. They are cast out of Eden because their banishment is necessary to fulfil the demands of divine justice. Their punishment is just, because God placed only one condition upon them and they failed to fulfil it, in spite of the fact that God gave them the means to do so. As Adam warns Eve, God's "creating hand / Nothing imperfect or deficient left/ Of all that he Created, much less Man. . ." (IX.344-346). By providing them with reason and free will, God gives humankind both the choice to obey or disobey, and the means by which to exercise that choice wisely, for "within himself / The danger lies, yet lies within his power: / Against his will he can receive no harm" (IX.347-348).

Having created man free to fall, yet able to resist, God goes one step further. He sends Raphael to warn Adam of the danger which threatens him, and to remind him of his duty of obedience. Adam is thus completely without excuse, and God himself reinforces Adam and Eve's responsibility for their own fall: "whose fault? / Whose but his own? . . . I made him just and right, / Sufficient to have stood, though free to fall" (III.95-98).

Once the Fall has occurred, the consequences are fixed. God set the rules when he pronounced his one prohibition: Adam and Eve are not to eat of the fruit of the Tree of Knowledge, or they will die. Having made the rules, God is now bound by them, and once Adam has eaten, he *must* die: "Die he or Justice must; unless for him / Some other able, and as willing, pay / The rigid satisfaction, death for death" (III.210-212). The Son's death, then, is freely offered out of mercy, to satisfy the demands of justice and offer grace. In the Incarnate Son, Jesus, "Man, as is most just, / Shall satisfy for Man" (III.295-6).

## Freedom

It is important that, while God made Adam and Eve "sufficient to have stood," he also created them "free to fall." This freedom is rooted in their very nature, for God "formed them free, and free they must remain" (III.124). For Milton, humankind's obedience is proof of their love and service to God, and obedience therefore *must* be free, for obedience which is not free is not obedience but slavery. It is for this reason that Adam is free to fall, and for this reason that he must leave Eve free to make her own choices, even if that choice be to leave him and work alone and vulnerable, "for thy stay, not free, absents thee more" (IX.372). But in this very freedom lies the possibility of disobedience, for in the freedom of will lies the possibility of choice.

## Choice and Consequences

The freedom of the will is associated with freedom of choice; yet freedom implies responsibility, and the freedom to choose brings with it the responsibility to choose correctly. It is reason which gives humans the ability to choose between obedience and disobedience and, after the fall, between good and evil. Thus, "Against his will he can receive no harm. But God left free the Will, for what obeys / Reason is free. . ." (IX.350-52). The Fall, then, is the *consequence* of failing to choose wisely. The events which follow are the logical consequences of the choice which Adam and Eve make when they choose "knowledge" over obedience. The full consequences of the Fall are made clear in the final vision of the future which Michael shows to Adam: the political upheaval, strife, toil, and anguish which result from being cast out of Eden, but also the redemption of humankind, which only the Fall makes possible.

## Obedience

The only condition placed on Adam and Eve is a simple prohibition: not to eat the fruit of the Tree of the Knowledge of good and evil. It is important, however, to recognize that it is not *knowledge* which causes the fall, it is disobedience. The commandment is not meant to *prevent* knowledge, but to provide the *opportunity* for obedience. As Adam reminds Eve, God "requires / From us no other service than to keep / This one, this easy charge, . . . The only sign of our obedience. . ."(IV.419-21, 428). Ironically, this "one easy prohibition" is both so easily kept and so easily broken, and man will ". . . easily transgress the sole Command, sole

# Topics for Further Study

- Milton presents the political consequences of the Fall in Michael's preview of human history (Book XII). Discuss this presentation in light of the Restoration of the monarchy in England and the political controversies surrounding the debate concerning the merits of monarchy vs. republic.

- Discuss Raphael's admonition to Adam concerning the limitations of human knowledge and his discouragement of Adam's inquiries into the movements of the heavenly spheres (Book VIII) in light of the advancements in science and the new "scientific" attitudes towards knowledge in the seventeenth century.

- Research the philosophical trend towards ration-

alism in the seventeenth century, and then discuss Milton's view of the Fall as a failure of reason and obedience, rather than as an acquisition of "forbidden knowledge."

- Book I, in part, describes the building of Pandemonium. Book IX describes the tending of Eden and the consequences of the Fall for nature. Both descriptions associate sin and the Fall with a disrupted natural affinity for the earth and the introduction of an indifference to the planet, which results in its "wounding." Discuss this in light of present-day arguments for humanity's responsibility toward environmental preservation.

---

pledge of his obedience'' (III.94-95) That the Fall must be understood as a failure of obedience, not the acquisition of forbidden knowledge, is made clear in the first lines of the poem, where Milton states his theme as being "Of Man's First Disobedience" (I.1).

Obedience is also an integral part of the maintenance of the natural hierarchy, which depends on the proper exercise of authority: God rules over Adam, and Adam must rule over both Eve and himself. The theme of obedience is thus tied to the question of authority, which is exercised through reason.

### Knowledge and Ignorance

The Fall, then, is not the acquisition of knowledge, but the failure of obedience, which is caused by the failure to exercise reason. The belief that it is knowledge itself which is forbidden is a misunderstanding of both the nature and purpose of the prohibition, and Milton emphasizes this by putting all his statements about forbidden knowledge into the mouth of Satan before the Fall, and into the mouths of Adam and Eve only after the Fall. In fact, it is *knowledge* which should prevent the Fall, and knowledge which Raphael imparts in his warning to

Adam. Satan's deception lies not in his claims that knowledge is a good thing and therefore to be desired, but in the idea that the knowledge of good and evil is enclosed within the tree and its fruit. Adam clearly knew of evil prior the Fall, and was well aware of the dangers of evil. The knowledge of good and evil which comes with the Fall, then, is not simply a new knowledge of evil, where before there was only the knowledge of good. What is gained is rather the "Knowledge of Good bought dear by knowing ill" (IV.220), or "knowledge of good lost, evil got." The consequence of eating the fruit is that the knowledge of good and of evil has become inseparable, and humankind can now know good only by knowing evil as well. This is consistent with Milton's conviction, expressed elsewhere, that *all* knowledge is valuable, and even necessary. After the Fall, the free choice with which humankind is endowed is exercised in the choice between good and evil, and that choice can only be established and maintained through the knowledge of both.

### The Human Condition

The human condition is thus the condition of fallen humanity, knowing not just "good and evil," but the inseparable nature of the two in a fallen world. Yet, humankind was created in the image of God, and still retains this innate characteristic. It is reason which is most fully the image of God in humankind, reason which enables humankind to choose between good and evil, reason which both establishes and preserves free will. Fallen humanity is thus characterized still by reason, but it is an impaired reason, for although God created humankind perfect, they are not immutable and the most obvious consequence of the Fall is indeed change. Even reason impaired, however, is still reason which need not fail, and Milton's final word is one of hope. Michael's revelation of God's redemptive purpose brings Adam to a new understanding of the proper role of obedience and virtue in a fallen world, reconciling him to his expulsion from Paradise and enabling him to possess "a paradise within, . . . happier far" (XII.587).

# Style

## Subject Matter

The standard definition of an epic, or heroic poem, is that it is a "noble story told in noble verse" (Hutson and McCoy, *Epics of the Western World*, p. 7), a continuous narrative concerning a heroic person from history or tradition. The epic uses historical and mythological material to exemplify a truth which is greater than both. The subject of an epic poem is to be a story which both delights and instructs, embodying the cultural and moral ideals of its time but with universal implications.

Milton chooses an unusual subject for his great epic poem, ostensibly shunning "Wars, hitherto the only Argument / Heroic deem'd" (IX.28-9), in favor of the sad task of relating an "argument / Not less but more Heroic than the wrath / Of Stern Achilles on his Foe pursu'd / Thrice Fugitive about Troy Wall" (IX. 13-15). The "higher argument" which Milton chooses is the story of the Creation, Fall, and Redemption of humankind, combining the epic conventions of high moral purpose with the conviction that in presenting a Biblical theme, he is also representing a higher truth. The fate of humankind thus becomes the unifying force of the poem, as Milton presents the ideals of private virtue and public rectitude by exploring both the nobility and weakness of fallen humanity.

## Poetic Style and Techniques

Milton's dramatic and magnificent manipulation of language in *Paradise Lost* has aroused the admiration of generations of readers. His choice of blank verse goes against the spirit of the times, which saw rhyme as the highest evidence of disciplined mastery of language, as well as a means of restraining an overactive fancy. This is typical of Milton's use of the classical poetic techniques associated with the epic form. The poem contains many formal parallels with classical forms: the beginning of the poem *in medias res;* the repetition of the formula "what cause?"; the epic games pursued by the rebel angels; the alternation of setting between earth and Heaven or Hell; lists of armies and the description of councils (both heavenly and demonic); wars and their descriptions; and the alternation of dialogue with description and narration. Yet, Milton consistently adapts these classical forms to his own purposes and style. For example, in his statement of theme and purpose, he follows the pattern of Homer and Virgil. However, he replaces the assertion of Fate with an assertion of Providence, and though he begins his poem with the standard invocation to the Muse, he alters that invocation. He appeals, not to Calliope, the traditional Muse of the epic poet, but to Urania, the Muse of astrology and the heavens, who, he asserts, inspired Moses. However, above Urania, he invokes the Holy Spirit (associated with heavenly light) as the true inspiration for his Christian epic.

## Character

The problem of the "epic hero" has plagued the analysis of *Paradise Lost*. The epic hero is generally defined as a hero of extraordinary magnitude, who is identified with a national or cult hero and exemplifies heroic and moral values. But there is no "real" hero of this world in Milton's poem. This has led to a debate as to who the "hero" of the piece really is. On the surface, it is humankind, represented by Adam and Eve. Yet it is Satan who displays the typical qualities of the classical hero, while Adam never really attains epic stature. To assume, however, that Satan is the "hero" is to misread Milton's assessment of both humanity and evil. Satan's character exposes the true danger of evil, which lies in the very fact that it is attractive. Through Satan, Milton exposes the false view of heroism as "egotistical magnificence" and the equally false idea that heroic energy is admirable, even when exercised in a bad cause (Daiches, *Milton* ).

Adam and Eve, on the other hand, reveal the central paradoxes of the human condition; capable of standing, yet free to fall. Humankind as a moral being is both noble and weak. Yet, this tragic ambiguity is balanced by the conclusion of the poem, which reveals humanity's capacity to derive hope from an exile which includes companionship and purpose. The story of fallen humankind may be a lament for a lost Eden, but it is also a challenge to triumph over despair and to explore an infinitely engaging new world.

### Setting

Like the classical epic, *Paradise Lost* alternates its setting between the world of men and the worlds of God and the angels (fallen and unfallen). The activities of God and the angels, both fallen and unfallen, project both the ideals and the realities of human behavior. The council of devils, for example, parallels the abuses of public ''reason'' and civil responsibility in the royalist parliament, as well as the secrecy and other sinister features which Milton attributes to the papacy. Eden is a real world, yet is described using classical imagery. It is the setting for the highest human ideals, such as perfect conjugal bliss, as well as extreme human weakness, such as recrimination and malice. Both heaven and earth are battlegrounds where virtue and vice, good and evil, fight for dominance.

### Epic Motifs

As well as the typical epic forms described above, a number of epic motifs are incorporated by Milton into the poem. For example, he incorporates mythology, though it is Biblical, not classical, myth which dominates *Paradise Lost.* Although he claims that war, the traditional subject matter of the epic, is not to be his theme, he does incorporate the motif of battle into the poem. The war in Heaven and Satan's subsequent fall and exile both prefigure and precipitate the central conflict of the poem, which takes place on earth. The conflict between Satan and God is continued in Eden and projected into conflict between human desire and God's command, between desire and reason, between Adam and Eve. Finally, after the Fall, the entire earth becomes the battleground for the ongoing conflict between good and evil. The epic motif of the journey as a symbol of life is also present. Again, the journey of Satan from Hell to earth both prefigures and contrasts humanity's journey out of Eden, and the progression of history presented to Adam by Michael as a panoramic journey through time.

## Historical Context

### The English Civil Wars, Interregnum, and Restoration

The civil wars of the 1640s in England were rooted in the conflicts between Charles I and his Parliament in the 1620s and the policies which were instituted in the 1630s, when Charles ruled without Parliament. His religious policies were resented: the apparently weakened stance regarding Catholics incensed the Puritans, as did the emphasis on the prayer book and its procedures, which curtailed the development of new religious practises and observances. In 1640-1642, a new Parliament was called which attempted religious and political reform, ultimately resulting in the first Civil War (1642-1646), which pitted king against parliament. The war was disorganized, and its outcome was determined not primarily by military factors, but by economic, religious, and political factors. The heavy taxation, extreme religious reform, and wide powers granted to parliamentary agents led to the second Civil War (1647-1649), which was primarily a revolt of the provinces against centralization and military rule, and which culminated in the beheading of Charles in 1649.

From 1649 to 1660, the period known as the Interregnum, England was a republic (though not a democracy). Cromwell governed from 1653 to 1658 as Lord Protector and Head of State. He saw England as representing God's chosen people, working towards a Promised Land where Church and State would be as one. His religious radicalism led to what was seen as undue control of individual behavior and arbitrary government. Cromwell's son had neither the strength nor the character to follow in his father's footsteps, and with Cromwell's death in 1658, the Republic collapsed. Eighteen months later free elections were held and Charles II was recalled unconditionally.

Milton's own disillusionment with the attempt to combine politics and religion and the collapse of the government which he served so loyally can be seen in *Paradise Lost,* as he outlines the political consequences of the fall in Michael's revelation to Adam in Book XII. Yet, the poem also conveys his conviction that political justice can be achieved in this world. The Puritan stress on overcoming temptation is also a theme which recurs throughout his work, and is especially dominant in *Paradise Lost.* Yet Milton's Puritanism is not as strict as that of many in his day; for example, Milton loves beauty

# Compare & Contrast

- **1642-1660:** The English civil wars resulted in an Interregnum, during which England was a republic, although not a democracy, ruled by Parliament alone. In 1660, the republic collapsed and the monarchy was restored.

  **1700s:** The late eighteenth century saw the French Revolution and the American Revolution, both of which sought to establish republics in the place of monarchies. The French Revolution was a civil war which toppled the French monarchy. The American Revolution was the revolt of a colony against England, and while the English monarchy survived intact, its colonies in what became the United States were lost.

  **Late twentieth century:** England is governed by a democratically elected parliament. Although the monarchy survives, the Queen, as head of state, has little real political power.

- **1600s:** The seventeenth century saw scientific advances which included William Harvey's discovery of the circulation of the blood, Isaac Newton's theory of gravity, and developments in chemistry (Robert Boyle) and geology (Robert Hooke). Science was only just beginning to be seen as a discipline divorced from theology and philosophy, based on empirical observation of ''objective fact'' rather than metaphysical speculation about ''truth.''

  **Late twentieth century:** The value of scientific and technological research is taken for granted, to the extent that more philosophical study of issues such as ethics is now being called for. Radical advances have occurred in all fields, producing results which would have been viewed as miraculous in Milton's day.

- **1600s:** In the field of astronomy, Galileo was transforming human knowledge of the heavens with his telescope, viewing the surface of the moon. Copernicus had developed an entirely new concept of the universe, in which the earth, like the other planets, revolved around the sun. This theory had not yet displaced the old Ptolemaic view, in which the sun and planets revolved around the earth. The Ptolemaic view was preferred by theologians, who wished to maintain man's place at the centre of creation, and Milton is carefully non-committal in his epic, relegating knowledge of the motions of the heavenly spheres to the category of unfathomable, and therefore not useful, knowledge against which Raphael warns Adam.

  **Late twentieth century:** While our knowledge of the universe is still in its infancy, technology has begun to open up ''the final frontier,'' and our knowledge of our own solar system is expanding. Space travel has become a reality, and satellites and space telescopes are expanding our knowledge of planets beyond the reach of space stations and shuttles.

- **1660s:** Milton's presentation of Eve assumes that women are naturally inferior to men in reason and intelligence, as well as physical strength. Eve is characterized by wanton beauty, physical desire, and domestic achievements.

  **Late twentieth century:** The feminist movement has exposed gender bias in society and literature, fighting for the recognition that women are not intrinsically inferior to men and striving for equal rights in the home and in the workplace.

- **1643:** Bitterly disillusioned with his own failed marriage, Milton published *On the Doctrine and Discipline of Divorce,* arguing that unsuccessful marriages should be dissolved. His arguments had little effect in an age where the Church had a large influence on public policy.

  **Late twentieth century:** Divorce, while not welcomed, is now publicly accepted.

and stresses both the beauty of Eden and the beauty and sexual bliss of Adam and Eve.

### Religious Thought

The civil wars produced a chaotic variety of sects which were never entirely rooted out. Although Charles II attempted to introduce the religious toleration which was lacking in both his father's reign and the Interregnum, he was not successful, and the entire period is characterized by religious intolerance and conflict. Yet, there are some general trends which can be traced through the seventeenth century.

In the early part of the century, scientific, philosophical, and political writings are infused with hope as scholarship, scientific inquiry, and Christian faith are combined. The Protestant commitment to the authority of Scripture is combined with a philosophical search for "truth," and perceived anomalies between science, philosophy, and religion are resolved in various ways. For example, some thinkers propose the existence of various orders of truth, separating reason and faith (which is informed by scripture and therefore above reason), while others argue that the Bible is to be read allegorically, since it conveys truth figuratively, rather than literally. Revelation, however, is not confined to Scripture. God's laws are revealed externally in the laws of nature, and internally through reason, or the moral law within. Milton shares these views, emphasizing moral guidance and free will. Scripture, passed down by human intermediaries, is less reliable than reason inspired by the Holy Spirit, which is the final authority.

There is also a stress on the combination of religious and political spheres, on God's activities within human history. It is this ideal which Cromwell attempted to realize in the Interregnum. After the Interregnum, however, the concept of the Kingdom of God was internalized, and the limitations of Church and State acknowledged. The search for peace and salvation became a personal, rather than collective, quest, and politics, science, and philosophy became increasingly secularized.

### Science

The seventeenth century was characterized by a new emphasis on empirical "truth" rather than metaphysical "reality." For example, Francis Bacon stressed the importance of observation and experimental science. These principles allowed many advances in the study of plant and animal life, and the study of physiology and anatomy progressed following William Harvey's discovery of the circulation of the blood. The seventeenth century also saw advances in physics (Isaac Newton), chemistry (Robert Boyle), and geology (Robert Hooke). Galileo transformed human knowledge of the heavens, showing change and mutability in heavenly bodies, arguing that perfection could no longer be identified with the incorruptible or the unalterable. Milton was ultimately uninterested in "scientific truth," and was indifferent to the ultimate success of either the old Ptolemaic model of the universe or the new Copernican model, yet he was fascinated by new scientific discoveries and their implications. He incorporated the separation between perfection and immutability in his portrait of unfallen humankind, created perfect but mutable, and therefore free to fall.

### Philosophy

Copernicus had shown that things are not necessarily what they seem, nor what they have been said to be, and scientific advances suggested that many things which had previously been attributed to God had new, natural explanations. Yet much remained unknown, and philosophy in the seventeenth century focused on the questions of epistemology, of what can truly be "known" about reality. René Descartes suggested that God and the Soul were the first "certainties." Yet both were ultimately reduced in Cartesian thought to intellectual abstractions: God no longer had any relationship to religious experience, and the "I" whose existence was proven by conscious thought ("I think, therefore I am") was only the *thinking* part of me. Thus, there was no certainty concerning either the properties or attributes of either God or the soul. Yet Descartes's break with the past is important, embodying a new appeal to the internal authority of reason, rather than the external authority of religion. Shaking off the influence of the past also enabled the growth of the idea of "progress" (both scientific and philosophical) which was rooted in Renaissance humanism and its celebration of human potential. The world was no longer constructed from "historical" realities, but rather from inner certainties, endorsed by reason. Thomas Hobbes went a step further, identifying the real with the material, reflecting the increasing secularization of politics and science. Hobbes replaced the divine justification of political authority with de facto power, and the sovereign's ability to protect his subjects. Religion was relegated to the realm of superstition, but religious beliefs were nonetheless valuable in forming attitudes and actions, in teaching humankind how to behave as subjects and citizens. The sovereign was thus viewed as God's earthly lieutenant; the laws of God were paralleled with the laws of nature and principles of morality; and scripture was granted a limited authority. With John Locke, a new emphasis on individualism and religious toleration became the groundwork for what would become modern liberal democracy.

# Critical Overview

Milton's poem has produced mixed reactions in the three centuries since its first publication. Much of the controversy surrounding the poem centers around two main issues: its style, and its content (specifically its religious subject matter and political overtones). Yet, it must be remembered, in the epic form style and content are closely related, and it is thus impossible to separate the two issues entirely.

Early reactions to the poem seem to have questioned Milton's use of blank verse in an epic poem, and the second and third issues of the first edition contain a note from ''The Printer to the Reader'' on this subject, as well as Milton's own justification of ''The Verse.'' However, the most intense reaction to the poem in its early days focused on its content. Nicholas von Maltzahn (''The First Reception of *Paradise Lost* (1667)'') summarizes the politics surrounding three early responses which typify its first reception. The episcopal licenser, Thomas Tomkins, was at first inclined to suppress the poem, finding evidence in it of the anti-royalist sentiments for which Milton was notorious after the publication of his tracts supporting the regicide of Charles I. After the Restoration, such opinions were, naturally, cause for profound concern. Tomkins disapproved of the emphasis on astrological omens, such as eclipses, which reflected a Puritan tendency to over-emphasize natural events, and which Tomkins feared would fuel dissent in the wake of numerous disasters which the English had suffered in the previous year (such as the Great Fire of London). Tomkins was also suspicious of Milton's elevation of private illumination or inspiration. However, other preoccupations also engaged Tomkins, and in a time of national crisis, Milton's emphasis on reason, first principles and common notions, and the poem's engaging development of sacred history were seen as contributing to, rather than detracting

from the stability and national unity which Tomkins sought to endorse. He therefore licensed the work, in spite of his misgivings.

The initial success of the poem is seen in the reactions of Sir John Hobart, who saw the Christian epic as a welcome balance to the decadent culture of the court. While joining in the (by now) almost universal condemnation of the politics represented in Milton's prose, Hobart praised Milton's humanism, as well as his style, which he stated was ''not only above alle moderne attempts in verse, but equall to any of the Antient Poets'' (letter, Bodl. Ms Tanner 45, cited by von Maltzahn). John Beale, however, had a more mixed reaction. Beale responded hopefully to Milton's claims to individual inspiration, and his elevation of the claims of conscience. Yet, he was wary of the politics of *Paradise Lost,* which he saw as openly republican, as well as its demonology, which was too Calvinist for his episcopal tastes.

Criticism of Milton's epic has continued to be divided. Early poets and critics who have praised Milton's style and content include John Dryden, who in 1688 placed Milton on a level with Homer and Virgil, Patrick Hume, who published an early annotated text of the poem in 1695, and Joseph Addison, who published a laudatory series of essays in 1712. Samuel Johnson, however, was less complimentary, writing, ''*Paradise Lost* is one of the books which the reader admires and lays down, and forgets to take up again. None ever wished it longer than it is. Its perusal is a duty rather than a pleasure.''

The greatness of Milton's verse was generally acknowledged in the nineteenth century, and his influence on poets such as William Wordsworth, Samuel Taylor Coleridge, Percy Bysshe Shelley, John Keats, Alfred, Lord Tennyson, and Matthew Arnold is clear, though all of these poets developed in their own distinctive ways. Yet, the twentieth century saw a continuation of the division which characterized early criticism. The ''attack'' on Milton was mounted by T. S. Eliot, who argued that Milton could only be a bad influence on later poets; that his visual imagination was flawed, and that he was not a great poet, but merely a great eccentric. Eliot's arguments, inconclusive in themselves, were taken up by F. R. Leavis, who argued that Milton has made a victim of the English language itself, and that his style is routine, monotonous and heavy. The case in Milton's defense was taken up by critics such as Basil Willey and C. S. Lewis, who argue that Milton's latinate vocabulary and syntax are highly appropriate to his subject matter and praise the broad sweep of the poem as well as its grand style. Later critics, such as Christopher Ricks and Frank Kermode, have defended Milton's style in detail and with force, and the attacks of Eliot and Leavis are now generally dismissed.

One final issue which cannot be ignored is the "split" which many critics have seen in the poem. The ostensible purpose of the poem is to expose Satan and "justify" God. However, it has been argued that Milton did precisely the opposite. In the Romantic period, criticism focused on the presentation of Satan, for which Milton has received both praise and blame. The Romantic poets, following Dryden, saw Satan as the true hero of *Paradise Lost,* and promoted the idea that Milton was "of the Devil's party without knowing it" (William Blake, *The Marriage of Heaven and Hell,* 1790). In this view, Milton projected his own revolutionary ideals onto Satan, presenting God (albeit unwittingly) in the image of the Stuart kings whom he so abhorred. This argument was picked up by twentieth century critics such as A. J. A. Waldock and John Peter, but its greatest champion is William Empson, who sees Milton's epic as a heroic struggle with the inner contradictions of the Christian faith itself, exposing God, in the end, as a tyrant.

There have been numerous responses to this view, but the most effective is by Stanley Fish. Fish argues that Milton's presentations of God and Satan are deliberate, and that the ambiguity of the poem represents the ambiguity of the human condition in its fallen state. The attraction of Satan and the remoteness of God thus reflect, not the true character of either, but the exile of fallen humanity, for whom Satan is a formidable enemy *because* of his compelling qualities, and God is alien because the fallen world is not in tune with its creator.

## Criticism

### Catherine Innes-Parker

*In the following essay, Innes-Parker studies Milton's struggle to reconcile the sinful nature of humankind with the inherent value of knowledge, assessing Adam and Eve's sin which results from eating from the Tree of Knowledge.*

*Paradise Lost* has been hailed as one of the greatest poems in the English language. While this acclaim is due in a large part to Milton's command of language and poetic style, much of the attraction of the poem lies in its content. The discussion of temptation and fall is rooted in universal questions concerning the nature of good and evil, the apparent injustice of a world where the wicked prosper and the good suffer, the nature and value of knowledge, and the nature of humankind.

Milton's struggle to reconcile the Genesis account of the Fall with his own deepest convictions and concerns is often attributed to a failure to come to terms with the particular demands of the epic form. However, in light of his prose treatments of similar themes, it becomes clear that the conflicts in *Paradise Lost* reflect a conflict between his understanding of the authority of scripture and his conviction that reason is the surest guide to truth. If reason represents the image of God in humankind, how can the Fall be attributed to knowledge, and, more important, how can knowledge be forbidden? Milton's struggle to reconcile his intellectual convictions with the text of Genesis reflects a conflict which remains to this day. The Genesis account of the creation and Fall remains one of the foundational myths of Western culture; yet, in our modern secular world, the intrinsic power of myth often collides with the demands of reason.

Milton's treatment of the Fall is, in fact, remarkably consistent with his understanding of the nature of humankind as created in the image of God and with his treatments of the nature and value of knowledge. The first question which must be asked, then, is what is the true nature of humankind? Or, what does it mean to be created in the image of God? In the first view of humankind (seen through Satan's eyes, but not described from his point of view) the omniscient narrator describes: "Two of far nobler shape erect and tall, / Godlike erect, with native Honor clad / In naked majesty seem'd Lords of all, / And worthy seem'd, for in their looks Divine / The image of their glorious maker shone, / Truth, Wisdom, Sanctitude severe and pure, / Severe, but in true filial freedom plac't; / Whence true authority in men. . ." (*PL* IV.287-294). Adam and Eve's outward appearance is characterized by nobility, and rectitude, reflecting the inward attributes of the image of God: truth, wisdom, sanctitude, purity and freedom. These attributes, or more accurately, the image of God which they represent, are the source of both human dignity and authority,

# What Do I Read Next?

- *Paradise Regained* (1671) is the sequel to *Paradise Lost*, in which Milton explores the temptation of Christ in the wilderness in order to show how redemption is achieved through the reversal of Adam's disobedience by Christ's obedience.

- Bitterly disappointed in his own first marriage, in 1643 Milton published *The Doctrine and Discipline of Divorce*, arguing that poor marriages should be dissolved. This essay provides an interesting contrast to the view of Adam and Eve's conjugal bliss in *Paradise Lost*.

- *Of Education* (1644) is a treatise in which Milton explores the contribution of education to mankind's ability to withstand temptation, examining many of the issues which resurface in the treatment of the temptation in *Paradise Lost*.

- *Areopagitica* (1644) is a treatise calling for freedom of the press and the removal of censorship. Here Milton develops many of the ideas concerning reason and knowledge developed in *Paradise Lost*, particularly the interdependence between the knowledge of good and evil and the folly of considering any knowledge "forbidden."

- *Samson Agonistes* (1671) is a verse drama in which Milton portrays the story of Samson and Delilah in true tragic style. The author presents Samson as engaged in a heroic conflict in which he conquers despair and triumphs over his foes.

- Mary Shelley's novel *Frankenstein* (1818) is deeply influenced by *Paradise Lost*, as she explores the problems of justice and the responsibility of the creator towards his creature through Victor Frankenstein's abandonment of his creature and the creature's subsequent "defense."

---

leading to the conclusion that they are rightly "Lords of all."

Similar motifs emerge in Raphael's description of the creation of humankind as "... a Creature who not prone / And Brute as other Creatures, but endu'd / With Sanctity of Reason, might erect / His Stature, and upright with front serene / Govern the rest, self-knowing..." (*PL* VII.506-510). Again, what distinguishes humans from the creatures which they will rule is their erect stature. This is specifically associated with that faculty which, above all others, Milton associates with the divine image: reason. But reason is associated with self-knowledge, and it is in Adam's ability to know himself (or failure to do so) that the success or failure of reason will ultimately lie.

Adam gives evidence of self-knowledge throughout *Paradise Lost*. He is aware of both his strengths and his weaknesses, as well as of his duties and obligations. This self-knowledge must be acquired by Adam through a process of growth, prompted by the reason which is innate to him.

Adam describes the learning process to Raphael in Book VIII as he describes his memories of his first awakening after his creation.

In addition to self-knowledge, Adam must acquire knowledge of the God whose image he bears. Adam intuitively deduces the existence of a creator from the fact of his own existence and seeks knowledge of the creator from the created world. In *Of Christian Doctrine,* Milton associates this intuitive knowledge of the existence of God with the possession of "right reason" or conscience, the moral sense which enables humankind to distinguish between right and wrong. In *Of Education,* therefore, Milton asserts that the purpose of education is to regain that knowledge possessed by Adam and lost in the Fall, "to know God aright," and out of that knowledge to love him, to imitate him, to be like him.

Humankind's knowledge of self, of creation, and of God is associated with rule or authority, not only over creation, but over the self. Self-rule, like self-knowledge, is based on reason, the chief faculty of the soul. Reason must rule over the lesser faculties, and, particularly, over the passions. As long as the natural order is maintained, the passions are kept under control and happiness prevails. For example, properly ruled, the attraction between Adam and Eve is expressed in love and mutual affection, governed by reason: ". . .for smiles from Reason flow / . . .and are of Love the food, Love not the lowest end of human life. / For not to irksome toil, but to delight / He made us, and delight to Reason joined." (*PL* IX.239f). Implicit in this, however, is also a warning. Reason is vulnerable to passion, and the disruption of the natural order is inherent in Adam's very nature if he fails to know and rule his own passion. The potential for disaster is evident in Adam's words to Raphael as he describes Eve: "All higher knowledge in her presence falls / Degraded, Wisdom in discourse with her / Loses Discount'nanc't, and like folly shows: / Authority and Reason on her wait." (*PL* VIII.551f). Adam blames the failure of his reason and authority in Eve's presence on his own nature and his love for Eve, foreshadowing his eventual fall. However, Raphael warns him, "Accuse not Nature, she hath done her part; / Do thou but thine, and be not diffident / Of Wisdom, she deserts thee not, if thou / Dismiss not her, when most thou need's her nigh" (*PL* VIII.560f). Adam must heed his own advice to Eve: the danger lies within himself, yet within his power, depending upon his ability to rule passion with reason.

Humankind can overcome the danger inherent within his own nature through the reason implanted in him by God. Reason, however, is vulnerable to deception: ". . .Reason he made right, / But bid her well beware, and still erect, / Lest by some fair appearing good surpris'd / She dictates false, and misinform the Will / To do what God expressly hath forbid. / . . . Firm we subsist, yet possible to swerve / Since Reason not impossible may meet / And fall into deception unaware." (*PL* IX.350-354, 359-362). This aspect of reason's vulnerability is represented by Eve, who succumbs to Satan's "persuasive words, impregn'd / With Reason, to her seeming, and with Truth" (*PL* IX.735-736).

Reason properly exercised, however, gives humankind the ability to choose between good and evil. Because humankind is created in the image of God, the natural disposition of humanity is toward what is right, good, and holy. Even after the Fall, this innate ability is retained, for the divine image is impaired, not destroyed. But the moral choice which reason enables is, necessarily, a free choice. Freedom is a natural consequence of reason and is rooted in the very nature of humankind, as God himself makes clear: "I formed them free, and free they must remain, / Till they enthral themselves: I else must change / Their nature. . ." (*PL* III.124f). The Fall, however, is rooted in free choice, and humankind is created with the ability to choose correctly: "Against his will he can receive no harm / But God left free the Will, for what obeys / Reason, is free, and Reason he made right." (*PL* IX.349f)

The choice which is faced by Adam and Eve in Eden is, quite simply, a question of obedience. Their obedience to God is proof of their love and service, and therefore, like the will, must be left free. The single commandment that God has given does not impair this freedom; rather it reflects it. Adam tells Eve that God "requires / From us no other service than to keep / This one, this easy charge" (*PL* IV.419f), and asserts that ". . . the rest, we live / Law to ourselves, our Reason is our Law" (*PL* IX.653-654). It is ironic that this "one easy prohibition" is both so easily kept and so easily broken.

The fact that the commandment is a pledge of obedience has enormous implications for the nature of the Fall. It is not the eating of the fruit *per se* that is wrong: it is the disobedience which that eating exhibits. As Milton states in *On Christian Doctrine,* "It was necessary that something should be forbidden or commanded as a test of fidelity, and that an act in its own nature indifferent, in order that man's obedience might thereby be manifested." The eating of the fruit is "an act in its own nature indifferent": the tree, in and of itself, is neither good nor evil, it is simply there. The eating of the fruit of the Tree of Knowledge is not forbidden because it is dangerous or wrong; it is wrong because it is forbidden. The Fall must therefore be understood as disobedience, not the acquisition of knowledge. It is not knowledge which is forbidden, but a particular action.

The Tree of Knowledge is thus a symbol of man's disobedience, the main subject of *Paradise Lost.* Milton states his theme as "Of Man's First Disobedience, and the Fruit / Of that Forbidden Tree, whose mortal taste, / Brought Death into the World, and all our woe" (*PL* I.1-3). The "woe" which is brought into the world is not the knowledge of good and evil, but death.

This has important implications for the understanding of the knowledge allegedly imparted by the tree. Since the Fall cannot be attributed to the acquisition of knowledge, either the tree did not impart any knowledge, or the knowledge which it did impart was not such as to lead to a "fall." In *Paradise Lost* Milton suggests that the knowledge of good and evil is not simply a new knowledge of evil where before was only knowledge of good. Adam clearly knew of evil prior to his Fall. Raphael has informed him of the fall of the angels and of the existence of his arch-enemy Satan. Adam shows himself to be well aware of the dangers of temptation in his exhortation to Eve as well as in his earlier reaction to Eve's dream, which he immediately identifies as having sprung from evil. Rather, what has occurred in the eating of the fruit is that the knowledge of good and of evil have become so intertwined as to become inseparable: humankind can now know good *only* by knowing evil.

This understanding of the Tree of Knowledge is dictated by Milton's convictions concerning knowledge and its value. Milton sees learning as itself the service of God and of truth. But, in order to attain true virtue, one must know not only good but also evil, for "good and evil we know in the field of this world grow up together almost inseparably; and the knowledge of good is so involved and interwoven with the knowledge of evil" (*Areopagitica*). Milton thus argues that all opinions, even those which reflect error, will eventually lead to the attainment of truth if the mind is correctly governed. Liberty of thought and speech are thus essential in the formation of virtue.

Virtue, like obedience, is rooted in freedom of choice. Yet, in order to choose, one must have alternative to choose from, for "what wisdom can there be to choose, what contingence to forbear without the knowledge of evil? . . . I cannot praise a fugitive and cloistered virtue" (*Areopagitica*). Choice becomes meaningless without the freedom to choose either good or evil, and that freedom to choose can only be established and maintained through the knowledge of both.

It follows, then, that the idea of forbidden knowledge is, for Milton, an absurdity. In fact, the quest for knowledge is closely tied to the quest for virtue, and thus with the highest achievements of humankind. Far from causing the Fall, the acquisition of knowledge is the only way of repairing the divine image which is impaired in the Fall, as reason is obscured. Milton asserts that "the end . . . of learning is to repair the ruins of our first parents by regaining to know God aright, and out of that knowledge to love him, to imitate him, to be like

him. . ." (*Of Education* ). The only limits to this quest are the limits of humanity's own capacity for knowledge.

**Source:** Catherine Innes-Parker, for *Epics for Students,* Gale Research, 1997.

### Lee M. Johnson

*In the following essay, Johnson examines ways that Milton uses such elements of language as symbolism, irony, ambiguity, and even puns in* Paradise Lost *to evoke images of innocence and the loss of innocence.*

We cannot enter the Garden of Eden in Book 4 of *Paradise Lost* and look upon the "mysterious parts" of the innocent Adam and Eve or upon Eve's "wanton ringlets" in a spirit of complete simplicity and purity: not only do we observe with the fallen Satan as our companion, but our perceptions, including those of the poet himself, are subject to the complex connotations and associations which characterize our use of language.[1] To some, "words alone are certain good"[2] but not to the epic's narrator, who, as if acknowledging the hopelessness of painting a credible verbal picture of innocent life, continually calls attention to the "guilty shame" and "dishonest shame" that evoke innocence only by contrast and by a sense of absence (4.313). As the unhappy turns in the careers of Satan, Adam, and Eve demonstrate, linguistic self-subversion, irony, and ambiguity, including, at its lowest, downright bad puns, inhere in the expression of fallen natures. Such a language drifts ineluctably into waywardness and perverse complexity and is, by definition, inadequate to the task of depicting innocent perfection on its own terms. But a poet need not be limited to the depiction of innocence solely by its absence: the illusion of its presence is within the domain of artistic symbolism.

It would appear that, for the purpose of dramatizing the state of innocence, Milton's poetic style displays a remarkable bond between his language and the use of uncomplicated symbolic formal patterns. In exploring the nature of those patterns, we find that they are restricted to books 4, 5, and 8 of *Paradise Lost:* precisely those portions of the epic in which Adam and Eve are described or act in their unfallen condition. We shall not come upon anything similar to Milton's art of innocence elsewhere in *Paradise Lost* or throughout *Paradise Regained* and *Samson Agonistes:* all such passages and works chiefly concern fallen experience and conditions and thus have their own appropriate modes of presentation.[3]

The symbolic patterns associated with the style and language of innocence lend a sense of authenticity to the early speeches of the innocent Adam and Eve. Among those early speeches, the one which displays the most concentrated example of the patterns we shall now consider is Eve's love-lyric "Sweet is the breath of morn":

> Sweet is the breath of morn, her rising sweet,
> With charm of earliest Birds; pleasant the Sun
> When first on this delightful Land he spreads
> His orient Beams, on herb, tree, fruit, and flow'r,
> Glist'ring with dew; fragrant the fertile earth
> After soft showers; and sweet the coming on
> Of grateful Ev'ning mild, then silent Night
> With this her solemn Bird and this fair Moon,
> And these the Gems of Heav'n, her starry train:
> But neither breath of Morn when she ascends
> With charm of earliest Birds, nor rising Sun
> On this delightful land, nor herb, fruit, flow'r,
> Glist'ring with dew, nor fragrance after showers,
> Nor grateful Ev'ning mild, nor silent Night
> With this her solemn Bird, nor walk by Moon,
> Or glittering Star-light without thee is sweet.

(4.641–56)

The principal effect of the passage is one of enclosure and depends on the careful placement of key words. The lyric's opening line, "Sweet is the breath of morn, her rising sweet," illustrates the effect in miniature by using the same word in its first and tenth syllables. The effect continues throughout the series of clauses that completes the initial part of the passage: "pleasant the Sun," "fragrant the fertile earth," and, finally, "sweet the coming on / Of grateful Ev'ning mild." What is being enclosed, of course, is the scale of creation from "morn" to "Ev'ning mild," settings for the sun and moon whose importance and interdependence are emphasized by their use as end-words in their respective lines.

The same phrases and images reappear in the second part of the lyric: the sun and moon again serve as end-words for their lines, but Eve's sense of the harmonious interrelationships among things would not be "sweet" without Adam as her companion. Eve's lyric on the mutual support and pairing of all things ends as it begins: the word "sweet" encloses the cycles and images of day and night in a circle, which, as a symbol of fullness and perfection, is appropriate to Eve's innocent state of being. The sixteen lines of Eve's lyric, which has been described mistakenly as a sonnet, are actually much more interesting and strictly unified in their use of key words to establish patterns of enclosure and circularity of evident symbolic value.[4]

By touching on the fullness of the scale of creation, such patterns of enclosure are notable, not for their exclusion or limitation of possibilities, but for their participation in a graceful range of complexity. In the verse paragraphs which immediately precede and follow Eve's love-lyric, Adam anticipates and echoes the imagery and form of Eve's speech. The phrase "Night bids us rest" concludes Adam's speech before Eve's lyric begins, and the words "night" and "rest" appear in the opening lines of Adam's verse paragraph as well, thereby encircling his thoughts on the mutually supportive cycles of their days and nights (4.610–33). As in Eve's lyric, so here the cyclical imagery and diction are at one with the formal design of the speech. After her lyric has ended and in response to her question about the role of starlight during their sleep, Adam considers the physical and spiritual natures of light and sound in relation to earth and earth's inhabitants. The speech is thirty lines long (4.659–88) and divides neatly into two fifteen-line halves (659–73; 674–88). In the first half, Adam notes the relationship of the stars to the sun: both sources of light, in a downward movement, irradiate the "earth," the word which appears prominently near the beginning (661) and end (672) of this portion of his speech. In the second half, he calls attention to the relationship of "Millions of spiritual Creatures," including perhaps angels, to their creator as the music of their praise rises from earth to "heaven," the word which surrounds this portion of the speech (676, 688). Thus, "Earth" and "Heaven" delimit their respective halves of the verse paragraph and, serving as end-words at the beginning (661) and conclusion (688) of the entire speech, circumscribe the mirror-effect of downward and upward motions of first physical and then spiritual forms of energy that ultimately "lift our thoughts to Heaven." Eve's love-lyric and the two surrounding speeches by Adam indicate that, to Milton, the presentation of the state of innocence is no mere study in reductive simplicity. Instead, the interaction of linguistic and formal symbols in these passages is sufficiently complex to create a coherent sense of an innocent reality that is complete in itself and that gives the impression of not needing to be encumbered with help from an additional and fallen level of discourse.

Opposed to the circles of perfection that befit the innocence of Adam and Eve is the surrounding presence of Satan, whose speeches and activities initiate and conclude book 4. Enclosing the perfection of Eden and its inhabitants is not enough, however: he needs to break through, as his attempt at the ear of Eve demonstrates. The measure of his success is suggested at the beginning of book 5 when Eve recounts her troubled dream, which begins with images similar to those of her love-lyric in book 4. The morning sun and evening moon with their attendant birds have been replaced by ''the night-warbling Bird, that now awake / Tunes sweetest his love-labor'd song'' and by a moon that shines ''with more pleasing light'' (5.40–42). In her dream, Eve says, ''I rose as at thy call, but found thee not'' (5.48). The theme of loving interdependence among all things has been replaced by Satan's theme of self-sufficiency.

Adam's explanation of the dream as a product of wayward faculties seems to satisfy Eve, but their restoration to untroubled innocence is completed by their morning-hymn which ensues shortly thereafter (5.153–208). Standing as the summation of Milton's art of innocence, the hymn, given its importance and complexity, is best seen whole with line-numbers and divisions noted in the margin:

These are thy glorious works, Parent of good,
Almighty, thine this universal Frame,
Thus wondrous fair; thyself how wondrous then!
Unspeakable, who sit'st above these Heavens
To us invisible or dimly seen
In these thy lowest works, yet these declare
Thy goodness beyond thought, and Power Divine:
Speak yee who best can tell, ye Sons of Light,
Angels, for yee behold him, and with songs
And choral symphonies, Day without Night,
Circle his Throne rejoicing, yee in Heav'n;
On Earth join all ye Creatures to extol
Him first, him last, him midst, and without end.
Fairest of Stars, last in the train of Night,
If better thou belong not to the dawn,
Sure pledge of day, that crown'st the smiling Morn
With thy bright Circlet, praise him in thy Sphere
While day arises, that sweet hour of Prime.
Thou Sun, of this great World both Eye and Soul,
Acknowledge him thy Greater, sound his praise
In thy eternal course, both when thou climb'st
And when high Noon hast gain'd, and when
        thou fall'st.
Moon, that now meet'st the orient Sun, now fli'st
With the fixt Stars, fixt in thir Orb that flies,
And yee five other wand'ring Fires that move
In mystic Dance not without Song, resound
His praise, who out of Darkness call'd up Light.
Air, and ye Elements the eldest birth
Of Nature's Womb, that in quaternion run
Perpetual Circle, multiform, and mix
And nourish all things, let your ceaseless change
Vary to our great Maker still new praise.
Ye Mists and Exhalations that now rise

From Hill or steaming Lake, dusky or grey,
Till the Sun paint your fleecy skirts with Gold,
In honor to the World's great Author rise,
Whether to deck with Clouds th' uncolor'd sky,
Or wet the thirsty Earth with falling showers,
Rising or falling still advance his praise.
His praise ye Winds, that from four Quarters blow,
Breathe soft or loud; and wave your tops, ye Pines,
With every Plant, in sign of Worship wave.
Fountains and yee, that warble, as ye flow,
Melodious murmurs, warbling tune his praise.
Join voices all ye living Souls; ye Birds,
That singing up to Heaven Gate ascend,
Bear on your wings and in your notes his praise;
Yee that in Waters glide, and yee that walk
The Earth, and stately tread, or lowly creep;
Witness if I be silent, Morn or Even,
To Hill, or Valley, Fountain, or fresh shade
Made vocal by my Song, and taught his praise.
Hail universal Lord, be bounteous still
To give us only good; and if the night
Have gather'd aught of evil or conceal'd,
Disperse it, as now light dispels the dark.

        (5.153–208)

Here patterns of enclosure and circles which symbolize innocent perfection receive their most highly developed expression in the entire epic. Direct addresses to the creator frame the hymn which in its body consists of direct addresses to different aspects of the creation. After the opening seven lines of praise to God and before the final four lines on the need for God's protective bounty, the hymn displays forty-five lines on the celestial and terrestrial elements of creation (160–204). These forty-five lines are symmetrically balanced: the first twenty address the celestial universe, then comes a middle section of five lines on the physical elements of the creation, and finally twenty more lines on the praise that comes from the earth. At the exact midpoint of these forty-five lines is the phrase ''Perpetual Circle,'' which describes how the elements intermix to form all things. Images and metaphors of circles dominate the hymn as well. The ''Sons of Light'' addressed at the beginning of the first twenty-line section ''Circle'' God's throne, the ''Fairest of Stars'' provides a ''bright Circlet'' to crown the morning, the fixed stars are whirled about in the moving ''Orb,'' and the entire passage is encircled by the word ''Light'' which serves as the end-word for lines one and twenty. The counter-balancing twenty-line section on the terrestrial scale of creation uses the word ''praise'' to end its major clauses, a praise that, according to other important words at the ends of lines, must ''rise'' and ''ascend'' as the passage touches on various aspects of earthly life associated with the springing forth of the morning light.

The symmetrical patterns of symbolic order just described would appear to counter the epic narrator's claim which immediately precedes the morning-hymn: namely, that such utterances from the innocent Adam and Eve are "Unmeditated" and spontaneous, occurring "in Prose or numerous Verse" (5.149,150). The "various style" (146) to which the narrator calls attention leads Joseph Summers to note the variety of strophic and syntactical lengths in the morning-hymn and to suggest that such variety is intrinsic to Milton's idea of perfection.[5] Now, it is demonstrably the case that the internal structure of the hymn is irregular and, by avoiding predictable lengths in its sections, fosters a sense of freedom; at the same time, it is equally demonstrable that the hymn fulfills strict patterns of symbolic order through its images, the placement of key words, and its overall design. Milton's articulation of the artistic principle in question also characterizes, of course, the "Mystical dance" of the angels and planets, whose motions are "regular / Then most, when most irregular they seem" (5.620–24). The striking conjunction of freedom and strict form in the morning-hymn, then, is no coincidence, as if we had simply caught Adam and Eve on a good day, but is one of Milton's most telling demonstrations of what characterizes the state of innocence: spontaneous perfection.

At the conclusion of Adam and Eve's morning-hymn, the epic's narrator observes, "So pray'd they innocent, and to thir thoughts / Firm peace recover'd soon and wonted calm" (5.209–10). Looking back, we have no difficulty in seeing how the morning-hymn accomplishes such a firm support to the theme of innocence. Its patterns of circular imagery and symmetry recall Eve's love-lyric in book 4 but on a larger scale and in a much more elaborate way, thereby reasserting the perfection of being assigned to Adam and Eve at the outset. The morning-hymn also recalls the scale of creation which here receives one of the most detailed and extensive treatments to be found in the epic. By this means, the theme of interdependence among all things is unequivocally restated and removes any traces of self-sufficiency as suggested by Satan to Eve in her dream. Looking ahead, we can anticipate Raphael's visit to Eden: in particular, his presentation of the scale of creation as a great tree of life (5.469–505). After listening to Raphael's speech, Adam provides a key to the symbolism with which we have been dealing: he is pleased with how the angel has

the scale of Nature set
From centre to circumference, whereon
In contemplation of created things
By steps we may ascend to God.

(5.509–12)

Of course, the orderliness of the spheres and circles of existence is a measure of the primal condition of perfection.

"So pray'd they innocent," but to read innocently is another matter. Even in the morning-hymn, the magnificent purity and control of style and expression cannot eliminate opportunities for verbal dissonance. When Adam and Eve call upon the "Fairest of Stars" to praise God with the planet's "bright Circlet" and "Sphere," it is difficult not to think of Venus as Lucifer, the morning star. Were Adam and Eve to know of Satan as the false Lucifer, as they will after the departure from Eden brings a tragic depth to their experience, they could not pray so confidently and avoid wrestling with language. For the reader, the problem is similar to that raised by Eve's "wanton ringlets" in book 4. The morning-hymn's "Mists and Exhalations" that nourish "the thirsty Earth with falling showers" and usher in the terrestrial praise of the creator present a related problem, given that in book 9 Satan enters Eden "involv'd in rising Mist" and moves about like "a black mist low creeping" (9.75,180). In the overall context of the poem, Milton's imagery seems designed to complicate and compromise depictions of innocence, leading to further considerations of what has been lost along with the simplicity of language.[6]

Within passages designed to express innocence, however, the function of circular patterns of enclosure is to temper linguistic complexity by supplying images of pure form that resist misinterpretation and by exemplifying those images through the symmetrical positioning of key words or other elements of poetic structure. The resulting language is purified, as it were, by the formal ritual of symbolic patterns, which are evident once more in our final example of dramatized innocence: Adam's account of his initial consciousness as a living being (8.249–91). The remarkable internal structure of the opening forty-three lines of Adam's long verse paragraph reveals a deft use of enclosure. The opening eight lines (249–56) and concluding nine lines (283–91) frame the central portion of twenty-six lines, which present Adam's first sensations and thoughts and which divide exactly in half. The key word in the framing lines around the central portion is "sleep," displayed prominently as the end-word of lines 253 and 287. Adam's account of his life's beginnings, which are thus literally and symbolically rounded with the word "sleep," then ensues (257–82), with each thirteen-line section being virtually the mirror-image of the other. In the first thirteen-line section, Adam's enchantment with the heavens prompts him to stand erect and then peruse the pastoral images around him before attending to his own physical abilities. What he has done is to go symbolically from the ethereal source of his being to an intuition of a scale of creation around him that ascends from "Hill, Dale, and shady Woods" to "Creatures that liv'd and mov'd" and, finally, to himself. In the second thirteen-line section, he is able to speak and name all that he perceives, repeat almost verbatim the images he has noted, and he concludes by inferring the existence of "some great Maker" to account for the existence and design of the world. The entire twenty-six lines thus end almost where they began. A sense of heavenly origins encircles Adam's creation, but the end has the additional creative glory of a self-reflexive and ordered language that enables him to express an exact sense of being happier than he knows. His first perceptions, first words, and first encircling sense of perfection all harmonize precisely to give the illusion of primordial innocence.

In the fallen world, however, great poets have repeatedly lamented the indeterminacy of language and have accordingly explored the greater precision which may be forged through symbolic form. Now, Milton is not unusual in employing symbolic form to control the waywardness of language when it relies on verbal meanings alone. Other instances pervade the history of poetry, and a few words should be added to distinguish between the tempering effect of symbolic form on language for general purposes in contrast to the depiction of innocence as a particular problem. Since we have been concerned with circles and spheres especially, let us use these figures to illustrate a few distinctions. Sometimes circles and spheres appear as basically uncomplicated descriptive images without having to perform larger tasks associated with symbolic form: such is their function, for example, in depicting elements of creation in book 7 of *Paradise Lost*. More often, though, their symbolic possibilities prove irresistible. To Ben Jonson, Donne, Herbert, Marvell, Dryden, and others in Milton's century, to name a few, circles and spheres have symbolic value that

focuses the themes of major poems. To T. S. Eliot in our century, the *Four Quartets* employ circles and patterns of enclosure to break away from the linear tyranny of time and the instability of words, which in "Burnt Norton" are said to

strain,
Crack and sometimes break, under the burden,
Under the tension, slip, slide, perish,
Decay with imprecision, will not stay in place,
Will not stay still.[7]

As a result, the *Four Quartets* attempt to set their images on a higher plane of symbolism in which beginnings and ends circle towards one another because

Only by the form, the pattern,
Can words or music reach
The stillness, as a Chinese jar still
Moves perpetually in its stillness.

("Burnt Norton," 5.140–43)

Thus, the word "stillness" is carefully positioned to enclose the simile of the Chinese jar in a demonstration of theme through the clarity of a formal pattern. To Eliot, circles are important for containing still, central points in a turning world of words. As such, the formal pattern uses language to evoke a sense of something beyond language, a transcendent order or symbol of permanence. There is necessarily a gap between temporal and symbolic realities as form supplements language. That gap or sense of dislocation is inherent in the nature of fallen language, which perforce relates to a fallen world, and is therefore characteristic of most symbolic discourse. By contrast, innocent perfection requires that there be no sense of dislocation.

The presentation of innocence presupposes acts of perception in which reality and appearance are indistinguishable in the union of language and symbolic form. In this respect, perhaps no poet since Milton has pondered the relationship of language to pure form so carefully as has Wordsworth, who, in his treatment of the theme of innocence, is even capable of expressing the process of perception by which innocence may be attained. An example of his ability to create a sense of innocence is in "Home at Grasmere" as the poet describes the sensation of living in that place:

'Tis, but I cannot name it, 'tis the sense
Of majesty, and beauty, and repose,
A blended holiness of earth and sky,
Something that makes this individual Spot,
This small Abiding-place of many Men,
A termination, and a last retreat,
A Centre, come from whereso'er you will,
A Whole without dependence or defect,

Made for itself; and happy in itself,
Perfect Contentment, Unity entire.[8]

The sensation Wordsworth cannot name is, of course, innocent perfection, which he is attempting to apply to his home ground. Language can only approximate that sensation, and so the passage, as it progresses, carefully refines its terms, using circles and patterns of enclosure to control the description, which becomes increasingly abstract and aligned with the purity of geometrical form, until it concludes in the line "Perfect Contentment, Unity entire" in which words of two syllables enclose those of three.[9] Here, as in the examples from *Paradise Lost*, all elements of language are coordinated to serve the symbolism of pure form and even express the process by which that coordination or union of perceptions is achieved. Wordsworth's memories of a more perfect state of being are, of course, at the heart of his endeavor to give them a life in the present throughout his major poetry, just as they are the source of the symbolic forms he employs in that endeavor. In *Paradise Lost*, Milton attempts a fiction which may seem even more daring: a sense that his innocent Eden is no mere memory but a perception of perfection on which memories will be based. For both Milton and Wordsworth, the results show, at the very least, how an illusion of perfection may be suggested beyond the capabilities of verbal meaning alone. At the most, a poignant sense of something ranging from the archetypal to the Platonic may be awakened as the particularities of language fade into insignificance.

[1] *John Milton: Complete Poems and Major Prose,* ed. Merritt Y. Hughes (New York: Odyssey Press, 1957), 285 (4.306, 312). Subsequent citations of *Paradise Lost* are from this edition and are indicated in the text by book and line numbers.

[2] W. B. Yeats, "The Song of the Happy Shepherd," *The Collected Poems of W. B. Yeats* (New York: Macmillan, 1956), 7.

[3] The difficulty of finding the right words and thoughts for paradise is admirably summarized by Ira Clark, "A Problem of Knowing Paradise in *Paradise Lost,*" *MS* 27 (1991): 183–207. Finding words and thoughts for fallen conditions leads A. Bartlett Giamatti to go so far as to posit a "Satanic style" of ambiguities and dissonance; see *The Earthly Paradise and the Renaissance Epic* (Princeton: Princeton Univ. Press, 1966), 303ff. Without pausing to qualify such views, we must respect the impulse that leads to them. Perhaps Peter Berek's

guidelines for a distinction between innocent and fallen language are as fair as anyone's:

> Milton, I suggest, has used a certain kind of 'poetical' manipulation of facts by means of language as a powerful metaphor for corruption, and, conversely, uses patterns of words that give the effect of imitating rather than manipulating reality as a way of presenting figures of innocence and perfection. ("'Plain' and 'Ornate' Styles and the Structure of *Paradise Lost,*" *PMLA* 85 [March, 1970]: 246)

Moving from questions of diction to the larger arena of forms, we might wish to consider the function of unrhymed sonnets and the divine proportion as ways of expressing and redeeming fallen language: see Lee Johnson, "Milton's Blank Verse Sonnets," *MS* 5 (1973): 129–53; for the divine proportion, see Lee Johnson, "Milton's Epic Style: The Invocations in *Paradise Lost,*" *The Cambridge Companion to Milton,* ed. Dennis Danielson (Cambridge: Cambridge Univ. Press, 1989), 65–78.

[4] For a discussion and notes on Eve's love-lyric as a Petrarchan-style sonnet, see Barbara K. Lewalski, *"Paradise Lost" and the Rhetoric of Literary Forms* (Princeton: Princeton Univ. Press, 1985), 188, 344 n. 42; also, Barbara K. Lewalski, "The Genres of *Paradise Lost,*" *The Cambridge Companion to Milton,* ed. Dennis Danielson (Cambridge: Cambridge Univ. Press, 1989), 88.

[5] Joseph H. Summers, *The Muse's Method: An Introduction to "Paradise Lost"* (London: Chatto and Windus, 1962), 77–78. For another way of dividing the morning-hymn, see John Hollander, *The Figure of Echo: A Mode of Allusion in Milton and After* (Berkeley: Univ. of California Press, 1981), 39.

[6] The expressive ambiguities and dissonances of Milton's style have long elicited first-rate comments; in addition to the items by Clark, Berek, and Giamatti cited in n. 3, Ricks, Swaim, and Leonard have provided astute and provocative observations on the complexity of Milton's words. When Christopher Ricks says, "with the Fall of Man, language falls too," he shows how corruptions infect words such as "wanton," "error," and numerous others: see *Milton's Grand Style* (Oxford: Clarendon Press, 1963), 109–11. In *Before and After the Fall: Contrasting Modes in "Paradise Lost"* (Amherst: Univ. of Massachusetts Press, 1986), Kathleen Swaim discusses the morning-hymn and its troublesome "Fairest of Stars" as well as adding to our sense of puns and ambiguities in Milton's diction (70, 185–86). Most thoroughly and admirably, John Leonard's *Naming in Paradise: Milton and the Lan-*

*guage of Adam and Eve* (Oxford: Clarendon Press, 1990) corroborates and extends Ricks's work: Leonard's final chapter, ''Prelapsarian Language and the Poet,'' is especially relevant throughout to our consideration of subtleties in the morning-hymn and in Edenic language generally (233–92).

[7] T. S. Eliot, ''Burnt Norton,'' *Four Quartets* (London: Faber and Faber, 1959), 19 (5.149–53). The subsequent citation of ''Burnt Norton'' is indicated in the text by section and line numbers.

[8] *Wordsworth's Poetical Works,* ed. Ernest de Selincourt and Helen Darbishire, 5 vols. (Oxford: Clarendon Press, 1949), 5:318.

[9] In this passage ''Home at Grasmere,'' the symbolism of geometrical form goes beyond the local qualities of diction to the design of the entire verse paragraph in which our passage serves as the conclusion. Echoing Milton's Edenic language, Wordsworth places his careful evocation of Grasmere in the overall pattern of a divine proportion, a geometrical way of interrelating smaller and larger sections of a verse paragraph into a symbol of interaction between temporal and timeless realities. The circles of innocent perfection which occupy us here thus reside in an overall context of geometrical symbolism which is suited to the fallen world and which, as indicated in n. 1, is also a key ingredient in Milton's art. Wordsworth's example, which blends a local pattern of innocence (the circle) with a larger design of experience (the divine proportion), is a superb triumph of his rational imagination that introduces rich complexities which deserve a separate discussion: see Lee Johnson, *Wordsworth's Metaphysical Verse: Geometry, Nature, and Form* (Toronto: Univ. of Toronto Press, 1982), 194–97.

**Source:** Lee M. Johnson, ''Language and the Illusion of Innocence in *Paradise Lost,*'' in *Of Poetry and Politics: New Essays on Milton and His World,* edited by P. G. Stanwood, *Medieval & Renaissance Texts and Studies ,* Vol. 126, 1995, pp. 47–58.

## *J. Martin Evans*

*In the following essay, the critic examines Milton's* Paradise Lost *for indications that it includes references to and thoughts on the colonization of the American continent by Europeans at the time it was written.*

In his comprehensive study of the North Atlantic world, K. G. Davies remarks that ''no major English literary work of the seventeenth century comes to mind that breathes an Atlantic air or takes the American empire for its theme.''[1] The purpose of this essay is to suggest that *Paradise Lost* constitutes at least a partial exception to Davies's generalization. Milton's epic, I believe, interacts continuously with the deeply ambivalent feelings which the conquest of the New World generated in seventeenth-century English culture. Like its closest classical model, the *Aeneid, Paradise Lost* seems to me to be, among other things, a poem about empire.[2]

Certainly, there were many reasons for pondering the colonization of America as Milton turned his attention back to his long-delayed plans for an epic poem in the mid-1650s. The Commonwealth's war with Spain had rekindled anti-Spanish sentiment, and writers in tune with the mood of the times were busy turning out works based on the so-called ''black legend'' of Spanish brutality in South America—Milton's nephew John Phillips, for instance, translated Las Casas' *Brevissima relacion de la destruycion de las Indias* into English in 1656, and in 1658 Sir William Davenant, the erstwhile governor-designate of Maryland, catered to prevailing English taste with his sensational play on the same subject, *The Cruelty of the Spaniards*. Still more to the point, Cromwell's ''Western Design'' and the conflict with Spain it precipitated served as a vivid reminder that England, too, was a major colonial power. Indeed, the crucial first phase of English empire-building in the New World coincided more or less exactly with Milton's lifetime. The year before he was born the first English settlers dispatched by the Virginia Company of London arrived in Chesapeake Bay. The establishment of the Plymouth colony took place when he was eleven, the widely publicized Virginia massacre when he was thirteen, and the great Puritan migration to Massachusetts Bay while he was in his twenties. He was thirty-five when the second Virginia massacre occurred, forty-six when Cromwell acquired Jamaica. By the time he had reached his fifties, England was the dominant colonial power in North America with between twenty-five and thirty thousand settlers in New England and thirty-six thousand or so in Virginia.[3]

What is more, by the time he began to work on *Paradise Lost* Milton had come into contact with numerous men who had promoted or emigrated to the colonies. Ralph Hamor, the author of *A True Discourse of the Present State of Virginia,* grew up in the house next to the Milton family home on Bread Street. Several of his Cambridge contemporaries emigrated to New England, and his longtime friend Samuel Hartlib produced a treatise on the

Virginian silk-worm. Sir Henry Vane, to whom Milton addressed an admiring sonnet in 1652, was a former governor of Massachusetts. And Roger Williams, the notorious champion of religious liberty and Indian property rights, gave him conversation lessons in Dutch in the early 1650s.[4] It is hardly surprising, then, that Milton's writings are liberally sprinkled with references to the colonization of the New World.

Not that Milton needed large numbers of close friends and acquaintances actively involved in the settlement of America in order to be vividly aware of its progress. For "this glorious business," as William Crashaw called it,[5] was deeply imprinted in the national consciousness of seventeenth-century England, inscribed there by dozens of promotional pamphlets, controversial tracts, personal histories, and economic analyses. From 1609 to 1624 the London bookstalls were inundated with sermons and treatises either prophesying or proclaiming the success of the English plantation in Virginia. Beginning with the publication of *Mourt's Relation* in 1622, there followed a steady stream of works recording the early history of New England, detailing the political and religious controversies going on there, and asserting the progress of the gospel among the Indians. Then in the mid-1650s came a spate of tracts reporting on the power struggle between the Catholic proprietor Lord Baltimore and his Puritan adversaries in Maryland. Whether or not he had a personal stake in the success of the American colonies, Milton could hardly avoid being aware of events taking place on the other side of the Atlantic.

With the exception of a handful of works by New England dissidents like Samuel Gorton and John Child, most of the literature I have just mentioned took a wholeheartedly positive view of England's transatlantic activities. Yet just beneath the surface of even the most optimistic evaluations of England's settlements in the New World there runs a powerful undercurrent of barely repressed anxiety concerning the entire colonial enterprise. For over and over again the promoters complain that Virginia and New England have been unjustly slandered by various unnamed detractors.

Few, if any, of these reported slanders were ever printed—like the heresies of the early Christian church they owe their preservation to the writers who endeavored to refute them—but they clearly constituted a powerful critique of England's activities across the Atlantic. As a result, whether they are excusing the failure of the New World to live up to expectations in some regard, or defending Virginia and New England against some allegedly unjustified criticism from their detractors, seventeenth-century English descriptions of America are relentlessly defensive. From Daniel Price's *Saul's Prohibition Staide. . . with a reproofe of those that traduce the Honourable Plantation of Virginia* (London, 1609) to John Hammond's *Leah and Rachel. . . With a Removall of such Imputations as are scandalously cast on those Countries* (London, 1656) justification is the keynote.

Nor is it difficult to understand why a seventeenth-century English protestant might have harbored deeply ambivalent feelings about his country's American colonies. To begin with, their history had hardly been a happy one. After a disastrous beginning, which cost many of the adventurers their investments and hundreds of planters their lives, Virginia had sided with the king during the civil war and only with the very greatest reluctance had accepted the authority of the Commonwealth commissioners dispatched by Cromwell. As John Hammond put it, England's first plantation was "whol for monarchy, and the last Country belonging to England that submitted to obedience of the Common-wealth of England."[6] Maryland, despite several attempts to reverse Lord Baltimore's policy of religious toleration, was still a haven for English Catholics, "a receptacle for Papists, and Priests, and Jesuites" as one writer called it.[7] New England, riven by internal disputes in the 1630s and 1640s, was regarded in many quarters as "a Nursery of Schismatickes,"[8] and had in any case lost a great deal of its ideological *raison d'être* now that the reform of the church had been accomplished in England. And finally, as the century wore on, English protestants were becoming increasingly concerned about the question of native American property rights and the failure of the English missionaries to convert the Indians to the reformed religion.

For all these reasons, then, the colonization of America stirred deeply ambivalent feelings in the collective consciousness of seventeenth-century England. *Paradise Lost,* I now want to suggest, not only registers many of these ambivalences, but plays them out in mythic form by reenacting on the cosmic stage many of the central events in the conquest of the New World. The argument is a complex one to which I am in the course of devoting an entire book, but in this brief "prospectus" I may be able to illustrate my general thesis by discussing the way in which Milton treats the central figure in the colonial drama, the colonist himself. He appears in *Paradise Lost* in various guises: most obviously as Satan, the diabolic deceiver who enslaves the inhabitants of the New World by cheating them out of their territory and replacing them with his own destructive plenipotentiaries; but also as Raphael, the divine missionary who brings to Adam and Eve the authentic word of God and instructs them in the history of the ancient rivalry of which their world is the focal point; then as Adam, the indentured servant placed in the paradisal garden by "the sovran Planter" (4.691) and destined for release from his labors after a fixed period of obedient toil; and finally as Michael, the representative of imperial authority who drives the rebellious natives out of their original home into the alien wilderness.

To begin with Satan, during the course of his triumphant speech in book 10 announcing the conquest of Eden, the devil sounds at times very much like Amerigo Vespucci reporting back to Lorenzo Pietro di Medici on his latest voyage to the New World. The echoes are probably accidental, but the general resemblance is not, for of the various roles that Satan plays in *Paradise Lost* none is more richly elaborated than his impersonation of a Renaissance explorer. It has often been noticed, for example, that Milton arranges the early part of the story so that we experience it as a diabolic voyage of discovery. Just as Columbus and his contemporaries heard rumors of the New World long before its existence had been confirmed, so we learn from Satan in book 1 that "a fame in Heav'n" has spread stories of "new Worlds" (650–51) elsewhere in the universe. In books 2 and 3 we then accompany him on the perilous "voyage" (2. 426, 919) across the "gulf" (2. 441) of chaos to "the coast of Earth" (3. 739). And at the beginning of book 4 we finally see the terrestrial paradise at least partially through the Devil's consciousness.

The motives which impel Satan on his voyage replicate, in turn, virtually all the social and political arguments advanced in favor of England's colonial expansion in the late sixteenth and early seventeenth centuries. The first of them emerges in Beelzebub's speech at the end of the infernal debate in book 2. After mentioning the rumors circulating in Heaven about the creation of the world, he proposes that even though

Heav'n be shut,
. . . this place may lie expos'd
The utmost border of his Kingdom, left
To their defense who hold it: here perhaps
Some advantageous act may be achiev'd

By sudden onset. . . .

(2. 358–64, Hughes edition)

This bears a startling resemblance to the political rationale for Elizabethan attacks on Spanish possessions in the New World a century before.[9] Indeed, Beelzebub's proposal momentarily transforms Satan into a demonic Sir Francis Drake setting off to singe God's beard. On one level, at least, the assault on Eden will be a daring naval raid by an infernal buccaneer.

The second motive for undertaking the journey across chaos is disclosed by Satan himself in his parting speech to his followers in Pandemonium, Oppressed by God's vengeance, he tells them, "I abroad / Through all the Coasts of dark destruction seek / Deliverance for us all" (2.464–65). In a diabolic parody of the pilgrims on the *Mayflower* he presents himself as the ultimate separatist, a victim of religious persecution in search of a new home where he and his fellow dissidents can practice their infernal rites in peace—in heaven, we have already been told by Mammon, the angels were constrained by "Strict Laws impos'd" to celebrate God's throne with Laudian ceremoniousness, worshipping their "envied Sovran" with "warbl'd Hymns" and "Forc'd Halleluiahs" (2.242–44). Like the faithful and freeborn Englishmen who, in Milton's words in *Of Reformation* "have bin constrained to forsake their dearest home, their friends and kindred, whom nothing but the wide Ocean, and the savage deserts of *America* could hide and shelter from the fury of the Bishops,"[10] the Devil claims to be seeking refuge from the oppression of a tyrannical power.

As Satan approaches the garden of Eden, however, a third motive makes its appearance. His underlying purpose, he now confesses, is territorial expansion. By raiding this vulnerable outpost of the heavenly kingdom he hopes to share at least "Divided Empire with Heav'ns King" (4.111). Hence the extraordinary scene in book 10 when Sin greets her triumphant parent at the foot of the "wondrous Pontifice" (348) which she and her son have constructed across chaos "by wonddrous Art / Pontifical" (312–13). Henceforth, she declares, let the Creator "Monarchy with thee divide / Of all things, parted by th'Empyreal bounds" (379–80). Cued by Milton's anti-papal puns, we seem to be witnessing a grotesque reenactment of Alexander VI's division of the western world between the Spanish and the Portuguese, a cosmic *inter caetera.*

During the course of the poem, then, Satan rehearses virtually all the major roles in the repertoire of English colonial discourse. By turns buccaneer, pilgrim, and empire-builder, he embodies not only the destructive potential of imperial conquest but its glamour and energy as well. It may well be no accident that the critical glorification of Milton's devil took place during the heyday of England's imperial power while his descent from hero to fool coincided with its decline.

Satan is not the only figure in the poem who embodies the colonial quest, however. God's emissaries, too, function as agents of imperial authority. Indeed, Raphael has in some ways even more in common with the explorers than his diabolical antagonist. For the extraordinary scene in which the archangel is greeted by two naked human beings as a ''Native of Heaven'' (5.361) reenacts an encounter which had been described in countless Renaissance descriptions of the discoverers' arrival in the New World. Like the ideally submissive and subservient Indians of those early narratives, Adam welcomes his ''god-like'' (351) visitor ''with submiss approach and reverence meek'' (359). Unquestioningly he agrees that he possesses the garden of Eden ''by sovran gift'' (366) from Raphael's divine master. Then he and Eve proceed to entertain the ''Heav'nly stranger'' (316, 397) in their ''Silvan Lodge'' (377) with all the bounty their world has to offer.

Unlike Columbus and his successors, of course, Adam's visitor really has come from heaven. As the ''Empyreal Minister'' (5.460) of the Almighty, his function is to instruct Adam and Eve in the indispensable colonial virtues of loyalty and obedience, to give them a brief lesson in the recent political history of the cosmos, and most important of all to alert them to the existence of an unfriendly rival power at large in the universe (5.233–41). In place of the Indians' tragic misconception of their future oppressors, the poem thus offers us an authentic encounter between man and angel, an encounter in which the problematic territorial and political claims of Spain and England have given way to the Creator's legitimate authority over his creation. In *Paradise Lost* the anxiety attaching to the discoveries has been relieved by the simple device of re-writing the scene as if the Indians and the Spanish had both been right. This visitor really does come from heaven, as the Indians believed, and the sovereign he represents really does own the land, as the Spanish, and later the English, insisted.

Thanks to Milton's revision of the primal imperial encounter, Adam and Eve are consequently spared the violent aftermath of Columbus's arrival in the New World. Unlike the Indians, they do not experience the horrors of Renaissance warfare at first hand; they learn about such murderous inventions as gunpowder only at second hand from their heavenly instructor. The appalling butchery and violence which characterized the Spanish conquest of America is thus projected onto Satan's campaign against his Maker.

When the natives do eventually rebel against their master, they receive a second visitor from heaven, with orders to drive them forth ''without remorse'' (11.105) from their terrestrial paradise into the wilderness beyond it. Michael's mission in books 11–12 thus recapitulates in mythic form not only Spain's campaigns in Mexico and Peru— Adam is shown the seats of Montezuma and Atabalipa (11.407–9)—but England's more recent dispossession of the Indians in New England and Virginia. The image of the colonist as a ruthless invader is too powerful to exclude entirely, and although Milton insists that the garden will remain empty once Adam and Eve have vacated it (11.101–3;123–25), their expulsion by a force of ''flaming Warriors'' (11.101) could hardly have failed to summon up in the minds of Milton's readers disquieting memories of the final act of the colonial drama.

The colonial figures we have considered so far were all, for one reason or another, eager to cross the Atlantic. A significant portion of the early emigrants to England's colonies, however, had to be actively recruited as indentured servants. Essentially indentured service was a mechanism which permitted potential emigrants to be shipped to America at the expense of a colonial landowner to whom they were subsequently bound as servants for a fixed term of years, usually four or five. In return for their transportation across the Atlantic and their food, lodging, and clothing in the colony, they worked on their master's property without wages until their term of service expired, at which time they received enough cash, provisions, and land to set up as independent smallholders themselves.[11]

Seen in this general context, Adam's situation in *Paradise Lost* resembles nothing so much as an idealized form of indentured servitude. Placed in an earthly paradise by the ''sovran Planter'' (4.691), he is destined to serve out a fixed term of ''pleasant labor'' (4.625) at the end of which, ''by long obedience tri'd'' (7.159), he may be given the status of an angel and allowed to dwell permanently in the terrestrial or the celestial paradise (5.500). His biblical counterpart, of course, had long been regarded as a paradigm of the colonial settler. In 1612 Robert Johnson, for example, commended "that most wholesome, profitable and pleasant work of planting in which it pleased God himself to set the first man and most excellent creature Adam in his innocencie."[12] But in *Paradise Lost* the current of correspondence between the two figures is reversed: the colonist doesn't resemble Adam so much as Adam resembles the colonist. The result is a vision of prelapsarian man unlike any other in the history of the Genesis myth. To take just one example, the concept of indentured labor may well be responsible for the quite unprecedented significance which Milton gives to Adam's daily toil in *Paradise Lost.* As I have shown elsewhere,[13] in no other version of the biblical story is the necessity of cultivating the garden so emphatically asserted.

When Adam and Eve eventually break the terms of their contract, moreover, they behave at first like run-away servants—they hide from their master and blame him for their disobedience. Adam, in particular, makes it sound as if he had been kidnapped by a "spirit," as the agents of the colonial landowners were called, and forced to work against his will on God's plantation:

> . . . did I solicit thee
> From darkness to promote me, or here place
> In this delicious Garden?

> (10.744–46)

In spite of the care with which the system of indentured labor has been purged of its most flagrant abuses—in Milton's definition of the human situation the master is benevolent and just, the servants are well fed and well lodged, the labor is strenuous but not backbreaking—a residue of uneasiness is still detectable in Adam's protest. He may admit that "then should have been refus'd / Those terms whatever, when they were propos'd" (10.756–57), but the lawyerly debating point cannot entirely dispose of the underlying objection. For when Adam was presented with the conditions of his contract, his existence was already a *fait accompli*. Like the convicted criminals who were beginning to be shipped to the New World in ever greater numbers as the seventeenth century wore on, Eden's original colonist had only two choices: indenture or death.

As these examples may suggest, Milton not only divides the role of colonist among the various characters in his poem. He associates the characters in his poem with different colonial roles at different points of the narrative. In some episodes, we have seen, Adam resembles the English settlers laboring in indentured servitude on a royal plantation; in others, he has more in common with the Indians welcoming Columbus to their American paradise. Clearly these contradictions and disjunctions do not permit a naive, uniplanar interpretation of the poem—we cannot simply equate God with James I, Eden with Virginia, and then read the poem as a straightforward political allegory about the conquest of America. My point is both simpler and more complicated. Milton's epic, I believe, not only breathes an Atlantic air but expresses in all their bewildering complexity the radically divided attitudes towards the American empire which existed in seventeenth-century English protestant culture.

[1] K. G. Davies, *The North Atlantic World in the Seventeenth Century* (Minneapolis: Univ. of Minnesota Press, 1974), 325.

[2] The word echoes and re-echoes throughout the text of *Paradise Lost.* See: 1.114; 2.296, 310, 315, 327, 378, 446; 4.145, 390; 5.724, 801; 7.96, 555, 585, 609; 10.389, 592; 12.32, 581.

[3] Davies, 63.

[4] See W. R. Parker, *John Milton: A Biography* (Oxford: Clarendon, 1968), 1.53, 410; 2.698, 1008.

[5] William Crashaw, Preface to Alexander Whitaker's *Good Newes from Virginia* (London, 1613), A2ʳ.

[6] *Leah and Rachel* (London, 1656), 22.

[7] Anon., *Virginia and Maryland* (London, 1655), 199–200.

[8] John White, *The Planter's Plea* (London, 1630), 37.

[9] See, for example, Hakluyt's *Discourse concerning Western Planting* (1584), chap. 5.

[10] CPW 3:49–50.

[11] For this account I have relied principally on: Abbott E. Smith, *Colonists in Bondage: White Servitude and Convict Labor in America* 1607–1776 (Chapel Hill: Univ. of North Carolina Press, 1965), chap. 1; Carl Bridenbaugh, *Vexed and Troubled Englishmen* 1590–1642 (New York: Oxford Univ. Press, 1968), chap. 11.

[12] Robert Johnson, *The New Life of Virginia* (London, 1612), 17.

[13] "Native Innocence" in *"Paradise Lost" and the Genesis Tradition* (Oxford: Clarendon, 1968).

**Source:** J. Martin Evans, "Milton's Imperial Epic," in *Of Poetry and Politics: New Essays on Milton and His World,* edited by P. G. Stanwood, *Medieval & Renaissance Texts and Studies,* Vol. 126, 1995, pp. 229–38.

## Sources for Further Study

Adams, Robert M. and George M. Logan, eds. "The Seventeenth Century" in *The Norton Anthology of English Literature,* 6th ed., Vol. I. Norton, 1993.

> Provides a good introduction to both the period and the poem, situating *Paradise Lost* in the context of Milton's life and works, the seventeenth century as a whole, and the epic tradition.

Berry, Boyd M. *Process of Speech: Puritan Religious Writings and "Paradise Lost".* Johns Hopkins University Press, 1976.

> Discusses *Paradise Lost* in the context of the English Civil Wars and Puritan ideology. He compares the battle scenes in heaven to the unheroic Puritan militarism of Cromwell's troops.

Christensen, Inger. "'Thy Great Deliverer': Christian Hero and Epic Convention in John Milton's *Paradise Lost* and C. S. Lewis's *Perelandra*," in Kennedy, Andrew and Overland, Orm (eds), *Excursions in Fiction,* pp. 68-88. Novus, 1994.

> Compares the presentation of the epic hero and the epic form in *Paradise Lost* to C. S. Lewis's science fiction trilogy, especially *Perelandra*

Daiches, David. *Milton.* Hutchinson and Co., 1957.

> Provides an excellent introduction to Milton's major works, including a general overview and reading of *Paradise Lost.*

DuRocher, Richard J. "Dante, Milton and the Art of Visual Speech," *Comparative Literature Studies,* Vol. 27, no. 3, 1990, pp. 157-71.

> Provides a comparison of Milton's use of the epic tradition in *Paradise Lost* with Dante's use of the same tradition in *The Divine Comedy*

Dyson, A.E. and Julian Lovelock, eds. *Milton: "Paradise Lost": A Casebook.* Macmillan, 1973.

> Provides a selection of critical responses to the poem, ranging from its earliest reception to 1973.

Eliot, T. S. "Milton," *The Sewanee Review,* Vol. LVI, no. 2, Spring 1948, pp. 185-209.

> Repeats but modifies his earlier claim that Milton was a bad influence on later writers, retracting this claim in part.

———. "Milton II," in his *On Poetry and Poets,* pp. 165-183. Farrar, Straus and Cudahy, 1957.

> Close analysis of Milton's versification, through which Eliot argues that Milton's influence on later authors and on the English language is a bad one.

Empson, William. *Milton's God.* Chatto and Windus, 1961.

> Studies Milton's major works for evidence of his beliefs about God. He develops the claim made by Blake and others that Milton unconsciously elevates Satan to the role of the epic hero, presenting God as, by contrast, a rather weak character. This is a classic study and well worth reading.

Evans, J. Martin. "Milton's Imperial Epic," in Stanwood, P.G., ed, *Of Poetry and Politics: New Essays on Milton and His World,* pp. 229-38. Medieval and Renaissance Texts and Studies, 1995.

> Studies *Paradise Lost* in relation to its historical context, relating it in particular to the imperialism and colonialism of seventeenth-century England.

Fish, Stanley. *Surprised by Sin: The Reader in "Paradise Lost".* Macmillan and St. Martin's, 1967.

> A classic study, in which Fish answers the arguments of critics who suggest that Satan is the true "hero" of the poem. Fish argues that Milton's presentations of Satan and God are deliberate attempts to manipulate the reader, thus showing both the attraction and the danger of evil.

Frye, Northrop. "Agon and Logos" in his *Spiritus Mundi: Essays on Literature, Myth, and Society,* pp. 201-27. Indiana University Press, 1970.

> Studies the use of classical genres in Milton's major poetry.

Gardner, Helen. *A Reading of "Paradise Lost".* Oxford University Press, 1965.

> A classic study by a leading Milton scholar. Gardner examines such issues as the subject matter of the poem, the character of Satan, Milton's personal comments through the voice of the narrator, and the human elements of the poem.

Golstein, Vladimir. "Tolstoj and Milton: How to Open an Epic," *Studies in Scottish Literature,* Vol. 40, 1994, pp. 23-36.

> Compares the use of the epic genre in *Paradise Lost* and Tolstoy's *War and Peace*

Hughes, Merritt Y., ed. *John Milton: Complete Poems and Major Prose.* Odyssey Press, 1957.

> The standard edition of Milton's poetry and translations of his major prose works. Hughes provides an excellent introduction to each piece, as well as extensive annotations to the texts.

Hutson, Arthur E. and McCoy, Patricia. *Epics of the Western World.* J.B. Lippincott, 1954.

> Provides a solid introduction to the epic form and to the major epics of western civilization, from Homer and Virgil to Dante and Milton.

Johnson, Lee M. "Language and the Illusion of Innocence in *Paradise Lost,*" in Stanwood, P.G., ed., *Of Poetry and Politics: New Essays on Milton and His World,* pp. 47-58. Medieval and Renaissance Texts and Studies, 1995.

> Explores Milton's use of language and symbolism in relation to themes of innocence and the loss thereof.

Kurth, Burton O. *Milton and Christian Heroism: Biblical Epic Themes and Forms in Seventeenth Century England,* University of California Publications, English Studies 20. University of California Press, 1959.

Explores the poem as a cosmic drama which exposes true and false heroism. He focuses on the idea of the Christian hero as a fallen hero.

Langford, Larry L. "Adam and the Subversion of Paradise," *Studies in English Literature,* Vol. 34, No. 1, Winter, 1994, pp. 119-34.
Studies the nature of humankind as expressed through Adam and the problems of man's relation to paradise.

Lewis, C. S. *A Preface to "Paradise Lost".* Oxford University Press, 1942.
A now-standard work which provides an excellent introduction to the poem, with a positive view of *Paradise Lost* as a great Christian epic as well as a classic of English literature.

Low, Lisa and Anthony John Harding, eds. *Milton, the Metaphysicals and Romanticism.* Cambridge University Press, 1994.
A new volume studying the influence of Milton on the romantic poets. A must for any student of literary heritage.

Martin, Roberta C. "'Thy Heart's Desire': God the Father and the Feminine Ideal in Milton's Perfect World," *English Language Notes,* Vol. 33, no. 4, June 1996, pp. 43- 52.
Provides a feminist reading of the character of God the father as it relates to the feminine ideal in the poem.

Norvell, Betty G. "Milton's Satan: Origins and Nomenclature," *The Bulletin of the West Virginia Association of College English Teachers,* Vol. 12, Fall, 1990, pp. 26- 34.
Provides a study of the sources for the presentation of Satan in *Paradise Lost.*

Pavlock, Barbara. "Milton's Criticism of Classical Epic in *Paradise Lost,*" in *The Classical Heritage: Vergil,* edited by Craig Kallendorf, pp. 291-314. Garland, 1993.
Shows how *Paradise Lost* can be read as a critique of the classical epic genre by comparing the poem to Virgil and Homer.

Peter, John. *A Critique of "Paradise Lost."* Columbia University Press and Longman, 1960.
Provides an insightful analysis of the "satanist" argument (that Milton was unintentionally of the devil's party), and continues the arguments begun by Waldock.

Porter, William M. *Reading the Classics and "Paradise Lost".* University of Nebraska Press, 1993.
Pedagogical approach to the relationship between *Paradise Lost* and the classics, providing a useful introduction for first-time students.

Ricks, Christopher. *Milton's Grand Style.* Oxford University Press, 1963.
Another now-standard study of Milton's epic style which is a fine analysis of the power of Milton's poetry and his command of language. This is a "must read."

———, Christopher, ed. *John Milton: "Paradise Lost" and "Paradise Regained".* Signet, 1968.

An inexpensive and extremely useful edition of the two poems, with a good introduction, a short bibliography, and brief but useful notes.

Rumrich, John. "Milton's God and the Matter of Chaos," *PMLA,* Vol. 110, no. 5, October, 1995, pp. 1035-46.
Examines the presentation of chaos and the story of the creation in *Paradise Lost* and compares it to the ancient Near Eastern creation story, *The Enuma Elish.*
This would be a useful study to those who are interested in the epic style in Milton and *The Epic of Gilgamesh.*

Sharratt, Bernard. "The Appropriation of Milton," *Essays and Studies,* Vol. 35, 1982, 30-44.
Studies the influence of Milton on later authors. This is an excellent source for students interested in the literary descendants of Milton and the lasting influence of his work.

Steadman, John M. "The Arming of an Archetype: Heroic Virtue and the Conventions of Literary Epic," in *Concepts of the Hero in the Middle Ages and the Renaissance,* ed. Norman T. Burns and Christopher J. Reagan, pp. 147-96. SUNY, 1975.
Explores the use of the Homeric epic tradition in *Paradise Lost* and *Paradise Regained,* arguing that both involve a reworking of the readers' expectations concerning the epic form.

Tillyard, E. M. W. *Studies in Milton.* Chatto and Windus, 1951.
A collection of Tillyard's major essays on Milton, and is a good representation of the thought of a major scholar in the field.

von Maltzahn, Nicholas. "The First Reception of *Paradise Lost,*" *The Review of English Studies,* Vol. XLVII, No. 188, November, 1986, pp. 479-99.
Provides an insightful study of the early reaction to *Paradise Lost* at the time of its publication, relating it to the social and political concerns of its day.

Waldock, A. J. A. *"Paradise Lost" and Its Critics.* Cambridge University Press, 1947.
Written by one of the first twentieth-century critics to take up the "satanist" argument. While not a particularly good analysis, and less insightful than Peter or Empson, Waldock was the first critic who attempted to "answer" C. S. Lewis, and is therefore interesting in terms of the history of criticism.

Webber, Joan Malory. *Milton and His Epic Tradition.* University of Washington Press, 1979.
Offers a fresh look at the relationship between *Paradise Lost* and the epic tradition, examining the poem in terms of seventeenth-century thought and concluding that it is a "subversive" epic.

Willey, Basil. *The Seventeenth-Century Background: Studies in the Thought of the Age in Relation to Poetry and Religion.* Routledge and Kegan Paul, 1934, repr. 1979.
An indispensable, now-standard study. Willey provides an extremely useful and insightful study of seventeenth–century religious, philosophical, and scientific thought, relating it to major authors of the time, including Milton.

# Sundiata

## Djeli Mamoudou Kouyaté

## c. 1200–1400

This tale tells of Sundiata, the great thirteenth-century ruler of Mali. The story comes to us through the centuries from a long line of oral historians, or *griots,* who are charged with keeping the memories of the past alive. Once only available to those who could understand the native language of the griot, which in the case of *Sundiata* is Malinké (or Mandingo), this epic tale intrigued Mali historian Djibril Tamsir Niane. He transcribed the words of the griot Djeli Mamoudou Kouyaté and produced a French translation in 1960. In 1965 an English translation by G. Pickett appeared.

*Sundiata* illustrates the anthropological importance of saving the words of the oral historians before the advent of literacy extinguishes their memories. Griots, like most oral historians, work for a particular patron, and as the patronage system falls into decline, these tale-weavers are less and less able to support themselves with their words. The significance of these oral historians is underlined in the epic itself: a griot plays an important role in helping Sundiata defeat his enemy Soumaoro.

In addition, the story of *Sundiata* contains important lessons for people of all times. Appearances can be deceiving, we learn: Sundiata's physically repulsive mother becomes an honored queen, and Sundiata himself overcomes a severe handicap to become a great warrior. Hospitality pays, as those rulers who receive Sundiata well during his period

as an outcast are rewarded under his reign. Above all, readers learn to respect their own history and ancestors, for they are the link to a glorious past.

## Author Biography

The story of *Sundiata,* the thirteenth-century ruler of Mali, came to the present through a familial line of *griots,* bards whose function in their society is to preserve the oral history of their people. This account was told from father to son for generations. It was first written down by the historian Djibril Tamsir Niane, who transcribed the story as it was recounted by Djeli Mamoudou Kouyaté.

The stories told by griots are not fixed in the way that written texts are: each recitation or performance may include additions or deletions, and can feature embellishment of some episodes and the downplaying of others. The griot may choose to play up the accomplishments of the distance ancestors of audience members as a sign of respect or to ensure that they will like what they are hearing. Thus, while the basic story derives from multiple storytellers who shaped it over time, the version that Niane wrote down is distinctly Kouyaté's. He is the modern-day griot of the Keita clan, which claims descent from Sundiata himself. Niane made the work available to a wide audience by publishing his version in French, and G. D. Pickett later translated the work into English. Pickett also collated his translation with the original Malinké (or Mandingo) version spoken by Kouyaté.

## Plot Summary

### Part I: The Buffalo Woman

After giving his lineage and justifying his right to tell the tale, the narrator begins the story of *Sundiata* by telling how Sundiata's mother and father came to be married. Sundiata's father, Maghan Kon Fatta, rules Mali. He has one wife, Sassouma Bérété, and a son named Dankaran Touman. One day a hunter comes to Maghan Kon Fatta's court,

bringing part of his catch in homage to the ruler, as was customary. The king asks the hunter, who is also a fortune-teller, to throw his cowry shells in a divination ceremony to reveal the future. Speaking in obscure language, the hunter reveals that the king's successor is not yet born, and that his heir will come from a hideous woman brought by two strangers.

Some time later, two hunters appear at court from the land of Do with a veiled woman hunchback. The brothers announce her to be a wife worthy of the king and proceeded to relate how they obtained her. The hunters had gone to search for a buffalo that was ravaging the countryside of Do. Great rewards had been promised to whoever killed the buffalo. They encountered an old woman who begged for food, which they gave her. In return for this kindness, she revealed that she is the buffalo in human form, and told them the secret of how to kill her animal form. She insisted that when the hunters were offered their choice from among the local maidens as their reward, they select the ugly hunchback named Sogolon Kedjou. Sogolon is the buffalo's wraith; that is, she embodies the soul of the shape-shifting buffalo. The hunters agree to all of this.

The spirit of the buffalo makes Sogolon strong, however, and she fights off the hunter who attempts to consummate his marriage with her. Unable to use her as they wish, the hunters thus bestow her on Maghan Kon Fatta, neglecting to tell him that she will not submit to any man.

Reminded of the fortune-teller's prophecy by his griot, Gnankouman Doua, the king takes Sogolon Kedjou as his second wife. On their marriage night, however, the king tries in vain to possess her, but with the strength of the buffalo spirit, she rebuffs him. After a week of such failures, the king tells her that he has discovered that he must sacrifice her. She faints from fear and he is able to consummate the marriage. Sundiata is conceived that very night.

### Part II: Sundiata's Childhood

Maghan Kon Fatta's first wife, Sassouma Bérété, fears that the prophecy, which seems to be coming true, will mean that her own son Dankaran Touman will not rule Mali after his father. She is pleased when it becomes evident that her rival's son cannot walk. Sogolon and the king tried remedies of all sorts, but Sundiata remains lame. The kind marries a

*Sundiata's father, King Maghan Kon Fatta of Mali, sitting in state. Papercut illustration by David Wisniewski.*

third wife, Namandjé, whose son Manding Bory becomes Sundiata's best friend. The king seeks more advice about his sons, and is reassured that Sundiata is the foretold heir. The king gives his own griot's son, Balla Fasséké, to Sundiata to be his griot.

The king died not long after this. Sassouma plots with the council of elders to have her son Dankaran Touman put on the throne. Sassouma encourages others to ridicule Sogolon and her other children, but especially Sundiata, who is still crawling at the age of seven. One day, in tears from being mocked, Sogolon laments to Sundiata that he can-

not not go and pick baobab leaves for her as other boys do for their mothers. Sundiata calls for an iron rod. He uses it to haul himself to his feet and takes his first steps. Striding to the baobab tree, he pulls it roots and all from the ground and brings it to his mother. From that day on, Sundiata excels at all physical pursuits, in particular hunting.

As the years pass, Sassouma grows more worried that Sundiata will take the throne from her son. When Sundiata is ten, she asks the nine great witches of Mali to kill him. They agree to try, but when Sundiata returns their deceit with kindness, they find they cannot harm him and instead offer their powers in protection.

Sundiata's mother Sogolon realizes that her family is in danger at the Mali court. When the regent prince Dankaran Touman sends Sundiata's griot, Balla Fasséké, to the court of the sorcerer king Soumaoro, Sogolon and her children leave. Sundiata vows to return and reclaim the throne someday.

## Part III: Sundiata in Exile

Sundiata and his family spent seven years in exile, sometimes finding welcome but more often finding that Sassouma has sent messages to other kingdoms urging that they turn the wanderers away. In the court of Djedeba, for example, the king Mansa Konkon challenges Sundiata to a life-or-death match of a word game called wori, which Sundiata wins by revealing that the king has accepted a bribe to kill Sundiata. When Sundiata wins, the king allows him to live, but expels him and his family from the court.

Next the family goes to Tabon, where one of Sundiata's childhood friends, Fran Kamara, is crown prince. The reunion is joyful, but the boy's father is afraid of Sassouma, and he insists that Sundiata and his family go elsewhere. They travel to Ghana, to the palace of the great Cissé clan. King Soumaba Cissé welcomes the visitors and treats Sundiata and his siblings as princes and princesses of his own realm. Sogolon falls ill, and the family must move to a more favorable climate. In Mema, the court of King Soumaba Cissé's cousin, Tounkara, the family thrives, and the youthful Sundiata becomes an important advisor to King Tounkara, even governing in the king's absence.

## Part IV: Soumaoro Kanté, the Sorcerer King

During Sundiata's years of exile, his griot, Balla Fasséké, had been at the court of Soumaoro Kanté. This evil king's power is legendary. His town of Sosso is fortified and invincible, his own palace a seven-story tower in the center of town. On the seventh floor he keeps his fetishes, magic charms that are the source of his evil power. Soumaoro Kanté has conquered all the surrounding peoples, including the people of Mali.

One day Balla Fasséké stumbles into the fetish room. Carpeted in human skins, the room contains the heads of the nine kings that Soumaoro had conquered. A giant snake, owls and fantastic weaponry also fill the room. The griot spotted a magic

balafon, or xylophone, that he began to play, bringing the ghoulish chamber to life. Soumaoro knows that someone had touched his xylophone, and he raced to the chamber to kill the intruder. Balla Fasséké, hearing the king's arrival, improvises a tune in honor of the sorcerer king. The song so pleases Soumaoro that he decided to make Balla Fasséké his own griot.

The evil king continues attacking and subjugating lands, ruling his people in terror. In an ultimate outrage, Soumaoro steals the wife of his own nephew and chief general, Fakoli Koroma. Fakoli swears revenge, and the men of many lands attacked by Soumaoro answered Fakoli's call to arms. As Dankaran Touman seeks to join the revolt, Soumaoro again invades Mali. Dankaran flees, leaving his villages to be pillaged and the capital city of Niani to be burned to the ground. Soumaoro proclaims himself king of Mali, but some villagers remember the words of the soothsayer and form resistance groups loyal to the prophesied king of Mali, Sundiata. No one knew where to find the exiled king, however.

## Part V: The Return of Sundiata

One day in Mema, Sundiata's sister Kolonkan sees a woman selling baobab leaves, a type of produce available only from Mali. She speaks to the woman, who is in fact one of the Malinké searching for Sundiata. Sogolon and Sundiata receives an embassy of notables from the court of Mali, learning of Soumaoro's depredations against their homeland. Sundiata vows to join the army of Fakoli to help defeat Soumaoro. The next morning, Sogolon dies. Sundiata leaves to join Fakoli, despite the protests of the king of Mema, who had considered Sundiata his heir.

Sundiata begins his march on Soumaoro by defeating the troops under the command of Soumaoro's son. Later he met Soumaoro's own troops, and though Sundiata and Fakoli's other allies fight well, they cannot take Soumaoro himself, for he has magical abilities and can vanish at will. Little by little, the allies drive back Soumaoro's troops, but he eludes them.

Reunited in battle with his griot, Balla Fasséké, Sundiata learns that Soumaoro's evil power can be destroyed if he is shot with an arrow tipped with a magical rooster's claw. During the next battle, Sundiata grazes Soumaoro with the magic weapon, depleting his powers enough so that he can be driven from the battlefield, though not killed. The victorious troops then march on Soumaoro's town

*Sundiata and his family, in exile, approach the city of Mema on the banks of the Niger River. Papercut illustration by David Wisniewski.*

of Sosso, take the fortified city, and find that the king's fetishes had lost their power. The Sorcerer King has been conquered.

### Part VI: Sundiata, Ruler of Mali

The allies go on to defeat all of Soumaoro's partisans. Sundiata travels back to Mali to rule. He appoints the descendants of Balla Fasséké, the Kouyatés, as the official griots to his heirs, the Keitas. He finds that the inhabitants of Niani have already started to rebuild their city, and Sundiata makes it his center of power. Here Sundiata rules justly and wisely for many years. Though many great rulers come after Sundiata, none equal the son of the Buffalo Woman and the Lion King. He left his mark on Mali for all time, Kouyaté reminds us, and his decrees still guide the citizens in their conduct.

## Characters

### Sosso Balla

Soumaoro's son, Sosso Balla leads his father's troops. When the sorcerer king flees at the battle of Krina, Sosso Balla is Sundiata's main captive.

### Sassouma Bérété

Maghan Kon Fatta's first wife, Sassouma Bérété expects her son to become the next king of Mali. When prophets foretell the marriage of the king and Sogolon and the birth of Sundiata, Sassouma is consumed with jealousy that haunts her throughout the epic. She taunts Sogolon when her son cannot walk, thus provoking Sundiata to raise himself to his feet to avenge his mother's honor. Plotting his death, she hires witches to kill him, but they are won over to his side because of his inherent goodness. Knowing that his family is in danger, Sundiata flees from the intrigues of Sassouma, but she continues to plague him. Sending sums of money to his hosts, she convinces them either to turn him away or try to kill him. In the end, however, Sassouma's plotting only serves to fulfill Sundiata's destiny, as the travels and travails she forces upon him cause him to develop into a strong, wise, cautious, and judicious person and mighty warrior.

### Manding Bory

Manding Bory, son of Namandjé, is Sundiata's step- or half-brother and best friend. The two boys grow up together, inseparable, and when Sogolon and her family go into exile, Manding Bory accompanies them. Later in life, when Sundiata becomes the commander of his own troops, he appoints Manding Bory as the head of his rear guard. Manding Bory continues to be Sundiata's most important general under the new Empire of Mali once Sundiata has taken the throne of his homeland, and he receives many honors in return for his services.

### Manding Boukari

*See* Manding Bory

### Buffalo of Do

When a buffalo terrorizes the countryside of Do, the king puts a bounty on its head. Many hunters try to kill the buffalo, and are killed in the process. Nonetheless, the hunters, Oulamba and Oulani, decide to try their hand at the task. On the trail of the buffalo, Oulamba sees an old woman lamenting her hunger and begging for food, and he responds by

# Media Adaptations

- The story of Sundiata is told in part by a master griot in the film *Keita!*. The griot teaches a young boy his own worth by sharing with him the story of his ancestor, Sundiata. The 1994 motion picture directed by Dani Kouyate is available on videocassette from California Newsreel. The film is in Jula and French with English subtitles.

- A children's retelling of the epic, *Sundiata: Lion King of Mali,* was written and beautifully illustrated by David Wisniewki in 1992. It was published by Clarion Books.

- The Disney full-length animated movie *The Lion King* incorporates many elements of traditional African oral narrative. The cartoon's plot resembles that of *Sundiata* in several respects.

---

sharing his food with her. She is in fact the Buffalo of Do in human form. Touched by his generosity, she tells him the magical method of killing her. In return, the Buffalo of Do asks that the hunter choose Sogolon Kedjou, her wraith, as his reward.

### Buffalo Woman

*See* Sogolon Kedjou

### Soumaba Cissé

The king of Ghana welcomes Sundiata and his family into his court for a year after they flee Mali. Hospitable to his guests, he treats the children like princes and princesses of his own country. When Sogolon falls ill in Ghana, the family must leave for the more healthful climate of Mema. The generosity and kindness of Soumaba Cissé ensure goodwill for his people when Sundiata becomes a great ruler.

### Do Mansa-Gnemo Diarra

Do Mansa-Gnemo Diarra is the king of the land of Do. When he grants the ugly hunchbacked woman Sogolon Kedjou as the prize to the hunters who kill the buffalo ravaging his lands, he starts the cycle of events that bring Sundiata's parents together. The people of Do join Sundiata in defeating the sorcerer-king Soumaoro.

### King Gnemo Diarra
*See* Do Mansa-Gnemo Diarra

### Manding Diara
*See* Sundiata

### Sogolon Djamarou
Sundiata's youngest sister, Sogolon Djamarou goes into exile with her family when her mother, Sogolon Kedjou, fears that Sundiata is in danger from the plotting of the king's first wife.

### Djata
*See* Sundiata

### Mari Djata
*See* Sundiata

### Naré Maghan Djata
*See* Sundiata

### Sogolon Djata
*See* Sundiata

### Gnankouman Doua
Griot to King Maghan Kon Fatta, Gnankouman Doua often advises the king when he must make important decisions. It is the griot who encourages the Hunter of Sangaran to reveal the prophecy about the king's future bride, Sogolon. Reminding the king of his duty to follow the prophecy of the hunter, Gnankouman Doua helps fulfill Sundiata's destiny. Gnankouman Doua's son, Balla Fasséké, continues his father's line, becoming griot for Sundiata.

### Balla Fasséké
Given to Sundiata by his father, Balla Fasséké is Sundiata's griot and the son of King Maghan Kon Fatta's griot Gnankouman Doua. Sundiata's half-brother Dankaran Touman sends Balla Fasséké to the court of the sorcerer-king Soumaoro. Having learned the secrets of Soumaoro's chamber of fetishes, Balla Fasséké, along with Nana Triban, advises Sundiata on the magic required to drain the sorcerer king's powers. Because he is instrumental in Sundiata's victory over Soumaoro, and the praise songs he sings about Sundiata, Balla Fasséké ensures that Sundiata's descendants, the Keita, will always chose their griots from his line, the Kouyaté. Djeli Mamoudou Kouyaté, who told the version of the epic that was transcribed by D. T. Niane, claims descent from Balla Fasséké.

### Maghan Kon Fatta
Sundiata's father, Maghan Kon Fatta, is known for his great physical attractiveness and his hunting skills. He is also considered to be a wise and kind ruler. Already married, he expects his first son, Dankaran Touman, to be his heir until the day that a soothsaying hunter tells him that another son, not yet born, had been foreseen to rule Mali. From this point on, Maghan Kon Fatta struggles between following that which was foretold and that which appears on the surface to be the natural way of things. When he sees the ugly hunchbacked woman Sogolon, he can hardly believe that he is to marry her, yet he fulfills the prophecy by their union. Even when their son, Sundiata, is born lame, Maghan Kon Fatta complies with the soothsayer and declares the child to be his heir. Each decision is difficult for Maghan Kon Fatta, but the fact that he follows the advice of the soothsayers and village wise men, rather than making the choices that his pride dictates, is held to be indicative of his wisdom and goodness as a ruler.

### Hunter from Sangaran
The Hunter from Sangaran shows up at Maghan Kon Fatta's court one day to give the king a portion of his catches, as custom dictates. Sangaran hunters were known to be great soothsayers, so Maghan Kon Fatta and his griot ask him to tell about the future of Mali. Divining with cowry shells, the hunter is the first to tell the king about Sogolon, her destined marriage with the king, and the remarkable destiny in store for the son they will have together.

### Fran Kamara
Son of the King of Tabon, Fran Kamara grows up in the court of King Maghan Kon Fatta together with Sundiata. When Sundiata's family flees Mali, they travel first to Tabon, but Fran Kamara's elderly father fears retribution from Sassouma Berete and her son Dankaran Touman and insists that the family stay only briefly before moving on. Once his father has died, Fran Kamara becomes an ally of Sundiata in his battle with Soumaoro.

## Soumaoro Kanté

The evil sorcerer-king Soumaoro subjugates the surrounding peoples and reigns over them. His strength derives from the powers of darkness. When he appropriates both Sundiata's griot and his nephew's wife, he angers these two warriors enough to encourage them to join forces to defeat him at the battle of Krina.

## Sogolon Kedjou

A hunchback, the ugly Sogolon is an unlikely choice as bride by the successful hunters of the Buffalo of Do. However, they promised the old woman who revealed the secret of hunting the buffalo to select Sogolon. Unable to consummate a sexual relationship with her, because she draws on the strength of the buffalo which she enbodies to fight them off, the hunters give Sogolon to the king of Mali, thus fulfilling the destiny prophesied by the hunter/soothsayer of Sangaran. The second wife of the king, Sogolon is mocked by the king's first wife when her son Sundiata turns out to be crippled. When Sogolon finally laments her son's condition in front of him, Sundiata finds within himself the strength and courage to walk. Sogolon flees with her family after the king's death to protect her son and eventually dies in exile.

## Frako Maghan Keigu
*See* Maghan Kon Fatta

## King of Ghana
*See* Soumaba Cissé

## King of Mali
*See* Maghan Kon Fatta

## King of Mema
*See* Mansa Tounkara

## King of Sosso
*See* Soumaoro Kanté

## Sogolon Kolonkan

Sogolon Kolonkan is Sundiata's oldest sister. While her family is in exile in Mema, it is Kolonkan who recognizes the baobab leaves from Mali in the market. Knowing that they are not locally available, she speaks with the woman selling them and learns that envoys from Mali have come searching for her brother Sundiata.

## Sogolon Kondouto
*See* Sogolon Kedjou

## Mansa Konkon

The first host of Sogolon and her family, Mansa Konkon welcomes the exiles from Mali at the royal court of Djedba until Sassouma Bérété bribes him to kill Sundiata. Mansa Konkon challenges Sundiata to a word game called wori, with the stakes being death to Sundiata if he loses. Sundiata, aware of the bribe, wins the game in revealing the king's treachery. Sundiata's life is spared, but he and his family must once again flee.

## Fakoli Koroma

Fakoli is Soumaoro's nephew and right-hand man until Soumaoro steals his wife. This so enrages Fakoli that he begins the revolt against the tyrant. Sundiata joins forces with this mighty warrior to defeat Soumaoro at Krina.

## Lion of Mali
*See* Sundiata

## Maghan the handsome
*See* Maghan Kon Fatta

## Naré Maghan
*See* Maghan Kon Fatta

## Namandjé

Namandjé is the third wife of Sundiata's father, King Maghan Kon Fatta. In sharp contrast to Sogolon, Namandjé's beauty is legendary. Namandjé's son, Manding Bory, becomes Sundiata's best friend.

## the old woman
*See* Buffalo of Do

## Oulamba

One of the two brothers who hunt and kill the Buffalo of Do. Their kindness to an old woman unlocks the secret of killing the buffalo. In return for the knowledge she gives them, they agree to select

Sogolon as their bounty. Unable to possess Sogolon sexually , Oulamba gives her to the king of Mali, Maghan Kon Fatta, forming the union that will produce the great king Sundiata.

## Oulani

One of the two brothers who hunt and kill the Buffalo of Do and bestow Sogolon on King Maghan kon Fatta.

## Sogo Simbon Salaba

*See* Sundiata

## Sundiata

Sundiata begins his life as an unlikely hero. Although soothsayers have predicted great things for this child, his body is crippled from birth and by the age of seven he has still not learned to walk. He was conceived in the union of the Buffalo Woman with the Lion King. Fortune tellers say that he will become the greatest ruler Mali has ever known. His mother's rival attempts to change his destiny and keep her son on the throne of Mali, but as the story shows, the rightful ruler of the Malinké eventually triumphs. Despite hardships, misfortune and physical infirmity, Sundiata grows to be the mighty warrior predicted by the prophets, saving his people from a tyrant.

## Dankaran Touman

Dankaran Touman, son of Sassouma Bérété, is Maghan Kon Fatta's first son and the heir to the throne before the birth of Sundiata. Even though the conflict between Dankaran Touman and Sundiata over the throne causes much hardship for Sundiata and his family, Dankaran Touman never proves himself to be a bad person. He would have been content to let Sundiata take his place as heir, but Dankaran's mother prods and goads him into an antagonistic relationship with his stepbrother. He proves to be a coward rather than a scoundrel, subjugating himself to the evil sorcerer king, Soumaoro, and fleeing from conflict when his attempt to revolt against Soumaoro meets with failure.

## Mansa Tounkara

The king of Mema hosts Sundiata and his family during their exile from Mali after they have been forced to leave several other courts due to the intrigues of Sassouma Bérété. Impressed by Sundiata's courage, he makes Sundiata his heir and

main general. When Sundiata decides to return to his people and try to free them from the tyranny of Soumaoro, the king grows angry and even refuses to let Sundiata bury his mother in his land. Tounkara and Sundiata are later reconciled. Tounkara is an ally during the fight with Soumauro, and is rewarded once Sundiata becomes ruler of Mali.

## Nana Triban

Nana Triban is the daughter of Maghan Kon Fatta's first wife Sassouma Bérété and the sister of Dankaran Touman. Because of the enmity between Sogolon and Sassouma, one would expect Nana Triban to join with her family in hating Sundiata. At an important moment, however, Nana Triban sides with Sundiata and is crucial in helping him overcome the sorcerer king, Soumaoro. Nana Triban had been given to Soumaoro as a wife by her brother during his rule of Mali. She helps Sundiata overcome the evil sorcerer king by telling him how to overcome Soumaoro's powers.

# Themes

*Sundiata* tells the story of the childhood and coming of age of one of Mali's greatest rulers, culminating with his defeat of the evil tyrant Soumaoro at the battle of Krina.

## Artists and Society

In the version of Sundiata collected by D. T. Niane, the narrating griot, Djeli Mamoudou Kouyaté, makes the role of the oral historian a primary theme of the work. One of the major characters in the story is Sundiata's griot, Balla Fasséké. *Sundiata* opens with the griot Kouyaté himself explaining his right to tell this epic story. At the point when the main battle is about to take place, the griot again pauses to commend the role of the oral historian in preserving the culture and history of his society. The importance of tradition and the griot's role in preserving memory emerges as a central concern of *Sundiata*.

## Physical Appearance

Sogolon, Sundiata's mother, is considered the ugliest woman in her village. When the hunters choose her as their bride, they are laughed at by the villagers. Yet the unattractive Sogolon is destined to carry the greatest ruler of Mali. While her lack of beauty makes her an unlikely consort for the king, the prophecies concerning her offspring prove strong-

# Topics for Further Study

- The griot plays an important role in Malinké society and in sustaining and developing the oral texts of such epics as *Sundiata*. Find one or more passages from the text of *Sundiata* in which the griot's art is discussed. Contrast that image with the image of the historian in American or European cultures.

- Explore expressions of friendship in the epic. Who are the important sets of friends? What traits are admired in friends? How do friends help Sundiata accomplish his destiny?

- Animal imagery plays an important role in the epic. What does this imagery add to your reading of the epic? Give examples from both this work and twentieth-century books or movies.

- Sundiata divides his empire into parts at the end of the text. Contrast his system of administration and justice with that of present-day Mali or that of your own country.

- Most of the women who appear in *Sundiata* are defined by their relationships to men. Their actions are considered important chiefly for the ways that they impact male characters. Are any of this epic's women characters defined wholly on their own terms? Consider some differences between the status of women in thirteenth-century Mali culture and late twentieth-century American culture. Is it ever appropriate to apply the standards of one culture to the literature of another? Can a modern American or European student find anything to value in a work of art produced by a culture that differs radically from the student's own?

- Compare the plot of the full-length animated Disney film *The Lion King* with that of *Sundiata*. Discuss what you see as similarities and differences between the thirteenth-century epic and the 1994 cartoon movie.

---

er than societal judgment. Sogolon, proves to be the most important wife of the king. Sogolon also proves to be intelligent, perceptive, and a good mother.

## *Coming of Age*

The first part of this epic concerns itself with the journey, both physical and spiritual, that Sundiata makes as he grows from a child into a man. While Sundiata always has the strength of a ruler within him, as was predicted from before his birth, he must change in several ways in order to claim that power. He must first learn to walk, and to lead his peer group in such traditional activities as hunting. Lame from birth, he finds the power within himself to stand up and walk in order to avenge his mother's honor. Made to leave his own country by the mother of his half-brother, Sundiata must learn how to be a warrior and how to comport himself in the courts of other rulers. He excels at hunting, and his feats in battle lead one foreign king to regard the exiled prince as his own Then, called to lead his people in a time of great trouble, Sundiata must leave this comfortable position and go forth on his own as a ruler. Finally Sundiata must learn when to make his stand, as he does on the battlefields of Krina. The warrior-king who emerges from this process is strong and wise, admired by all. This king will establish the administrative and justice system for the great empire of Mali.

## *Limitations and Opportunities*

Stricken from birth with a disability that prevents him from walking, Sundiata seems far from the great leader foreseen by the soothsayers. His father doubts whether a boy who cannot even walk can be the predicted savior of the Malinké. Sundiata must overcome both his physical handicap and the perception that it renders him unfit to rule.

While his victory over the tyrant Soumaoro gains Sundiata immediate acclaim and the throne of

Mali, his lasting accomplishments are his establishment of a system of administration and justice for his vast kingdom. Sundiata's truest strength comes from within.

### Mystery and Intrigue

The intrigues of the Mali king Maghan Kon Fatta's first wife, Sassouma Bérété, against Sundiata plague his childhood. Sundiata and his family leave their home because of the danger that Sassouma represents, but even at a distance she remains a threat, attempting to bribe others to kill Sundiata while he is with them. Sassouma never tires in her quest to undo Sundiata, but ultimately, her son's cowardice leaves the throne of Mali vacant for Sundiata to assume after his victory against Soumaoro.

### Magic and the Supernatural

Magic and supernatural events surround Sundiata even before he is born. Soothsayers predict the circumstances of his parentage and birth, and that he will become Mali's ruler. Sundiata's parents are brought together by the hunters of a supernatural buffalo, and his mother magically partakes of the spirit and strength of the buffalo. In an attempt to thwart Sundiata's predicted destiny and ensure that her own son will inherit the throne of his father, Sassouma hires witches to kill him by supernatural means. Her plan backfires: their malevolent powers cannot work against anyone with a truly pure and good heart. The sorcerer king Soumaoro derives his evil power from his room of magic fetishes, and Sundiata eventually overcomes him with the aid of magic.

### Strength and Weakness

The epic calls into question traditional perceptions of strength and weakness. The buffalo ravages the lands of Do, but when the hunters give hospitality and kindness to an old woman, she unlocks the secret of the buffalo's power and they easily defeat it. When Sassouma Bérété sends the most powerful witches in Mali to kill him, Sundiata's kindness overcomes their power, leaving them unable (and unwilling) to harm him. The kings who are kind to Sundiata and his family during their years of wandering are repaid by being made allies of this powerful kingdom once Sundiata takes the throne of Mali. The sorcerer Soumaoro derives great strength from his evil fetishes, but the scratch of a magic arrow is enough to leave him powerless. In *Sundiata,* great power can be overcome by simple acts of kindness.

## Style

The story of *Sundiata* has been handed through generations of griots. These oral historians form their own caste, and they alone are authorized to tell the history that has been entrusted to them by their forefathers. The griot Djeli Mamoudou Kouyaté, who recounted the version of *Sundiata* transcribed by D. T. Niane, claims descent from Sundiata's griot Balla Faséké.

Young people from this caste are screened for storytelling and other performance abilities and taught to sing or speak tales or play musical instruments. Women can also be griots. The spoken word is considered suspect in Malinké culture, because language can be used to distort or misrepresent the truth, so griots have an ambiguous place in society. They are entrusted with history, yet their words are never fully believed. Each griot possesses a precious secret: the truth of history; yet each is known to intentionally modify each story in the telling, in order to make the story appeal to a particular audience. The story of *Sundiata* enters into the historical and fictional realm simultaneously, and these two aspects of the tale cannot be separated from each other.

### Form and Style

Like many epics, *Sundiata* is meant to be sung and performed. The role of the griot in the production of the epic is paramount; he or she must embellish the language and make the story pleasing to the listeners. *Sundiata* does not appear to adhere to any regular meter of stresses or syllables, and most versions are told in everyday vernacular language. The audience does not participate, except to honor the griot with gifts at the end of the performance.

### Language

The story of *Sundiata* appears in the oral literature of many West African tribes and in many languages. Djeli Mamoudou Kouyaté recounted the tale to Djibril Tamsir Niane in Malinké, or Mandingo. Niane wrote down his words in that language, then translated the tale into French for its initial publication in 1960. G. D. Pickett translated the epic into English in 1965, working from Niane's published French text as well as his original Malinké transcription.

### Point of View

The point of view of the narrator, griot Mamoudou Kouyaté, plays a crucial role in the epic. He states again and again his inherited right to tell the history of the Keita ruler, because he is descended from the griot who served Sundiata. Several times in the course of the story, the griot makes reference to himself and to the importance of the griot's art. The griot functions as an omniscient narrator, able to adopt shifting points of view, to describe the thoughts and feelings as well as the actions of every character, and even to step back and comment about the meaning or importance of what is unfolding.

### Foreshadowing

The technique of literary foreshadowing is used to hint at something that is yet to come, preparing the reader or viewer for later revelations. In *Sundiata,* prophecy plays a similar but even more direct role. Most of the major events are foretold by seers or fortune-tellers before they take place. One tells the King of Mali that his heir will be born of an ugly woman who will be brought to his court. Other soothsayers tell the king that his crippled son is the future savior of Mali, unlikely as that seems. Prophecies do not hint at what is to come the way that foreshadowing does. Rather, these prophecies indicate the path of destiny. The king may choose not to follow the path indicated, but then he will not produce the heir that had been predicted. Further, indigenous African cultures are replete with cautionary tales about the bad luck that commonly befalls those who chose to disregard such prophecies and to forge their own destinies in defiance of what has been foretold.

### Grotesque

Elements of the grotesque plays a role in the epic. Sogolon's deformity, a hump that makes her resemble a buffalo, makes her repulsive to men. Nonetheless, she is the only woman who can transmit the spirit of the buffalo to the son she will bear. Soumaoro's chamber of fetishes also enters into the grotesque. The heads of the kings he has conquered as well as human skins of his victims line the chamber. Soumaoro derives his magic power from these symbols or emblems of evil. This power,

however, is not permanent; more magic can break its spell. The grotesque images in the epic serve to cover forms of power: Sogolon's serving good and Soumaoro's pledged to do evil.

### Imagery and Symbolism

Animals serve as symbols for many of the characters in the tale. Sogolon is the Buffalo Woman, strong and unattractive. Maghan Kon Fatta is compared to a lion, and he is handsome and a good hunter. Sundiata combines the qualities of his two parents and of the animals that represent them. Soumaoro's den of fetishes includes a giant snake, a sign of evil. Owls represent the night-flying witches of Mali.

## Historical Context

### Sundiata's Dynasty: the Keita Clan

Sundiata was not the first Keita to rule the Malinké people. The Keita dynasty began sometime in the eighth century and continues into the late twentieth century: the Keita are still chiefs of the Kangaba province. Rule passes from father to son, but if the child is too young to rule, a close family member from the father's side will rule until the child is of age. This appears to have been the case with the son of Sundiata himself. Manding Bory, Sundiata's step-brother and best friend, ruled Mali for a period of time after the death of Sundiata in 1255.

Islam was introduced into Mali with the conversion of a Malinké king around 1050, and Malinké griots have long claimed that the Keitas descend from Muhammad's companion Bilal ibn Rabah, the first mu'adhdhin (the man who issues the call to prayer). Forming a link between the Keitas and the companion of the Prophet makes their rule seem divinely ordained. According to the griots, the grandson of Bilal ibn Rabah came to Mali and was the first of the Keita.

### The Rise of the Empire of Mali

Until the time of Sundiata, Mali was a minor kingdom owing allegiance first to the King of Ghana and later to the king of Sosso, Soumaoro Kanté. Most of the history that is available to the present comes via the epic *Sundiata* in its many forms and across many nations. Over the years,

# Compare & Contrast

- **1200s:** Sundiata consolidates a vast empire stretching over most of West Africa and including many different peoples.

  **1900s:** A colony for many years, Mali receives her independence from France in 1960. The former French colonies are divided into many different countries, often with disputed borders. An ongoing border conflict with Burkina is not resolved until 1986.

- **1200s:** The Keita clan rules the Malinké people, and Sundiata's empire includes many ethnic groups throughout West Africa. Sundiata divides Mali into administrative regions, remaining chief ruler of the region.

  **1900s:** Members of the Keita clan remain chiefs of a province in Mali, but the government is now a republic.

  **1990s:** President Alpha Oumar Konaré is elected in 1992. Prime Minister Ibrahim Boubacar Keita heads the government elected in 1994..

- **1200s:** Mali is largely an agricultural state, with gold and salt mining later providing additional trading materials. The unit of exchange is most often the cowry shell, occasionally gold.

  **1900s:** Mali remains an agricultural state, with gold, cotton, and livestock being the main export commodities.

  **1990s:** The currency used in Mali today is the CFA, shared with most countries in the former French West Africa.

- **1200s:** Hunting is the main occupation of the ruling class. The Keitas are known to be great hunters, and Sundiata and his father are often referred to as "lions" for their hunting ability.

  **1900s:** Expanding human population, over-hunting, and poaching by Africans and Europeans depletes much of Mali's wildlife.

  **1990s:** Significant conservation efforts, including two national wild game preserves, aim at preserving Mali's wildlife heritage.

many additions have been made to the Sundiata story, giving him credit for the actions of previous or later Malinké kings. One story tells that Sundiata was the twelfth son of Maghan Kon Fatta. Soumaoro Kanté is said to have killed the other eleven, leaving the sickly Sundiata alive because he did not appear to be a potential threat. In this version, Sundiata recovers the use of his legs just in time to defeat Soumaoro at the battle of Krina.

The battle of Krina is estimated to have taken place in 1235. With this battle, Sundiata became the leader of a vast empire that covered much of present-day West Africa. Less clear is what happened to Sundiata following the victory at Krina. Some say he was killed by an arrow at an exhibition of arms while others relate that he was drowned near his home-town of Niani. Also unknown are the exact descendants of Sundiata. In order to please the patrons of a performance, griots will often add the names of those in the audience to the list of Sundiata's sons. In this way, a prominent family can gain even more prestige by claiming to be descended from the great Sundiata himself.

## Sundiata's Times: 1230-1255

Sundiata played such a vital role in the history of Mali that the entire thirteenth century is referred to as "Sundiata's Time" by the Malinké. After the battle at Krina, the conquered countries were divided into administrative units. Soumaoro's people were made slaves. Some of them took flight, settling in what later became Ivory Coast. Some of the Keita clan remained loyal to Sundiata's half-brother Dankaran Touman, and these peoples fled to the south. Sundiata's empire spread the Malinké language throughout West Africa.

## Life at Court

The extended family has always formed the basic social unit of the Malinké. The head of the family filled many roles. Among them, he had certain priestly powers and acted as judge, administering communal property and making decisions on relationships within the family. The head of the village was simply the head of the family that was thought to have been in the village for the longest period of time. He performed as village chief and priest. Different villages were also sometimes linked into one group, as was the case with the Keita clan. With time, the leader of a large group of villages became called a king. He usually had several wives, with the senior of them receiving the most societal respect.

Commoners paid great respect to their king. The king usually ate in private, his meals surrounded by mystery. When a subject was in the royal presence, he or she would lie prostrate and put dust and ashes on his or her head. The king had a spokesman who did all of his public speaking. The etiquette of the court demanded distance and respect from the king's subjects.

Subjects could appeal to the king for justice. The court usually had scribes, but most of the king's decrees were transmitted orally. The king consolidated his strength by making sure that his vassals paid him strict obedience. The sons of vassal kings were often sent to court to live, as seen in *Sundiata* at the court of Mema. The court was filled with slaves loyal to the king, and at times the slaves were given positions more powerful than some of the noblemen. Another caste important to the court were the *jelis,* or griots. These men served as close confidants to the king and transmitted the oral history of the monarch.

## Economy and Daily Life

Salt and gold mines brought wealth to the people of Mali. Generally, the king exacted a tax from the miners, often enough to make him quite rich. Mali was an important trading center during Sundiata's time. Most of the populace, however, were farmers and had little to do with external trade. Some of their crops included millet and sorghum. Often the slave caste worked the land. Another of the castes were the blacksmiths, but they were noblemen. Other artisans such as tanners and carpenters were also respected. Textile manufacture eventually developed into an art form. Along with gold, cowry shells were used as currency in Mali. By the time of Sundiata, some historians believe

that the kola nut, which when chewed has the effect of a stimulant, had already attained the ceremonial significance that it enjoys today in West Africa.

## Critical Overview

The story of *Sundiata* has attracted little critical interest among speakers of English. This can be attributed to two main reasons, the first being the lack of interest in African texts until recent decades. Only now are literature departments including courses and specialists in African literature. The critical world had privileged the Western literary canon for many years. Those wanting to see other texts undergo mainstream critical analysis had a hard battle to fight. With the development of professorships in African literature throughout the world, this problem is being overcome.

The second, and still relevant, problem is that of linguistic and social accessibility. Many stories from Africa are oral, told in indigenous languages. Those outside the small language-speaking community are unable to access the tale until it is transcribed and then translated into a common language. In addition, many of the guardians of African oral tradition do not wish to communicate their words outside of their own communities. They feel, perhaps rightly so, that in fixing their stories in written form they will lose control over the production of the text. The important element of performance is always lost in the written version of any oral tale. Little by little, many of the oral texts of Africa are being recorded and eventually transcribed. Even so, much of African oral literature remains unknown outside of its small community of production. *Sundiata* was largely unfamiliar outside Mali before D. T. Niane's version was published in French in 1960. The English-speaking world had to wait until G. D. Pickett's translation appeared in 1973.

*Sundiata* is now known as an excellent example of West African epic. A children's version, with beautiful papercut illustrations, has been produced by David Wisniewski. The first steps have thus been taken, spreading knowledge of this epic throughout different communities of readers. During this first phase, critical attention has been focused on the anthropological and historical detail found in *Sundiata*. Critics have tended to read the tale as history rather than literature, although it of course enters into both realms. As a piece of history,

*Sundiata* tells us much about life in thirteenth-century Mali and the reign of the great king Sundiata.

But *Sundiata* is equally a literary text. The part the griot plays in shaping history to please his audience cannot be overlooked. Each griot plays the roles of both historian and artist. More studies on both the oral and literary functions of *Sundiata* are certainly in order.

Post-colonial criticism has flourished in the late twentieth century, and can be used to help non-African readers of traditional African texts gain insights and understanding. Problems such as audience (is the text meant for those inside a specific cultural community or open to universal interpretation?) and applicability of Western critical theory (for instance, can an ancient African text ever be called ''feminist''?) are two of the many questions that must be raised and answered by readers of *Sundiata.* These issues have been initially addressed in *The Post-Colonial Studies Reader* published in 1995.

Other forms of criticism available to the reader of epic will also prove invaluable for reading *Sundiata.* The oral aspect of epic has been examined, with one of the first and outstanding examples being that of Alfred Lord's *Singer of Tales* (1960), which looks at contemporary Serbo-Croatian epic. Questions of nationalism and nation-forming have been long associated with epic, and current critical approaches to the epic and history should be examined to see if they shed light on reading the West African epic as well. One thing is certain, however. *Sundiata* is the epic recounting the pinnacle of an important dynasty in West Africa, and it tells us much about the heritage, literary and cultural, of a population still vital today. With that in mind, it seems certain that only toward the end of the twentieth century is the critical history of the thirteenth-century epic story of *Sundiata* beginning.

## Criticism

### Lynn T. Ramey

*In the following essay, Ramey focuses on the role of the griot in crafting a unique, individualized version of the story each time it is retold, and comments on the atypical nature of a written and published version of* Sundiata.

When reading an epic like *Sundiata,* the reader must realize that the tale was designed to be performed for a certain audience at a specific time. Most stories that we read today have one, fixed version. However, *Sundiata* is an oral tale, carefully passed down through the centuries by a segment of African society charged with preserving the collective memory. Many different tribes will have griots that tell the story slightly differently, from the perspective of their own people's history. For instance, we would not expect the griots of Soumaoro's descendants to tell of the battle of Krina in the same manner as do the Kouyatés, griots to Sundiata's ancestral line. In addition, different griots in the same family will have various strengths, some perhaps preferring to leave out battle scenes while others relish in the gory details. Likewise, the same griot may tailor his or her story to various audiences. If one of Manding Bory's descendants is the guest of honor, perhaps the griot will emphasize his role in Sundiata's reign. No two oral versions of *Sundiata* will ever be the same.

However, *Sundiata* is a living history text. The story tells of the beginning of the high-point of the great African empire of Mali. Still performed today, the epic conveys to the people of Mali where they came from and what makes them special. The goal of the storyteller is not necessarily to tell the facts of history in a concise and meticulous fashion. Rather, like the author of a literary text, the aim of the griot is to please the audience at the same time that he or she instructs. This technique involves, of course, attention to aesthetic properties of speech, including metaphor, descriptive passages and building to climactic moments. The content, too, is subject to manipulation in the repertoire of the well-trained oral historian. While the backbone of the tale remains constant, slight changes in the content can pique the audience's interest. The ''truth'' of history takes a backseat at times to artistic production.

In fact, Christopher Miller maintains, factual truth *always* gives way to the creativity of the griot. Miller notes that in Malinké society silence is revered. Kings and noblemen, therefore, show their status by maintaining silence whenever possible. The griot caste functions in society precisely to allow the speech necessary and desirable for social interaction to take place. The griot speaks for the king on occasions where public speaking is needed, such as speeches, judicial declarations, and historical recitations. Because the griot is so gifted with words, his status is ambiguous. He has power to create or recite the history of important deed, yet by

# What Do I Read Next?

- Nigerian novelist Chinua Achebe's *Things Fall Apart* (1958) relates the clash between African and European culture during colonial days, using a style very similar to that of the oral historian.

- Camara Laye recounts another version of the Sundiata story in his *The Guardian of the Word: Kouma Lafôlô Kouma*, translated from French into English in 1980.

- *The Children of Segu*, translated into English in 1989, is Maryse Condé's fictional account of the Bambara kingdom in Mali at the end of the late eighteenth century.

- A collection titled *West African Folktales* (1993) by Jack Berry introduces the reader to the spoken art of West Africa in a series of short tales.

---

speaking aloud he has lowered himself. His rhetorical agility leads the Malinké to suspect his every word, and yet his pronouncements carry important weight. For instance, if the oral historian says that a piece of property was given to someone by another's ancestor, his words are often heeded.

Djeli Mamoudou Kouyaté's task in recounting the story of *Sundiata* has very real implications for today. Because the epic is about origins, the tale treats carefully the people and places where each event occurred. As if to answer questions that members of the audience might ask, the epic provides the genealogy of the mighty Keita clan and the feats performed by the clan and its friendly neighbors. How did the Kouyaté clan come to be the griots for the ruling Keita clan, someone might inquire. Kouyaté responds by telling how Sundiata's father, Maghan Kon Fatta, gave Balla Fasséké of the Kouyaté family to his son as griot. Then when Balla Fasséké performed extraordinary service at the battle of Krina, Sundiata decreed that the Kouyatés would always be griots to the Keitas. Out of self-interest, the story of Balla Fasséké is probably always recounted when a Kouyaté tells of Sundiata. By telling of his auspicious origins and authority, the griot raises the worth of both his story and his position. When a griot from Ghana tells the story of *Sundiata,* however, Balla Fasséké might well be altogether absent from his account.

Djeli Mamoudou Kouyaté not only elevates himself in *Sundiata,* he does the same for many members of Malinké society. In the opening of the epic, he recounts the origin of the Keitas and the Malinké people, claiming that they are descended from the black companion of Muhammad, Bilali Bounama. Since the Malinké converted to Islam in the eleventh century, great prestige comes from having a close connection to the Prophet. The factual truth of this claimed lineage bears no significance to either the audience or the griot. The griot's word is always suspect, but it carries authority nonetheless. History once again defers to the larger goal of the griot, which in this case might be to create pride and unity among the Malinké people.

The Malinké people gain as well a sense that they are unique and special, distinct from their neighbors. Mamoudou Kouyaté states his goal at the beginning of the text: ''By my mouth you will get to know the story of the ancestor of great Mali, the story of him who, by his exploits, surpassed even Alexander the Great; he who, from the East, shed his rays upon all the countries of the West.'' When he gives their ancestor as Bilali, the griot states that the inhabitants of Mali are not indigenous, that they come from the East. They are a people blessed by the Prophet and not simply converted Muslims like those around them. Because they are not from the land they conquered and rule, they are above the other tribes. The hunter divines for Maghan Kon Fatta and reports that a light is coming from the east. This light is Sundiata, who like Bilali has a divine presence and spreads his aura among all the Malinké. Finally, when Sundiata is born the griot tells that ''great clouds coming from the east hid the sun'' and a flash of lightning "lit up the whole sky as far as the west.'' This stormy sky mirrors the birth of Sundiata, who comes with fury from the East and gives light to an entire community.

Griot Mamoudou Kouyaté is also a man of his own times. As he tells his version of the story to Niane, he incorporates his own concerns and those of his audience. Griots often include the names of their patrons in the lists of illustrious men at battles, much as Jacques Louis David painted his contemporaries into the *Coronation of Emperor Napoleon and Empress Josephine* (1804-07). Such additions are not considered to radically alter the account of history, but are rather whimsical touches that please the author and audience. Inspiration comes from the patronage system, which ensures that those storytellers who flatter the audience will receive the most gifts in return. As Kouyaté summarizes, "the generosity of kings makes griots eloquent.''

Kouyaté's privileging of the East over the West, as he repeatedly gives the origin of the great Sundiata as Eastern, may well stem from the concerns of the 1950s when Niane collected the griot's words. After World War II, as the world seemed to organize itself into Eastern and Western blocs, Africa had to find its place. US and Soviet interests began competing in Africa, trying to win access to rich mineral deposits. A former colony of France, Mali harbored some resentment against the intrusion of Western culture. In 1961, Mali began cooperative agreements with the Soviet Union to locate mineral deposits. Mamoudou Kouyaté's insistence on the supremacy of the East over the West held not only historical significance for Mali, but also a clear message for his listeners in the late 1950s.

The epic is a living text. Djeli Mamoudou Kouyaté claims that his oral history is superior to written history, for those people with a written history "do not feel the past any more, for writing lacks the warmth of the human voice.'' Part of feeling the past is participating in it. *Sundiata* allows its Malinké audience to become a part of the past. The griot creates an illustrious history for his listeners. By making reference to the present within the past, history becomes alive. The ability (and necessity) for the historical text to change with each telling is part of what makes oral history fascinating and ever-relevant. Our text of *Sundiata* is simply one version, rooted in a specific time and place. If and when oral history disappears from Mali, it will be a truly great loss.

**Source:** Lynn T. Ramey, for *Epics for Students*, Gale Research, 1997.

## Daniel P. Biebuyck

*In the following excerpt, the critic discusses characteristics of African heroic epics and notes ways that Sundiata (here called Sunjata) both conforms to and differs from other such epics.*

[For] each epic tradition there seems to be a central core. In the various known versions of the Sunjata epic, [there] is a clear-cut central core of thematic material. It includes events leading to the birth of the hero, the hero's youth and exile from the Mande, and the hero's return to reconquer the Mande from Sumanguru. Each major set includes a recurring number of episodes.

Underlying the various epics are, of course, many of the quasi-universal epic patterns, with many variations from culture to culture and within the same culture. To give a few examples, the epics illustrate many different cases of a miraculous conception and birth. One hero is born the same day that he was conceived, another is born after the one hundred-fifty year long pregnancy of his mother, still another is born through parthenogenesis. Some of the heroes are active and can talk while they are still in their mother's womb. They leave and reenter the womb freely and also decide autonomously the manner and moment of birth. One is born from the palm of his mother's hand, another through his mother's medius, another one by ripping her belly open. The heroes are born possessing certain gifts (the capacity to walk and talk, the foreknowledge of events, and invulnerability) and holding certain objects (knives, scepters, spears, shoulderbags). Most heroes are ready for great action right after birth, but Sunjata is weak and cannot walk for many years after his birth. There are numerous other common patterns: Herculean deeds; extraterrestrial journeys; fierce individual battles with heroes, with divinities, with animals, dragons, and monsters; possession of extraordinary magical devices; tests of strength and intelligence; games. Some of the heroes are quasi-invulnerable and invincible; others have the capacity to resuscitate themselves and to revivify others, to make themselves invisible, and so on. Whereas most of the main heroes are fierce warriors and ruthless fighters possessing superhuman strength, there are exceptions to this pattern. Mwindo, the hero of the Nyanga, is a small being; he is not a great killer or fighter; he pays great attention to revivifying his defeated enemies, and becomes, through purification in the celestial sphere, a poised, peace-minded, and balanced leader of his people.

African epics present extremely significant testimonies about the value systems and patterns of thought of African peoples. Several authors have pointed out that in the Sunjata epic the main hero is depicted as a good leader whose destiny it is to make immortal the name of the Mali Empire. He is a good leader because by going into exile he avoids bringing to a climax the intense rivalry between himself and his father's son. He returns only after the throne has been left vacant and has been usurped by a foreigner. [Some critics see] a political charter underlying the Sunjata epic: it instructs the king in how to deal with people, and the people about their rights and their duties towards the king. The king can be harsh and severe, but not unjust; he must respect the forces of love, trust, allegiance, that keep society together. In a certain sense the hero, Sunjata, is a spiritual more than a physical force.

**Source:** Daniel P. Biebuyck, ''The African Heroic Epic,'' in *Heroic Epic and Saga: An Introduction to the World's Great Folk Epics,* edited by Felix J. Oinas, Indiana University Press, 1978, pp. 336–38.

## Sources for Further Study

Biebuyck, Daniel P. ''Heroic Songs of the Mande Hunters,'' in *African Folklore,* edited by Richard M. Dorson, Doubleday, 1972, pp. 275-93.
  Biebuyck explores *Sundiata* and other African epics in detail.

Camara Laye, *The Guardian of the Word:Kouma Lafolo Kouma,* translated by James Kirkup, Aventura, 1984, 223 p.
  Examination of African oral traditions, forcusing on the role of the griot in Mandigo culture.

Imperato, Pascal James. *Historical Dictionary of Mali,* Scarecrow Press, 1996, 362 p.
  Many of the characters in *Sundiata* are included as entries in this dictionary. Imperato's chronology of Mali shows the political and social changes that have taken place in Mali from its early history. The Introduction supplies information about present-day Mali, including data about resources, economy, and politics.

——. *Mali: A Search for Direction,* Westview Press, 1989, 170 p.
  Imperato takes particular interest in the political climate of present-day Mali and its relationship with its neighbors and the global community, including U.S.-Malian relations.

Levtzion, Nehemia. *Ancient Ghana and Mali ,* New York, N.Y. : Africana Publishing Company, 1980, 289 p.
  One of the few sources on the historical period of Sundiata written in English. Levtzion treats all aspects of society, from life at court to the economy and religion.

Miller, Christopher. ''Orality Through Literacy: Mande Verbal Art after the Letter,'' in *The Southern Review,* Vol. 23, no. 1, Winter, 1987, pp. 84- 105.
  Miller explores the role of the griot in Malian society and as represented in various versions of *Sundiata.*

Niane, Djibril Tamsir. *Recherches sur l'Empire du Mali au Moyen Age,* Présence Africaine, 1975, 112 p.
  This short book, as of 1997 only available in French, gives an account of Niane's historical research before his eventual transcription of Kouyaté's version of *Sundiata.* He chronicles the history of the Keita dynasty and the impressive accomplishments of Sundiata.

Pickett, G. D., translator. *Sundiata: an epic of old Mali.* Longman, 1973.
  Pickett translated the epic from D.T. Niane's French version with reference to Niane's original Malinké notes. He includes a short preface from Niane's edition that explains the art of the griot.

Shelton, A. J. ''The Problem of Griot Interpretation and the Actual Causes of War in Soundjata'' in *Présence Africaine,* n.s. 66, 1968, pp. 145- 52.
  Contrasts the historical and literary accounts of Sundiata's battles.

# Glossary of Literary Terms

## A

**Abstract:** Used as a noun, the term refers to a short summary or outline of a longer work. Used as an adjective, abstract refers to concepts not knowable through the five senses. Examples of abstracts (n) include the synopsis that appear in front of the critical essays in each *Epics for Students* entry. Examples of abstract concepts (adj) include "idea," "guilt" "honesty," and "loyalty."

**Accent:** The emphasis or stress placed on a syllable in poetry. Traditional poetry, including epic poetry, commonly uses patterns of accented and unaccented syllables (known as feet) that create distinct rhythms. Much modern poetry uses less formal arrangements that create a sense of freedom and spontaneity. The opening line of the Dorothy Sayers translation of *The Divine Comedy*: "Midway this way of life we're bound upon" has five accents: on the second syllable of the first word ("-way) and on "way," "life," "bound," and the last syllable of the last work ("–on").

**Allegory:** A narrative technique in which characters represent things or abstract ideas and are used to convey a message or teach a lesson. Allegory is typically used to teach moral, ethical, or religious lessons but is sometimes used for satiric or political purposes. Examples of allegorical works include Dante's *Divine Comedy* and John Bunyan's *The Pilgrim's Progress.*

**Alliteration:** The repetition of vowel sounds as a poetic device.

**Allusion:** A reference to a familiar character, real person, event, or concept, used to make an idea more easily understood. Describing someone as a "Romeo" makes an allusion to William Shakespeare's famous young lover in *Romeo and Juliet.*

**Analogy:** A comparison of two unlike things. An analogy appears in Book 9 of *The Aeneid,* when the sounds of battle are described in one translation as being "like a great shower from the west drumming on the earth in the rainy season ... or like hailstones dropping from the clouds into the sea when the south wind in blowing."

**Antagonist:** The character in a narrative or drama who works against or stands in opposition to the hero or protagonist. An example of an antagonist is Ganelon in *The Song of Roland.*

**Anthropomorphism:** The presentation of animals or objects in human shape or with human characteristics. The term is derived from the Greek word for "human form." The fables of Aesop and many of the animated films of Walt Disney feature anthropomorphic characters.

**Anti-hero:** A central character in a work of literature who lacks traditional heroic qualities such as courage, physical prowess, and fortitude. Anti-heros typically distrust conventional values and are unable to commit themselves to any ideals. They generally feel helpless in a world over which they have no control. Anti-heroes usually accept, and often celebrate, their positions as social outcasts.

**Antithesis:** Direct opposite. In literature, the use of antithesis as a figure of speech results in two statements that show a contrast through the balancing of two opposite ideas. Technically, the second portion of the statement is the ''antithesis''; the first portion is the ''thesis.'' An example of antithesis is found in the following portion of Abraham Lincoln's ''Gettysburg Address'': ''The world will little note nor long remember what we say here, but it can never forget what they did here.''

**Apocrypha:** Writings tentatively attributed to an author but not proven or universally accepted to be their works. The term was originally applied to certain books of the Bible that were not considered inspired and so were not included in the ''sacred canon.'' Geoffrey Chaucer, William Shakespeare, Thomas Kyd, Thomas Middleton, and John Marston all have apocrypha. Apocryphal books of the Bible include the Old Testament's Book of Enoch and New Testament's Gospel of Peter.

**Apostrophe:** A statement, question, or request addressed to an inanimate object or concept or to a nonexistent or absent person. Requests for inspiration from the muses in poetry are examples of apostrophe.

**Archetype:** In literature, a universal type of recurring image, character, plot device, or action. This term was introduced to literary criticism from the psychology of Carl Jung. It expresses Jung's theory that behind every person's ''unconscious,'' or repressed memories of the past, lies the ''collective unconscious'' of the human race: memories of the countless typical experiences of our ancestors. These memories are said to prompt associations that trigger powerful emotions. Examples of literary archetypes include the theme of birth and death and the figure of the war hero. The term is used more generally to mean the first or best example of its kind: Gilgamesh and Enkidu are sometimes described as the archetypal best friends, for example.

**Argument:** The argument of a work is the author's subject matter or principal idea. Examples of defined ''argument'' portions of works include John Milton's *Arguments* to each of the books of *Paradise Lost.*

**Assonance:** The repetition of similar vowel sounds in poetry.

**Audience:** The people for whom a piece of literature is written. Authors usually write with a certain audience in mind: for example, children, members of a religious or ethnic group, or colleagues in a professional field. The term ''audience'' also applies to the people who gather to see or hear any performance, including plays, poetry readings, speeches, and concerts.

# B

**Ballad:** A short poem that tells a simple story and has a repeated refrain. Ballads were originally intended to be sung. Early ballads, known as folk ballads, were passed down through generations, so their authors are often unknown. Later ballads composed by known authors are called literary ballads.

**Blank Verse:** Loosely, any unrhymed poetry, but more generally, unrhymed iambic pentameter verse (composed of lines of five two-syllable feet with the first syllable accented, the second unaccented). Blank verse has been used by poets since the Renaissance for its flexibility and its graceful, dignified tone. John Milton's *Paradise Lost* is in blank verse, as are most of William Shakespeare's plays.

# C

**Cadence:** The natural rhythm of language caused by the alternation of accented and unaccented syllables.

**Caesura:** A pause in a line of poetry, usually occurring near the middle. It typically corresponds to a break in the natural rhythm or sense of the line but is sometimes shifted to create special meanings or rhythmic effects.

**Character:** Broadly speaking, a figure in a literary work. The actions of characters are what constitute the plot of a story, novel, or poem. There are numerous types of characters, ranging from simple, stereotypical figures to intricate, multifaceted ones. In the techniques of anthropomorphism and personification, animals—and even places or things—can assume aspects of character.

**Chronicle:** A record of events presented in chronological order. Although the scope and level of detail provided varies greatly among the chronicles surviving from ancient times, some, such as the *Anglo-Saxon Chronicle,* feature vivid descriptions and a lively recounting of events. During the Elizabethan

Age, many dramas—appropriately called "chronicle plays"—were based on material from chronicles.

**Classical:** In its strictest definition in literary criticism, classicism refers to works of ancient Greek or Roman literature. The term may also be used to describe a literary work of recognized importance (a "classic") from any time period or literature that exhibits the traits of classicism.

**Classicism:** A term used in literary criticism to describe critical doctrines that have their roots in ancient Greek and Roman literature, philosophy, and art. Works associated with classicism typically exhibit restraint on the part of the author, unity of design and purpose, clarity, simplicity, logical organization, and respect for tradition.

**Climax:** The turning point in a narrative, the moment when the conflict is at its most intense. Typically, the structure of stories, novels, and plays is one of rising action, in which tension builds to the climax, followed by falling action, in which tension lessens as the story moves to its conclusion.

**Colloquialism:** A word, phrase, or form of pronunciation that is acceptable in casual conversation but not in formal, written communication. It is considered more acceptable than slang.

**Concrete:** As a literary term, concrete is the opposite of abstract, and refers to a thing that actually exists or a description that allows the reader to experience an object or concept with the senses.

**Conflict:** The conflict in a work of fiction is the issue to be resolved in the story. It usually occurs between two characters, the protagonist and the antagonist, or between the protagonist and society or the protagonist and himself or herself.

**Consonance:** Consonance occurs in poetry when words appearing at the ends of two or more verses have similar final consonant sounds but have final vowel sounds that differ, as with "stuff" and "off."

**Convention:** Any widely accepted literary device, style, or form. An authorial aside, in which an omniscient narrator reveals something to the reader that the characters in the literary work do not yet know, is an example of a literary convention.

**Couplet:** Two lines of poetry with the same rhyme and meter, often expressing a complete, self-contained thought.

**Criticism:** The systematic study and evaluation of literary works, usually based on a specific method or set of principles. An important part of literary studies since ancient times, the practice of criticism has given rise to numerous theories, methods, and "schools," sometimes producing conflicting, even contradictory, interpretations of literature in general as well as of individual works. Even such basic issues as what constitutes a poem or a novel have been the subject of much criticism over the centuries.

# D

**Dactyl:** See *Foot*

**Denotation:** The definition of a word, apart from the impressions or feelings it creates in the reader.

**Denouement:** A French word meaning "the unknotting." In literary criticism, it denotes the resolution of conflict in fiction or drama. The *denouement* follows the climax and provides an outcome to the primary plot situation as well as an explanation of secondary plot complications. The *denouement* often involves a character's recognition of his or her state of mind or moral condition.

**Dialogue:** In its widest sense, dialogue is simply conversation between people in a literary work; in its most restricted sense, it refers specifically to the speech of characters in a drama. As a specific literary genre, a "dialogue" is a composition in which characters debate an issue or idea.

**Diction:** The selection and arrangement of words in a literary work. Either or both may vary depending on the desired effect. There are four general types of diction: "formal," used in scholarly or lofty writing; "informal," used in relaxed but educated conversation; "colloquial," used in everyday speech; and "slang," containing newly coined words and other terms not accepted in formal usage.

**Didactic:** A term used to describe works of literature that aim to teach some moral, religious, political, or practical lesson. Although didactic elements are often found in artistically pleasing works, the term "didactic" usually refers to literature in which the message is more important than the form. The term may also be used to criticize a work that the critic finds "overly didactic," that is, heavy-handed in its delivery of a lesson.

**Dissonance:** A combination of harsh or jarring sounds, especially in poetry. Although such combinations may be accidental, poets sometimes intentionally make them to achieve particular effects. Dissonance is also sometimes used to refer to close but not identical rhymes. When this is the case, the word functions as a synonym for consonance.

**Drama:** In its widest sense, a drama is any work designed to be presented by actors on a stage. Similarly, "drama" denotes a broad literary genre that includes a variety of forms, from pageant and spectacle to tragedy and comedy, as well as countless types and subtypes. More commonly in modern usage, however, a drama is a work that treats serious subjects and themes but does not aim at the grandeur of tragedy.

**Dramatic Monologue:** See *Monologue*

# E

**Eclogue:** A poem featuring rural themes and structured as a dialogue among shepherds. Eclogues often took specific poetic forms, such as elegies or love poems. Some were written as the soliloquy of a shepherd. In later centuries, "eclogue" came to refer to any poem that was in the pastoral tradition or that had a dialogue or monologue structure. The form takes its name from Virgil's *Eclogues,* also known as *Bucolics.*

**Epic:** A long narrative poem about the adventures of a hero, usually a person of great nationalistic, historic, or legendary importance. The setting is vast and the action is often given cosmic significance through the intervention of supernatural forces such as gods, angels, or demons. Epics are typically written in a classical style with elaborate metaphors and allusions that enhance the symbolic importance of a hero's adventures.

**Epic Simile:** See *Homeric Simile*

**Epilogue:** A concluding statement or section of a literary work. In dramas, particularly those of the seventeenth and eighteenth centuries, the epilogue is a closing speech, often in verse, delivered by an actor at the end of a play and spoken directly to the audience.

**Episode:** An incident that forms part of a story and is significantly related to it. Episodes may be either self-contained narratives or events that depend on a larger context for their sense and importance.

# F

**Fable:** A prose or verse narrative intended to convey a moral. Animals or inanimate objects with human characteristics often serve as characters in fables.

**Feet:** See *Foot*

**Fiction:** Any story that is the product of imagination rather than a documentation of fact. Characters and events in such narratives may be based in real life but their ultimate form and configuration is a creation of the author.

**Figurative Language:** A technique in writing in which the author temporarily interrupts the order, construction, or meaning of the writing for a particular effect. This interruption takes the form of one or more figures of speech such as hyperbole, irony, or simile. Figurative language is the opposite of literal language, in which every word is truthful, accurate, and free of exaggeration or embellishment.

**Figures of Speech:** Language that differs from customary conventions of construction, meaning, order, or significance for the purpose of a special meaning or effect. There are two major types of figures of speech: rhetorical figures, which do not make changes in the meaning of the words, and tropes, which do. Types of figures of speech include simile, hyperbole, alliteration, and pun, among many others.

**Flashback:** A device used in literature to present action that occurred before the beginning of the story.

**Foil:** A character in a work of literature whose physical or psychological qualities contrast strongly with, and therefore highlight, the corresponding qualities of another character. In *The Song of Roland,* for example, the cautious Olivier serves as a foil to the hot-blooded and impetuous hero Roland.

**Folk Ballad:** See *Ballad*

**Folklore:** Traditions and myths preserved in a culture or group of people. Typically, these are passed on by word of mouth in various forms—such as legends, songs, and proverbs—or preserved in customs and ceremonies. This term was first used by W. J. Thoms in 1846. *The Kalevala* incorporates many elements of traditional Finnish folklore.

**Folktale:** A story originating in oral tradition. Folktales fall into a variety of categories, including legends, ghost stories, fairy tales, fables, and anecdotes based on historical figures and events.

**Foot:** The smallest unit of rhythm in a line of poetry. In English-language poetry, a foot is typically one accented syllable combined with one or two unaccented syllables. There are many different types of feet. When the accent is on the second syllable of a two syllable word (con-*tort*), the foot is an "iamb"; the reverse accentual pattern (*tor*-ture) is a "trochee." Other feet that commonly occur in poetry in English are "anapest", two unaccented syllables followed by an accented syllable as in inter-*cept*, and "dactyl", an accented syllable followed by two unaccented syllables as in *su*-i-cide.

**Foreshadowing:** A device used in literature to create expectation or to set up an explanation of later developments.

**Form:** The pattern or construction of a work which identifies its genre and distinguishes it from other genres.

# G

**Genre:** A category of literary work. In critical theory, genre may refer to both the content of a given work—tragedy, comedy, pastoral—and to its form, such as epic, poetry, novel, or drama. This term also refers to types of popular literature, as in the genres of science fiction or the detective story.

**Georgic:** A poem about farming and the farmer's way of life. The genre is named after Virgil's *Georgics,* written before the *Aeneid.*

# H

**Half Rhyme:** See *Consonance*

**Hamartia:** In tragedy, the event or act that leads to the hero's or heroine's downfall. This term is often incorrectly used as a synonym for tragic flaw.

**Hellenism:** Imitation of ancient Greek thought or styles. Also, an approach to life that focuses on the growth and development of the intellect. "Hellenism" is sometimes used to refer to the belief that reason can be applied to examine all human experience

**Heptameter:** See *Meter*

**Hero/Heroine:** The principal sympathetic character (male or female) in a literary work. Heroes and heroines typically exhibit admirable traits: idealism, courage, and integrity, for example. Epic heroes and heroines include Aeneas in the *Aeneid,* Gilgamesh in *The Epic of Gilgamesh,* and Kriemhild in the *Nibelungenlied.*

**Heroic Couplet:** A rhyming couplet written in iambic pentameter (a verse with five iambic feet).

**Heroic Line:** The meter and length of a line of verse in epic or heroic poetry. This varies by language and time period. For example, in English poetry, the heroic line is iambic pentameter (a verse with five iambic feet). In French, it is the alexandrine (a verse with six iambic feet); in classical literature, dactylic hexameter (a verse with six dactylic feet).

**Heroine:** See *Hero/Heroine*

**Hexameter:** See *Meter*

**Historical Criticism:** The study of a work based on its impact on the world of the time period in which it was written.

**Homeric Simile:** An elaborate, detailed comparison written as a simile many lines in length.

**Humanism:** A philosophy that places faith in the dignity of humankind and rejects the medieval perception of the individual as a weak, fallen creature. Humanists typically believe in the perfectibility of human nature and view reason and education as the means to that end.

**Hyperbole:** In literary criticism, deliberate exaggeration used to achieve an effect.

# I

**Iamb:** See *Foot*

**Idiom:** A word construction or verbal expression closely associated with a given language. Idioms pose particular problems to translators.

**Image:** A concrete representation of an object or sensory experience. Typically, such a representation helps evoke the feelings associated with the object or experience itself. Images are either "literal" or "figurative." Literal images are especially concrete and involve little or no extension of the obvious meaning of the words used to express them. Figurative images do not follow the literal meaning of the words exactly. Images in literature are usually visual, but the term "image" can also refer to the representation of any sensory experience.

**Imagery:** The array of images in a literary work. Also, figurative language.

**In medias res:** A Latin term meaning "in the middle of things." It refers to the technique of beginning a story at its midpoint and then using various flashback devices to reveal previous action. This technique originated in such epics as Virgil's *Aeneid.*

**Induction:** The process of reaching a conclusion by reasoning from specific premises to form a general premise. Also, an introductory portion of a work of literature, especially a play.

**Intentional Fallacy:** The belief that judgments of a literary work based solely on an author's stated or implied intentions are false and misleading. Critics who believe in the concept of the intentional fallacy typically argue that the work itself is sufficient matter for interpretation, even though they may concede that an author's statement of purpose can be useful.

**Interior Monologue:** A narrative technique in which characters' thoughts are revealed in a way that appears to be uncontrolled by the author. The interior monologue typically aims to reveal the inner self of a character. It portrays emotional experiences as they occur at both a conscious and unconscious level. images are often used to represent sensations or emotions.

**Internal Rhyme:** Rhyme that occurs within a single line of verse.

**Irony:** In literary criticism, the effect of language in which the intended meaning is the opposite of what is stated.

# L

**Lay:** A song or simple narrative poem. The form originated in medieval France. Early French *lais* were often based on the Celtic legends and other tales sung by Breton minstrels. In fourteenth-century England, the term ''lay'' was used to describe short narratives written in imitation of the Breton lays.

**Literal Language:** An author uses literal language when he or she writes without exaggerating or embellishing the subject matter and without any tools of figurative language.

**Literature:** Literature is broadly defined as any written or spoken material, but the term most often refers to creative works. Literature includes poetry, drama, fiction, and many kinds of nonfiction writing, as well as oral, dramatic, and broadcast compositions not necessarily preserved in a written format, such as films and television programs.

# M

**Measure:** The foot, verse, or time sequence used in a literary work, especially a poem. Measure is often used somewhat incorrectly as a synonym for meter.

**Metaphor:** A figure of speech that expresses an idea through the image of another object. Metaphors suggest the essence of the first object by identifying it with certain qualities of the second object.

**Meter:** In literary criticism, the repetition of sound patterns that creates a rhythm in poetry. The patterns are based on the number of syllables and the presence and absence of accents. The unit of rhythm in a line is called a foot. Types of meter are classified according to the number of feet in a line. These are the standard English lines: Monometer, one foot; Dimeter, two feet; Trimeter, three feet; Tetrameter, four feet; Pentameter, five feet; Hexameter, six feet (also called the Alexandrine); Heptameter, seven feet (also called the ''Fourteener'' when the feet are iambic). The most common English meter is the iambic pentameter, in which each line contains ten syllables, or five iambic feet, which individually are composed of an unstressed syllable followed by an accented syllable.

**Monologue:** A composition, written or oral, by a single individual. More specifically, a speech given by a single individual in a drama or other public entertainment. It has no set length, although it is usually several or more lines long.

**Mood:** The prevailing emotions of a work or of the author in his or her creation of the work. The mood of a work is not always what might be expected based on its subject matter.

**Motif:** A theme, character type, image, metaphor, or other verbal element that recurs throughout a single work of literature or occurs in a number of different works over a period of time.

**Muses:** In Greek mythology, nine goddesses, the daughters of Zeus and Mnemosyne (Memory). Each muse patronized a specific area of the liberal arts and sciences. Calliope presided over epic poetry, Clio over history, Erato over love poetry, Euterpe over music or lyric poetry, Melpomene over tragedy, Polyhymnia over hymns to the gods, Terpsichore over dance, Thalia over comedy, and Urania over astronomy. Poets and writers traditionally made appeals to the Muses for inspiration in their work. John Milton invokes the aid of a muse at the beginning of the first book of his *Paradise Lost,* and Homer's *Odyssey* beings ''Tell me, Muse, the story of that resourceful man.''

**Myth:** An anonymous tale emerging from the traditional beliefs of a culture or social unit. Myths use supernatural explanations for natural phenomena.

They may also explain cosmic issues like creation and death. Collections of myths, known as mythologies, are common to all cultures and nations.

# N

**Narration:** The telling of a series of events, real or invented. A narration may be either a simple narrative, in which the events are recounted chronologically, or a narrative with a plot, in which the account is given in a style reflecting the author's artistic concept of the story. Narration is sometimes used as a synonym for "storyline."

**Narrative:** A verse or prose accounting of an event or sequence of events, real or invented. The term is also used as an adjective in the sense "method of narration." For example, in literary criticism, the expression "narrative technique" usually refers to the way the author structures and presents his or her story.

**Narrative Poetry:** A nondramatic poem in which the author tells a story. Such poems may be of any length or level of complexity. Epics are examples of narrative poetry.

**Narrator:** The teller of a story. The narrator may be the author or a character in the story through whom the author speaks.

# O

**Objectivity:** A quality in writing characterized by the absence of the author's opinion or feeling about the subject matter. Objectivity is an important factor in criticism.

**Omniscience:** See *Point of View*

**Onomatopoeia:** The use of words whose sounds express or suggest their meaning. In its simplest sense, onomatopoeia may be represented by words that mimic the sounds they denote such as "hiss" or "meow." At a more subtle level, the pattern and rhythm of sounds and rhymes of a line or poem may be onomatopoeic.

**Oral Transmission:** A process by which songs, ballads, folklore, and other material are transmitted by word of mouth. The tradition of oral transmission predates the written record systems of literate society. Oral transmission preserves material sometimes over generations, although usually with variations. Breton lays, Native American legends, French *fabliaux,* and many national epics (including the Anglo-Saxon *Beowulf,* the Finnish *Kalevala* and the Mali *Sundiata*), are examples of orally transmitted literature.

**Oration:** Formal speaking intended to motivate the listeners to some action or feeling. Such public speaking was much more common before the development of timely printed communication such as newspapers.

# P

**Parable:** A story intended to teach a moral lesson or answer an ethical question.

**Pastoral:** A term derived from the Latin word "pastor," meaning shepherd. A pastoral is a literary composition on a rural theme. The conventions of the pastoral were originated by the third-century Greek poet Theocritus, who wrote about the experiences, love affairs, and pastimes of Sicilian shepherds. In a pastoral, characters and language of a courtly nature are often placed in a simple setting. The term pastoral is also used to classify dramas, elegies, and lyrics that exhibit the use of country settings and shepherd characters.

**Pathetic Fallacy:** A term coined by English critic John Ruskin to identify writing that falsely endows nonhuman things with human intentions and feelings, such as "angry clouds" and "sad trees."

**Pen Name:** See *Pseudonym*

**Persona:** A Latin term meaning "mask." *Personae* are the characters in a fictional work of literature. The *persona* generally functions as a mask through which the author tells a story in a voice other than his or her own. A *persona* is usually either a character in a story who acts as a narrator or an "implied author," a voice created by the author to act as the narrator for himself or herself.

**Personification:** A figure of speech that gives human qualities to abstract ideas, animals, and inanimate objects.

**Plagiarism:** Claiming another person's written material as one's own. Plagiarism can take the form of direct, word-for-word copying or the theft of the substance or idea of the work.

**Plot:** In literary criticism, this term refers to the pattern of events in a narrative or drama. In its simplest sense, the plot guides the author in composing the work and helps the reader follow the work. Typically, plots exhibit causality and unity and have a beginning, a middle, and an end.

Sometimes, however, a plot may consist of a series of disconnected events, in which case it is known as an "episodic plot."

**Poem:** In its broadest sense, a composition utilizing rhyme, meter, concrete detail, and expressive language to create a literary experience with emotional and aesthetic appeal. Typical poems include epics, sonnets, odes, elegies, *haiku,* ballads, and free verse.

**Poet:** An author who writes poetry or verse. The term is also used to refer to an artist or writer who has an exceptional gift for expression, imagination, and energy in the making of art in any form.

**Poetics:** This term has two closely related meanings. It denotes (1) an aesthetic theory in literary criticism about the essence of poetry or (2) rules prescribing the proper methods, content, style, or diction of poetry. The term poetics may also refer to theories about literature in general, not just poetry.

**Poetry:** In its broadest sense, writing that aims to present ideas and evoke an emotional experience in the reader through the use of meter, imagery, connotative and concrete words, and a carefully constructed structure based on rhythmic patterns. Poetry typically relies on words and expressions that have several layers of meaning. It also makes use of the effects of regular rhythm on the ear and may make a strong appeal to the senses through the use of imagery.

**Point of View:** The narrative perspective from which a literary work is presented to the reader. There are four traditional points of view. The "third person omniscient" gives the reader a "godlike" perspective, unrestricted by time or place, from which to see actions and look into the minds of characters. This allows the author to comment openly on characters and events in the work. The "third person" point of view presents the events of the story from outside of any single character's perception, much like the omniscient point of view, but the reader must understand the action as it takes place and without any special insight into characters' minds or motivations. The "first person" or "personal" point of view relates events as they are perceived by a single character. The main character "tells" the story and may offer opinions about the action and characters which differ from those of the author. Much less common than omniscient, third person, and first person is the "second person" point of view, wherein the author tells the story as if it is happening to the reader.

**Polemic:** A work in which the author takes a stand on a controversial subject, such as abortion or religion. Such works are often extremely argumentative or provocative. Classic examples of polemics include John Milton's *Aeropagitica* and Thomas Paine's *The American Crisis.*.

**Prologue:** An introductory section of a literary work. It often contains information establishing the situation of the characters or presents information about the setting, time period, or action. In drama, the prologue is spoken by a chorus or by one of the principal characters.

**Prose:** A literary medium that attempts to mirror the language of everyday speech. It is distinguished from poetry by its use of unmetered, unrhymed language consisting of logically related sentences. Prose is usually grouped into paragraphs that form a cohesive whole such as an essay or a novel.

**Protagonist:** The central character of a story who serves as a focus for its themes and incidents and as the principal rationale for its development. The protagonist is sometimes referred to in discussions of modern literature as the hero or anti-hero.

**Pseudonym:** A name assumed by a writer, most often intended to prevent his or her identification as the author of a work.

**Pun:** A play on words that have the same or similar sounds but different meanings.

**Pure Poetry:** poetry written without instructional intent or moral purpose that aims only to please a reader by its imagery or musical flow. The term pure poetry is used as the antonym (opposite) of the term "didacticism."

# Q

**Quatrain:** A four-line stanza of a poem or an entire poem consisting of four lines.

# R

**Refrain:** A phrase repeated at intervals throughout a poem. A refrain may appear at the end of each stanza or at less regular intervals. It may be altered slightly at each appearance.

**Resolution:** The portion of a narrative following the climax, in which the conflict is resolved.

**Rhyme:** When used as a noun in literary criticism, this term generally refers to a poem in which words sound identical or very similar and appear in parallel positions in two or more lines. Rhymes are classified into different types according to where they fall in a line or stanza or according to the degree of similarity they exhibit in their spellings and sounds. Some major types of rhyme are ''masculine'' rhyme, ''feminine'' rhyme, and ''triple'' rhyme. In a masculine rhyme, the rhyming sound falls in a single accented syllable, as with ''heat'' and ''eat.'' Feminine rhyme is a rhyme of two syllables, one stressed and one unstressed, as with ''merry'' and ''tarry.'' Triple rhyme matches the sound of the accented syllable and the two unaccented syllables that follow: ''narrative'' and ''declarative.''

**Rhyme Royal:** A stanza of seven lines composed in iambic pentameter and rhymed *ababbcc.* The name is said to be a tribute to King James I of Scotland, who used it in his poetry.

**Rhythm:** A regular pattern of sound, time intervals, or events occurring in writing, most often and most discernably in poetry. Regular, reliable rhythm is known to be soothing to humans, while interrupted, unpredictable, or rapidly changing rhythm is disturbing. These effects are known to authors, who use them to produce a desired reaction in the reader.

**Rising Action:** The part of a drama where the plot becomes increasingly complicated. Rising action leads up to the climax, or turning point, of a drama.

**Romance:** A broad term, usually denoting a narrative with exotic, exaggerated, often idealized characters, scenes, and themes.

# S

**Scansion:** The analysis or ''scanning'' of a poem to determine its meter and often its rhyme scheme. The most common system of scansion uses accents (slanted lines drawn above syllables) to show stressed syllables, breves (curved lines drawn above syllables) to show unstressed syllables, and vertical lines to separate each foot.

**Semiotics:** The study of how literary forms and conventions affect the meaning of language.

**Sestet:** Any six-line poem or stanza.

**Setting:** The time, place, and culture in which the action of a narrative takes place. The elements of setting may include geographic location, characters' physical and mental environments, prevailing cultural attitudes, or the historical time in which the action takes place.

**Simile:** A comparison, usually using ''like'' or ''as,'' of two essentially dissimilar things, as in ''coffee as cold as ice'' or ''He sounded like a broken record.''

**Slang:** A type of informal verbal communication that is generally unacceptable for formal writing. Slang words and phrases are often colorful exaggerations used to emphasize the speaker's point; they may also be shortened versions of an often-used word or phrase.

**Spondee:** In poetry meter, a foot consisting of two long or stressed syllables occurring together. This form is quite rare in English verse, and is usually composed of two monosyllabic words.

**Sprung Rhythm:** Versification using a specific number of accented syllables per line but disregarding the number of unaccented syllables that fall in each line, producing an irregular rhythm in the poem.

**Stanza:** A subdivision of a poem consisting of lines grouped together, often in recurring patterns of rhyme, line length, and meter. Stanzas may also serve as units of thought in a poem much like paragraphs in prose.

**Stereotype:** A stereotype was originally the name for a duplication made during the printing process; this led to its modern definition as a person or thing that is (or is assumed to be) the same as all others of its type. Stereotypical characters who appear in both ancient and modern literature include the bragging soldier, the wise old advisor, the young people who fall madly in love at first sight, and the nagging wife.

**Structure:** The form taken by a piece of literature. The structure may be made obvious for ease of understanding, as in nonfiction works, or may be obscured for artistic purposes, as in some poetry or seemingly ''unstructured'' prose. Examples of common literary structures include the plot of a narrative, the acts and scenes of a drama, and such poetic forms as the Shakespearean sonnet and the Pindaric ode.

**Style:** A writer's distinctive manner of arranging words to suit his or her ideas and purpose in writing. The unique imprint of the author's personality upon his or her writing, style is the product of an author's way of arranging ideas and his or her use of diction, different sentence structures, rhythm, figures of speech, rhetorical principles, and other elements of composition.

**Subject:** The person, event, or theme at the center of a work of literature. A work may have one or more subjects of each type, with shorter works tending to have fewer and longer works tending to have more.

**Subplot:** A secondary story in a narrative. A subplot may serve as a motivating or complicating force for the main plot of the work, or it may provide emphasis for, or relief from, the main plot. The efforts of retired Major Plunkett to assimilate himself into the culture and history of his adopted home of St. Lucia is a subplot of Derek Walcott's *Omeros*.

**Suspense:** A literary device in which the author maintains the audience's attention through the build-up of events which are intended—but may fail—to result in a specific outcome.

**Syllogism:** A method of presenting a logical argument. In its most basic form, the syllogism consists of a major premise, a minor premise, and a conclusion.

**Symbol:** Something that suggests or stands for something else without losing its original identity. In literature, symbols combine their literal meaning with the suggestion of an abstract concept. Literary symbols are of two types: those that carry complex associations of meaning no matter what their contexts, and those that derive their suggestive meaning from their functions in specific literary works.

# T

**Terza Rima:** A three-line stanza form in poetry in which the rhymes are made on the last word of each line in the following manner: the first and third lines of the first stanza, then the second line of the first stanza and the first and third lines of the second stanza, and so on with the middle line of any stanza rhyming with the first and third lines of the following stanza.

**Textual Criticism:** A branch of literary criticism that seeks to establish the authoritative text of a literary work. Textual critics typically compare all known manuscripts or printings of a single work in order to assess the meanings of differences and revisions. This procedure allows them to arrive at a definitive version that (supposedly) corresponds to the author's original intention.

**Tone:** The author's attitude toward his or her audience may be deduced from the tone of the work. A formal tone may create distance or convey politeness, while an informal tone may encourage a friendly, intimate, or intrusive feeling in the reader. The author's attitude toward his or her subject matter may also be deduced from the tone of the words he or she uses in discussing it.

**Tragedy:** A drama in prose or poetry about a noble, courageous hero of excellent character who, because of some tragic character flaw or *hamartia*, brings ruin upon him- or herself. Tragedy treats its subjects in a dignified and serious manner, using poetic language to help evoke pity and fear and bring about catharsis, a purging of these emotions. The tragic form was practiced extensively by the ancient Greeks.

**Tragic Flaw:** In a tragedy, the quality within the hero or heroine which leads to his or her downfall. Some critics have charged that Roland's excessive pride, which prevents him from calling for help until it is too late, is the tragic flaw of the hero of *The Song of Roland*.

**Trimeter:** See *Meter*

**Triple Rhyme:** See *Rhyme*

**Trochee:** See *Foot*

# U

**Unities:** Strict rules of dramatic structure, formulated by Italian and French critics of the Renaissance and based loosely on the principles of drama discussed by Aristotle in his *Poetics*. Foremost among these rules were the three unities of action, time, and place that compelled a dramatist to: (1) construct a single plot with a beginning, middle, and end that details the causal relationships of action and character; (2) restrict the action to the events of a single day; and (3) limit the scene to a single place or city. The unities were observed faithfully by continental European writers until the Romantic Age, but they were never regularly observed in English drama. Modern dramatists are typically more concerned with a unity of impression or emotional effect than with any of the classical unities.

# V

**Verisimilitude:** Literally, the appearance of truth. In literary criticism, the term refers to aspects of a work of literature that seem true to the reader.

**Versification:** The writing of verse. Versification may also refer to the meter, rhyme, and other mechanical components of a poem.

# Z

**Zeitgeist:** A German term meaning ''spirit of the time.'' It refers to the moral and intellectual trends of a given era.

# Author/Title Index

# Nationality/Ethnicity Index

**English**

Milton, John
*Paradise Lost*

**Finnish**

Lönnrot, Elias
*Kalevala*

**Greek**

Homer
*Iliad*
*Odyssey*

**Italian**

Alighieri, Dante
*Divina Commedia (The Divine Comedy)*

**Malian**

Kouyaté, Djeli Mamoudou
*Sundiata*

**Roman**

Virgil
*Aeneid*

**West Indian**

Walcott, Derek
*Omeros*

# Subject/Theme Index